GUARDIANS OF THE GALAXY & X-MEN

THE BLACK VORTEX

PREVIOUSLY...

Vhen a blood bounty was placed on Peter Quill's head, Peter found himself hounded by a group of mercenaries :alled the Slaughter Squad, henchmen of the mysterious Mister Knife. Upon being captured by the Squad, Peter 'ound himself face-to-face with Knife, who he discovered was, in fact, his father, J'Son, the deposed Emperor of ;partax. Though Kitty Pryde, Peter's new girlfriend, arrived in time to save Peter from being brainwashed by his father, they both remain unaware of Knife's true plan.

Having obtained an object of unimaginable cosmic power known as the Black Vortex and after recruiting the son of Thanos, Thane, to his cause, it looks like Mister Knife's quest to reclaim control of the galaxy may be a greater threat than they know.

Guardians of the Galaxy & X-Men: The Black Vortex Alpha #1
Writer: Sam Humphries
Penciler: Ed McGuinness
Additional Pencils: Kris Anka
Inkers: Kris Anka, Mark Farmer, Jay Leisten & Mark Morales
Colorists: Marte Gracia & Marcelo Maiolo
Letterer: VC's Travis Lanham
Cover Art: Ed McGuinness & Justin Ponsor

Guardians of the Galaxy #24-25
Writer: Brian Michael Bendis
Artist: Valerio Schiti
Colorist: Jason Keith
Letterer: VC's Cory Petit
Cover Art: Valerio Schiti & Jason Keith

Legendary Star-Lord #9-11
Writer: Sam Humphries
Penciler: Paco Medina
Inkers: Juan Vlasco & Paco Medina
Colorist: David Curiel
Letterer: VC's Joe Caramagna
Cover Art: Paco Medina

All-New X-Men #38-39
Writer: Brian Michael Bendis
Artist: Andrea Sorrentino
Colorist: Marcelo Maiolo
Letterer: VC's Cory Petit
Cover Art: Andrea Sorrentino & Marcelo Maiolo

Guardians Team-Up #3
Writer: Sam Humphries
Artist: Mike Mayhew
Colorist: Rain Beredo
Letterer: VC's Cory Petit
Cover Art: Mike Mayhew & Rain Beredo

Nova #28
Writer: Gerry Duggan
Artist: David Baldeon
Inker: Terry Pallot
Colorist: David Curiel
Letterer: Comicraft's Albert Deschesne
Cover Art: Orphans Cheeps

Cyclops #12
Writer: John Layman
Art: Javier Garrón
Colorist: Chris Sotomayor
Letterer: VC's Joe Caramagna
Cover Art: Alexander Lozano

Captain Marvel #14
Writer: Kelly Sue DeConnick
Artist: David Lopez
Colorist: Lee Loughridge
Letterer: VC's Joe Caramagna
Cover Art: David Lopez

Guardians of the Galaxy & X-Men: The Black Vortex Omega #1
Writer: Sam Humphries
Pencilers: Ed McGuinness & Javier Garrón
Inkers: Mark Farmer, Javier Garrón & Ed McGuinness
Colorist: Marte Gracia
Letterer: VC's Travis Lanham
Cover Art: Ed McGuinness, Mark Farmer & Marte Gracia

Assistant Editors: Xander Jarowey, Christina Harrington, Devin Lewis & Charles Beacham
Editors: Mike Marts, Katie Kubert, Nick Lowe & Sana Amanat

X-Men created by Stan Lee & Jack Kirby

Collection Editor: Jennifer Grünwald
Assistant Editor: Sarah Brunstad
Associate Managing Editor: Alex Starbuck
Editor, Special Projects: Mark D. Beazley
Senior Editor, Special Projects: Jeff Youngquist
SVP Print, Sales & Marketing: David Gabriel
Book Designer: Adam Del Re

Editor in Chief: Axel Alonso
Chief Creative Officer: Joe Quesada
Publisher: Dan Buckley
Executive Producer: Alan Fine

ARDIANS OF THE GALAXY & X-MEN: THE BLACK VORTEX. Contains material originally published in magazine form as GUARDIANS OF THE GALAXY & X-MEN: THE BLACK VORTEX ALPHA #1, GUARDIANS OF THE GALAXY #24-25, LEGENDARY R-LORD #9-11, ALL-NEW X-MEN #38-39, GUARDIANS TEAM-UP #3, NOVA #28, CYCLOPS #12, CAPTAIN MARVEL #14 and GUARDIANS OF THE GALAXY & X-MEN: THE BLACK VORTEX OMEGA #1. First printing 2016. ISBN# 978-0-7851-9909-0. lished by MARVEL WORLDWIDE, INC., a subsidiary of MARVEL ENTERTAINMENT, LLC. OFFICE OF PUBLICATION: 135 West 50th Street, New York, NY 10020. **Printed in the U.S.A.** ALAN FINE, President, Marvel Entertainment; DAN BUCKLEY, sident, TV, Publishing and Brand Management; JOE QUESADA, Chief Creative Officer; TOM BREVOORT, SVP of Publishing; DAVID BOGART, SVP of Operations & Procurement, Publishing; C.B. CEBULSKI, VP of International Development & Brand nagement; DAVID GABRIEL, SVP Print, Sales & Marketing; JIM O'KEEFE, VP of Operations & Logistics; DAN CARR, Executive Director of Publishing Technology; SUSAN CRESPI, Editorial Operations Manager; ALEX MORALES, Publishing Operations nager; STAN LEE, Chairman Emeritus. For information regarding advertising in Marvel Comics or on Marvel.com, please contact Jonathan Rheingold, VP of Custom Solutions & Ad Sales, at jrheingold@marvel.com. For Marvel subscription inquiries, ase call 800-217-9158. **Manufactured between 1/1/2016 and 2/8/2016 by R.R. DONNELLEY, INC., SALEM, VA, USA.**

987654321

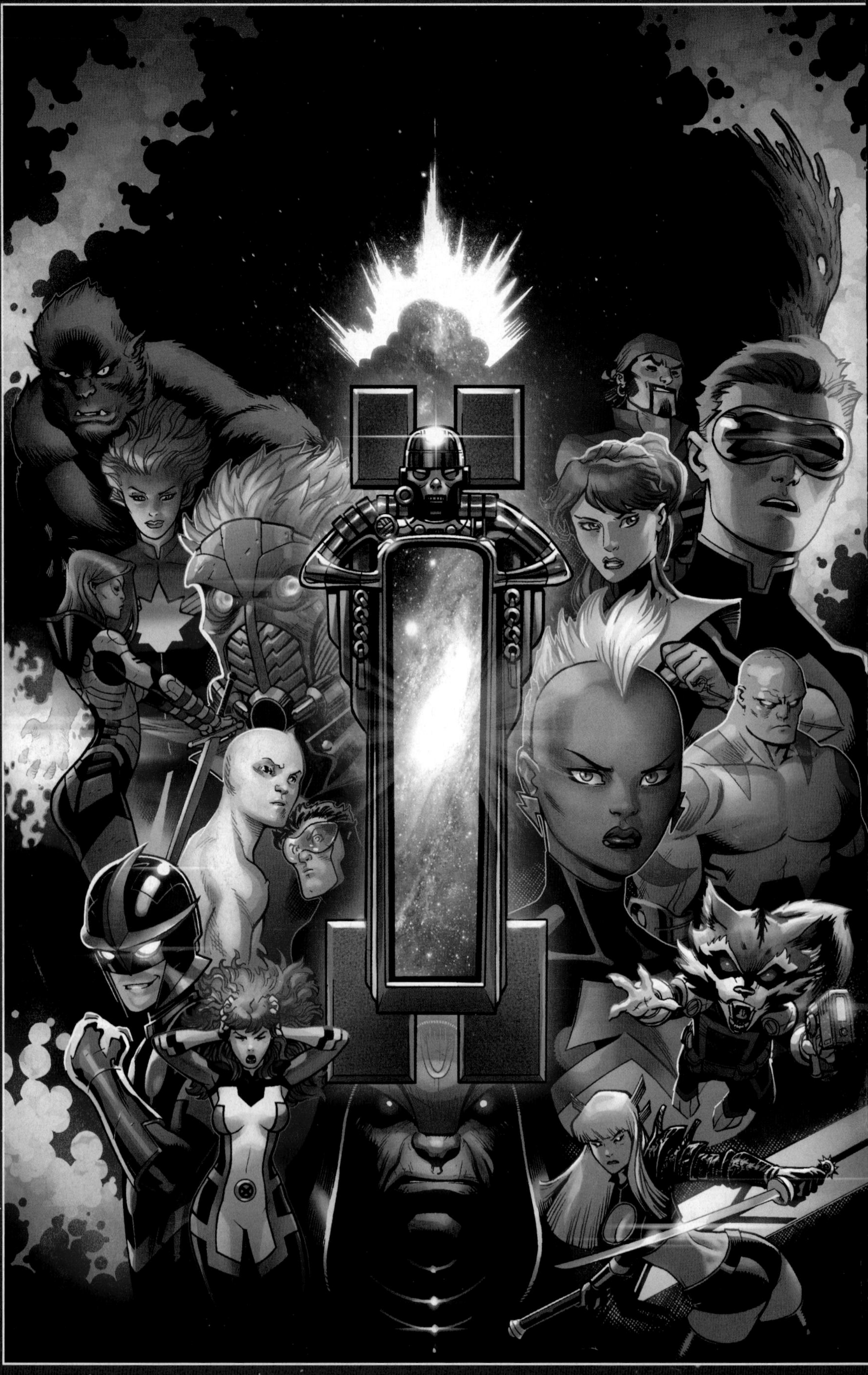

GUARDIANS OF THE GALAXY & X-MEN: THE BLACK VORTEX ALPHA #1

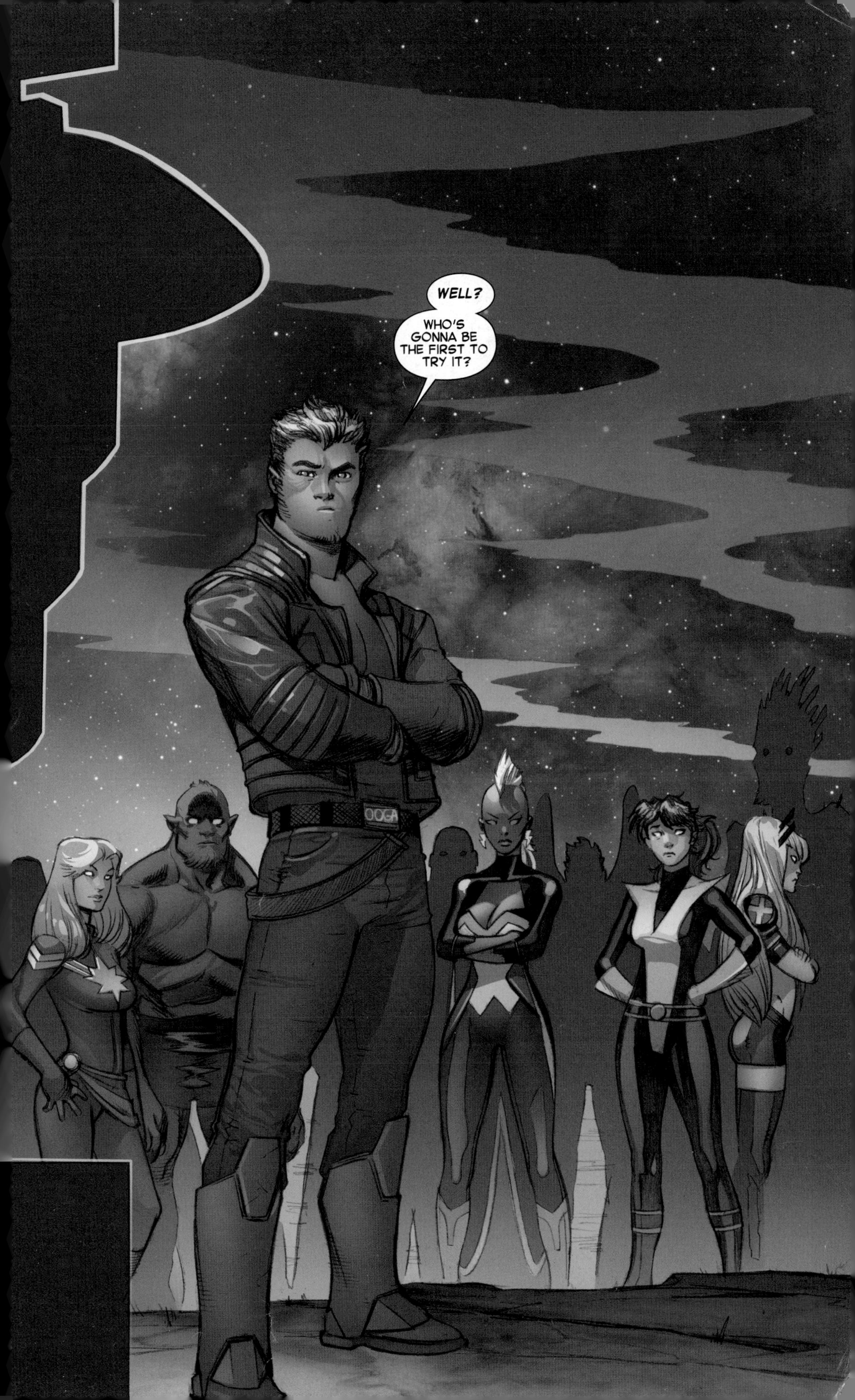
WELL?
WHO'S GONNA BE THE FIRST TO TRY IT?

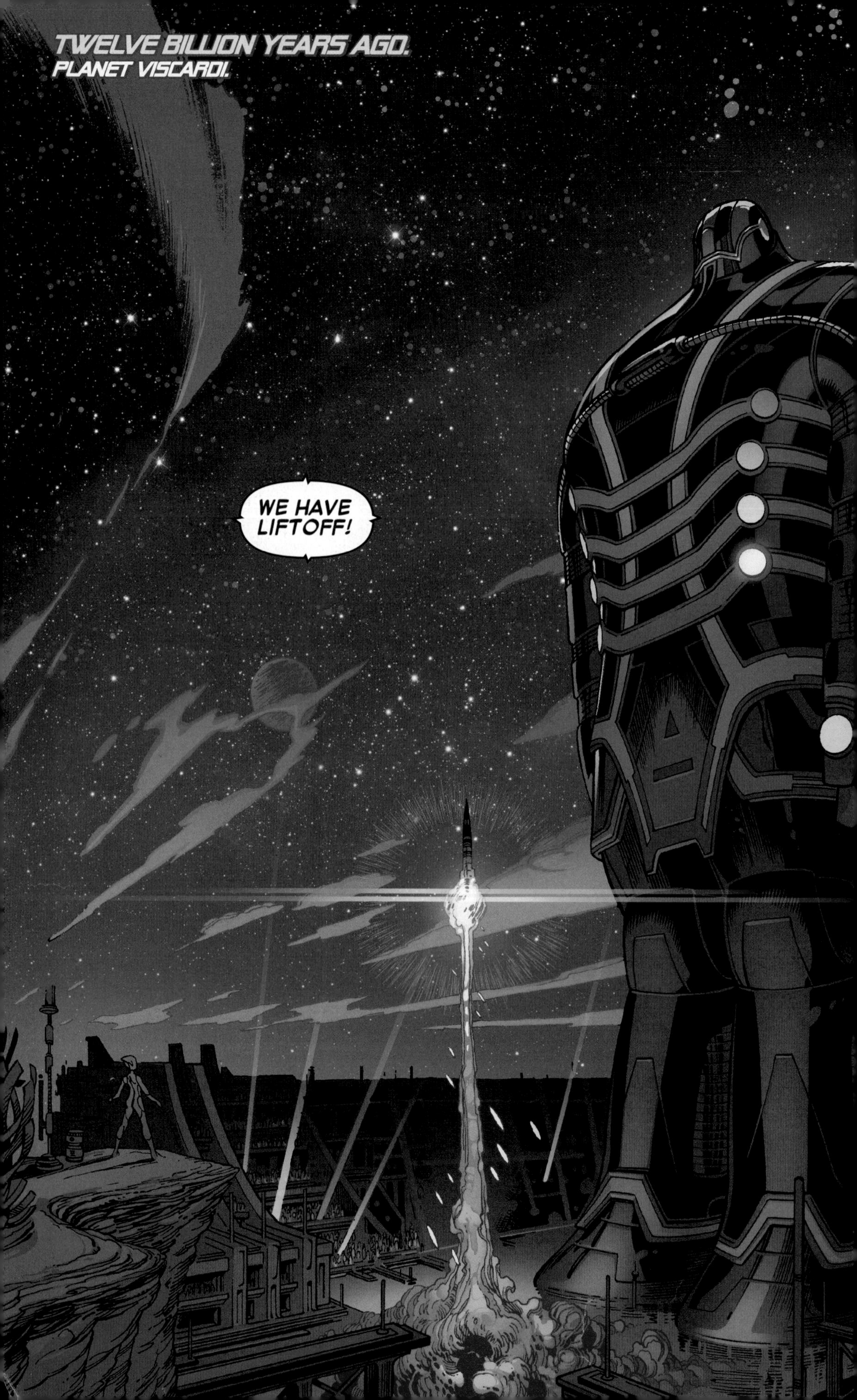
TWELVE BILLION YEARS AGO.
PLANET VISCARDI.
WE HAVE LIFTOFF!

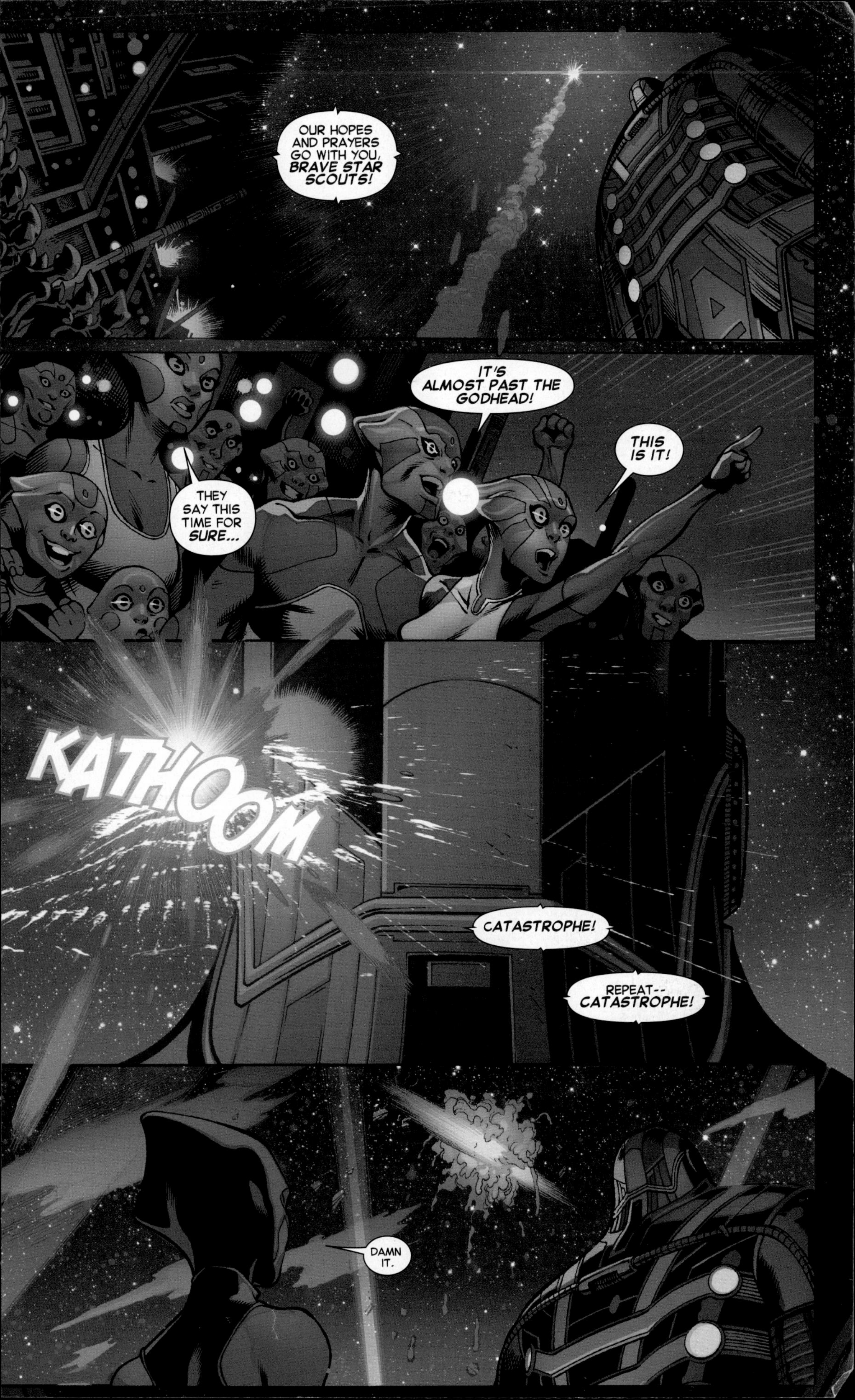
OUR HOPES AND PRAYERS GO WITH YOU, BRAVE STAR SCOUTS!
THEY SAY THIS TIME FOR SURE...
IT'S ALMOST PAST THE GODHEAD!
THIS IS IT!
KATHOOM
CATASTROPHE!
REPEAT-- CATASTROPHE!
DAMN IT.

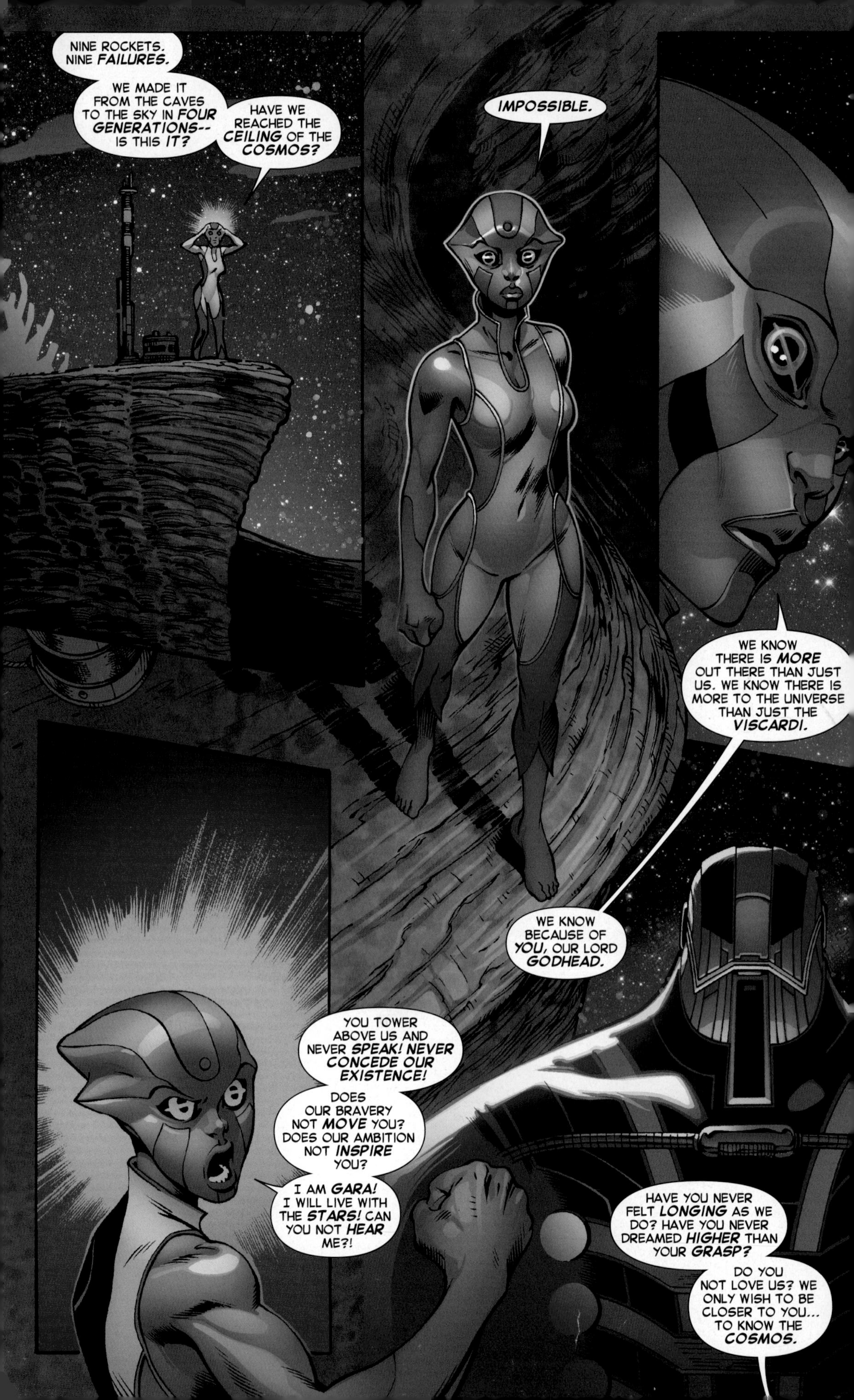
NINE ROCKETS. NINE FAILURES.
WE MADE IT FROM THE CAVES TO THE SKY IN FOUR GENERATIONS-- IS THIS IT?
HAVE WE REACHED THE CEILING OF THE COSMOS?
IMPOSSIBLE.
WE KNOW THERE IS MORE OUT THERE THAN JUST US. WE KNOW THERE IS MORE TO THE UNIVERSE THAN JUST THE VISCARDI.
WE KNOW BECAUSE OF YOU, OUR LORD GODHEAD.
YOU TOWER ABOVE US AND NEVER SPEAK! NEVER CONCEDE OUR EXISTENCE!
DOES OUR BRAVERY NOT MOVE YOU? DOES OUR AMBITION NOT INSPIRE YOU?
I AM GARA! I WILL LIVE WITH THE STARS! CAN YOU NOT HEAR ME?!
HAVE YOU NEVER FELT LONGING AS WE DO? HAVE YOU NEVER DREAMED HIGHER THAN YOUR GRASP?
DO YOU NOT LOVE US? WE ONLY WISH TO BE CLOSER TO YOU... TO KNOW THE COSMOS.

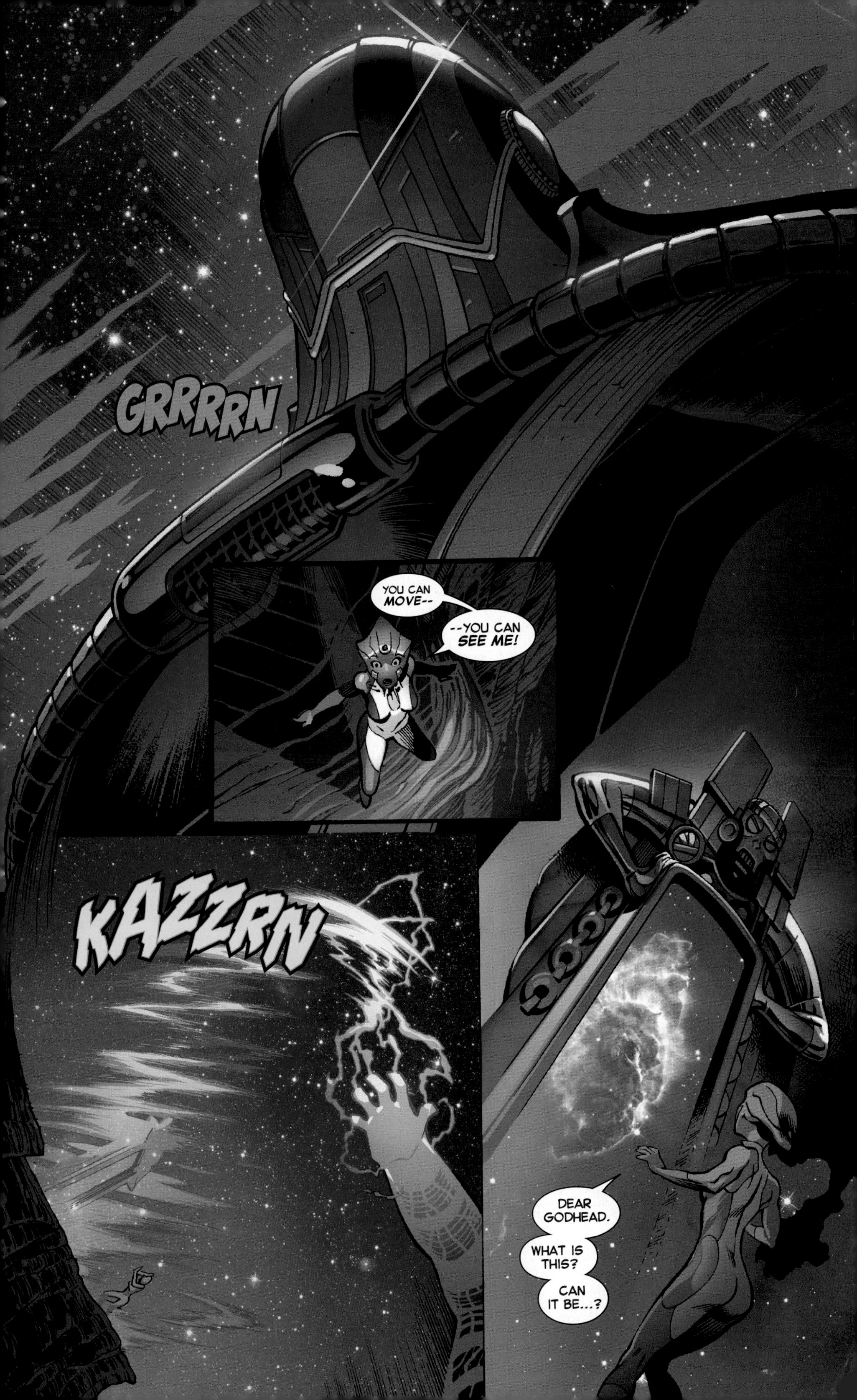
GRRRRN
YOU CAN MOVE--
--YOU CAN SEE ME!
KAZZRN
DEAR GODHEAD.
WHAT IS THIS?
CAN IT BE...?

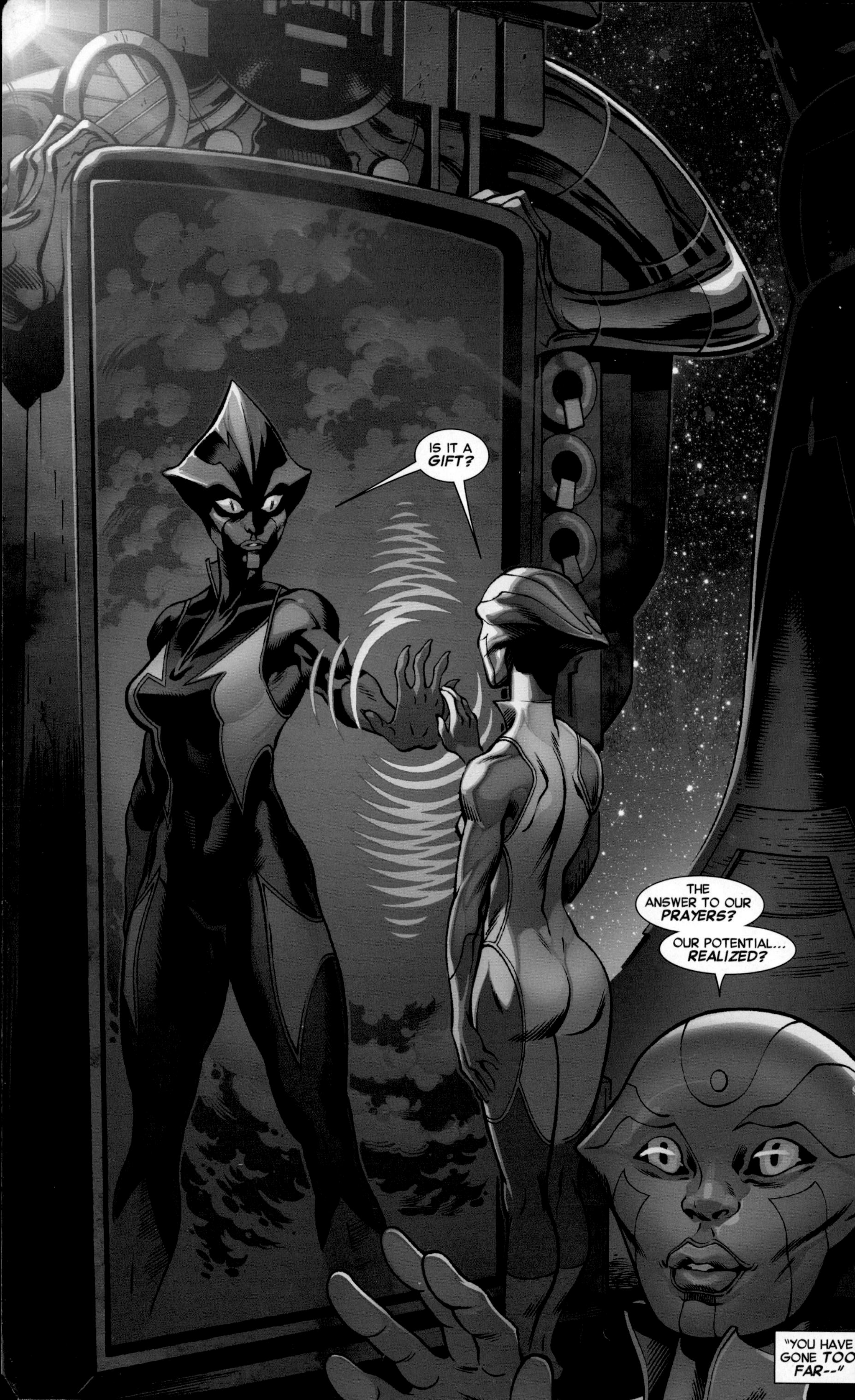
IS IT A GIFT?
THE ANSWER TO OUR PRAYERS?
OUR POTENTIAL... REALIZED?
"YOU HAVE GONE TOO FAR--"

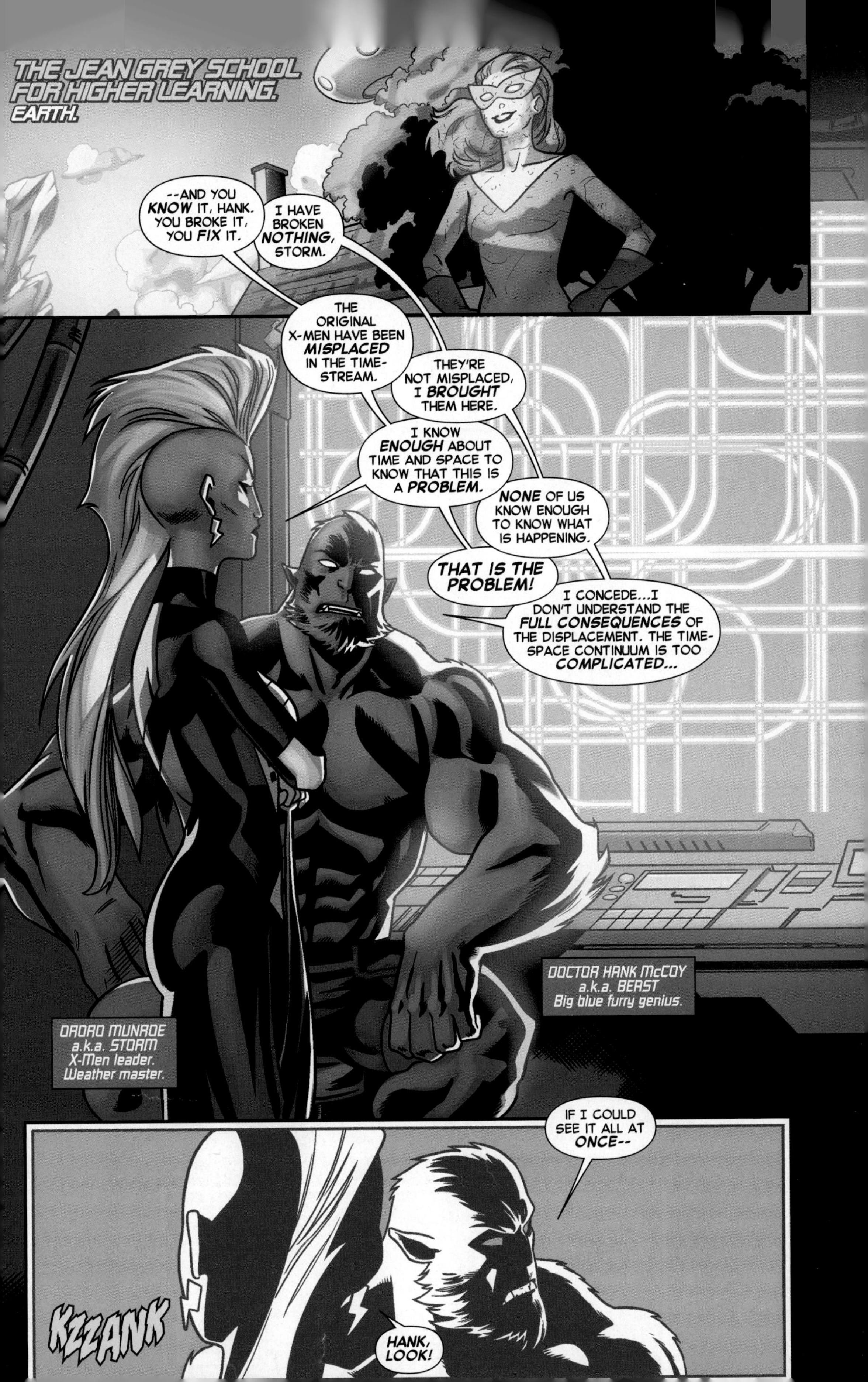
THE JEAN GREY SCHOOL FOR HIGHER LEARNING. EARTH.
--AND YOU KNOW IT, HANK. YOU BROKE IT, YOU FIX IT.
I HAVE BROKEN NOTHING, STORM.
THE ORIGINAL X-MEN HAVE BEEN MISPLACED IN THE TIME-STREAM.
THEY'RE NOT MISPLACED, I BROUGHT THEM HERE.
I KNOW ENOUGH ABOUT TIME AND SPACE TO KNOW THAT THIS IS A PROBLEM.
NONE OF US KNOW ENOUGH TO KNOW WHAT IS HAPPENING.
THAT IS THE PROBLEM!
I CONCEDE...I DON'T UNDERSTAND THE FULL CONSEQUENCES OF THE DISPLACEMENT. THE TIME-SPACE CONTINUUM IS TOO COMPLICATED...
DOCTOR HANK McCOY a.k.a. BEAST Big blue furry genius.
ORORO MUNROE a.k.a. STORM X-Men leader. Weather master.
IF I COULD SEE IT ALL AT ONCE--
KZZANK
HANK, LOOK!

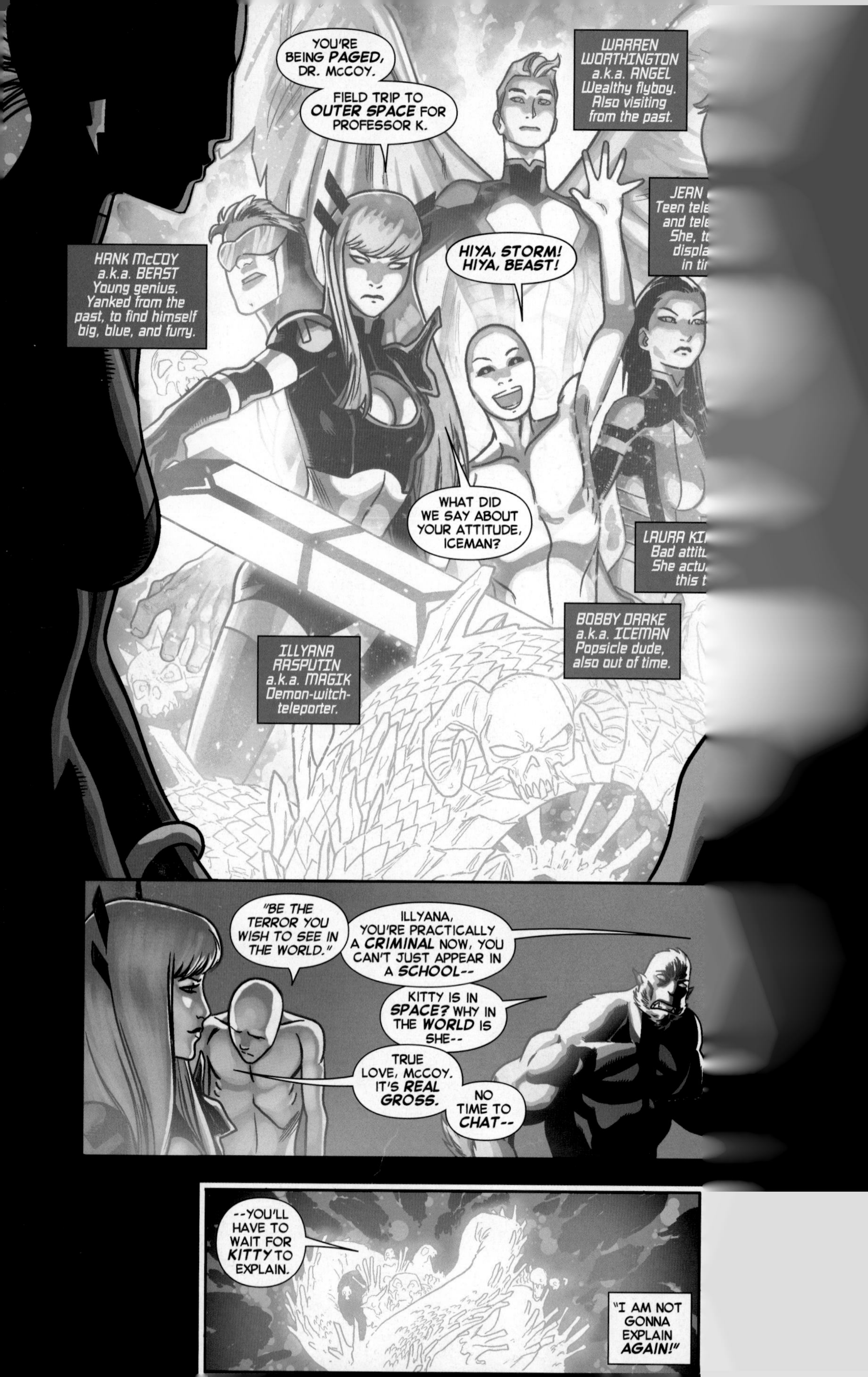
YOU'RE BEING PAGED, DR. McCOY.
FIELD TRIP TO OUTER SPACE FOR PROFESSOR K.
WARREN WORTHINGTON a.k.a. ANGEL Wealthy flyboy. Also visiting from the past.
HANK McCOY a.k.a. BEAST Young genius. Yanked from the past, to find himself big, blue, and furry.
HIYA, STORM! HIYA, BEAST!
WHAT DID WE SAY ABOUT YOUR ATTITUDE, ICEMAN?
BOBBY DRAKE a.k.a. ICEMAN Popsicle dude, also out of time.
ILLYANA RASPUTIN a.k.a. MAGIK Demon-witch-teleporter.
"BE THE TERROR YOU WISH TO SEE IN THE WORLD."
ILLYANA, YOU'RE PRACTICALLY A CRIMINAL NOW, YOU CAN'T JUST APPEAR IN A SCHOOL--
KITTY IS IN SPACE? WHY IN THE WORLD IS SHE--
TRUE LOVE, McCOY. IT'S REAL GROSS.
NO TIME TO CHAT--
--YOU'LL HAVE TO WAIT FOR KITTY TO EXPLAIN.
"I AM NOT GONNA EXPLAIN AGAIN!"

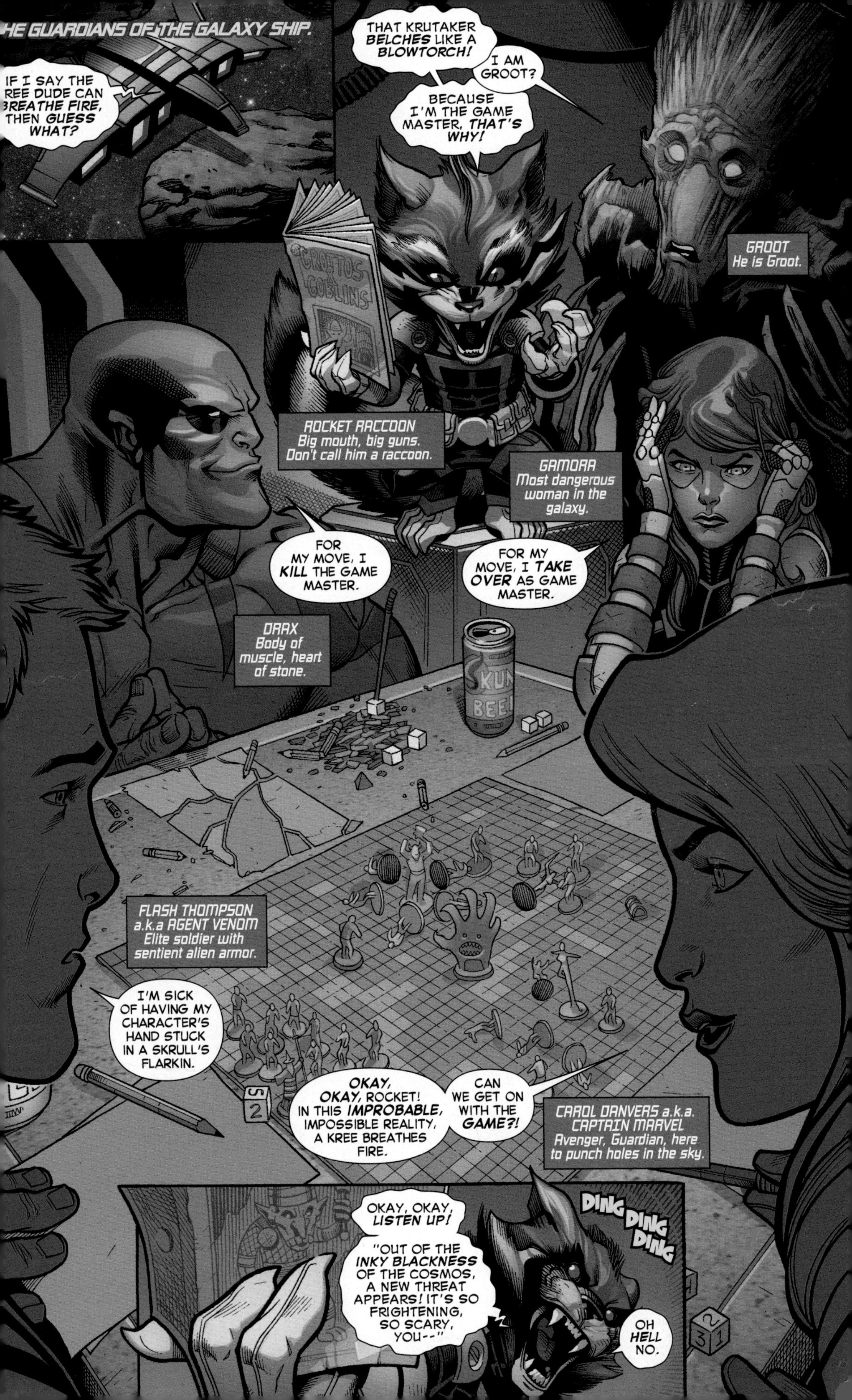
HE GUARDIANS OF THE GALAXY SHIP.
IF I SAY THE REE DUDE CAN BREATHE THE FIRE, THEN GUESS WHAT?
THAT KRUTAKER BELCHES LIKE A BLOWTORCH!
I AM GROOT?
BECAUSE I'M THE GAME MASTER, THAT'S WHY!
GROTTOS & GOBLINS
GROOT He is Groot.
ROCKET RACCOON Big mouth, big guns. Don't call him a raccoon.
GAMORA Most dangerous woman in the galaxy.
FOR MY MOVE, I KILL THE GAME MASTER.
FOR MY MOVE, I TAKE OVER AS GAME MASTER.
DRAX Body of muscle, heart of stone.
FLASH THOMPSON a.k.a AGENT VENOM Elite soldier with sentient alien armor.
I'M SICK OF HAVING MY CHARACTER'S HAND STUCK IN A SKRULL'S FLARKIN.
OKAY, OKAY, ROCKET! IN THIS IMPROBABLE, IMPOSSIBLE REALITY, A KREE BREATHES FIRE.
CAN WE GET ON WITH THE GAME?!
CAROL DANVERS a.k.a. CAPTAIN MARVEL Avenger, Guardian, here to punch holes in the sky.
OKAY, OKAY, LISTEN UP!
"OUT OF THE INKY BLACKNESS OF THE COSMOS, A NEW THREAT APPEARS! IT'S SO FRIGHTENING, SO SCARY, YOU--"
DING DING DING
OH HELL NO.

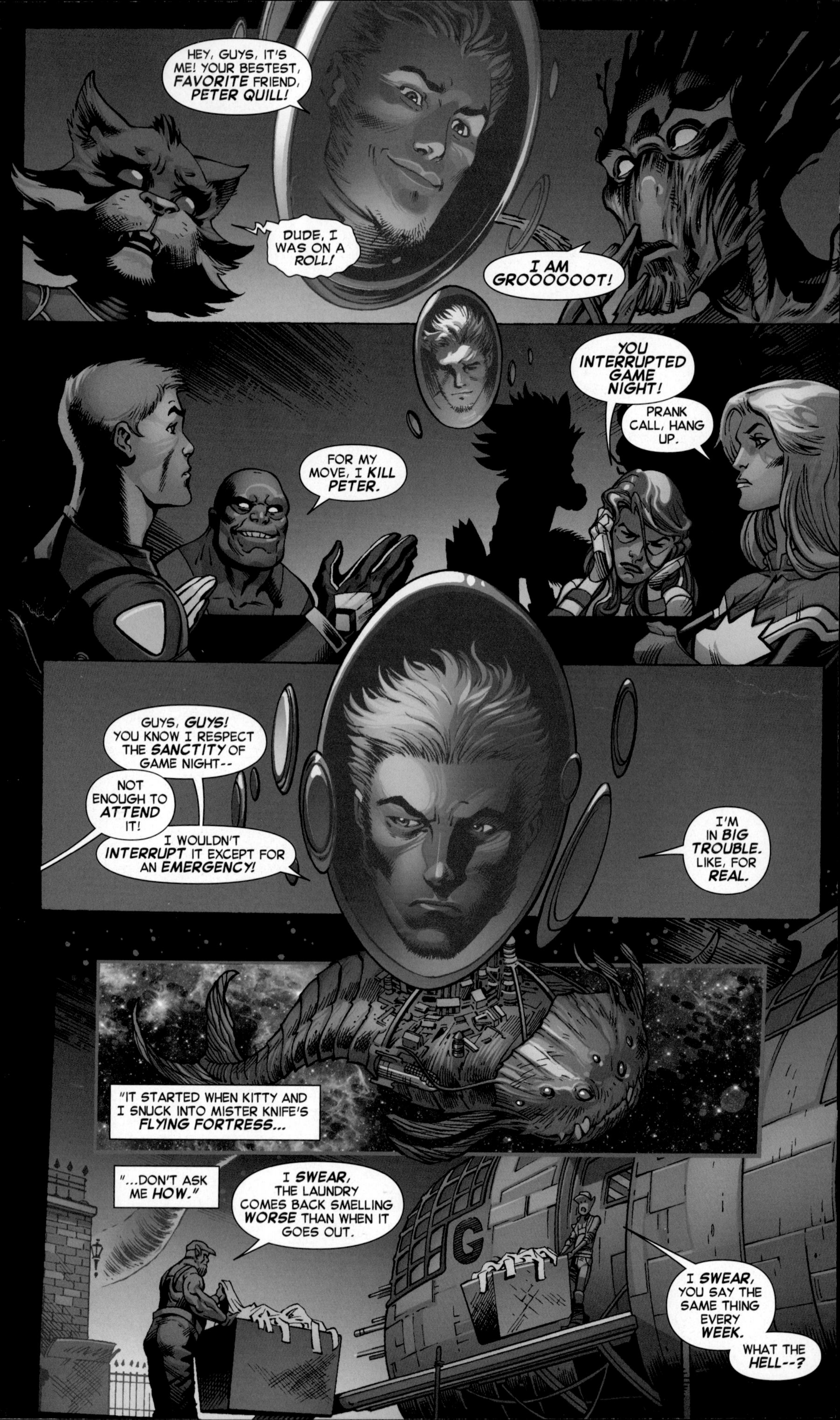
HEY, GUYS, IT'S ME! YOUR BESTEST, FAVORITE FRIEND, PETER QUILL!
DUDE, I WAS ON A ROLL!
I AM GROOOOOOT!
YOU INTERRUPTED GAME NIGHT!
PRANK CALL, HANG UP.
FOR MY MOVE, I KILL PETER.
GUYS, GUYS! YOU KNOW I RESPECT THE SANCTITY OF GAME NIGHT--
NOT ENOUGH TO ATTEND IT!
I WOULDN'T INTERRUPT IT EXCEPT FOR AN EMERGENCY!
I'M IN BIG TROUBLE. LIKE, FOR REAL.
"IT STARTED WHEN KITTY AND I SNUCK INTO MISTER KNIFE'S FLYING FORTRESS...
"...DON'T ASK ME HOW."
I SWEAR, THE LAUNDRY COMES BACK SMELLING WORSE THAN WHEN IT GOES OUT.
I SWEAR, YOU SAY THE SAME THING EVERY WEEK.
WHAT THE HELL--?

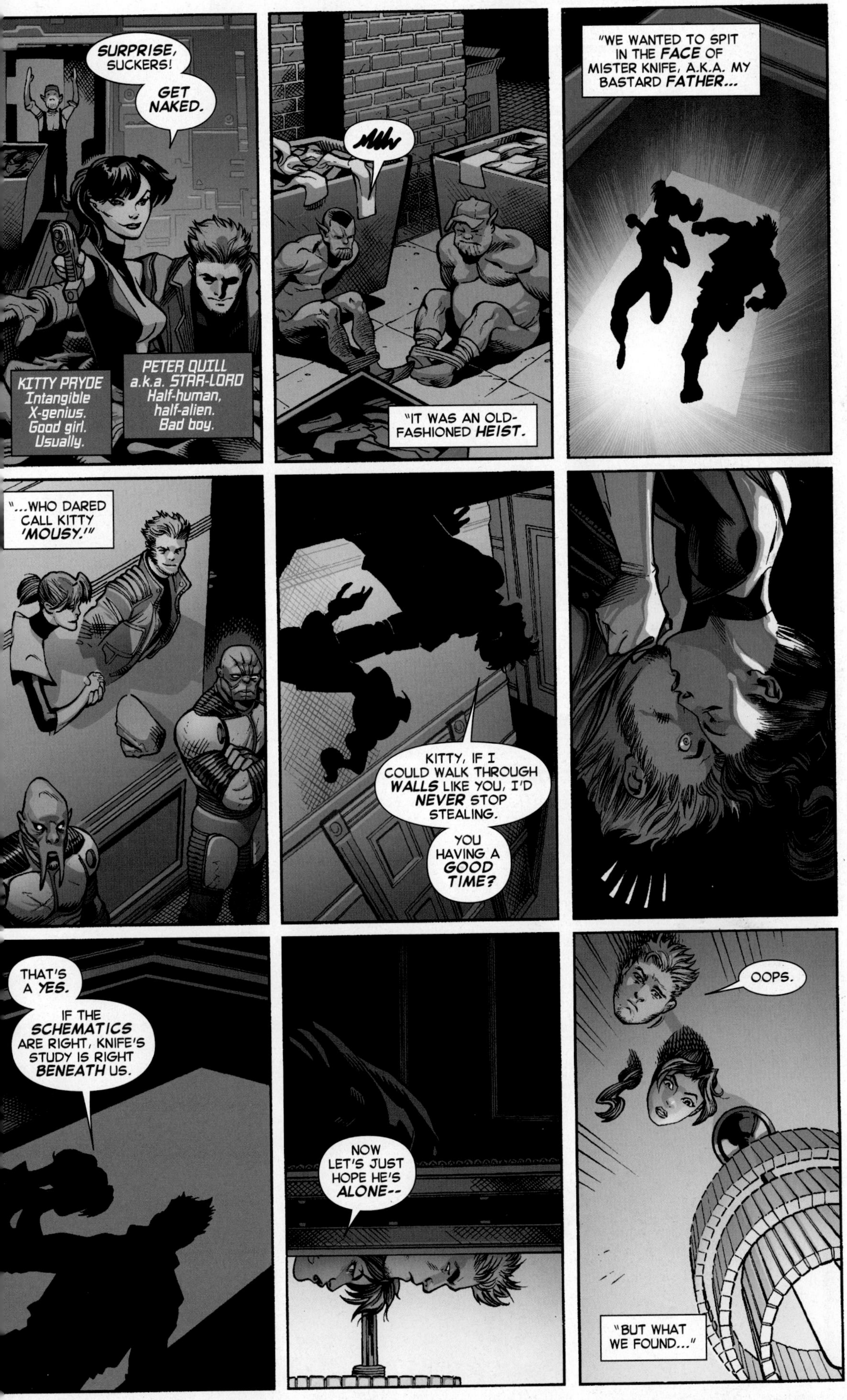
SURPRISE, SUCKERS!
GET NAKED.
KITTY PRYDE Intangible X-genius. Good girl. Usually.
PETER QUILL a.k.a. STAR-LORD Half-human, half-alien. Bad boy.
"IT WAS AN OLD-FASHIONED HEIST.
"WE WANTED TO SPIT IN THE FACE OF MISTER KNIFE, A.K.A. MY BASTARD FATHER...
"...WHO DARED CALL KITTY 'MOUSY.'"
KITTY, IF I COULD WALK THROUGH WALLS LIKE YOU, I'D NEVER STOP STEALING.
YOU HAVING A GOOD TIME?
THAT'S A YES.
IF THE SCHEMATICS ARE RIGHT, KNIFE'S STUDY IS RIGHT BENEATH US.
NOW LET'S JUST HOPE HE'S ALONE--
OOPS.
"BUT WHAT WE FOUND..."

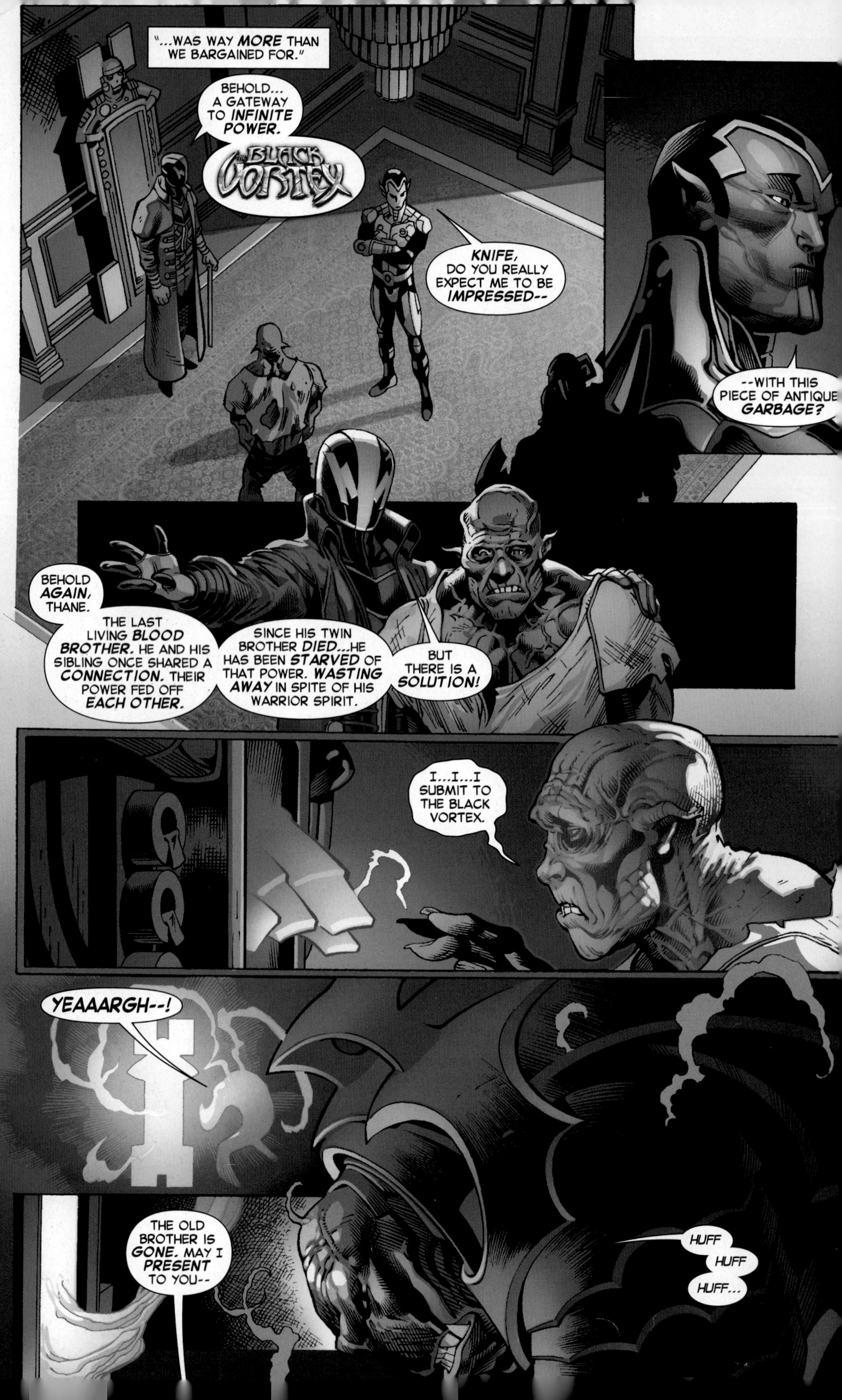
"...WAS WAY MORE THAN WE BARGAINED FOR."
BEHOLD... A GATEWAY TO INFINITE POWER.
THE BLACK VORTEX
KNIFE, DO YOU REALLY EXPECT ME TO BE IMPRESSED--
--WITH THIS PIECE OF ANTIQUE GARBAGE?
BEHOLD AGAIN, THANE.
THE LAST LIVING BLOOD BROTHER. HE AND HIS SIBLING ONCE SHARED A CONNECTION. THEIR POWER FED OFF EACH OTHER.
SINCE HIS TWIN BROTHER DIED...HE HAS BEEN STARVED OF THAT POWER. WASTING AWAY IN SPITE OF HIS WARRIOR SPIRIT.
BUT THERE IS A SOLUTION!
I...I...I SUBMIT TO THE BLACK VORTEX.
YEAAARGH--!
THE OLD BROTHER IS GONE. MAY I PRESENT TO YOU--
HUFF
HUFF
HUFF...

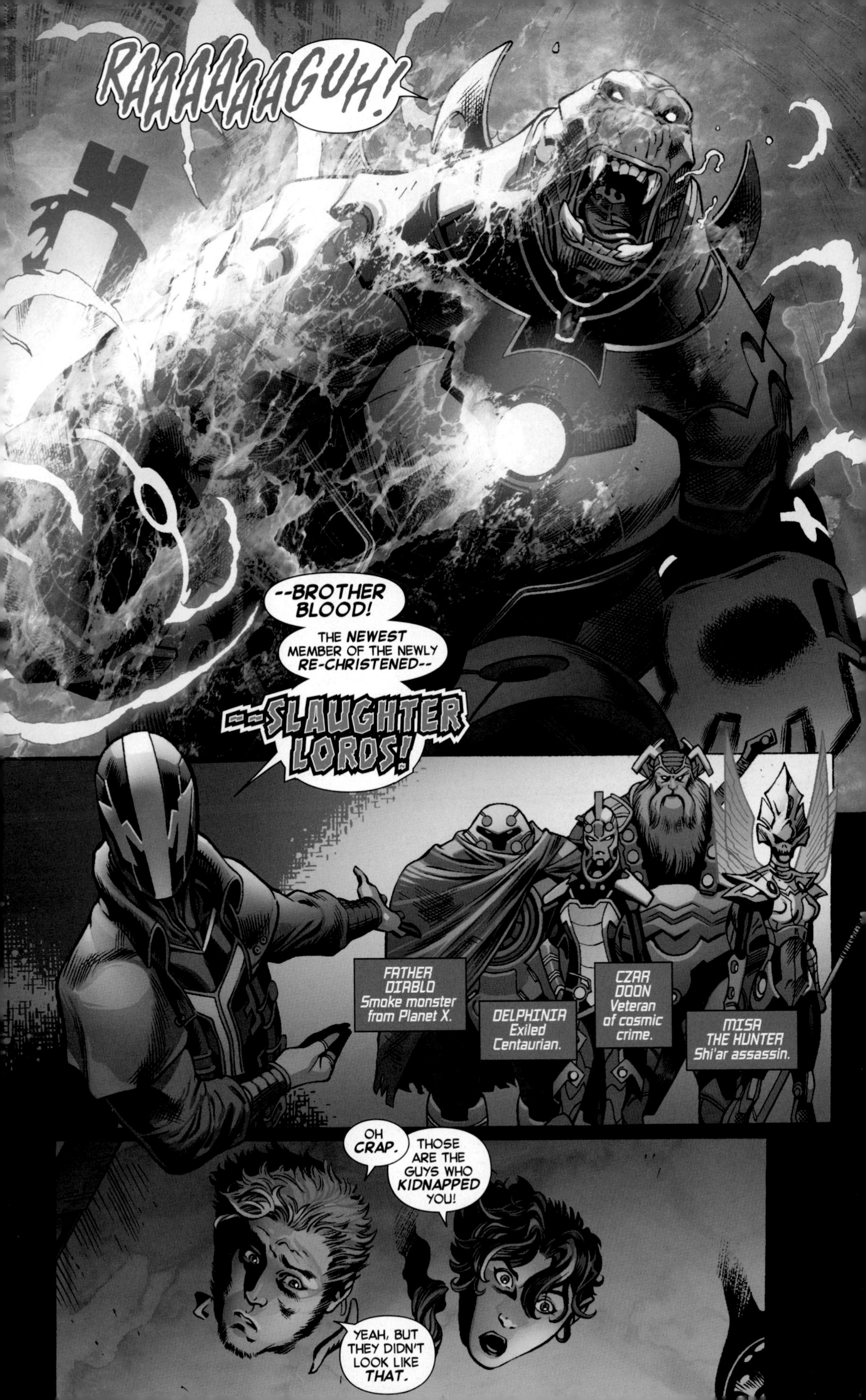
RAAAAAAAGUH!
--BROTHER BLOOD!
THE NEWEST MEMBER OF THE NEWLY RE-CHRISTENED--
--SLAUGHTER LORDS!
FATHER DIABLO Smoke monster from Planet X.
DELPHINIA Exiled Centaurian.
CZAR DOON Veteran of cosmic crime.
MISA THE HUNTER Shi'ar assassin.
OH CRAP.
THOSE ARE THE GUYS WHO KIDNAPPED YOU!
YEAH, BUT THEY DIDN'T LOOK LIKE THAT.

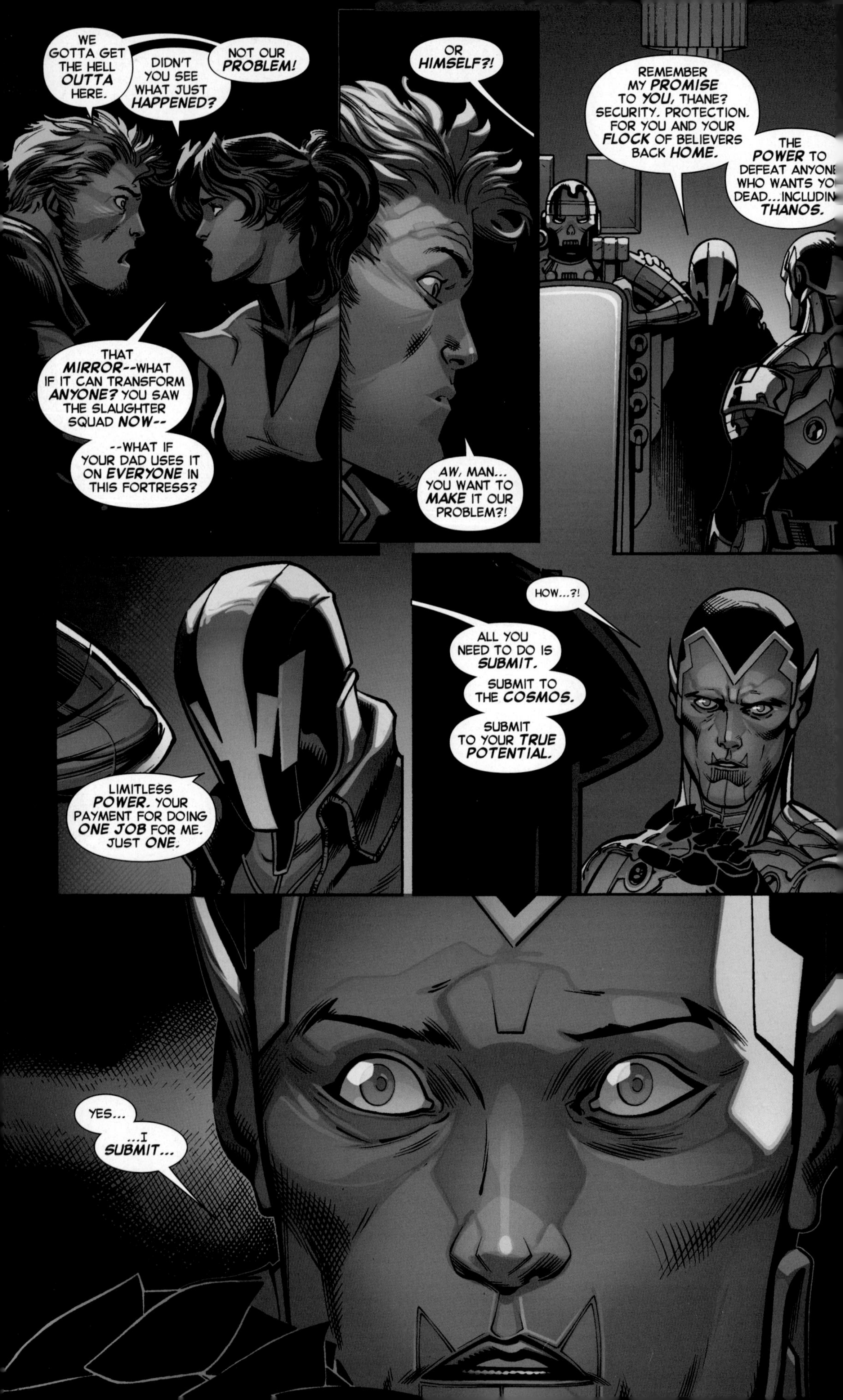

WE GOTTA GET THE HELL OUTTA HERE.
NOT OUR PROBLEM!
DIDN'T YOU SEE WHAT JUST HAPPENED?
THAT MIRROR--WHAT IF IT CAN TRANSFORM ANYONE? YOU SAW THE SLAUGHTER SQUAD NOW--
--WHAT IF YOUR DAD USES IT ON EVERYONE IN THIS FORTRESS?
OR HIMSELF?!
AW, MAN... YOU WANT TO MAKE IT OUR PROBLEM?!
REMEMBER MY PROMISE TO YOU, THANE? SECURITY. PROTECTION. FOR YOU AND YOUR FLOCK OF BELIEVERS BACK HOME.
THE POWER TO DEFEAT ANYONE WHO WANTS YOU DEAD...INCLUDING THANOS.
LIMITLESS POWER. YOUR PAYMENT FOR DOING ONE JOB FOR ME. JUST ONE.
HOW...?!
ALL YOU NEED TO DO IS SUBMIT.
SUBMIT TO THE COSMOS.
SUBMIT TO YOUR TRUE POTENTIAL.
YES...
...I SUBMIT...

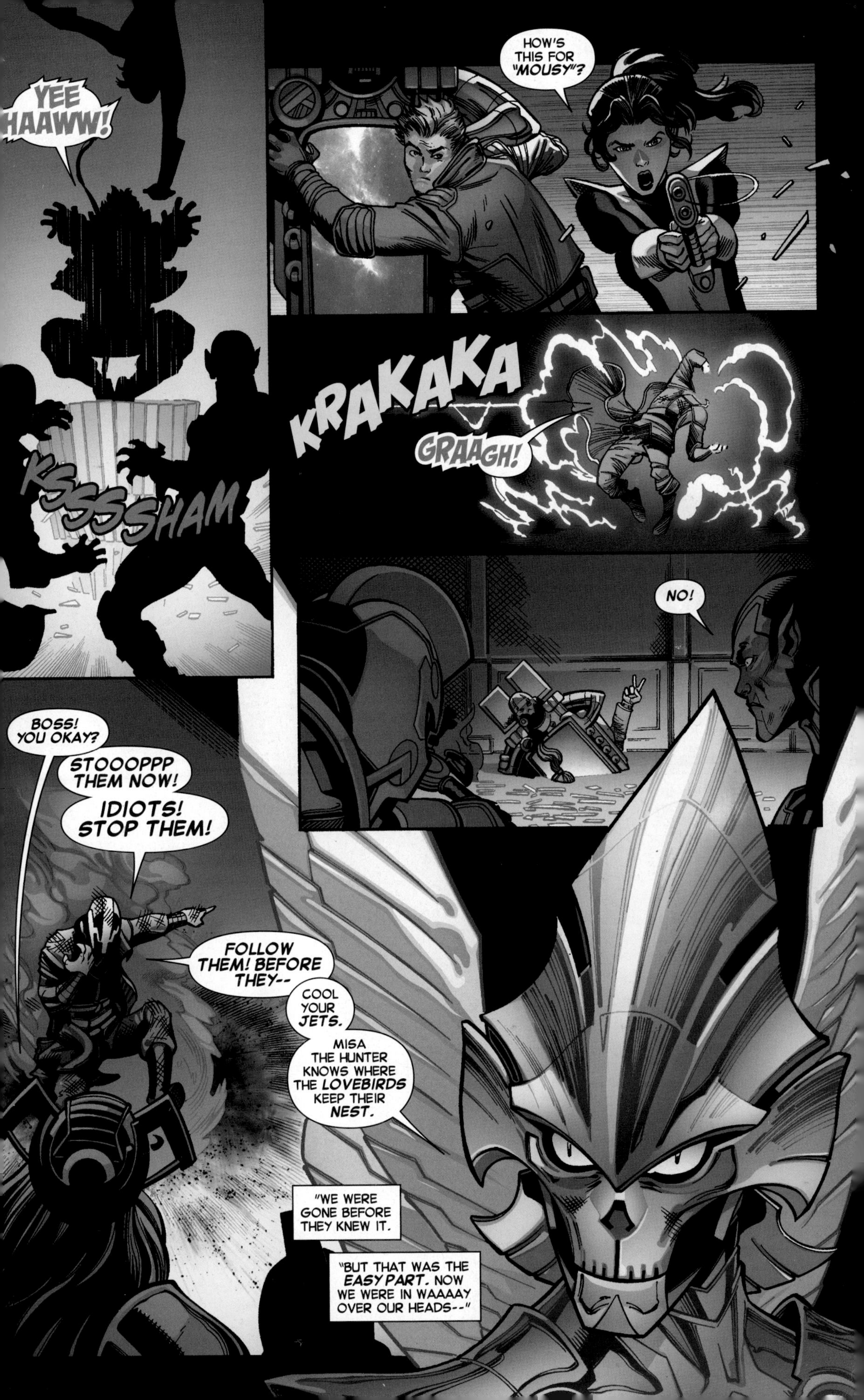
YEE HAAWW!
HOW'S THIS FOR "MOUSY"?
KSSSSSHAM
KRAKAKA
GRAAGH!
NO!
BOSS! YOU OKAY?
STOOOPPP THEM NOW!
IDIOTS! STOP THEM!
FOLLOW THEM! BEFORE THEY--
COOL YOUR JETS.
MISA THE HUNTER KNOWS WHERE THE LOVEBIRDS KEEP THEIR NEST.
"WE WERE GONE BEFORE THEY KNEW IT.
"BUT THAT WAS THE EASY PART. NOW WE WERE IN WAAAAY OVER OUR HEADS--"

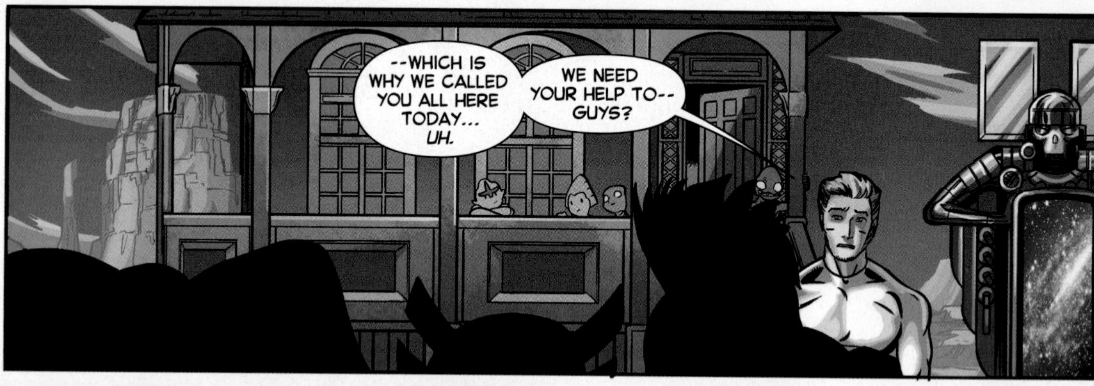
--WHICH IS WHY WE CALLED YOU ALL HERE TODAY... UH.
WE NEED YOUR HELP TO-- GUYS?

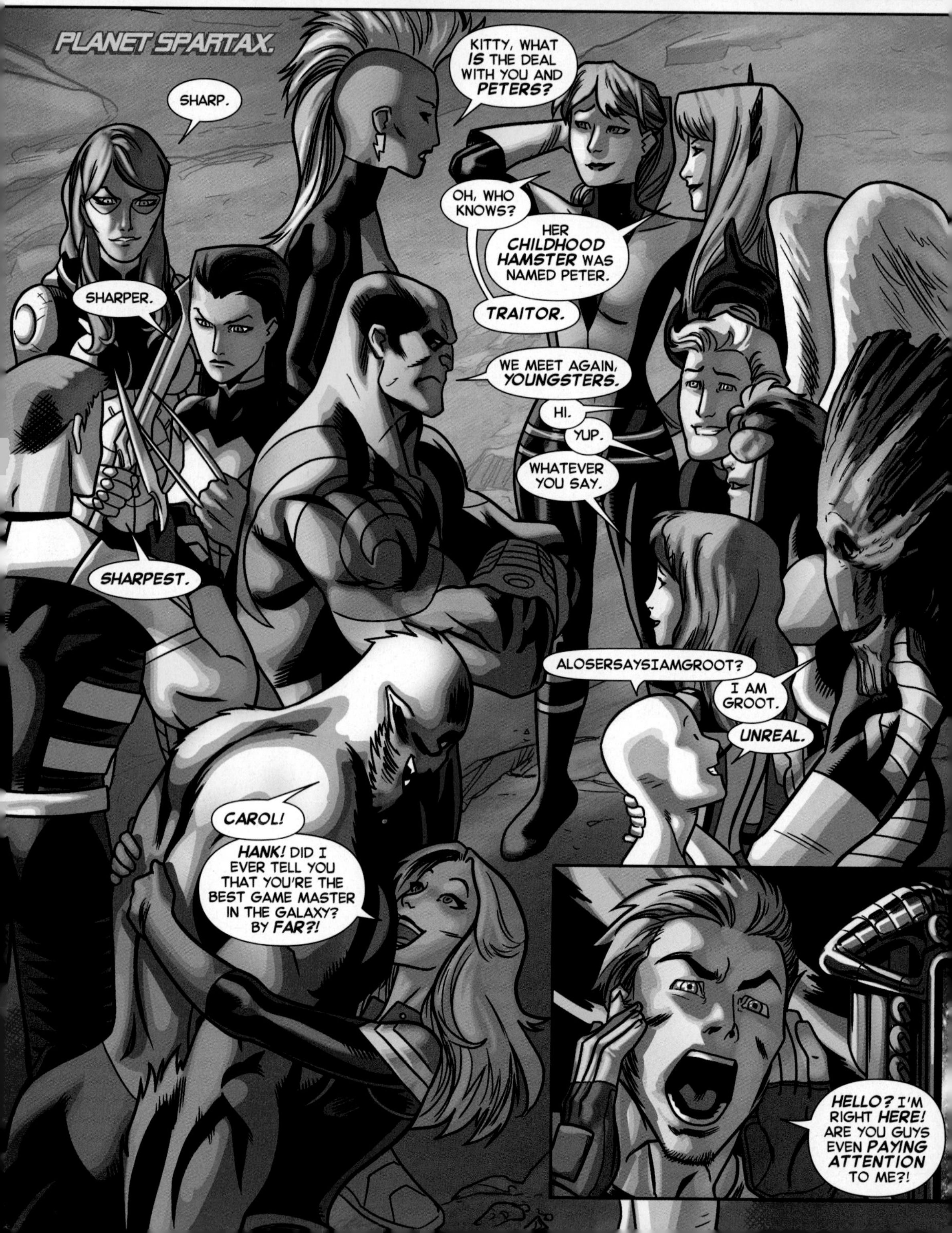
PLANET SPARTAX.
SHARP.
KITTY, WHAT IS THE DEAL WITH YOU AND PETERS?
OH, WHO KNOWS?
HER CHILDHOOD HAMSTER WAS NAMED PETER.
TRAITOR.
SHARPER.
WE MEET AGAIN, YOUNGSTERS.
HI.
YUP.
WHATEVER YOU SAY.
SHARPEST.
ALOSERSAYSIAMGROOT?
I AM GROOT.
UNREAL.
CAROL!
HANK! DID I EVER TELL YOU THAT YOU'RE THE BEST GAME MASTER IN THE GALAXY? BY FAR?!
HELLO? I'M RIGHT HERE! ARE YOU GUYS EVEN PAYING ATTENTION TO ME?!

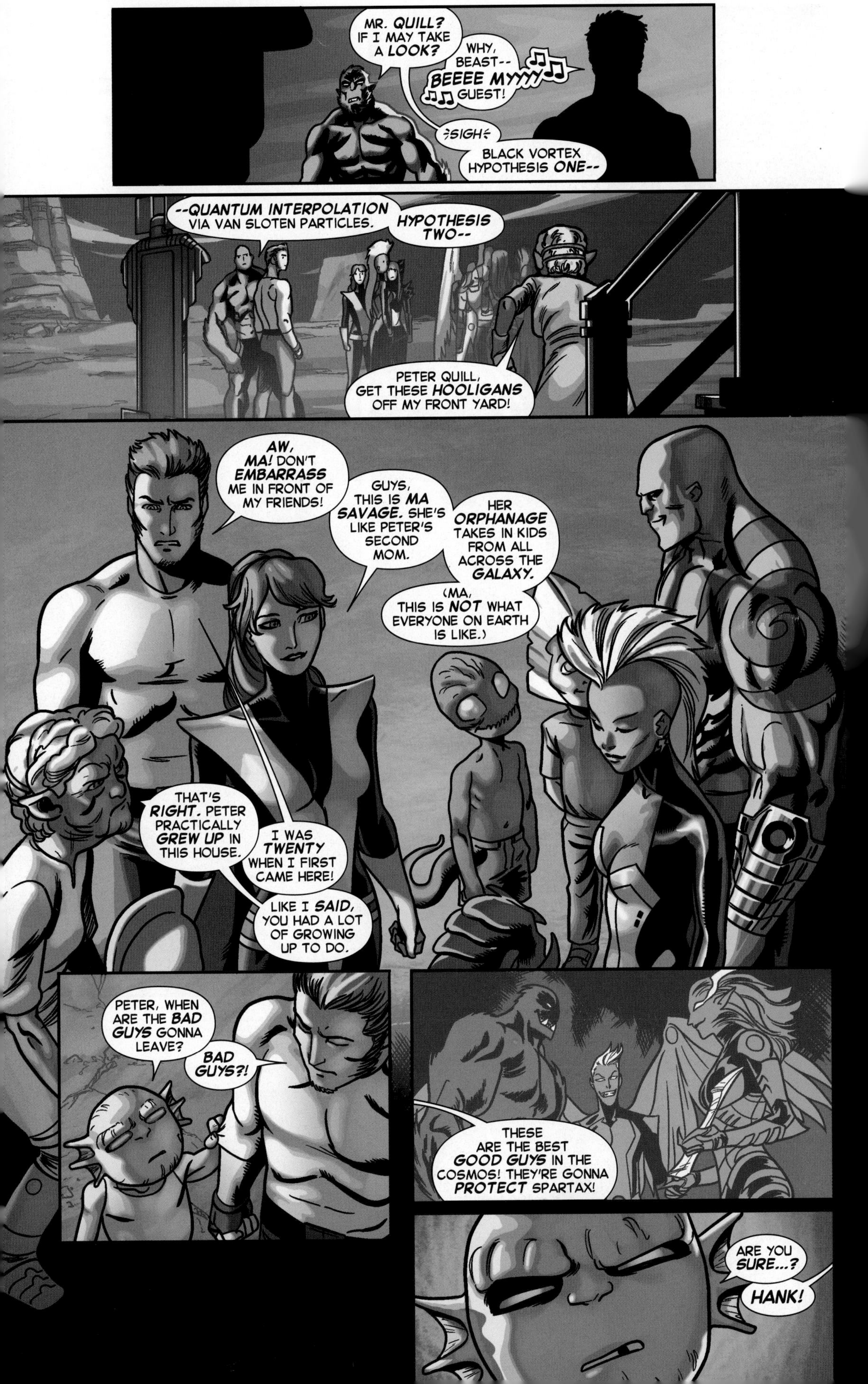
MR. QUILL? IF I MAY TAKE A LOOK?
WHY, BEAST-- BEEEE MYYYY GUEST!
SIGH
BLACK VORTEX HYPOTHESIS ONE--
--QUANTUM INTERPOLATION VIA VAN SLOTEN PARTICLES.
HYPOTHESIS TWO--
PETER QUILL, GET THESE HOOLIGANS OFF MY FRONT YARD!
AW, MA! DON'T EMBARRASS ME IN FRONT OF MY FRIENDS!
GUYS, THIS IS MA SAVAGE. SHE'S LIKE PETER'S SECOND MOM.
HER ORPHANAGE TAKES IN KIDS FROM ALL ACROSS THE GALAXY.
(MA, THIS IS NOT WHAT EVERYONE ON EARTH IS LIKE.)
THAT'S RIGHT. PETER PRACTICALLY GREW UP IN THIS HOUSE.
I WAS TWENTY WHEN I FIRST CAME HERE!
LIKE I SAID, YOU HAD A LOT OF GROWING UP TO DO.
PETER, WHEN ARE THE BAD GUYS GONNA LEAVE?
BAD GUYS?!
THESE ARE THE BEST GOOD GUYS IN THE COSMOS! THEY'RE GONNA PROTECT SPARTAX!
ARE YOU SURE...?
HANK!

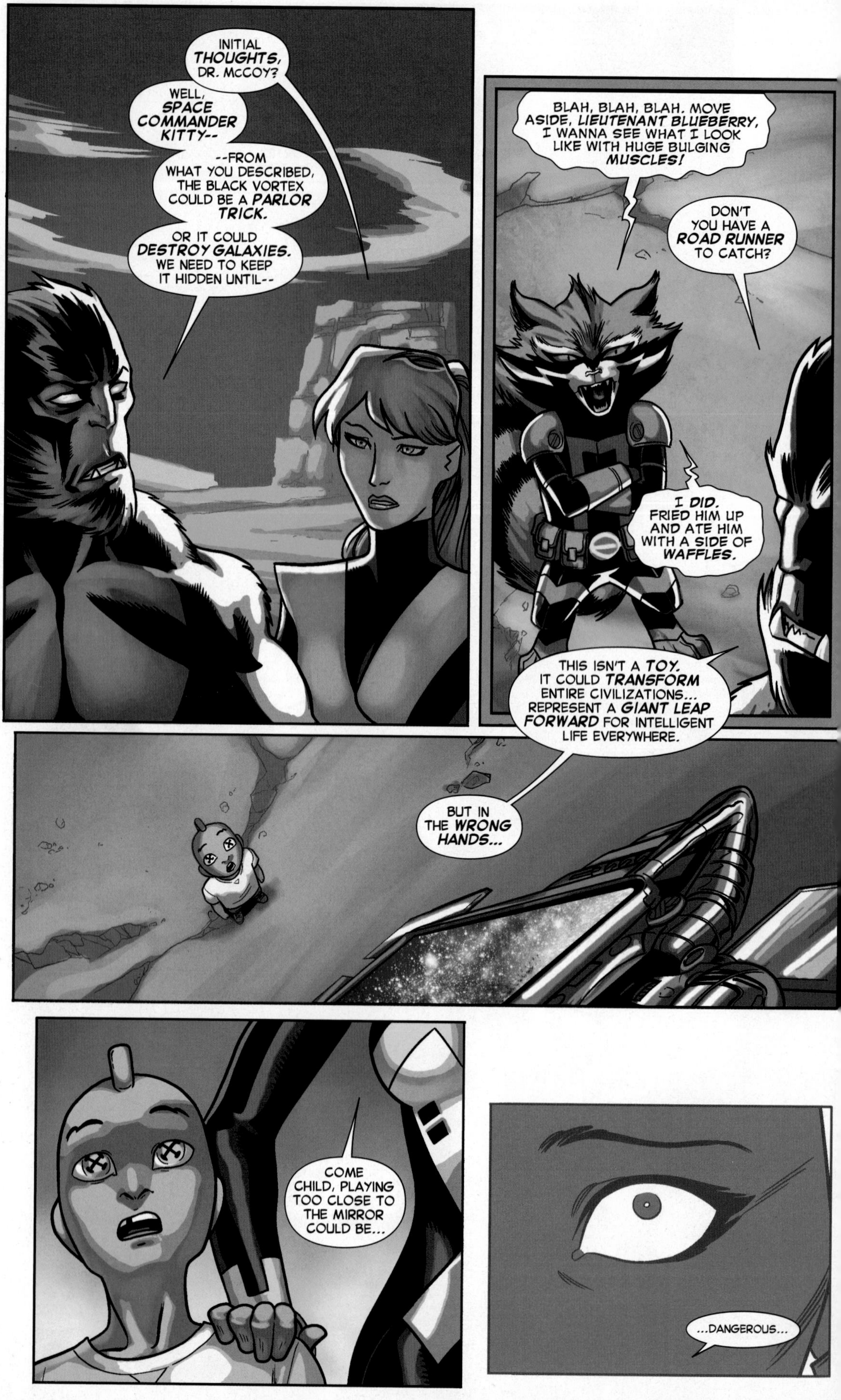
INITIAL THOUGHTS, DR. McCOY?
WELL, SPACE COMMANDER KITTY--
--FROM WHAT YOU DESCRIBED, THE BLACK VORTEX COULD BE A PARLOR TRICK.
OR IT COULD DESTROY GALAXIES. WE NEED TO KEEP IT HIDDEN UNTIL--
BLAH, BLAH, BLAH. MOVE ASIDE, LIEUTENANT BLUEBERRY, I WANNA SEE WHAT I LOOK LIKE WITH HUGE BULGING MUSCLES!
DON'T YOU HAVE A ROAD RUNNER TO CATCH?
I DID. FRIED HIM UP AND ATE HIM WITH A SIDE OF WAFFLES.
THIS ISN'T A TOY. IT COULD TRANSFORM ENTIRE CIVILIZATIONS... REPRESENT A GIANT LEAP FORWARD FOR INTELLIGENT LIFE EVERYWHERE.
BUT IN THE WRONG HANDS...
COME CHILD, PLAYING TOO CLOSE TO THE MIRROR COULD BE...
...DANGEROUS...

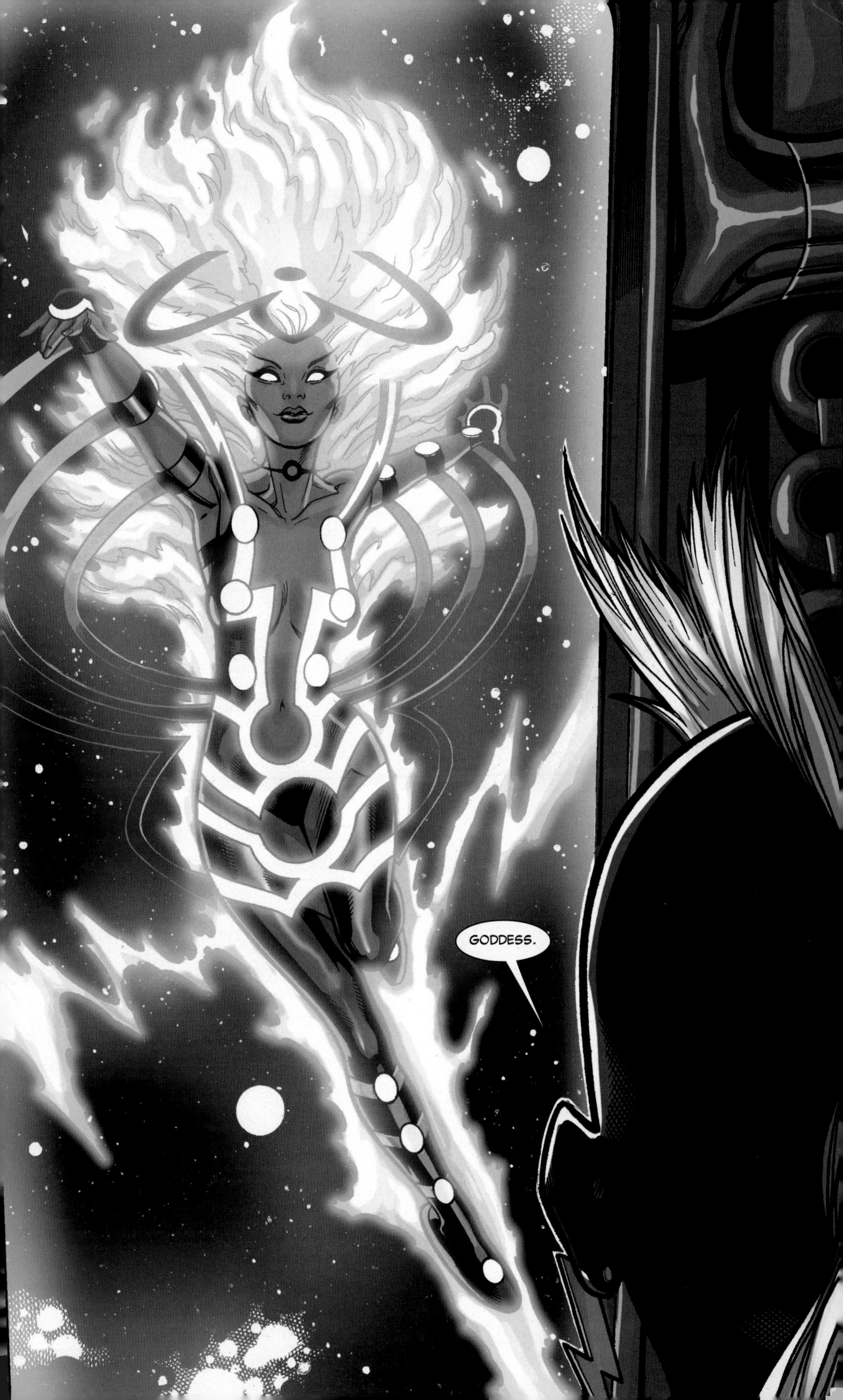
GODDESS.

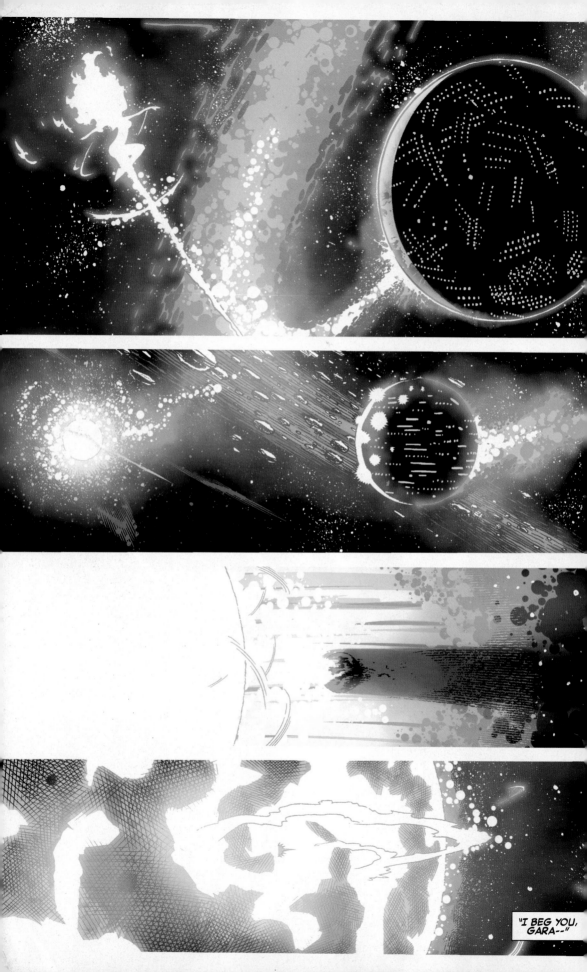

"I BEG YOU, GARA--"

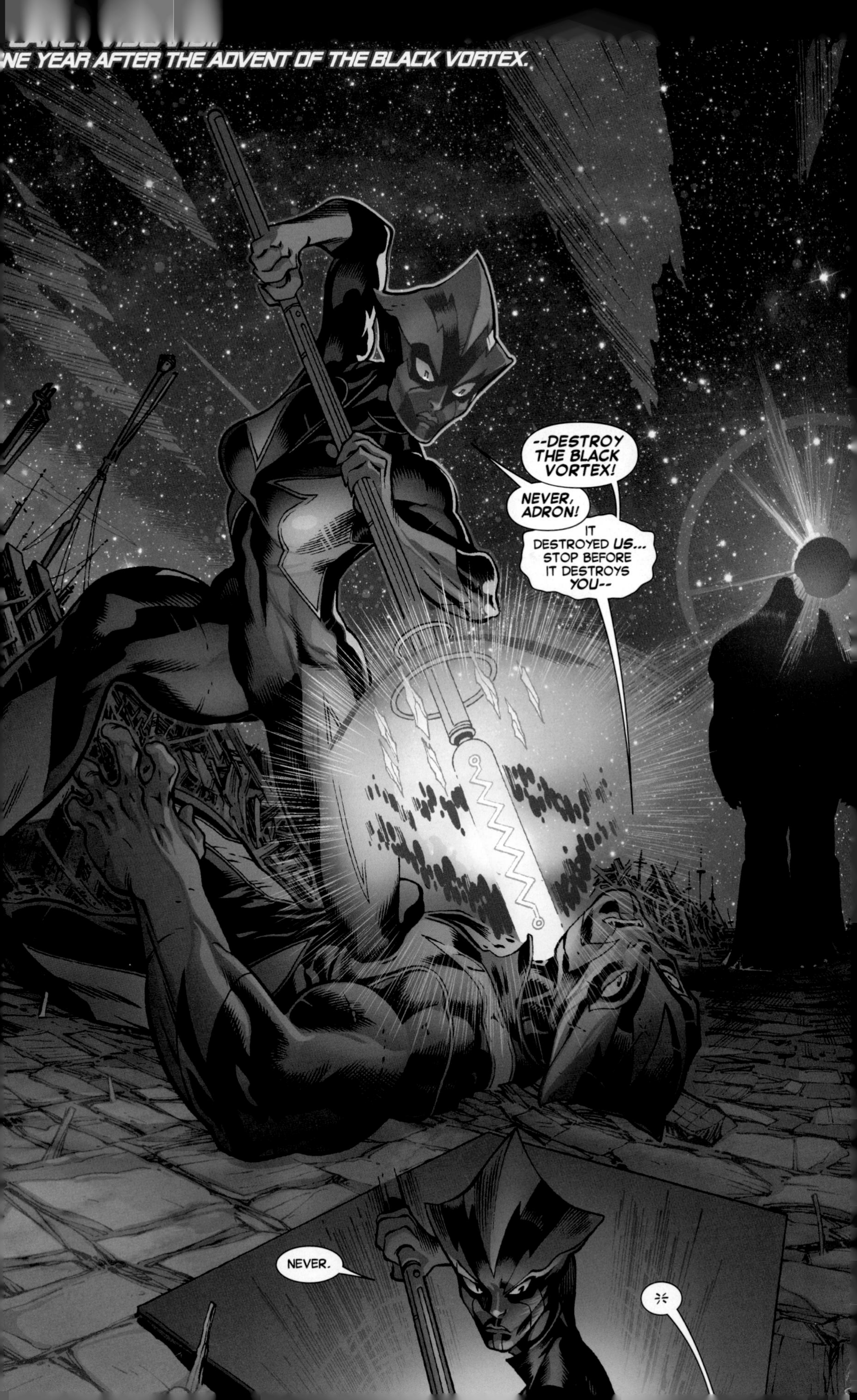
NE YEAR AFTER THE ADVENT OF THE BLACK VORTEX.
--DESTROY THE BLACK VORTEX!
NEVER, ADRON!
IT DESTROYED US... STOP BEFORE IT DESTROYS YOU--
NEVER.

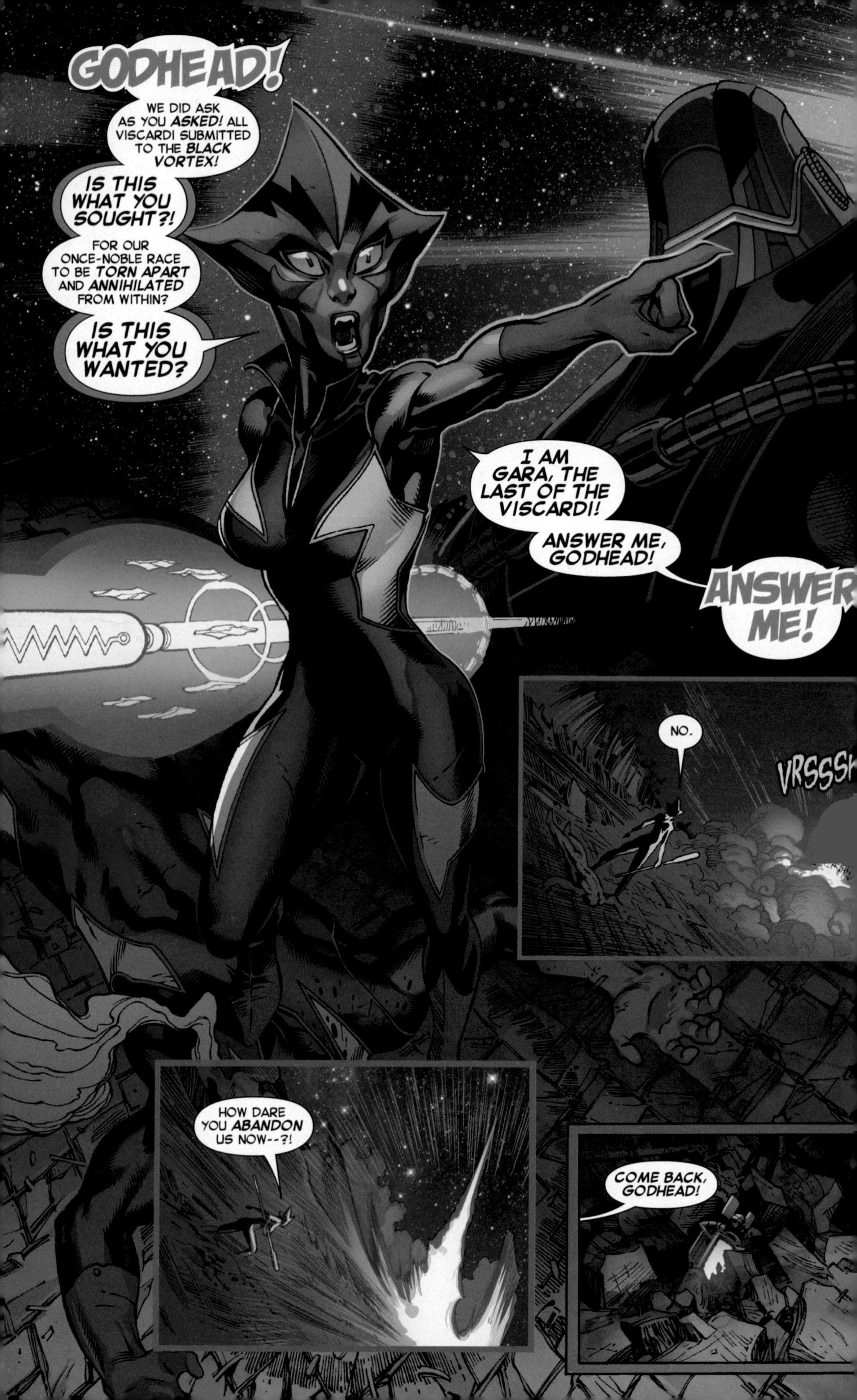
GODHEAD!
WE DID ASK AS YOU ASKED! ALL VISCARDI SUBMITTED TO THE BLACK VORTEX!
IS THIS WHAT YOU SOUGHT?!
FOR OUR ONCE-NOBLE RACE TO BE TORN APART AND ANNIHILATED FROM WITHIN?
IS THIS WHAT YOU WANTED?
I AM GARA, THE LAST OF THE VISCARDI!
ANSWER ME, GODHEAD!
ANSWER ME!
NO.
VRSSSH
HOW DARE YOU ABANDON US NOW--?!
COME BACK, GODHEAD!

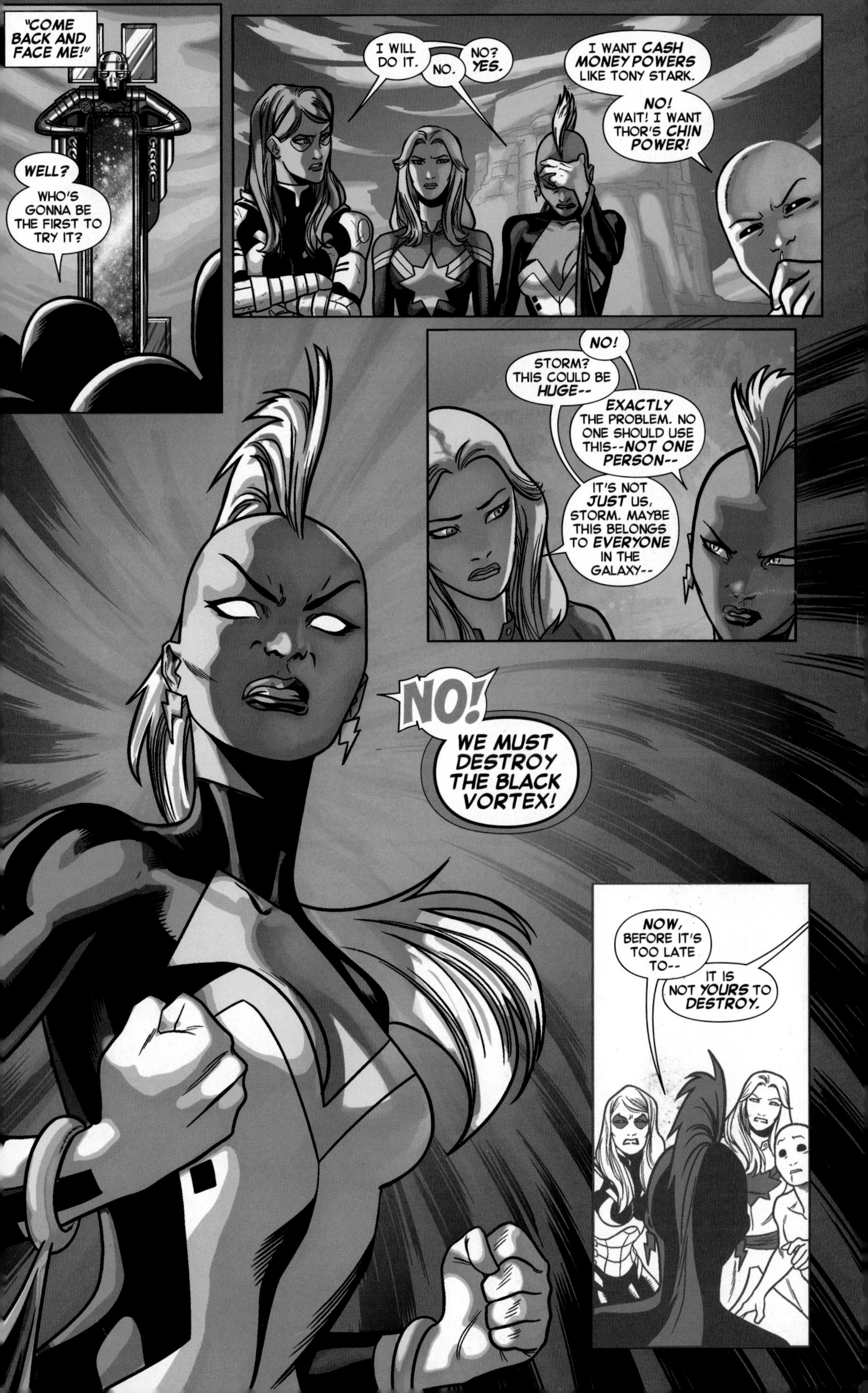

"COME BACK AND FACE ME!"
WELL?
WHO'S GONNA BE THE FIRST TO TRY IT?
I WILL DO IT.
NO.
NO? YES.
I WANT CASH MONEY POWERS LIKE TONY STARK.
NO! WAIT! I WANT THOR'S CHIN POWER!
NO!
STORM? THIS COULD BE HUGE--
EXACTLY THE PROBLEM. NO ONE SHOULD USE THIS--NOT ONE PERSON--
IT'S NOT JUST US, STORM. MAYBE THIS BELONGS TO EVERYONE IN THE GALAXY--
NO!
WE MUST DESTROY THE BLACK VORTEX!
NOW, BEFORE IT'S TOO LATE TO--
IT IS NOT YOURS TO DESTROY.

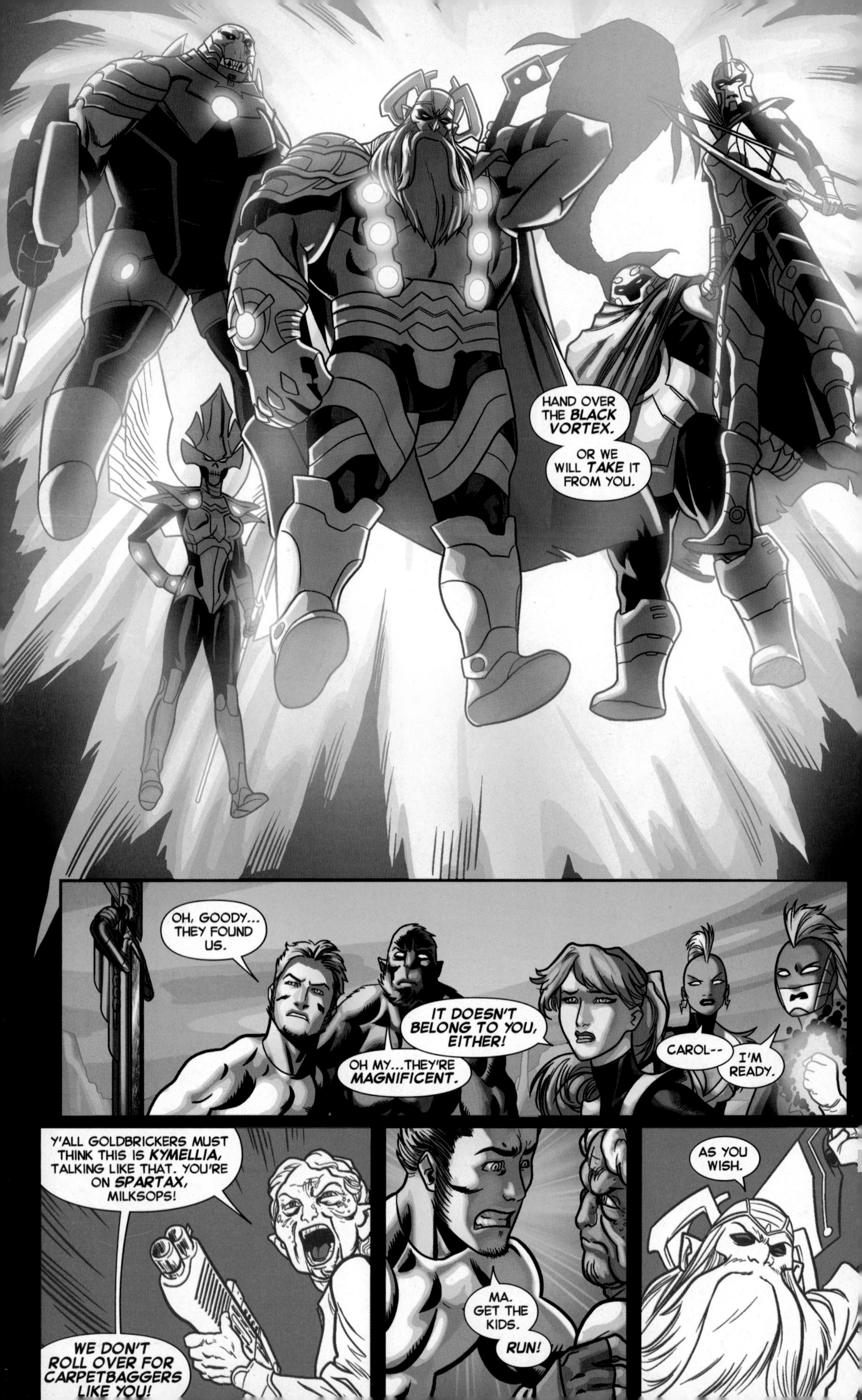
HAND OVER THE BLACK VORTEX.
OR WE WILL TAKE IT FROM YOU.
OH, GOODY... THEY FOUND US.
IT DOESN'T BELONG TO YOU, EITHER!
OH MY...THEY'RE MAGNIFICENT.
CAROL--
I'M READY.
Y'ALL GOLDBRICKERS MUST THINK THIS IS KYMELLIA, TALKING LIKE THAT. YOU'RE ON SPARTAX, MILKSOPS!
WE DON'T ROLL OVER FOR CARPETBAGGERS LIKE YOU!
MA. GET THE KIDS.
RUN!
AS YOU WISH.

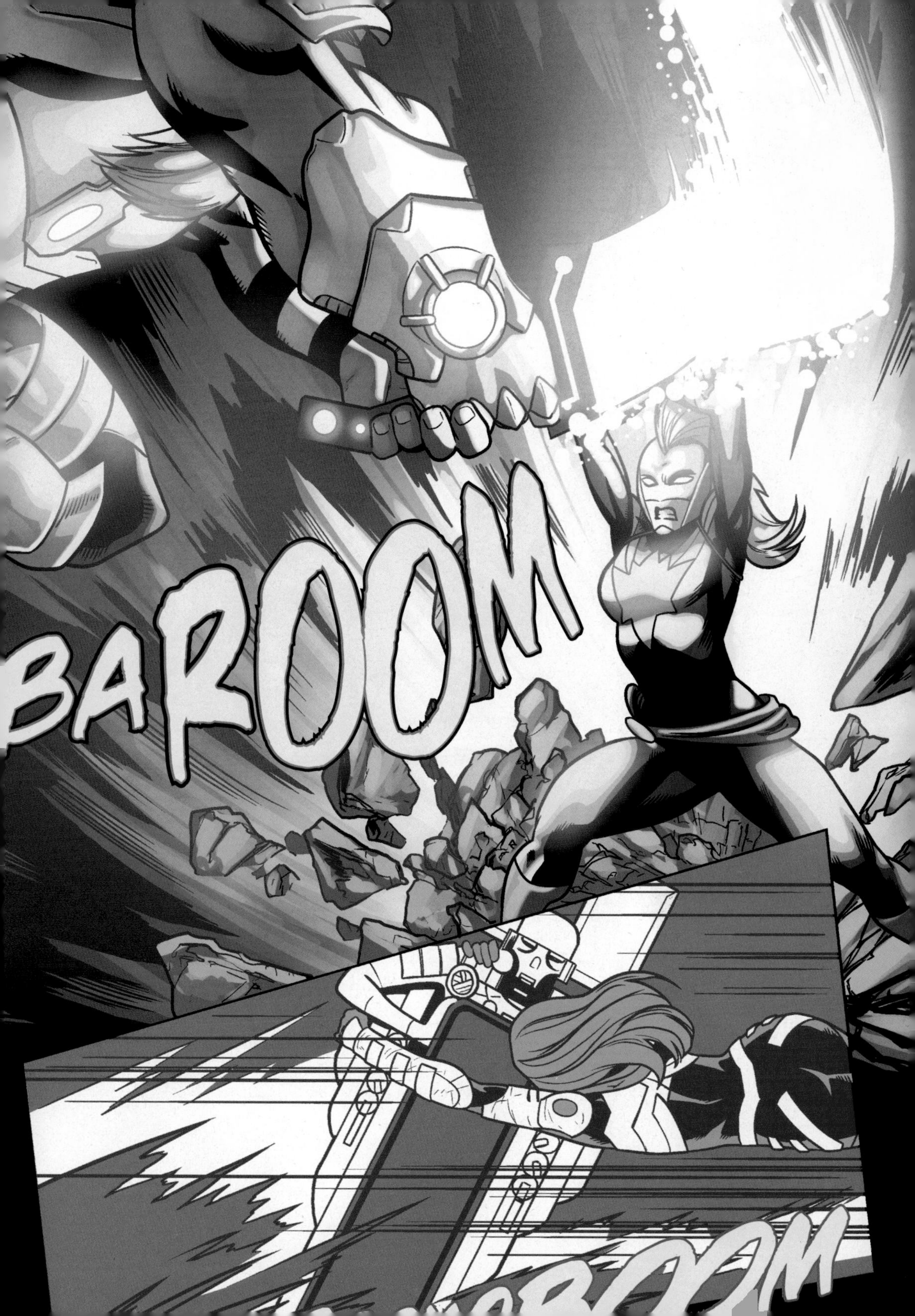
BAROOM

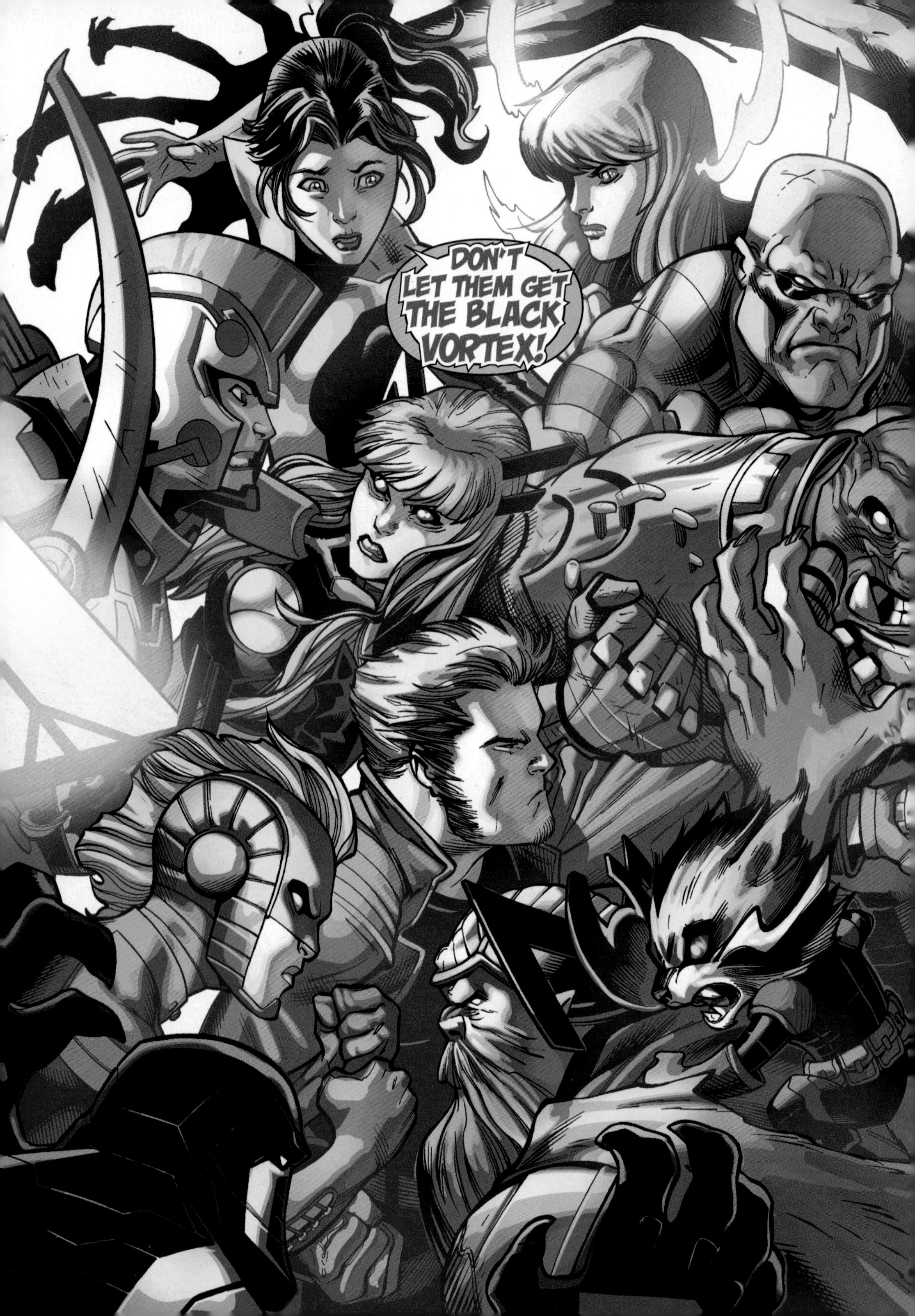
DON'T LET THEM GET THE BLACK VORTEX!

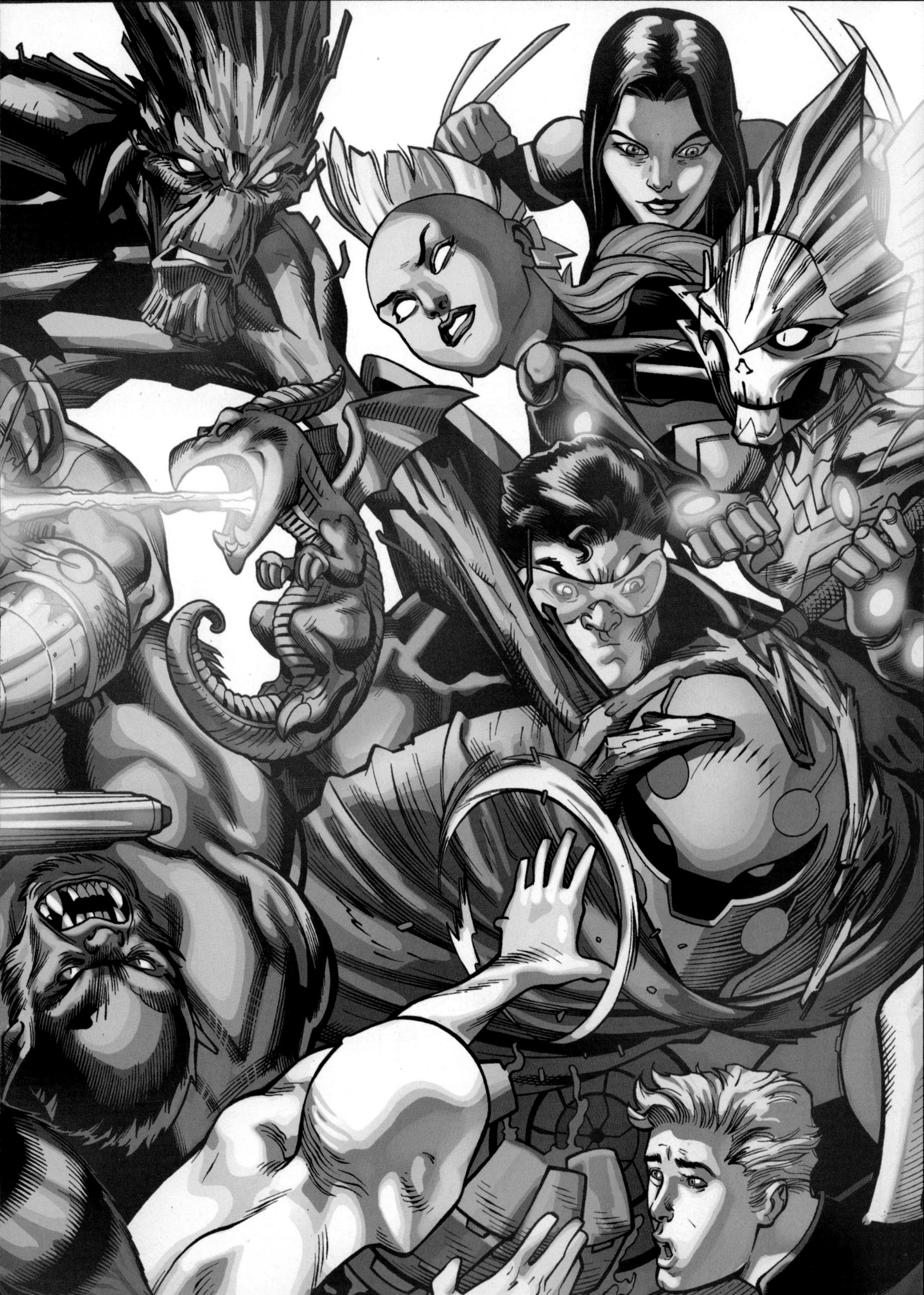

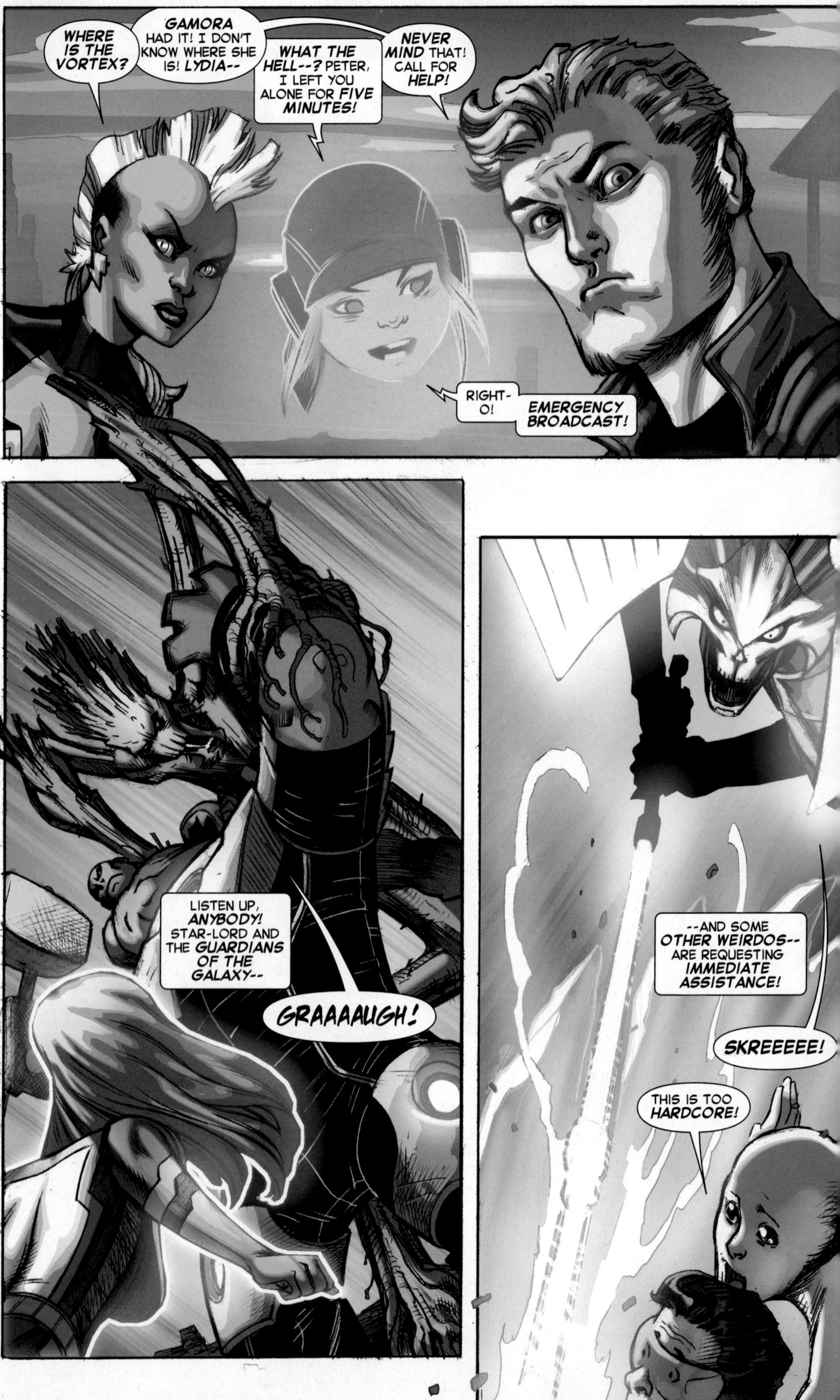
WHERE IS THE VORTEX?
GAMORA HAD IT! I DON'T KNOW WHERE SHE IS! LYDIA--
WHAT THE HELL--? PETER, I LEFT YOU ALONE FOR FIVE MINUTES!
NEVER MIND THAT! CALL FOR HELP!
RIGHT-O!
EMERGENCY BROADCAST!
LISTEN UP, ANYBODY! STAR-LORD AND THE GUARDIANS OF THE GALAXY--
GRAAAAUGH!
--AND SOME OTHER WEIRDOS-- ARE REQUESTING IMMEDIATE ASSISTANCE!
SKREEEEE!
THIS IS TOO HARDCORE!

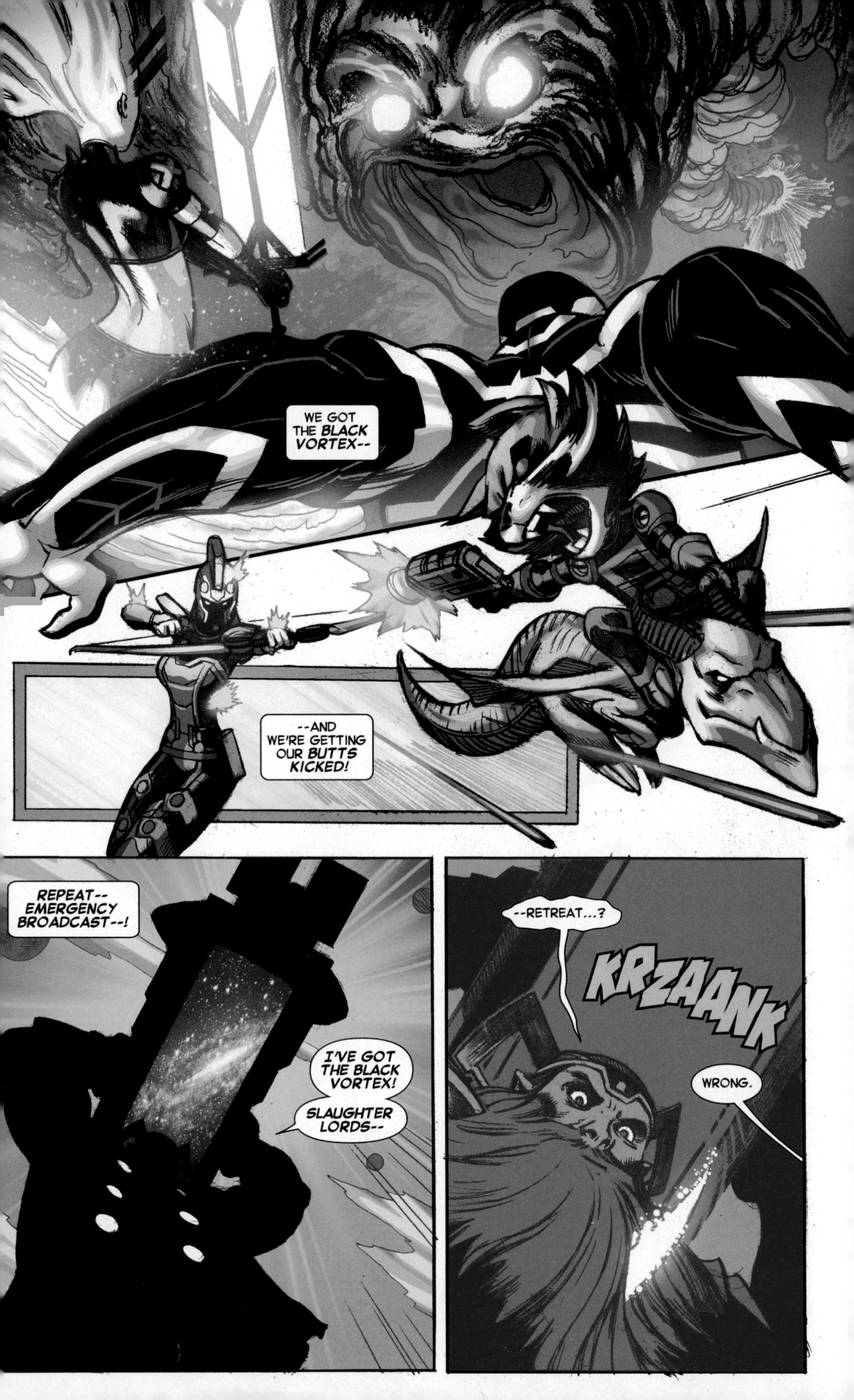
WE GOT THE BLACK VORTEX--
--AND WE'RE GETTING OUR BUTTS KICKED!
REPEAT-- EMERGENCY BROADCAST--!
I'VE GOT THE BLACK VORTEX!
SLAUGHTER LORDS--
--RETREAT...?
KRZAANK
WRONG.

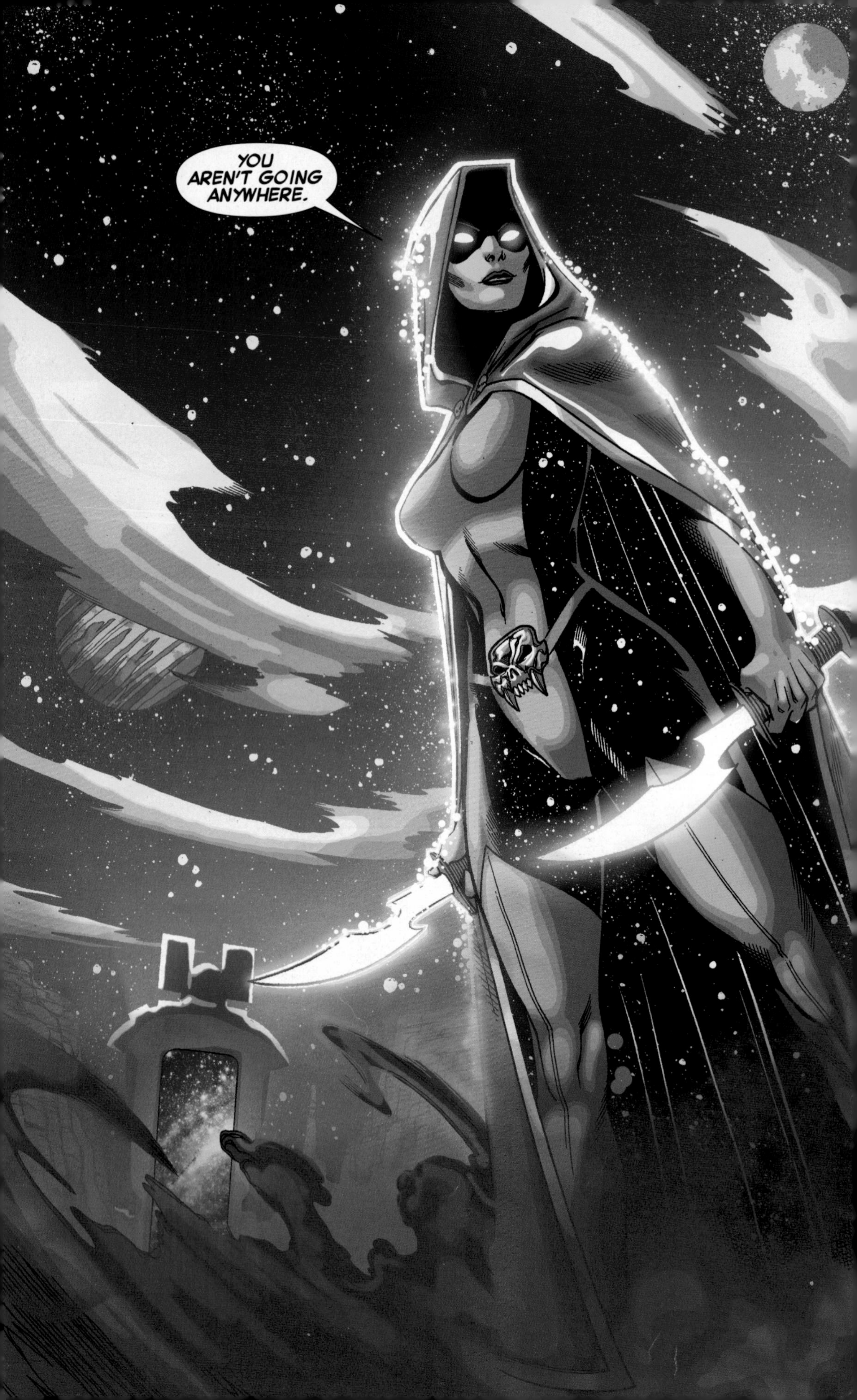
YOU AREN'T GOING ANYWHERE.

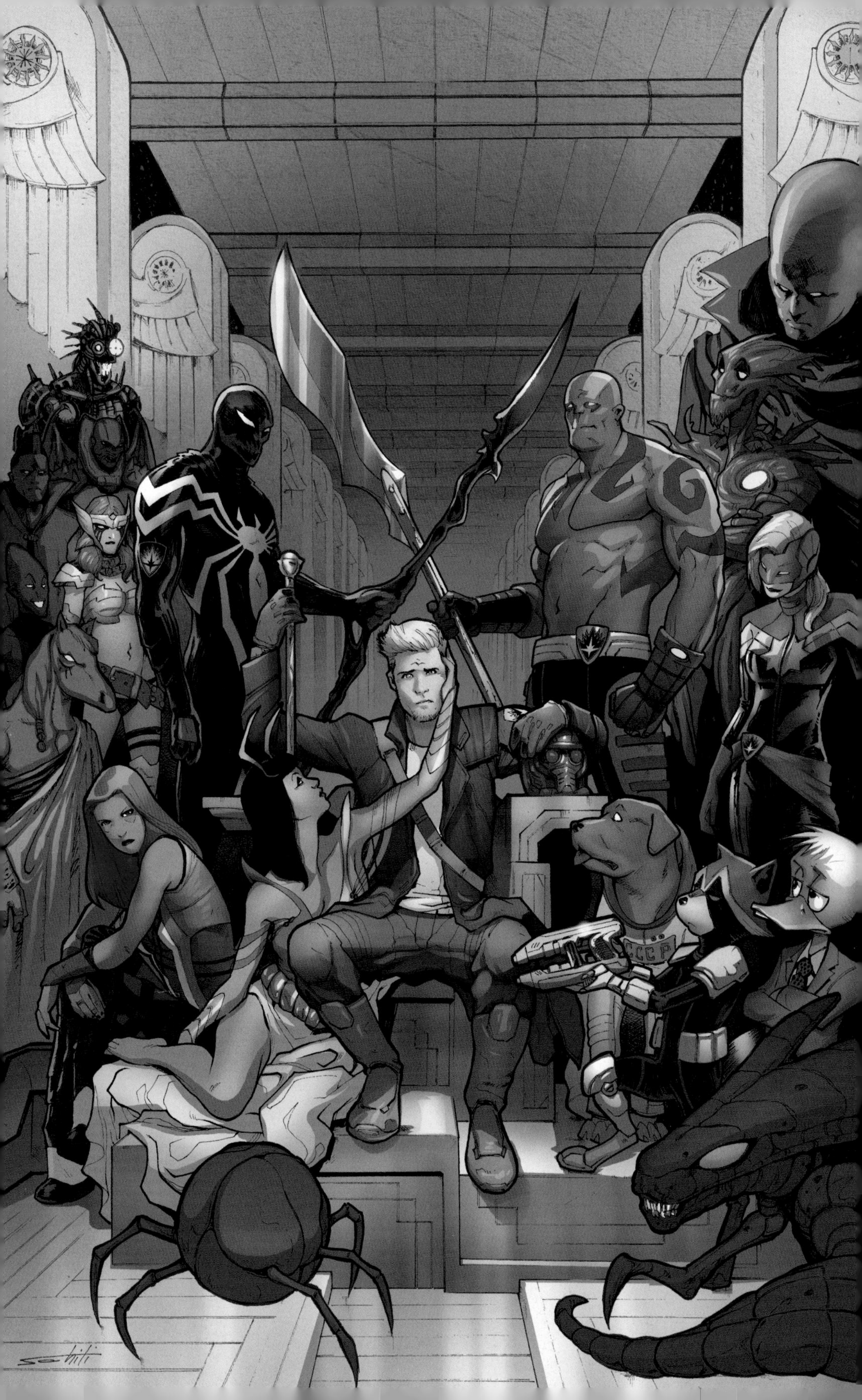

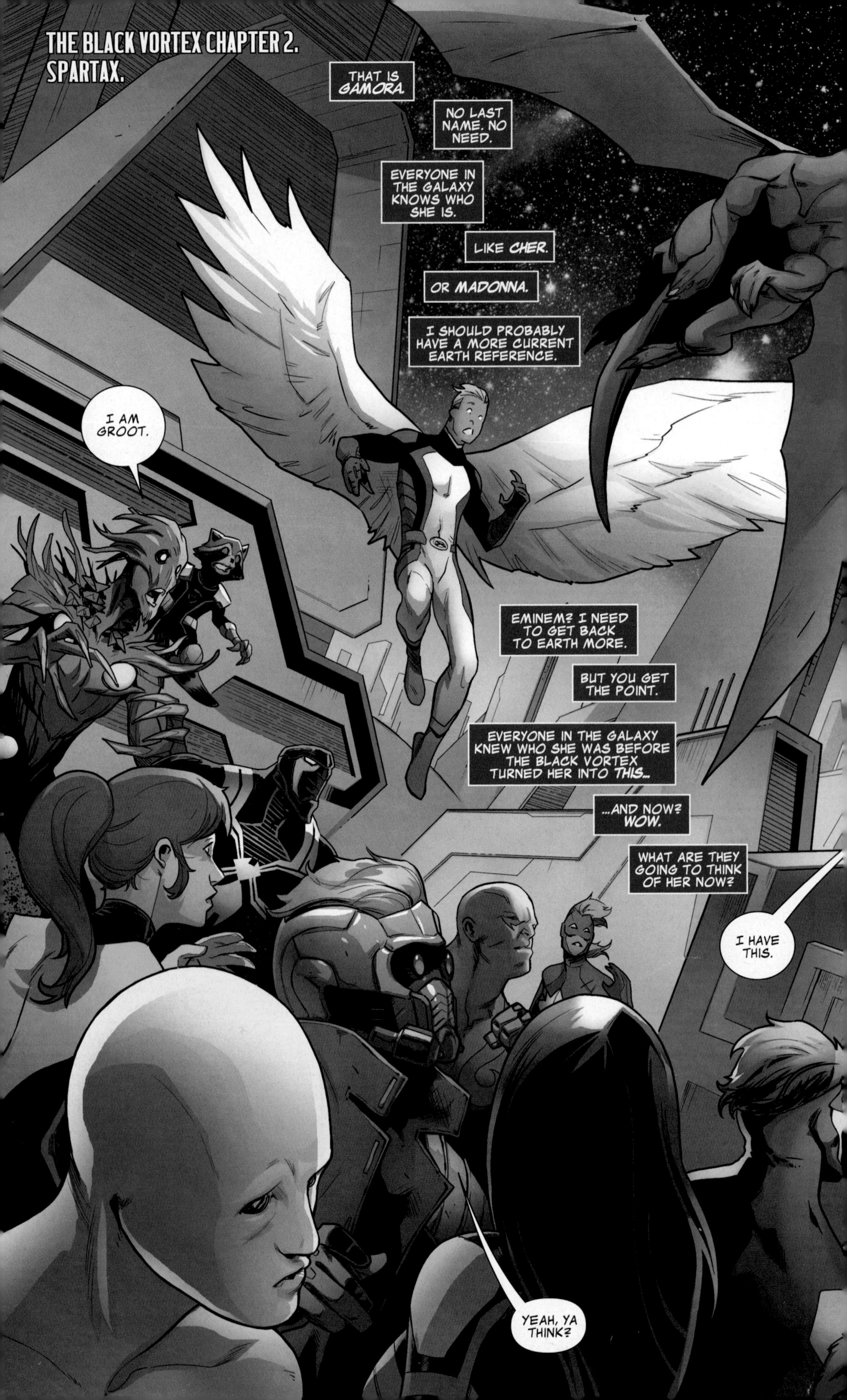
THE BLACK VORTEX CHAPTER 2.
SPARTAX.
THAT IS GAMORA.
NO LAST NAME. NO NEED.
EVERYONE IN THE GALAXY KNOWS WHO SHE IS.
LIKE CHER.
OR MADONNA.
I SHOULD PROBABLY HAVE A MORE CURRENT EARTH REFERENCE.
I AM GROOT.
EMINEM? I NEED TO GET BACK TO EARTH MORE.
BUT YOU GET THE POINT.
EVERYONE IN THE GALAXY KNEW WHO SHE WAS BEFORE THE BLACK VORTEX TURNED HER INTO THIS...
...AND NOW? WOW.
WHAT ARE THEY GOING TO THINK OF HER NOW?
I HAVE THIS.
YEAH, YA THINK?

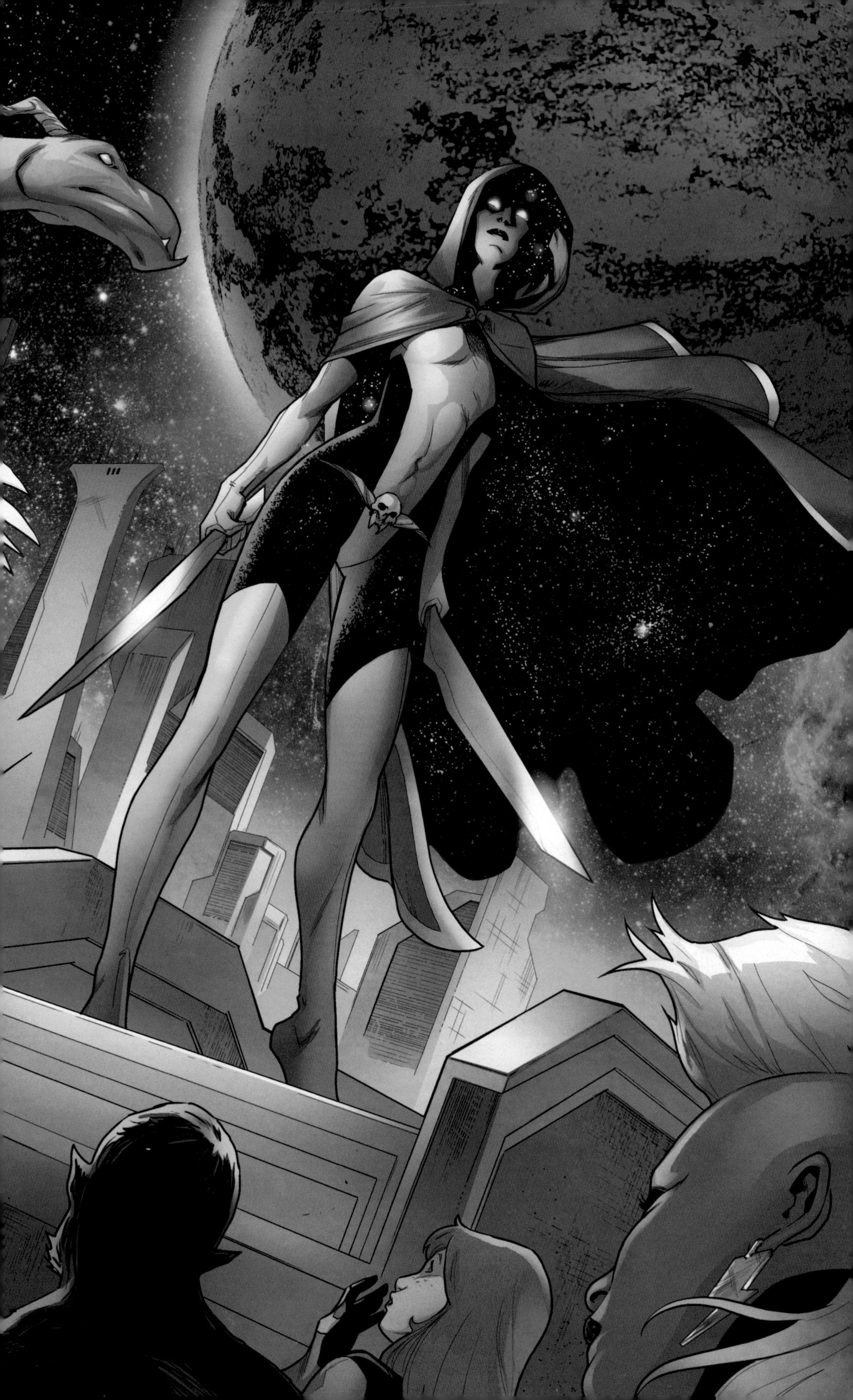

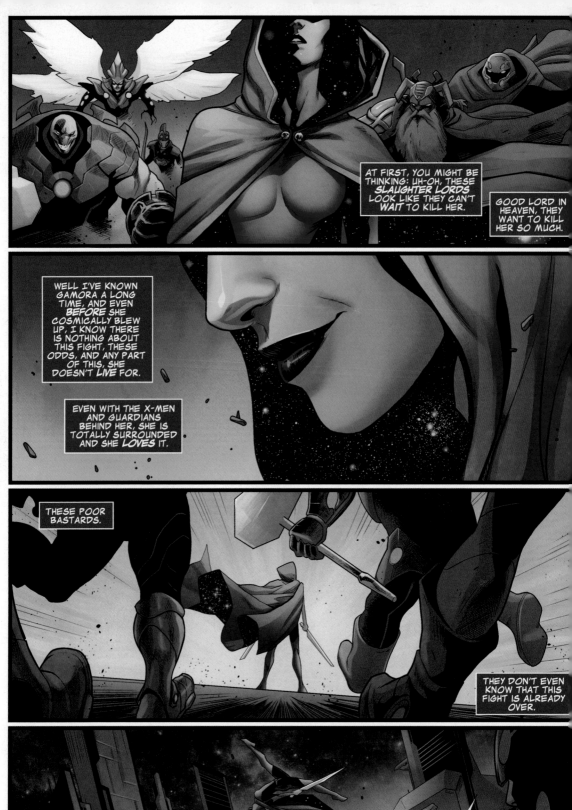

AT FIRST, YOU MIGHT BE THINKING: UH-OH, THESE *SLAUGHTER LORDS* LOOK LIKE THEY CAN'T *WAIT* TO KILL HER.

GOOD LORD IN HEAVEN, THEY WANT TO KILL HER SO MUCH.

WELL I'VE KNOWN GAMORA A LONG TIME, AND EVEN *BEFORE* SHE COSMICALLY BLEW UP, I KNOW THERE IS NOTHING ABOUT THIS FIGHT, THESE ODDS, AND ANY PART OF THIS, SHE DOESN'T *LIVE* FOR.

EVEN WITH THE X-MEN AND GUARDIANS BEHIND HER, SHE IS TOTALLY SURROUNDED AND SHE *LOVES* IT.

THESE POOR BASTARDS.

THEY DON'T EVEN KNOW THAT THIS FIGHT IS ALREADY OVER.

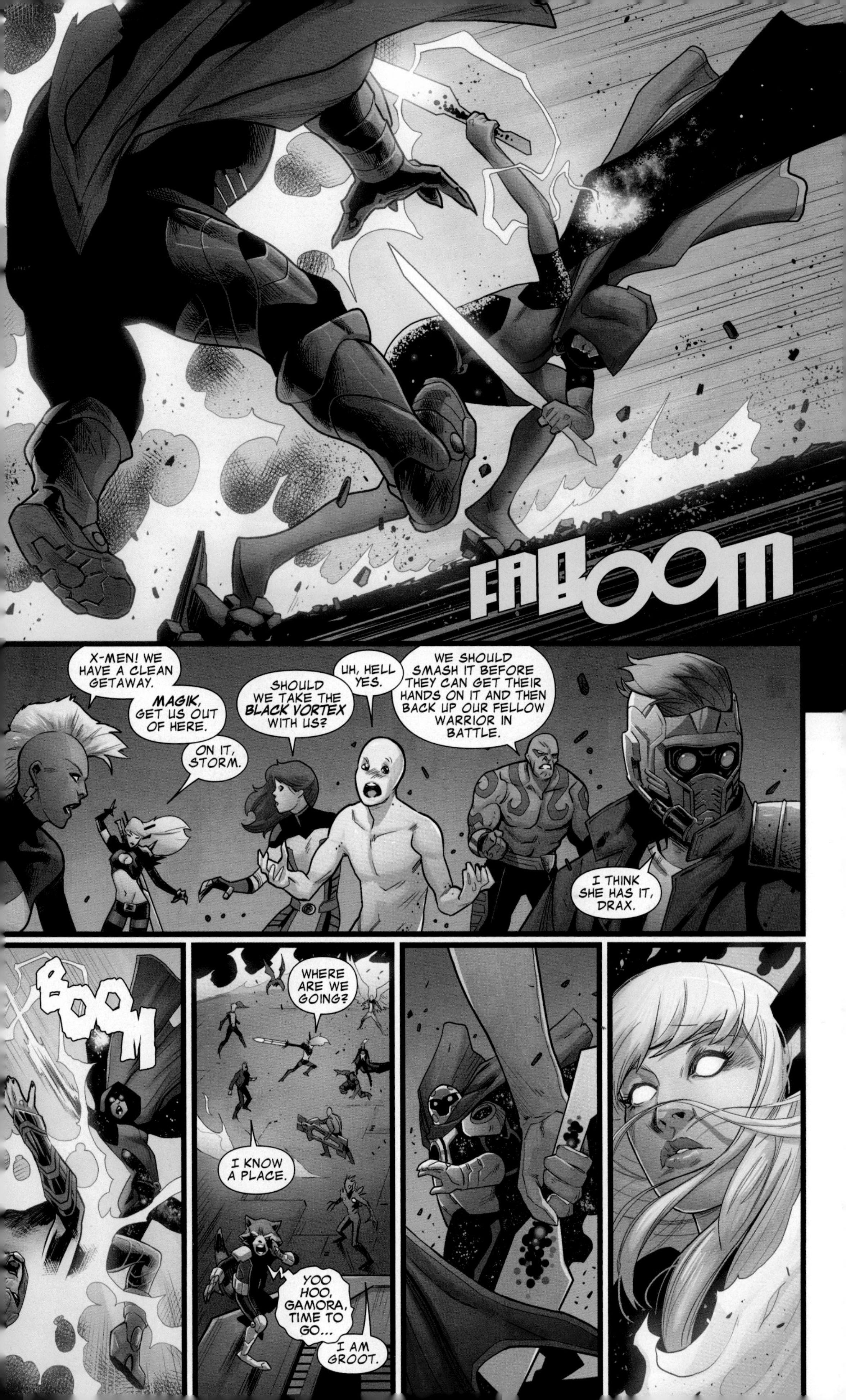
FABOOM
X-MEN! WE HAVE A CLEAN GETAWAY.
MAGIK, GET US OUT OF HERE.
ON IT, STORM.
SHOULD WE TAKE THE BLACK VORTEX WITH US?
UH, HELL YES.
WE SHOULD SMASH IT BEFORE THEY CAN GET THEIR HANDS ON IT AND THEN BACK UP OUR FELLOW WARRIOR IN BATTLE.
I THINK SHE HAS IT, DRAX.
BOOM
WHERE ARE WE GOING?
I KNOW A PLACE.
YOO HOO, GAMORA, TIME TO GO...
I AM GROOT.

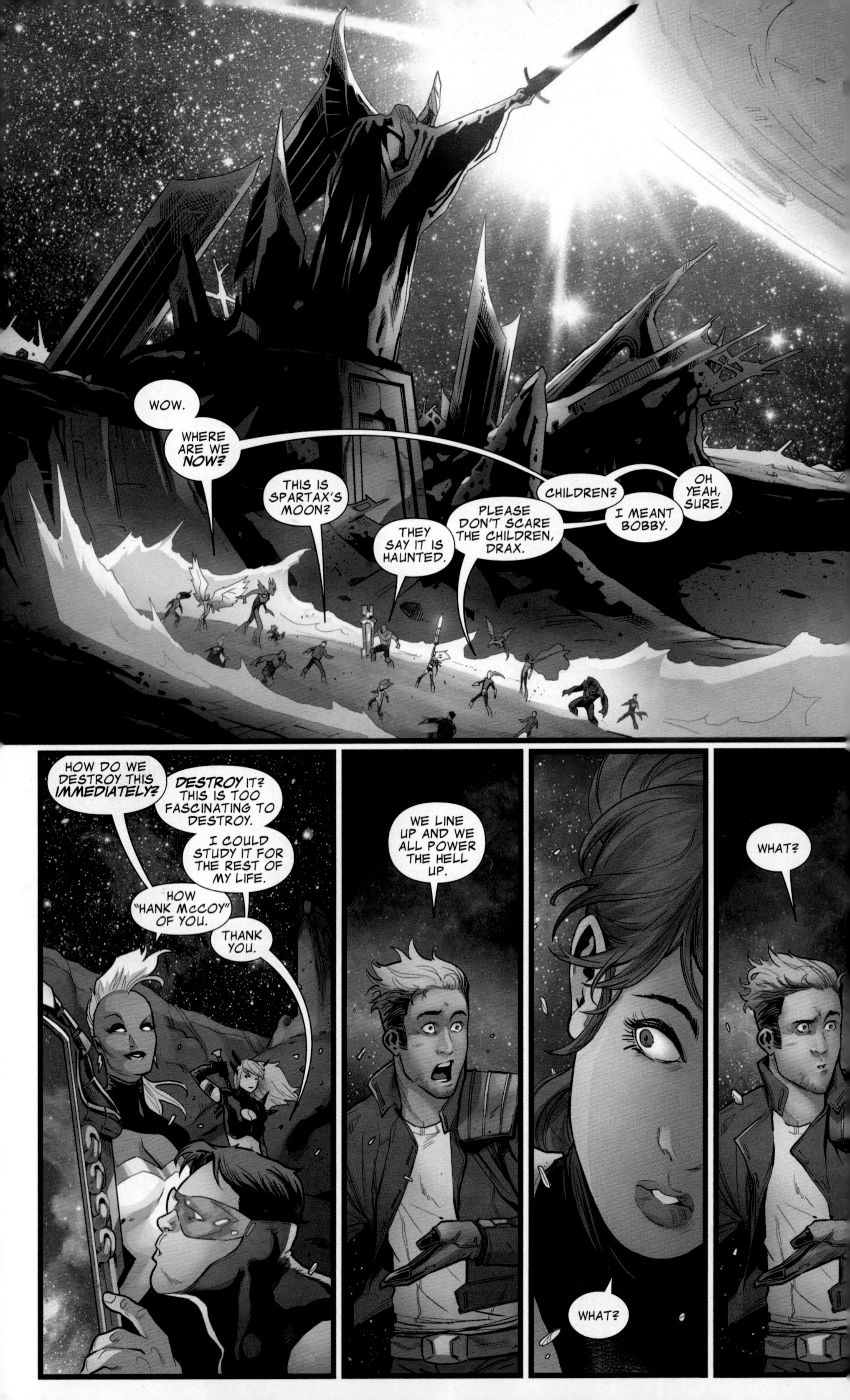
WOW.
WHERE ARE WE NOW?
THIS IS SPARTAX'S MOON?
THEY SAY IT IS HAUNTED.
PLEASE DON'T SCARE THE CHILDREN, DRAX.
CHILDREN?
I MEANT BOBBY.
OH YEAH, SURE.
HOW DO WE DESTROY THIS IMMEDIATELY?
DESTROY IT? THIS IS TOO FASCINATING TO DESTROY.
I COULD STUDY IT FOR THE REST OF MY LIFE.
HOW "HANK McCOY" OF YOU.
THANK YOU.
WE LINE UP AND WE ALL POWER THE HELL UP.
WHAT?
WHAT?

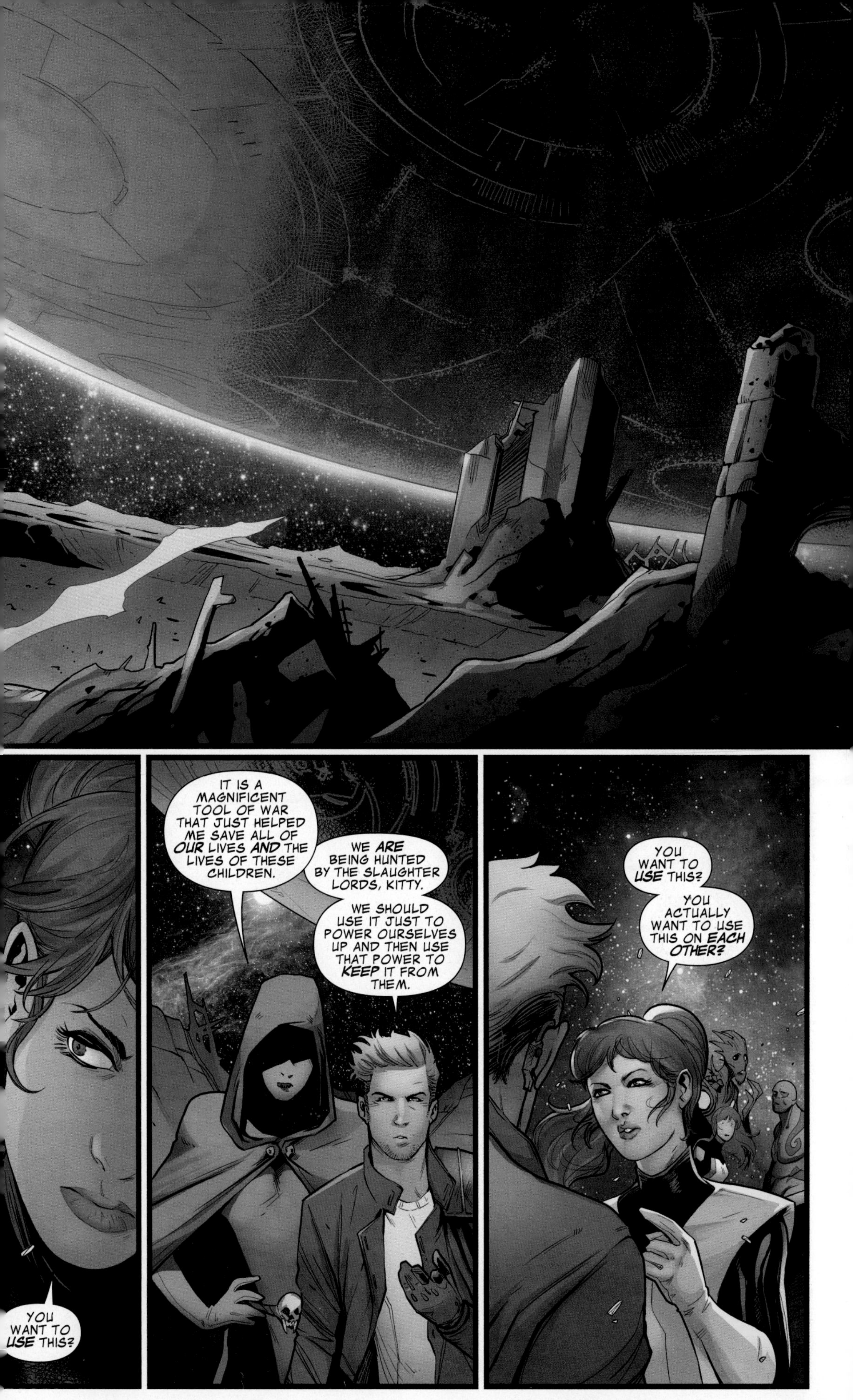
YOU WANT TO USE THIS?
IT IS A MAGNIFICENT TOOL OF WAR THAT JUST HELPED ME SAVE ALL OF OUR LIVES AND THE LIVES OF THESE CHILDREN.
WE ARE BEING HUNTED BY THE SLAUGHTER LORDS, KITTY.
WE SHOULD USE IT JUST TO POWER OURSELVES UP AND THEN USE THAT POWER TO KEEP IT FROM THEM.
YOU WANT TO USE THIS?
YOU ACTUALLY WANT TO USE THIS ON EACH OTHER?

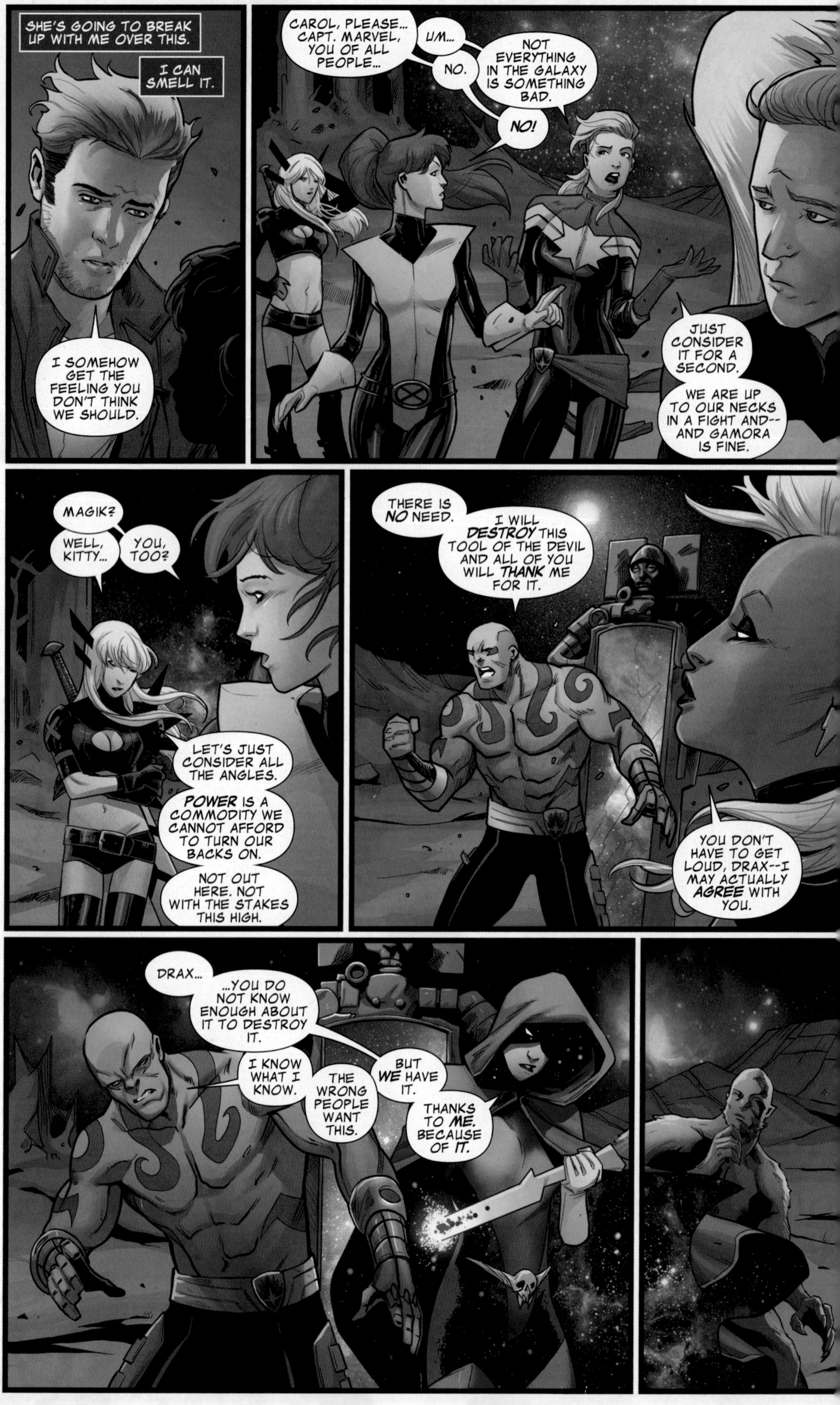

SHE'S GOING TO BREAK UP WITH ME OVER THIS.
I CAN SMELL IT.
I SOMEHOW GET THE FEELING YOU DON'T THINK WE SHOULD.
CAROL, PLEASE... CAPT. MARVEL, YOU OF ALL PEOPLE...
UM...
NO.
NOT EVERYTHING IN THE GALAXY IS SOMETHING BAD.
NO!
JUST CONSIDER IT FOR A SECOND.
WE ARE UP TO OUR NECKS IN A FIGHT AND-- AND GAMORA IS FINE.
MAGIK?
WELL, KITTY...
YOU, TOO?
LET'S JUST CONSIDER ALL THE ANGLES.
POWER IS A COMMODITY WE CANNOT AFFORD TO TURN OUR BACKS ON.
NOT OUT HERE. NOT WITH THE STAKES THIS HIGH.
THERE IS NO NEED.
I WILL DESTROY THIS TOOL OF THE DEVIL AND ALL OF YOU WILL THANK ME FOR IT.
YOU DON'T HAVE TO GET LOUD, DRAX--I MAY ACTUALLY AGREE WITH YOU.
DRAX...
...YOU DO NOT KNOW ENOUGH ABOUT IT TO DESTROY IT.
I KNOW WHAT I KNOW.
THE WRONG PEOPLE WANT THIS.
BUT WE HAVE IT.
THANKS TO ME. BECAUSE OF IT.

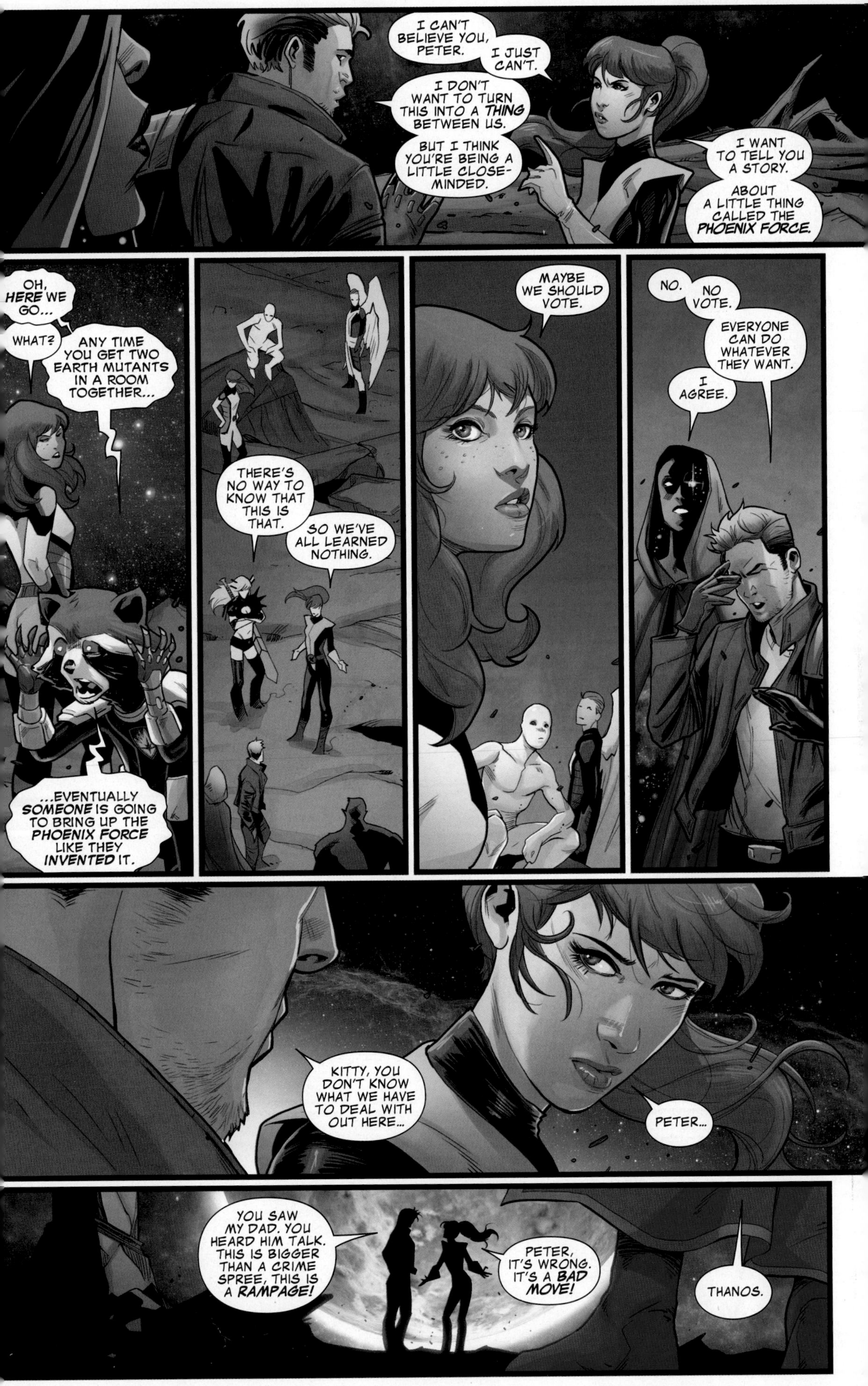
I CAN'T BELIEVE YOU, PETER.
I JUST CAN'T.
I DON'T WANT TO TURN THIS INTO A THING BETWEEN US.
BUT I THINK YOU'RE BEING A LITTLE CLOSE-MINDED.
I WANT TO TELL YOU A STORY.
ABOUT A LITTLE THING CALLED THE PHOENIX FORCE.
OH, HERE WE GO...
WHAT?
ANY TIME YOU GET TWO EARTH MUTANTS IN A ROOM TOGETHER...
...EVENTUALLY SOMEONE IS GOING TO BRING UP THE PHOENIX FORCE LIKE THEY INVENTED IT.
THERE'S NO WAY TO KNOW THAT THIS IS THAT.
SO WE'VE ALL LEARNED NOTHING.
MAYBE WE SHOULD VOTE.
NO.
NO VOTE.
EVERYONE CAN DO WHATEVER THEY WANT.
I AGREE.
KITTY, YOU DON'T KNOW WHAT WE HAVE TO DEAL WITH OUT HERE...
PETER...
YOU SAW MY DAD. YOU HEARD HIM TALK. THIS IS BIGGER THAN A CRIME SPREE, THIS IS A RAMPAGE!
PETER, IT'S WRONG. IT'S A BAD MOVE!
THANOS.

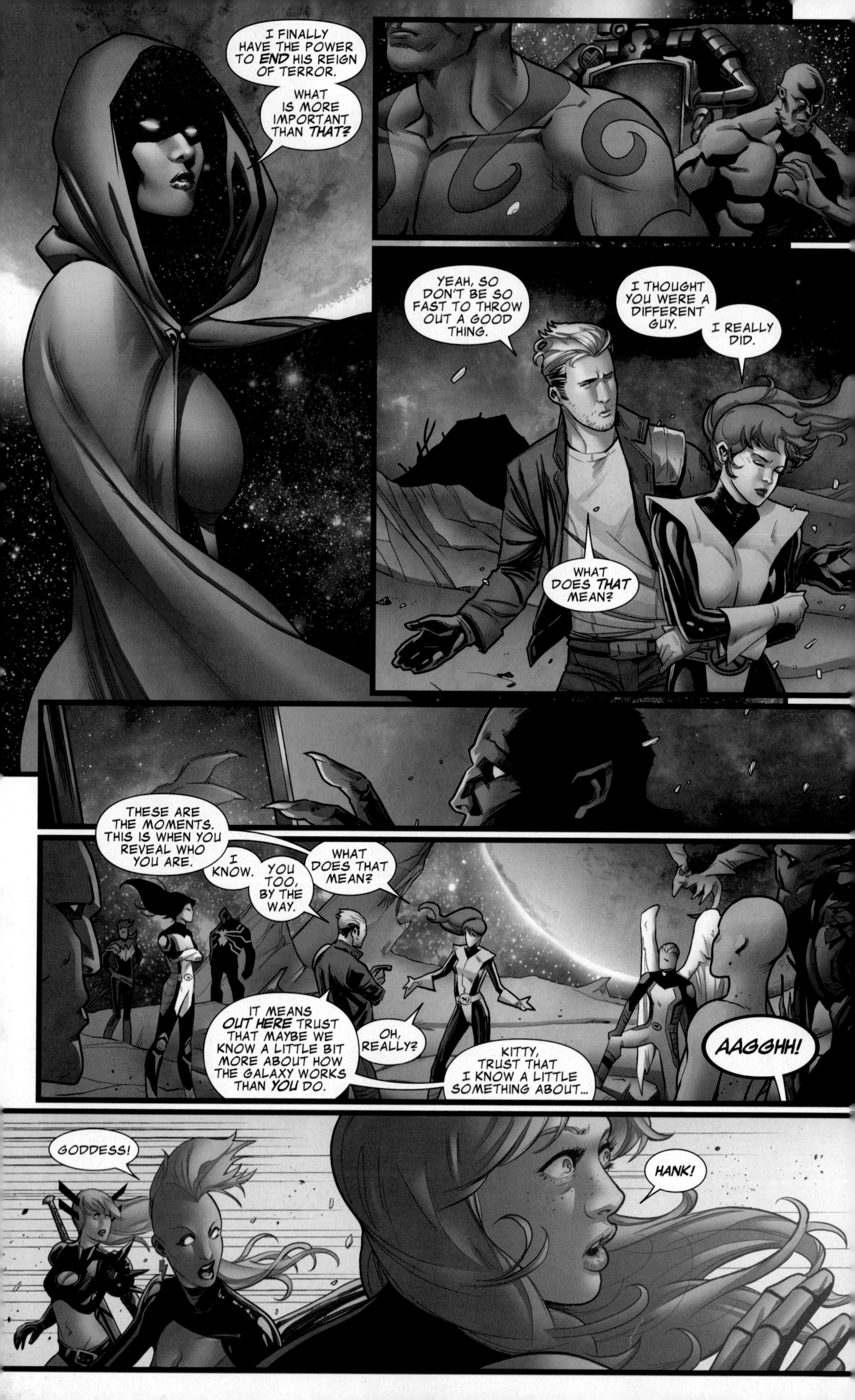
I FINALLY HAVE THE POWER TO END HIS REIGN OF TERROR.
WHAT IS MORE IMPORTANT THAN THAT?
YEAH, SO DON'T BE SO FAST TO THROW OUT A GOOD THING.
I THOUGHT YOU WERE A DIFFERENT GUY.
I REALLY DID.
WHAT DOES THAT MEAN?
THESE ARE THE MOMENTS. THIS IS WHEN YOU REVEAL WHO YOU ARE.
I KNOW.
YOU TOO, BY THE WAY.
WHAT DOES THAT MEAN?
IT MEANS OUT HERE TRUST THAT MAYBE WE KNOW A LITTLE BIT MORE ABOUT HOW THE GALAXY WORKS THAN YOU DO.
OH, REALLY?
KITTY, TRUST THAT I KNOW A LITTLE SOMETHING ABOUT...
AAGGHH!
GODDESS!
HANK!

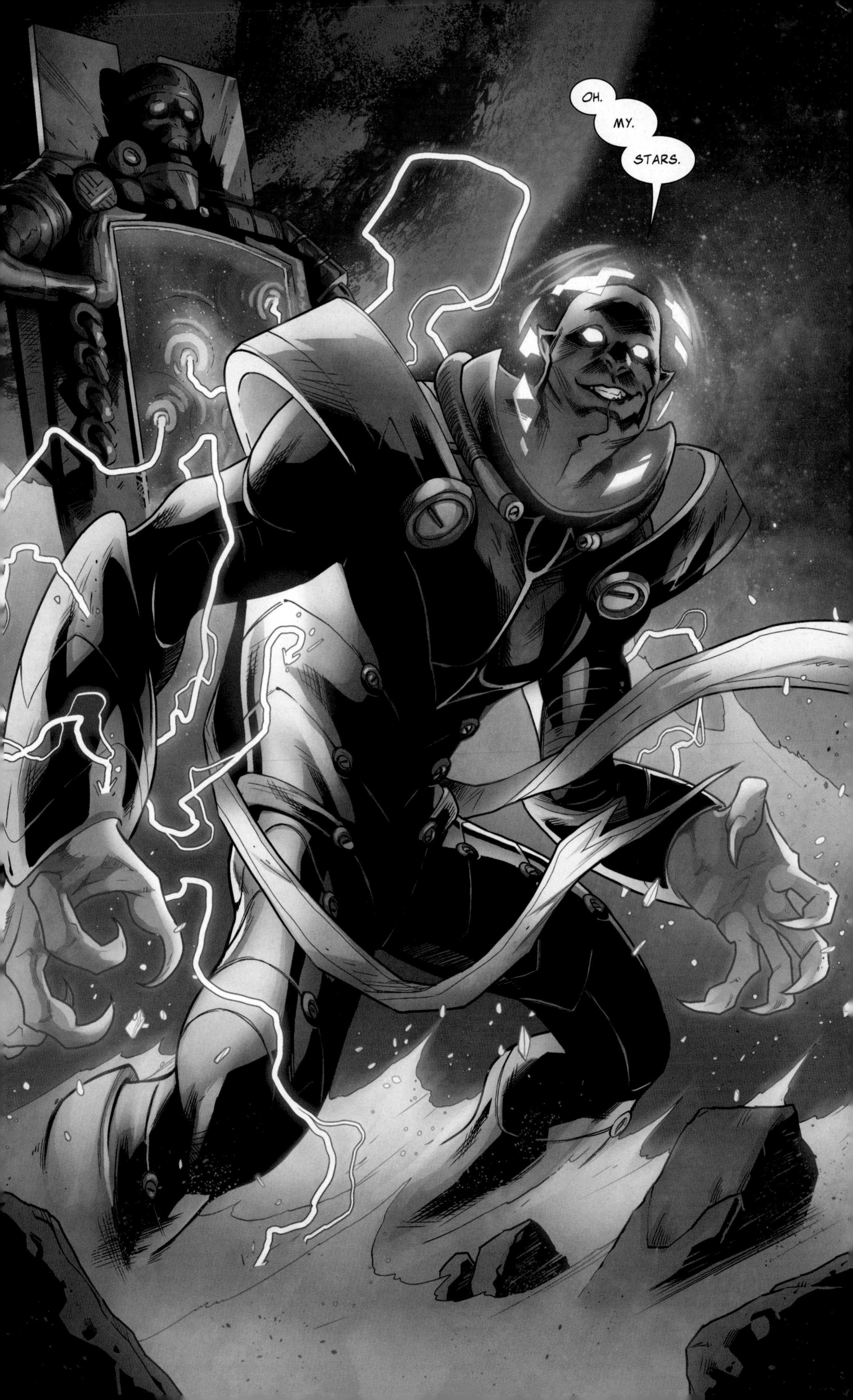
OH.
MY.
STARS.

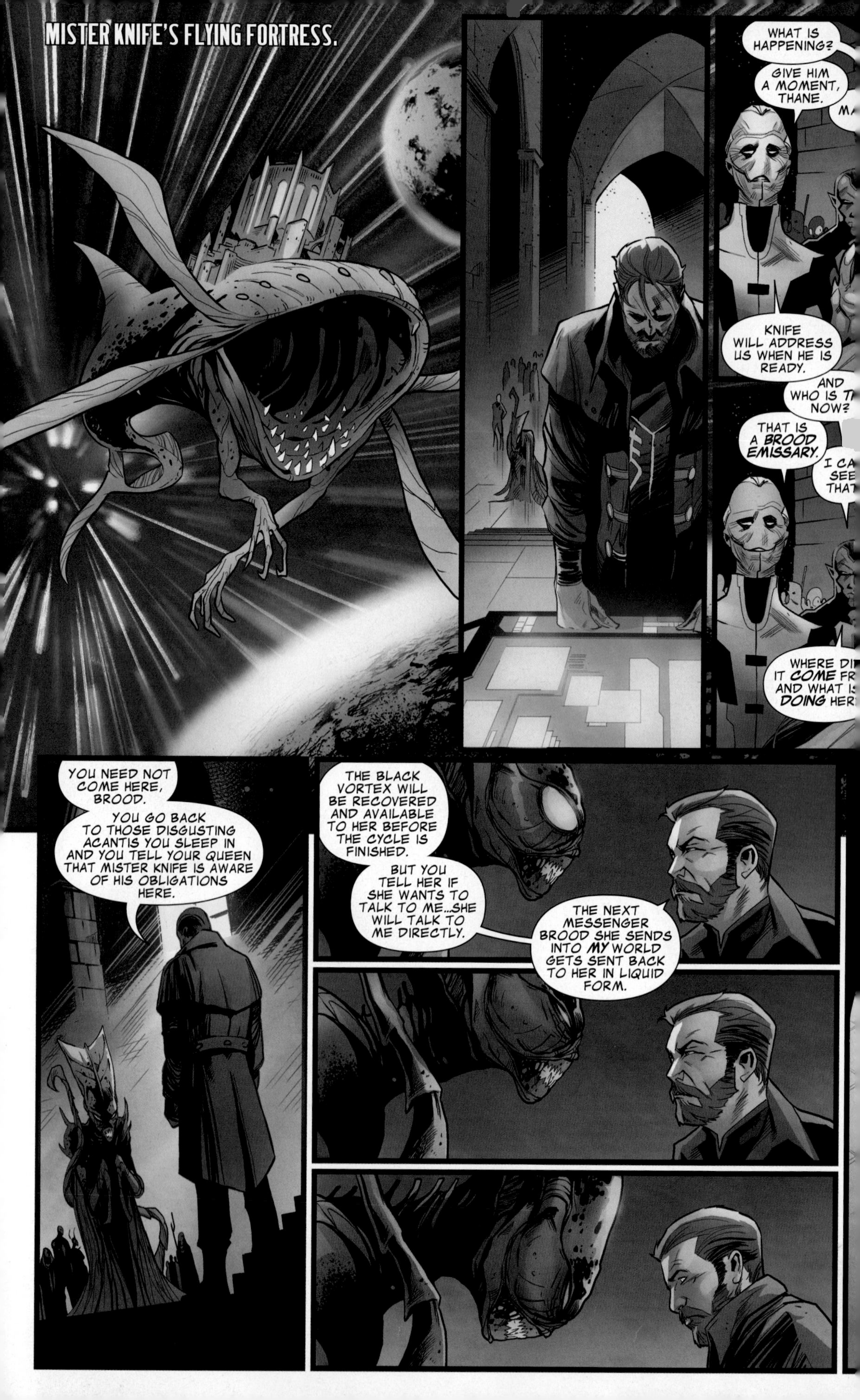
MISTER KNIFE'S FLYING FORTRESS.
WHAT IS HAPPENING?
GIVE HIM A MOMENT, THANE.
KNIFE WILL ADDRESS US WHEN HE IS READY.
AND WHO IS T NOW?
THAT IS A BROOD EMISSARY.
I CA SEE THAT
WHERE DI IT COME FR AND WHAT I DOING HER
YOU NEED NOT COME HERE, BROOD.
YOU GO BACK TO THOSE DISGUSTING ACANTIS YOU SLEEP IN AND YOU TELL YOUR QUEEN THAT MISTER KNIFE IS AWARE OF HIS OBLIGATIONS HERE.
THE BLACK VORTEX WILL BE RECOVERED AND AVAILABLE TO HER BEFORE THE CYCLE IS FINISHED.
BUT YOU TELL HER IF SHE WANTS TO TALK TO ME...SHE WILL TALK TO ME DIRECTLY.
THE NEXT MESSENGER BROOD SHE SENDS INTO MY WORLD GETS SENT BACK TO HER IN LIQUID FORM.

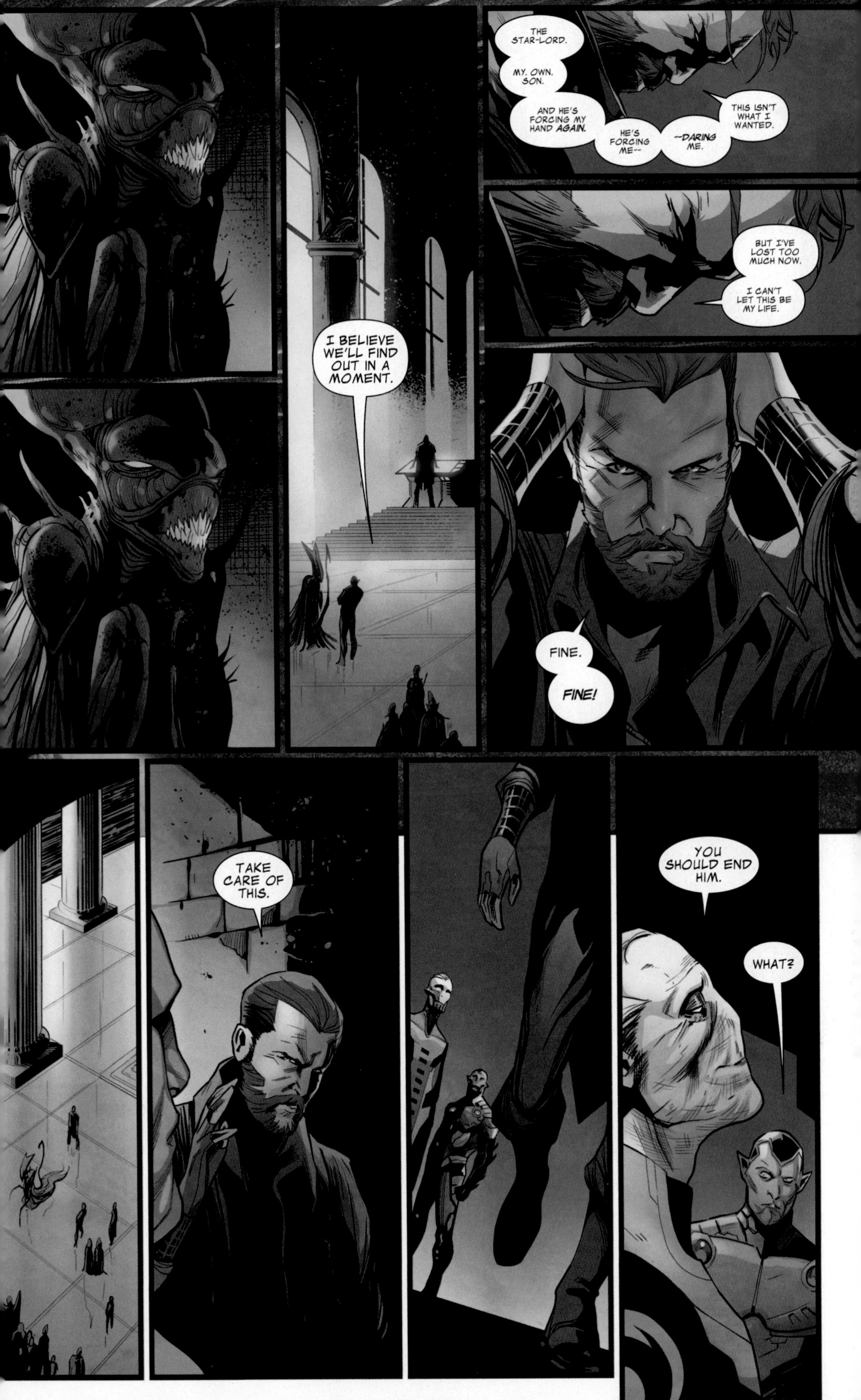
I BELIEVE WE'LL FIND OUT IN A MOMENT.
THE STAR-LORD.
MY. OWN. SON.
AND HE'S FORCING MY HAND AGAIN.
HE'S FORCING ME--
--DARING ME.
THIS ISN'T WHAT I WANTED.
BUT I'VE LOST TOO MUCH NOW.
I CAN'T LET THIS BE MY LIFE.
FINE.
FINE!
TAKE CARE OF THIS.
YOU SHOULD END HIM.
WHAT?

YOU HEARD ME.

WE ARE BUILDING SOMETHING HERE.

SOMETHING TO FEAR. SOMETHING OF MATTER.

OF IMPORT.

WE ARE CHANGING THE BALANCE OF POWER IN THE GALAXY AND THAT IS SOMETHING THIS GALAXY *DESPERATELY* NEEDS.

AND HE, THAT *MAN*, WITH EVERY STEP FORWARD IS REVEALING THAT HE IS NOT THE MAN TO TAKE US THERE.

SO WE *KILL* HIM?

THAT'S NOT NICE.

YOUR FATHER IS A MAD TITAN. NO ONE WOULD ARGUE THAT.

BUT IF HE HAD THE VISION AND CLARITY YOU HAVE...HE WOULD OWN THIS GALAXY.

HE WOULD ABSOLUTELY *OWN* IT.

THANE... YOU HAVE ALL OF YOUR FATHER'S *STRENGTH OF SPIRIT* AND NONE OF HIS *DEFECTS*.

YOU...CAN *LEAD*.

GO BACK TO WHEREVER YOU *DISAPPEAR* TO.

YOU WILL NOT SPEAK THESE WORDS TO ME AGAIN.

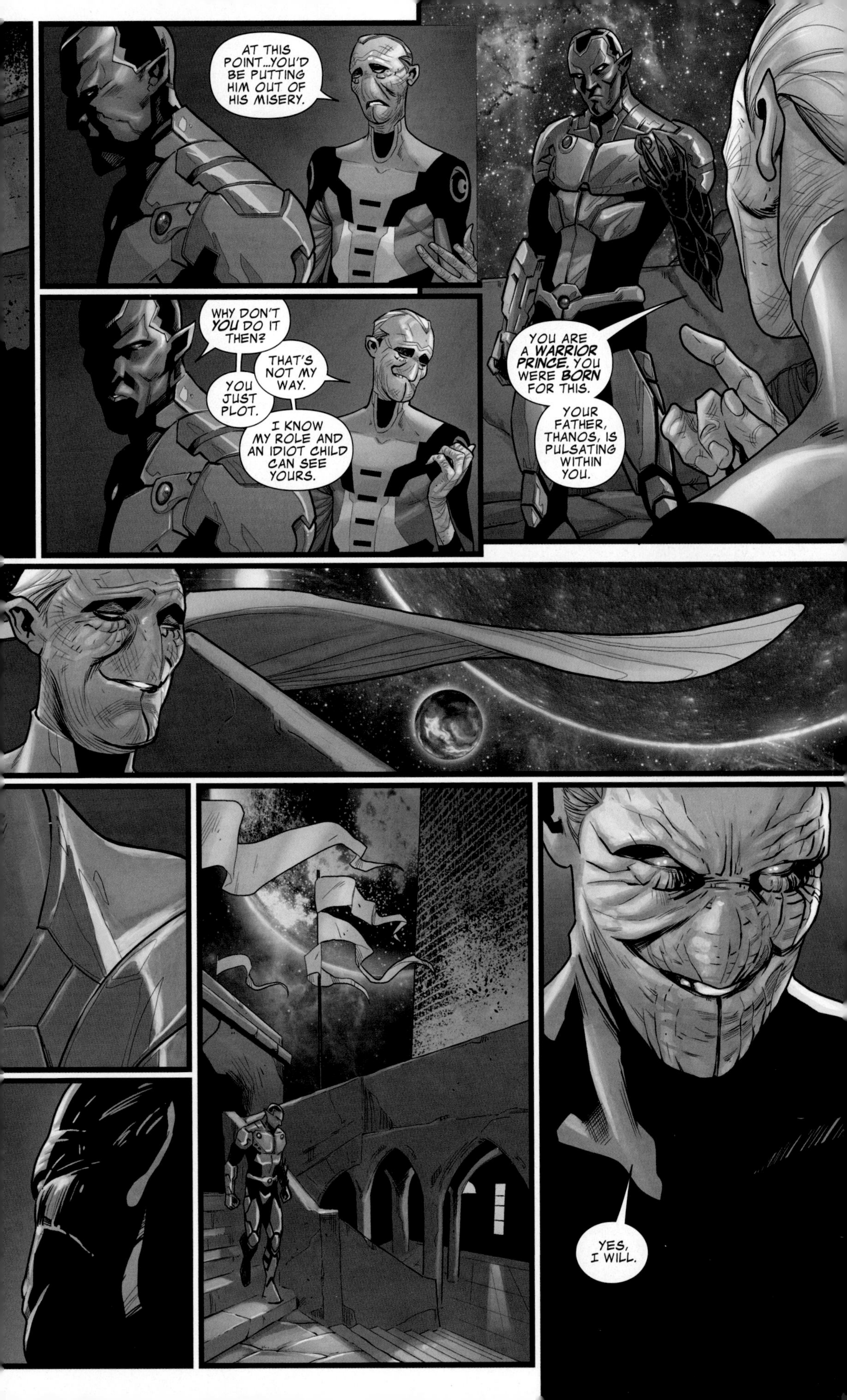
AT THIS POINT...YOU'D BE PUTTING HIM OUT OF HIS MISERY.
WHY DON'T *YOU* DO IT THEN?
THAT'S NOT MY WAY.
YOU JUST PLOT.
I KNOW MY ROLE AND AN IDIOT CHILD CAN SEE YOURS.
YOU ARE A **WARRIOR PRINCE.** YOU WERE **BORN** FOR THIS.
YOUR FATHER, THANOS, IS PULSATING WITHIN YOU.
YES, I WILL.

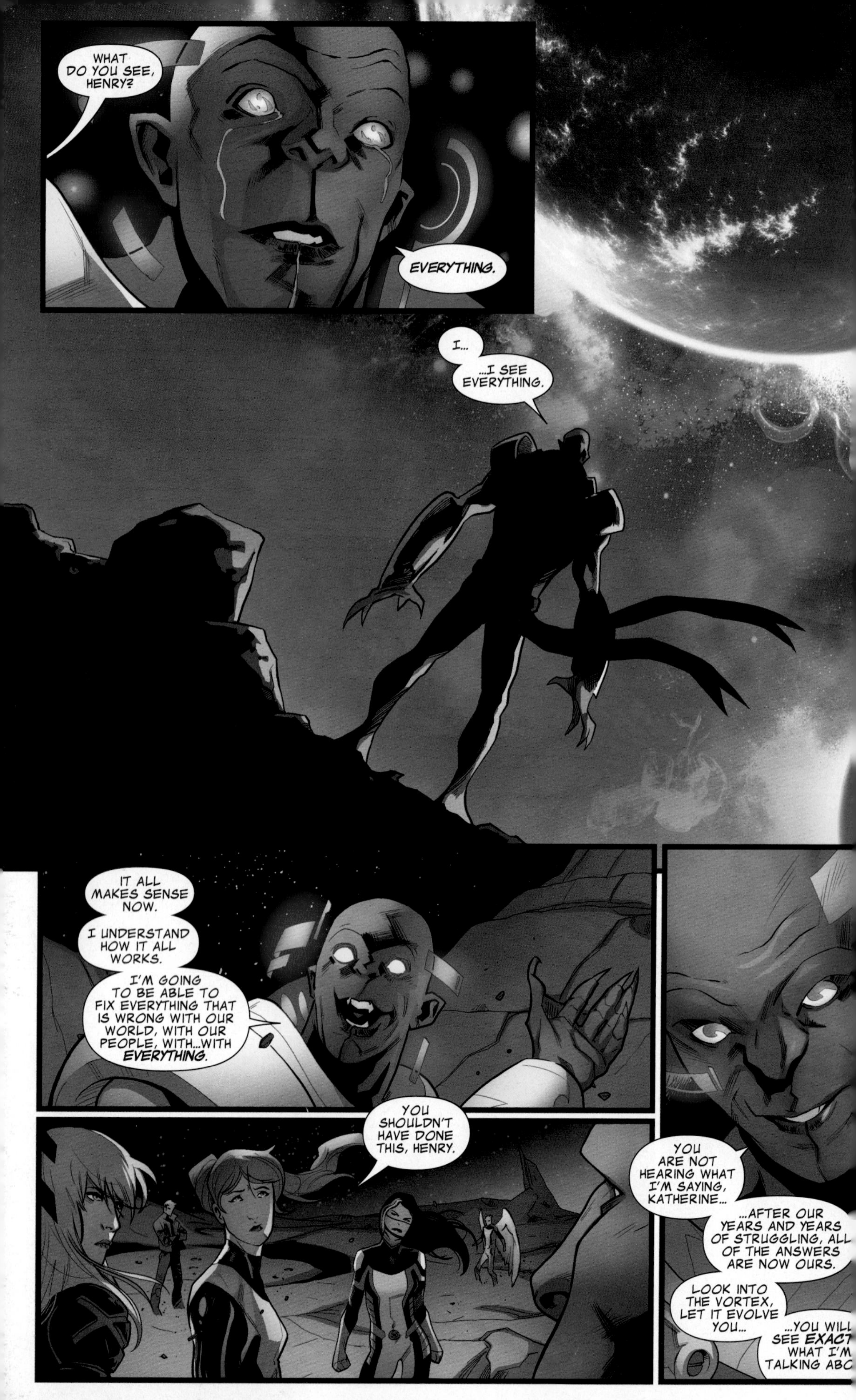

WHAT DO YOU SEE, HENRY?
EVERYTHING.
I...
...I SEE EVERYTHING.
IT ALL MAKES SENSE NOW.
I UNDERSTAND HOW IT ALL WORKS.
I'M GOING TO BE ABLE TO FIX EVERYTHING THAT IS WRONG WITH OUR WORLD, WITH OUR PEOPLE, WITH...WITH EVERYTHING.
YOU SHOULDN'T HAVE DONE THIS, HENRY.
YOU ARE NOT HEARING WHAT I'M SAYING, KATHERINE...
...AFTER OUR YEARS AND YEARS OF STRUGGLING, ALL OF THE ANSWERS ARE NOW OURS.
LOOK INTO THE VORTEX, LET IT EVOLVE YOU...
...YOU WILL SEE EXACT WHAT I'M TALKING ABC

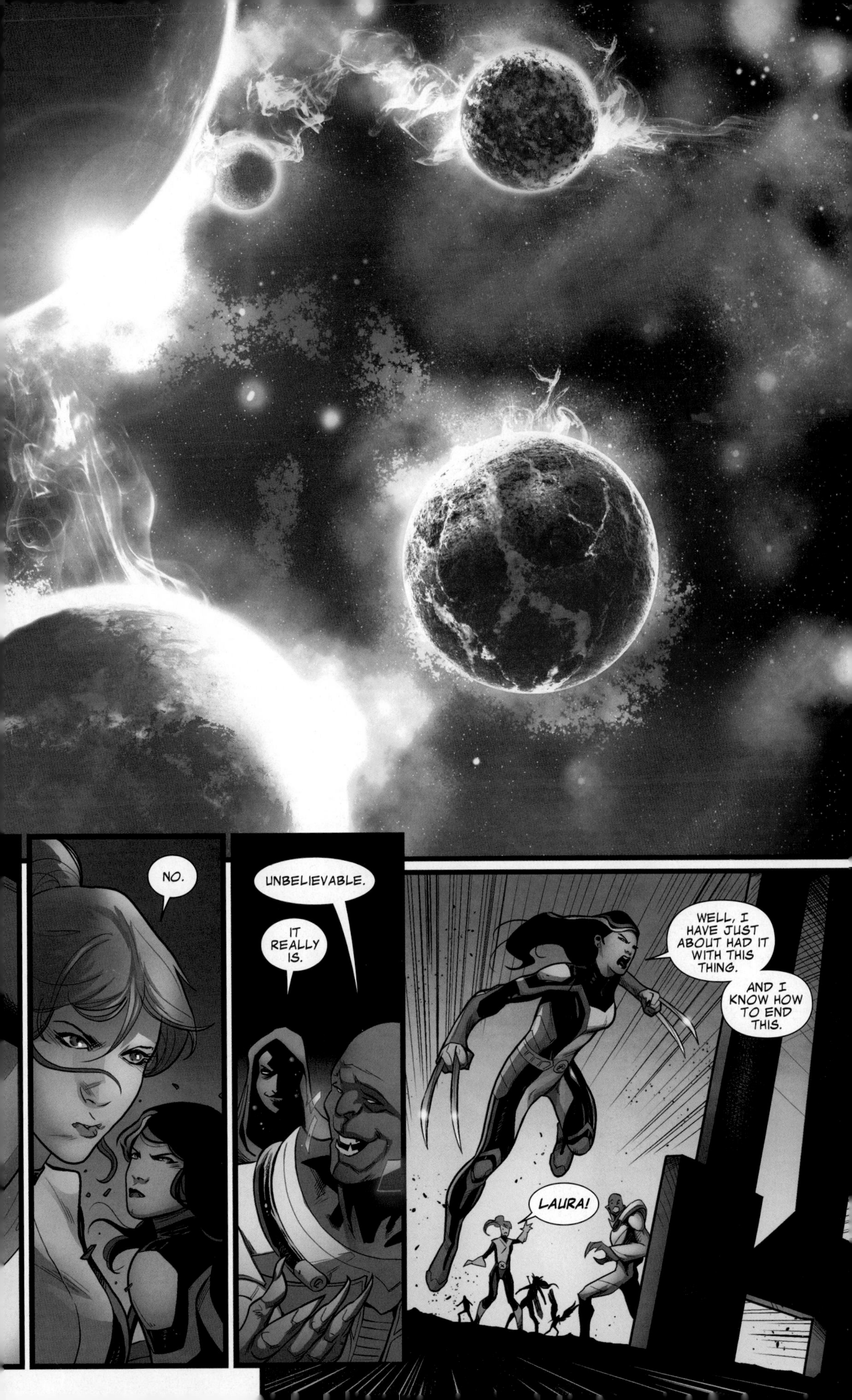
NO.
UNBELIEVABLE.
IT REALLY IS.
WELL, I HAVE JUST ABOUT HAD IT WITH THIS THING.
AND I KNOW HOW TO END THIS.
LAURA!

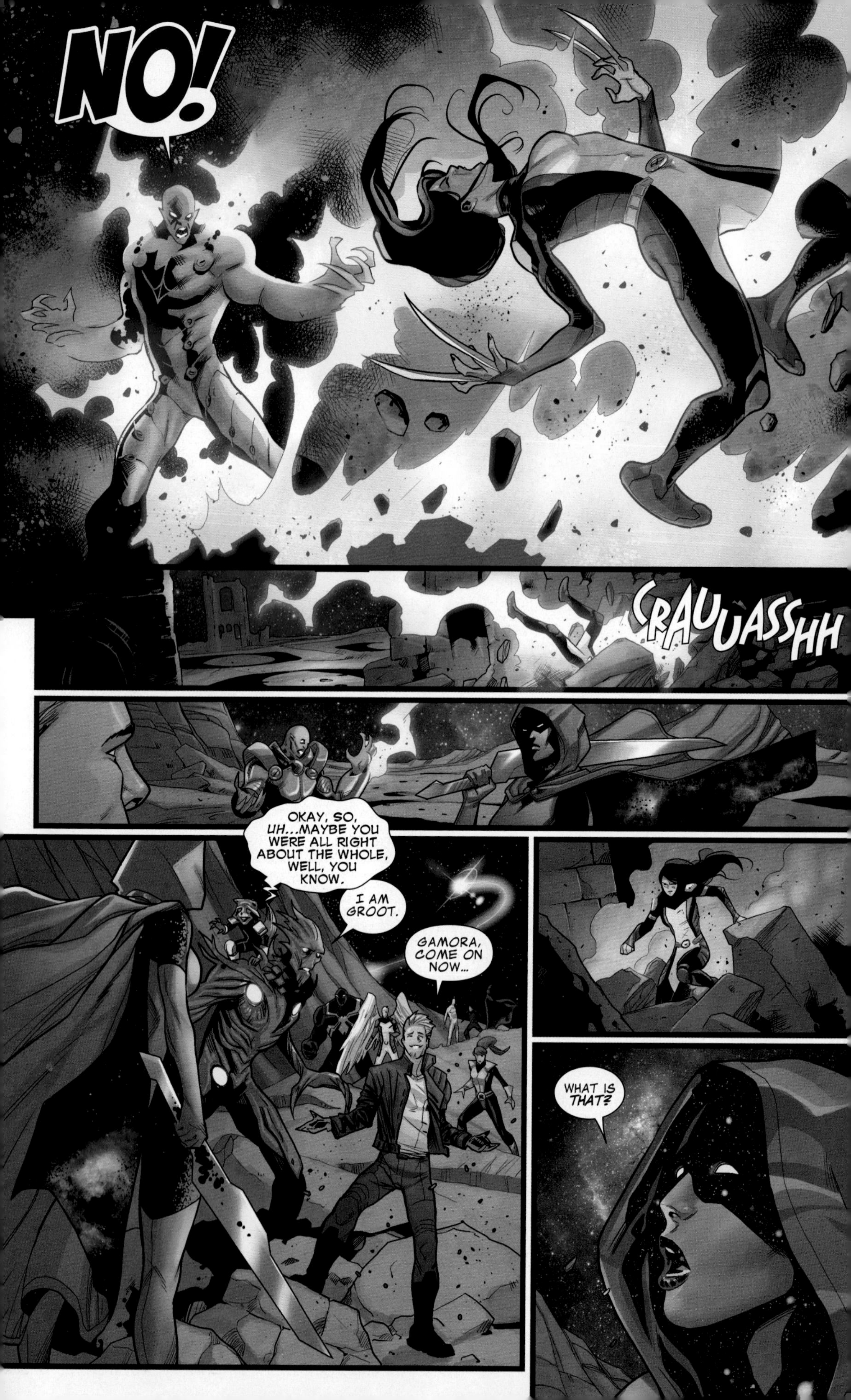
NO!
CRAUUASSHH
OKAY, SO, UH...MAYBE YOU WERE ALL RIGHT ABOUT THE WHOLE, WELL, YOU KNOW.
I AM GROOT.
GAMORA, COME ON NOW...
WHAT IS THAT?

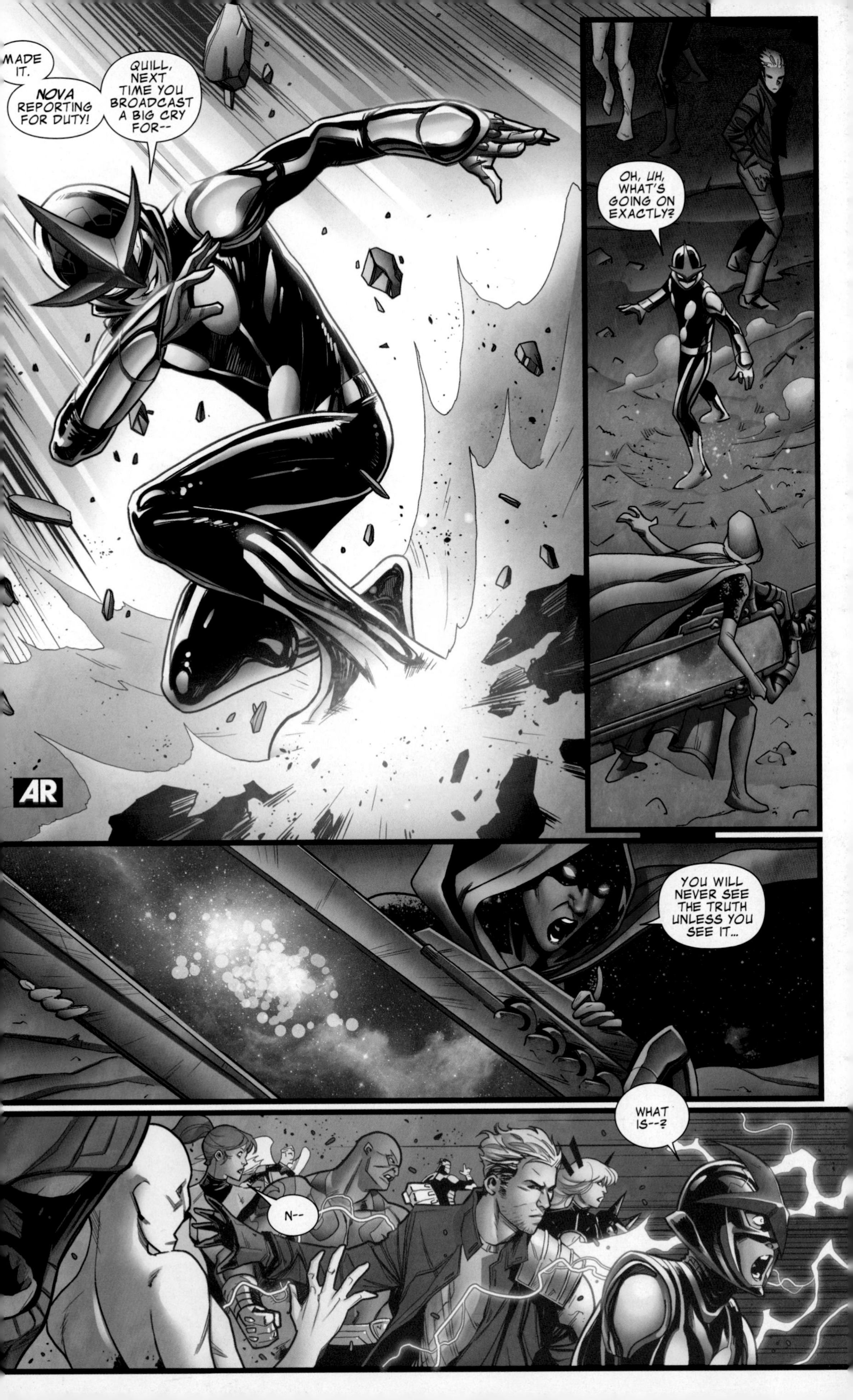
MADE IT.
NOVA REPORTING FOR DUTY!
QUILL, NEXT TIME YOU BROADCAST A BIG CRY FOR--
AR
OH, UH, WHAT'S GOING ON EXACTLY?
YOU WILL NEVER SEE THE TRUTH UNLESS YOU SEE IT...
WHAT IS--?
N--

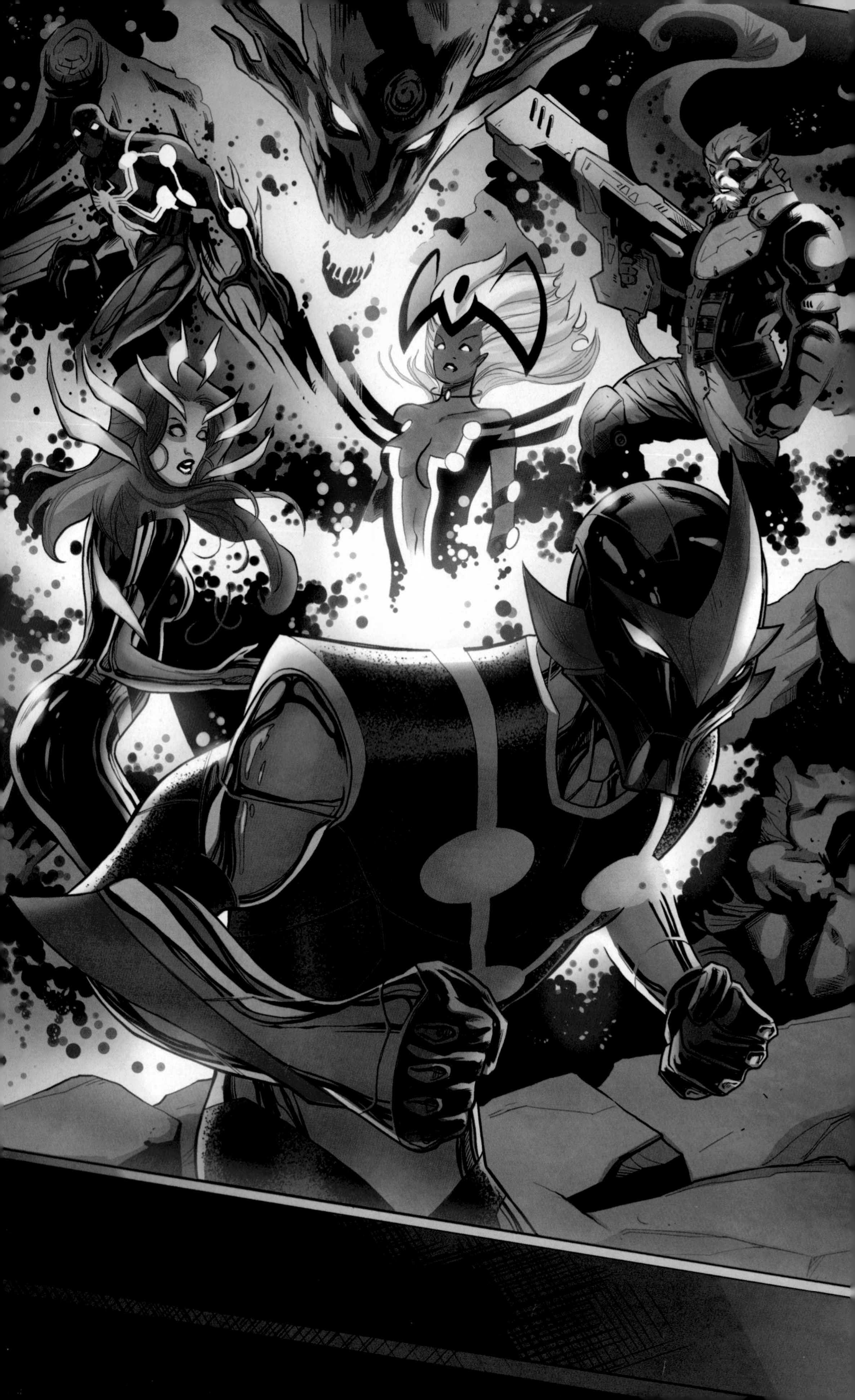

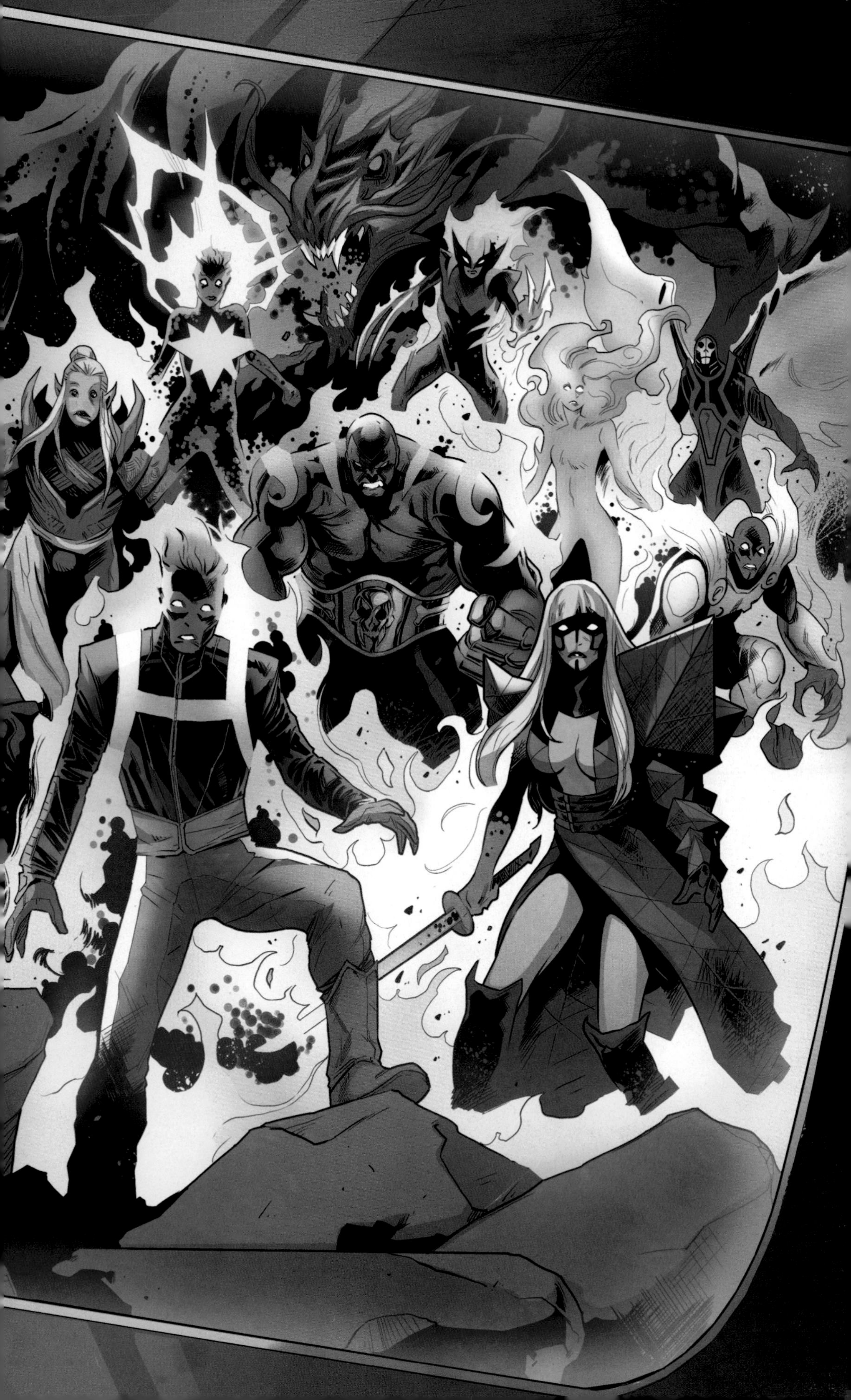

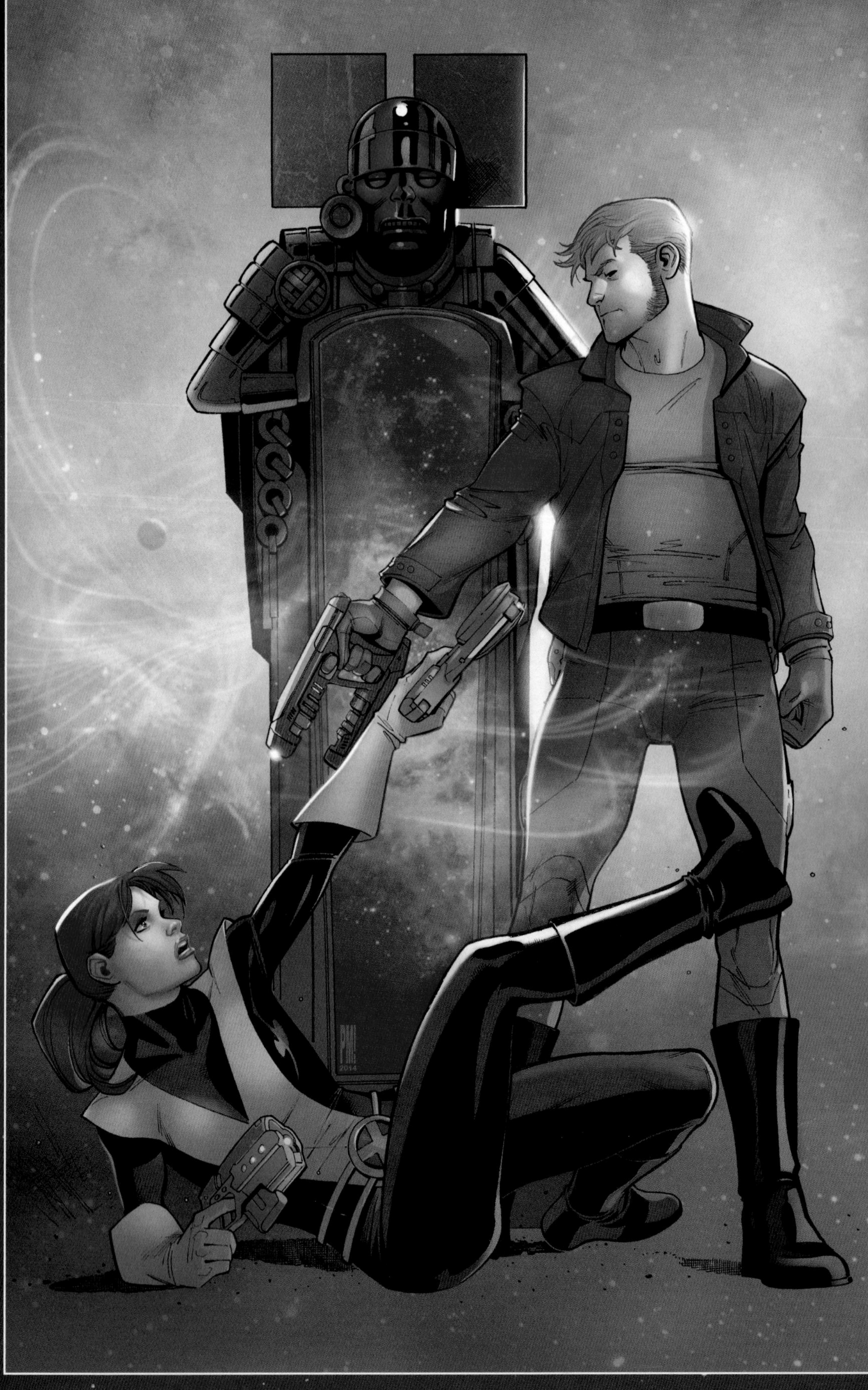
PM
2014

LEGENDARY STAR-LORD #9

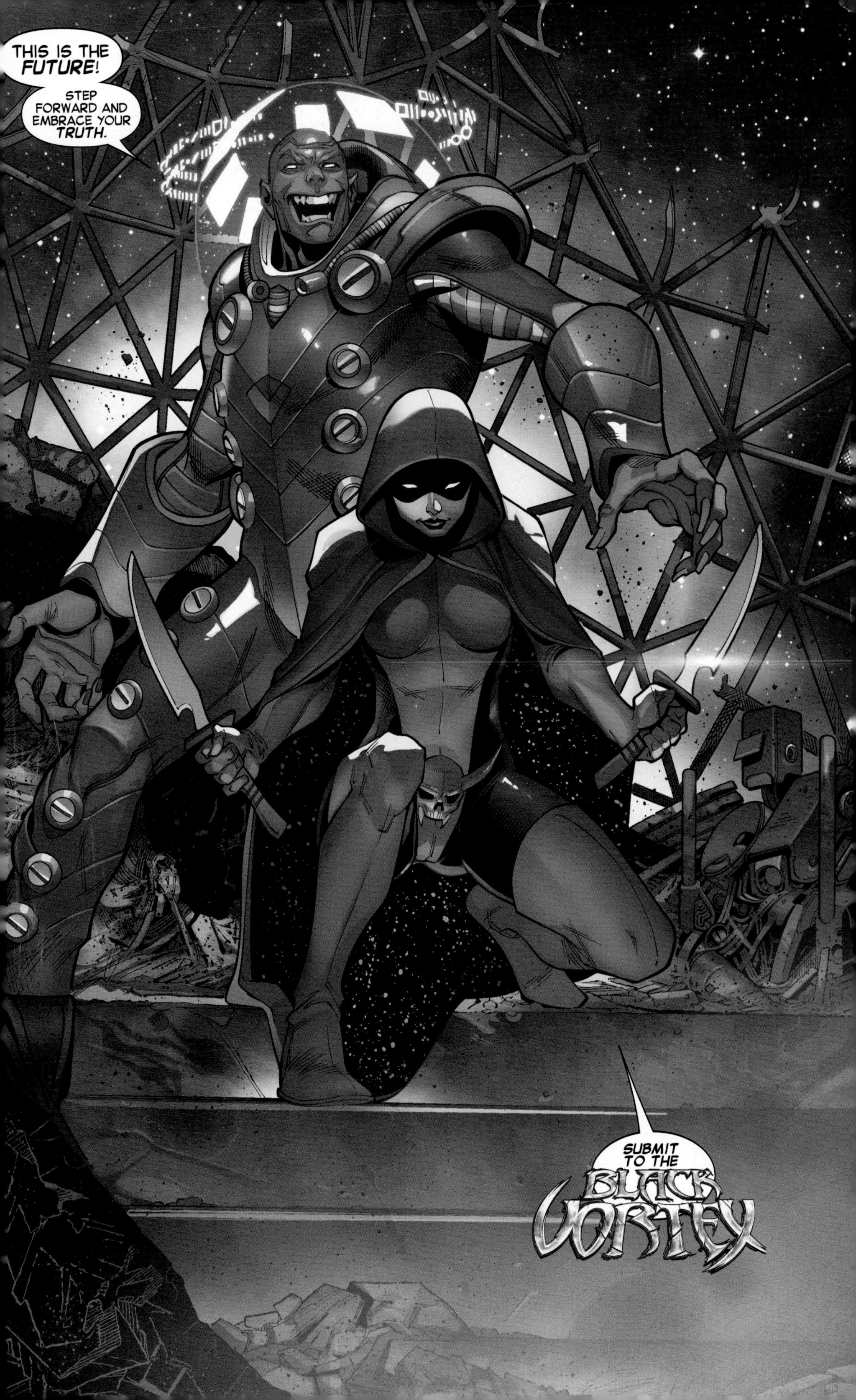
THIS IS THE FUTURE!
STEP FORWARD AND EMBRACE YOUR TRUTH.
SUBMIT TO THE
BLACK VORTEX

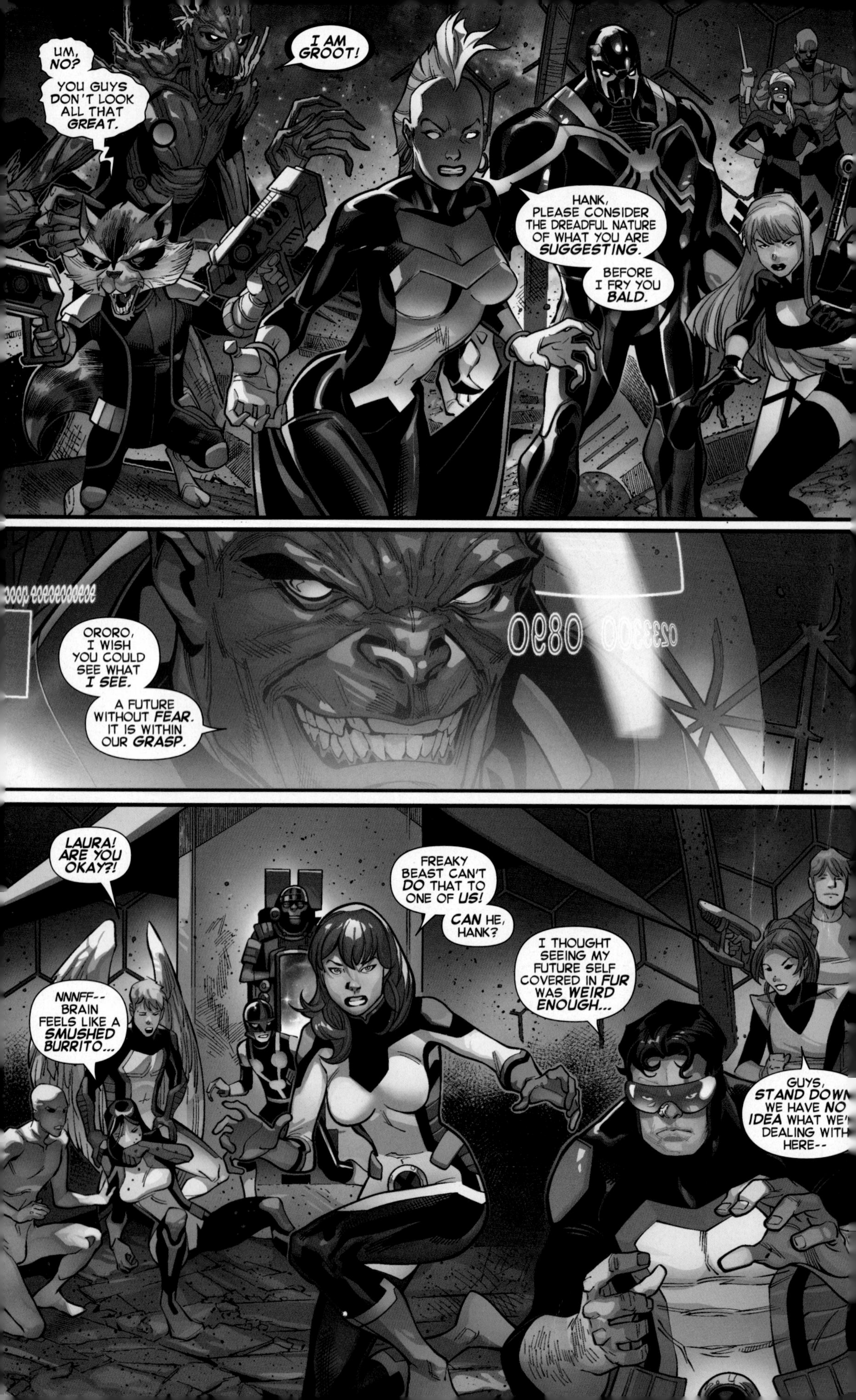
UM, NO?
YOU GUYS DON'T LOOK ALL THAT GREAT.
I AM GROOT!
HANK, PLEASE CONSIDER THE DREADFUL NATURE OF WHAT YOU ARE SUGGESTING.
BEFORE I FRY YOU BALD.
ORORO, I WISH YOU COULD SEE WHAT I SEE.
A FUTURE WITHOUT FEAR. IT IS WITHIN OUR GRASP.
LAURA! ARE YOU OKAY?!
NNNFF-- BRAIN FEELS LIKE A SMUSHED BURRITO...
FREAKY BEAST CAN'T DO THAT TO ONE OF US!
CAN HE, HANK?
I THOUGHT SEEING MY FUTURE SELF COVERED IN FUR WAS WEIRD ENOUGH...
GUYS, STAND DOWN WE HAVE NO IDEA WHAT WE' DEALING WITH HERE--

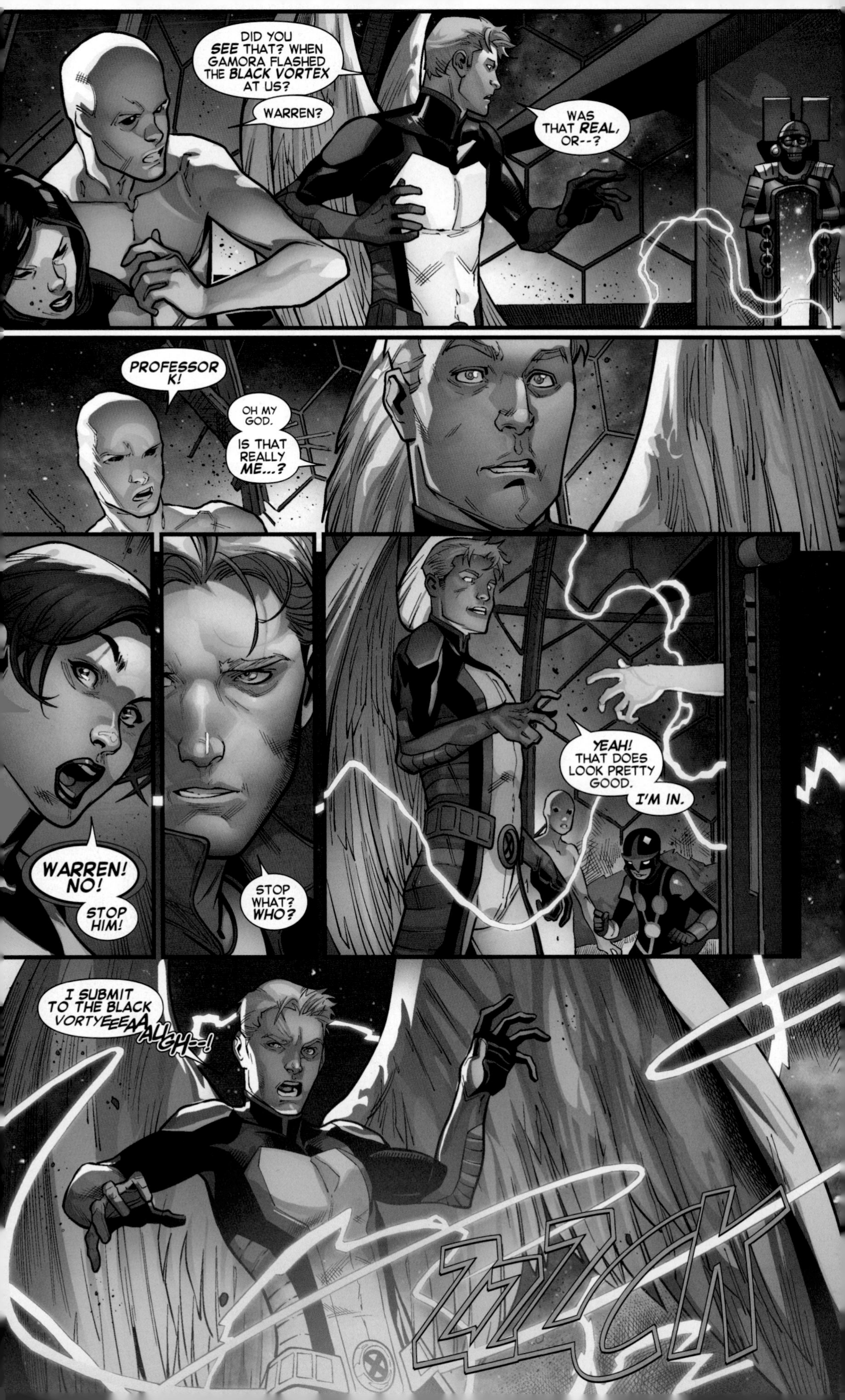
DID YOU SEE THAT? WHEN GAMORA FLASHED THE BLACK VORTEX AT US?
WARREN?
WAS THAT REAL, OR--?
PROFESSOR K!
OH MY GOD.
IS THAT REALLY ME...?
WARREN! NO!
STOP HIM!
STOP WHAT? WHO?
YEAH! THAT DOES LOOK PRETTY GOOD.
I'M IN.
I SUBMIT TO THE BLACK VORTYEEEAAAUGH--!
ZZZCH

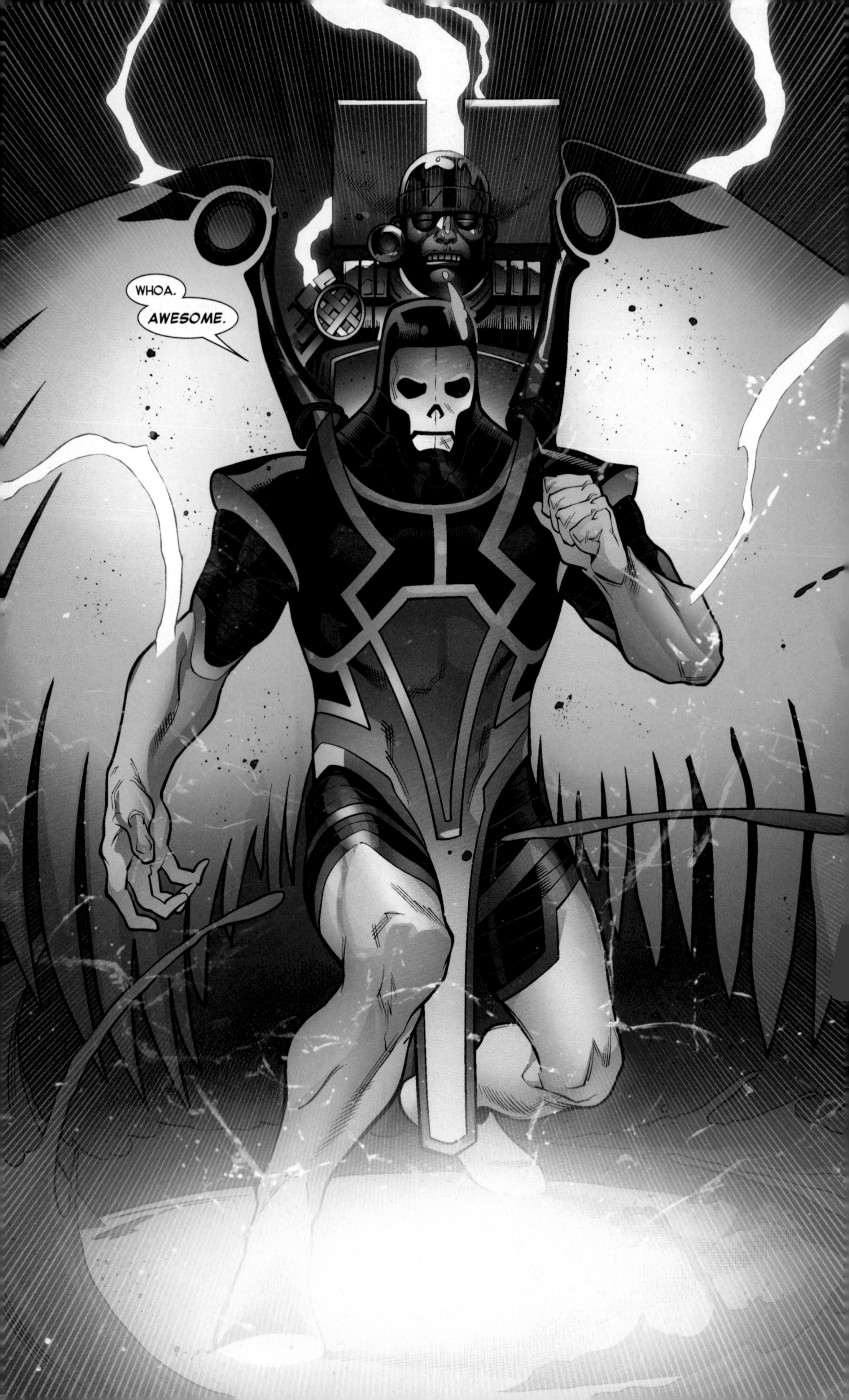
WHOA.
AWESOME.

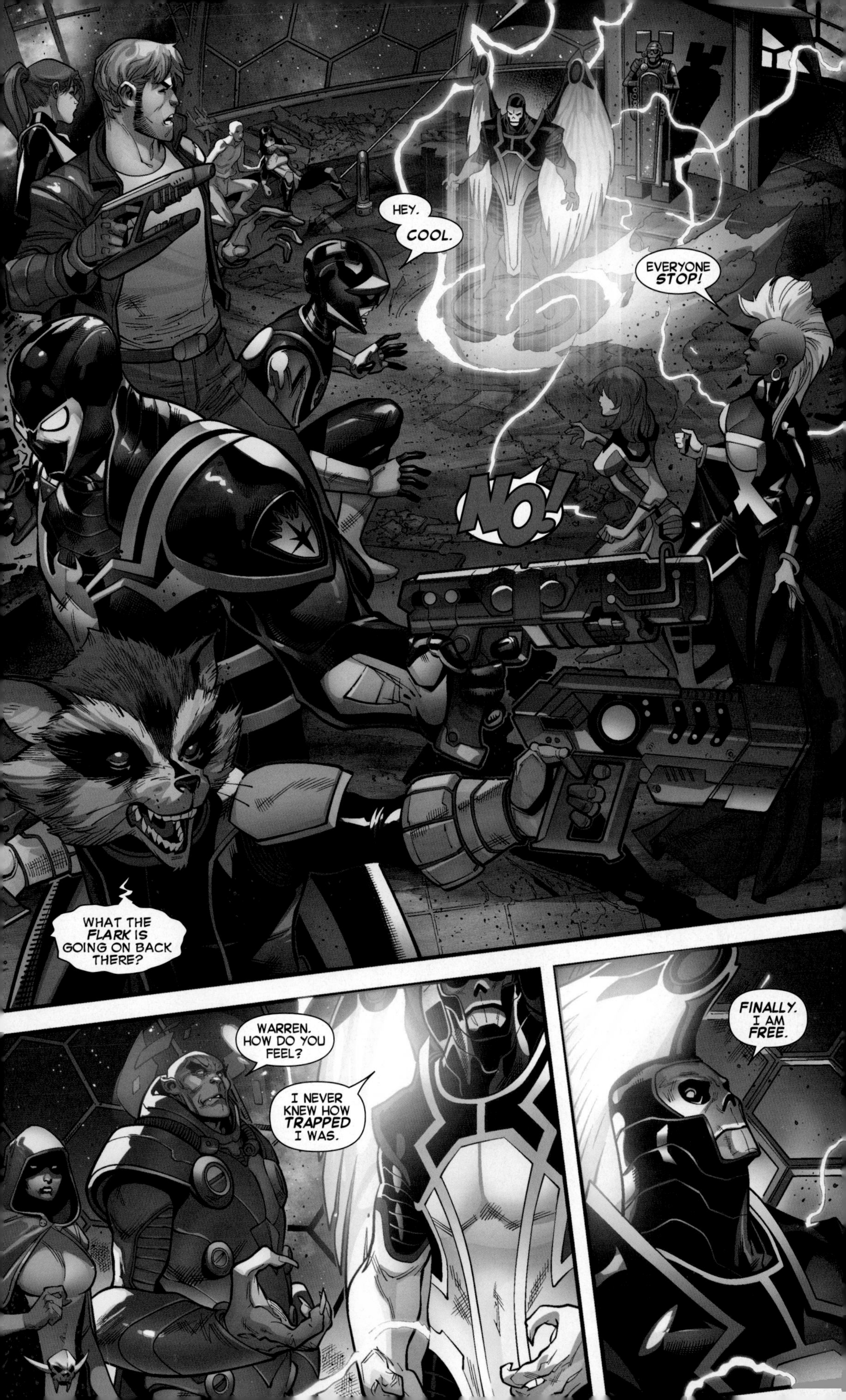
HEY.
COOL.
EVERYONE STOP!
NO!
WHAT THE FLARK IS GOING ON BACK THERE?
WARREN. HOW DO YOU FEEL?
I NEVER KNEW HOW TRAPPED I WAS.
FINALLY. I AM FREE.

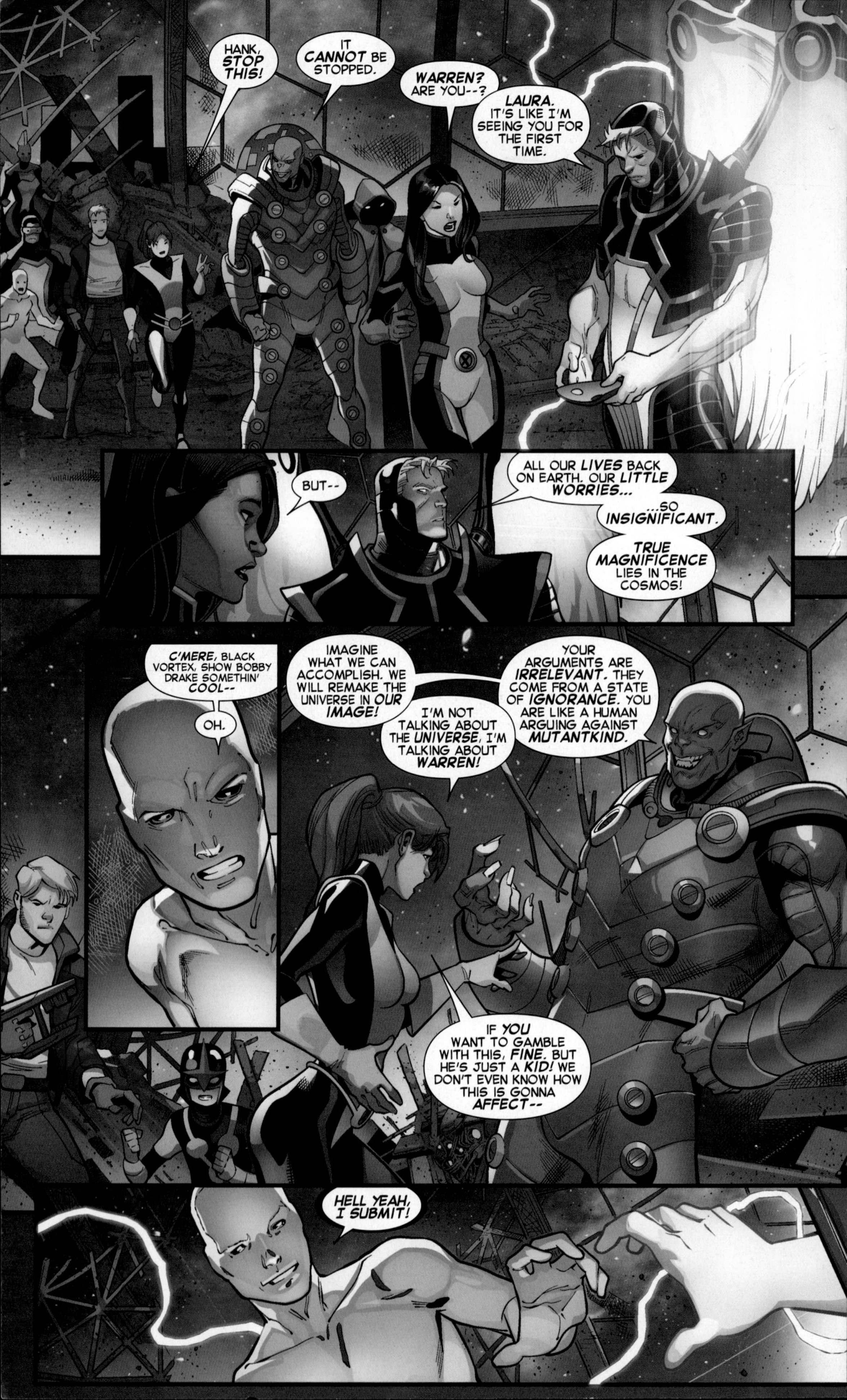
HANK, STOP THIS!
IT CANNOT BE STOPPED.
WARREN? ARE YOU--?
LAURA. IT'S LIKE I'M SEEING YOU FOR THE FIRST TIME.
BUT--
ALL OUR LIVES BACK ON EARTH. OUR LITTLE WORRIES...
...SO INSIGNIFICANT.
TRUE MAGNIFICENCE LIES IN THE COSMOS!
C'MERE, BLACK VORTEX, SHOW BOBBY DRAKE SOMETHIN' COOL--
OH.
IMAGINE WHAT WE CAN ACCOMPLISH. WE WILL REMAKE THE UNIVERSE IN OUR IMAGE!
I'M NOT TALKING ABOUT THE UNIVERSE, I'M TALKING ABOUT WARREN!
YOUR ARGUMENTS ARE IRRELEVANT. THEY COME FROM A STATE OF IGNORANCE. YOU ARE LIKE A HUMAN ARGUING AGAINST MUTANTKIND.
IF YOU WANT TO GAMBLE WITH THIS, FINE. BUT HE'S JUST A KID! WE DON'T EVEN KNOW HOW THIS IS GONNA AFFECT--
HELL YEAH, I SUBMIT!

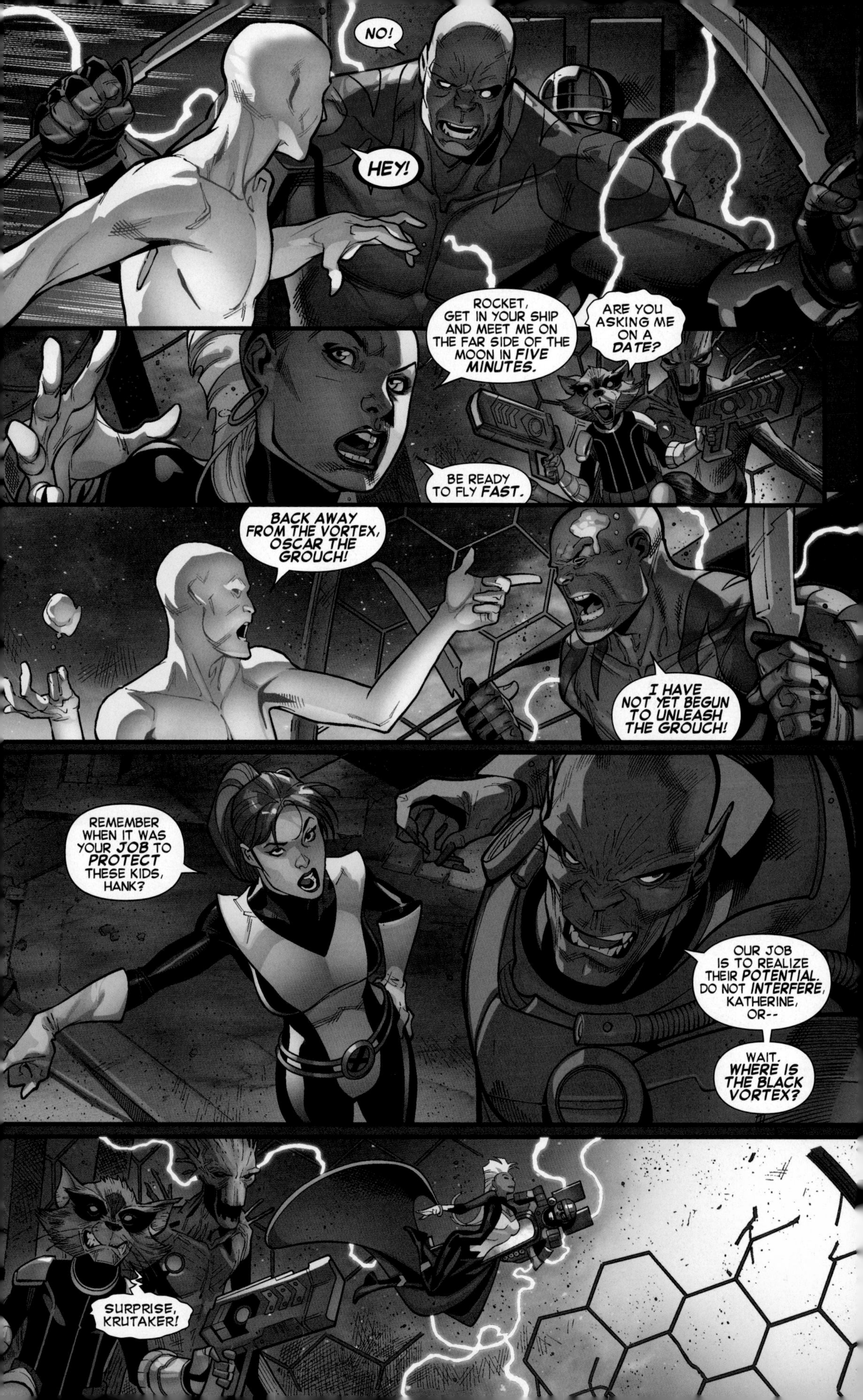
NO!
HEY!
ROCKET, GET IN YOUR SHIP AND MEET ME ON THE FAR SIDE OF THE MOON IN FIVE MINUTES.
ARE YOU ASKING ME ON A DATE?
BE READY TO FLY FAST.
BACK AWAY FROM THE VORTEX, OSCAR THE GROUCH!
I HAVE NOT YET BEGUN TO UNLEASH THE GROUCH!
REMEMBER WHEN IT WAS YOUR JOB TO PROTECT THESE KIDS, HANK?
OUR JOB IS TO REALIZE THEIR POTENTIAL. DO NOT INTERFERE, KATHERINE, OR--
WAIT. WHERE IS THE BLACK VORTEX?
SURPRISE, KRUTAKER!

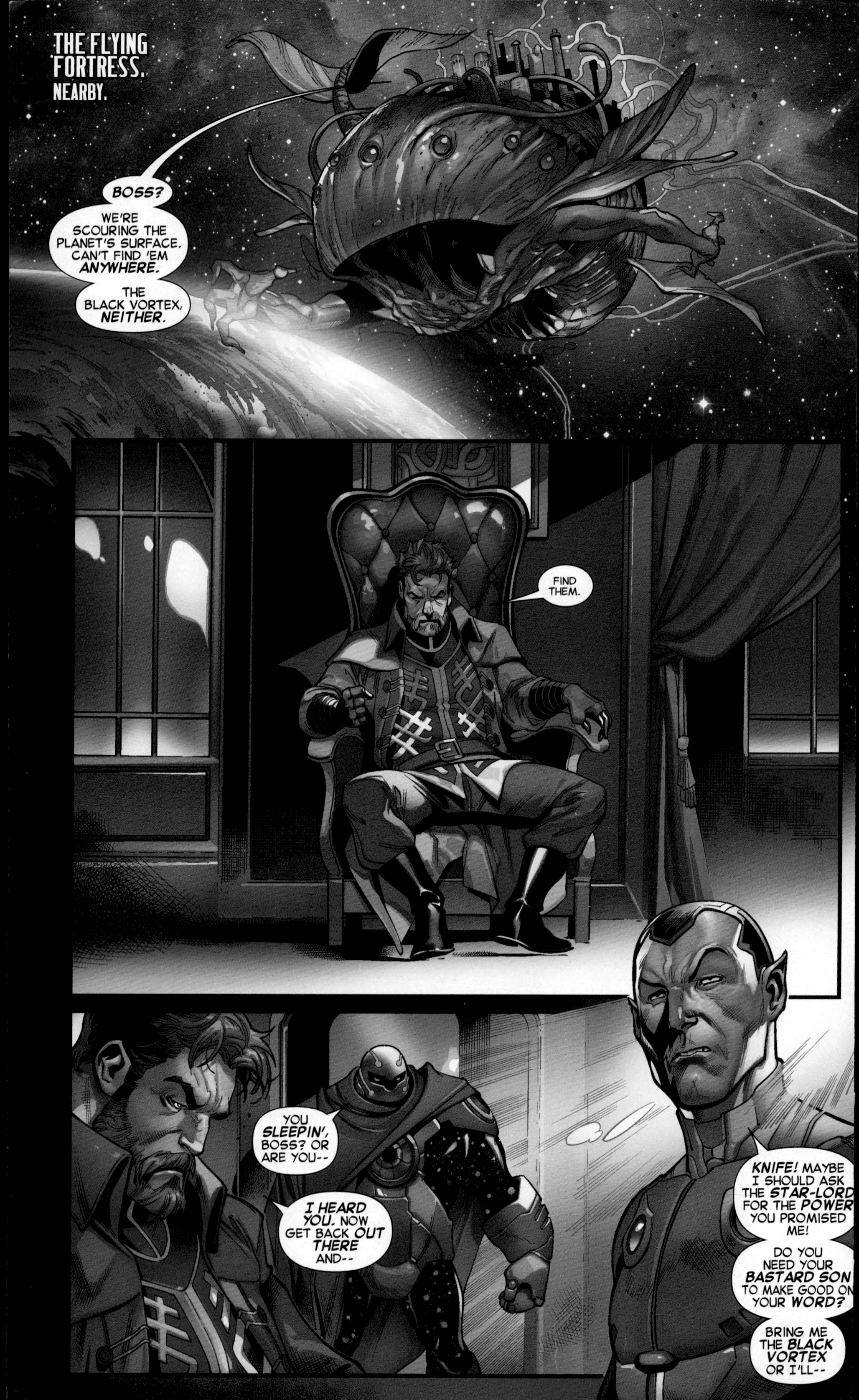
THE FLYING FORTRESS. NEARBY.
BOSS?
WE'RE SCOURING THE PLANET'S SURFACE. CAN'T FIND 'EM ANYWHERE.
THE BLACK VORTEX, NEITHER.
FIND THEM.
YOU SLEEPIN', BOSS? OR ARE YOU--
I HEARD YOU. NOW GET BACK OUT THERE AND--
KNIFE! MAYBE I SHOULD ASK THE STAR-LORD FOR THE POWER YOU PROMISED ME!
DO YOU NEED YOUR BASTARD SON TO MAKE GOOD ON YOUR WORD?
BRING ME THE BLACK VORTEX OR I'LL--

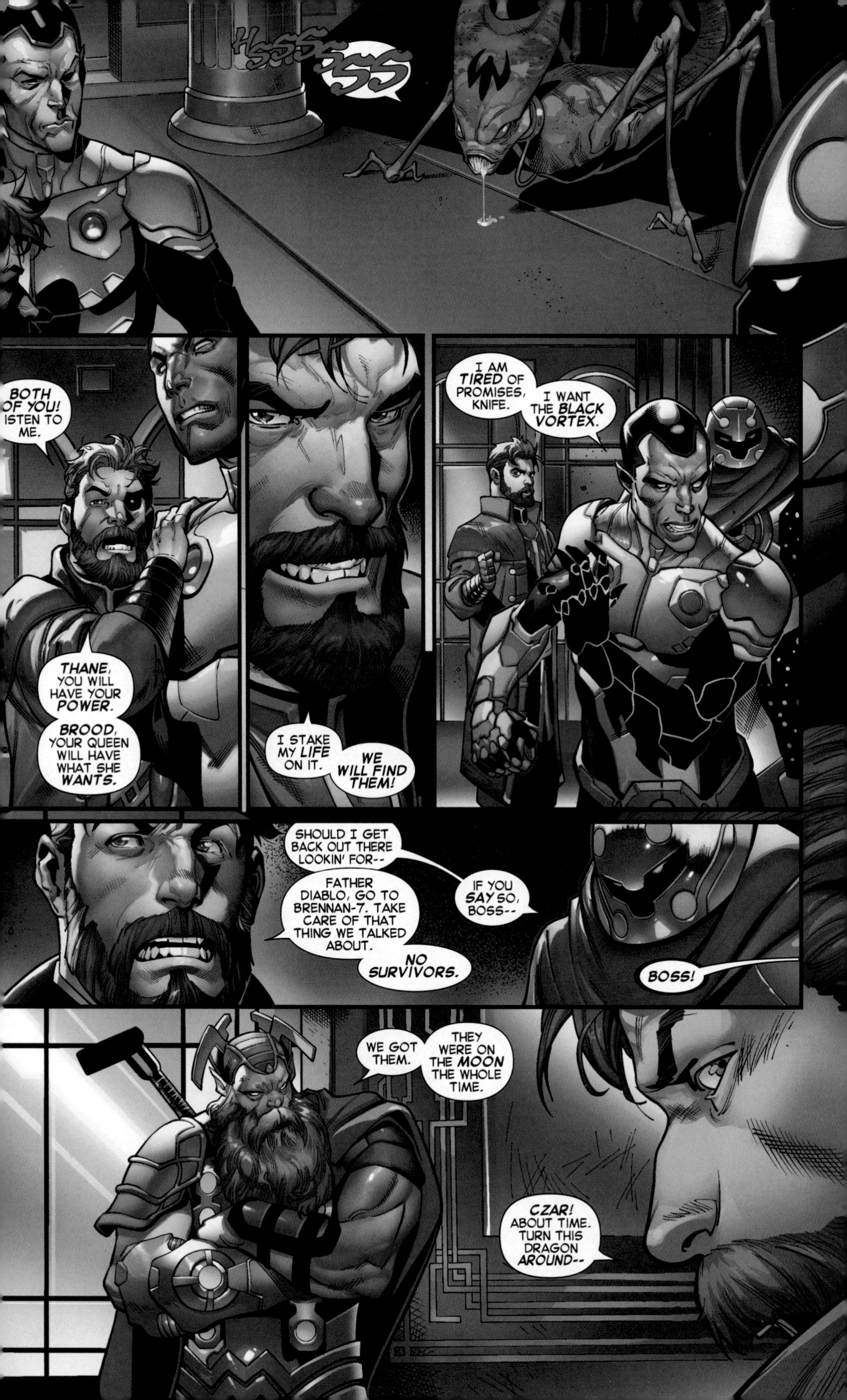
HSSSSSSS
BOTH OF YOU! LISTEN TO ME.
THANE, YOU WILL HAVE YOUR POWER.
BROOD, YOUR QUEEN WILL HAVE WHAT SHE WANTS.
I STAKE MY LIFE ON IT.
WE WILL FIND THEM!
I AM TIRED OF PROMISES, KNIFE.
I WANT THE BLACK VORTEX.
SHOULD I GET BACK OUT THERE LOOKIN' FOR--
FATHER DIABLO, GO TO BRENNAN-7. TAKE CARE OF THAT THING WE TALKED ABOUT.
NO SURVIVORS.
IF YOU SAY SO, BOSS--
BOSS!
WE GOT THEM.
THEY WERE ON THE MOON THE WHOLE TIME.
CZAR! ABOUT TIME. TURN THIS DRAGON AROUND--

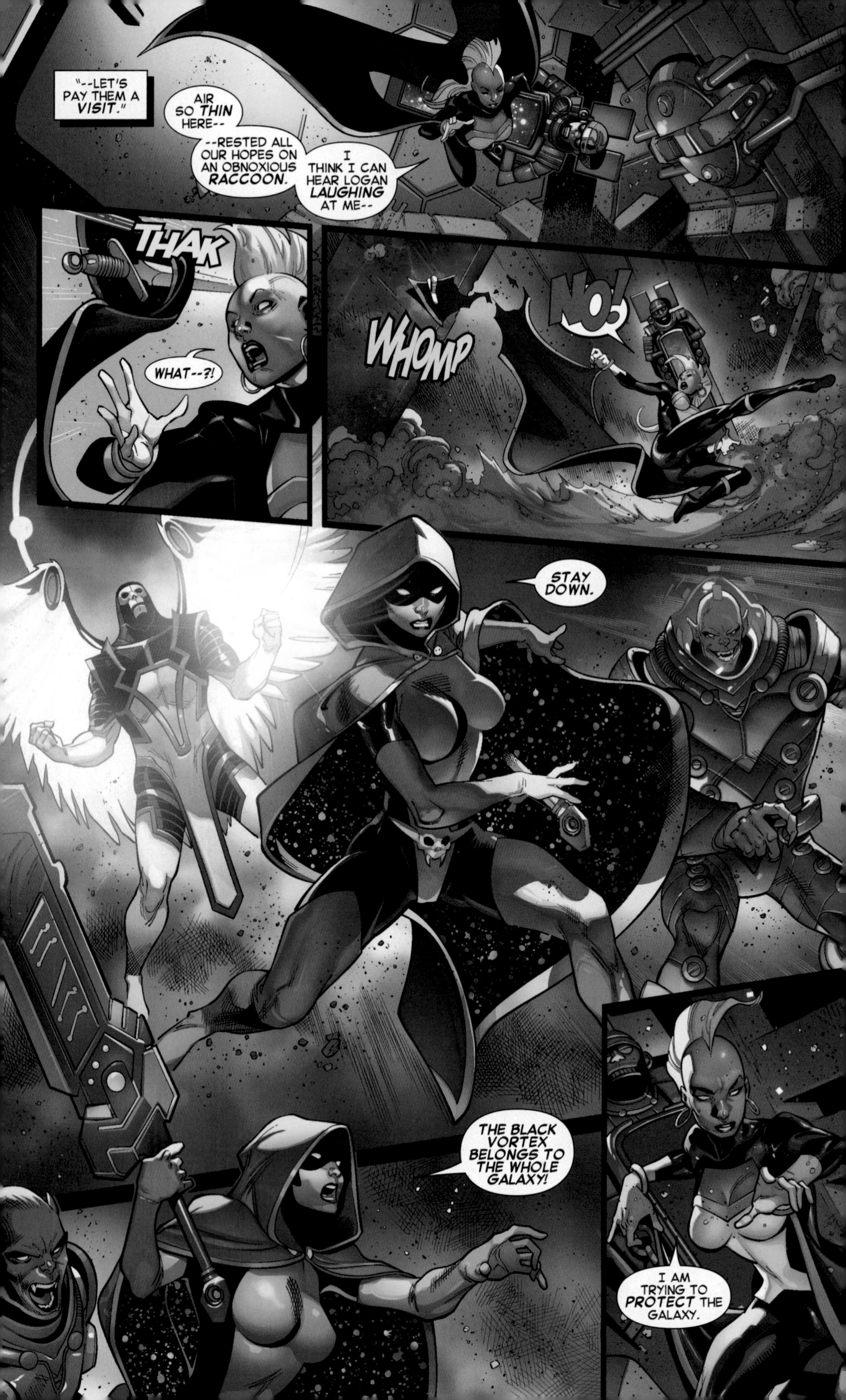
"--LET'S PAY THEM A VISIT."
AIR SO THIN HERE--
--RESTED ALL OUR HOPES ON AN OBNOXIOUS RACCOON.
I THINK I CAN HEAR LOGAN LAUGHING AT ME--
THAK
WHAT--?!
WHOMP
NO!
STAY DOWN.
THE BLACK VORTEX BELONGS TO THE WHOLE GALAXY!
I AM TRYING TO PROTECT THE GALAXY.

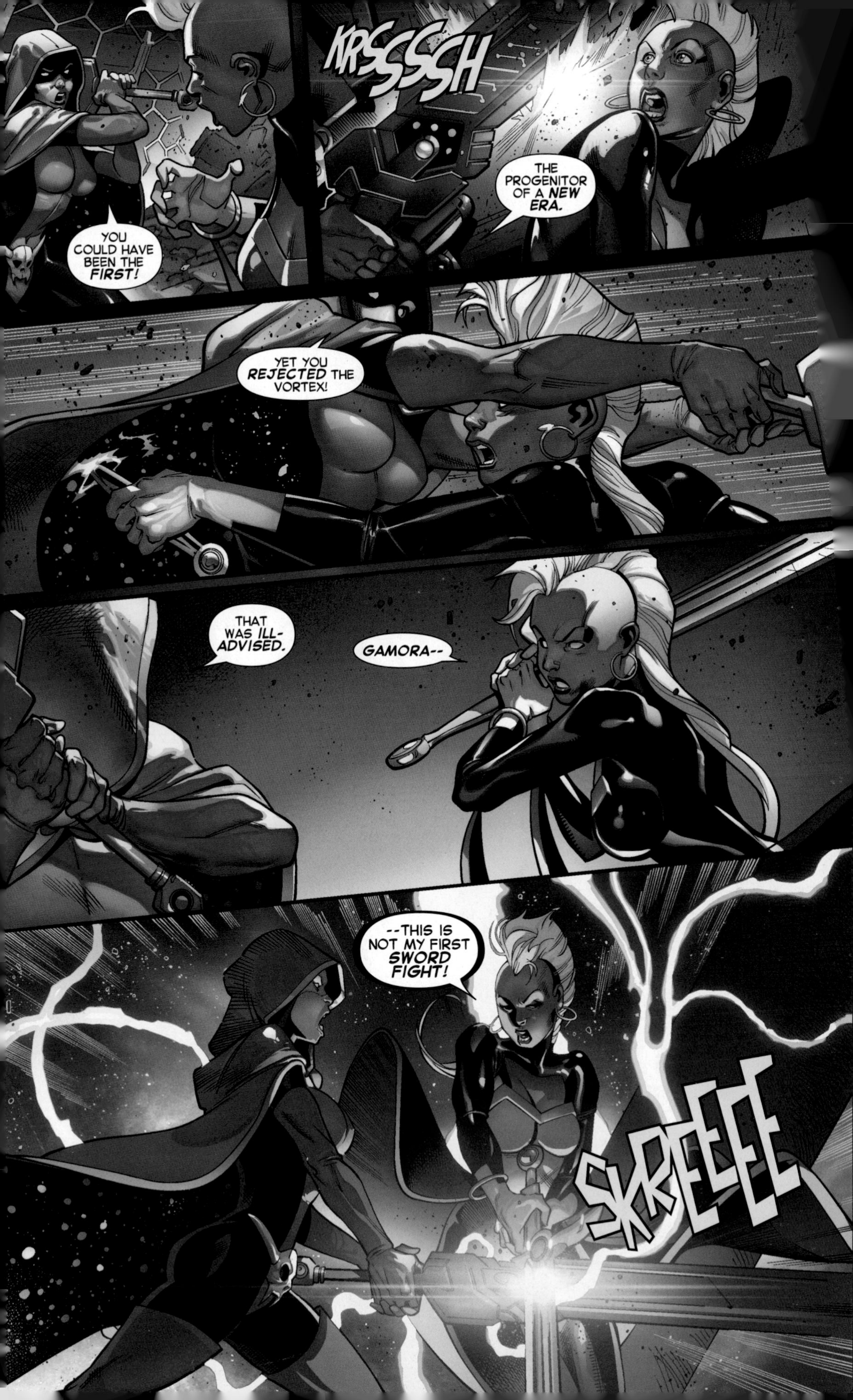
YOU COULD HAVE BEEN THE FIRST!
KRSSSSH
THE PROGENITOR OF A NEW ERA.
YET YOU REJECTED THE VORTEX!
THAT WAS ILL-ADVISED.
GAMORA--
--THIS IS NOT MY FIRST SWORD FIGHT!
SKREEEE

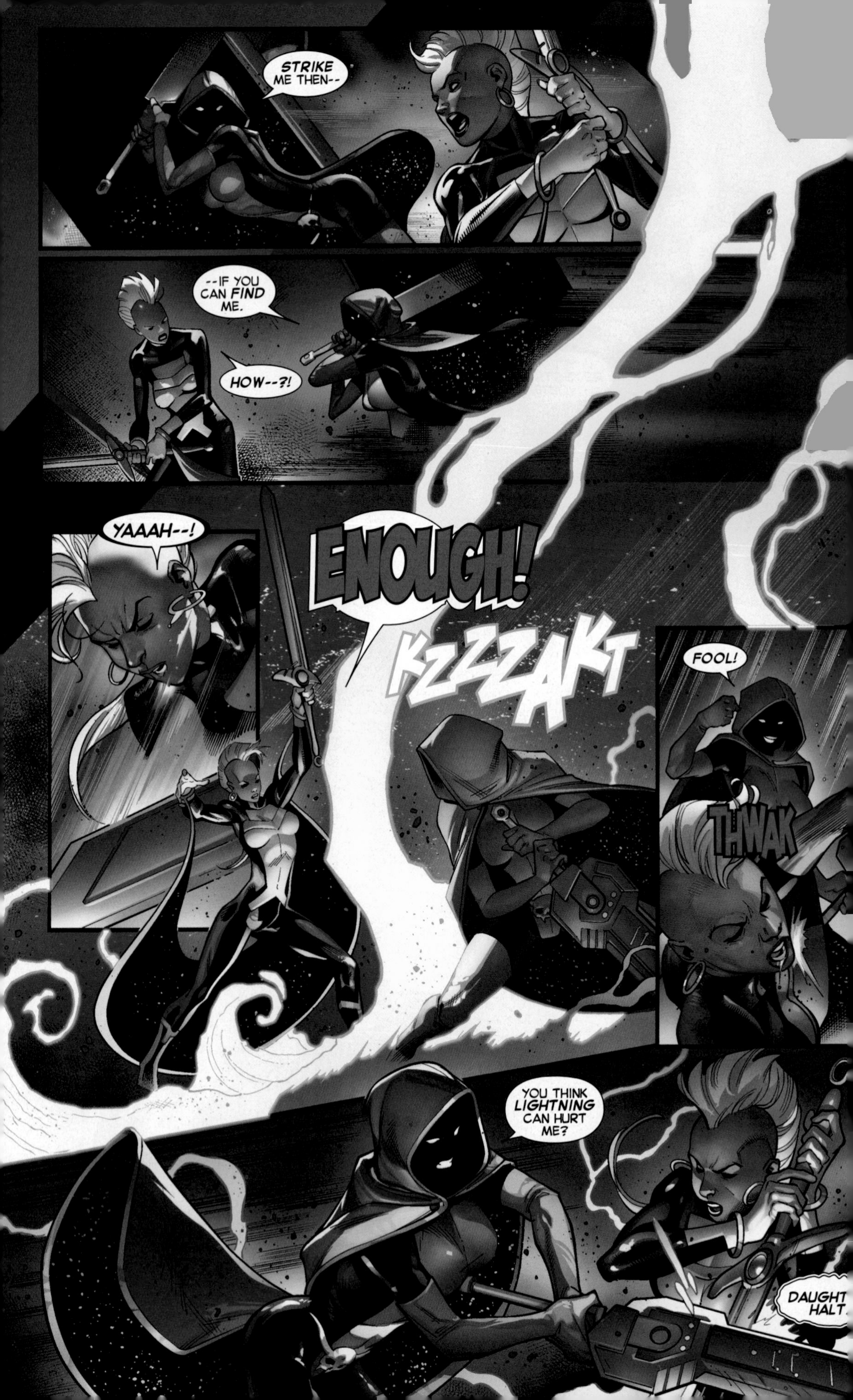
STRIKE ME THEN--
--IF YOU CAN FIND ME.
HOW--?!
YAAAH--!
ENOUGH!
KZZZZAKT
FOOL!
THWAK
YOU THINK LIGHTNING CAN HURT ME?
DAUGHT HALT

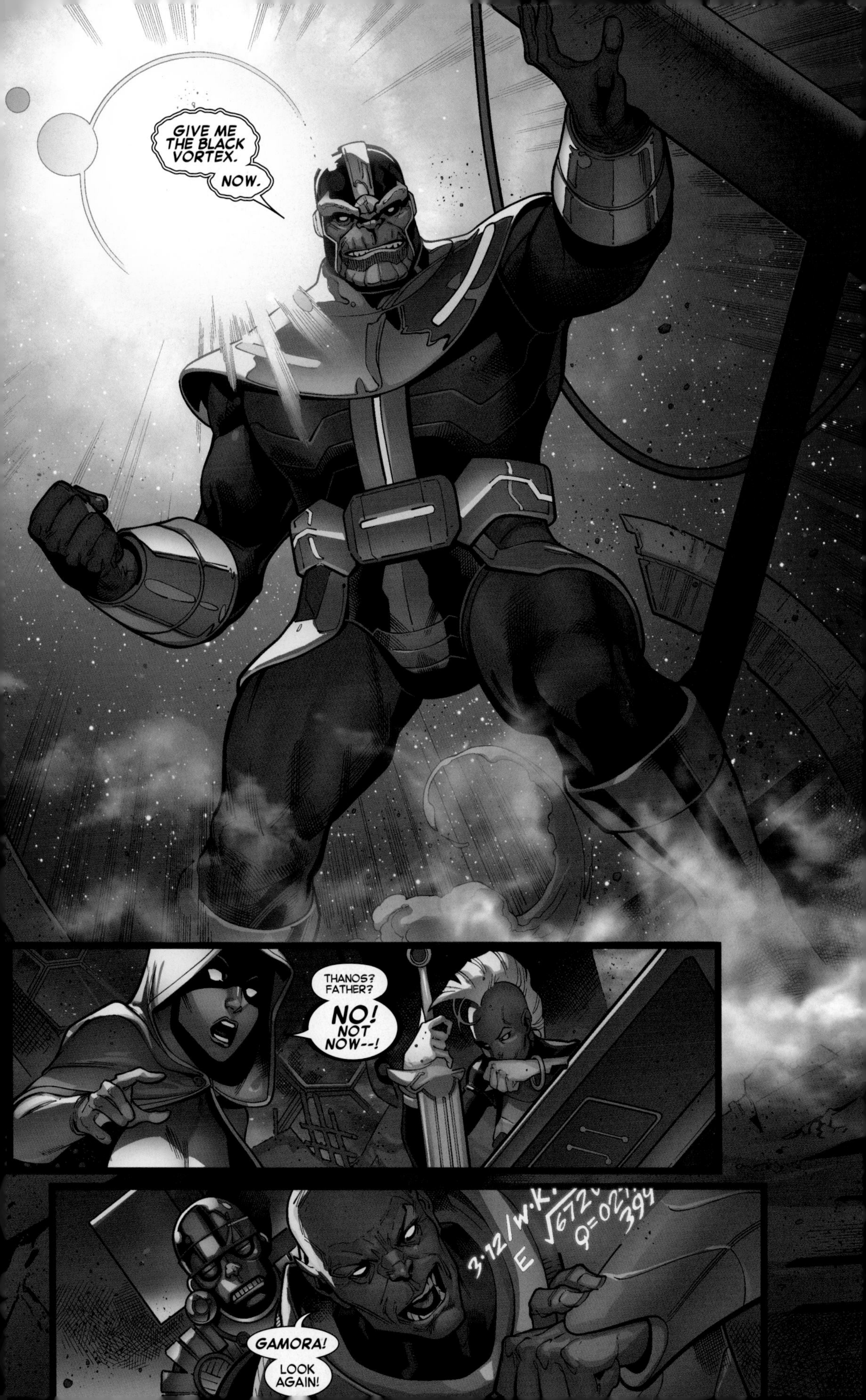
GIVE ME THE BLACK VORTEX.
NOW.
THANOS? FATHER?
NO! NOT NOW--!
GAMORA!
LOOK AGAIN!

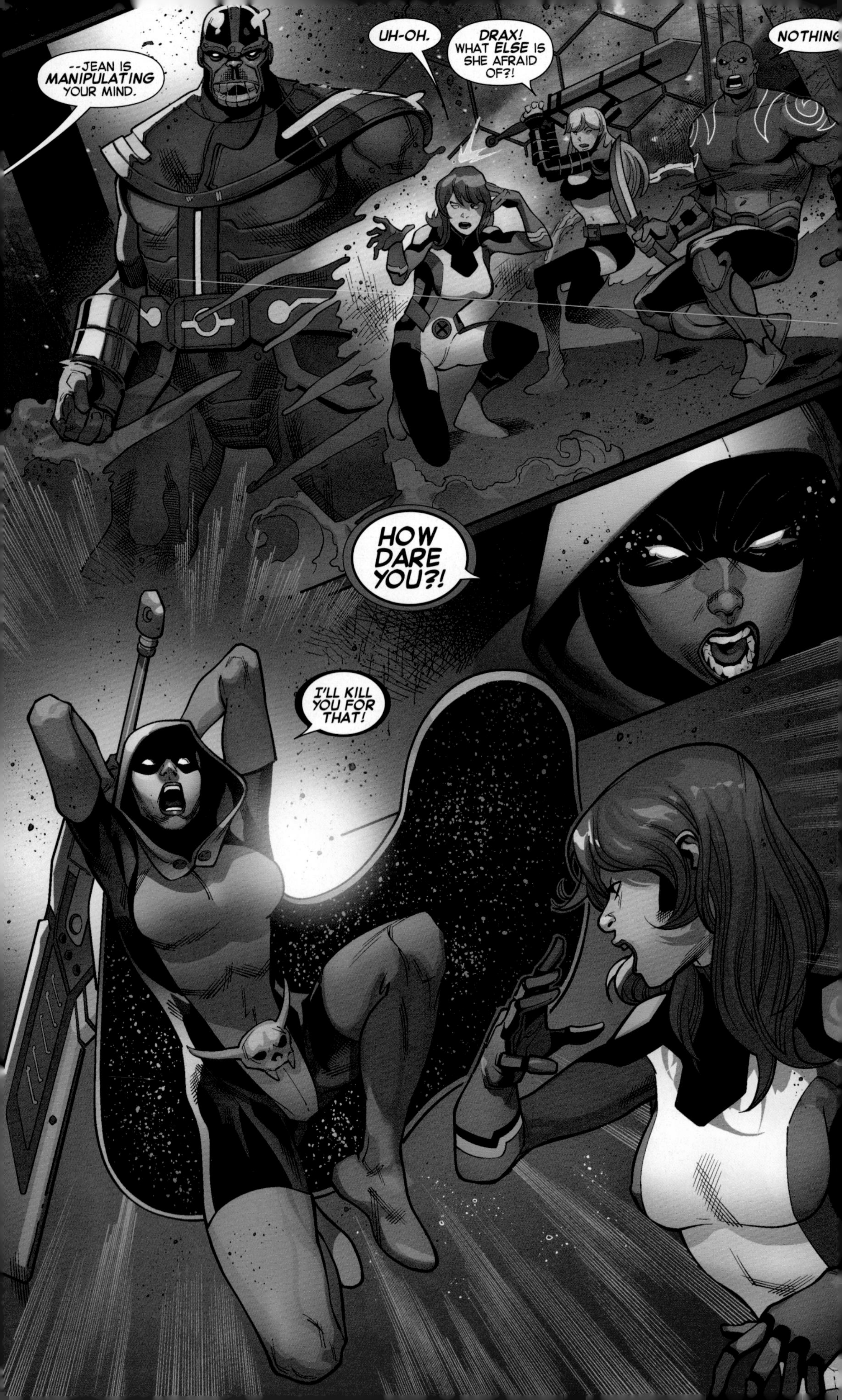
--JEAN IS MANIPULATING YOUR MIND.
UH-OH.
DRAX! WHAT ELSE IS SHE AFRAID OF?!
NOTHING
HOW DARE YOU?!
I'LL KILL YOU FOR THAT!

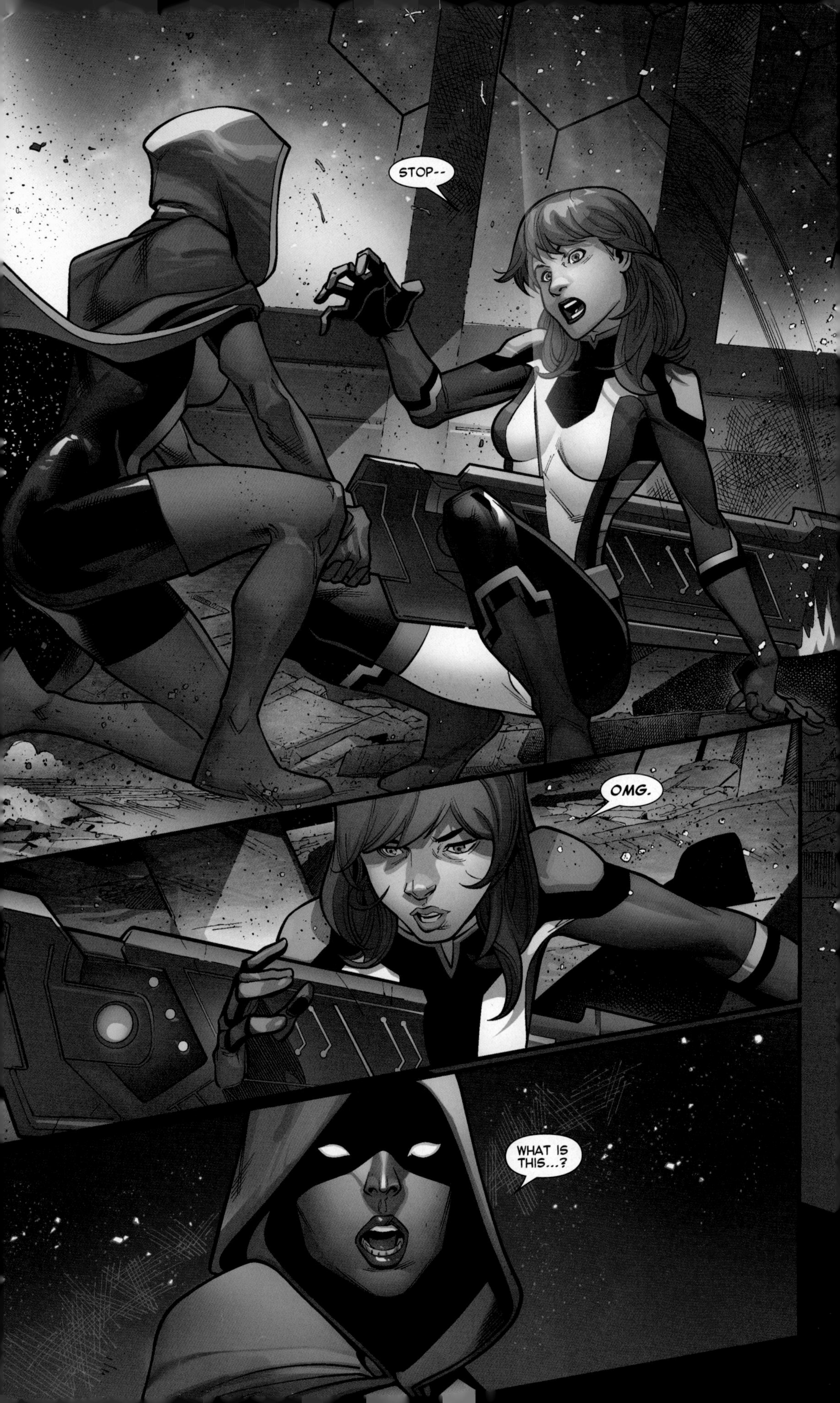
STOP--
OMG.
WHAT IS THIS...?

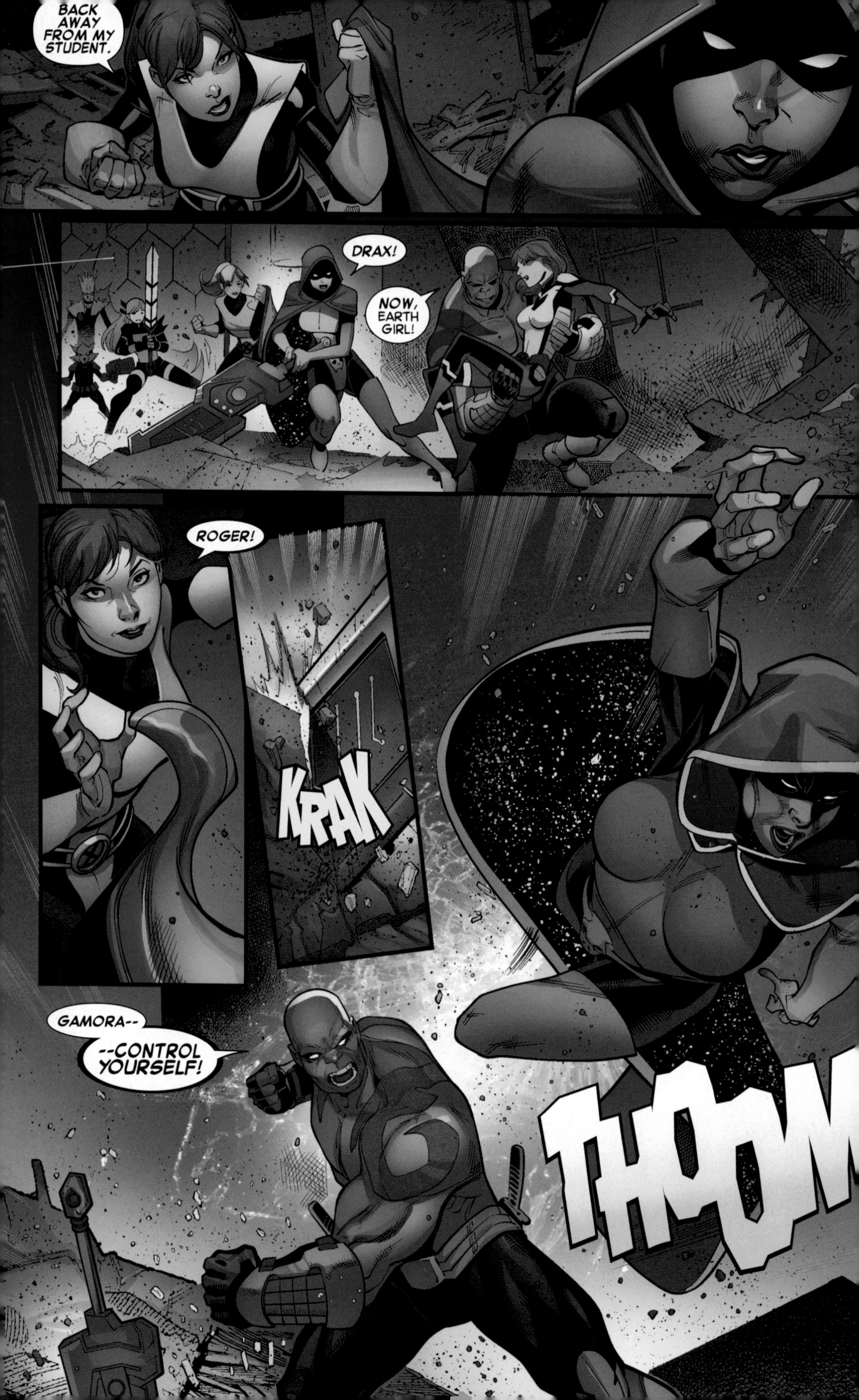
BACK AWAY FROM MY STUDENT.
DRAX!
NOW, EARTH GIRL!
ROGER!
KRAK
GAMORA--
--CONTROL YOURSELF!
THOOM

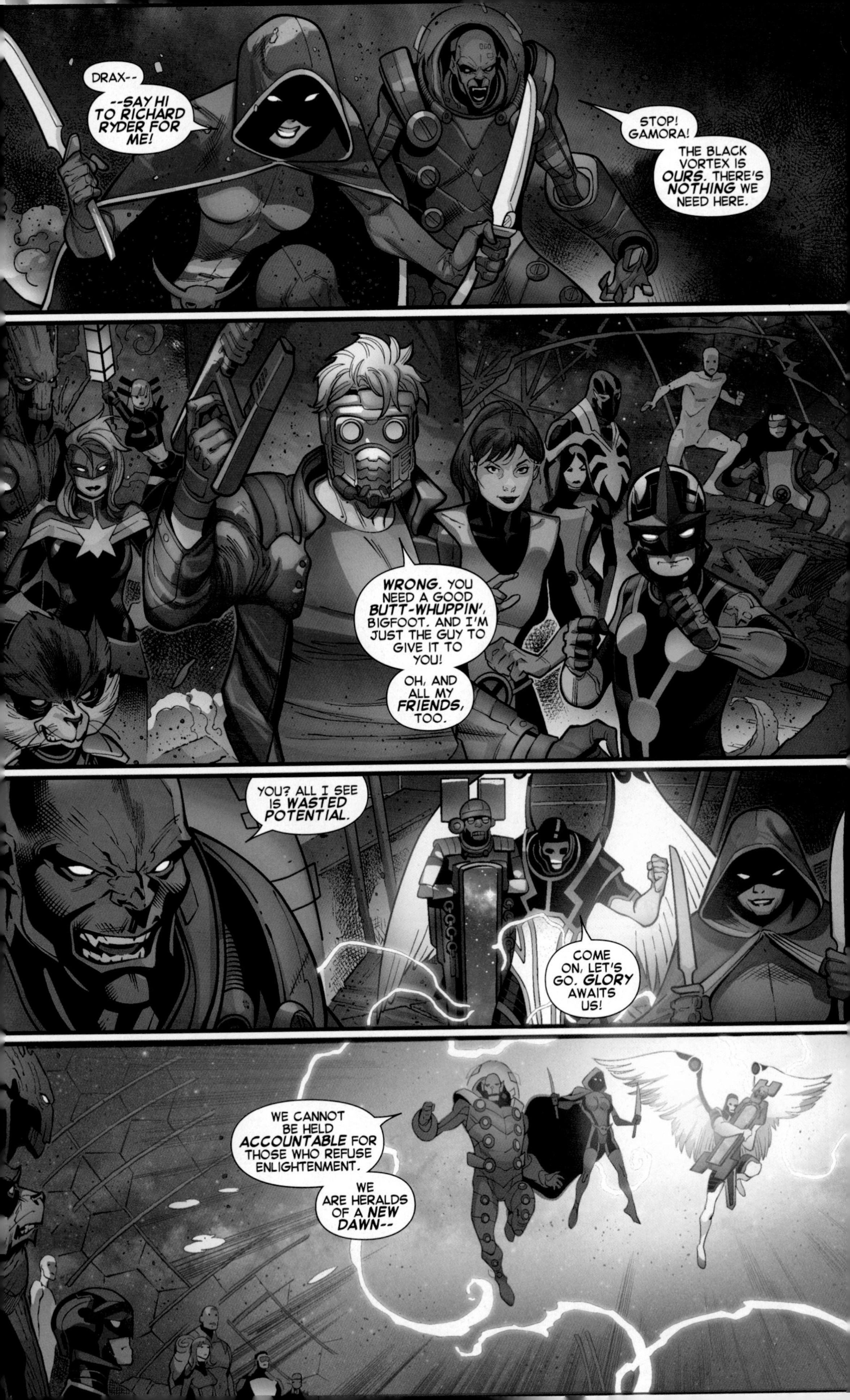
DRAX--
--SAY HI TO RICHARD RYDER FOR ME!
STOP! GAMORA!
THE BLACK VORTEX IS OURS. THERE'S NOTHING WE NEED HERE.
WRONG. YOU NEED A GOOD BUTT-WHUPPIN', BIGFOOT. AND I'M JUST THE GUY TO GIVE IT TO YOU!
OH, AND ALL MY FRIENDS, TOO.
YOU? ALL I SEE IS WASTED POTENTIAL.
COME ON, LET'S GO. GLORY AWAITS US!
WE CANNOT BE HELD ACCOUNTABLE FOR THOSE WHO REFUSE ENLIGHTENMENT.
WE ARE HERALDS OF A NEW DAWN--

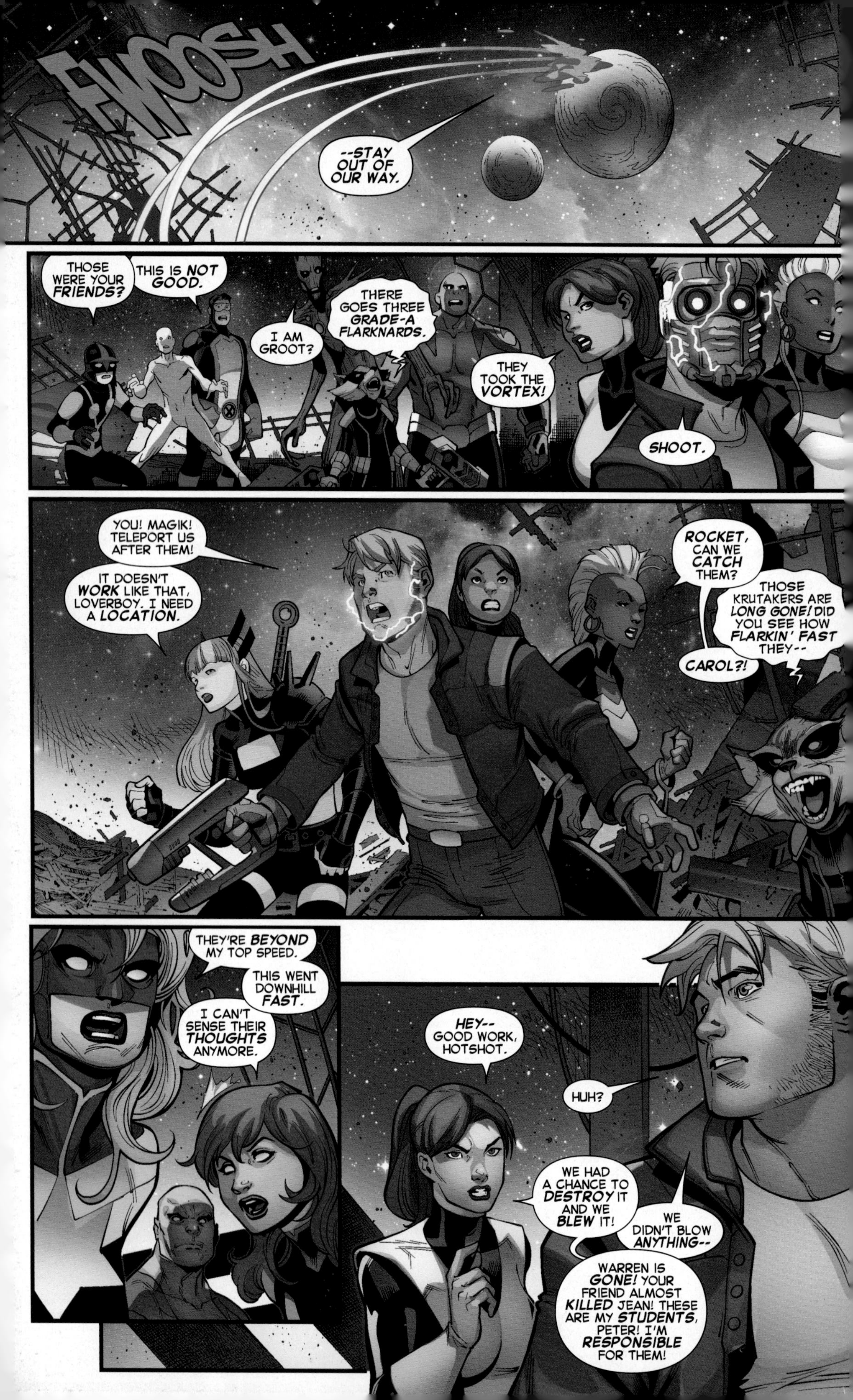

FWOOSH
--STAY OUT OF OUR WAY.
THOSE WERE YOUR FRIENDS?
THIS IS NOT GOOD.
I AM GROOT?
THERE GOES THREE GRADE-A FLARKNARDS.
THEY TOOK THE VORTEX!
SHOOT.
YOU! MAGIK! TELEPORT US AFTER THEM!
IT DOESN'T WORK LIKE THAT, LOVERBOY. I NEED A LOCATION.
ROCKET, CAN WE CATCH THEM?
THOSE KRUTAKERS ARE LONG GONE! DID YOU SEE HOW FLARKIN' FAST THEY--
CAROL?!
THEY'RE BEYOND MY TOP SPEED.
THIS WENT DOWNHILL FAST.
I CAN'T SENSE THEIR THOUGHTS ANYMORE.
HEY-- GOOD WORK, HOTSHOT.
HUH?
WE HAD A CHANCE TO DESTROY IT AND WE BLEW IT!
WE DIDN'T BLOW ANYTHING--
WARREN IS GONE! YOUR FRIEND ALMOST KILLED JEAN! THESE ARE MY STUDENTS, PETER! I'M RESPONSIBLE FOR THEM!

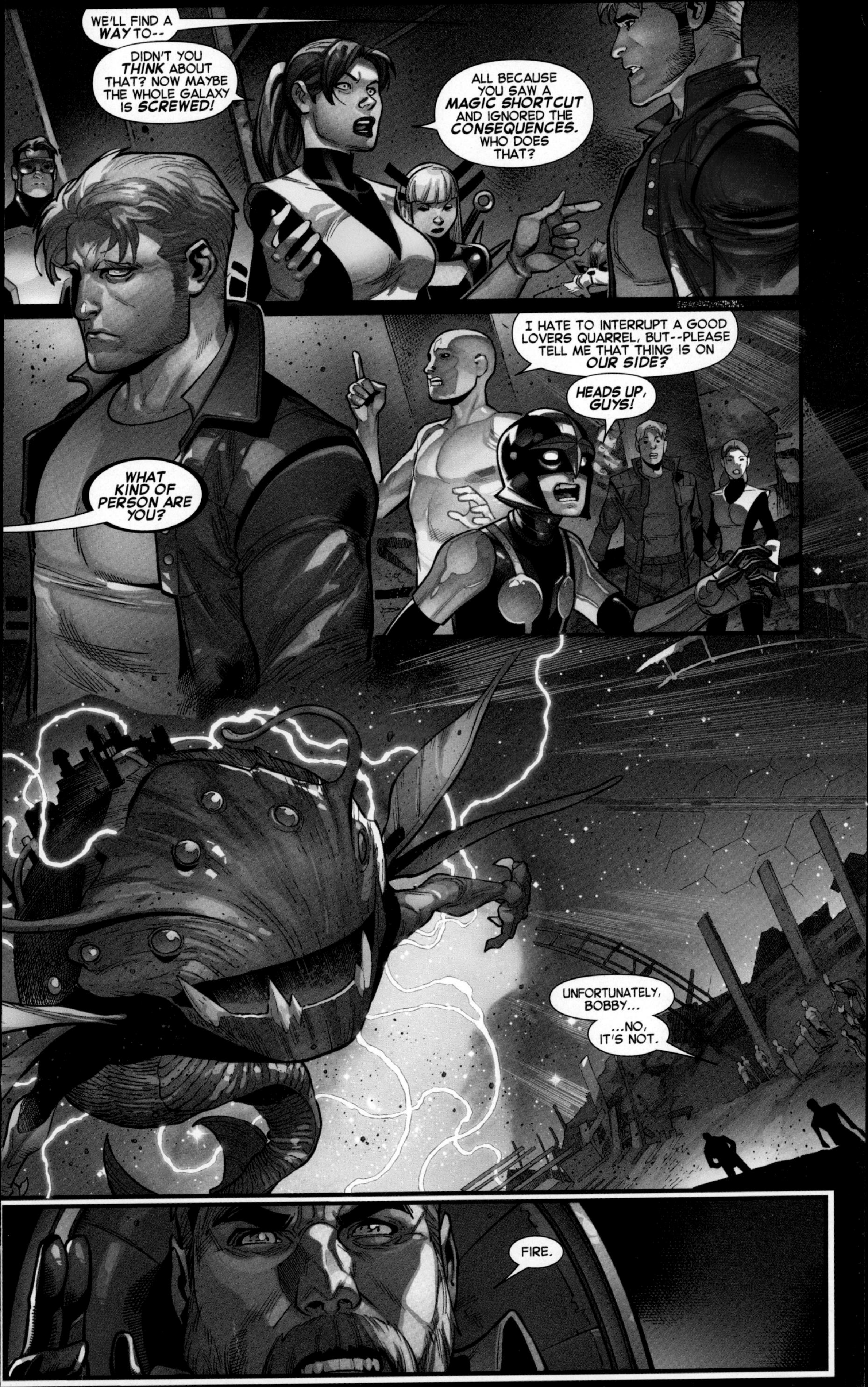
WE'LL FIND A WAY TO--
DIDN'T YOU THINK ABOUT THAT? NOW MAYBE THE WHOLE GALAXY IS SCREWED!
ALL BECAUSE YOU SAW A MAGIC SHORTCUT AND IGNORED THE CONSEQUENCES. WHO DOES THAT?
WHAT KIND OF PERSON ARE YOU?
I HATE TO INTERRUPT A GOOD LOVERS QUARREL, BUT--PLEASE TELL ME THAT THING IS ON OUR SIDE?
HEADS UP, GUYS!
UNFORTUNATELY, BOBBY...
...NO, IT'S NOT.
FIRE.

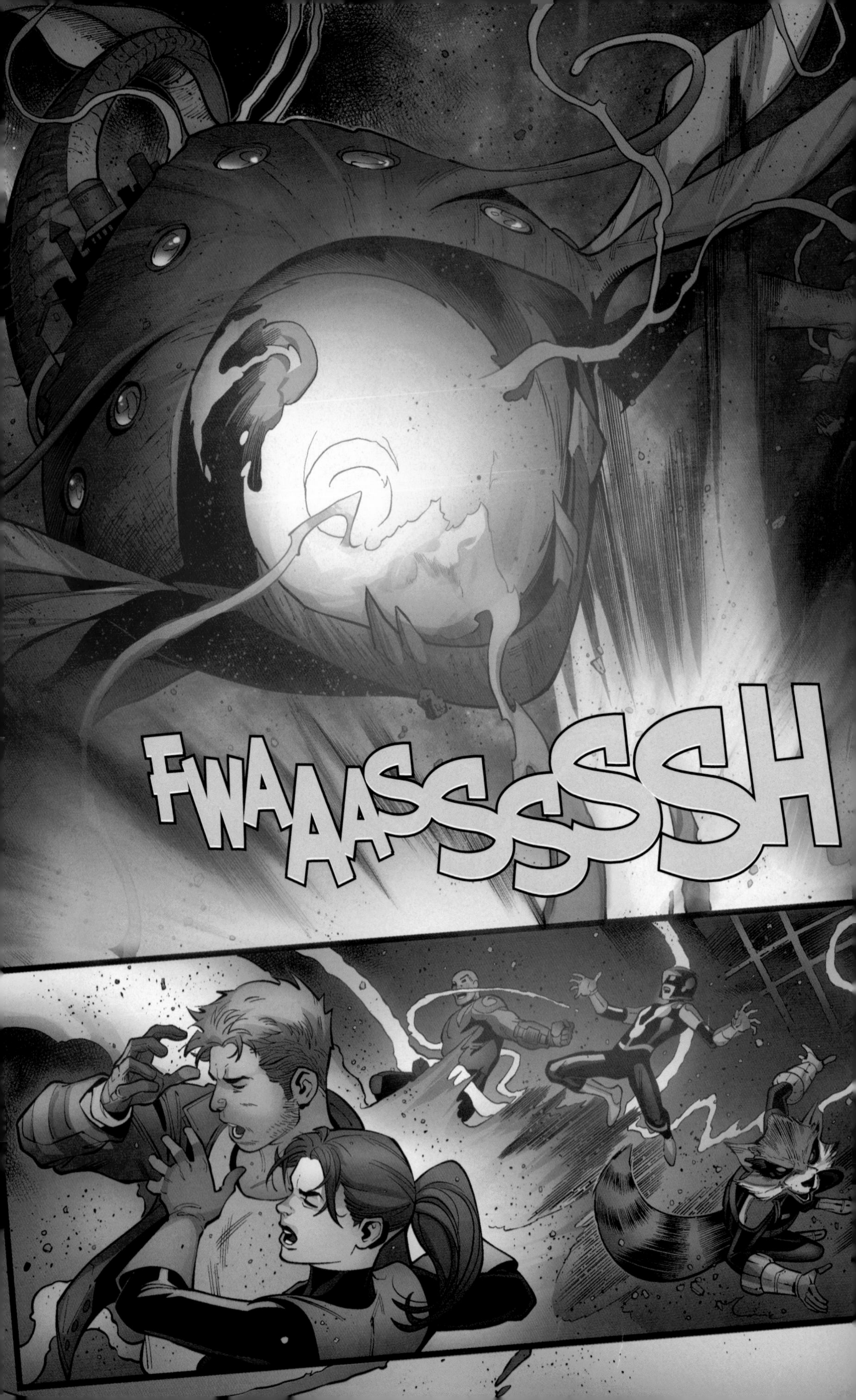
FWAAASSSSH

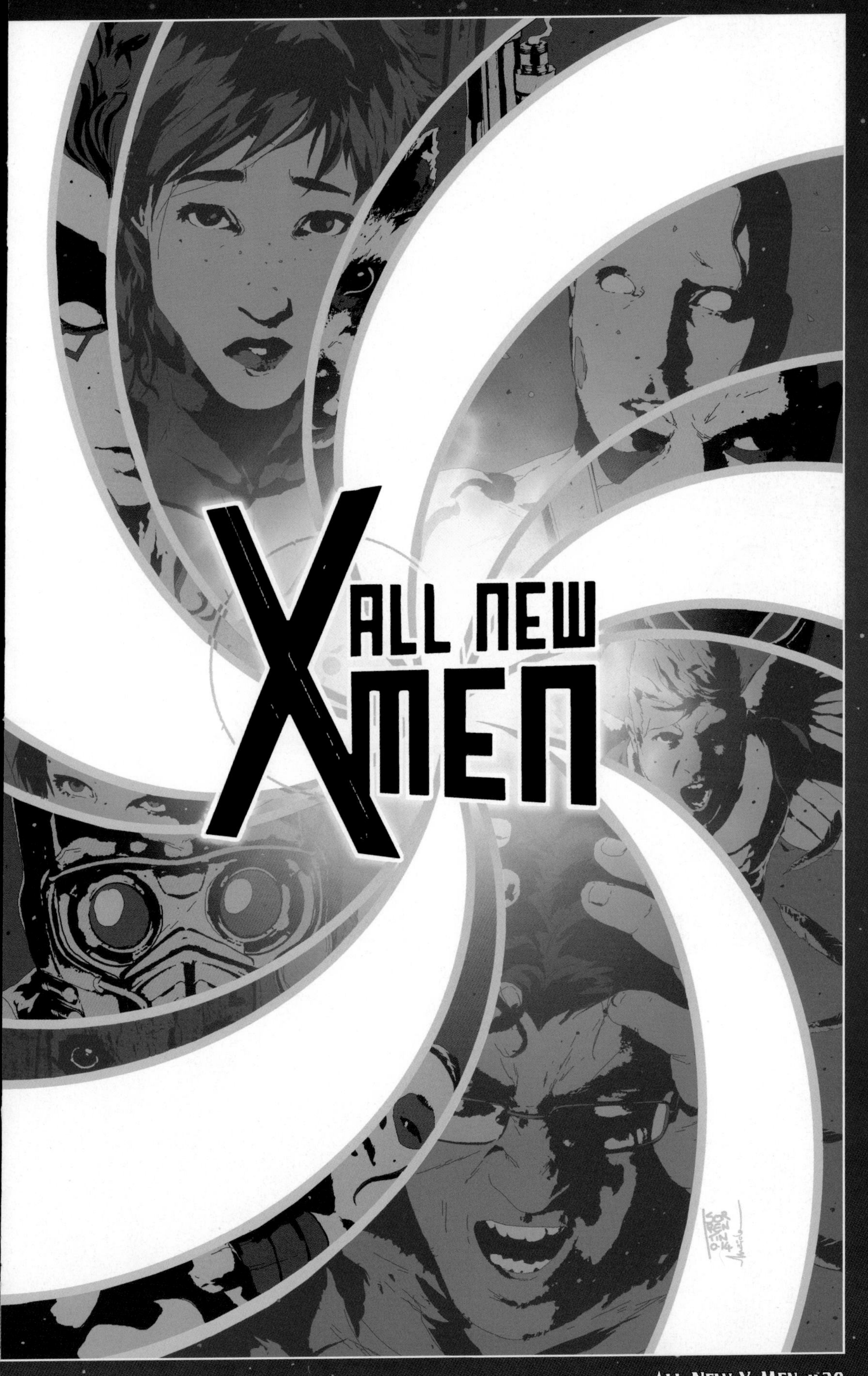
ALL NEW
X
MEN

ALL-NEW X-MEN #38

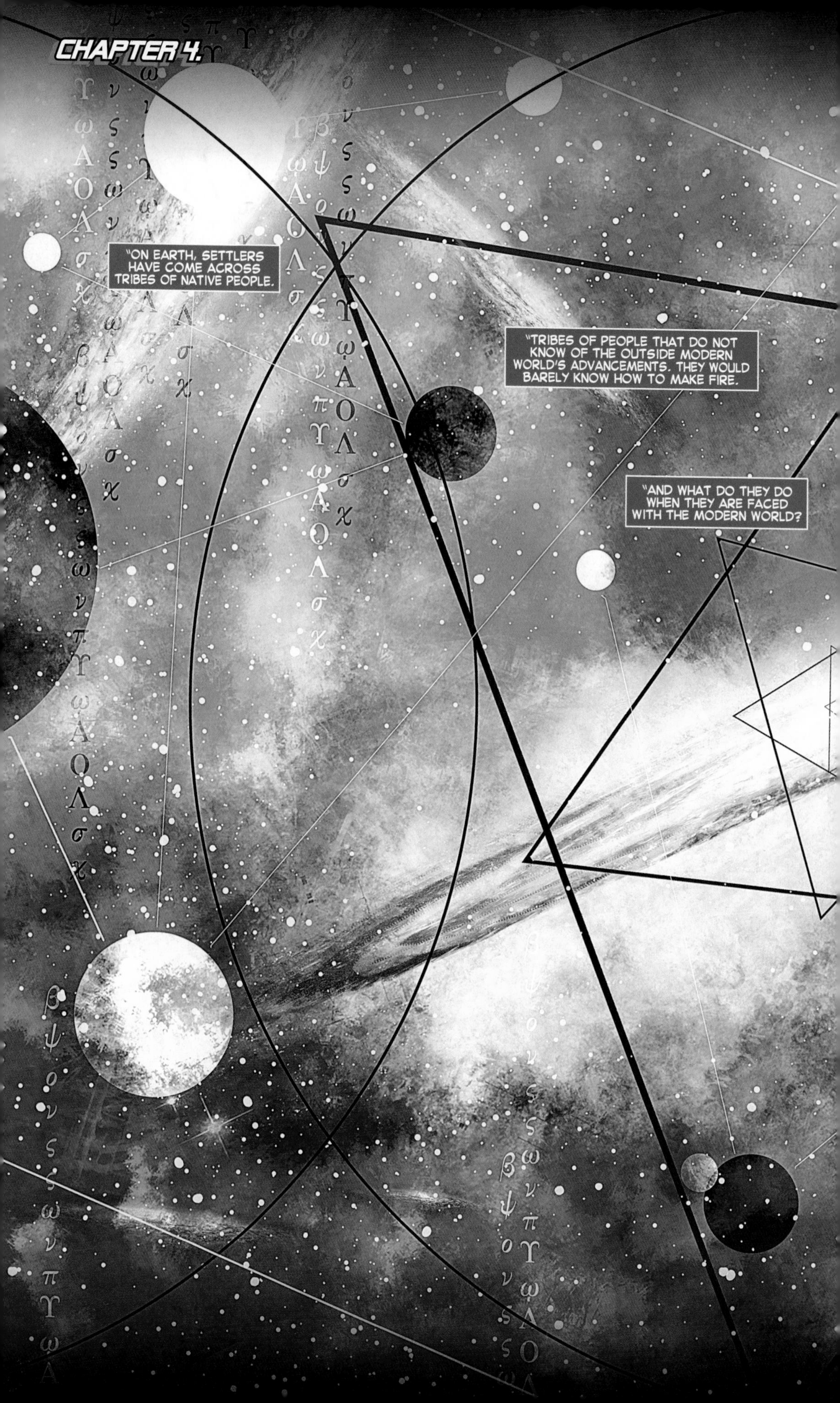
CHAPTER 4.
"ON EARTH, SETTLERS HAVE COME ACROSS TRIBES OF NATIVE PEOPLE.
"TRIBES OF PEOPLE THAT DO NOT KNOW OF THE OUTSIDE MODERN WORLD'S ADVANCEMENTS. THEY WOULD BARELY KNOW HOW TO MAKE FIRE.
"AND WHAT DO THEY DO WHEN THEY ARE FACED WITH THE MODERN WORLD?

"THEY SEE SORCERY. THEY SEE DEMONS. THEY ATTACK IT.
"THIS IS WHAT IS HAPPENING NOW.
"THEY CAN'T SEE WHAT WE SEE, THEY CAN'T FEEL WHAT WE FEEL.
"CHANGE TERRIFIES THE WEAK.
"WE HAVE TO SHOW THEM THIS IS FOR THEIR OWN GOOD.
"WE HAVE TO SHOW THEM WHAT WE SEE.
"WE HAVE TO SHOW THEM THEY ARE PRIMITIVE CAVE PEOPLE AND THAT WE..."

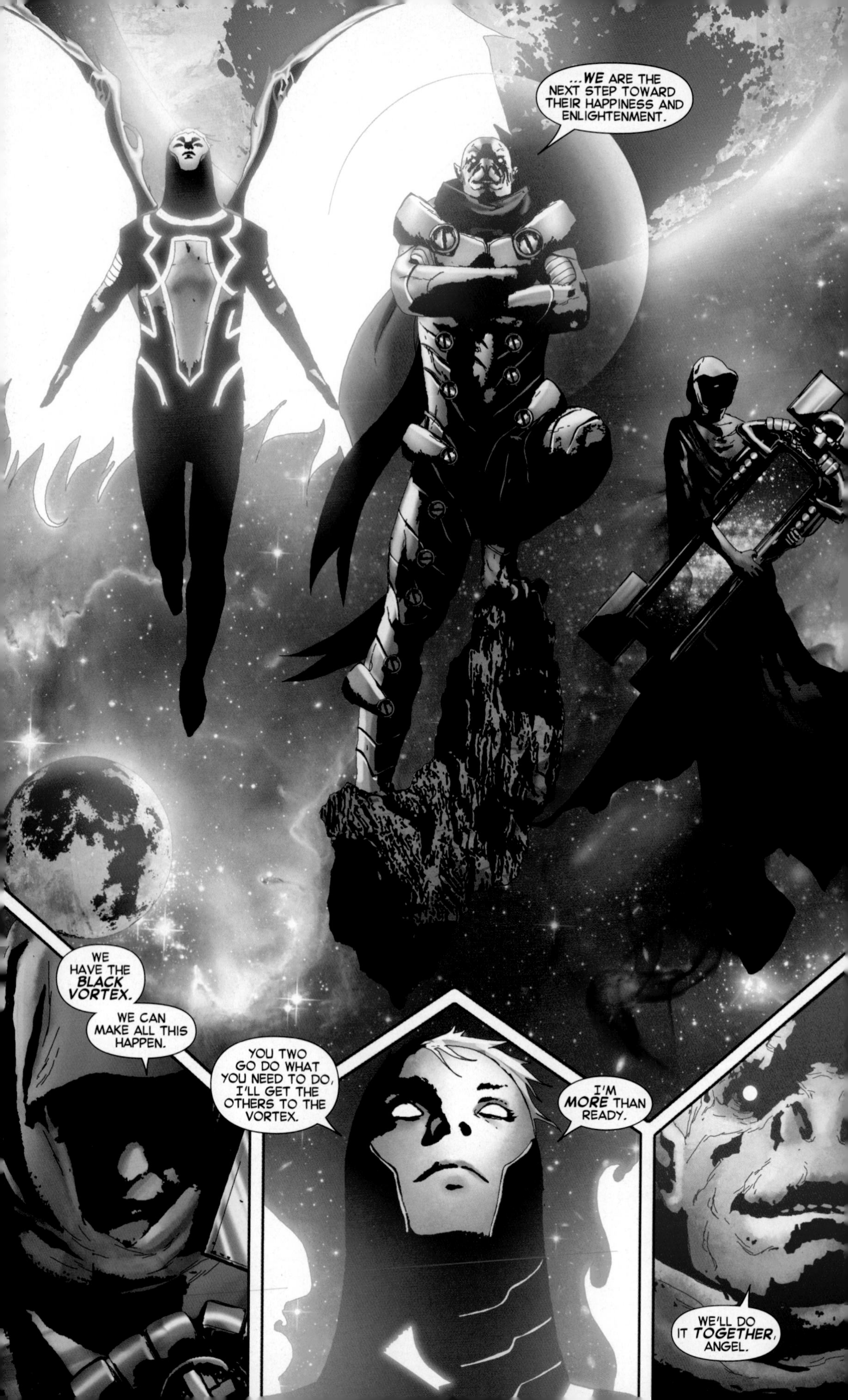
...WE ARE THE NEXT STEP TOWARD THEIR HAPPINESS AND ENLIGHTENMENT.
WE HAVE THE BLACK VORTEX.
WE CAN MAKE ALL THIS HAPPEN.
YOU TWO GO DO WHAT YOU NEED TO DO, I'LL GET THE OTHERS TO THE VORTEX.
I'M MORE THAN READY.
WE'LL DO IT TOGETHER, ANGEL.

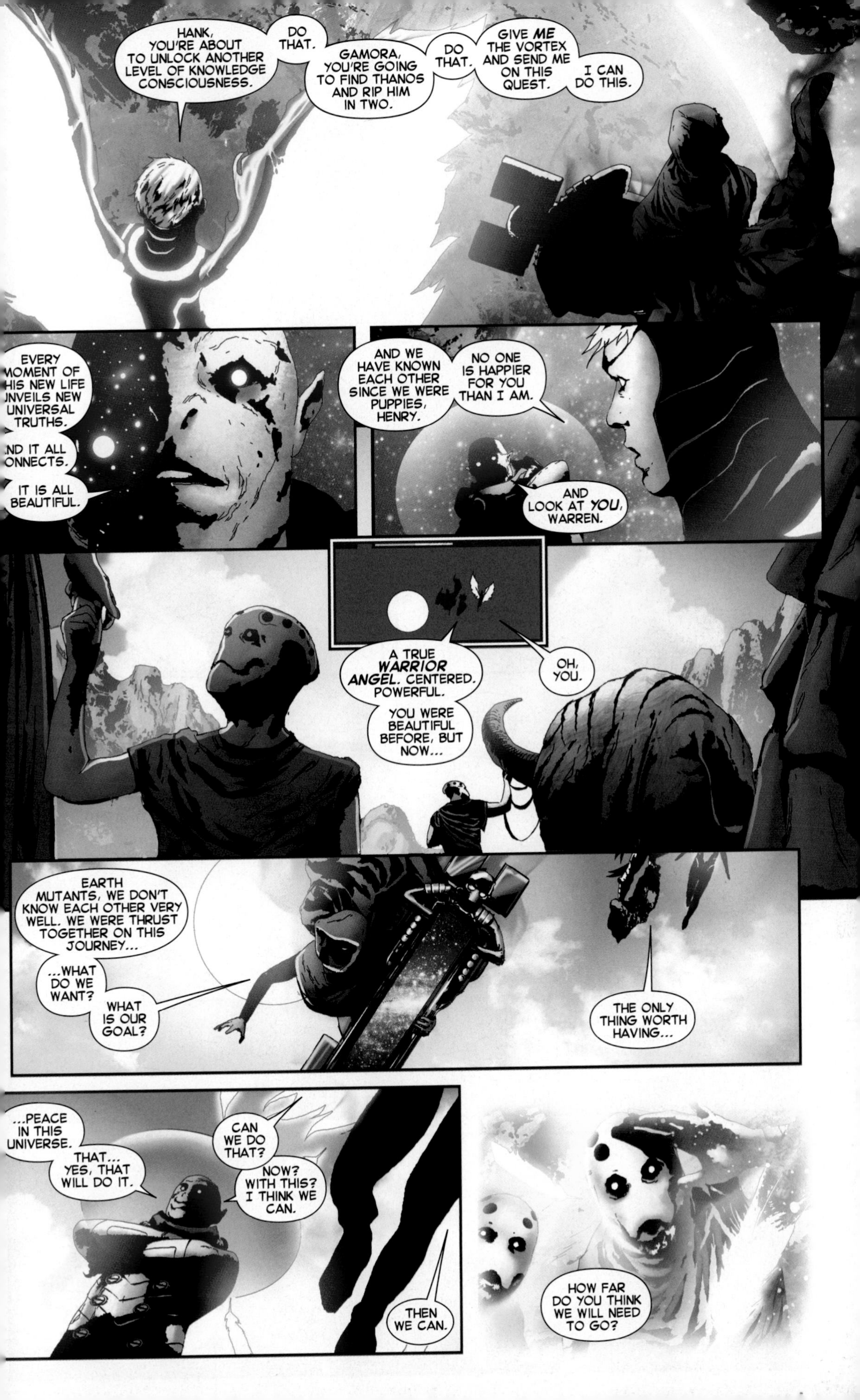
HANK, YOU'RE ABOUT TO UNLOCK ANOTHER LEVEL OF KNOWLEDGE CONSCIOUSNESS.
DO THAT.
GAMORA, YOU'RE GOING TO FIND THANOS AND RIP HIM IN TWO.
DO THAT.
GIVE ME THE VORTEX AND SEND ME ON THIS QUEST.
I CAN DO THIS.
EVERY MOMENT OF HIS NEW LIFE UNVEILS NEW UNIVERSAL TRUTHS.
AND IT ALL CONNECTS.
IT IS ALL BEAUTIFUL.
AND WE HAVE KNOWN EACH OTHER SINCE WE WERE PUPPIES, HENRY.
NO ONE IS HAPPIER FOR YOU THAN I AM.
AND LOOK AT YOU, WARREN.
A TRUE WARRIOR ANGEL. CENTERED. POWERFUL.
YOU WERE BEAUTIFUL BEFORE, BUT NOW...
OH, YOU.
EARTH MUTANTS, WE DON'T KNOW EACH OTHER VERY WELL. WE WERE THRUST TOGETHER ON THIS JOURNEY...
...WHAT DO WE WANT?
WHAT IS OUR GOAL?
THE ONLY THING WORTH HAVING...
...PEACE IN THIS UNIVERSE.
THAT... YES, THAT WILL DO IT.
CAN WE DO THAT?
NOW? WITH THIS? I THINK WE CAN.
THEN WE CAN.
HOW FAR DO YOU THINK WE WILL NEED TO GO?

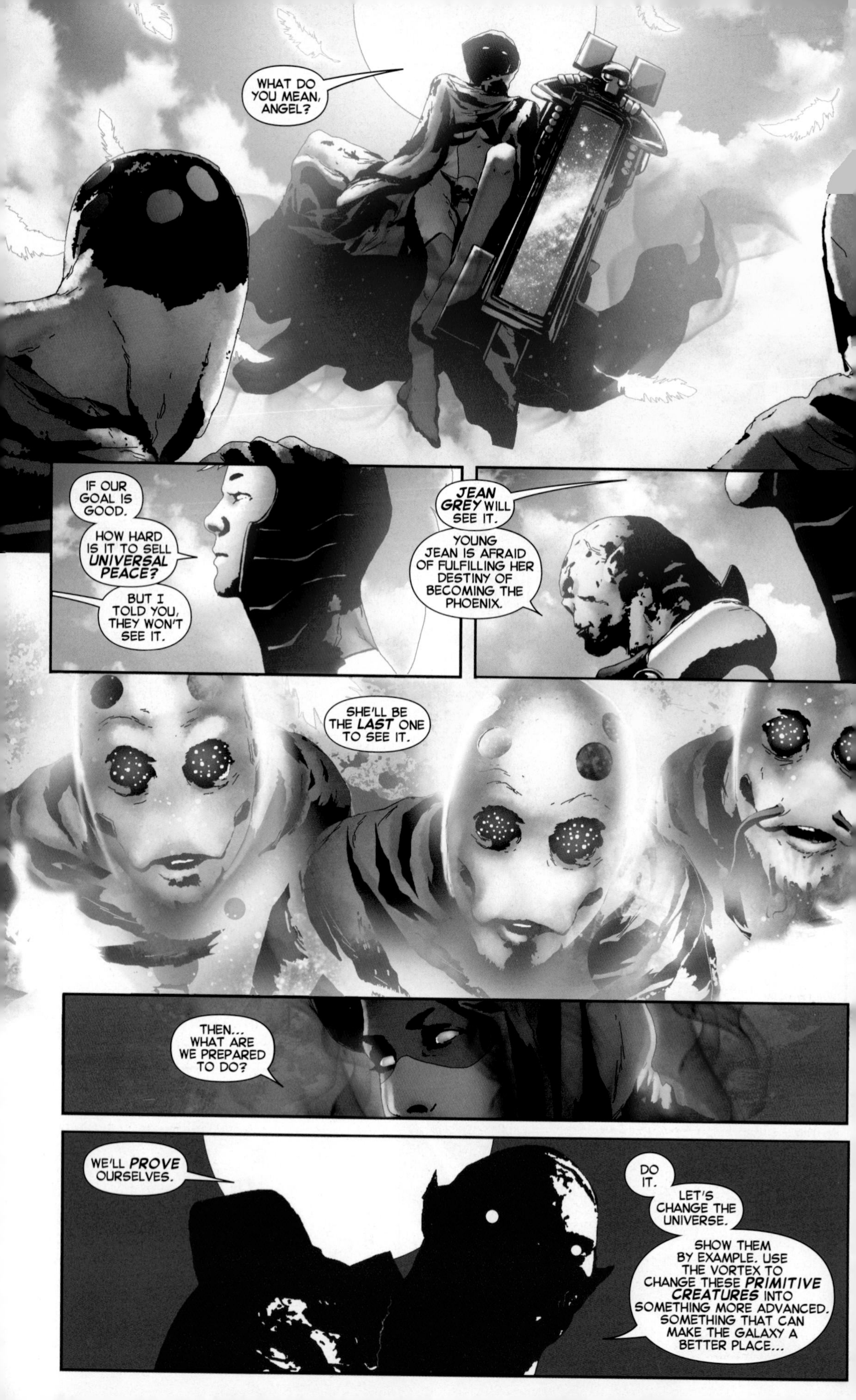
WHAT DO YOU MEAN, ANGEL?
IF OUR GOAL IS GOOD.
HOW HARD IS IT TO SELL UNIVERSAL PEACE?
BUT I TOLD YOU, THEY WON'T SEE IT.
JEAN GREY WILL SEE IT.
YOUNG JEAN IS AFRAID OF FULFILLING HER DESTINY OF BECOMING THE PHOENIX.
SHE'LL BE THE LAST ONE TO SEE IT.
THEN... WHAT ARE WE PREPARED TO DO?
WE'LL PROVE OURSELVES.
DO IT.
LET'S CHANGE THE UNIVERSE.
SHOW THEM BY EXAMPLE. USE THE VORTEX TO CHANGE THESE PRIMITIVE CREATURES INTO SOMETHING MORE ADVANCED. SOMETHING THAT CAN MAKE THE GALAXY A BETTER PLACE...

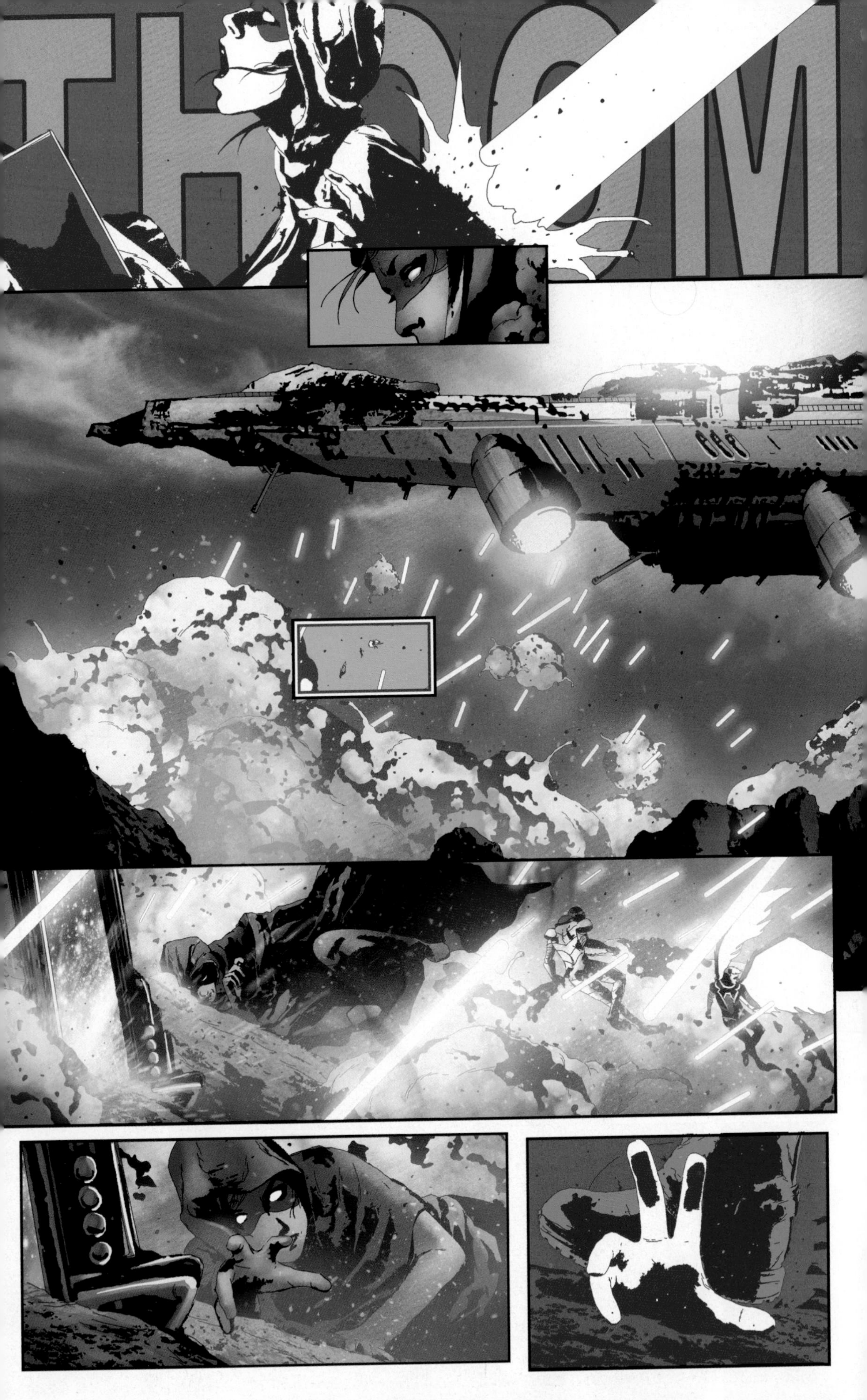
THOOM

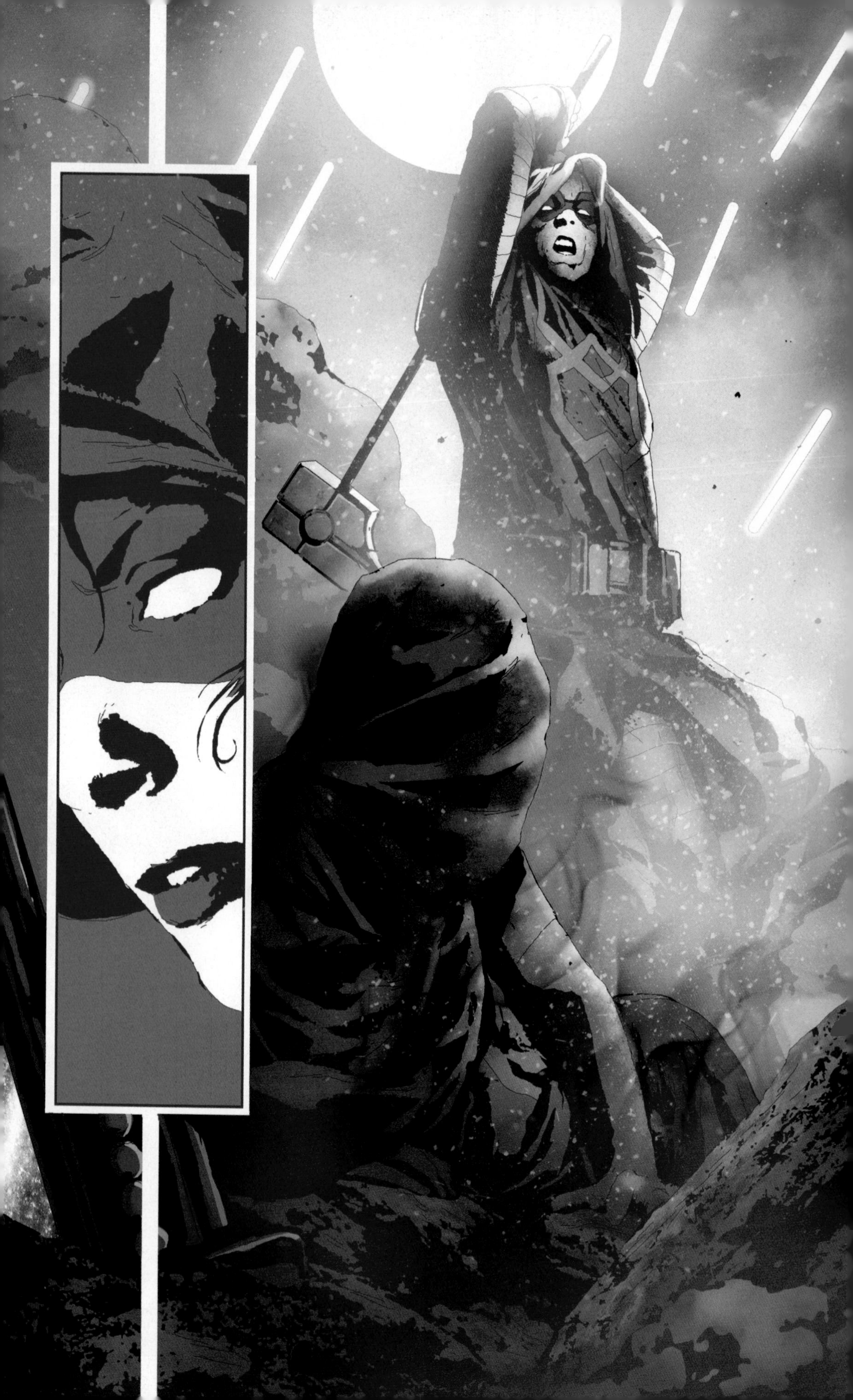

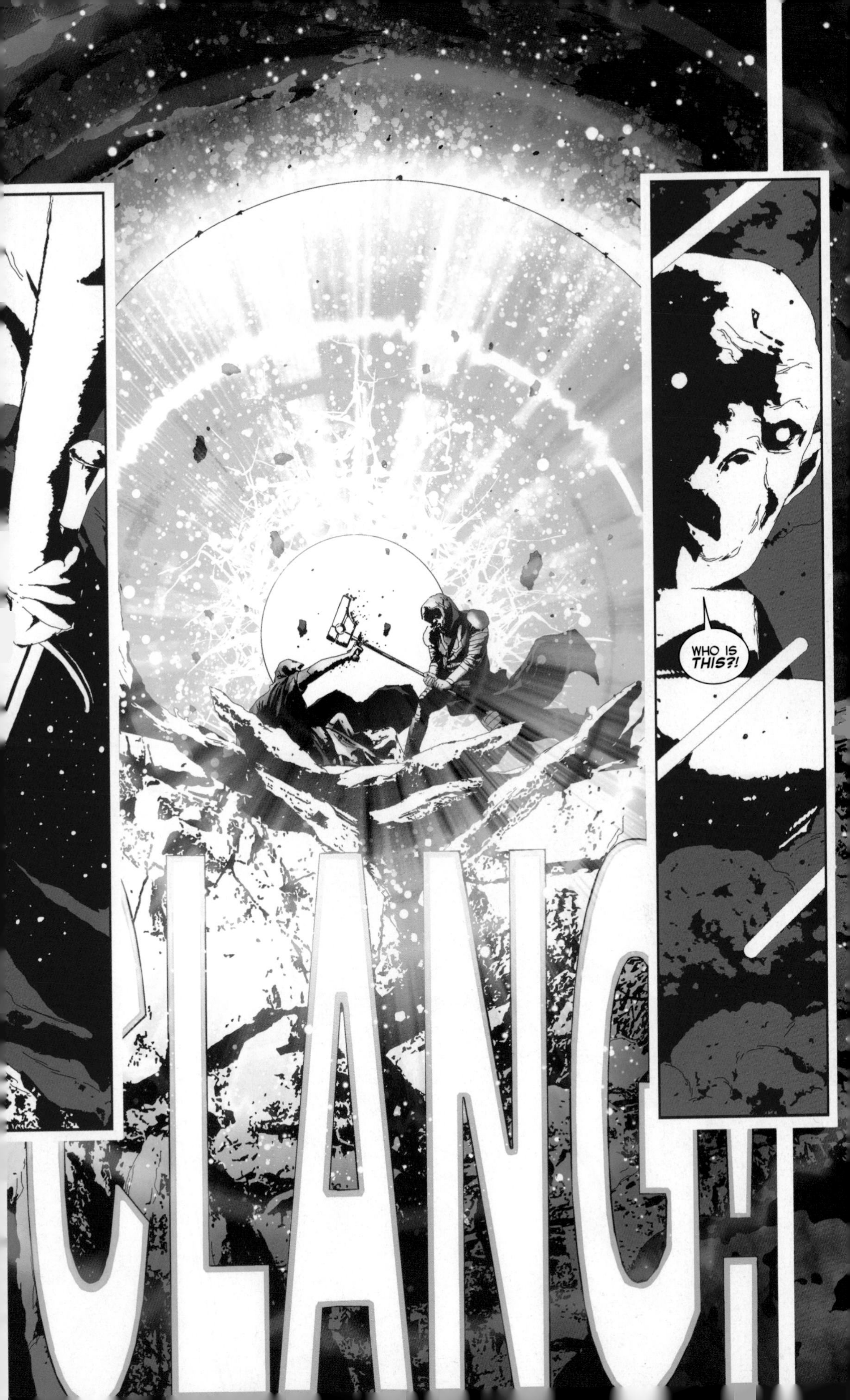

WHO IS THIS?!
CLANCH!

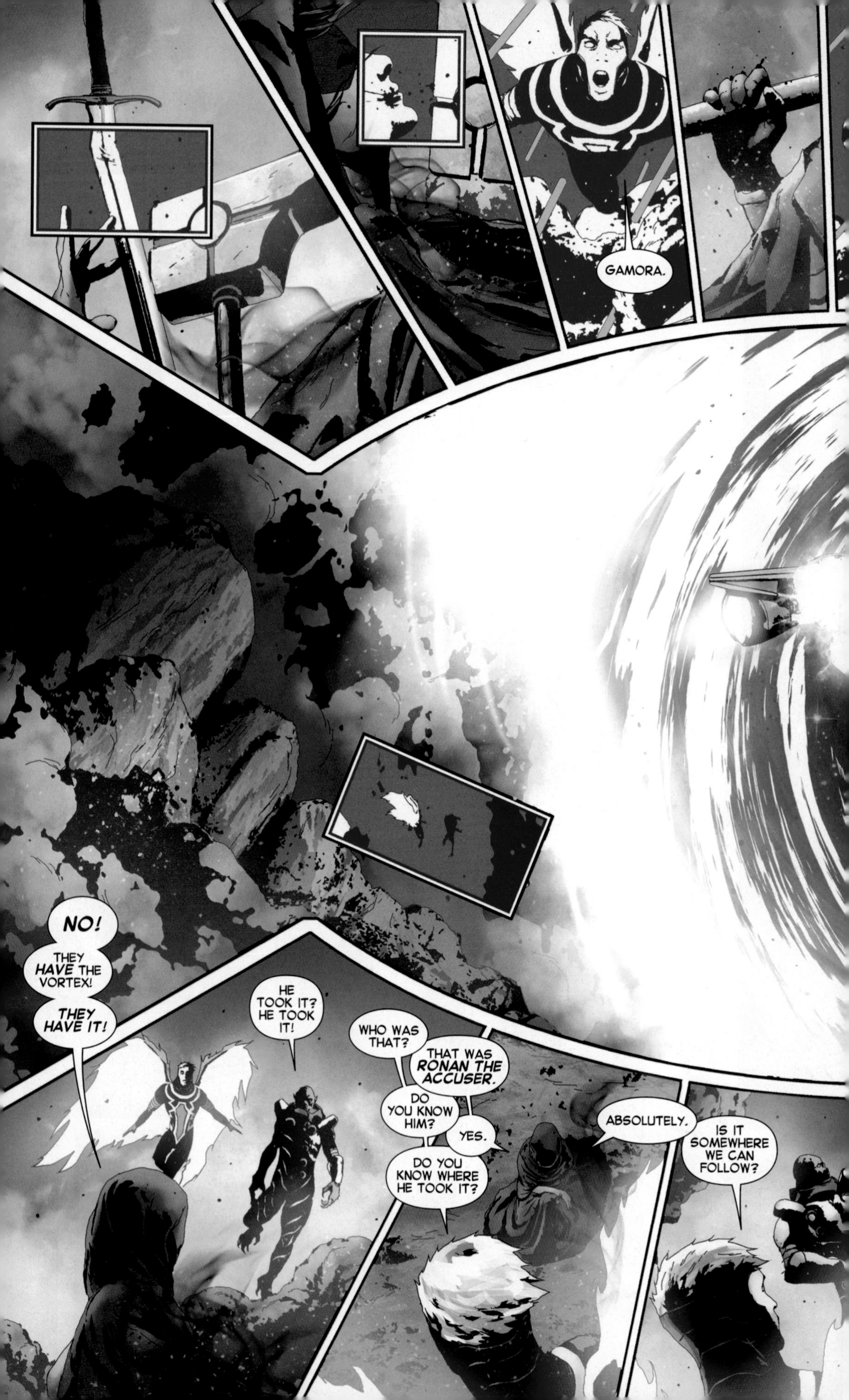
GAMORA.
NO!
THEY HAVE THE VORTEX!
THEY HAVE IT!
HE TOOK IT? HE TOOK IT!
WHO WAS THAT?
THAT WAS RONAN THE ACCUSER.
DO YOU KNOW HIM?
YES.
DO YOU KNOW WHERE HE TOOK IT?
ABSOLUTELY.
IS IT SOMEWHERE WE CAN FOLLOW?

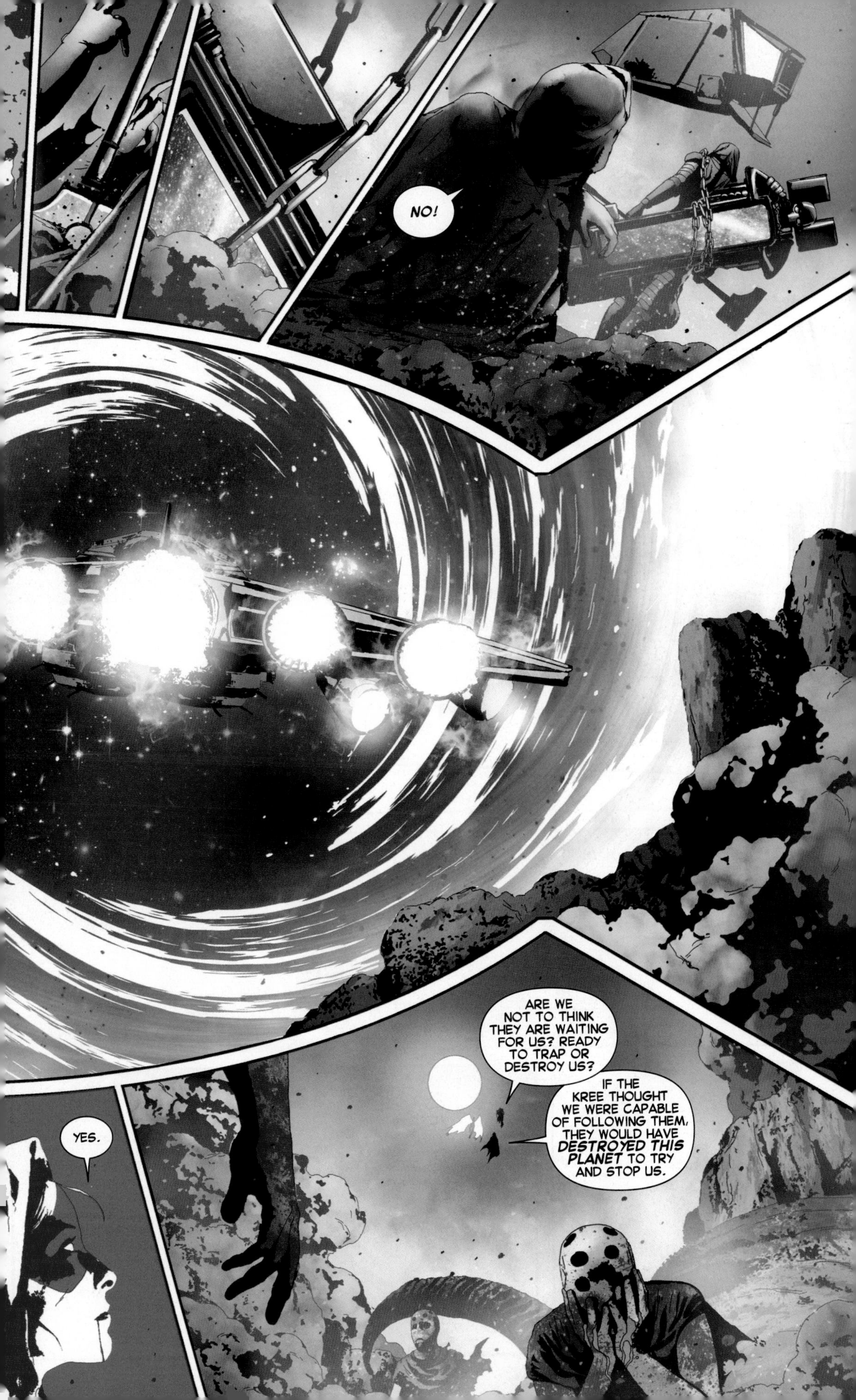
NO!
ARE WE NOT TO THINK THEY ARE WAITING FOR US? READY TO TRAP OR DESTROY US?
IF THE KREE THOUGHT WE WERE CAPABLE OF FOLLOWING THEM, THEY WOULD HAVE **DESTROYED THIS PLANET** TO TRY AND STOP US.
YES.

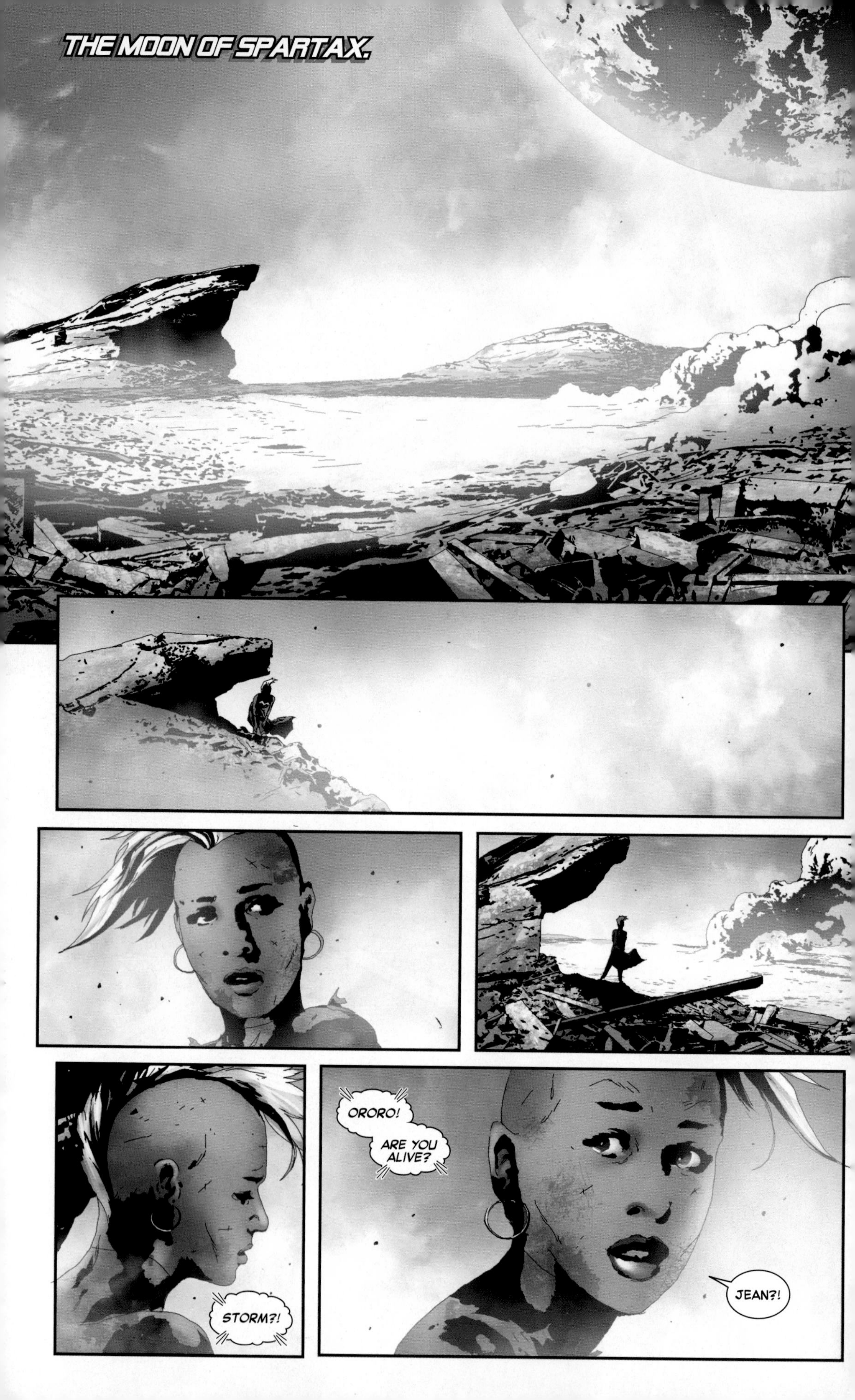
THE MOON OF SPARTAX.
ORORO!
ARE YOU ALIVE?
STORM?!
JEAN?!

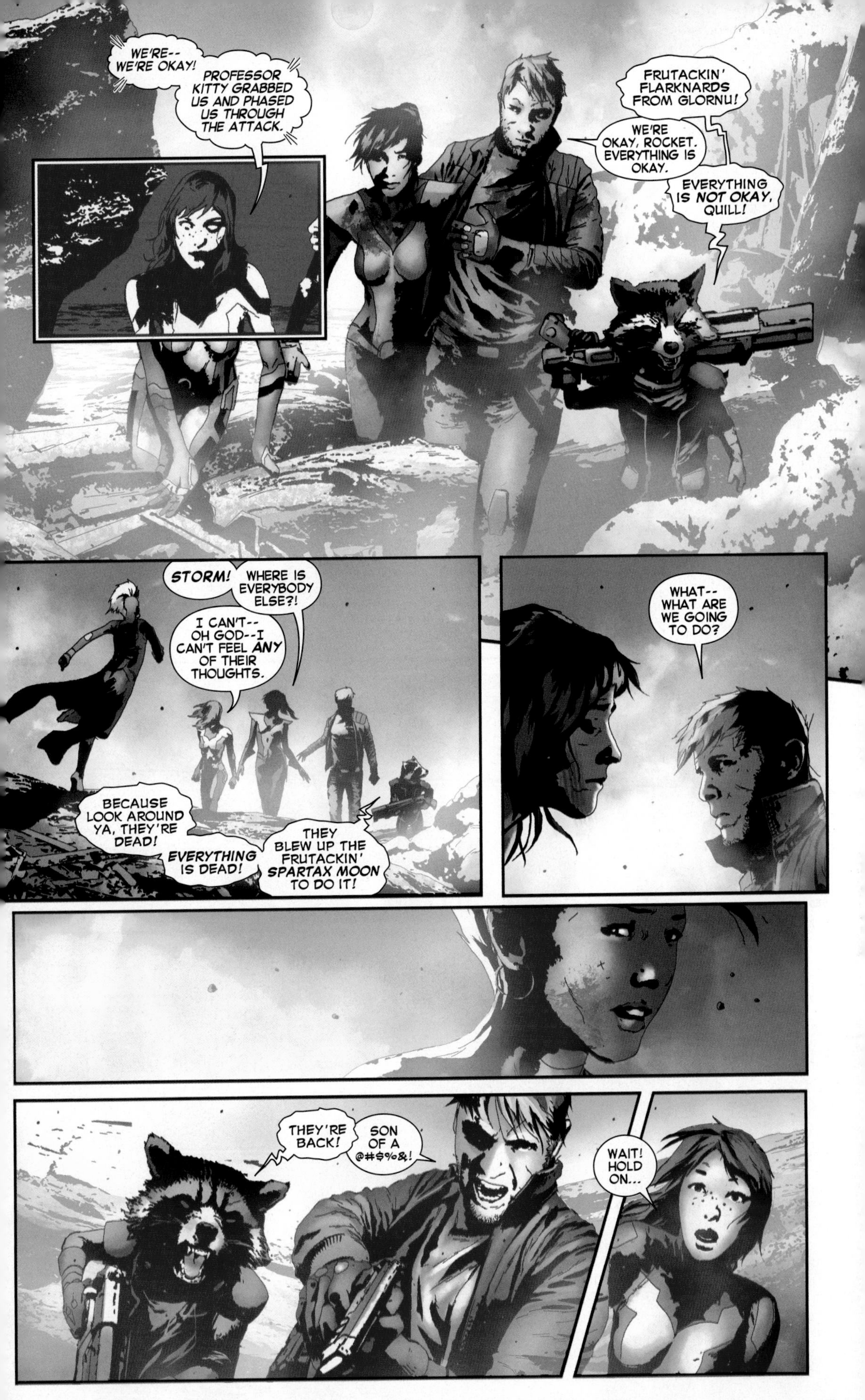
WE'RE--
WE'RE OKAY!
PROFESSOR KITTY GRABBED US AND PHASED US THROUGH THE ATTACK.
FRUTACKIN' FLARKNARDS FROM GLORNU!
WE'RE OKAY, ROCKET. EVERYTHING IS OKAY.
EVERYTHING IS NOT OKAY, QUILL!
STORM!
WHERE IS EVERYBODY ELSE?!
I CAN'T-- OH GOD--I CAN'T FEEL ANY OF THEIR THOUGHTS.
BECAUSE LOOK AROUND YA, THEY'RE DEAD!
EVERYTHING IS DEAD!
THEY BLEW UP THE FRUTACKIN' SPARTAX MOON TO DO IT!
WHAT-- WHAT ARE WE GOING TO DO?
THEY'RE BACK!
SON OF A @#$%&!
WAIT! HOLD ON...

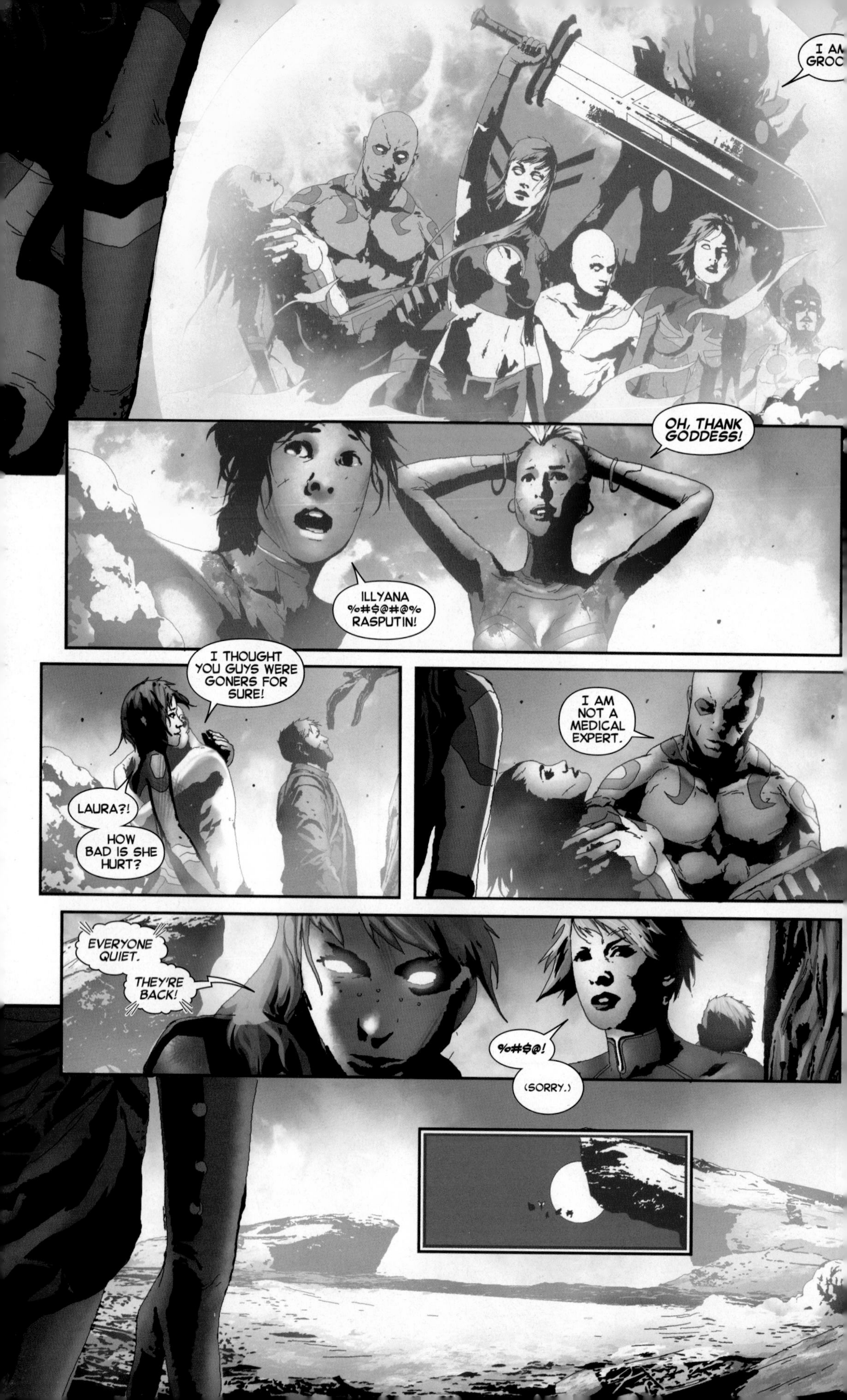
I AM GROO
OH, THANK GODDESS!
ILLYANA %#$@#@% RASPUTIN!
I THOUGHT YOU GUYS WERE GONERS FOR SURE!
LAURA?!
HOW BAD IS SHE HURT?
I AM NOT A MEDICAL EXPERT.
EVERYONE QUIET.
THEY'RE BACK!
%#$@!
(SORRY.)

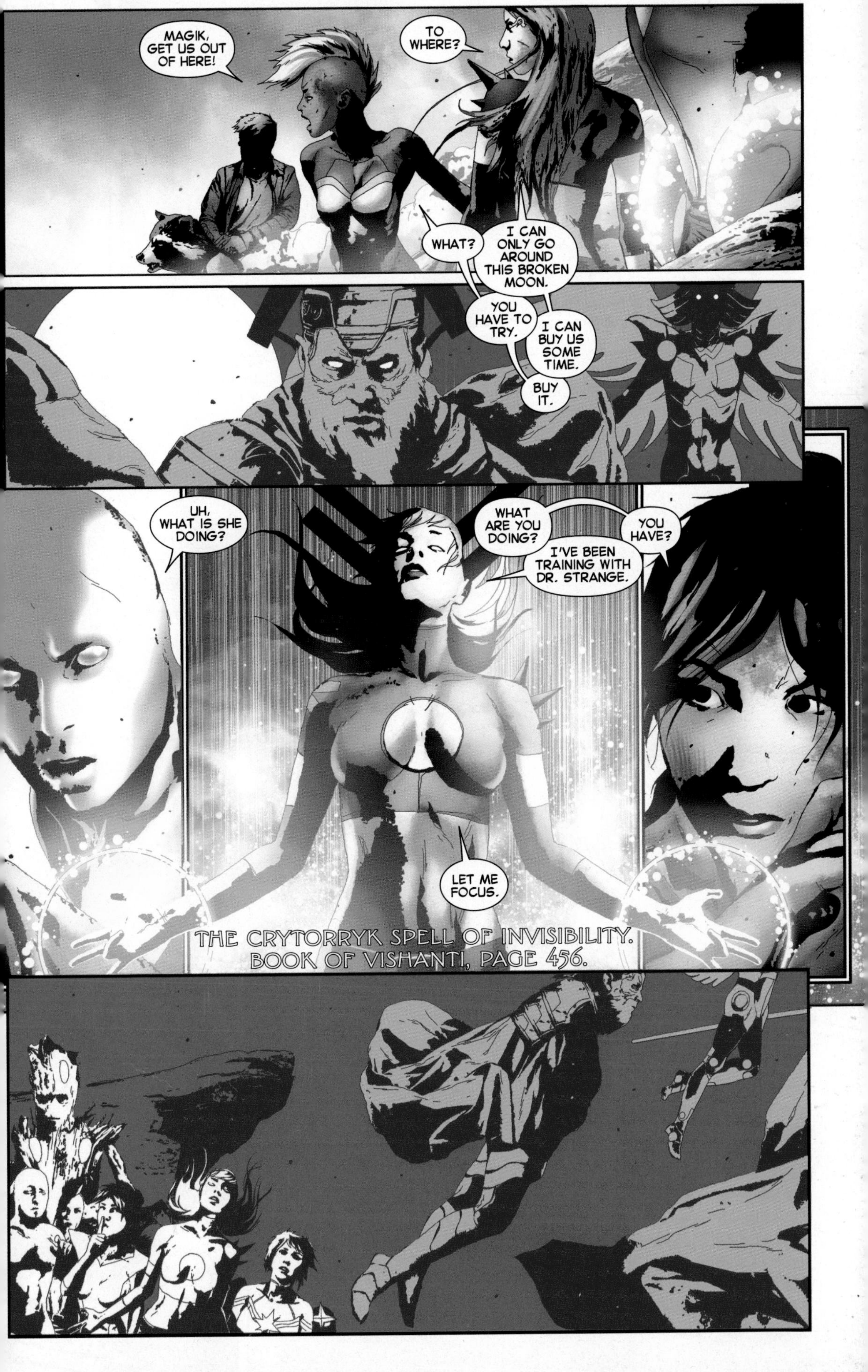
MAGIK, GET US OUT OF HERE!
TO WHERE?
WHAT?
I CAN ONLY GO AROUND THIS BROKEN MOON.
YOU HAVE TO TRY.
I CAN BUY US SOME TIME.
BUY IT.
UH, WHAT IS SHE DOING?
WHAT ARE YOU DOING?
YOU HAVE?
I'VE BEEN TRAINING WITH DR. STRANGE.
LET ME FOCUS.
THE CRYTORRYK SPELL OF INVISIBILITY.
BOOK OF VISHANTI, PAGE 456.

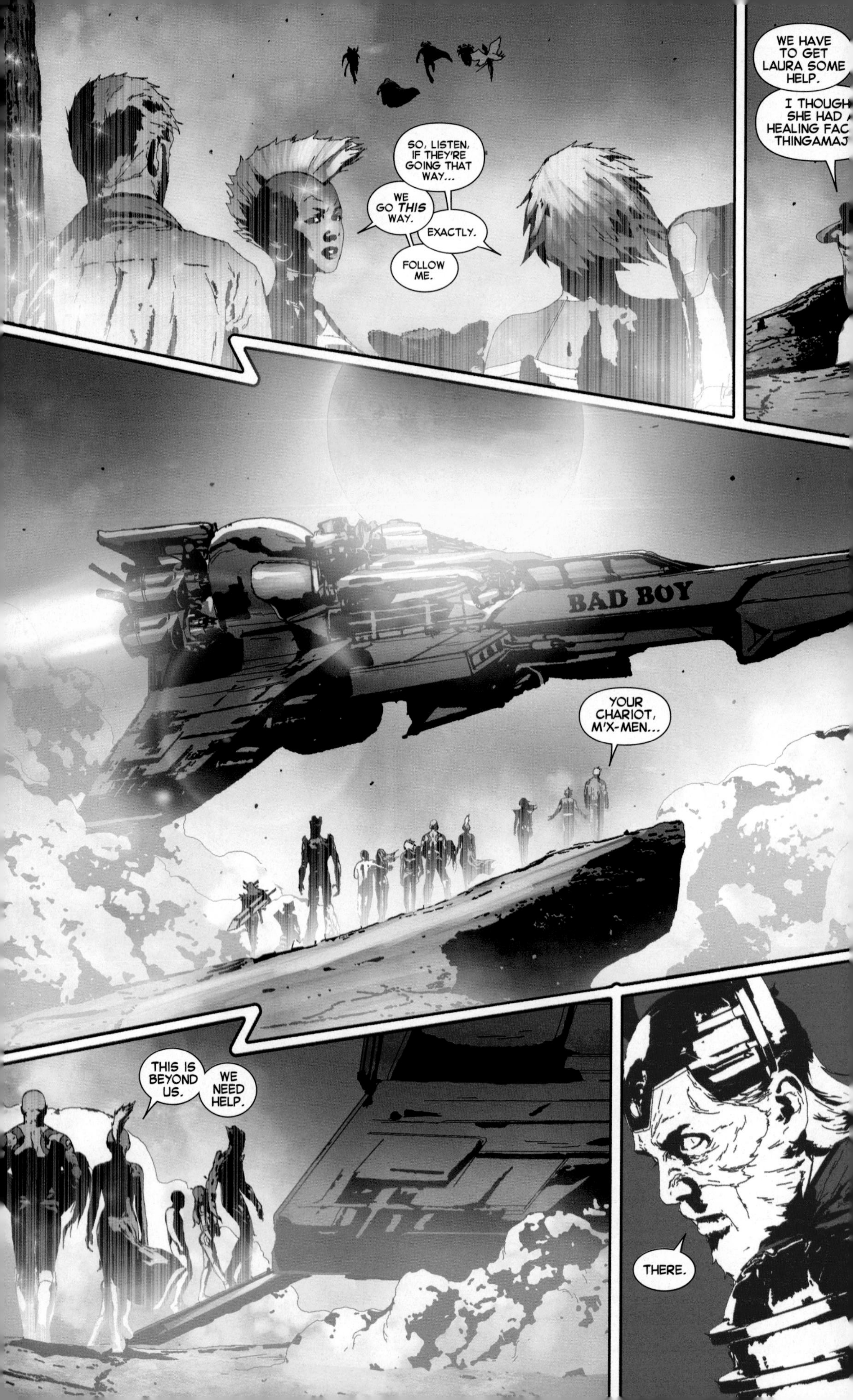
SO, LISTEN, IF THEY'RE GOING THAT WAY...
WE GO *THIS* WAY.
EXACTLY.
FOLLOW ME.
WE HAVE TO GET LAURA SOME HELP.
I THOUGH SHE HAD HEALING FAC THINGAMAJ
BAD BOY
YOUR CHARIOT, M'X-MEN...
THIS IS BEYOND US.
WE NEED HELP.
THERE.

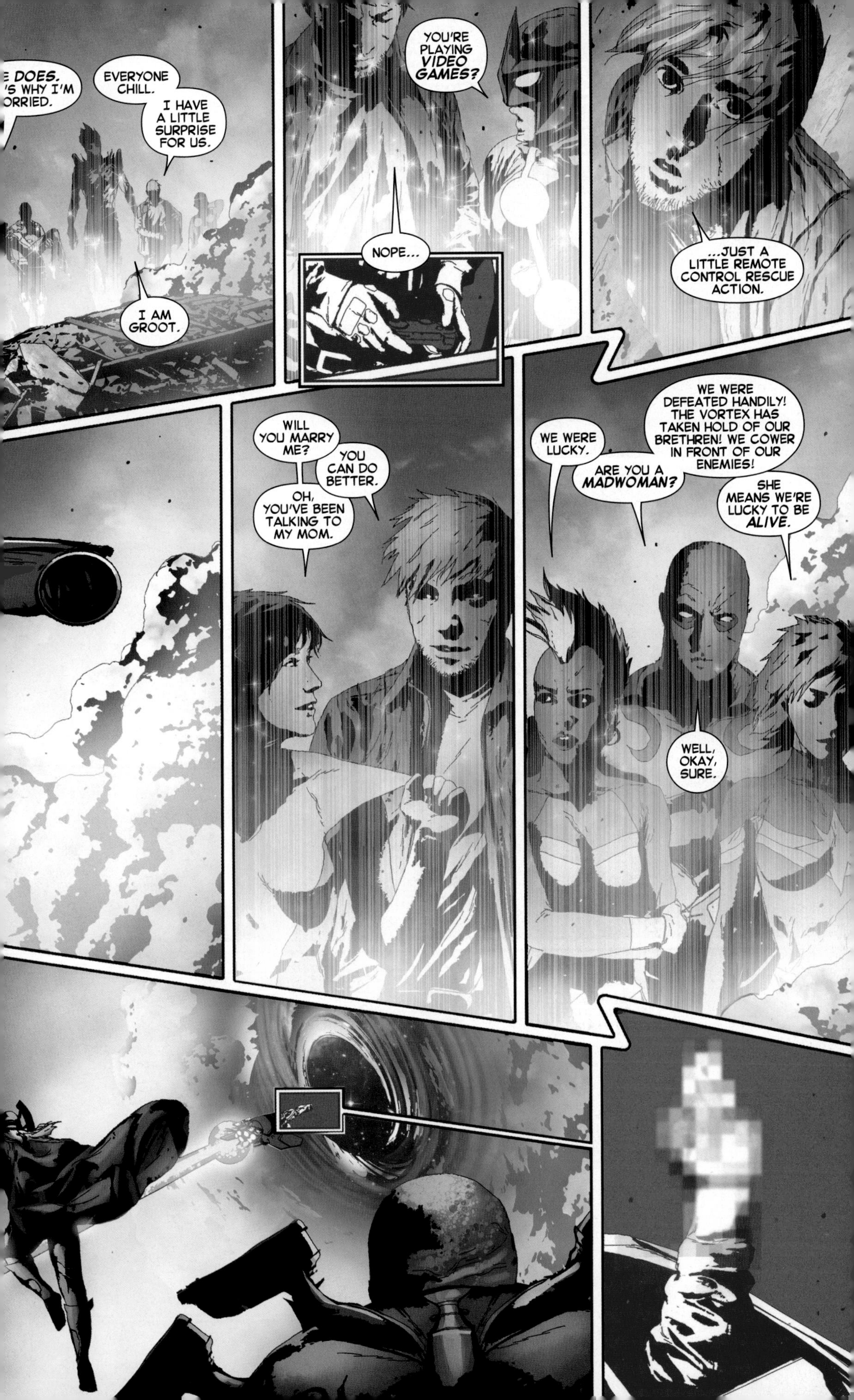
E DOES. 'S WHY I'M ORRIED.
EVERYONE CHILL.
I HAVE A LITTLE SURPRISE FOR US.
I AM GROOT.
YOU'RE PLAYING VIDEO GAMES?
NOPE...
...JUST A LITTLE REMOTE CONTROL RESCUE ACTION.
WILL YOU MARRY ME?
YOU CAN DO BETTER.
OH, YOU'VE BEEN TALKING TO MY MOM.
WE WERE LUCKY.
WE WERE DEFEATED HANDILY! THE VORTEX HAS TAKEN HOLD OF OUR BRETHREN! WE COWER IN FRONT OF OUR ENEMIES!
ARE YOU A MADWOMAN?
SHE MEANS WE'RE LUCKY TO BE ALIVE.
WELL, OKAY, SURE.

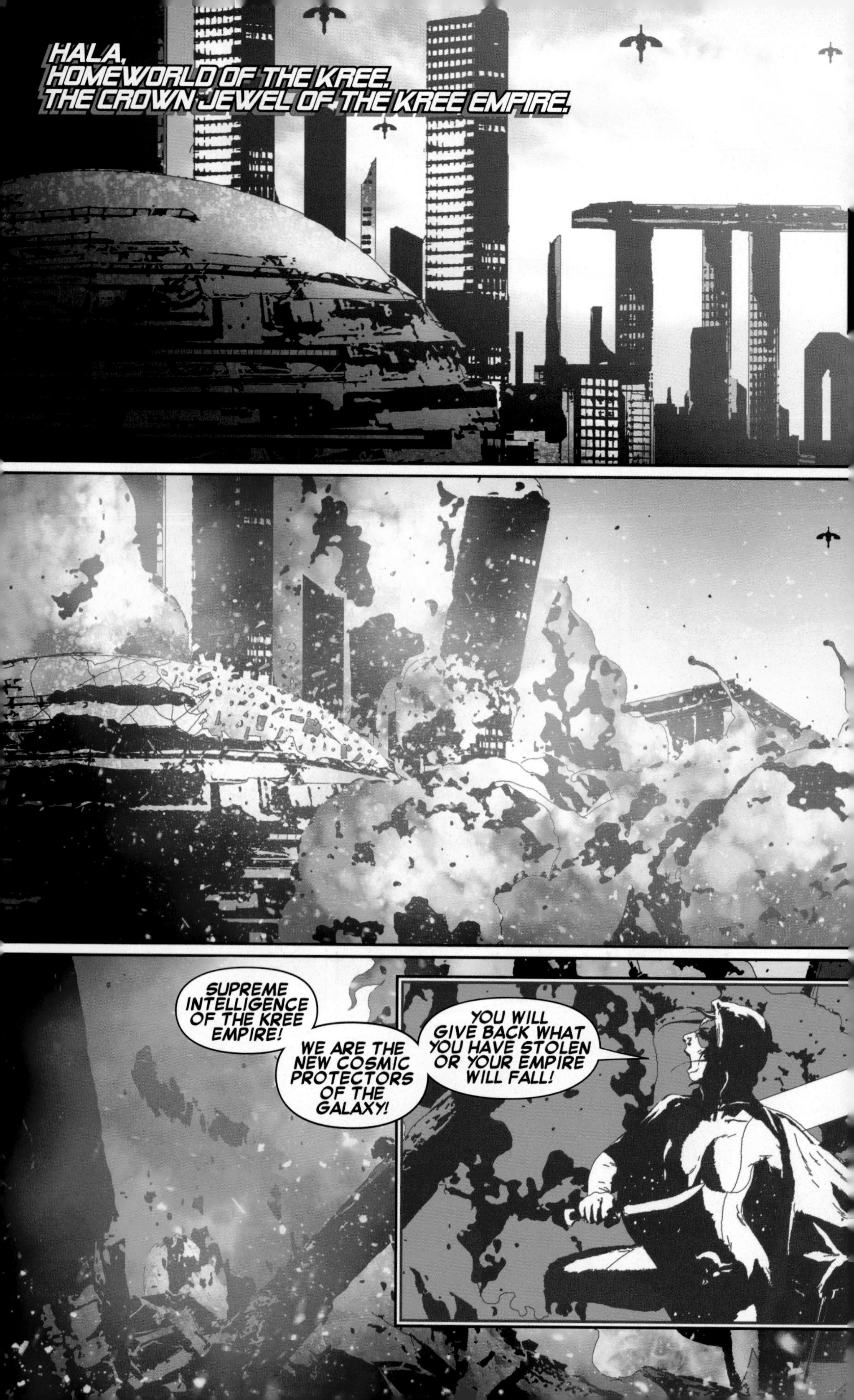
HALA,
HOMEWORLD OF THE KREE.
THE CROWN JEWEL OF THE KREE EMPIRE.
SUPREME INTELLIGENCE OF THE KREE EMPIRE!
WE ARE THE NEW COSMIC PROTECTORS OF THE GALAXY!
YOU WILL GIVE BACK WHAT YOU HAVE STOLEN OR YOUR EMPIRE WILL FALL!

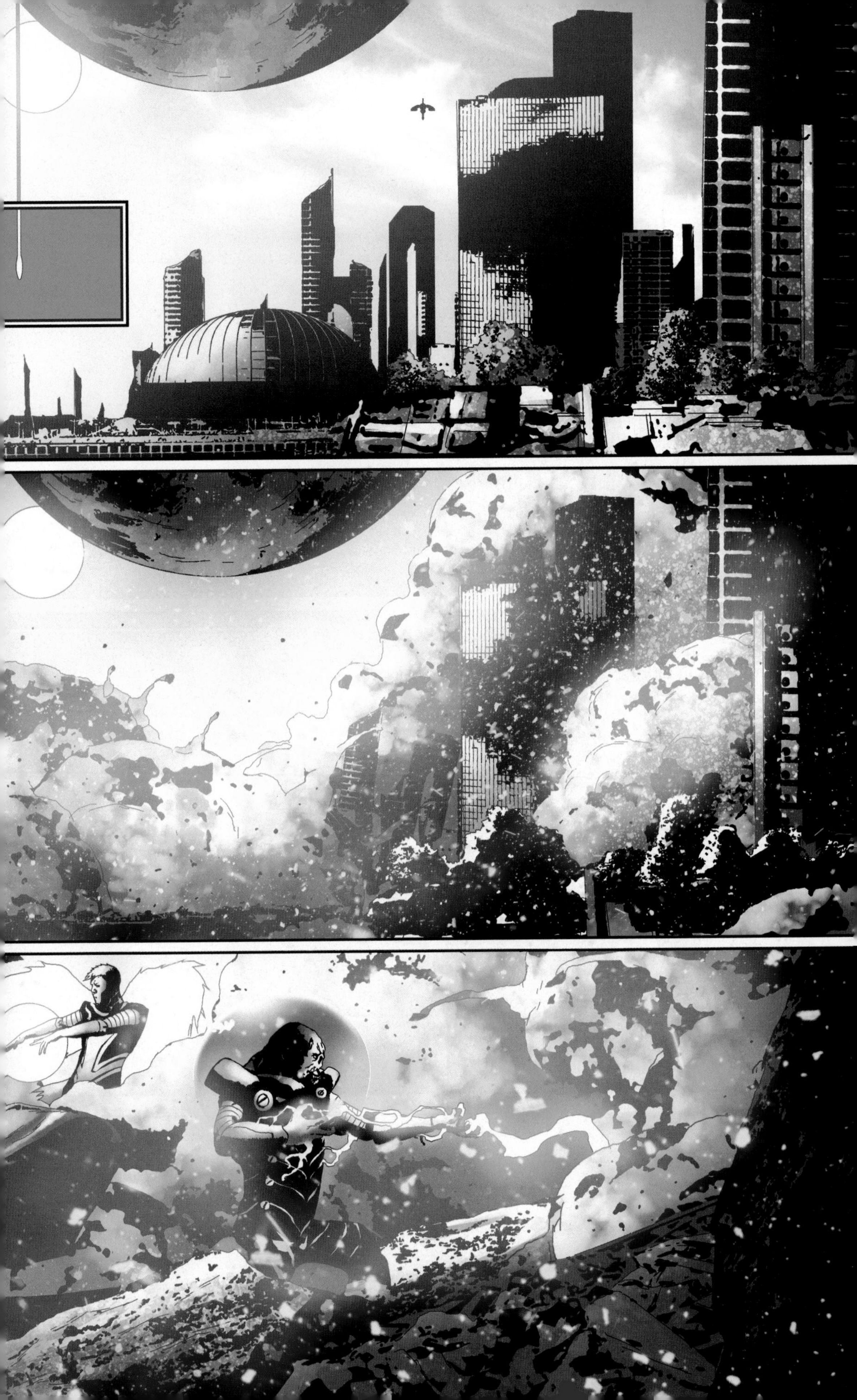

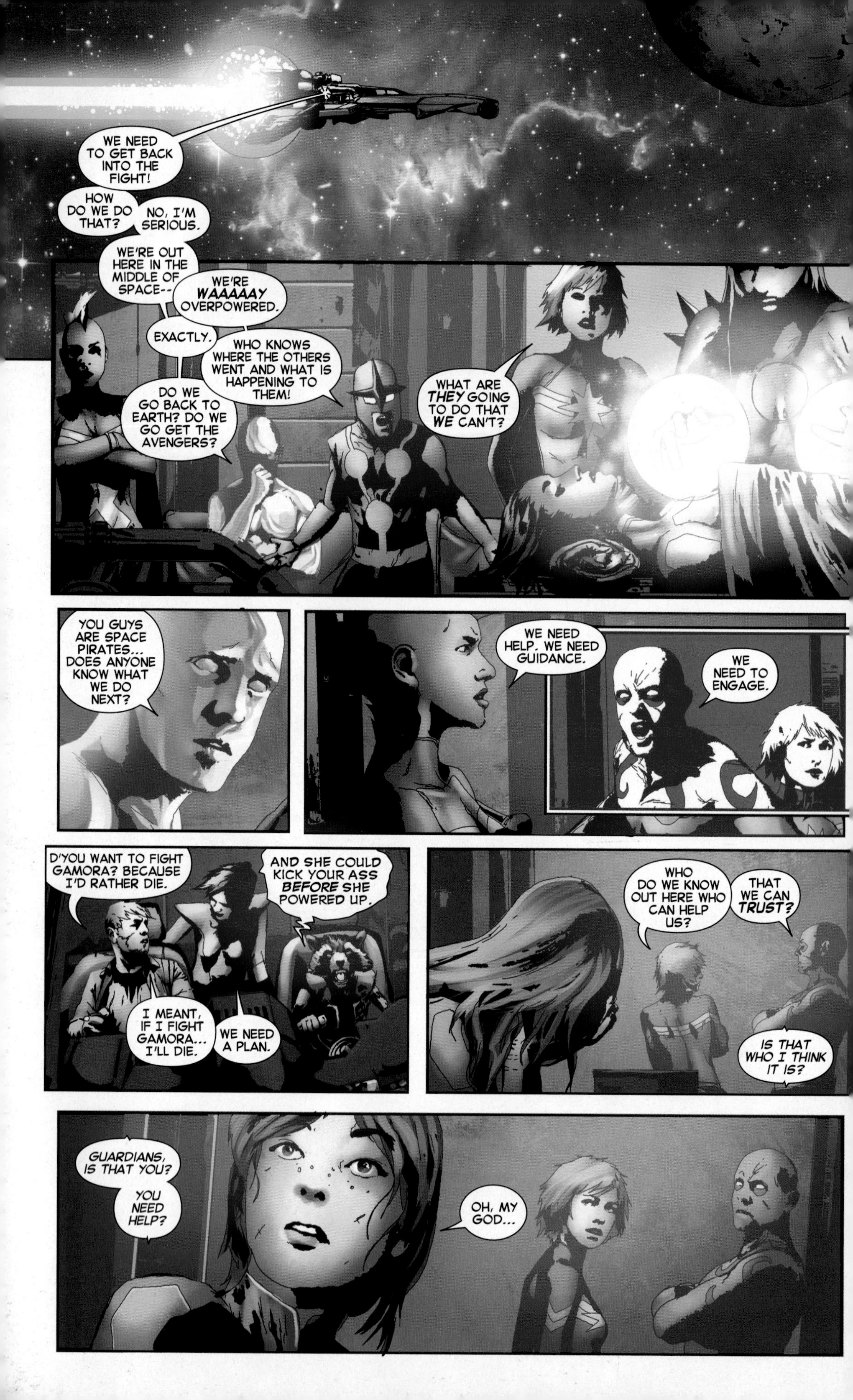
WE NEED TO GET BACK INTO THE FIGHT!
HOW DO WE DO THAT?
NO, I'M SERIOUS.
WE'RE OUT HERE IN THE MIDDLE OF SPACE--
WE'RE WAAAAAY OVERPOWERED.
EXACTLY.
WHO KNOWS WHERE THE OTHERS WENT AND WHAT IS HAPPENING TO THEM!
DO WE GO BACK TO EARTH? DO WE GO GET THE AVENGERS?
WHAT ARE THEY GOING TO DO THAT WE CAN'T?
YOU GUYS ARE SPACE PIRATES... DOES ANYONE KNOW WHAT WE DO NEXT?
WE NEED HELP. WE NEED GUIDANCE.
WE NEED TO ENGAGE.
D'YOU WANT TO FIGHT GAMORA? BECAUSE I'D RATHER DIE.
AND SHE COULD KICK YOUR ASS BEFORE SHE POWERED UP.
I MEANT, IF I FIGHT GAMORA... I'LL DIE.
WE NEED A PLAN.
WHO DO WE KNOW OUT HERE WHO CAN HELP US?
THAT WE CAN TRUST?
IS THAT WHO I THINK IT IS?
GUARDIANS, IS THAT YOU?
YOU NEED HELP?
OH, MY GOD...

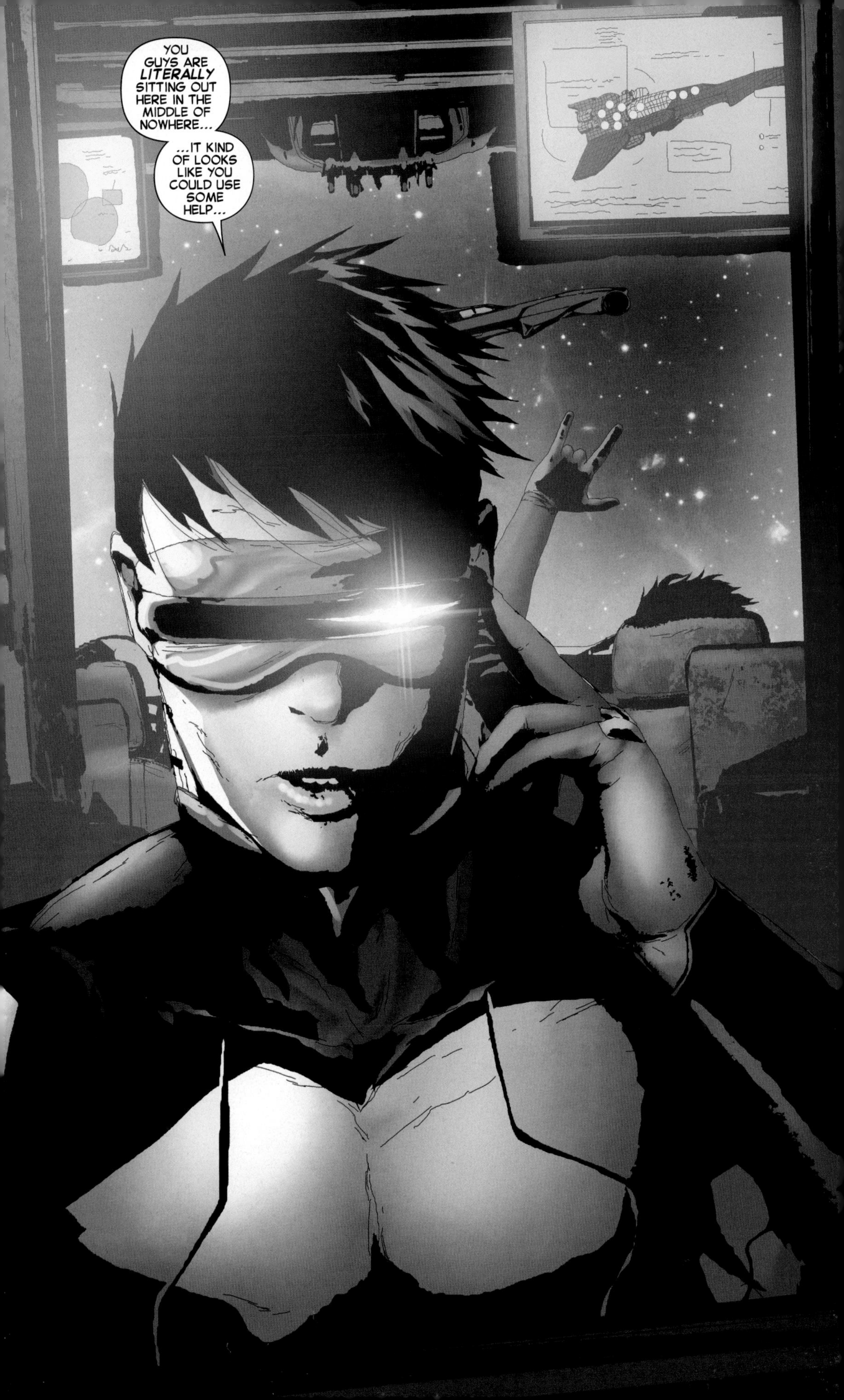
YOU GUYS ARE *LITERALLY* SITTING OUT HERE IN THE MIDDLE OF NOWHERE...
...IT KIND OF LOOKS LIKE YOU COULD USE SOME HELP...

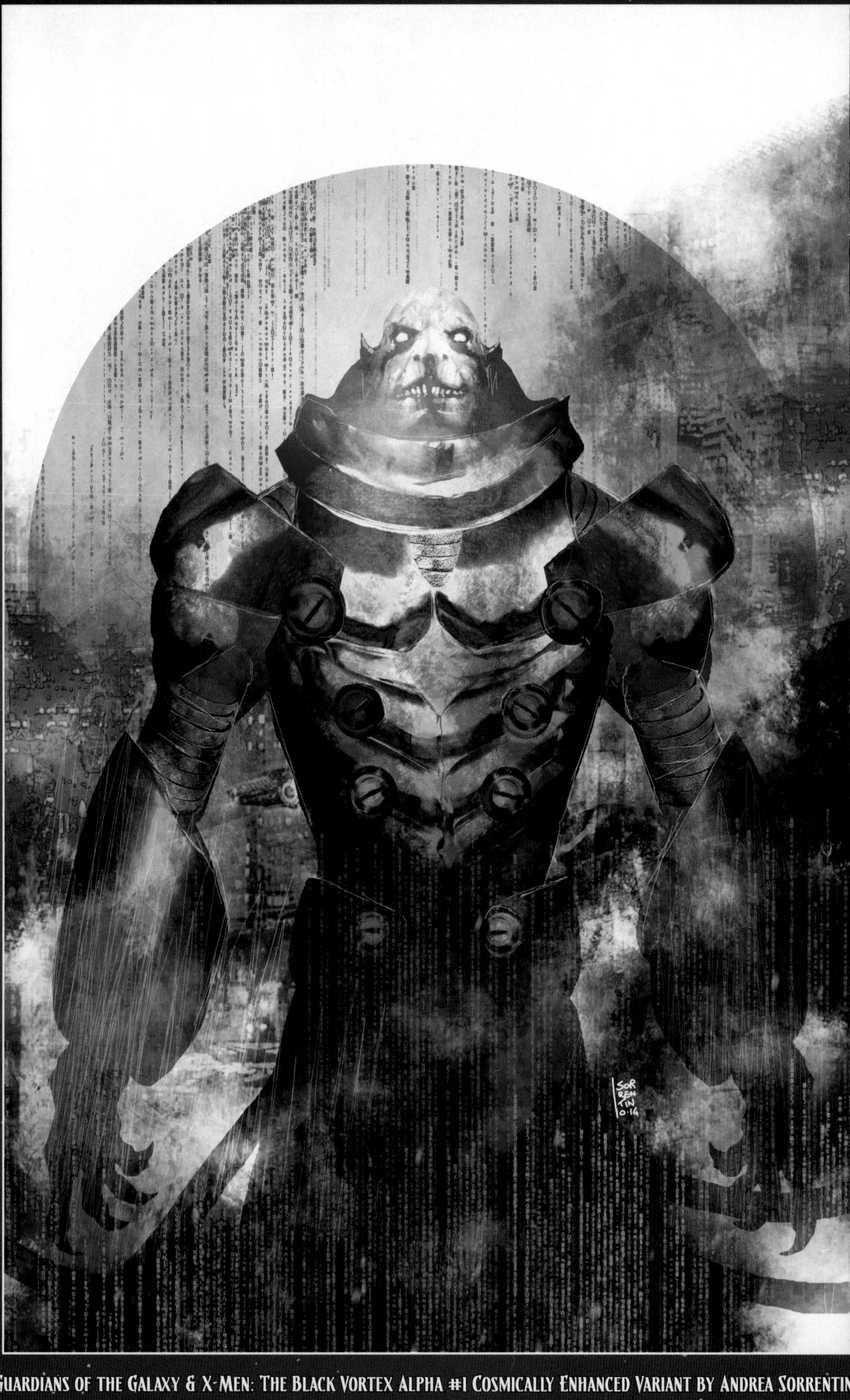
SOR
REN
TIN
O·14

GUARDIANS OF THE GALAXY & X-MEN: THE BLACK VORTEX ALPHA #1 COSMICALLY ENHANCED VARIANT BY ANDREA SORRENTIN

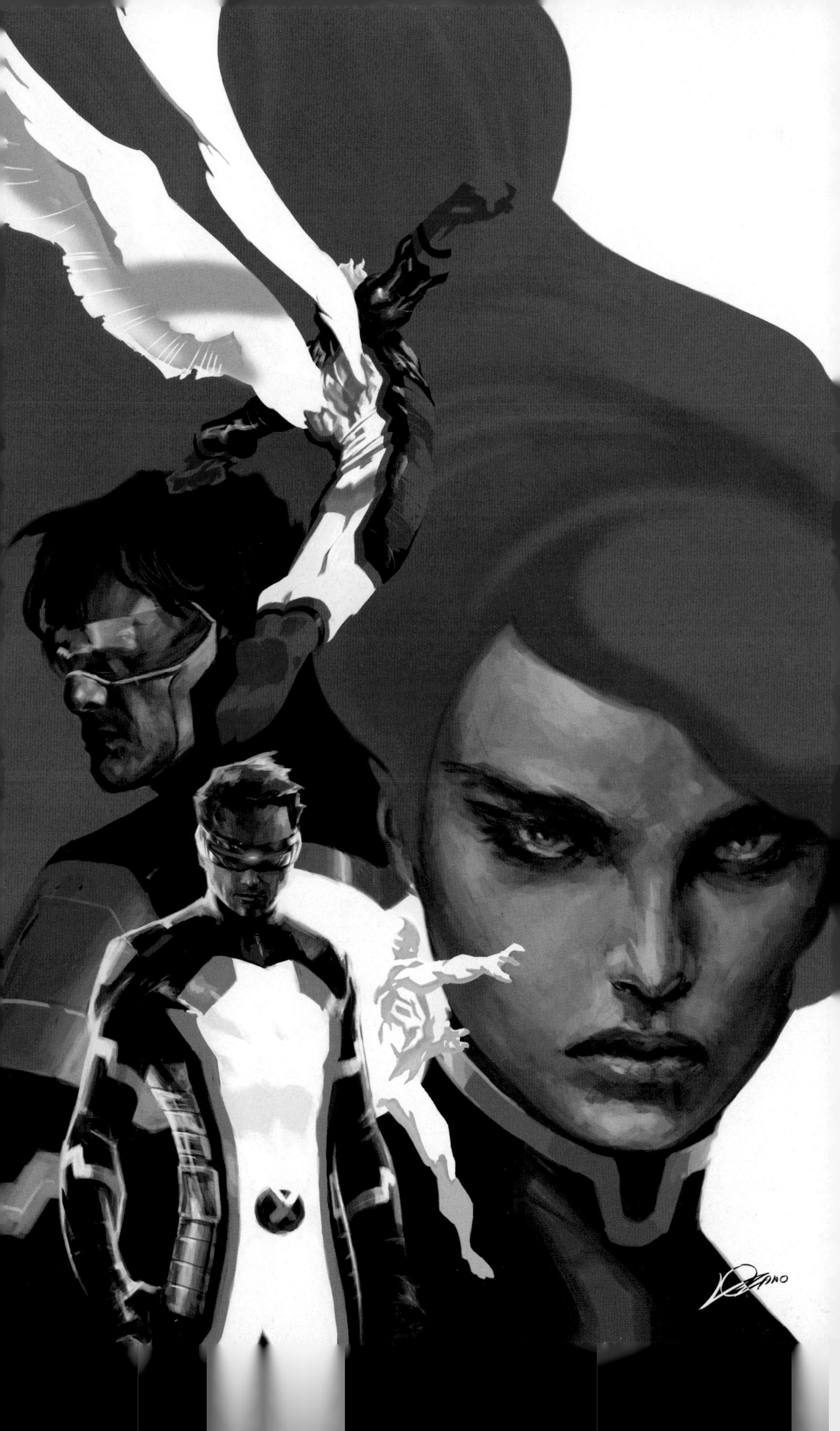

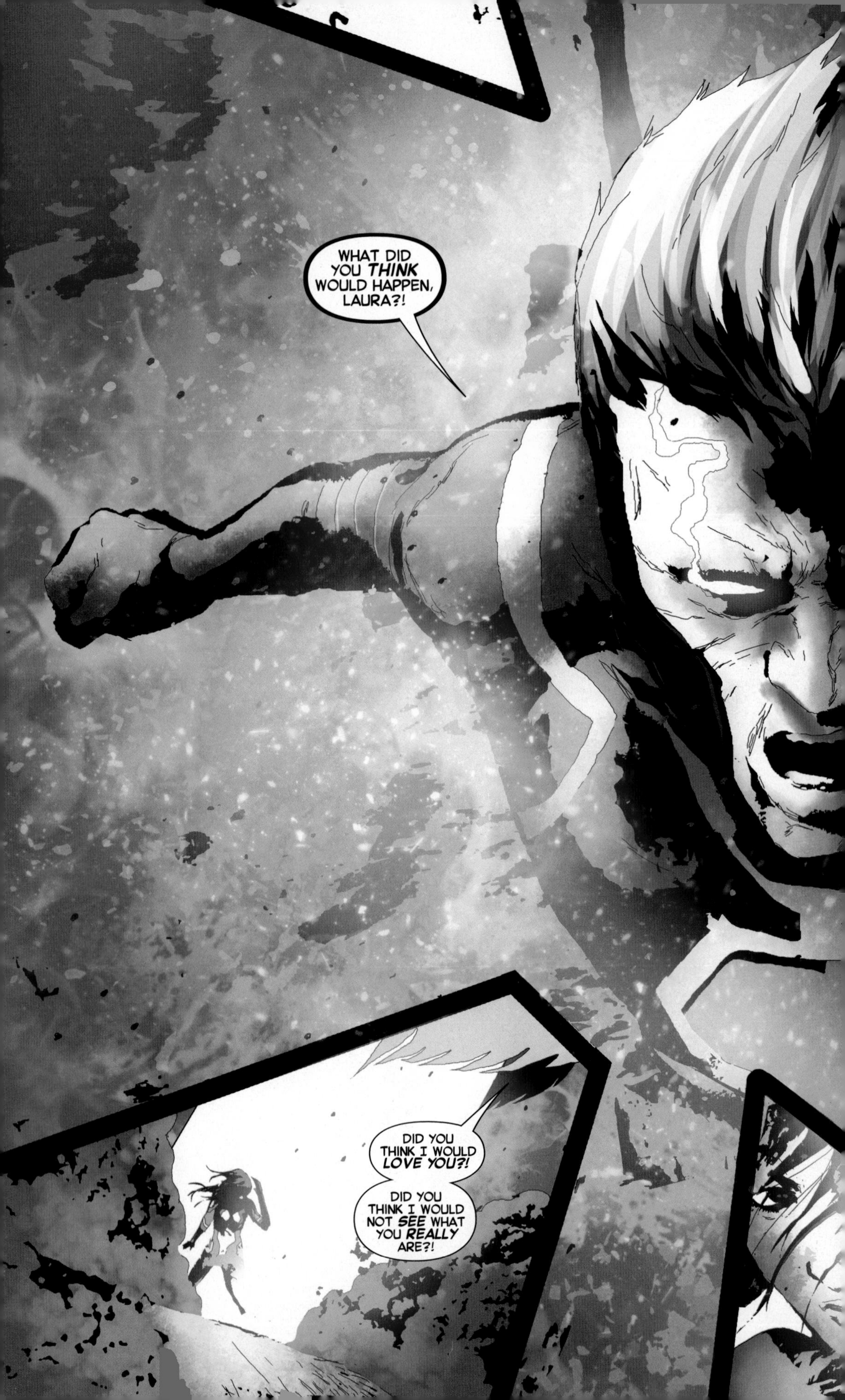
WHAT DID YOU THINK WOULD HAPPEN, LAURA?!
DID YOU THINK I WOULD LOVE YOU?!
DID YOU THINK I WOULD NOT SEE WHAT YOU REALLY ARE?!

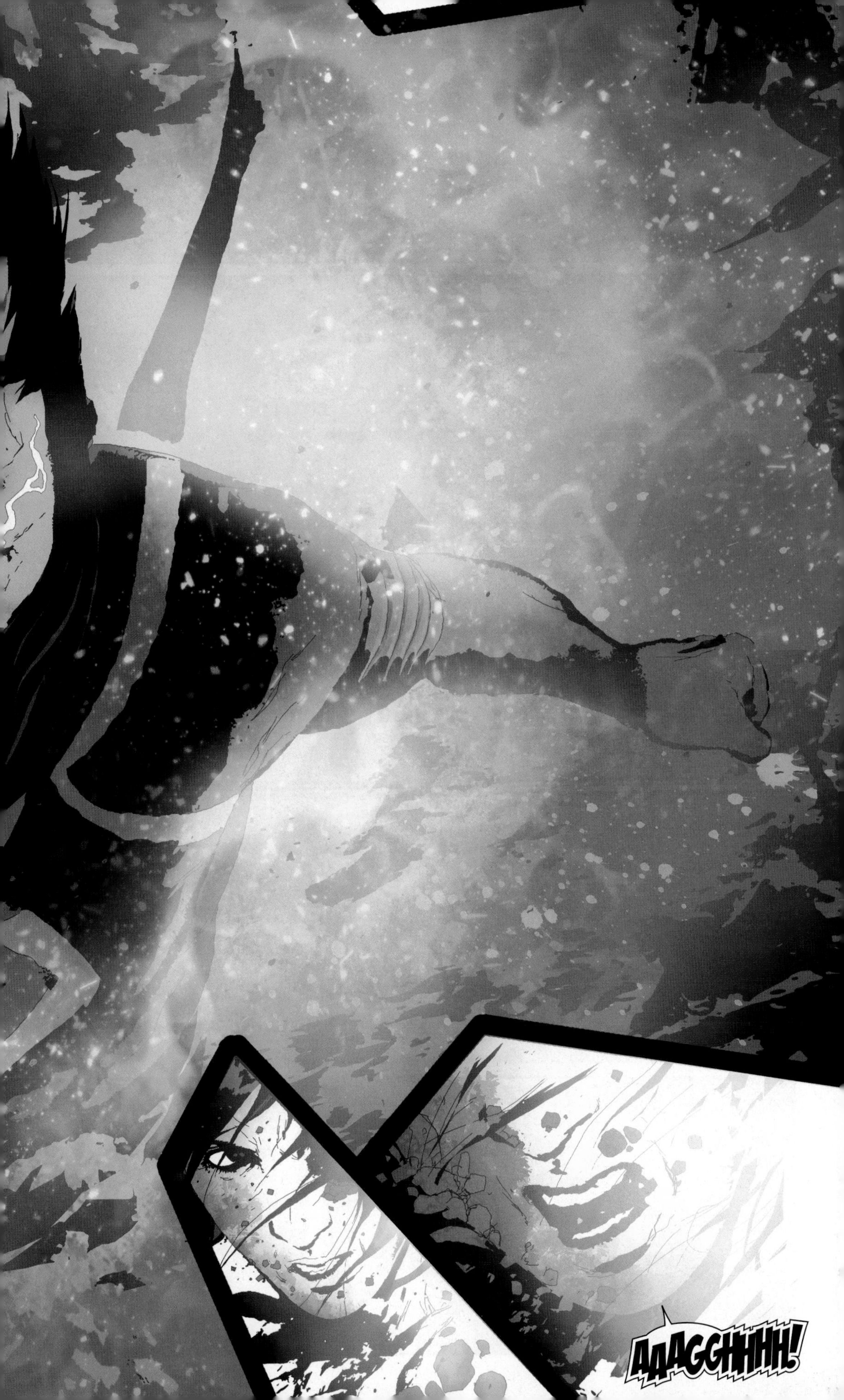
AAAGGHHHH!

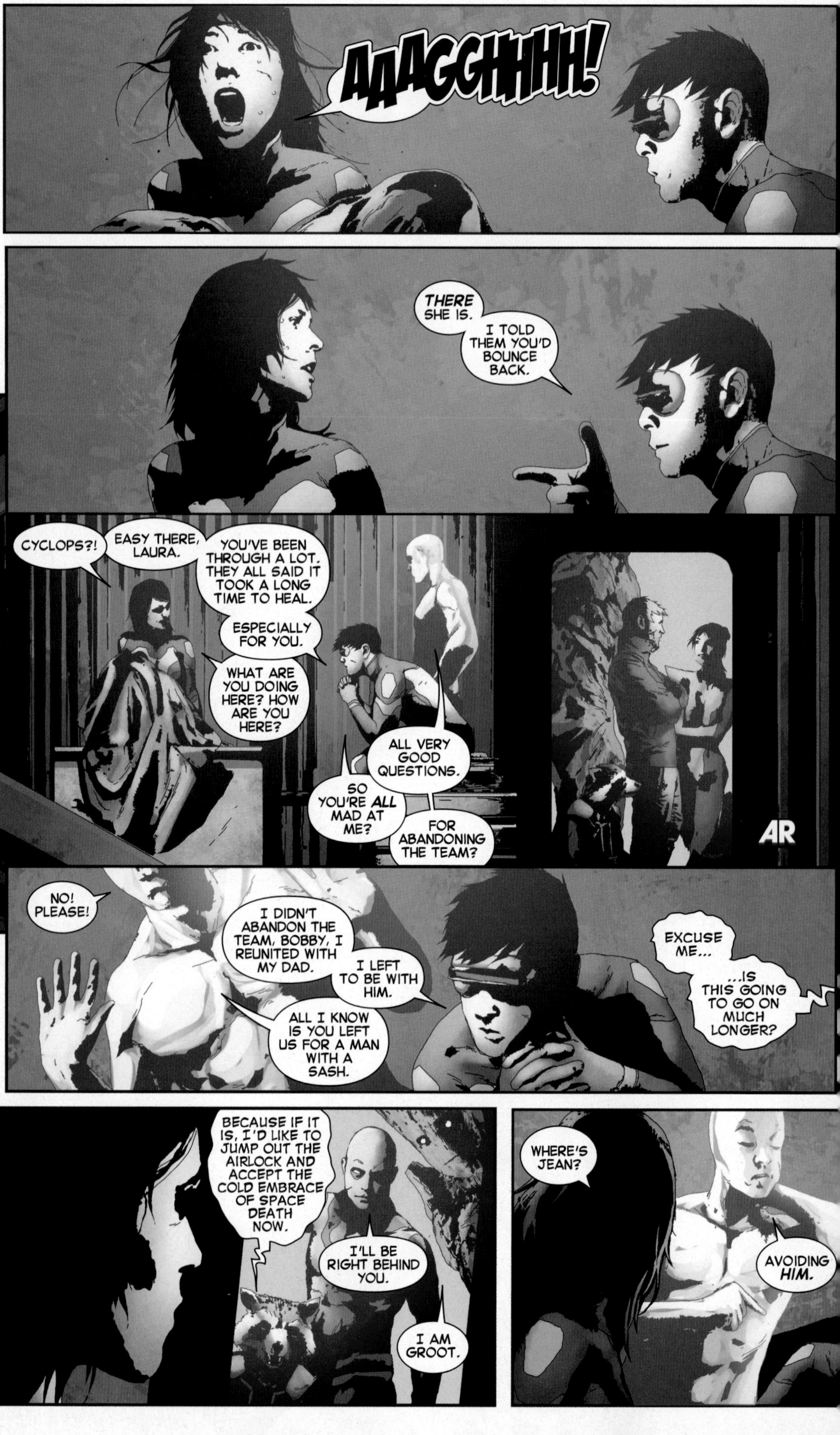
AAAGGHHHH!
THERE SHE IS.
I TOLD THEM YOU'D BOUNCE BACK.
CYCLOPS?!
EASY THERE, LAURA.
YOU'VE BEEN THROUGH A LOT. THEY ALL SAID IT TOOK A LONG TIME TO HEAL.
ESPECIALLY FOR YOU.
WHAT ARE YOU DOING HERE? HOW ARE YOU HERE?
ALL VERY GOOD QUESTIONS.
SO YOU'RE ALL MAD AT ME?
FOR ABANDONING THE TEAM?
AR
NO! PLEASE!
I DIDN'T ABANDON THE TEAM, BOBBY, I REUNITED WITH MY DAD.
I LEFT TO BE WITH HIM.
ALL I KNOW IS YOU LEFT US FOR A MAN WITH A SASH.
EXCUSE ME...
...IS THIS GOING TO GO ON MUCH LONGER?
BECAUSE IF IT IS, I'D LIKE TO JUMP OUT THE AIRLOCK AND ACCEPT THE COLD EMBRACE OF SPACE DEATH NOW.
I'LL BE RIGHT BEHIND YOU.
I AM GROOT.
WHERE'S JEAN?
AVOIDING HIM.

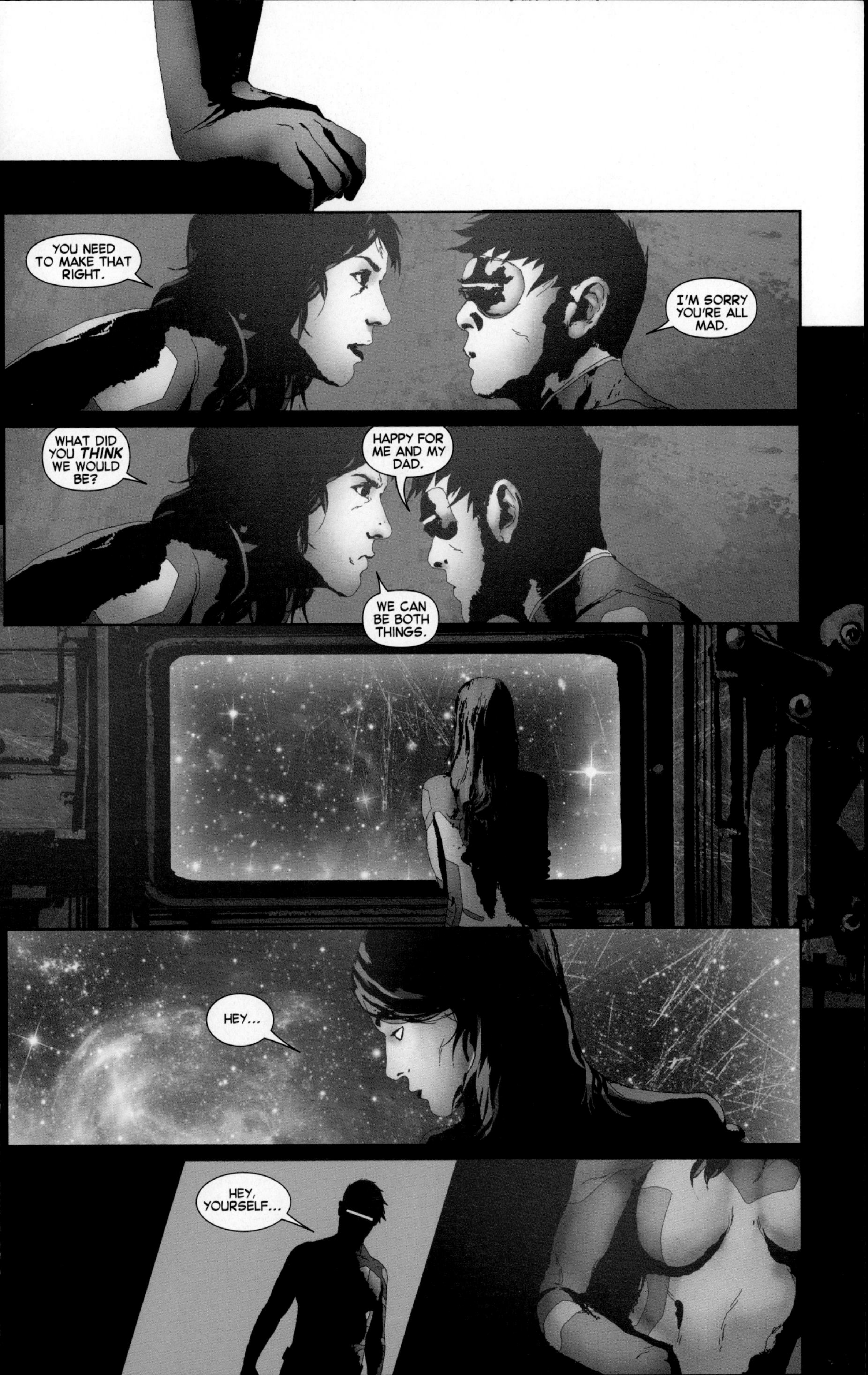
YOU NEED TO MAKE THAT RIGHT.
I'M SORRY YOU'RE ALL MAD.
WHAT DID YOU *THINK* WE WOULD BE?
HAPPY FOR ME AND MY DAD.
WE CAN BE BOTH THINGS.
HEY...
HEY, YOURSELF...

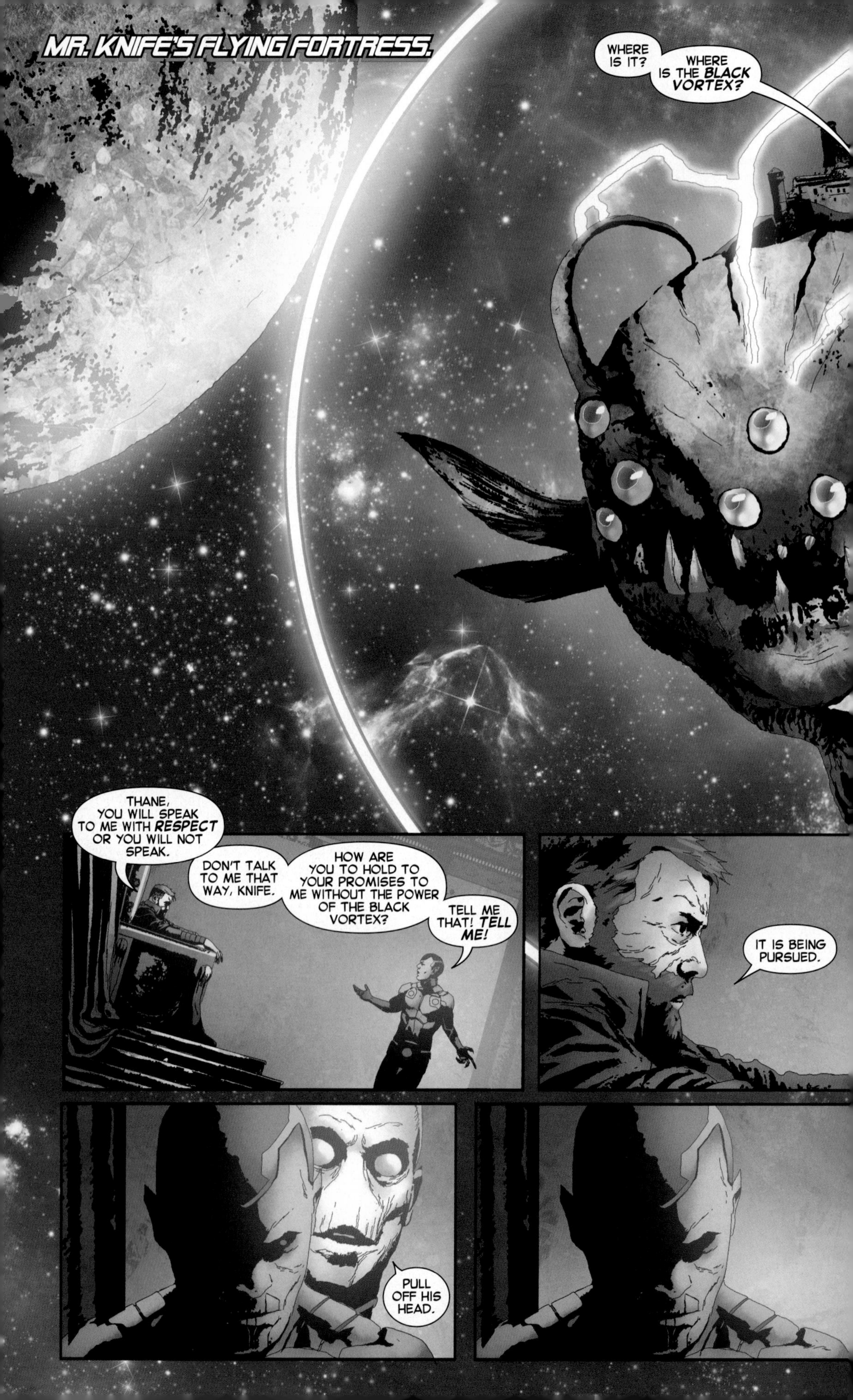
MR. KNIFE'S FLYING FORTRESS.
WHERE IS IT?
WHERE IS THE BLACK VORTEX?
THANE, YOU WILL SPEAK TO ME WITH RESPECT OR YOU WILL NOT SPEAK.
DON'T TALK TO ME THAT WAY, KNIFE.
HOW ARE YOU TO HOLD TO YOUR PROMISES TO ME WITHOUT THE POWER OF THE BLACK VORTEX?
TELL ME THAT! TELL ME!
IT IS BEING PURSUED.
PULL OFF HIS HEAD.

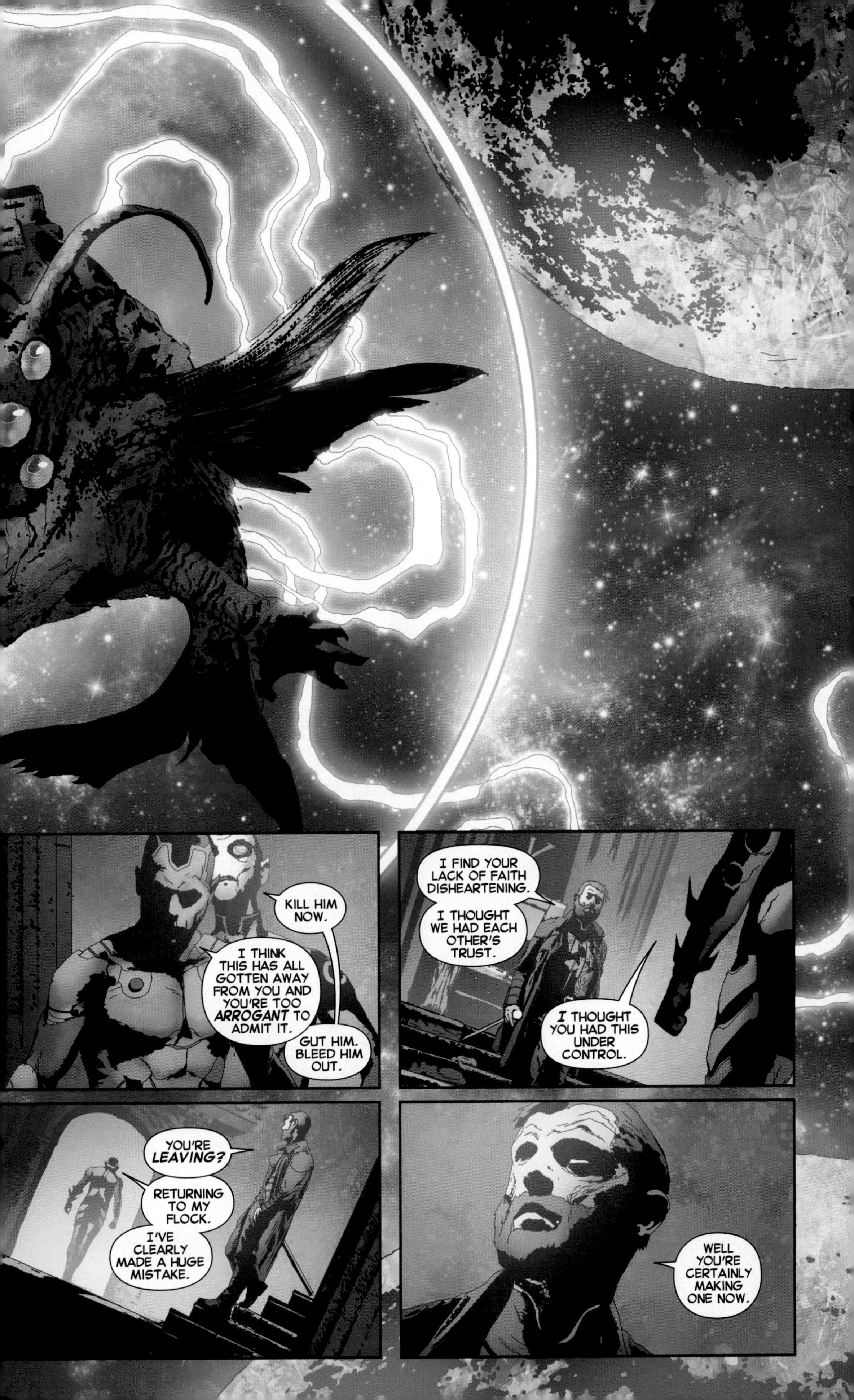
KILL HIM NOW.
I THINK THIS HAS ALL GOTTEN AWAY FROM YOU AND YOU'RE TOO ARROGANT TO ADMIT IT.
GUT HIM. BLEED HIM OUT.
I FIND YOUR LACK OF FAITH DISHEARTENING.
I THOUGHT WE HAD EACH OTHER'S TRUST.
I THOUGHT YOU HAD THIS UNDER CONTROL.
YOU'RE LEAVING?
RETURNING TO MY FLOCK.
I'VE CLEARLY MADE A HUGE MISTAKE.
WELL YOU'RE CERTAINLY MAKING ONE NOW.

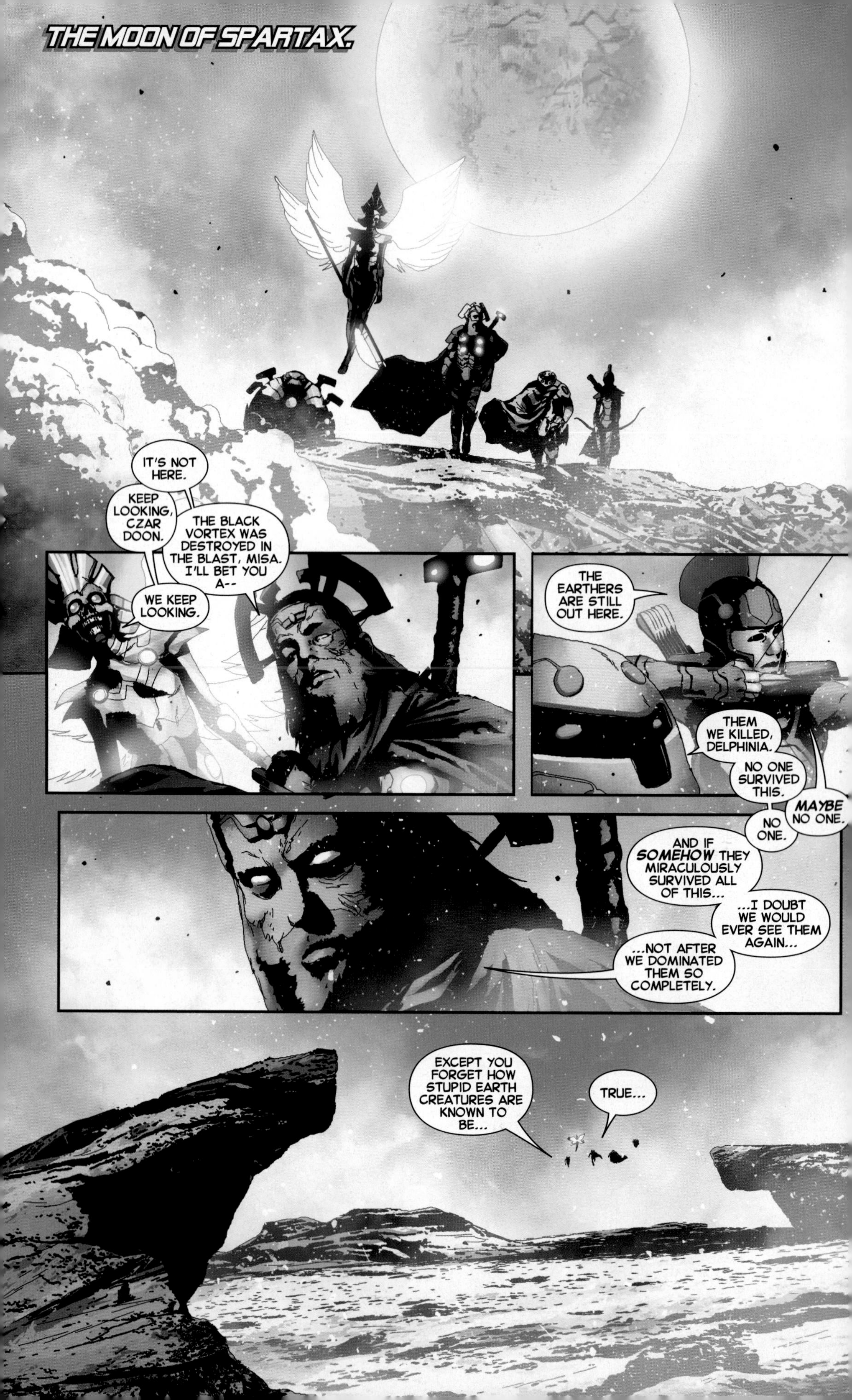
THE MOON OF SPARTAX.
IT'S NOT HERE.
KEEP LOOKING, CZAR DOON.
THE BLACK VORTEX WAS DESTROYED IN THE BLAST, MISA. I'LL BET YOU A--
WE KEEP LOOKING.
THE EARTHERS ARE STILL OUT HERE.
THEM WE KILLED, DELPHINIA.
NO ONE SURVIVED THIS.
NO ONE.
MAYBE NO ONE.
AND IF SOMEHOW THEY MIRACULOUSLY SURVIVED ALL OF THIS...
...I DOUBT WE WOULD EVER SEE THEM AGAIN...
...NOT AFTER WE DOMINATED THEM SO COMPLETELY.
EXCEPT YOU FORGET HOW STUPID EARTH CREATURES ARE KNOWN TO BE...
TRUE...

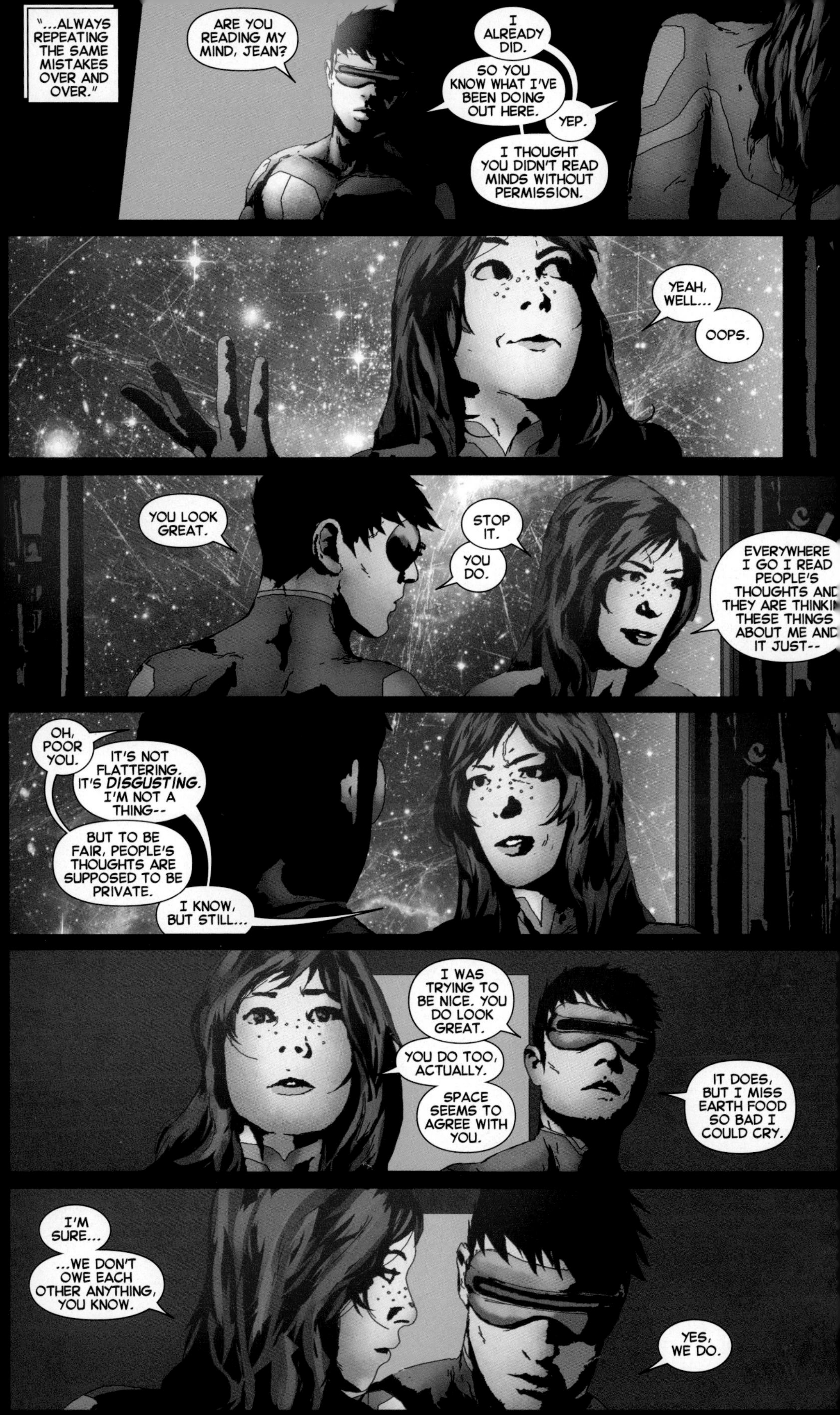
"...ALWAYS REPEATING THE SAME MISTAKES OVER AND OVER."
ARE YOU READING MY MIND, JEAN?
I ALREADY DID.
SO YOU KNOW WHAT I'VE BEEN DOING OUT HERE.
YEP.
I THOUGHT YOU DIDN'T READ MINDS WITHOUT PERMISSION.
YEAH, WELL...
OOPS.
YOU LOOK GREAT.
STOP IT.
YOU DO.
EVERYWHERE I GO I READ PEOPLE'S THOUGHTS AND THEY ARE THINKI THESE THINGS ABOUT ME AND IT JUST--
OH, POOR YOU.
IT'S NOT FLATTERING. IT'S *DISGUSTING.* I'M NOT A THING--
BUT TO BE FAIR, PEOPLE'S THOUGHTS ARE SUPPOSED TO BE PRIVATE.
I KNOW, BUT STILL...
I WAS TRYING TO BE NICE. YOU DO LOOK GREAT.
YOU DO TOO, ACTUALLY.
SPACE SEEMS TO AGREE WITH YOU.
IT DOES, BUT I MISS EARTH FOOD SO BAD I COULD CRY.
I'M SURE...
...WE DON'T OWE EACH OTHER ANYTHING, YOU KNOW.
YES, WE DO.

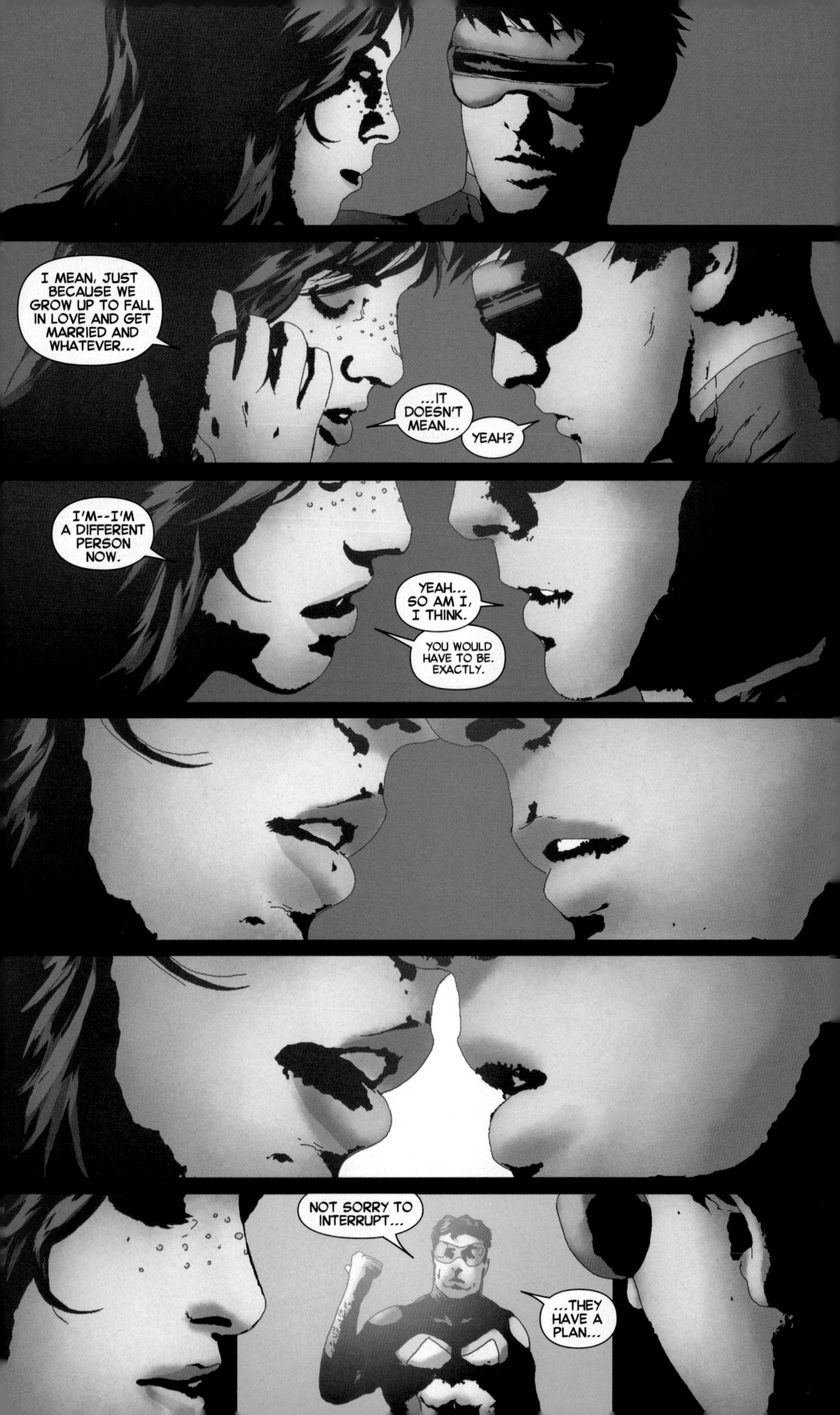
I MEAN, JUST BECAUSE WE GROW UP TO FALL IN LOVE AND GET MARRIED AND WHATEVER...
...IT DOESN'T MEAN...
YEAH?
I'M--I'M A DIFFERENT PERSON NOW.
YEAH... SO AM I, I THINK.
YOU WOULD HAVE TO BE. EXACTLY.
NOT SORRY TO INTERRUPT...
...THEY HAVE A PLAN...

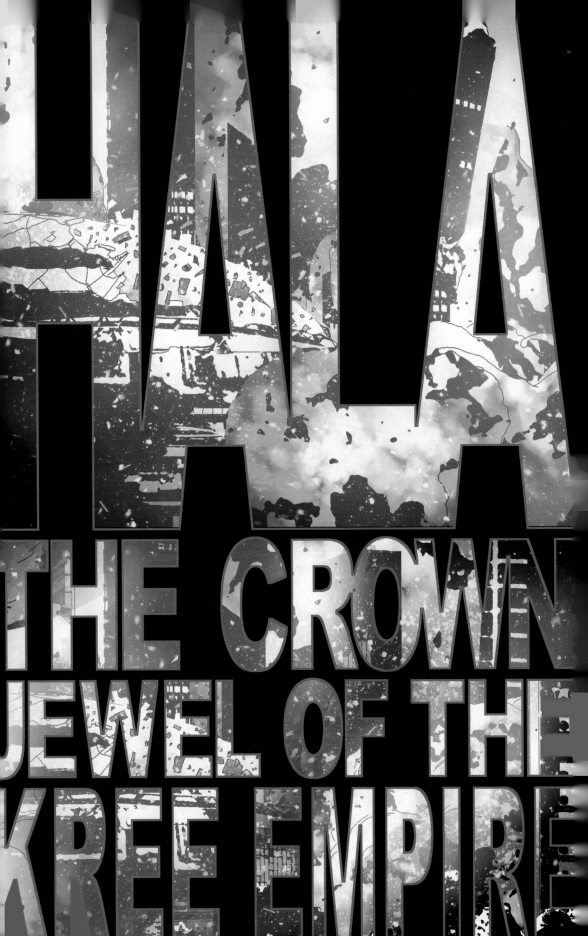

HALA

THE CROWN
JEWEL OF THE
KREE EMPIRE

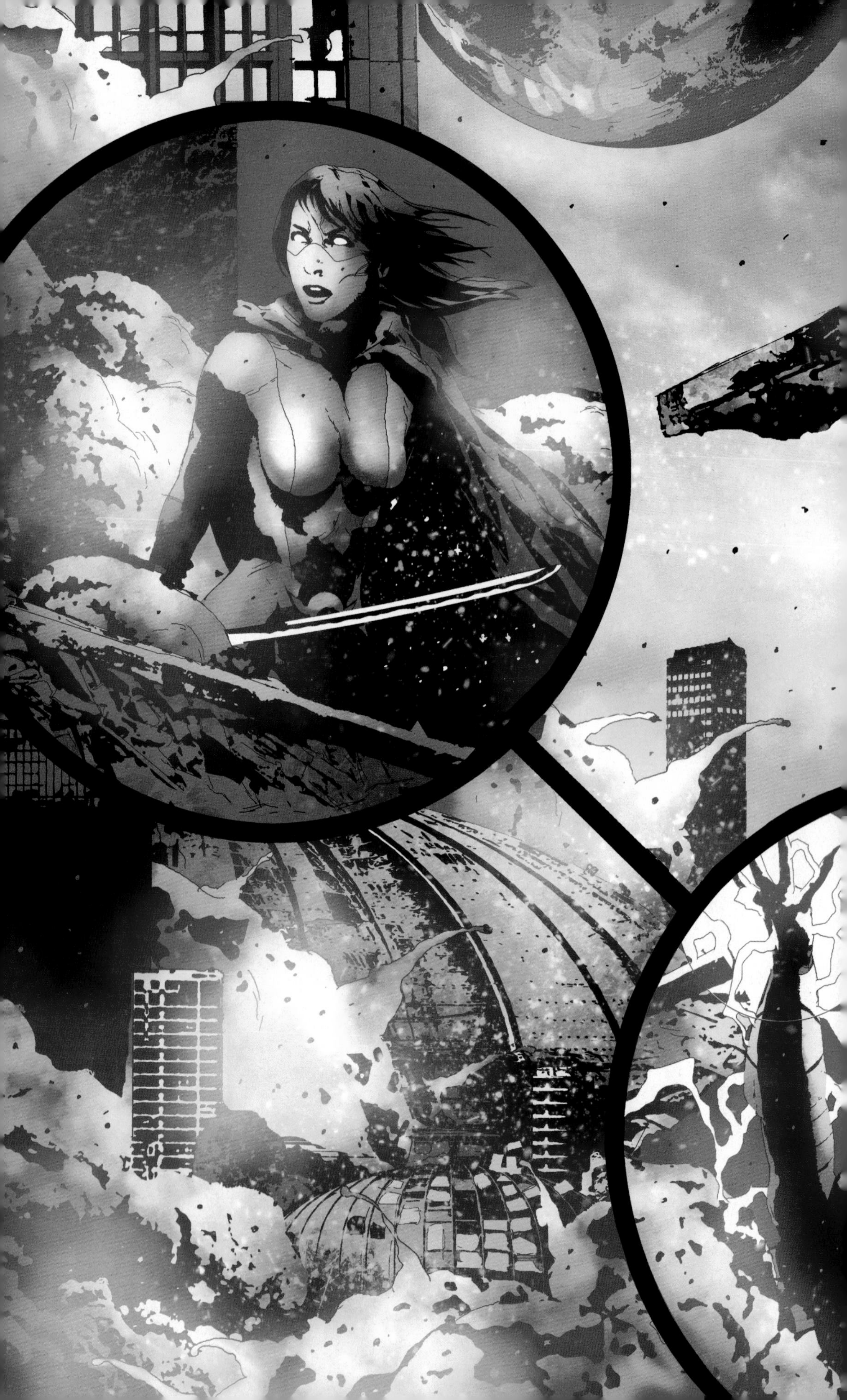

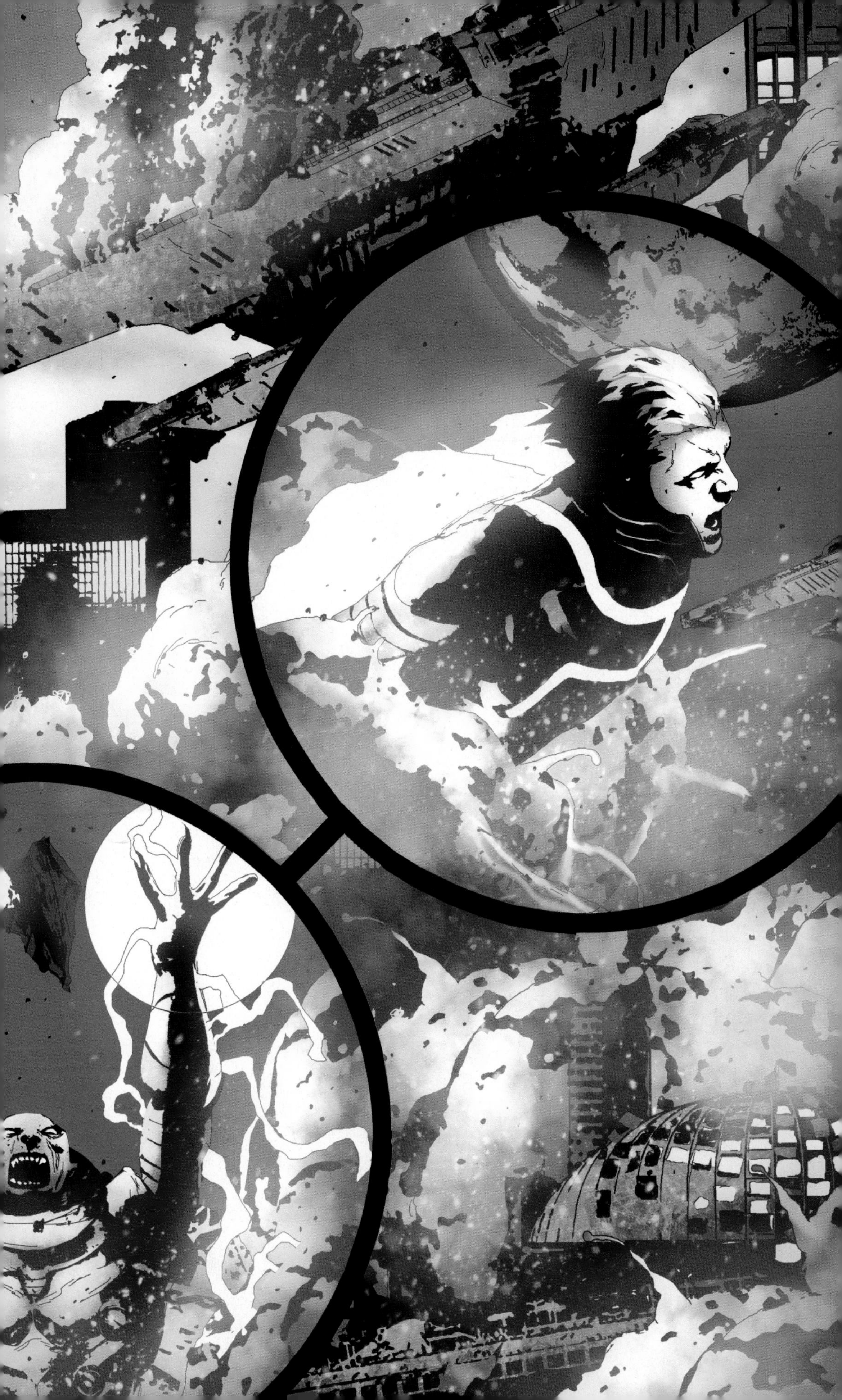

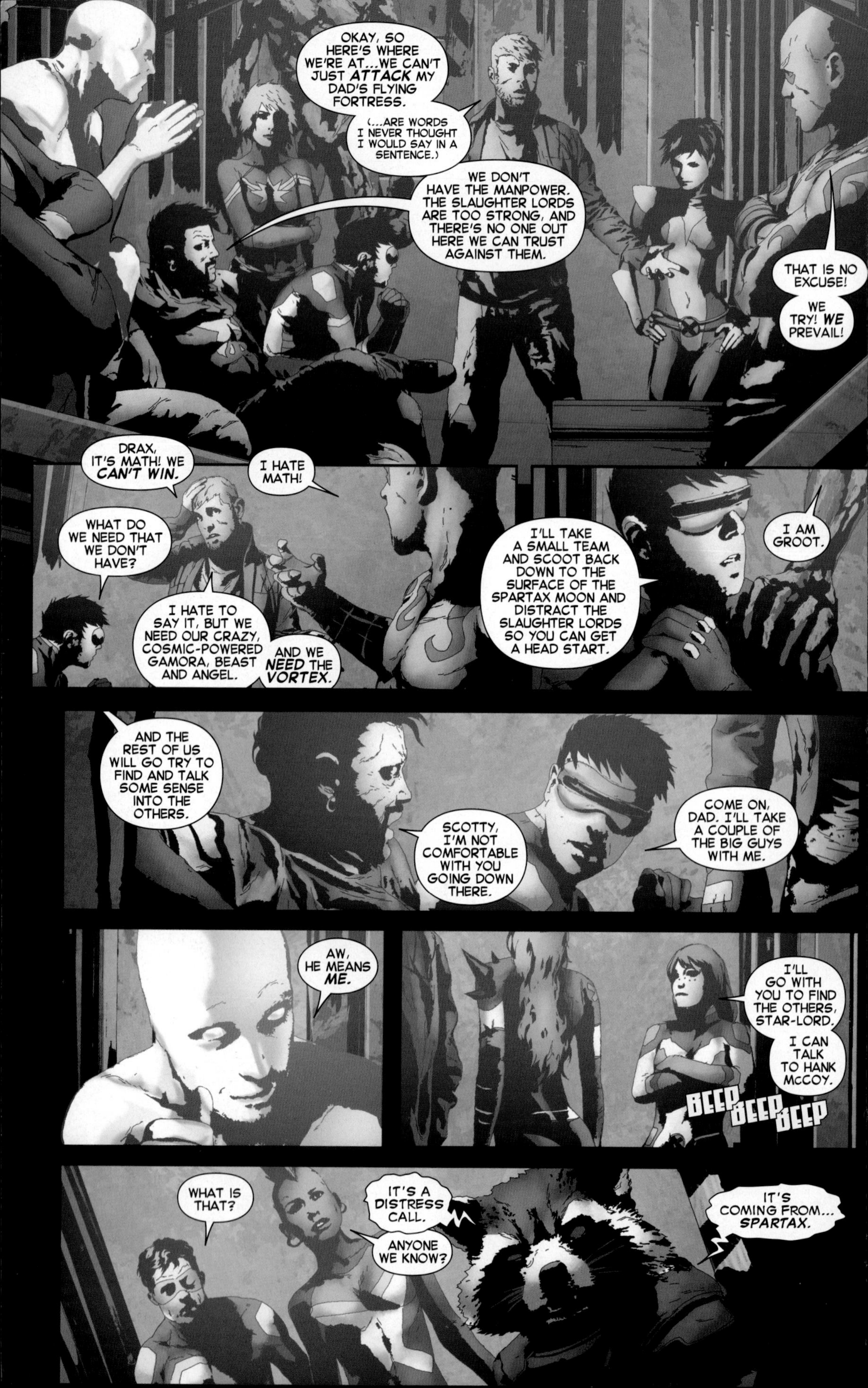

OKAY, SO HERE'S WHERE WE'RE AT...WE CAN'T JUST ATTACK MY DAD'S FLYING FORTRESS.
(...ARE WORDS I NEVER THOUGHT I WOULD SAY IN A SENTENCE.)
WE DON'T HAVE THE MANPOWER. THE SLAUGHTER LORDS ARE TOO STRONG, AND THERE'S NO ONE OUT HERE WE CAN TRUST AGAINST THEM.
THAT IS NO EXCUSE!
WE TRY! WE PREVAIL!
DRAX, IT'S MATH! WE CAN'T WIN.
I HATE MATH!
WHAT DO WE NEED THAT WE DON'T HAVE?
I HATE TO SAY IT, BUT WE NEED OUR CRAZY, COSMIC-POWERED GAMORA, BEAST AND ANGEL.
AND WE NEED THE VORTEX.
I'LL TAKE A SMALL TEAM AND SCOOT BACK DOWN TO THE SURFACE OF THE SPARTAX MOON AND DISTRACT THE SLAUGHTER LORDS SO YOU CAN GET A HEAD START.
I AM GROOT.
AND THE REST OF US WILL GO TRY TO FIND AND TALK SOME SENSE INTO THE OTHERS.
SCOTTY, I'M NOT COMFORTABLE WITH YOU GOING DOWN THERE.
COME ON, DAD. I'LL TAKE A COUPLE OF THE BIG GUYS WITH ME.
AW, HE MEANS ME.
I'LL GO WITH YOU TO FIND THE OTHERS, STAR-LORD.
I CAN TALK TO HANK McCOY.
BEEP BEEP BEEP
WHAT IS THAT?
IT'S A DISTRESS CALL.
ANYONE WE KNOW?
IT'S COMING FROM... SPARTAX.

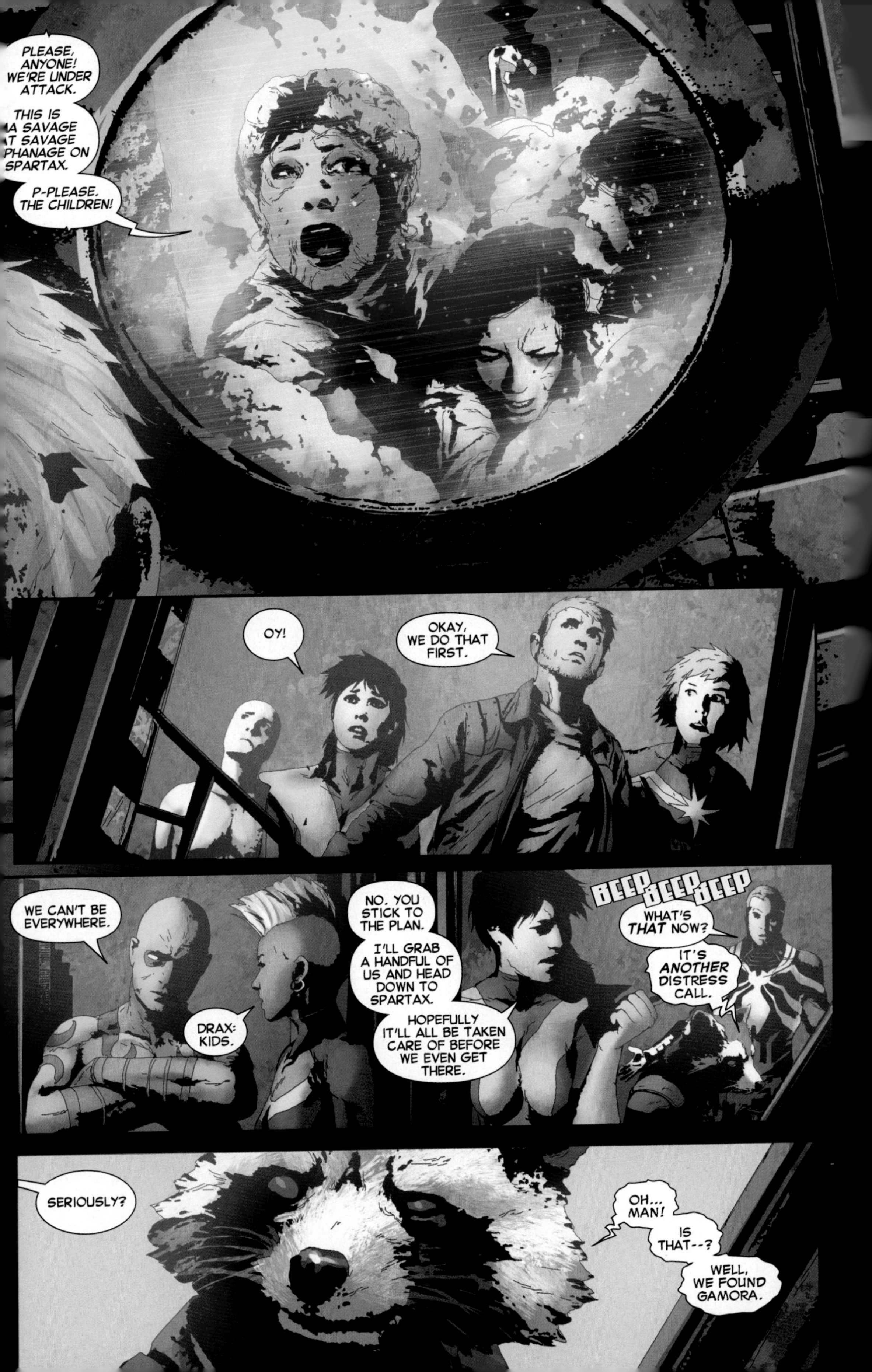

PLEASE, ANYONE! WE'RE UNDER ATTACK.
THIS IS A SAVAGE AT SAVAGE PHANAGE ON SPARTAX.
P-PLEASE. THE CHILDREN!
OY!
OKAY, WE DO THAT FIRST.
WE CAN'T BE EVERYWHERE.
DRAX: KIDS.
NO. YOU STICK TO THE PLAN.
I'LL GRAB A HANDFUL OF US AND HEAD DOWN TO SPARTAX.
HOPEFULLY IT'LL ALL BE TAKEN CARE OF BEFORE WE EVEN GET THERE.
BEEP BEEP BEEP
WHAT'S THAT NOW?
IT'S ANOTHER DISTRESS CALL.
SERIOUSLY?
OH... MAN!
IS THAT--?
WELL, WE FOUND GAMORA.

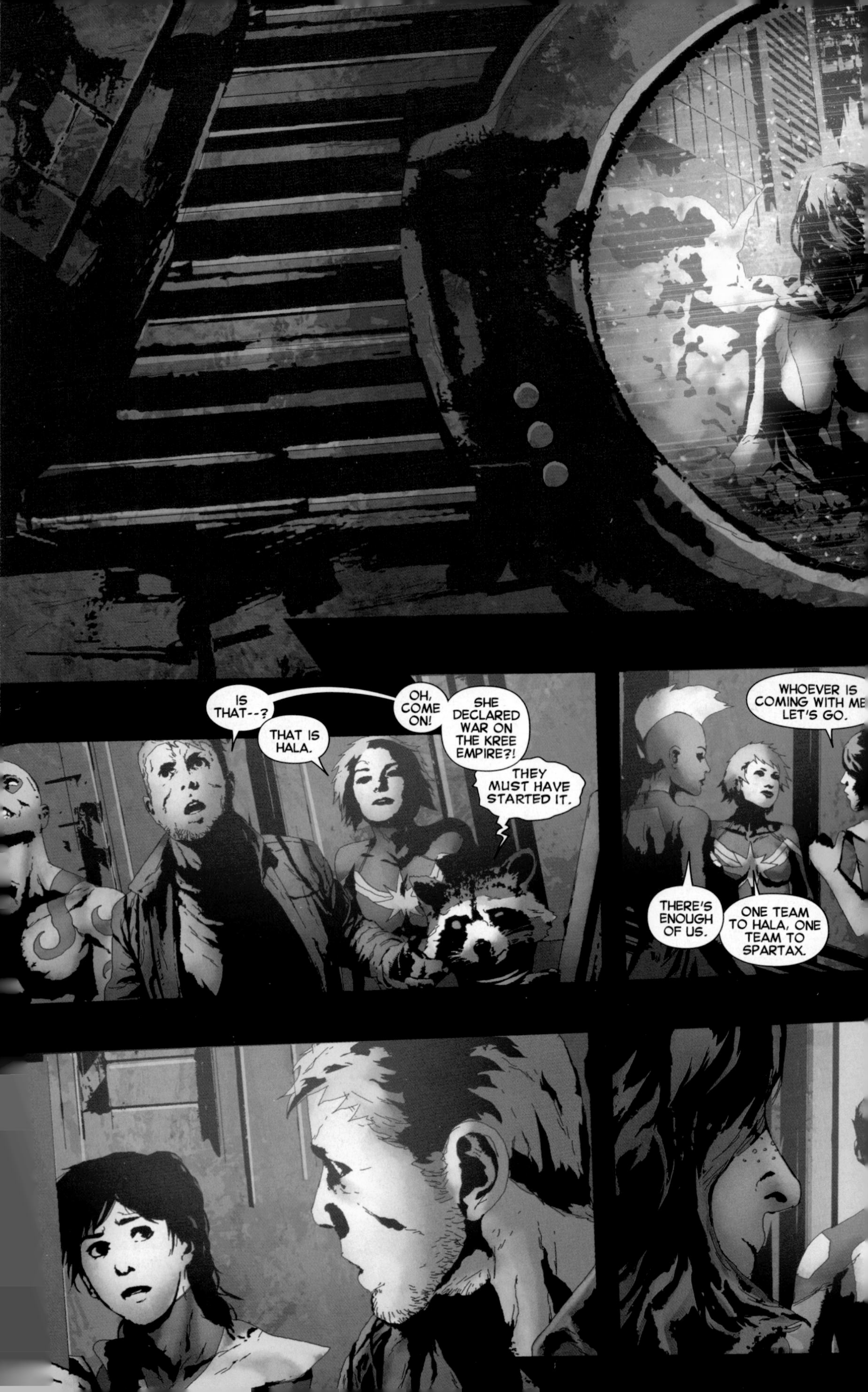
IS THAT--?
THAT IS HALA.
OH, COME ON!
SHE DECLARED WAR ON THE KREE EMPIRE?!
THEY MUST HAVE STARTED IT.
WHOEVER IS COMING WITH ME LET'S GO.
THERE'S ENOUGH OF US.
ONE TEAM TO HALA, ONE TEAM TO SPARTAX.

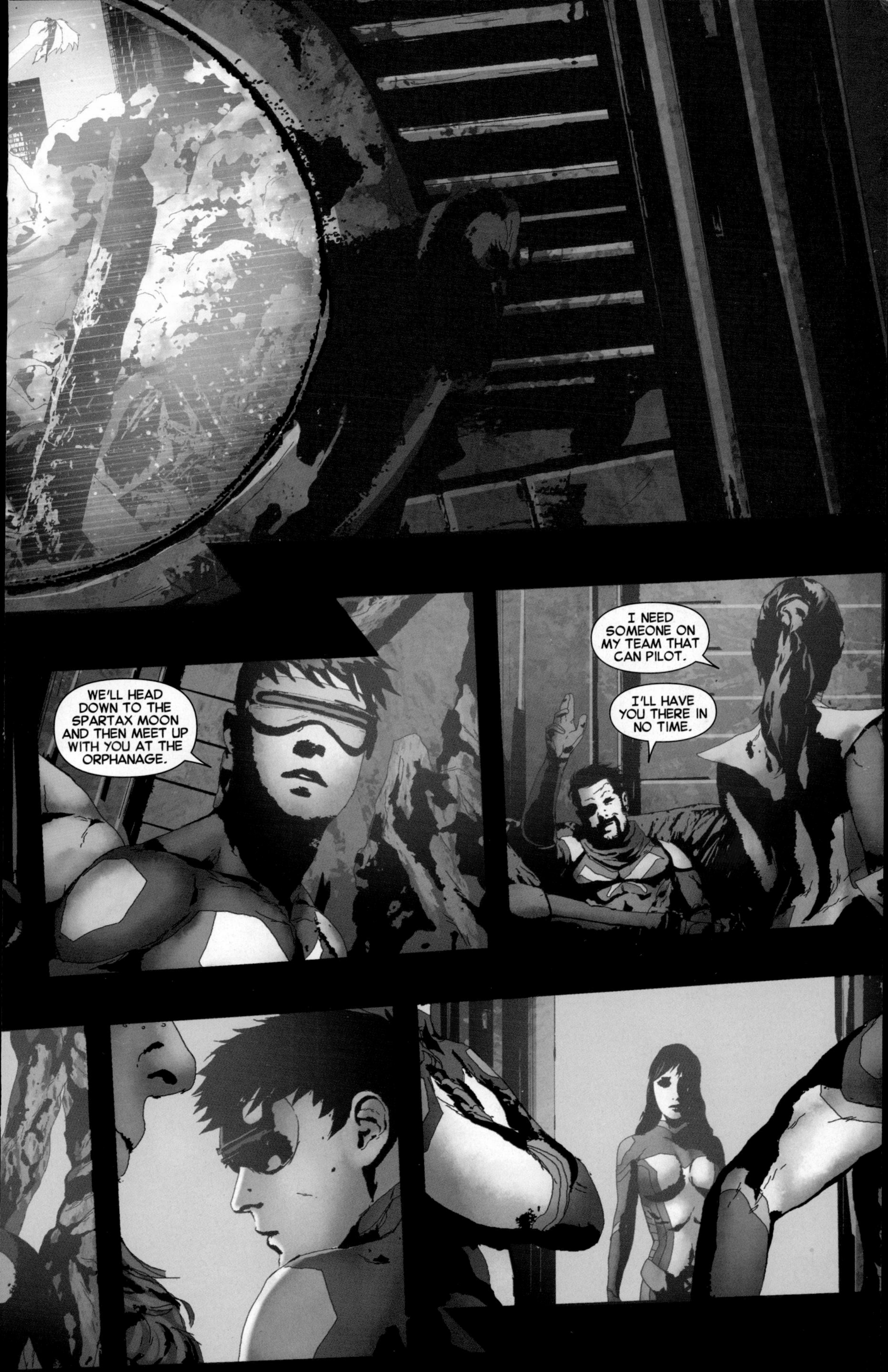
WE'LL HEAD DOWN TO THE SPARTAX MOON AND THEN MEET UP WITH YOU AT THE ORPHANAGE.
I NEED SOMEONE ON MY TEAM THAT CAN PILOT.
I'LL HAVE YOU THERE IN NO TIME.

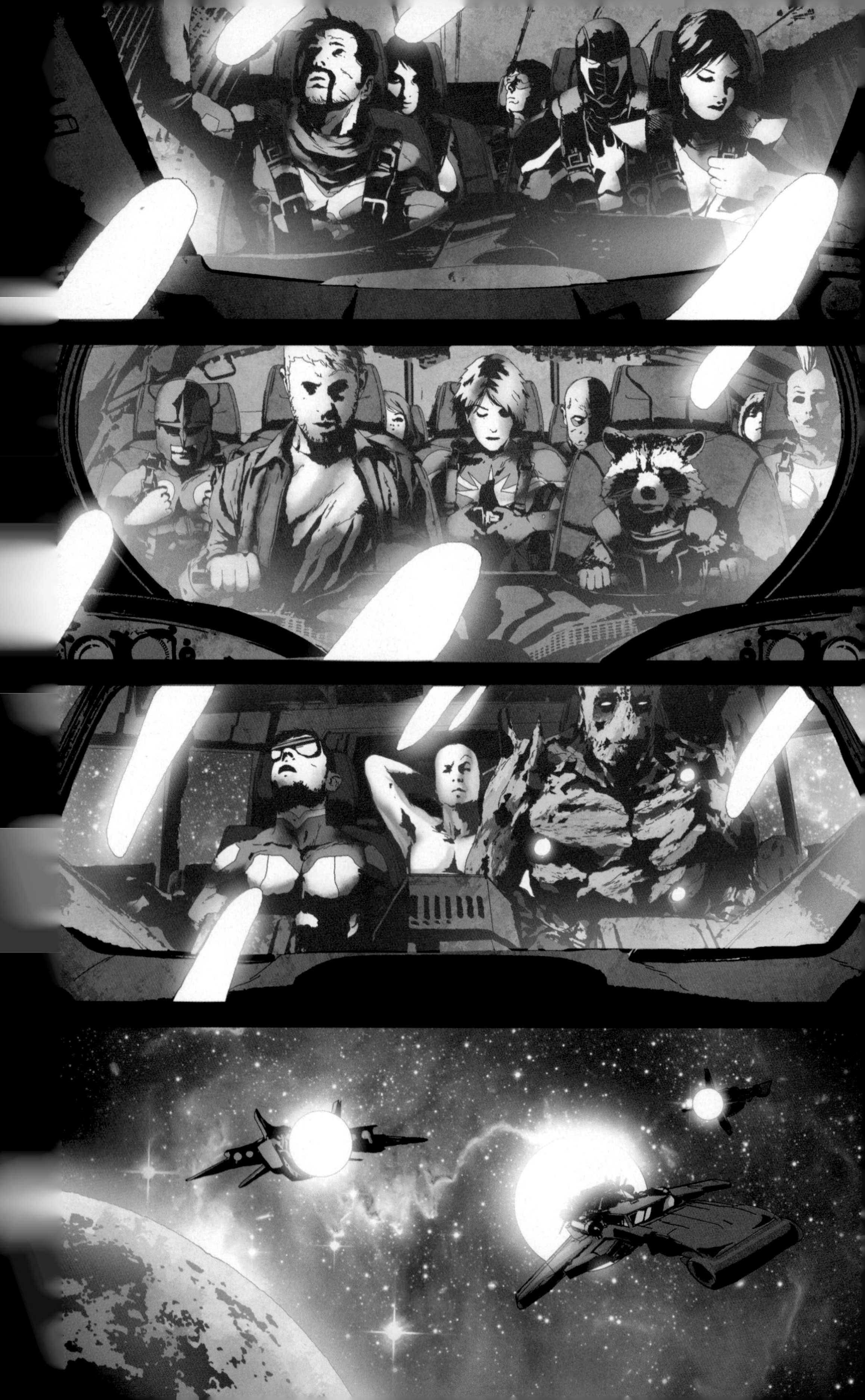

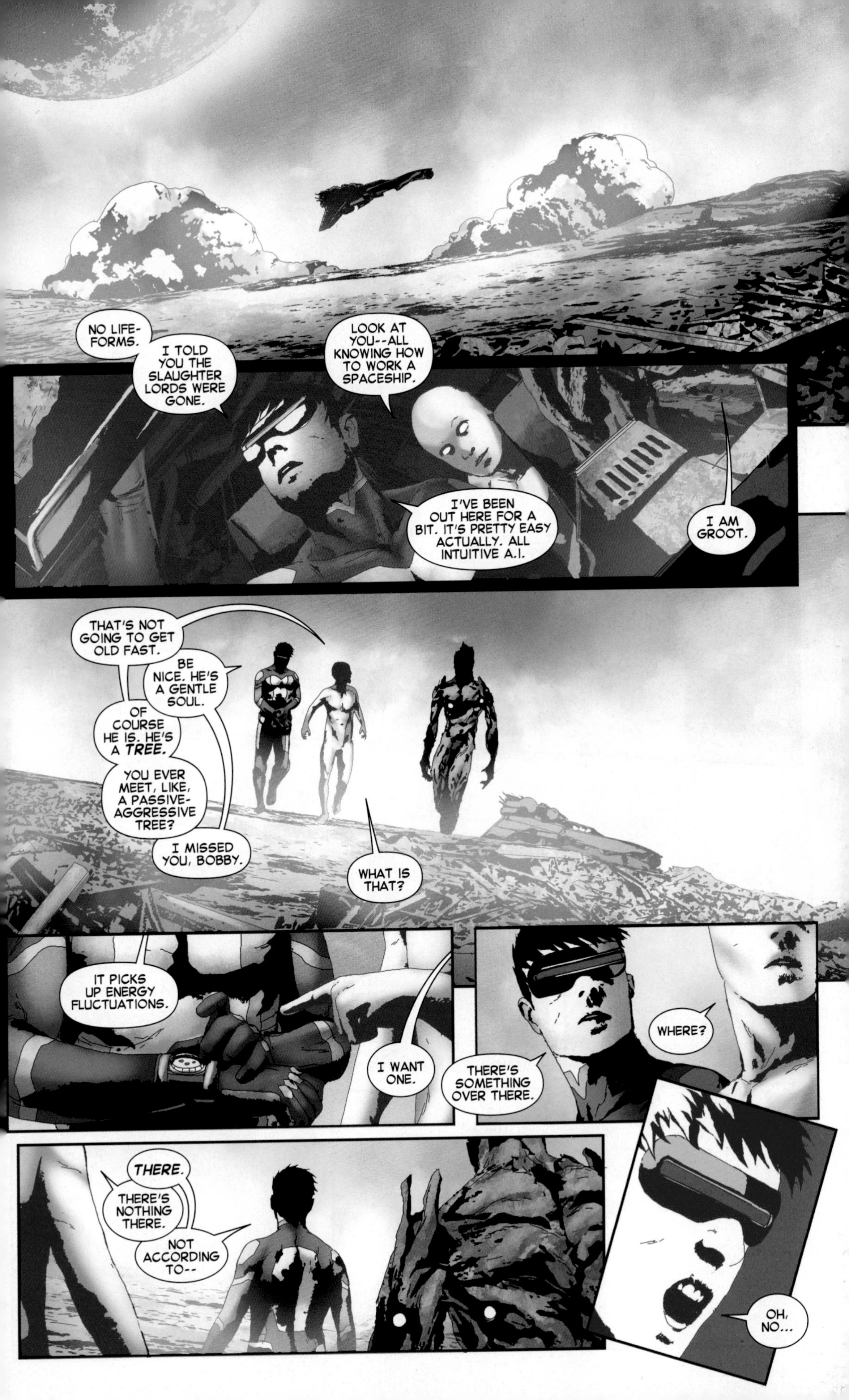
NO LIFE-FORMS.
I TOLD YOU THE SLAUGHTER LORDS WERE GONE.
LOOK AT YOU--ALL KNOWING HOW TO WORK A SPACESHIP.
I'VE BEEN OUT HERE FOR A BIT. IT'S PRETTY EASY ACTUALLY. ALL INTUITIVE A.I.
I AM GROOT.
THAT'S NOT GOING TO GET OLD FAST.
BE NICE. HE'S A GENTLE SOUL.
OF COURSE HE IS. HE'S A *TREE.*
YOU EVER MEET, LIKE, A PASSIVE-AGGRESSIVE TREE?
I MISSED YOU, BOBBY.
WHAT IS THAT?
IT PICKS UP ENERGY FLUCTUATIONS.
I WANT ONE.
THERE'S SOMETHING OVER THERE.
WHERE?
THERE.
THERE'S NOTHING THERE.
NOT ACCORDING TO--
OH, NO...

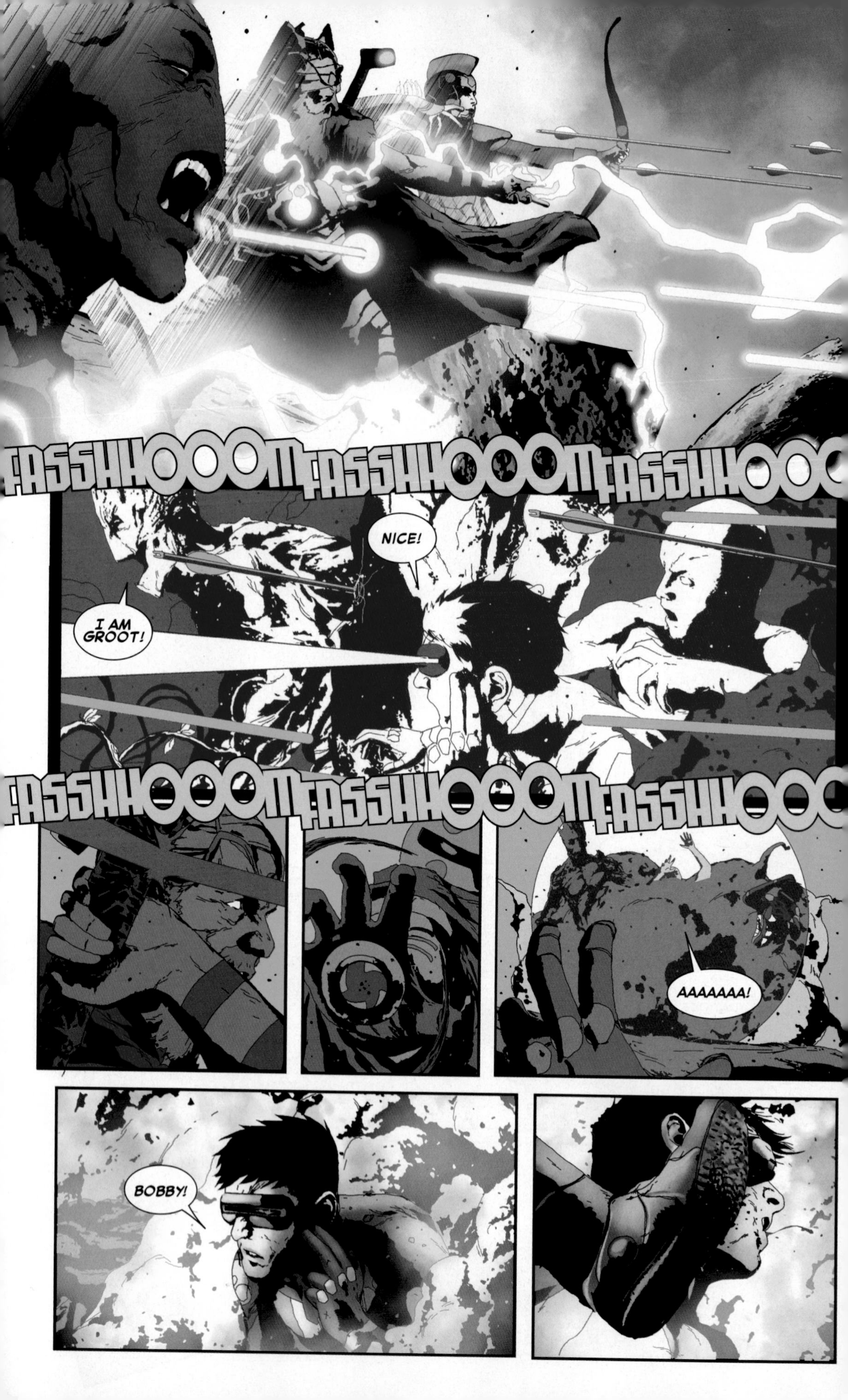
FASSHHOOOM FASSHHOOOM FASSHHOOO
NICE!
I AM GROOT!
FASSHHOOOM FASSHHOOOM FASSHHOOO
AAAAAAA!
BOBBY!

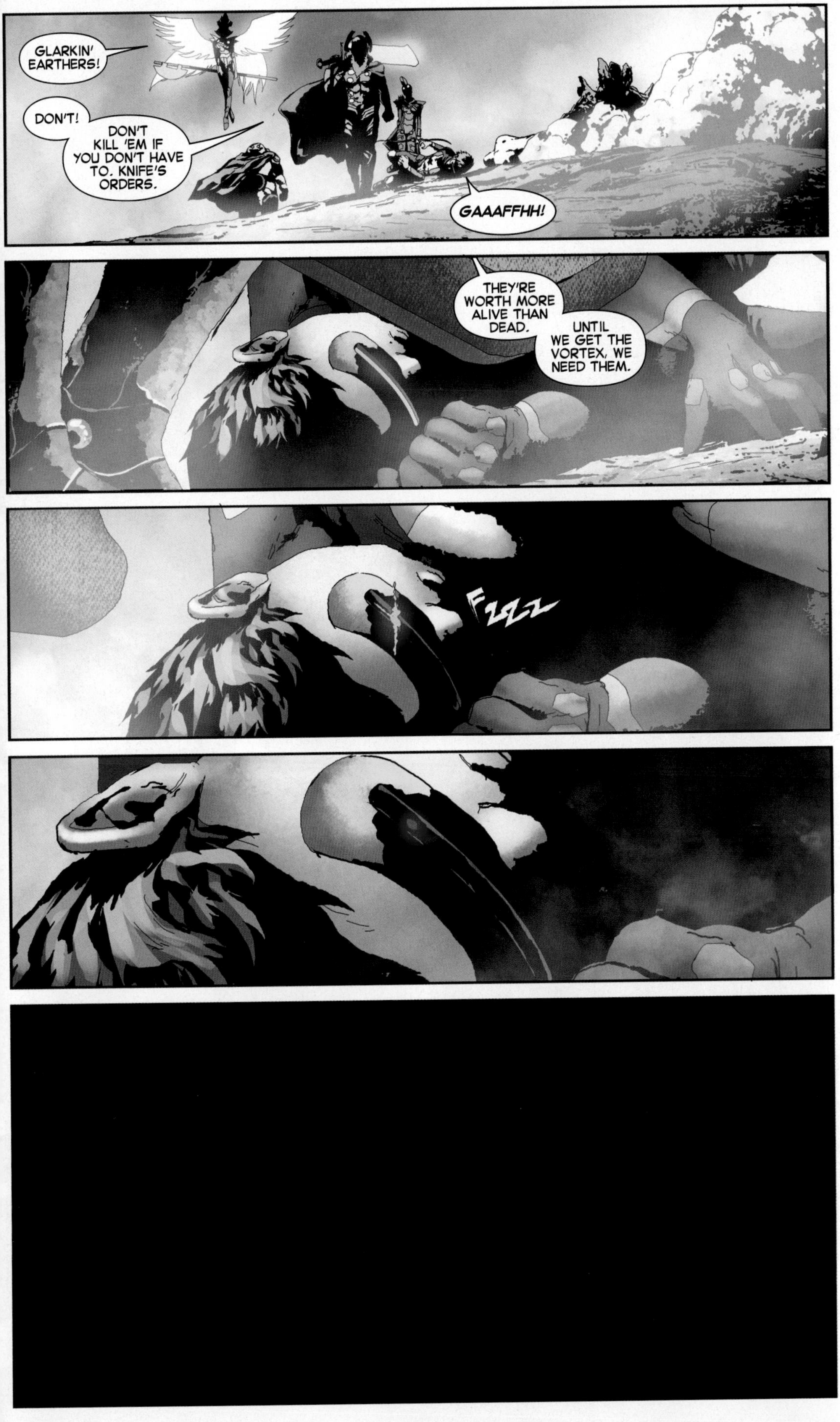
GLARKIN' EARTHERS!
DON'T!
DON'T KILL 'EM IF YOU DON'T HAVE TO. KNIFE'S ORDERS.
GAAAFFHH!
THEY'RE WORTH MORE ALIVE THAN DEAD.
UNTIL WE GET THE VORTEX, WE NEED THEM.
FZZZ

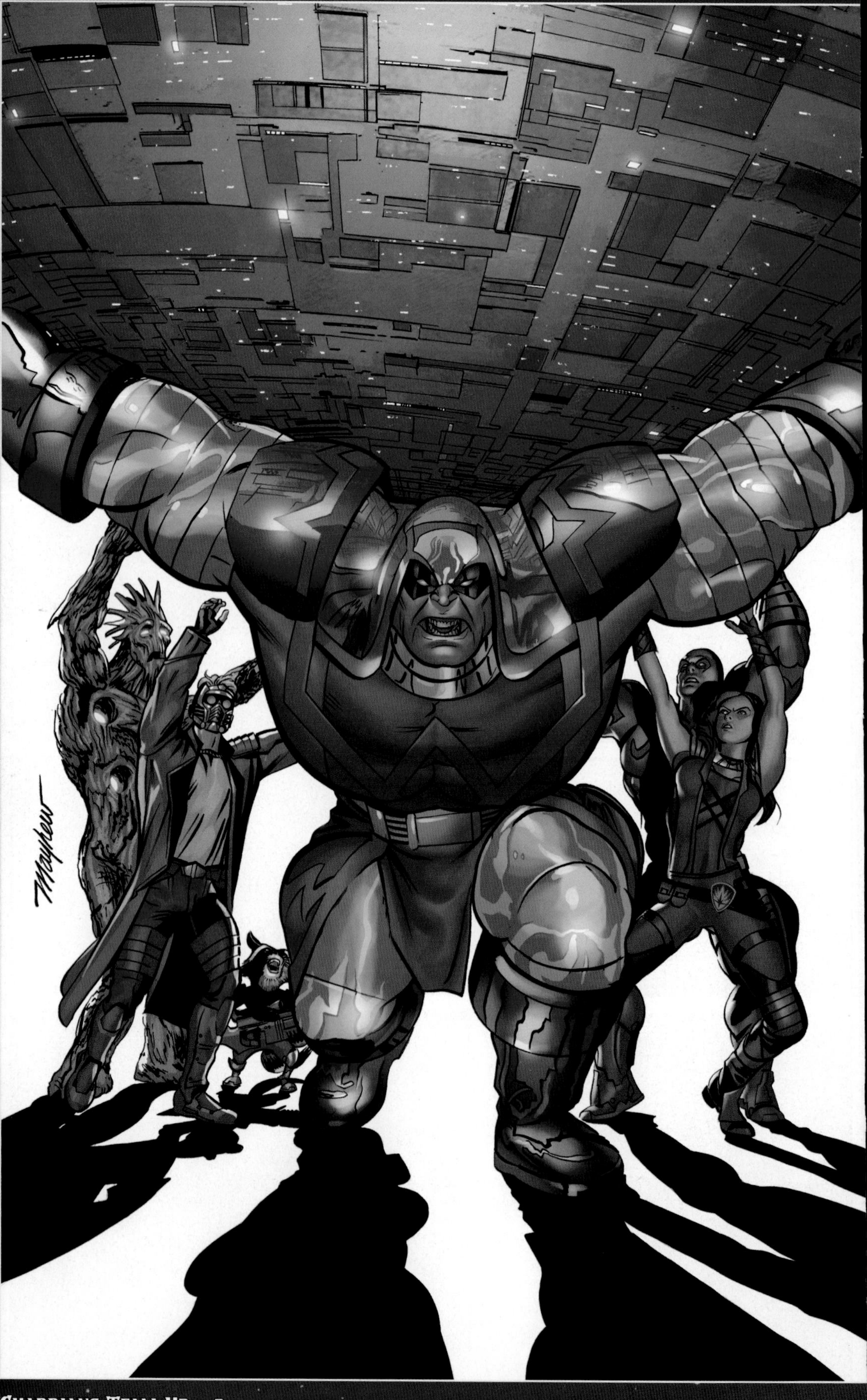
Mayhew

GUARDIANS TEAM-UP #3

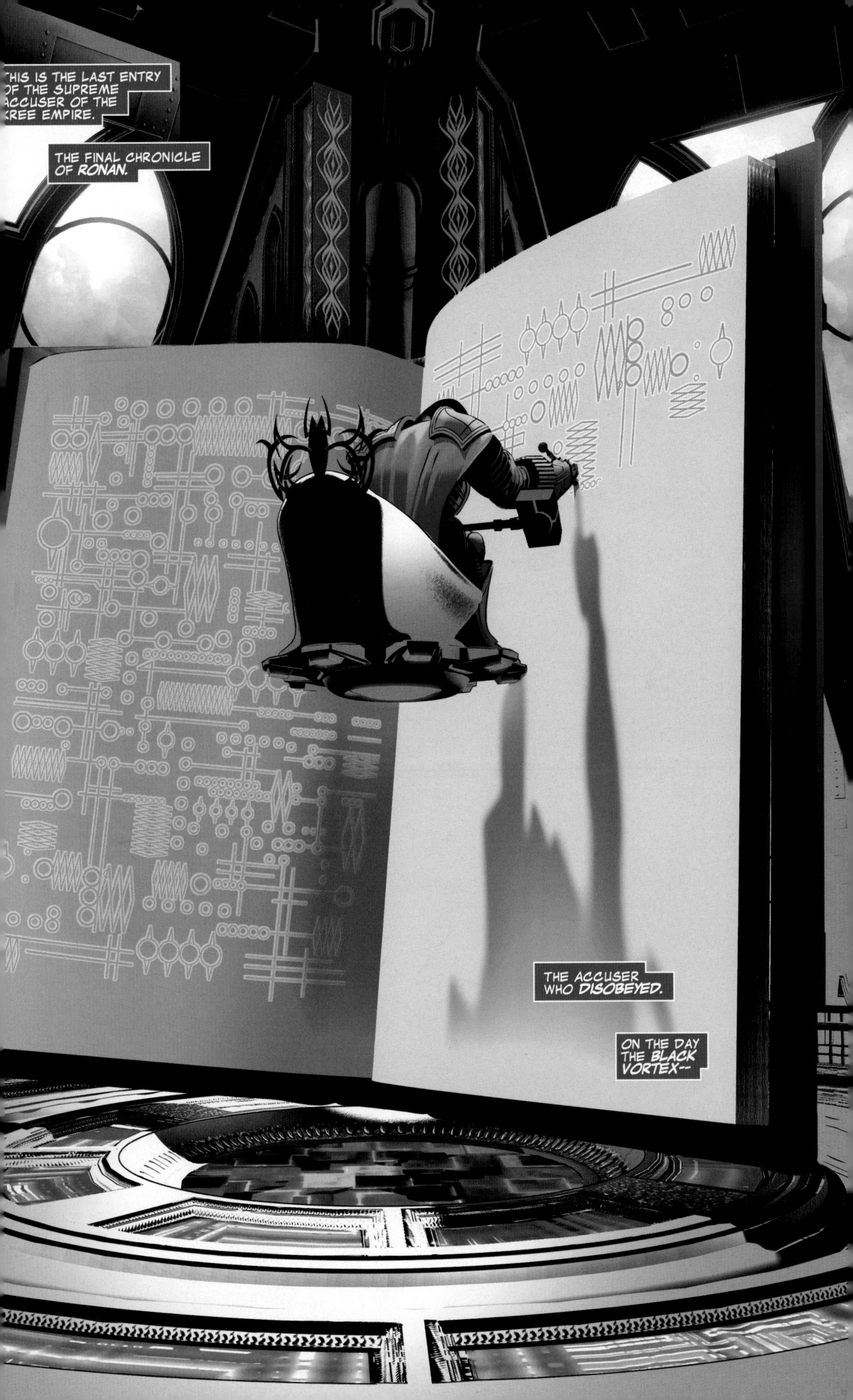
THIS IS THE LAST ENTRY OF THE SUPREME ACCUSER OF THE KREE EMPIRE.
THE FINAL CHRONICLE OF RONAN.
THE ACCUSER WHO DISOBEYED.
ON THE DAY THE BLACK VORTEX--

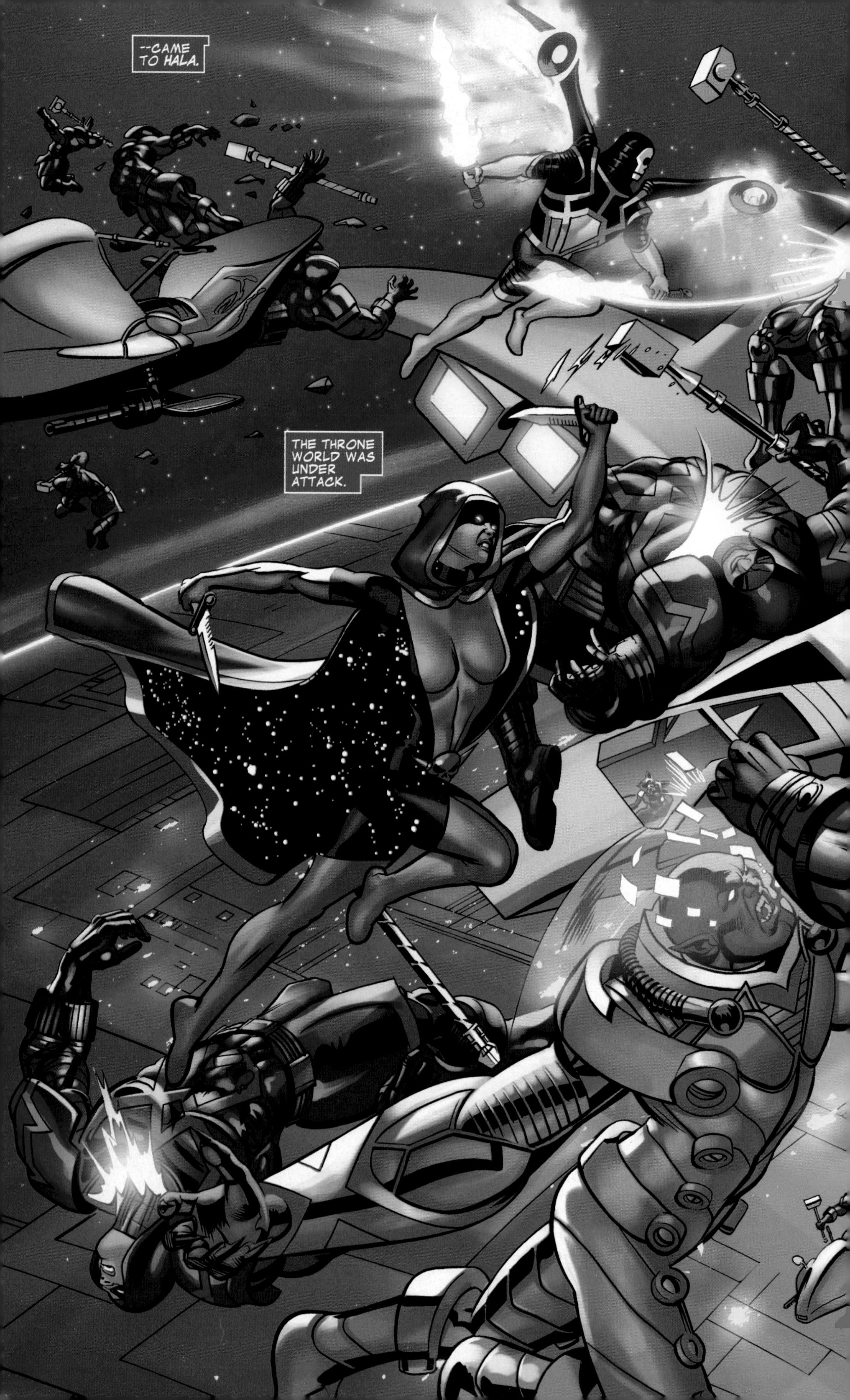
--CAME TO HALA.
THE THRONE WORLD WAS UNDER ATTACK.

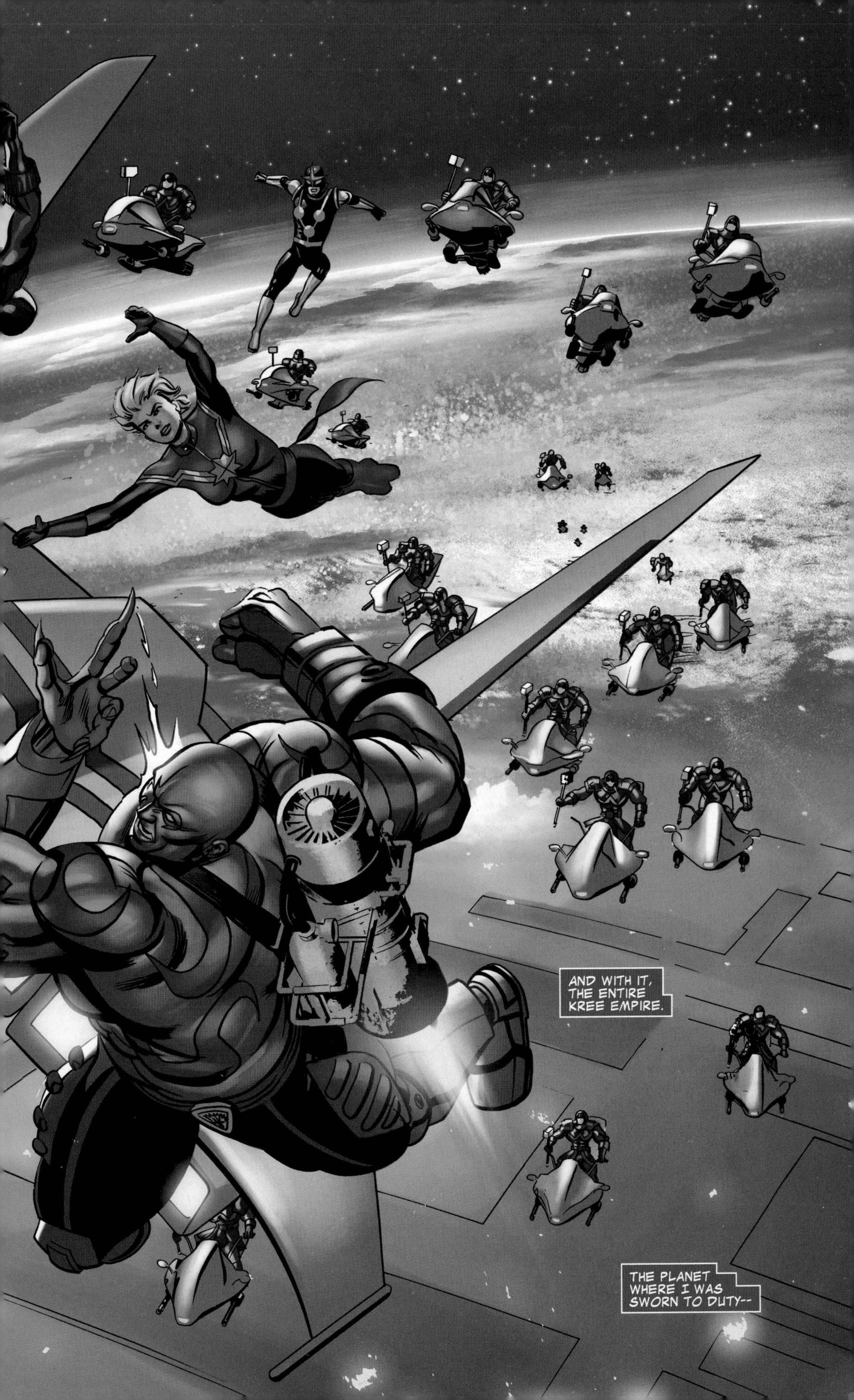
AND WITH IT, THE ENTIRE KREE EMPIRE.
THE PLANET WHERE I WAS SWORN TO DUTY--

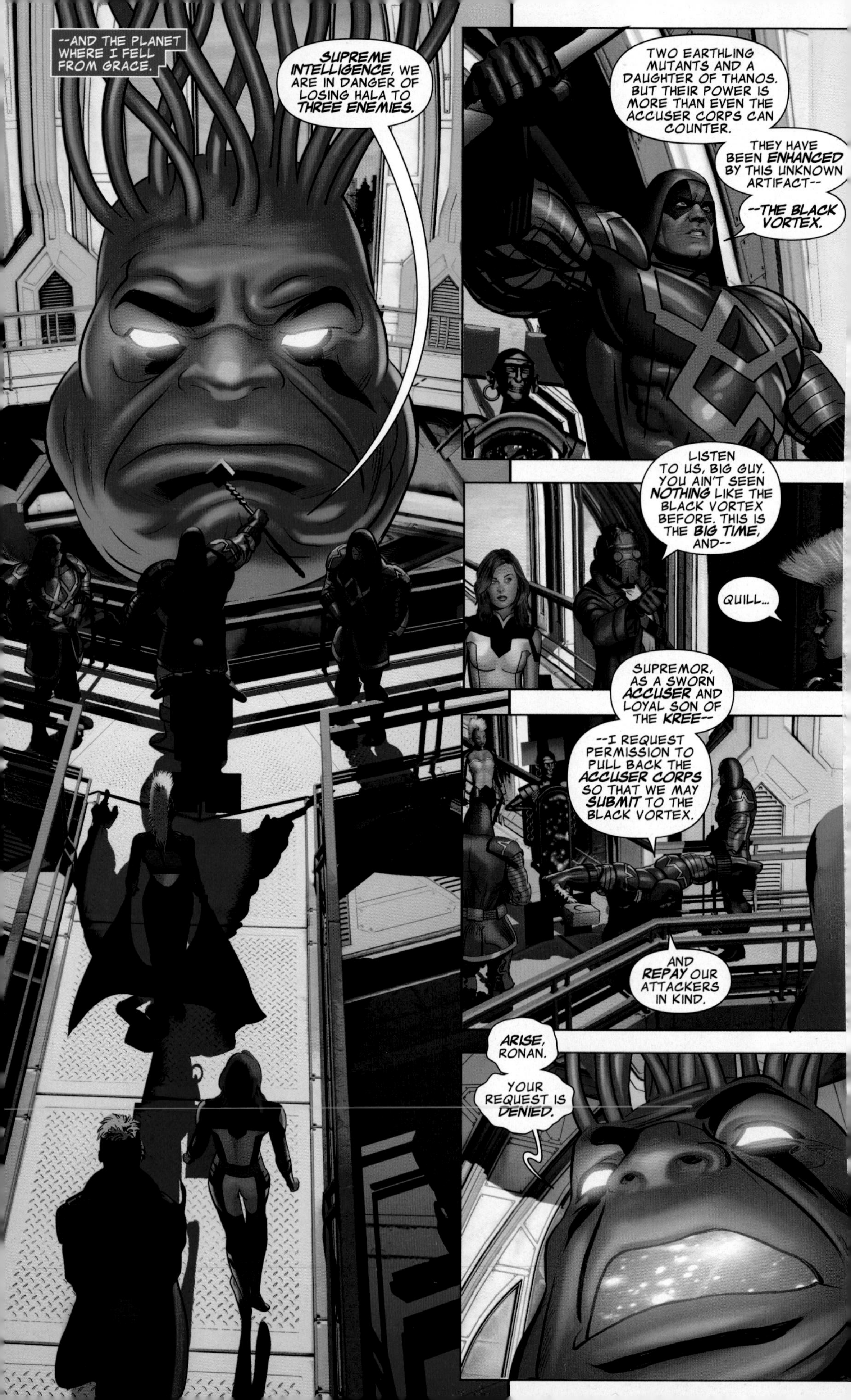
--AND THE PLANET WHERE I FELL FROM GRACE.
SUPREME INTELLIGENCE, WE ARE IN DANGER OF LOSING HALA TO THREE ENEMIES.
TWO EARTHLING MUTANTS AND A DAUGHTER OF THANOS. BUT THEIR POWER IS MORE THAN EVEN THE ACCUSER CORPS CAN COUNTER.
THEY HAVE BEEN ENHANCED BY THIS UNKNOWN ARTIFACT--
--THE BLACK VORTEX.
LISTEN TO US, BIG GUY. YOU AIN'T SEEN NOTHING LIKE THE BLACK VORTEX BEFORE. THIS IS THE BIG TIME, AND--
QUILL...
SUPREMOR, AS A SWORN ACCUSER AND LOYAL SON OF THE KREE--
--I REQUEST PERMISSION TO PULL BACK THE ACCUSER CORPS SO THAT WE MAY SUBMIT TO THE BLACK VORTEX.
AND REPAY OUR ATTACKERS IN KIND.
ARISE, RONAN.
YOUR REQUEST IS DENIED.

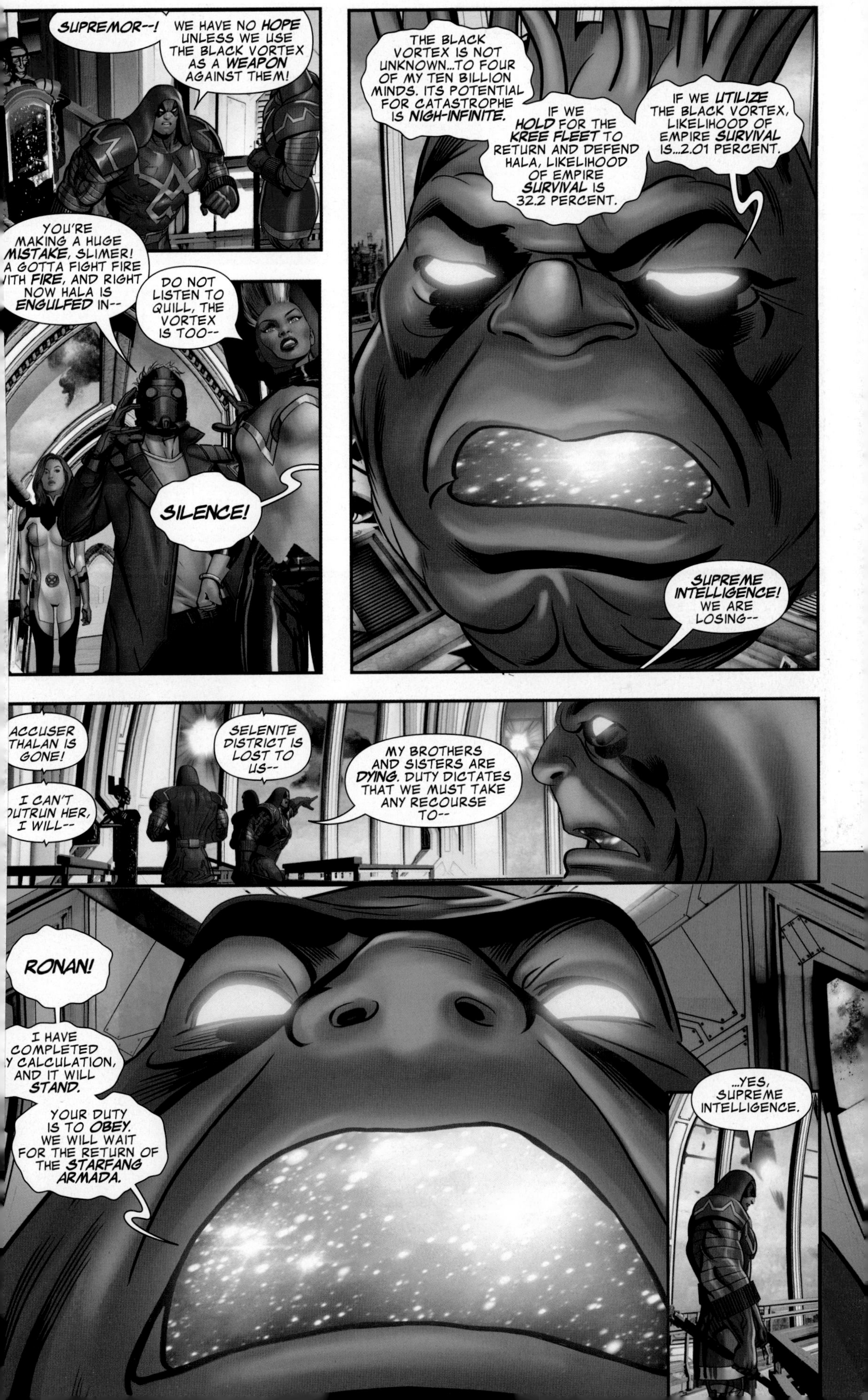
SUPREMOR--!
WE HAVE NO HOPE UNLESS WE USE THE BLACK VORTEX AS A WEAPON AGAINST THEM!
THE BLACK VORTEX IS NOT UNKNOWN...TO FOUR OF MY TEN BILLION MINDS. ITS POTENTIAL FOR CATASTROPHE IS NIGH-INFINITE.
IF WE HOLD FOR THE KREE FLEET TO RETURN AND DEFEND HALA, LIKELIHOOD OF EMPIRE SURVIVAL IS 32.2 PERCENT.
IF WE UTILIZE THE BLACK VORTEX, LIKELIHOOD OF EMPIRE SURVIVAL IS...2.01 PERCENT.
YOU'RE MAKING A HUGE MISTAKE, SLIMER! GOTTA FIGHT FIRE WITH FIRE, AND RIGHT NOW HALA IS ENGULFED IN--
DO NOT LISTEN TO QUILL, THE VORTEX IS TOO--
SILENCE!
SUPREME INTELLIGENCE! WE ARE LOSING--
ACCUSER THALAN IS GONE!
I CAN'T OUTRUN HER, I WILL--
SELENITE DISTRICT IS LOST TO US--
MY BROTHERS AND SISTERS ARE DYING. DUTY DICTATES THAT WE MUST TAKE ANY RECOURSE TO--
RONAN!
I HAVE COMPLETED CALCULATION, AND IT WILL STAND.
YOUR DUTY IS TO OBEY. WE WILL WAIT FOR THE RETURN OF THE STARFANG ARMADA.
...YES, SUPREME INTELLIGENCE.

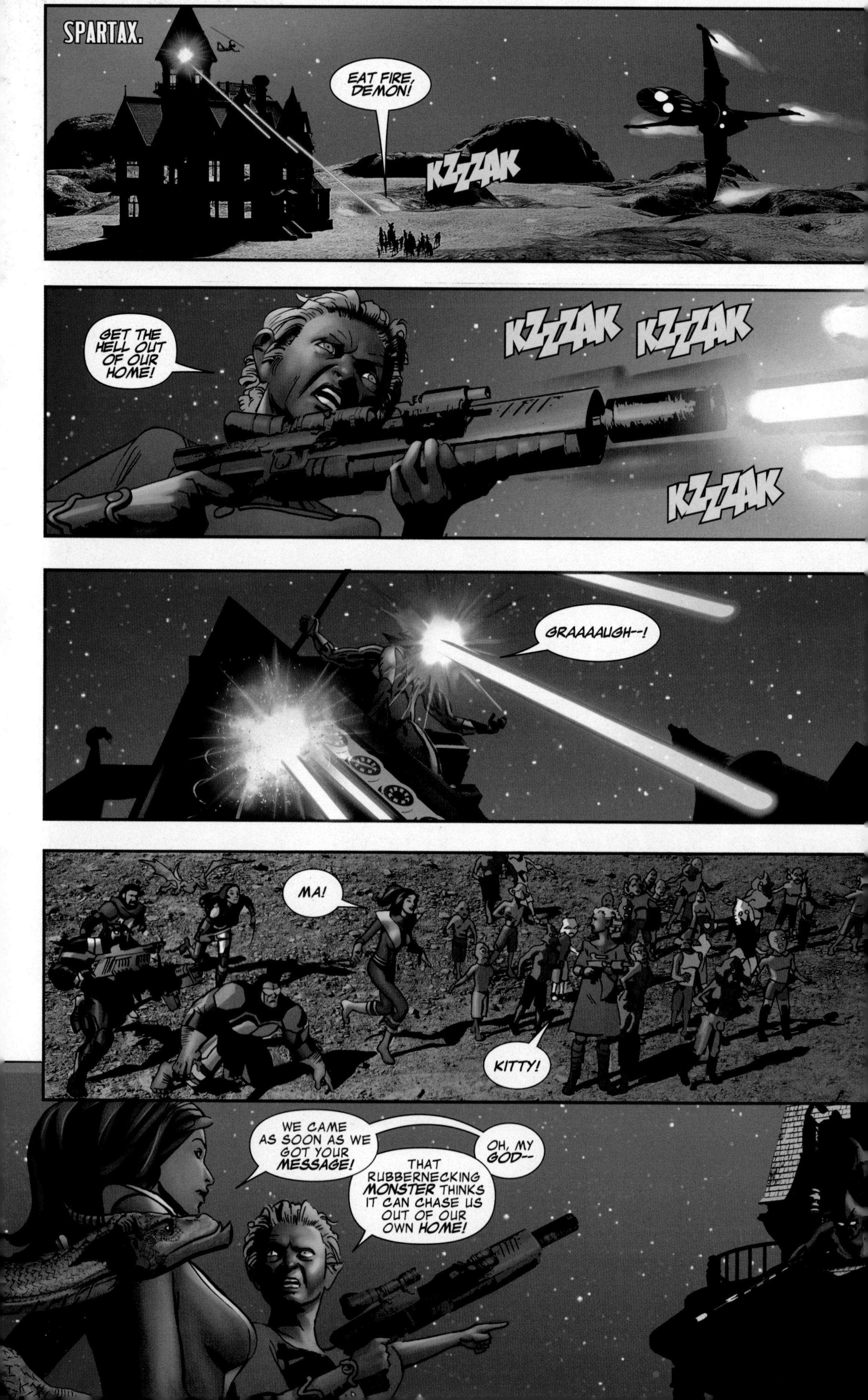
SPARTAX.
EAT FIRE, DEMON!
KZZZAK
GET THE HELL OUT OF OUR HOME!
KZZZAK KZZZAK
KZZZAK
GRAAAAUGH--!
MA!
KITTY!
WE CAME AS SOON AS WE GOT YOUR MESSAGE!
OH, MY GOD--
THAT RUBBERNECKING MONSTER THINKS IT CAN CHASE US OUT OF OUR OWN HOME!

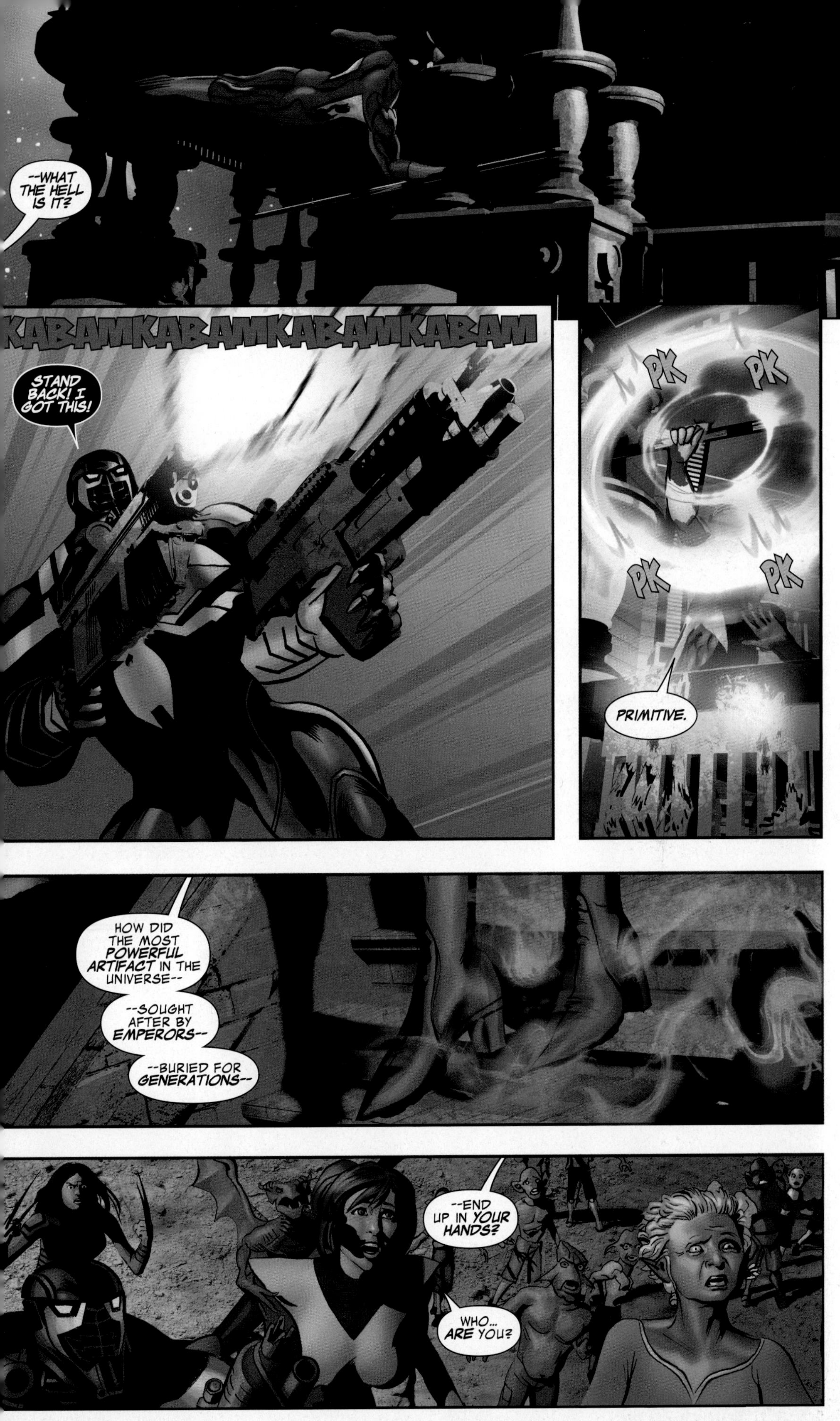
--WHAT THE HELL IS IT?
KABAMKABAMKABAMKABAM
STAND BACK! I GOT THIS!
PK PK PK PK
PRIMITIVE.
HOW DID THE MOST POWERFUL ARTIFACT IN THE UNIVERSE--
--SOUGHT AFTER BY EMPERORS--
--BURIED FOR GENERATIONS--
--END UP IN YOUR HANDS?
WHO... ARE YOU?

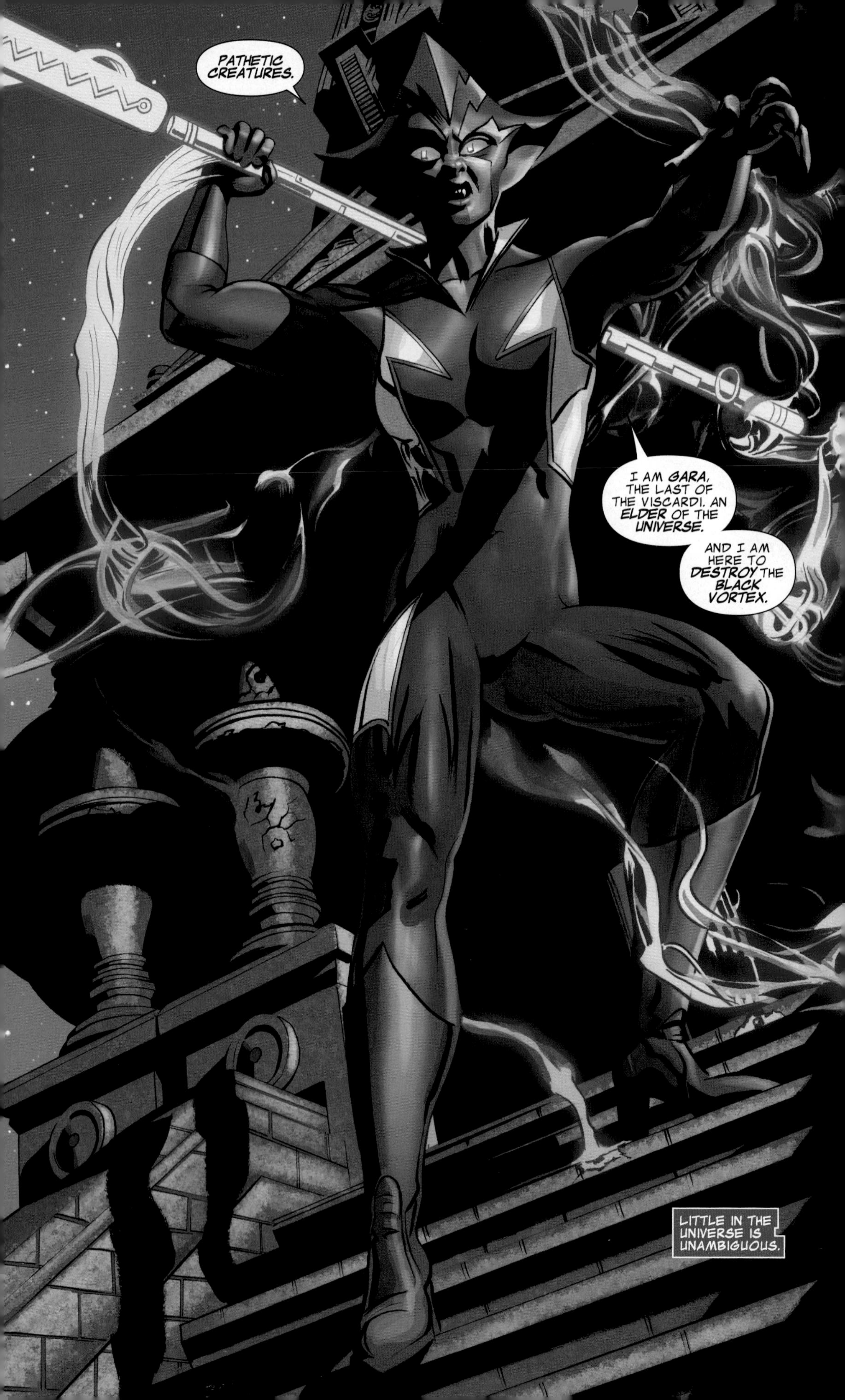

PATHETIC CREATURES.
I AM GARA, THE LAST OF THE VISCARDI. AN ELDER OF THE UNIVERSE.
AND I AM HERE TO DESTROY THE BLACK VORTEX.
LITTLE IN THE UNIVERSE IS UNAMBIGUOUS.

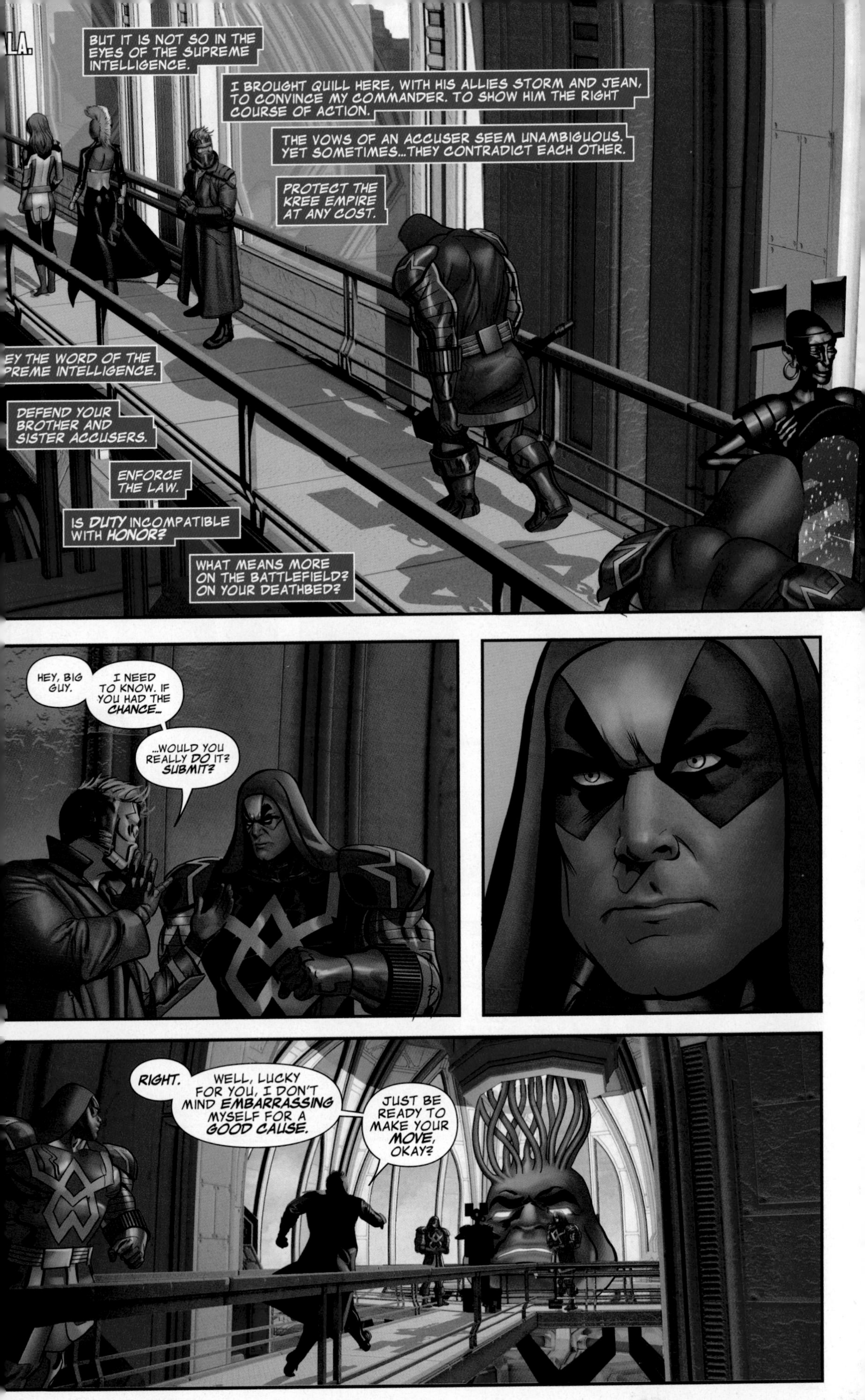
LA.
BUT IT IS NOT SO IN THE EYES OF THE SUPREME INTELLIGENCE.
I BROUGHT QUILL HERE, WITH HIS ALLIES STORM AND JEAN, TO CONVINCE MY COMMANDER. TO SHOW HIM THE RIGHT COURSE OF ACTION.
THE VOWS OF AN ACCUSER SEEM UNAMBIGUOUS. YET SOMETIMES...THEY CONTRADICT EACH OTHER.
PROTECT THE KREE EMPIRE AT ANY COST.
EY THE WORD OF THE PREME INTELLIGENCE.
DEFEND YOUR BROTHER AND SISTER ACCUSERS.
ENFORCE THE LAW.
IS DUTY INCOMPATIBLE WITH HONOR?
WHAT MEANS MORE ON THE BATTLEFIELD? ON YOUR DEATHBED?
HEY, BIG GUY.
I NEED TO KNOW. IF YOU HAD THE CHANCE...
...WOULD YOU REALLY DO IT? SUBMIT?
RIGHT.
WELL, LUCKY FOR YOU, I DON'T MIND EMBARRASSING MYSELF FOR A GOOD CAUSE.
JUST BE READY TO MAKE YOUR MOVE, OKAY?

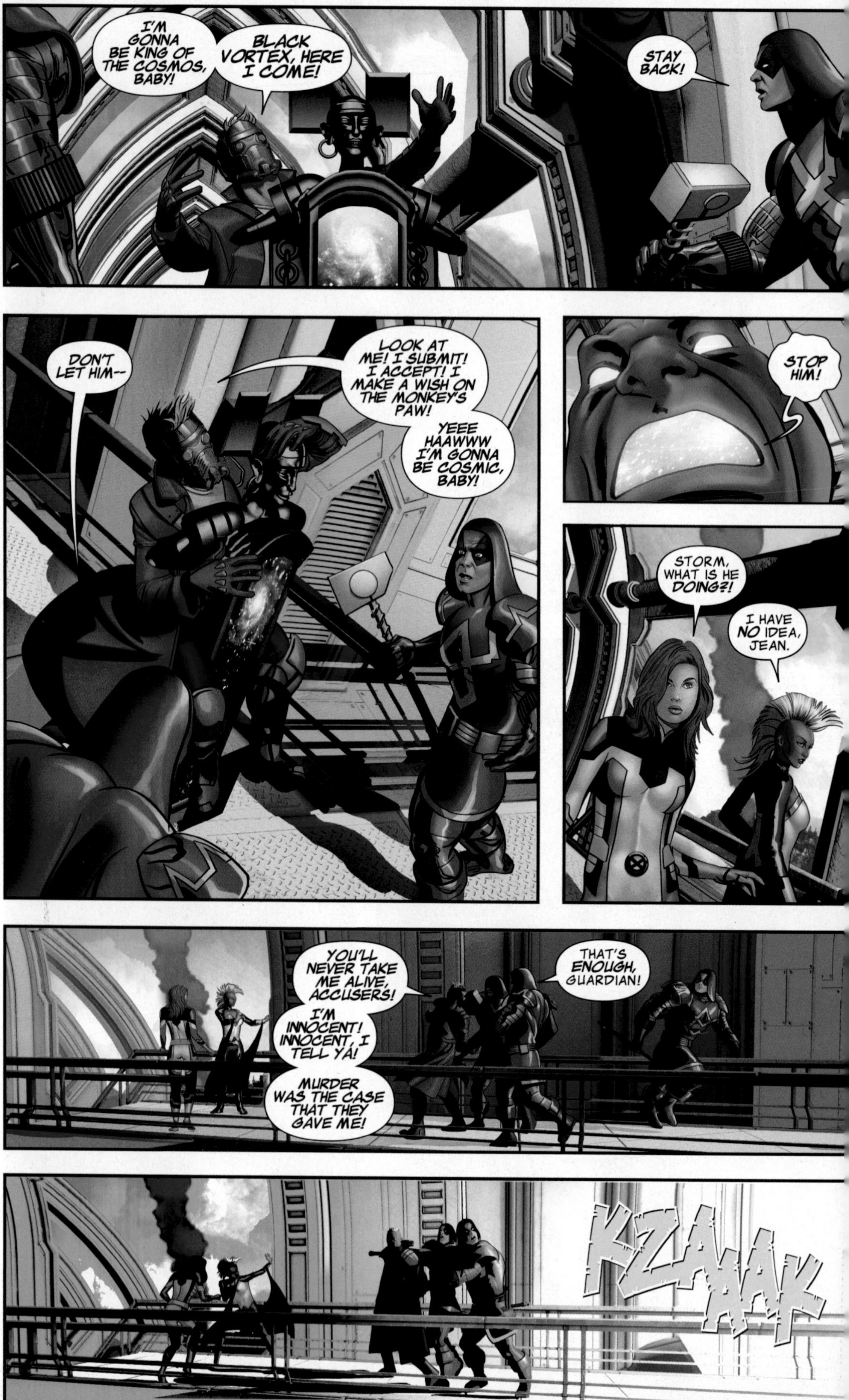
I'M GONNA BE KING OF THE COSMOS, BABY!
BLACK VORTEX, HERE I COME!
STAY BACK!
DON'T LET HIM--
LOOK AT ME! I SUBMIT! I ACCEPT! I MAKE A WISH ON THE MONKEY'S PAW!
YEEE HAAWWW I'M GONNA BE COSMIC, BABY!
STOP HIM!
STORM, WHAT IS HE DOING?!
I HAVE NO IDEA, JEAN.
YOU'LL NEVER TAKE ME ALIVE, ACCUSERS!
I'M INNOCENT! INNOCENT, I TELL YA!
MURDER WAS THE CASE THAT THEY GAVE ME!
THAT'S ENOUGH, GUARDIAN!
KZAAAK

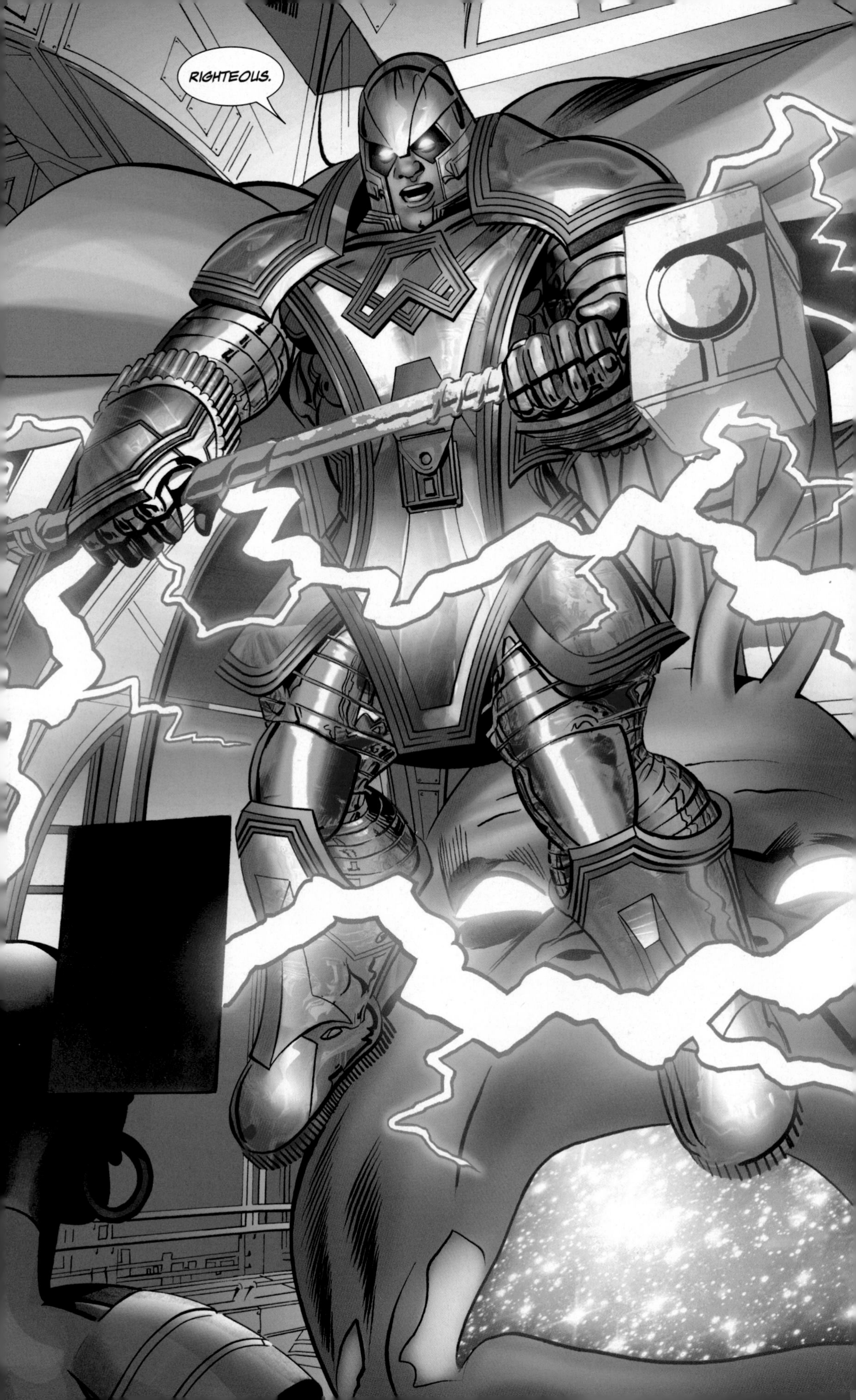
RIGHTEOUS.

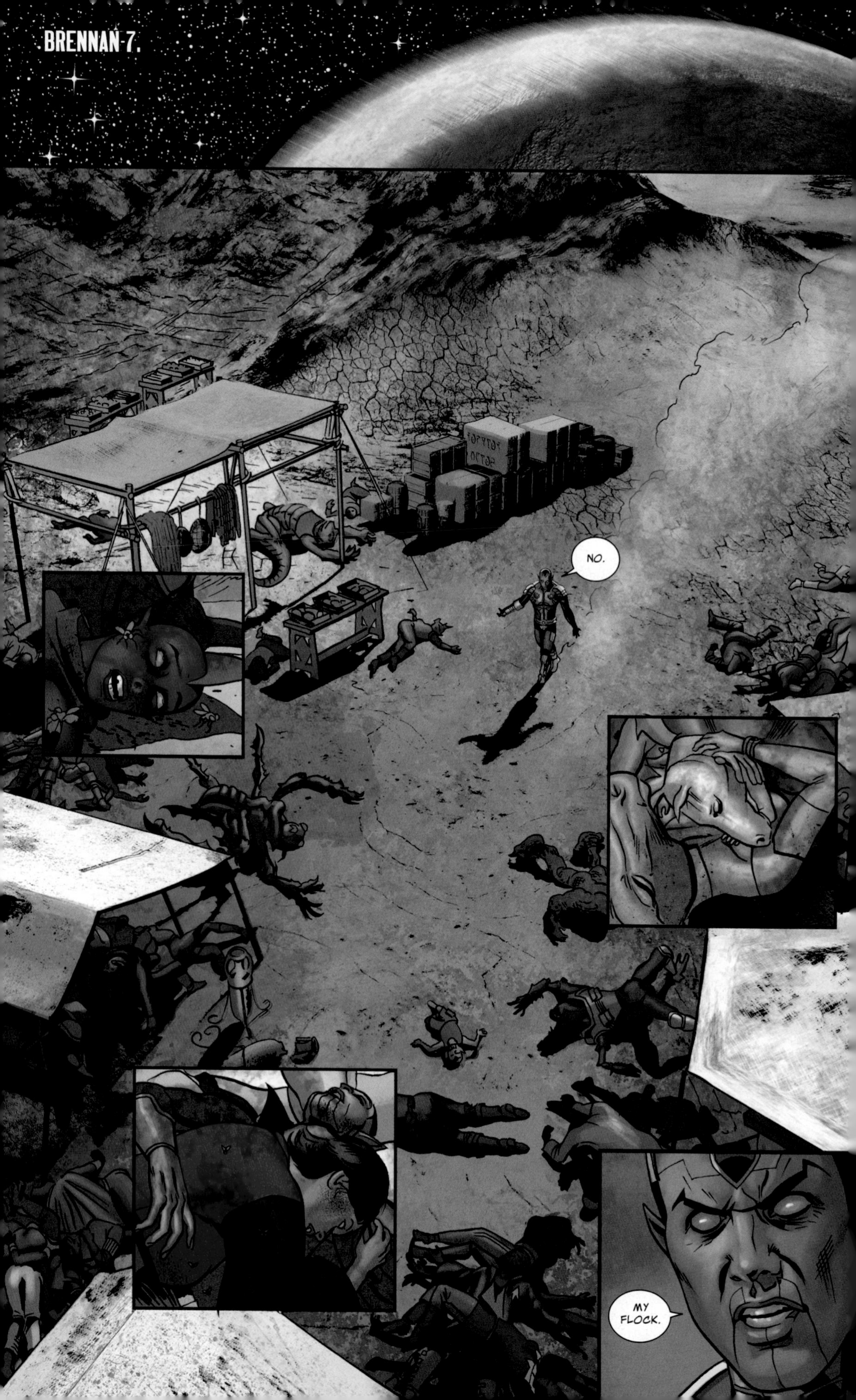
BRENNAN-7.
NO.
MY FLOCK.

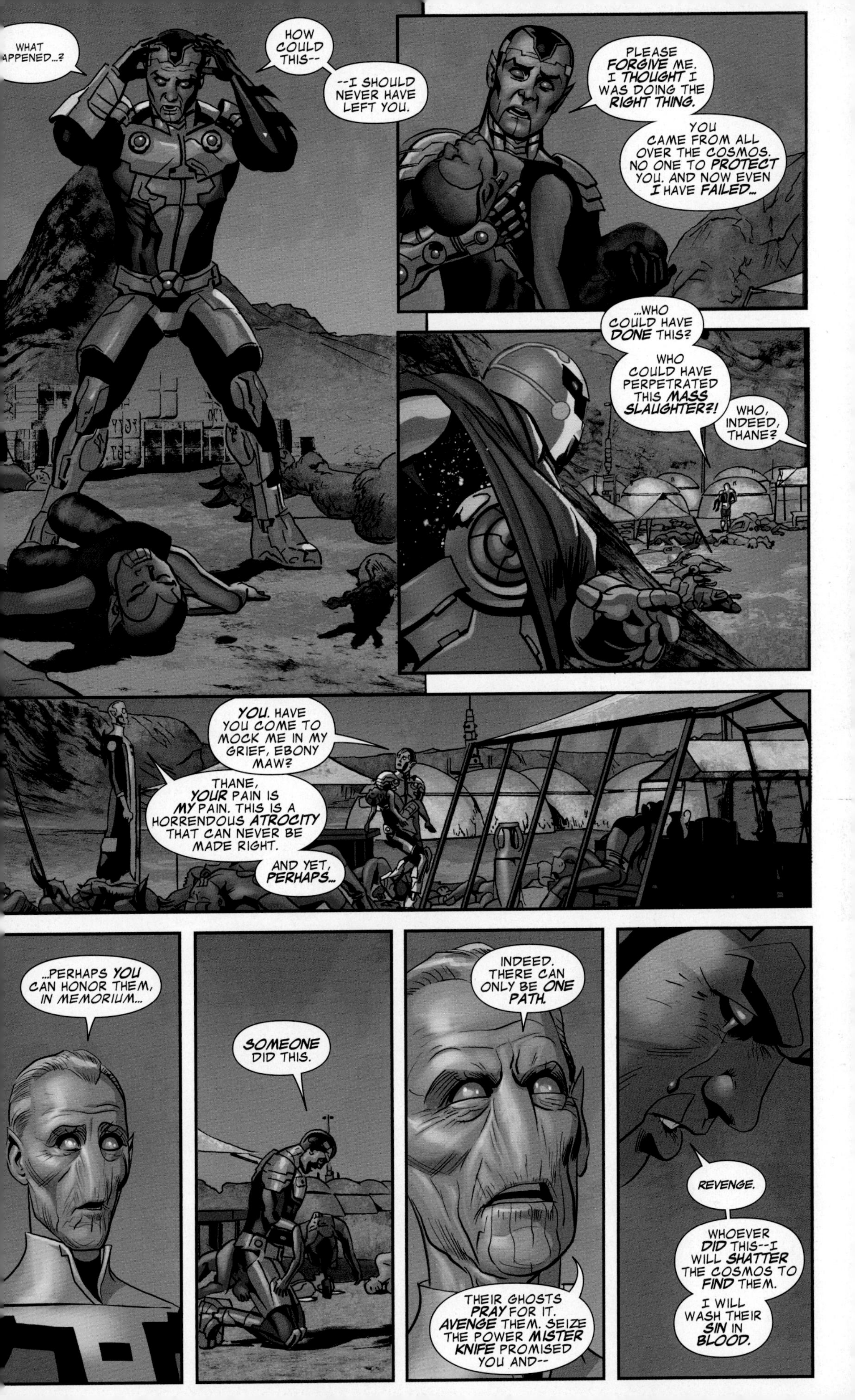
WHAT HAPPENED...?
HOW COULD THIS--
--I SHOULD NEVER HAVE LEFT YOU.
PLEASE FORGIVE ME. I THOUGHT I WAS DOING THE RIGHT THING.
YOU CAME FROM ALL OVER THE COSMOS. NO ONE TO PROTECT YOU. AND NOW EVEN I HAVE FAILED...
...WHO COULD HAVE DONE THIS?
WHO COULD HAVE PERPETRATED THIS MASS SLAUGHTER?!
WHO, INDEED, THANE?
YOU. HAVE YOU COME TO MOCK ME IN MY GRIEF, EBONY MAW?
THANE, YOUR PAIN IS MY PAIN. THIS IS A HORRENDOUS ATROCITY THAT CAN NEVER BE MADE RIGHT.
AND YET, PERHAPS...
...PERHAPS YOU CAN HONOR THEM, IN MEMORIUM...
SOMEONE DID THIS.
INDEED. THERE CAN ONLY BE ONE PATH.
THEIR GHOSTS PRAY FOR IT. AVENGE THEM. SEIZE THE POWER MISTER KNIFE PROMISED YOU AND--
REVENGE.
WHOEVER DID THIS--I WILL SHATTER THE COSMOS TO FIND THEM.
I WILL WASH THEIR SIN IN BLOOD.

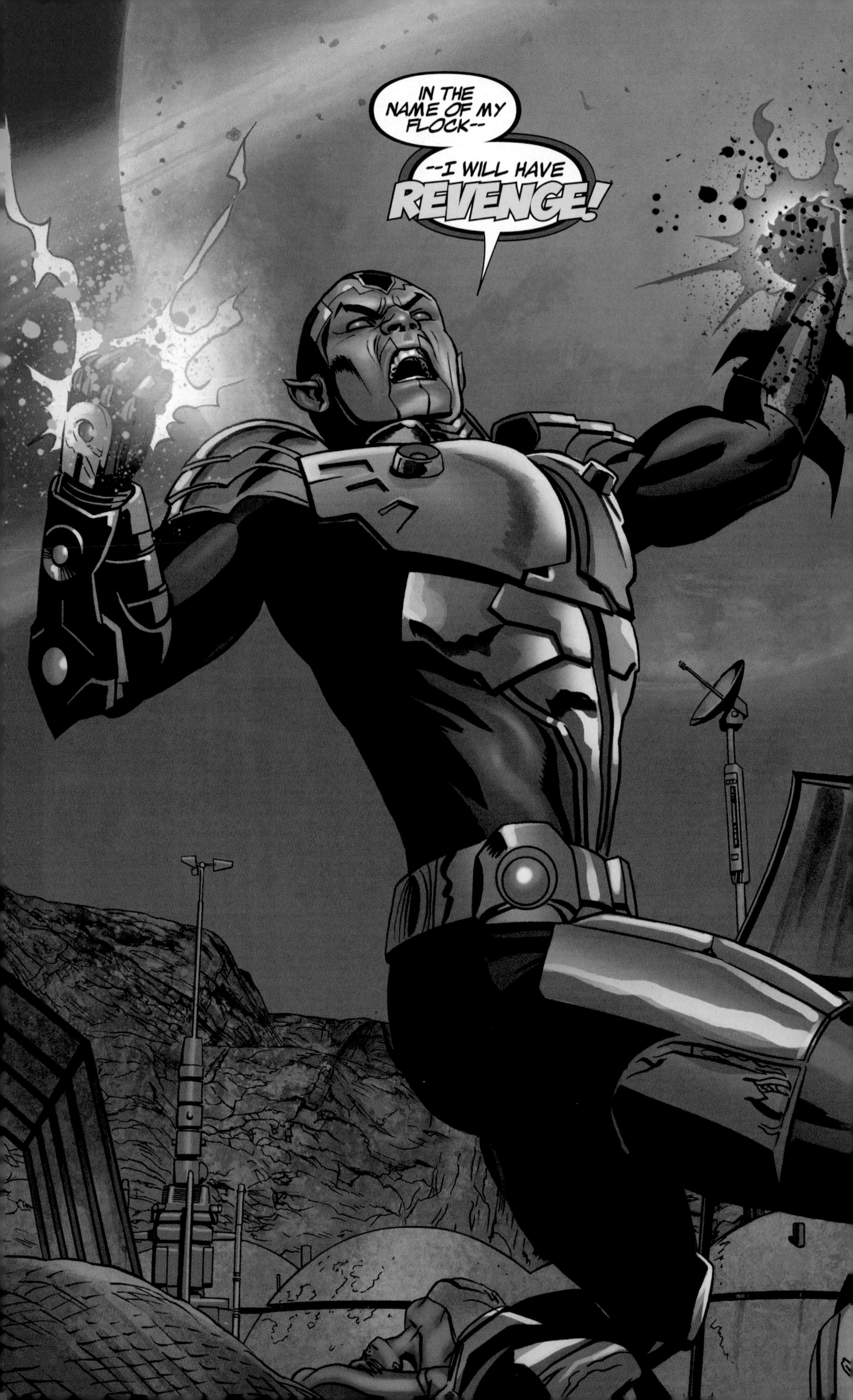
IN THE NAME OF MY FLOCK--
--I WILL HAVE REVENGE!

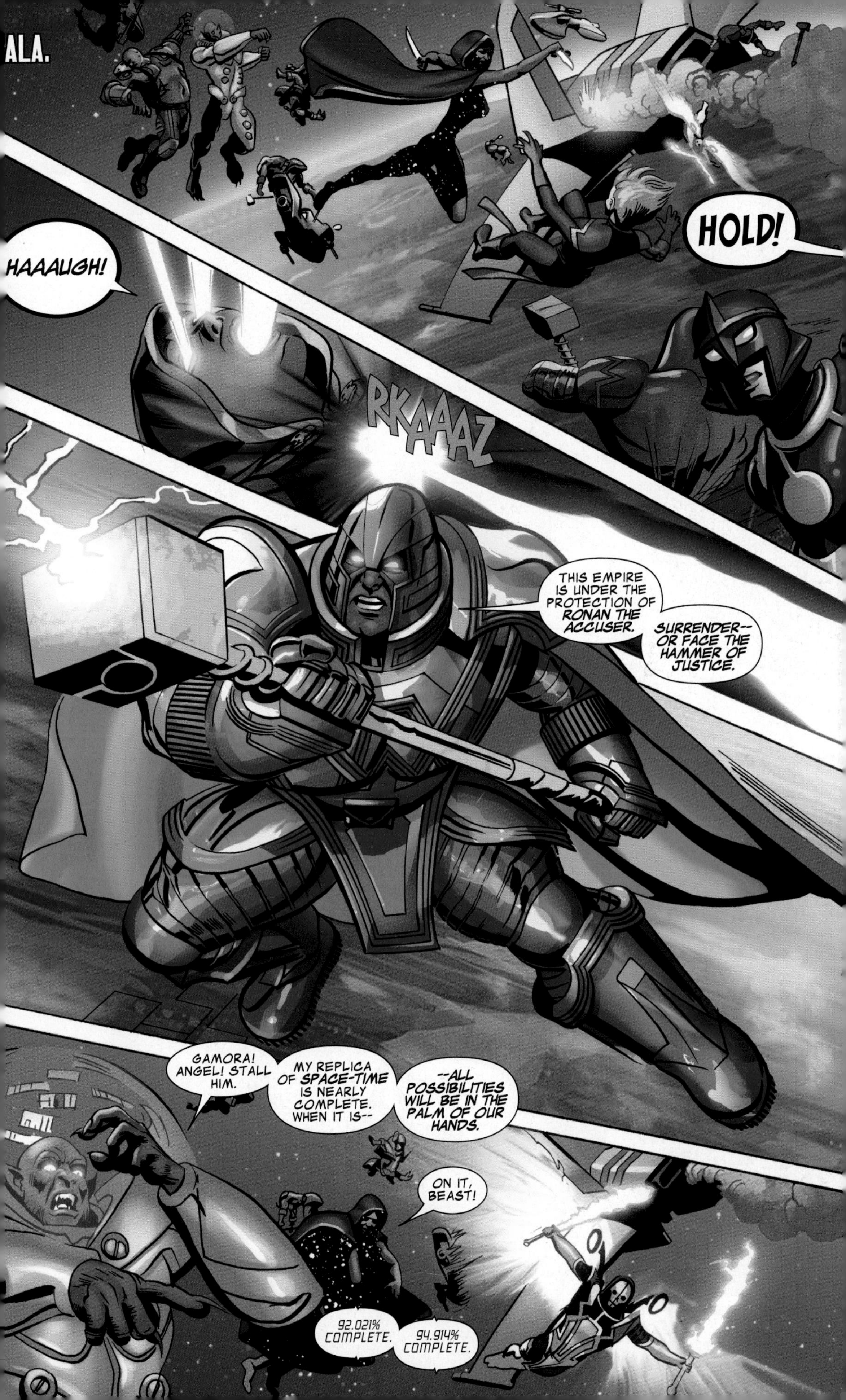
ALA.
HAAAUGH!
HOLD!
RKAAAZ
THIS EMPIRE IS UNDER THE PROTECTION OF RONAN THE ACCUSER.
SURRENDER-- OR FACE THE HAMMER OF JUSTICE.
GAMORA! ANGEL! STALL HIM.
MY REPLICA OF SPACE-TIME IS NEARLY COMPLETE. WHEN IT IS--
--ALL POSSIBILITIES WILL BE IN THE PALM OF OUR HANDS.
ON IT, BEAST!
92.021% COMPLETE.
94.914% COMPLETE.

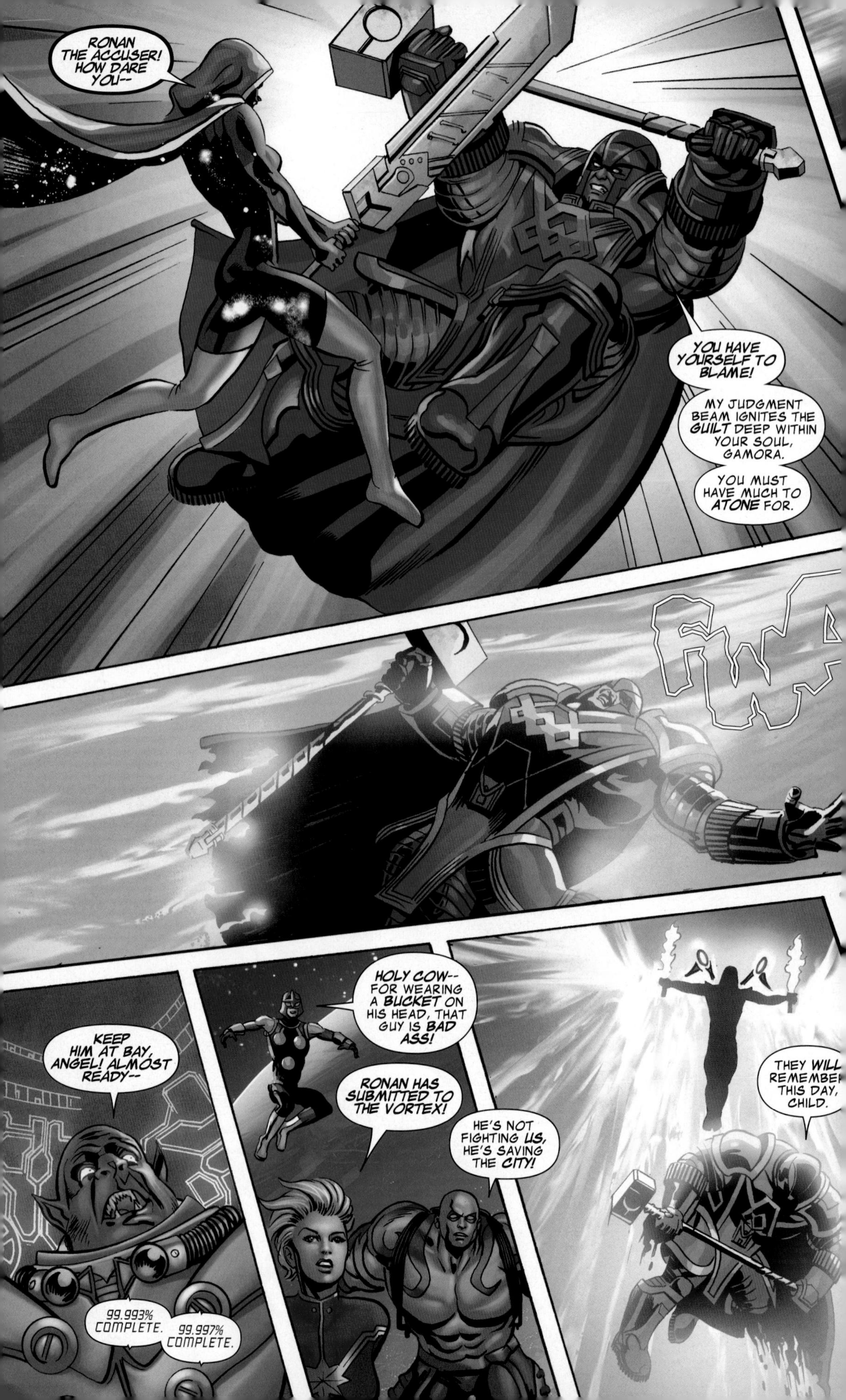
RONAN THE ACCUSER! HOW DARE YOU--
YOU HAVE YOURSELF TO BLAME!
MY JUDGMENT BEAM IGNITES THE GUILT DEEP WITHIN YOUR SOUL, GAMORA.
YOU MUST HAVE MUCH TO ATONE FOR.
KEEP HIM AT BAY, ANGEL! ALMOST READY--
99.993% COMPLETE.
99.997% COMPLETE.
HOLY COW-- FOR WEARING A BUCKET ON HIS HEAD, THAT GUY IS BAD ASS!
RONAN HAS SUBMITTED TO THE VORTEX!
HE'S NOT FIGHTING US, HE'S SAVING THE CITY!
THEY WILL REMEMBER THIS DAY, CHILD.

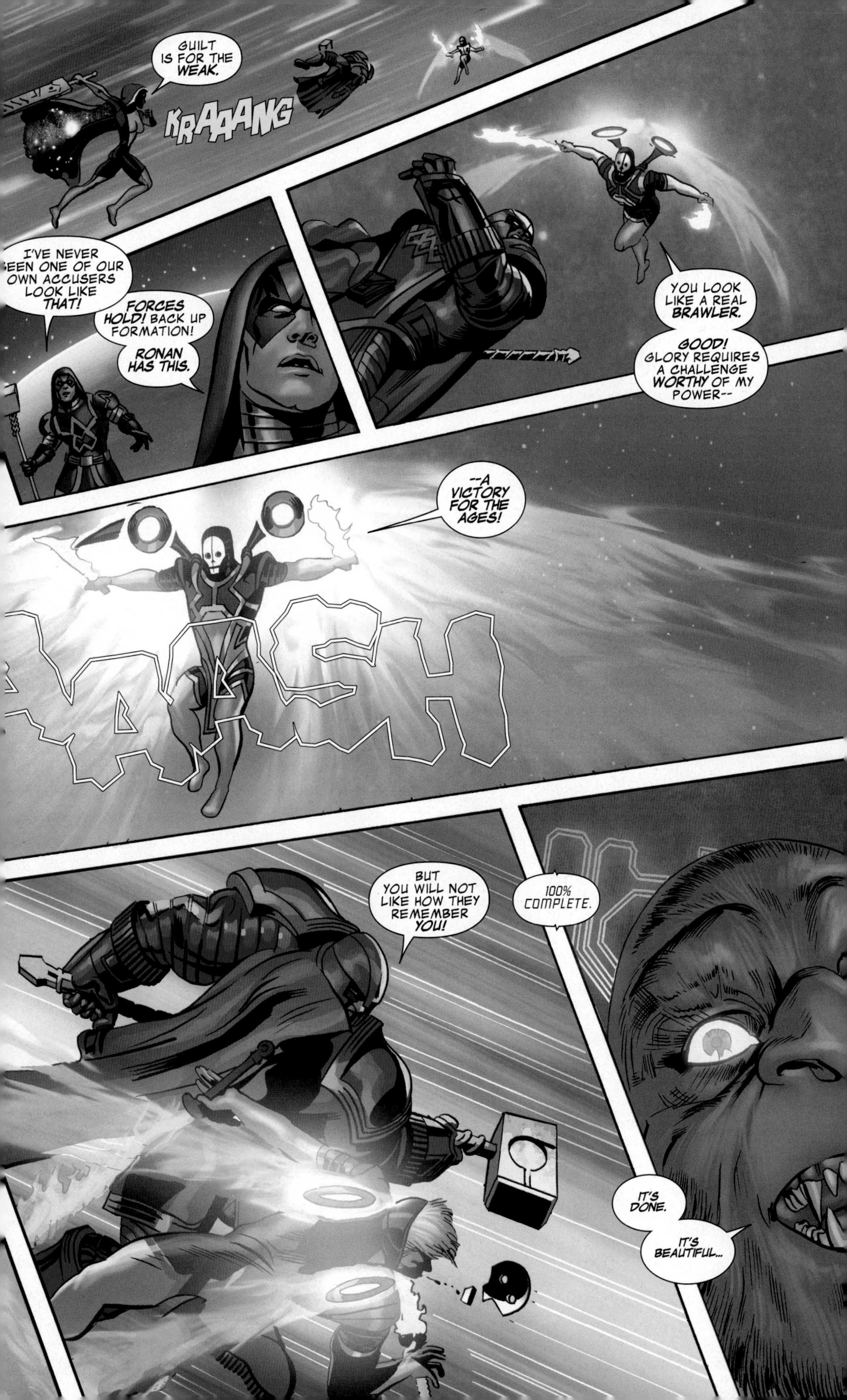
GUILT IS FOR THE WEAK.
KRAAANG
I'VE NEVER SEEN ONE OF OUR OWN ACCUSERS LOOK LIKE THAT!
FORCES HOLD! BACK UP FORMATION!
RONAN HAS THIS.
YOU LOOK LIKE A REAL BRAWLER.
GOOD! GLORY REQUIRES A CHALLENGE WORTHY OF MY POWER--
--A VICTORY FOR THE AGES!
BUT YOU WILL NOT LIKE HOW THEY REMEMBER YOU!
100% COMPLETE.
IT'S DONE.
IT'S BEAUTIFUL...

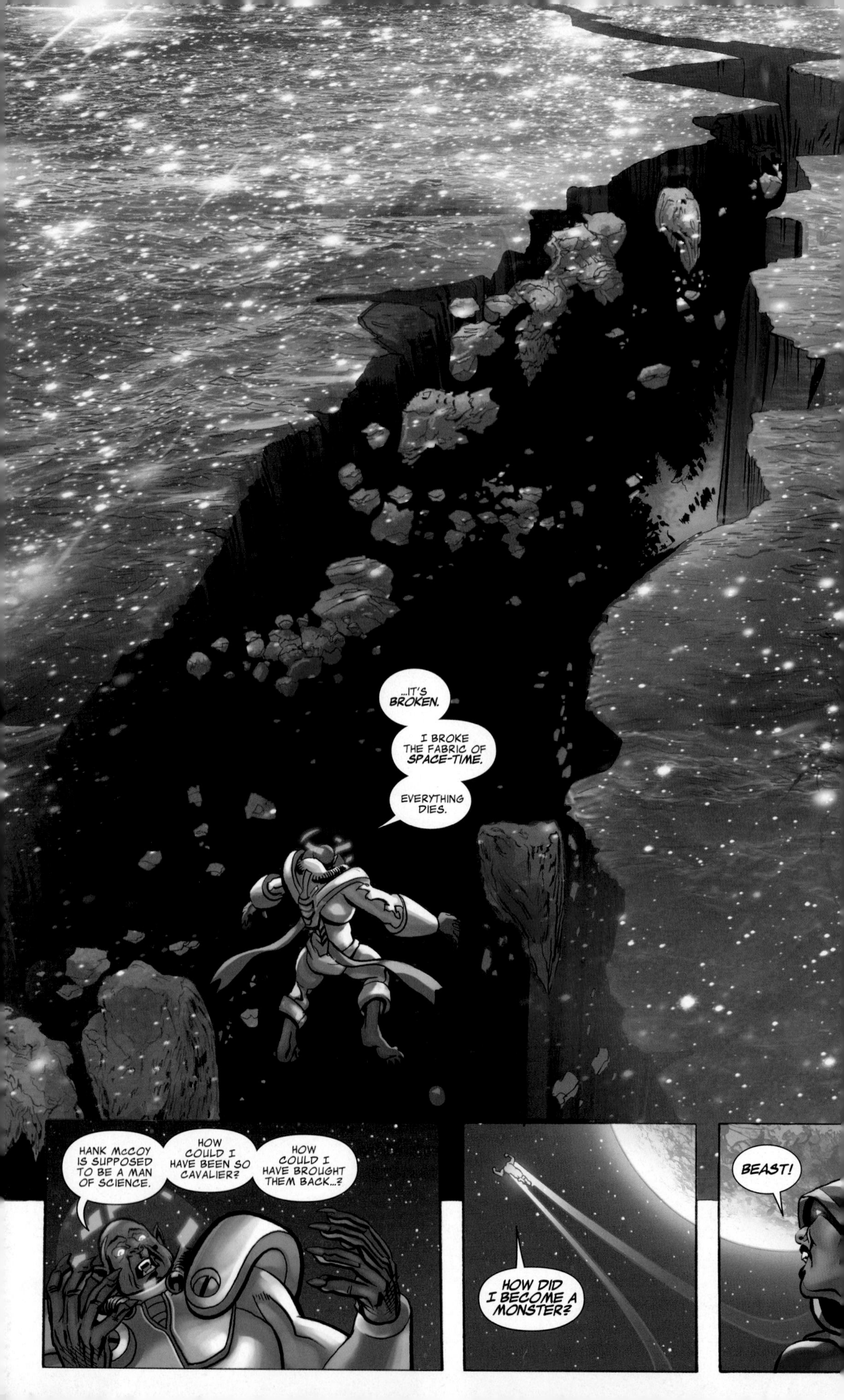

...IT'S BROKEN.
I BROKE THE FABRIC OF SPACE-TIME.
EVERYTHING DIES.
HANK McCOY IS SUPPOSED TO BE A MAN OF SCIENCE.
HOW COULD I HAVE BEEN SO CAVALIER?
HOW COULD I HAVE BROUGHT THEM BACK...?
HOW DID I BECOME A MONSTER?
BEAST!

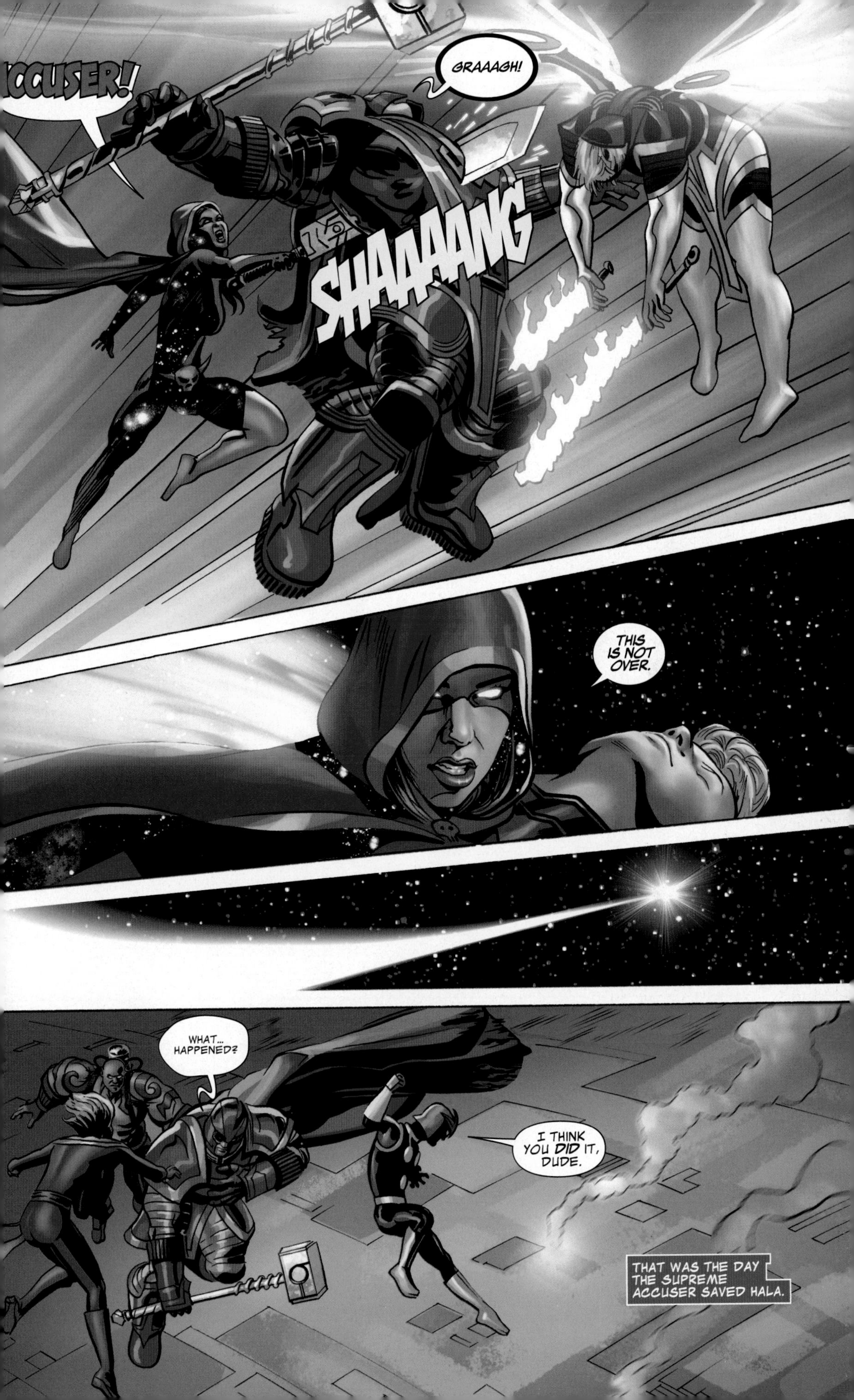
CCUSER!
GRAAAGH!
SHAAAANG
THIS IS NOT OVER.
WHAT... HAPPENED?
I THINK YOU DID IT, DUDE.
THAT WAS THE DAY THE SUPREME ACCUSER SAVED HALA.

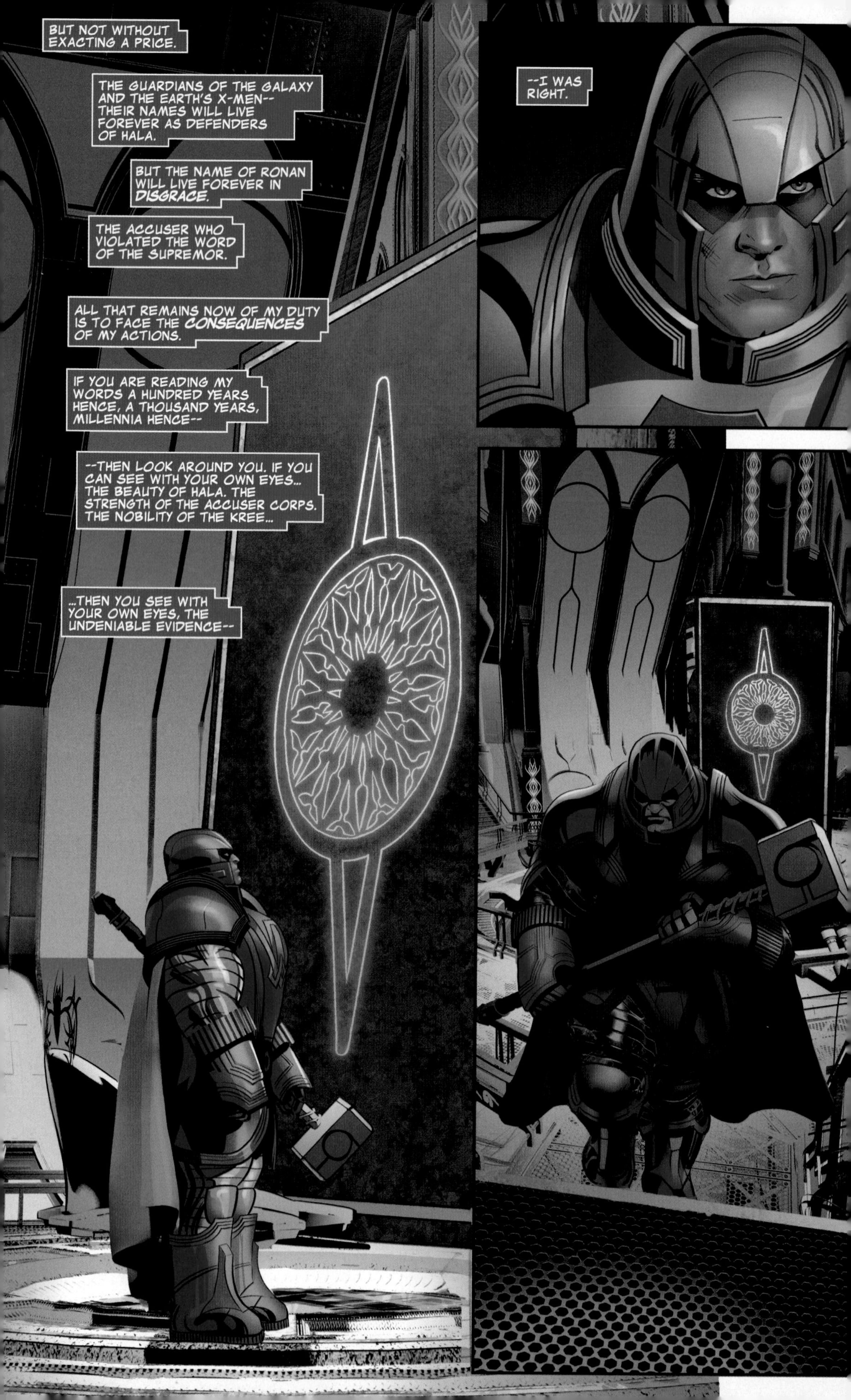

BUT NOT WITHOUT EXACTING A PRICE.
THE GUARDIANS OF THE GALAXY AND THE EARTH'S X-MEN-- THEIR NAMES WILL LIVE FOREVER AS DEFENDERS OF HALA.
BUT THE NAME OF RONAN WILL LIVE FOREVER IN DISGRACE.
THE ACCUSER WHO VIOLATED THE WORD OF THE SUPREMOR.
ALL THAT REMAINS NOW OF MY DUTY IS TO FACE THE CONSEQUENCES OF MY ACTIONS.
IF YOU ARE READING MY WORDS A HUNDRED YEARS HENCE, A THOUSAND YEARS, MILLENNIA HENCE--
--THEN LOOK AROUND YOU. IF YOU CAN SEE WITH YOUR OWN EYES... THE BEAUTY OF HALA. THE STRENGTH OF THE ACCUSER CORPS. THE NOBILITY OF THE KREE...
...THEN YOU SEE WITH YOUR OWN EYES, THE UNDENIABLE EVIDENCE--
--I WAS RIGHT.

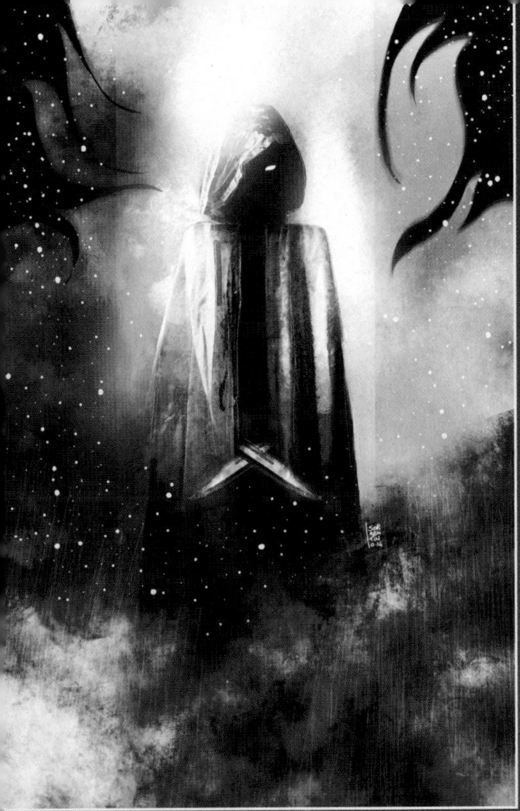

UARDIANS OF THE GALAXY #24 COSMICALLY ENHANCED VARIANT
BY ANDREA SORRENTINO

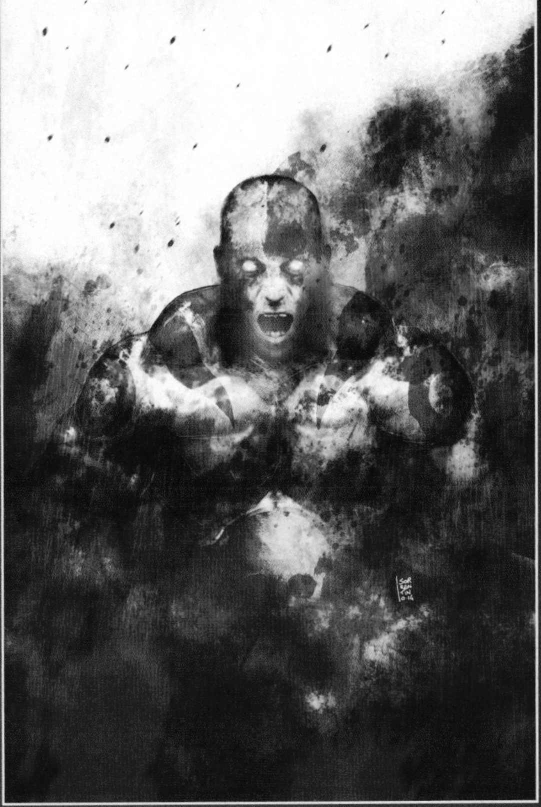

LEGENDARY STAR-LORD #9 COSMICALLY ENHANCED VARIANT
BY ANDREA SORRENTINO

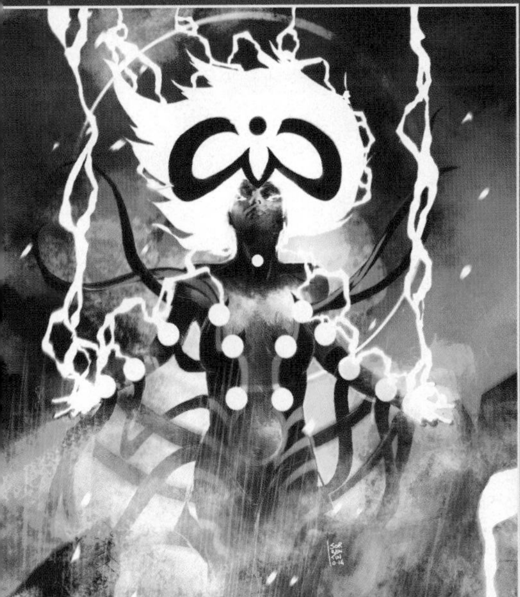

ALL NEW X-MEN #38 COSMICALLY ENHANCED VARIANT

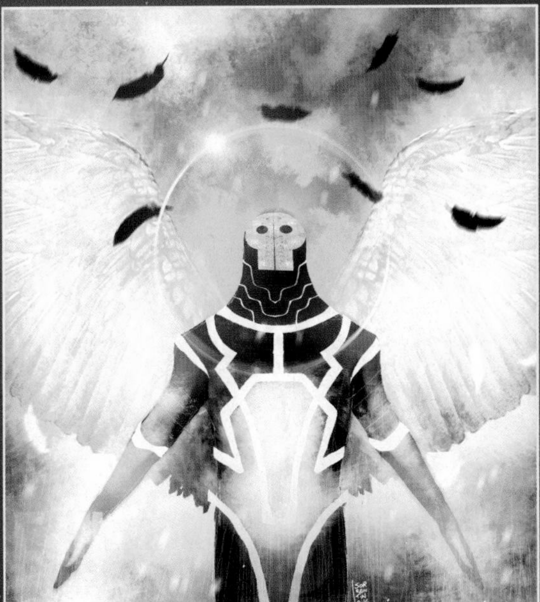

ALL NEW X-MEN #39 COSMICALLY ENHANCED VARIANT

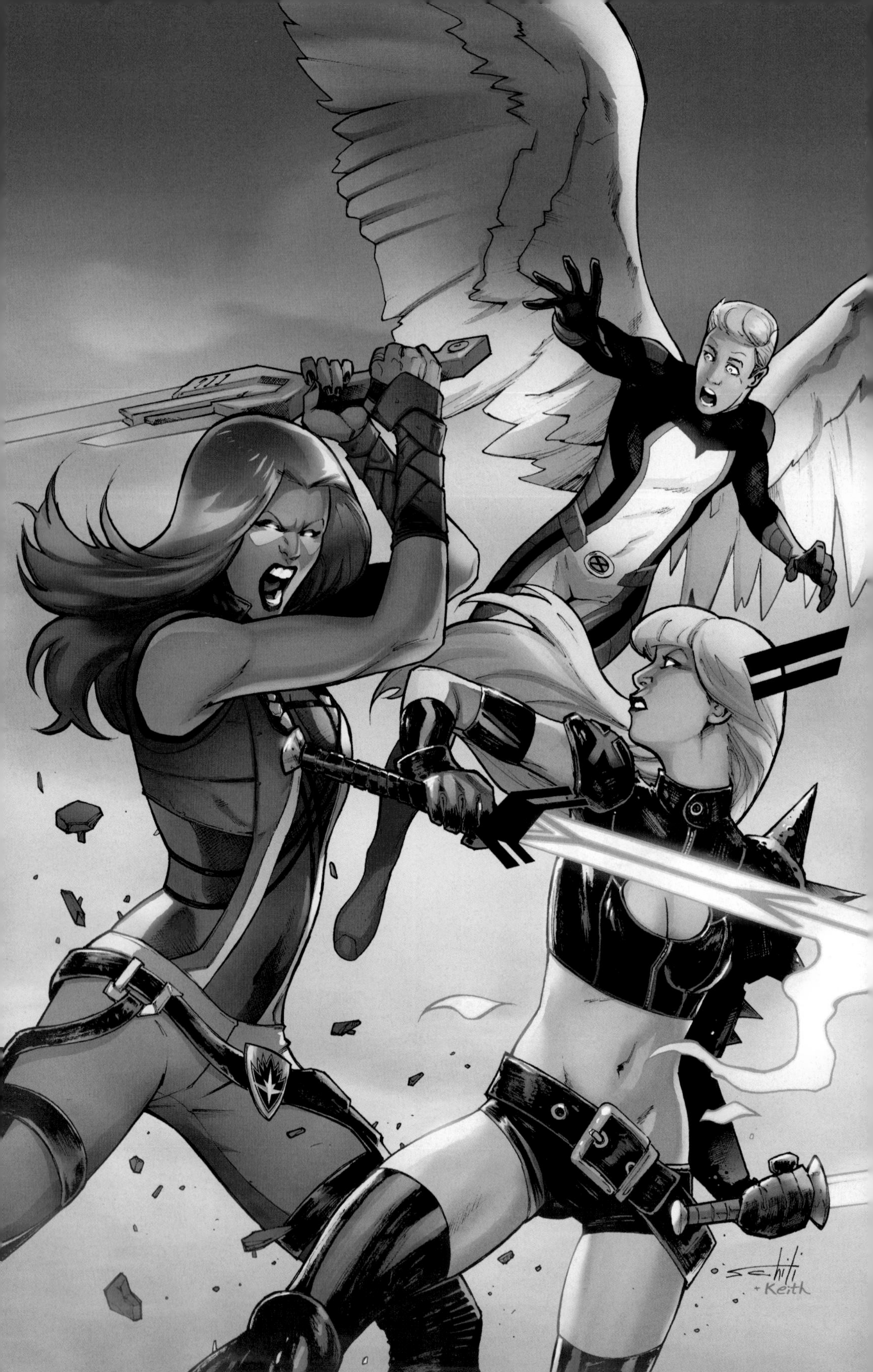
schiti
+ Keith

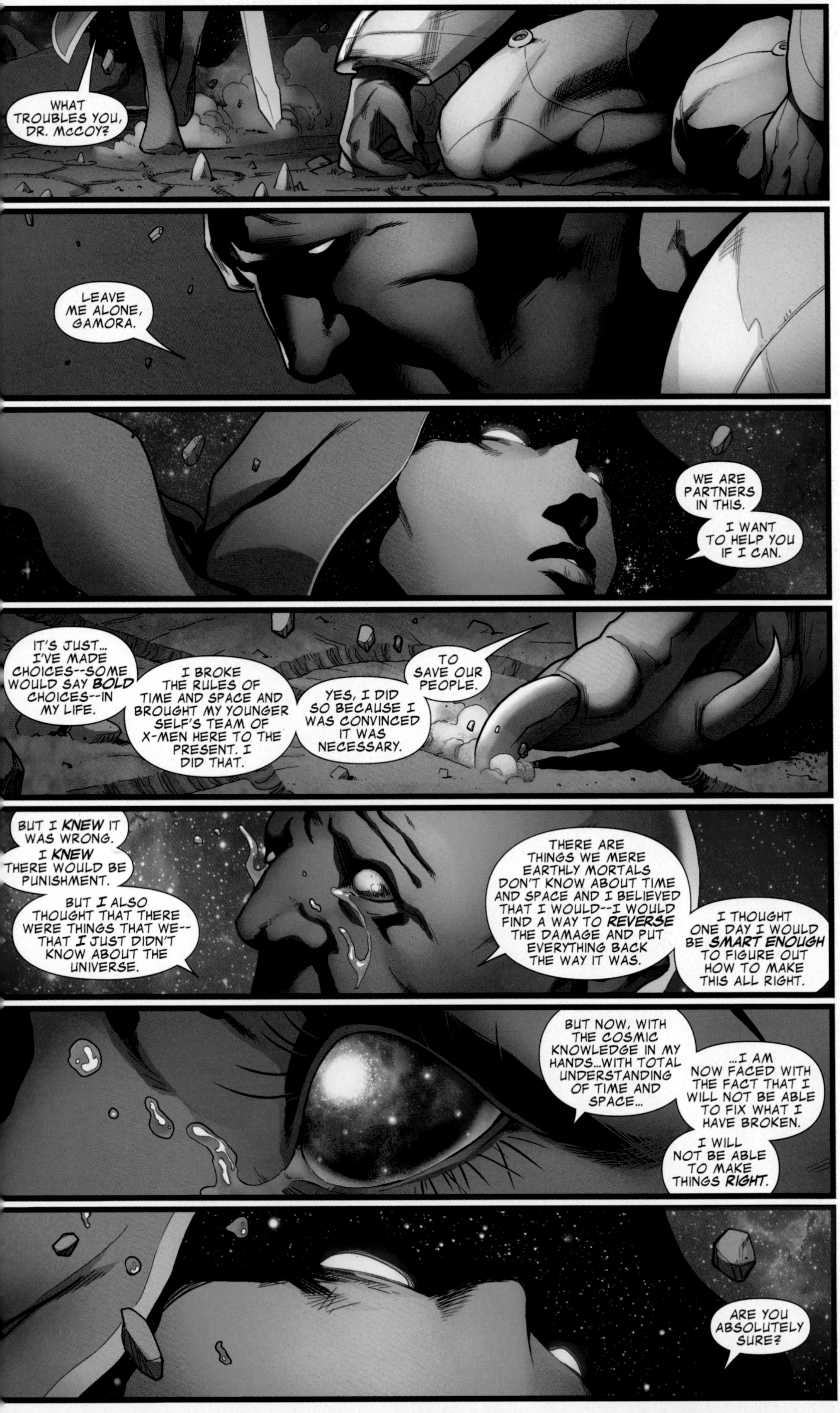
WHAT TROUBLES YOU, DR. McCOY?
LEAVE ME ALONE, GAMORA.
WE ARE PARTNERS IN THIS.
I WANT TO HELP YOU IF I CAN.
IT'S JUST... I'VE MADE CHOICES--SOME WOULD SAY BOLD CHOICES--IN MY LIFE.
I BROKE THE RULES OF TIME AND SPACE AND BROUGHT MY YOUNGER SELF'S TEAM OF X-MEN HERE TO THE PRESENT. I DID THAT.
YES, I DID SO BECAUSE I WAS CONVINCED IT WAS NECESSARY.
TO SAVE OUR PEOPLE.
BUT I KNEW IT WAS WRONG.
I KNEW THERE WOULD BE PUNISHMENT.
BUT I ALSO THOUGHT THAT THERE WERE THINGS THAT WE-- THAT I JUST DIDN'T KNOW ABOUT THE UNIVERSE.
THERE ARE THINGS WE MERE EARTHLY MORTALS DON'T KNOW ABOUT TIME AND SPACE AND I BELIEVED THAT I WOULD--I WOULD FIND A WAY TO REVERSE THE DAMAGE AND PUT EVERYTHING BACK THE WAY IT WAS.
I THOUGHT ONE DAY I WOULD BE SMART ENOUGH TO FIGURE OUT HOW TO MAKE THIS ALL RIGHT.
BUT NOW, WITH THE COSMIC KNOWLEDGE IN MY HANDS...WITH TOTAL UNDERSTANDING OF TIME AND SPACE...
...I AM NOW FACED WITH THE FACT THAT I WILL NOT BE ABLE TO FIX WHAT I HAVE BROKEN.
I WILL NOT BE ABLE TO MAKE THINGS RIGHT.
ARE YOU ABSOLUTELY SURE?

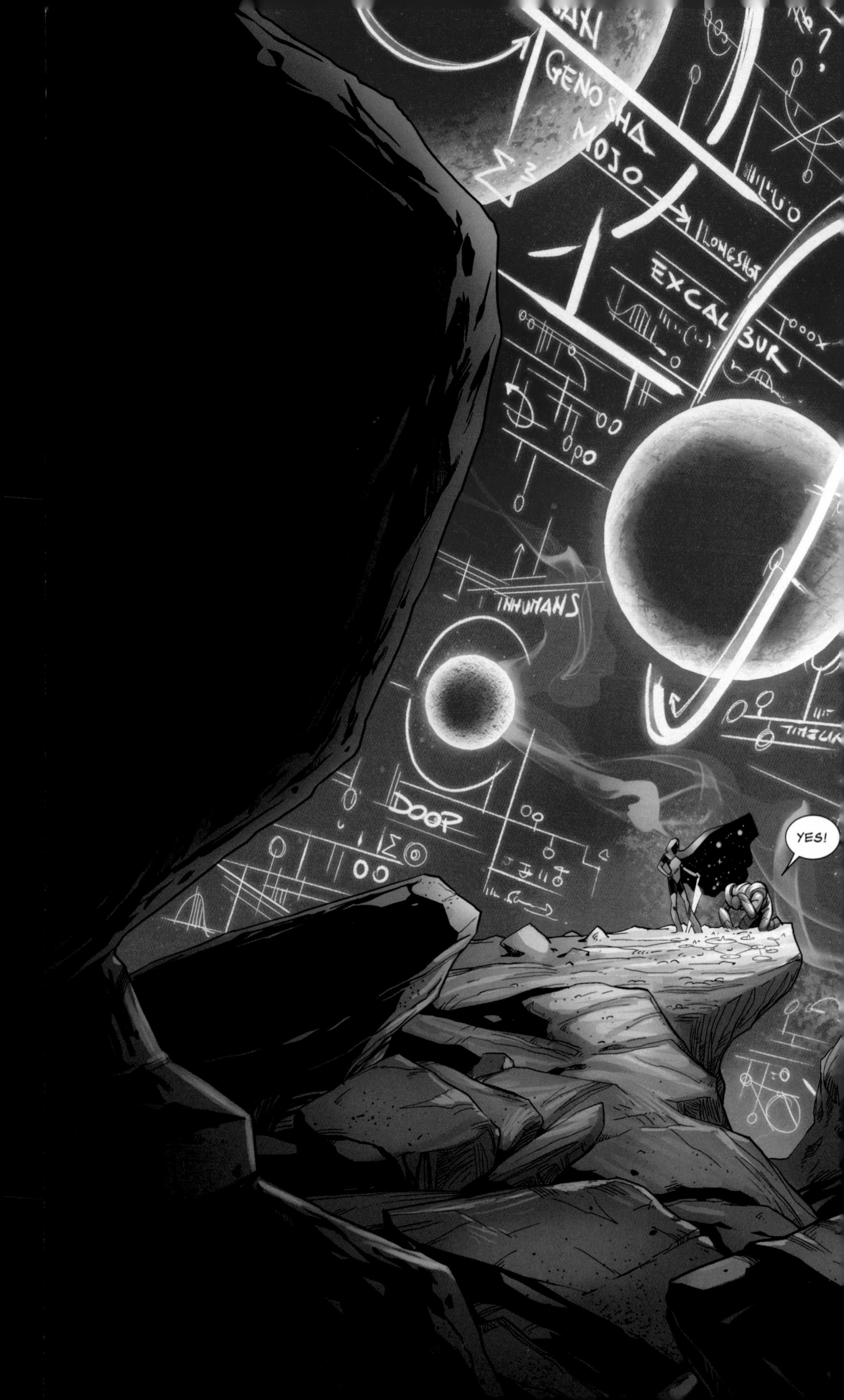
GENOSHA
MOJO
LONGSHOT
EXCALIBUR
INHUMANS
DOOP
YES!

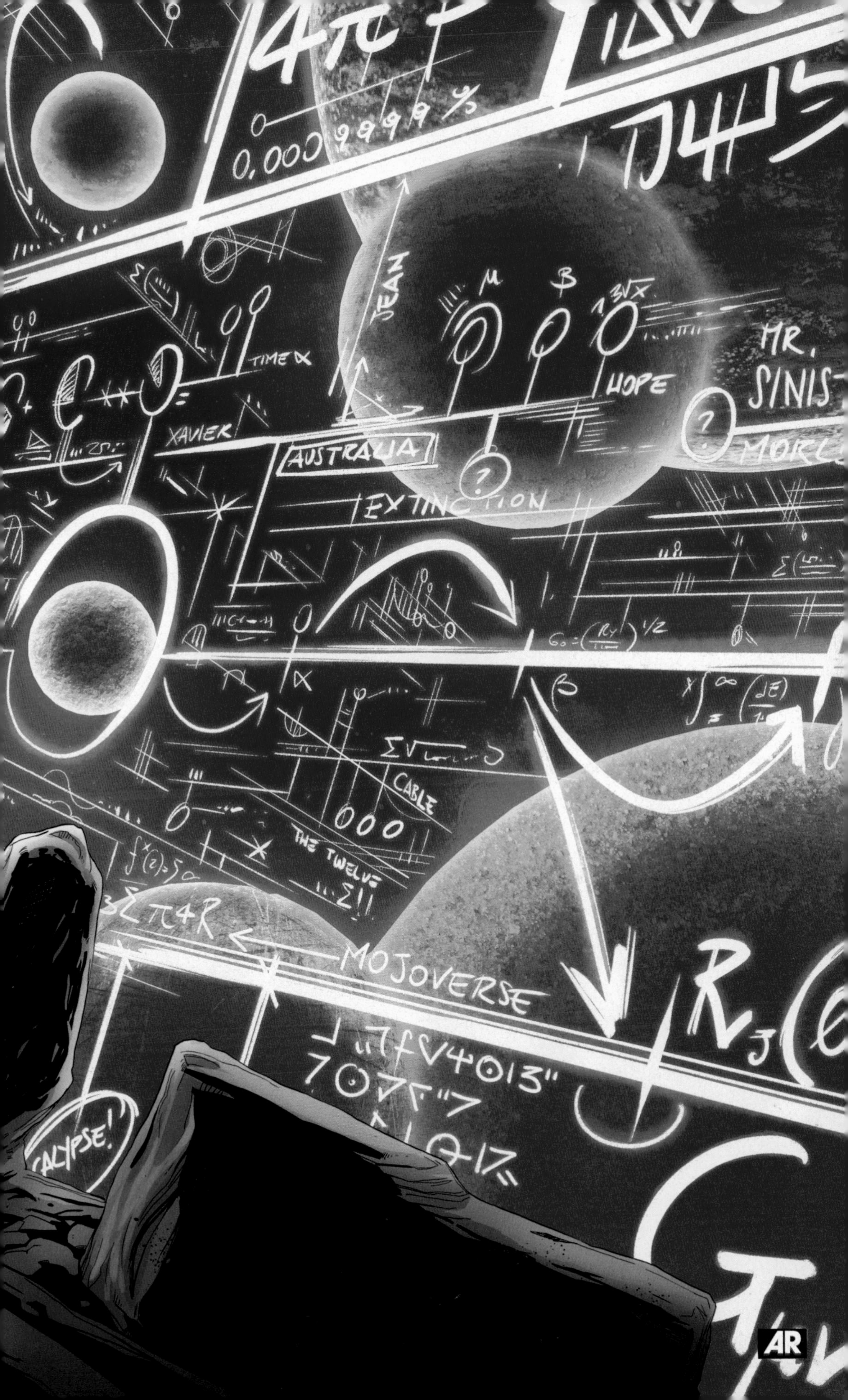
0,000 9999 %
JEAN
HOPE
MR. SINIS-
MORL
TIME
XAVIER
AUSTRALIA
EXTINCTION
CABLE
THE TWELVE
MOJOVERSE
CALYPSE!

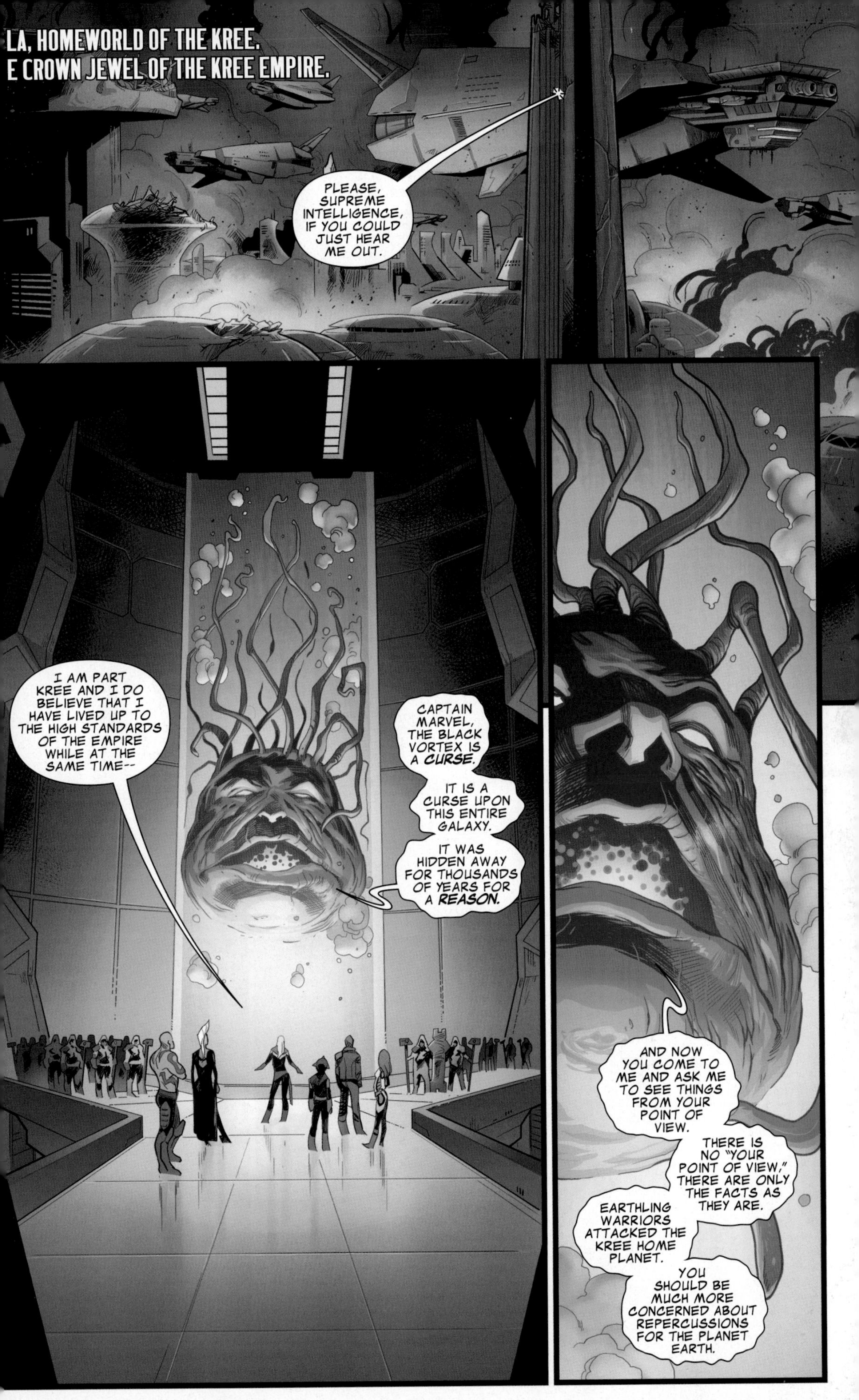
LA, HOMEWORLD OF THE KREE.
E CROWN JEWEL OF THE KREE EMPIRE.
PLEASE, SUPREME INTELLIGENCE, IF YOU COULD JUST HEAR ME OUT.
I AM PART KREE AND I DO BELIEVE THAT I HAVE LIVED UP TO THE HIGH STANDARDS OF THE EMPIRE WHILE AT THE SAME TIME--
CAPTAIN MARVEL, THE BLACK VORTEX IS A CURSE.
IT IS A CURSE UPON THIS ENTIRE GALAXY.
IT WAS HIDDEN AWAY FOR THOUSANDS OF YEARS FOR A REASON.
AND NOW YOU COME TO ME AND ASK ME TO SEE THINGS FROM YOUR POINT OF VIEW.
THERE IS NO "YOUR POINT OF VIEW," THERE ARE ONLY THE FACTS AS THEY ARE.
EARTHLING WARRIORS ATTACKED THE KREE HOME PLANET.
YOU SHOULD BE MUCH MORE CONCERNED ABOUT REPERCUSSIONS FOR THE PLANET EARTH.

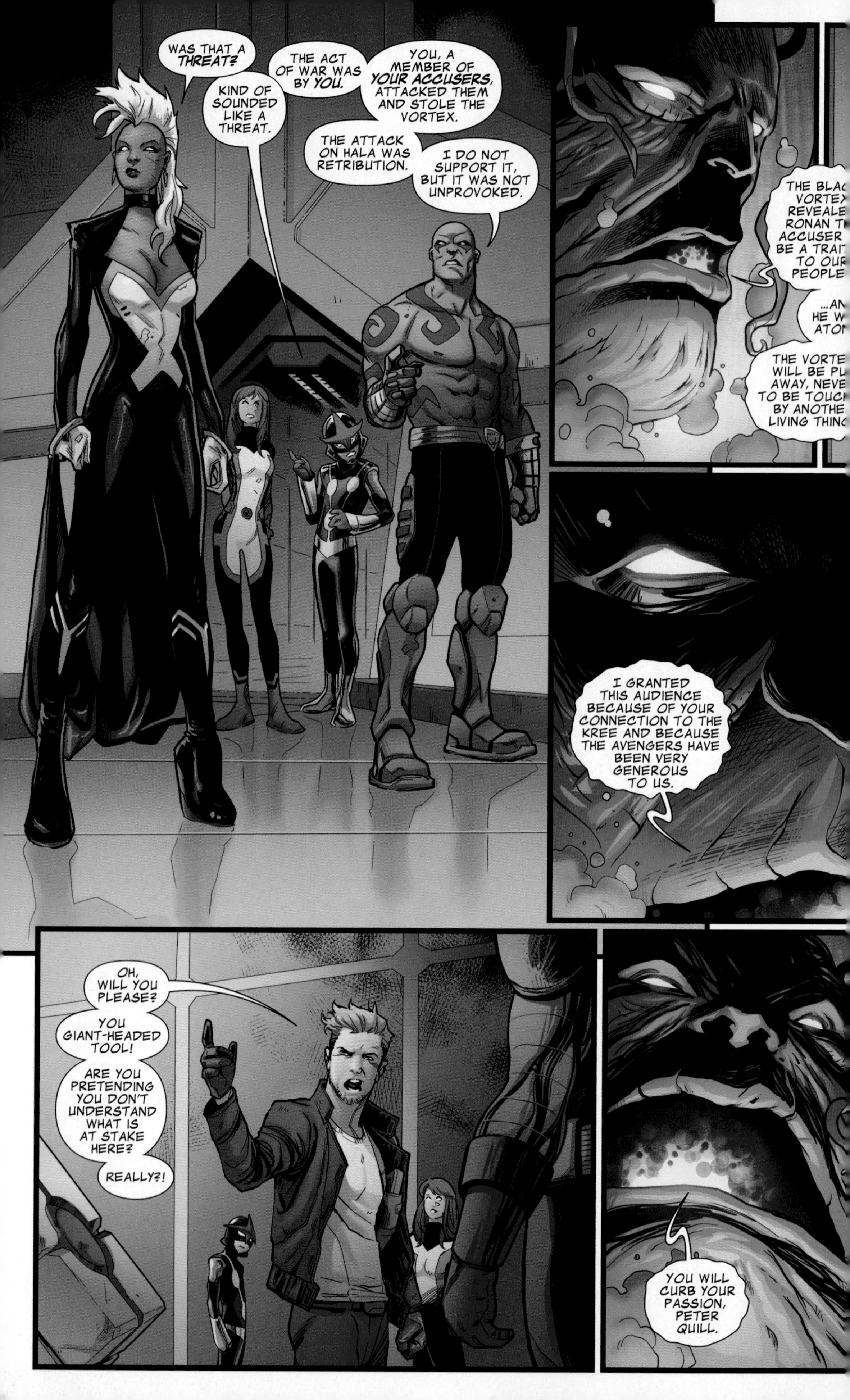

WAS THAT A THREAT?
KIND OF SOUNDED LIKE A THREAT.
THE ACT OF WAR WAS BY YOU.
YOU, A MEMBER OF YOUR ACCUSERS, ATTACKED THEM AND STOLE THE VORTEX.
THE ATTACK ON HALA WAS RETRIBUTION.
I DO NOT SUPPORT IT, BUT IT WAS NOT UNPROVOKED.
THE BLAC VORTEX REVEALE RONAN T ACCUSER BE A TRAIT TO OUR PEOPLE
...AN HE W ATON
THE VORTE WILL BE PL AWAY, NEVE TO BE TOUCH BY ANOTHE LIVING THIN
I GRANTED THIS AUDIENCE BECAUSE OF YOUR CONNECTION TO THE KREE AND BECAUSE THE AVENGERS HAVE BEEN VERY GENEROUS TO US.
OH, WILL YOU PLEASE?
YOU GIANT-HEADED TOOL!
ARE YOU PRETENDING YOU DON'T UNDERSTAND WHAT IS AT STAKE HERE?
REALLY?!
YOU WILL CURB YOUR PASSION, PETER QUILL.

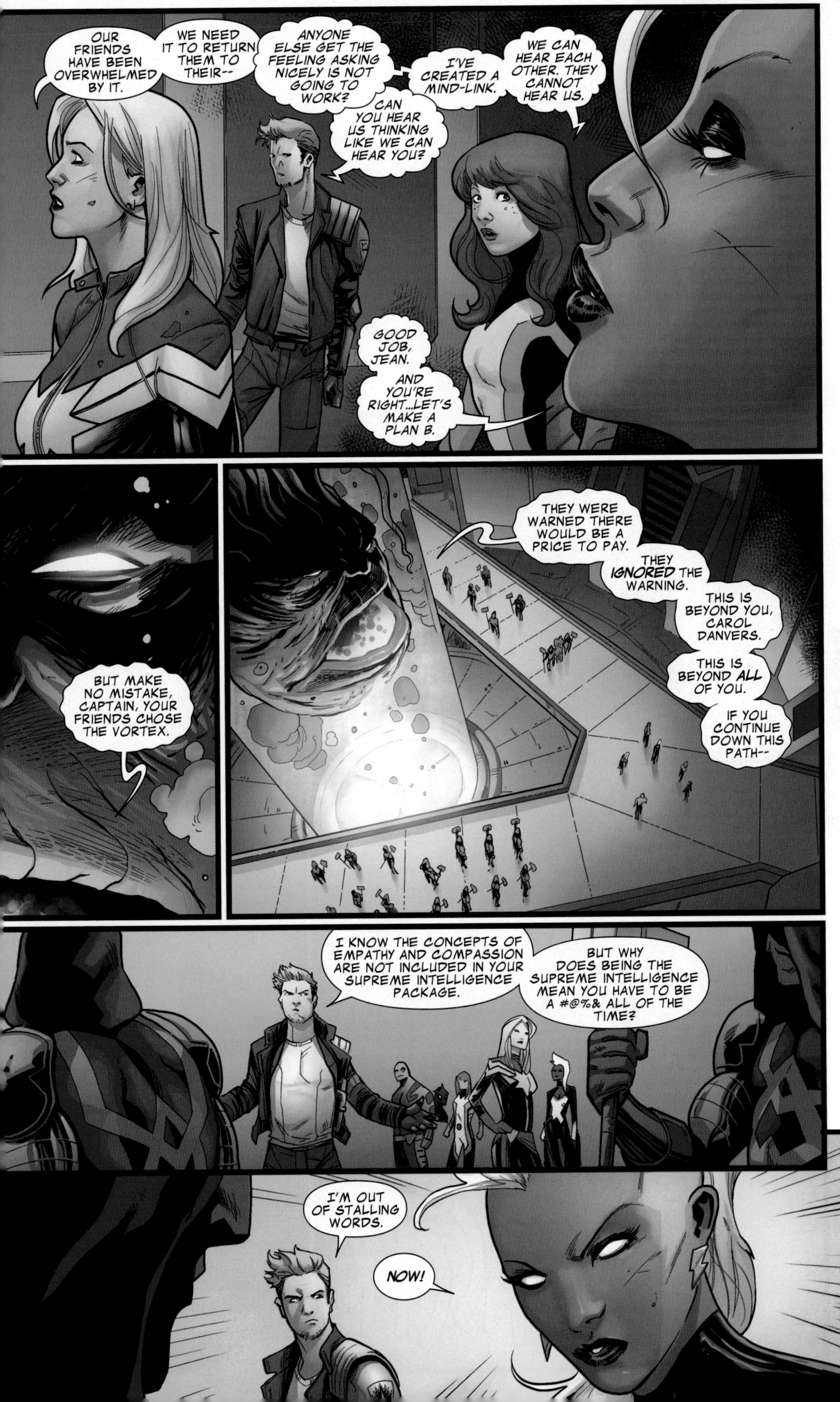

OUR FRIENDS HAVE BEEN OVERWHELMED BY IT.
WE NEED IT TO RETURN THEM TO THEIR--
ANYONE ELSE GET THE FEELING ASKING NICELY IS NOT GOING TO WORK?
I'VE CREATED A MIND-LINK.
WE CAN HEAR EACH OTHER. THEY CANNOT HEAR US.
CAN YOU HEAR US THINKING LIKE WE CAN HEAR YOU?
GOOD JOB, JEAN.
AND YOU'RE RIGHT...LET'S MAKE A PLAN B.
BUT MAKE NO MISTAKE, CAPTAIN, YOUR FRIENDS CHOSE THE VORTEX.
THEY WERE WARNED THERE WOULD BE A PRICE TO PAY.
THEY IGNORED THE WARNING.
THIS IS BEYOND YOU, CAROL DANVERS.
THIS IS BEYOND ALL OF YOU.
IF YOU CONTINUE DOWN THIS PATH--
I KNOW THE CONCEPTS OF EMPATHY AND COMPASSION ARE NOT INCLUDED IN YOUR SUPREME INTELLIGENCE PACKAGE.
BUT WHY DOES BEING THE SUPREME INTELLIGENCE MEAN YOU HAVE TO BE A #@%& ALL OF THE TIME?
I'M OUT OF STALLING WORDS.
NOW!

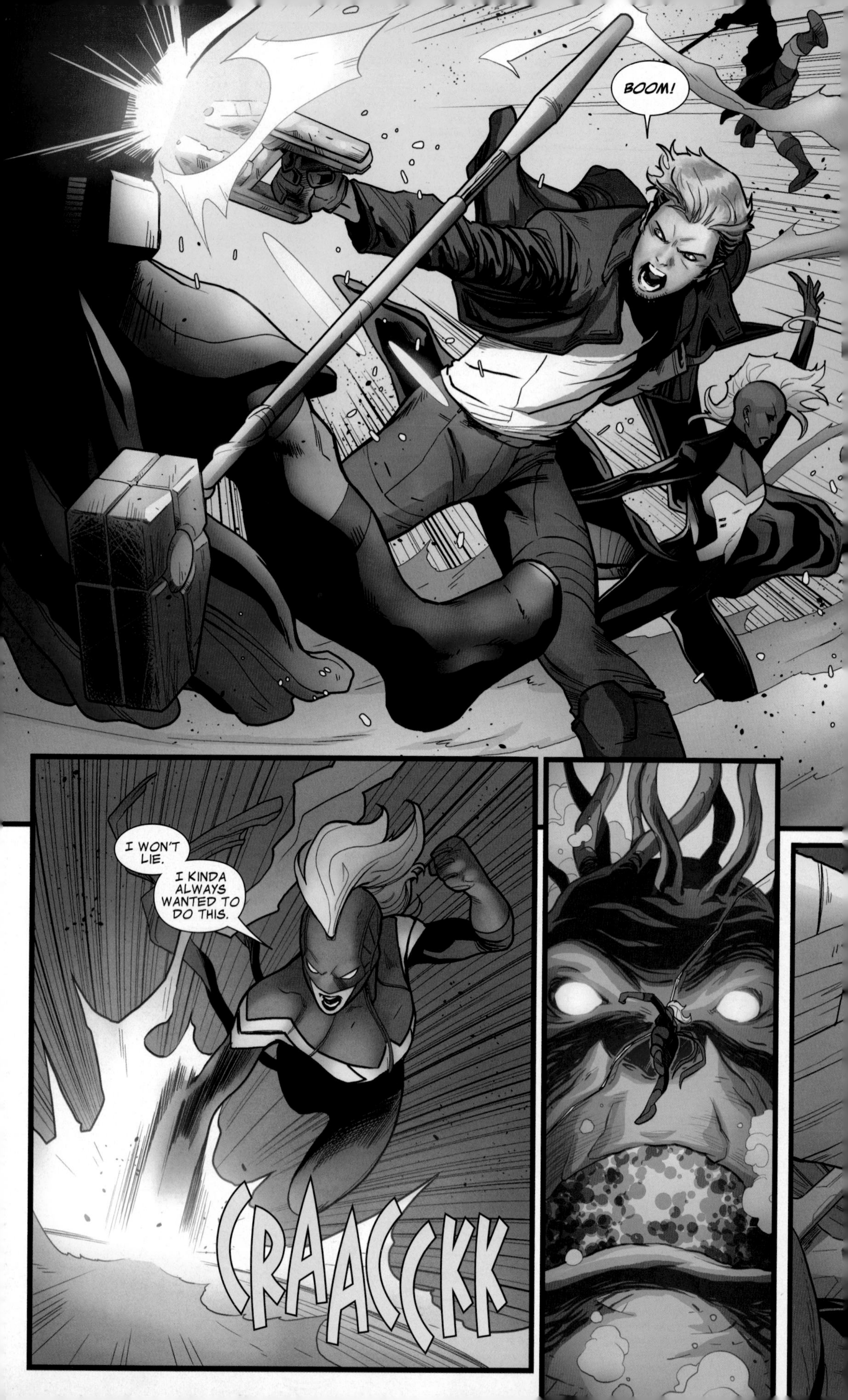
BOOM!
I WON'T LIE.
I KINDA ALWAYS WANTED TO DO THIS.
CRAACCKK

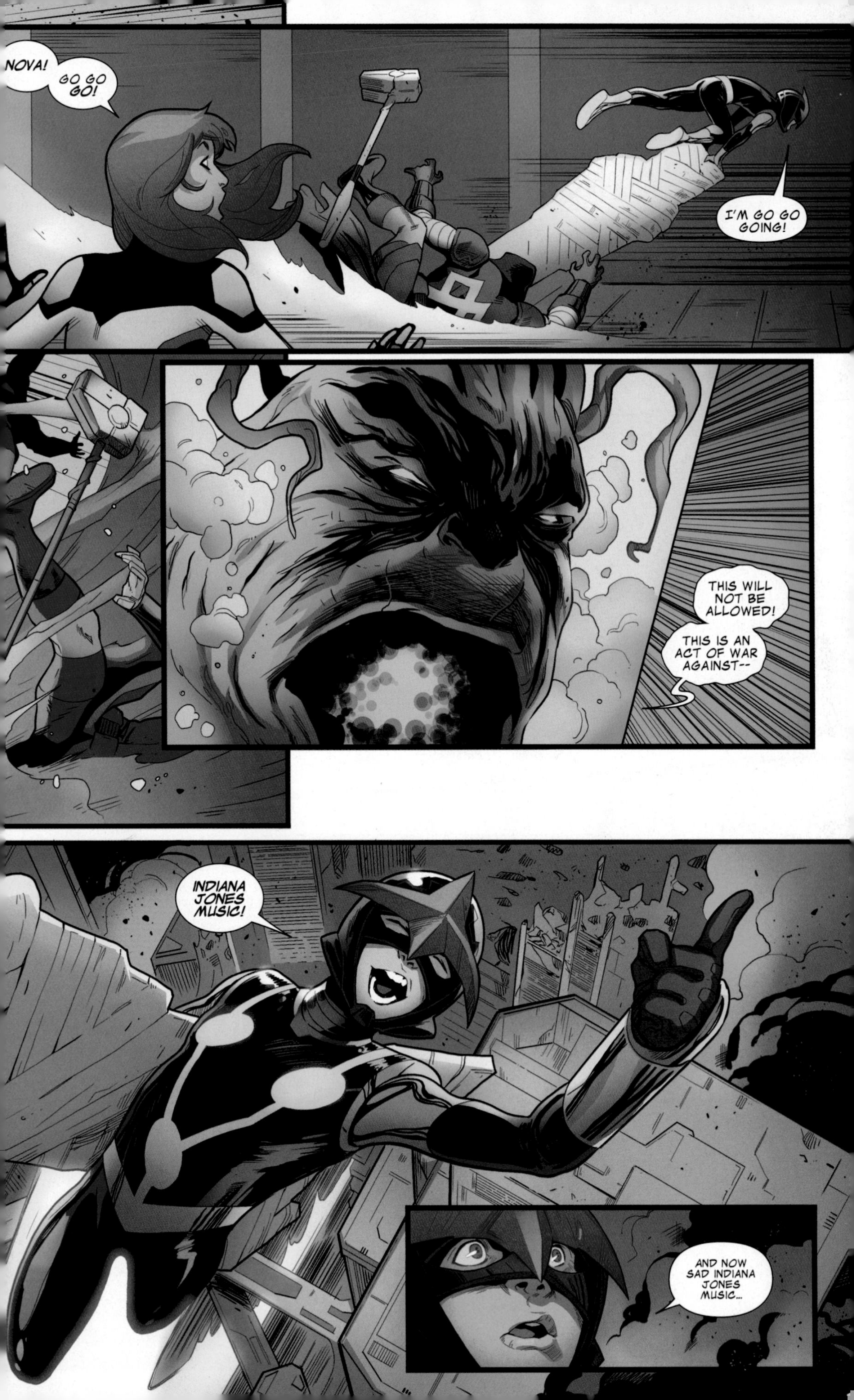
NOVA!
GO GO GO!
I'M GO GO GOING!
THIS WILL NOT BE ALLOWED!
THIS IS AN ACT OF WAR AGAINST--
INDIANA JONES MUSIC!
AND NOW SAD INDIANA JONES MUSIC...

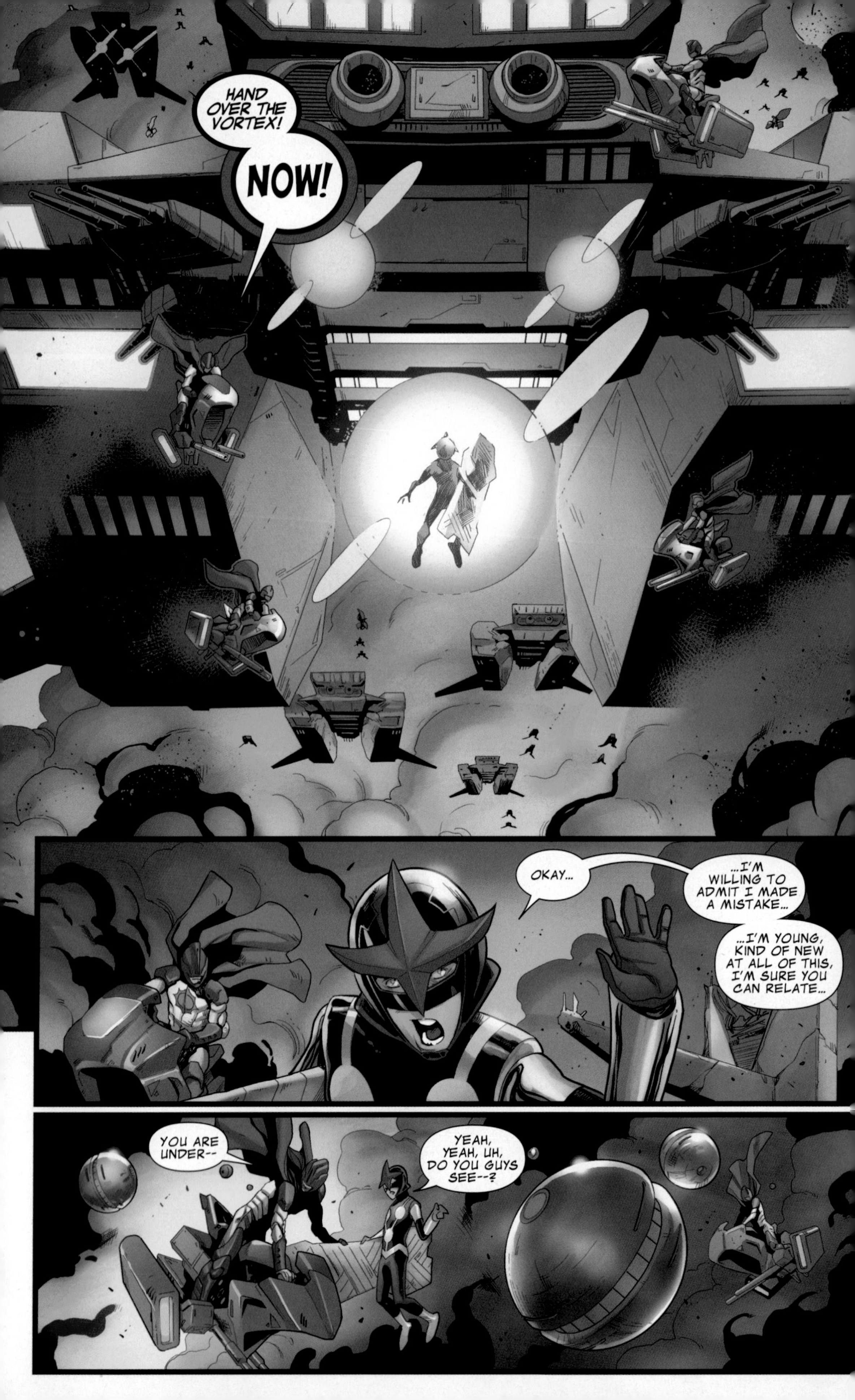
HAND OVER THE VORTEX!
NOW!
OKAY...
...I'M WILLING TO ADMIT I MADE A MISTAKE...
...I'M YOUNG, KIND OF NEW AT ALL OF THIS, I'M SURE YOU CAN RELATE...
YOU ARE UNDER--
YEAH, YEAH, UH, DO YOU GUYS SEE--?

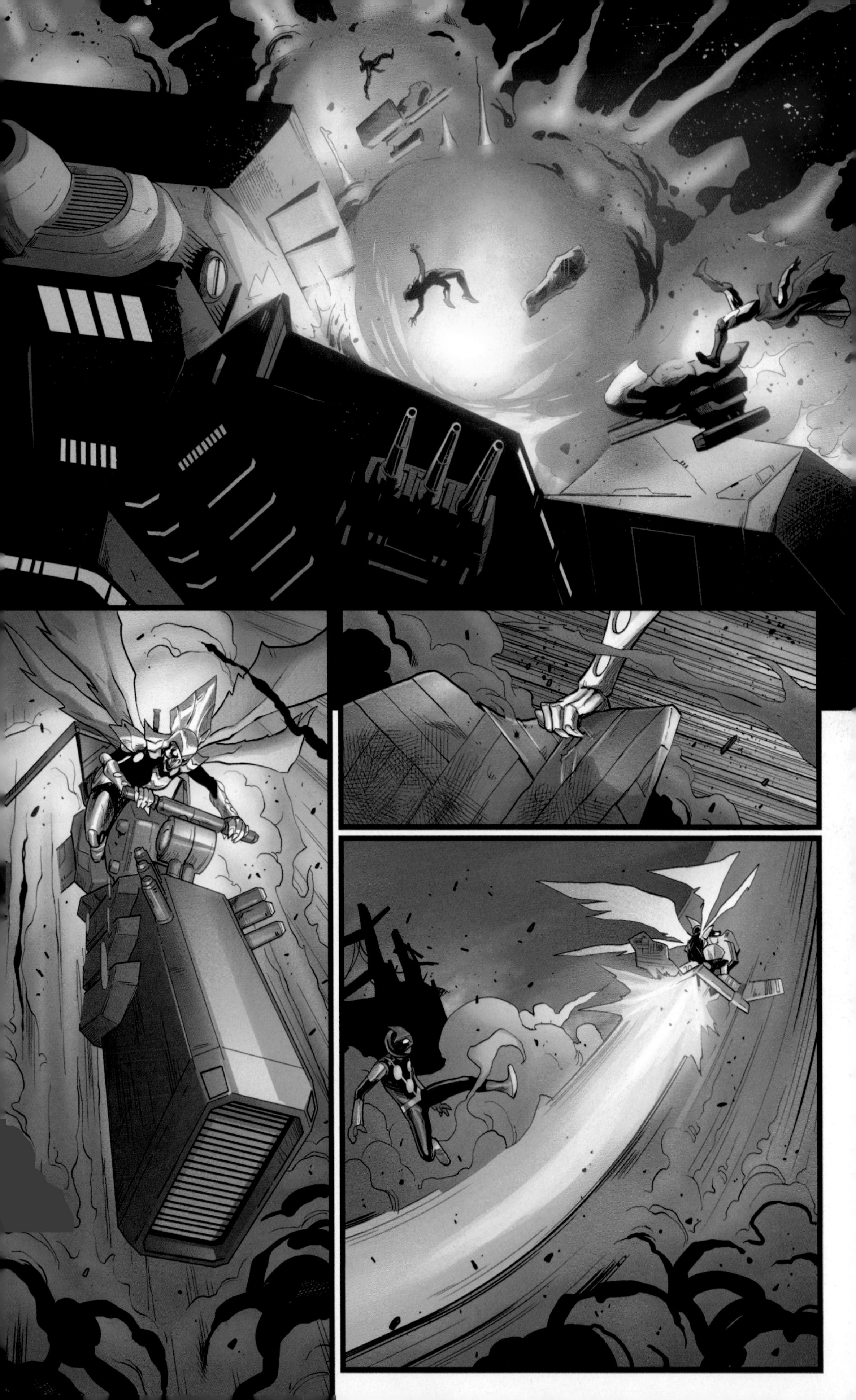

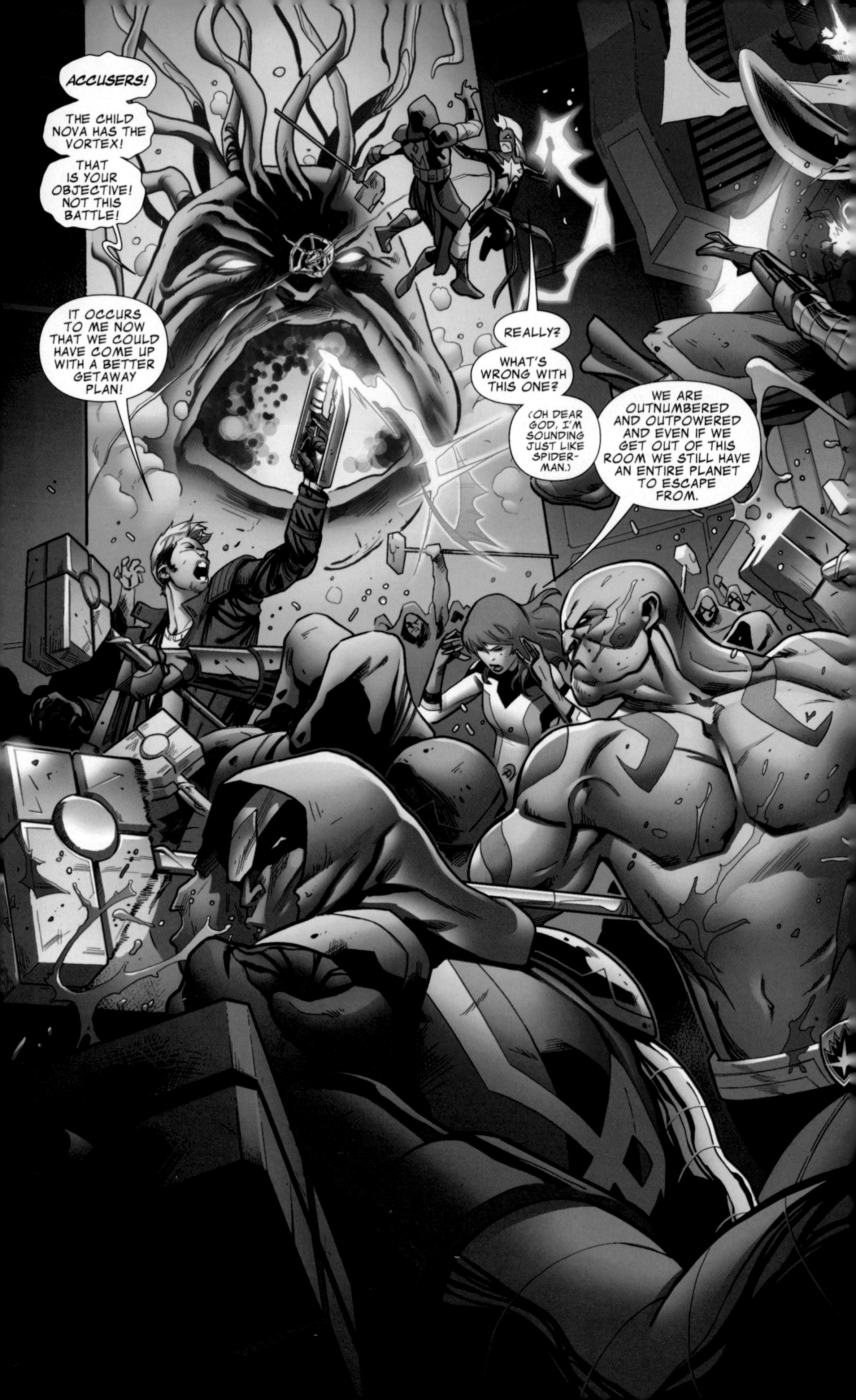
ACCUSERS!
THE CHILD NOVA HAS THE VORTEX!
THAT IS YOUR OBJECTIVE! NOT THIS BATTLE!
IT OCCURS TO ME NOW THAT WE COULD HAVE COME UP WITH A BETTER GETAWAY PLAN!
REALLY?
WHAT'S WRONG WITH THIS ONE?
(OH DEAR GOD, I'M SOUNDING JUST LIKE SPIDER-MAN.)
WE ARE OUTNUMBERED AND OUTPOWERED AND EVEN IF WE GET OUT OF THIS ROOM WE STILL HAVE AN ENTIRE PLANET TO ESCAPE FROM.

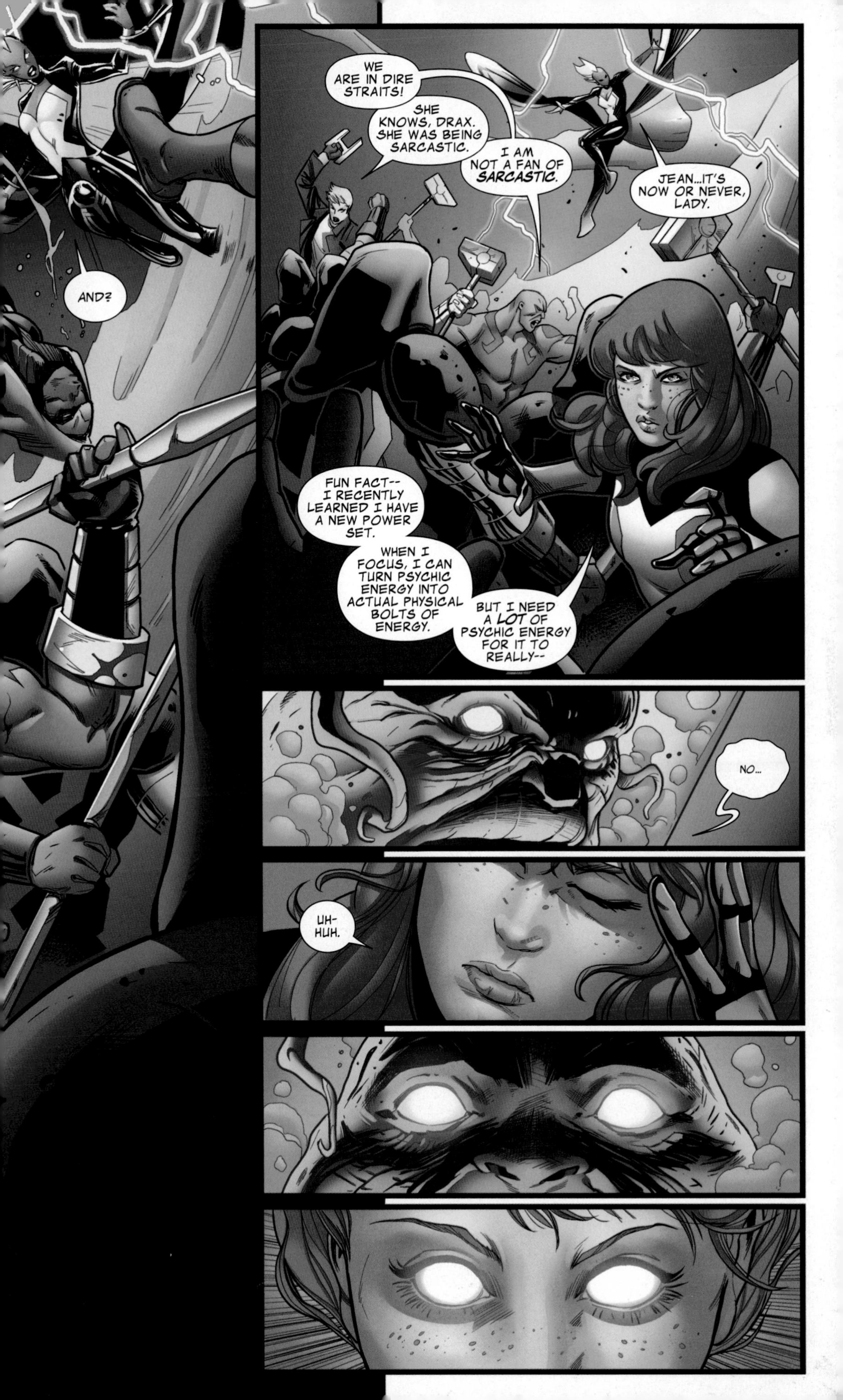
WE ARE IN DIRE STRAITS!
SHE KNOWS, DRAX. SHE WAS BEING SARCASTIC.
I AM NOT A FAN OF SARCASTIC.
JEAN...IT'S NOW OR NEVER, LADY.
AND?
FUN FACT-- I RECENTLY LEARNED I HAVE A NEW POWER SET.
WHEN I FOCUS, I CAN TURN PSYCHIC ENERGY INTO ACTUAL PHYSICAL BOLTS OF ENERGY.
BUT I NEED A LOT OF PSYCHIC ENERGY FOR IT TO REALLY--
NO...
UH-HUH.

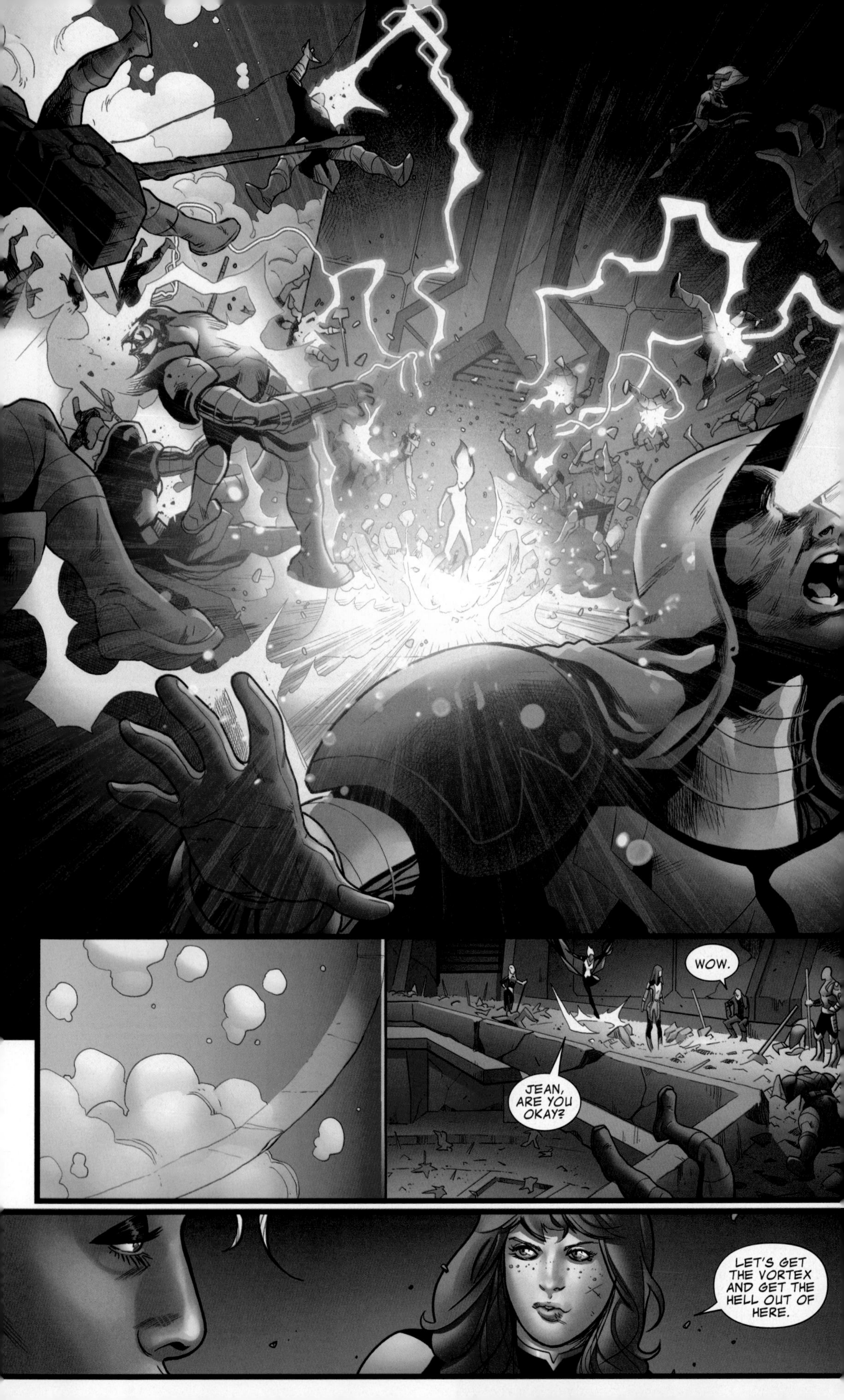
WOW.
JEAN, ARE YOU OKAY?
LET'S GET THE VORTEX AND GET THE HELL OUT OF HERE.

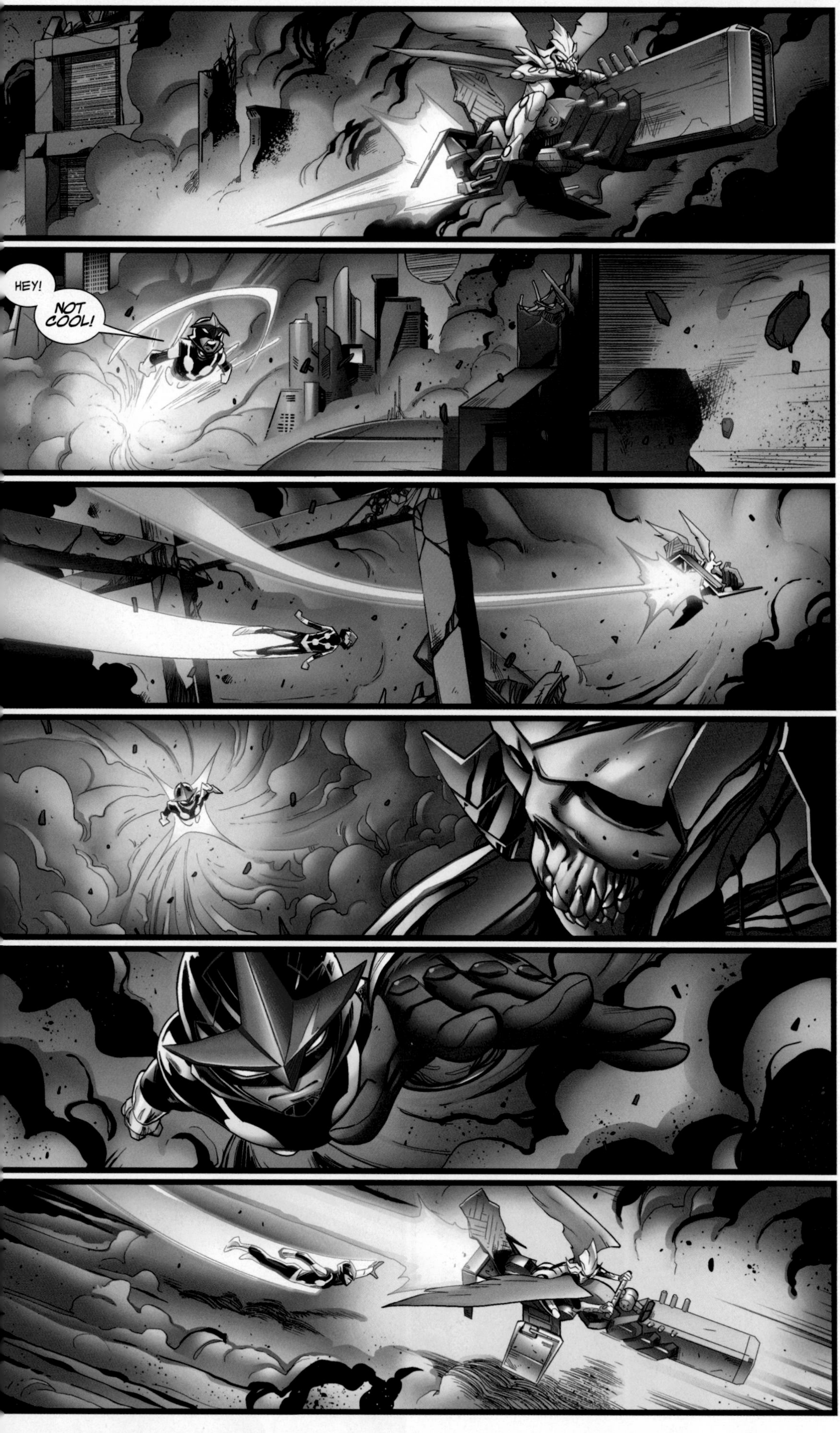
HEY!
NOT COOL!

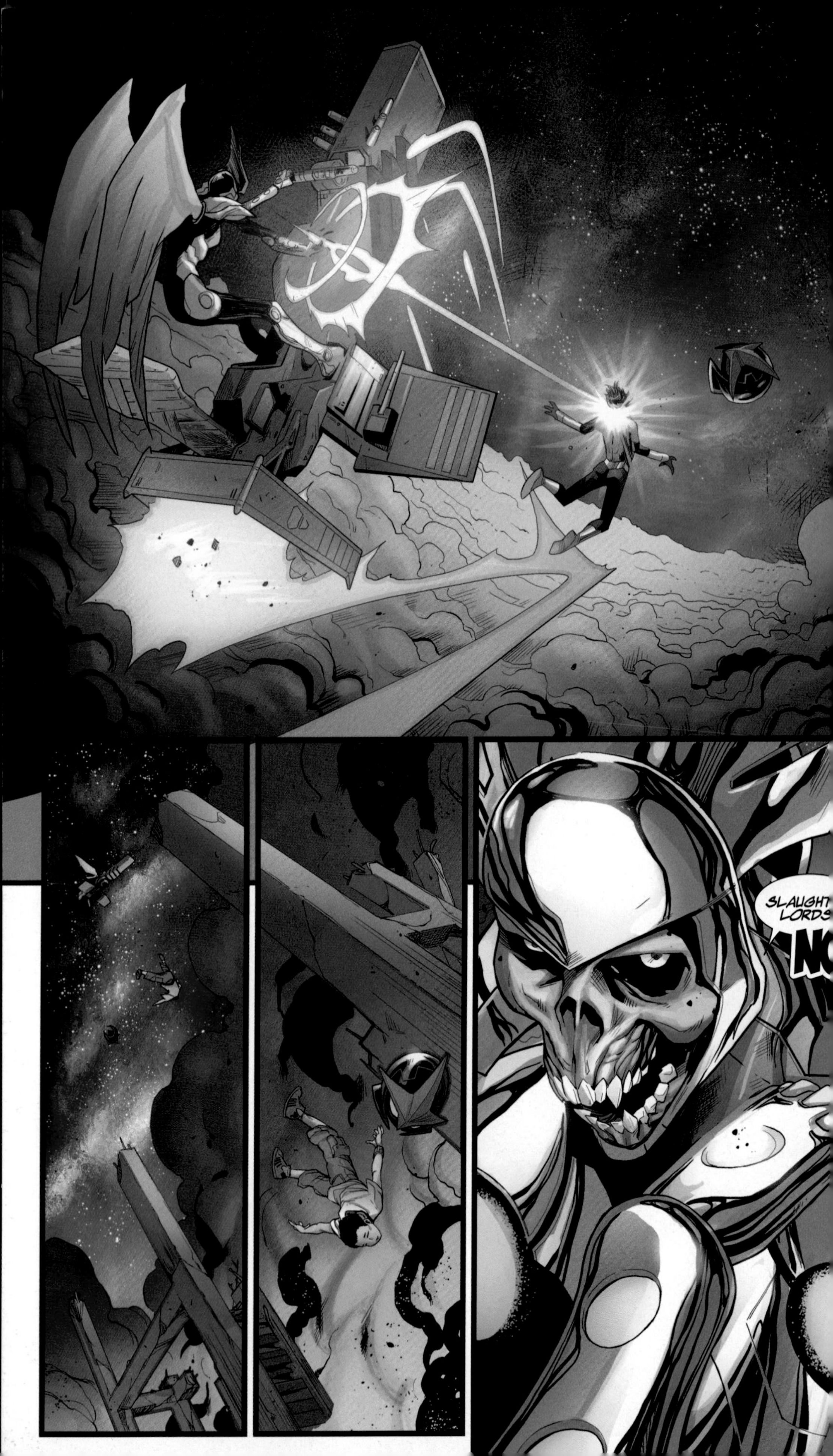
SLAUGHT
LORDS
N

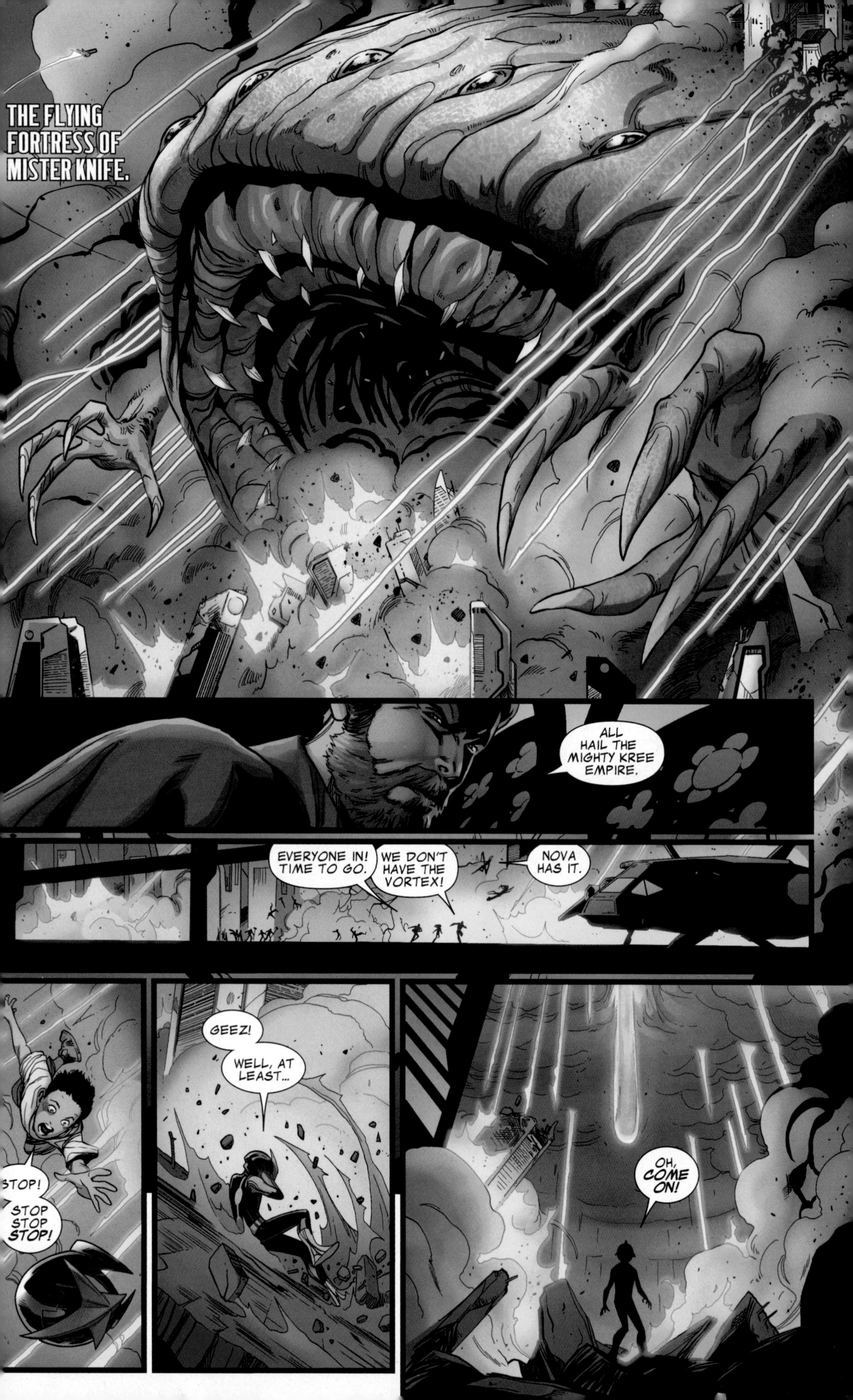
THE FLYING FORTRESS OF MISTER KNIFE.
ALL HAIL THE MIGHTY KREE EMPIRE.
EVERYONE IN! TIME TO GO.
WE DON'T HAVE THE VORTEX!
NOVA HAS IT.
STOP!
STOP STOP STOP!
GEEZ!
WELL, AT LEAST...
OH, COME ON!

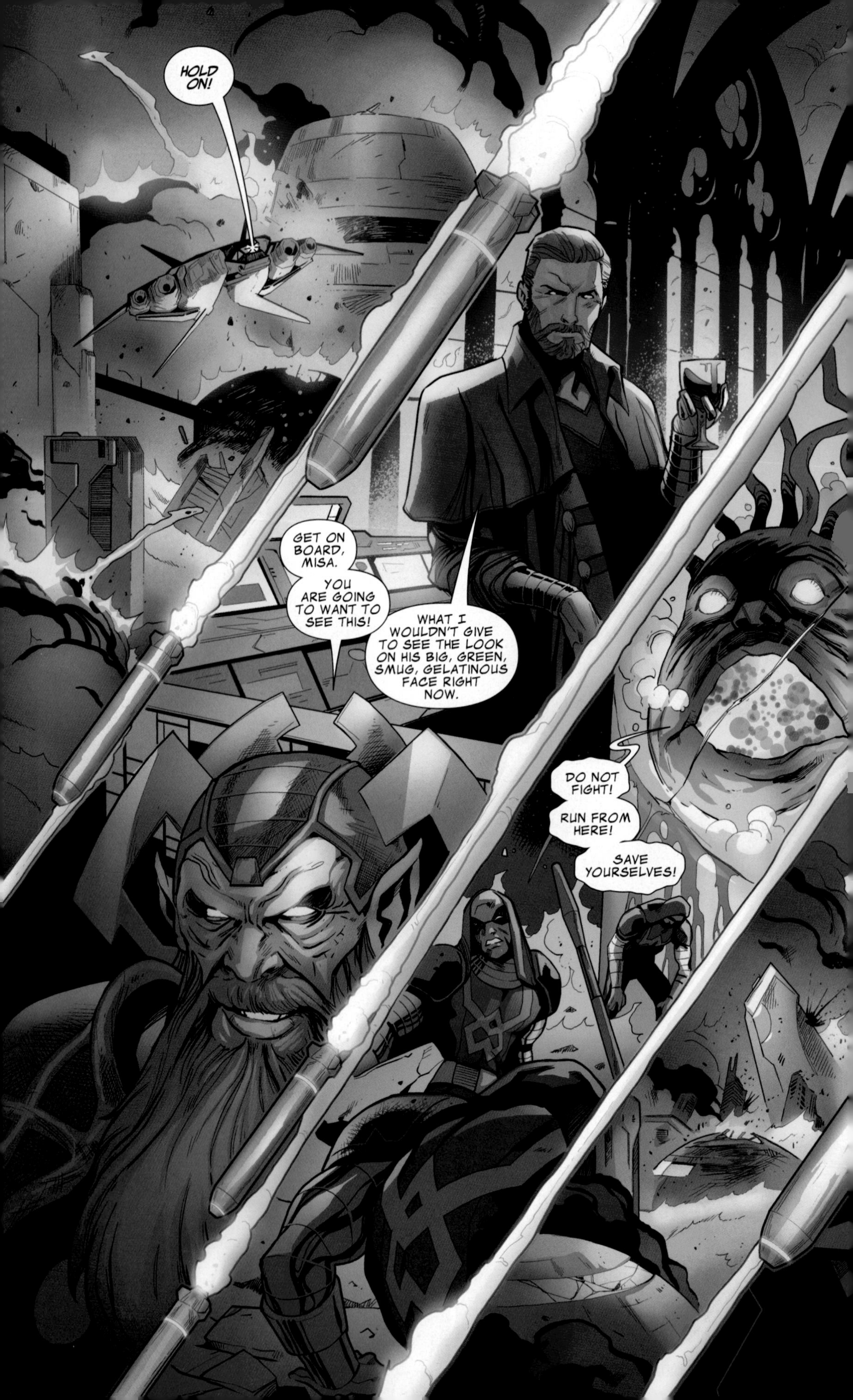
HOLD ON!
GET ON BOARD, MISA.
YOU ARE GOING TO WANT TO SEE THIS!
WHAT I WOULDN'T GIVE TO SEE THE LOOK ON HIS BIG, GREEN, SMUG, GELATINOUS FACE RIGHT NOW.
DO NOT FIGHT!
RUN FROM HERE!
SAVE YOURSELVES!

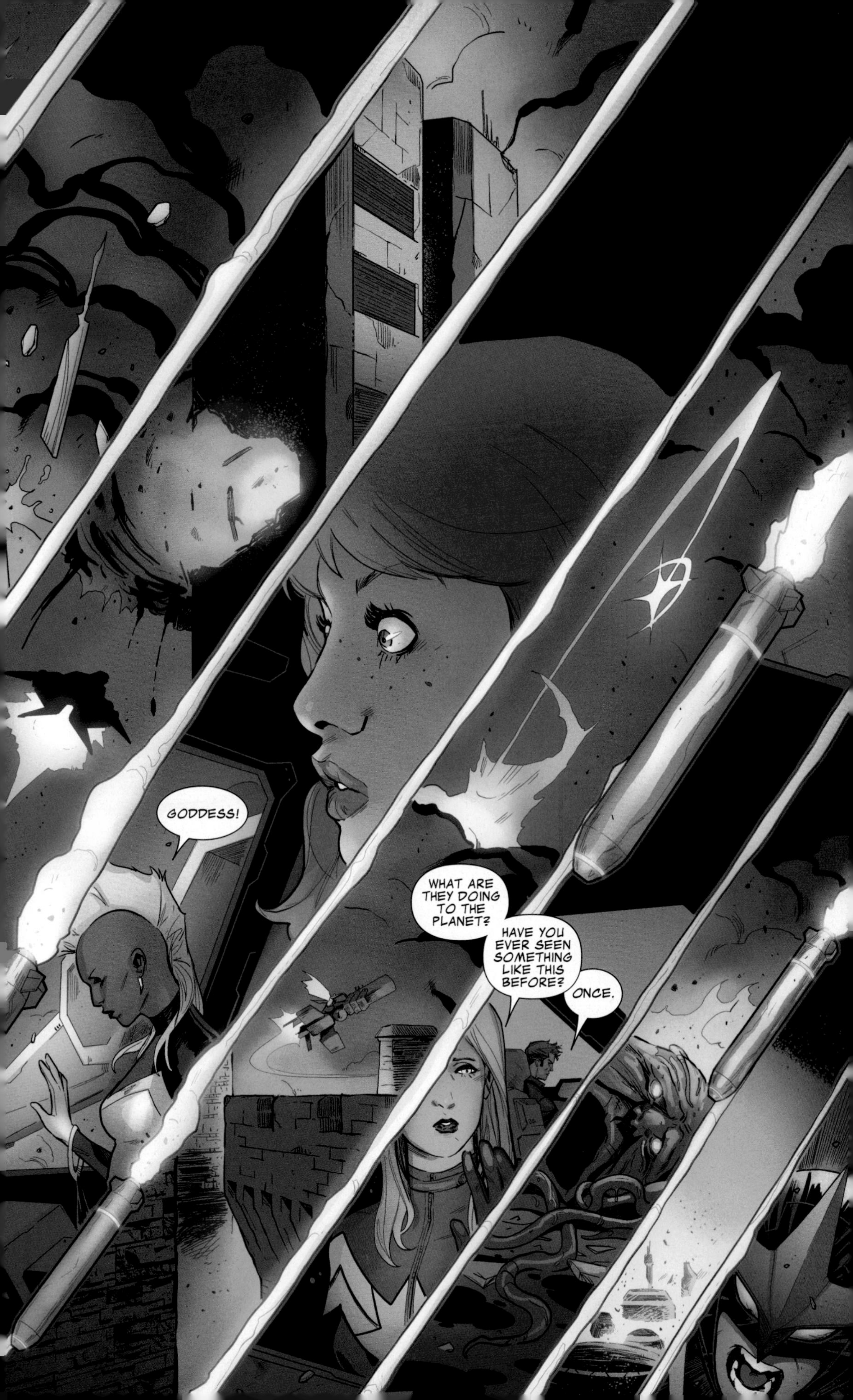
GODDESS!
WHAT ARE THEY DOING TO THE PLANET?
HAVE YOU EVER SEEN SOMETHING LIKE THIS BEFORE?
ONCE.

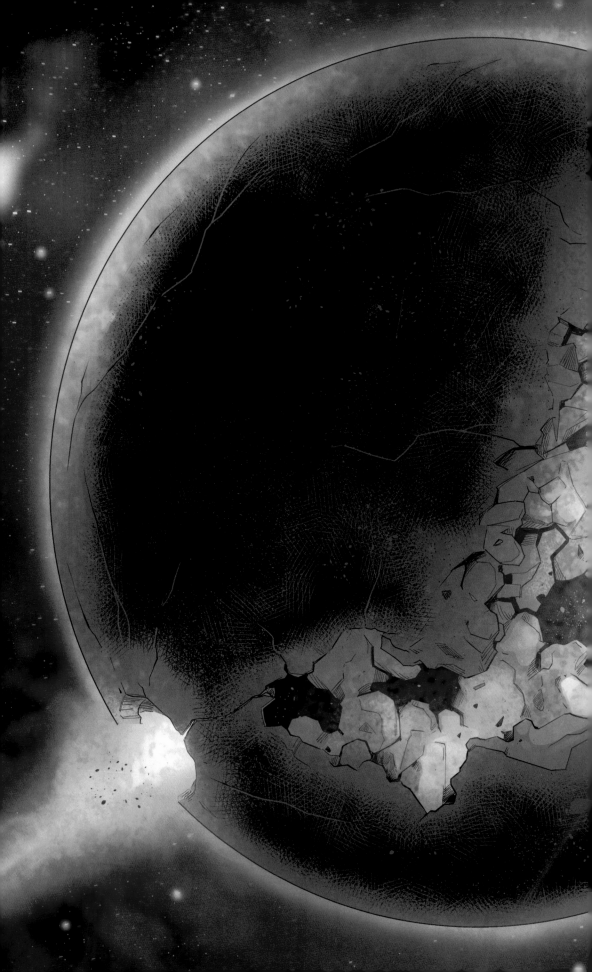

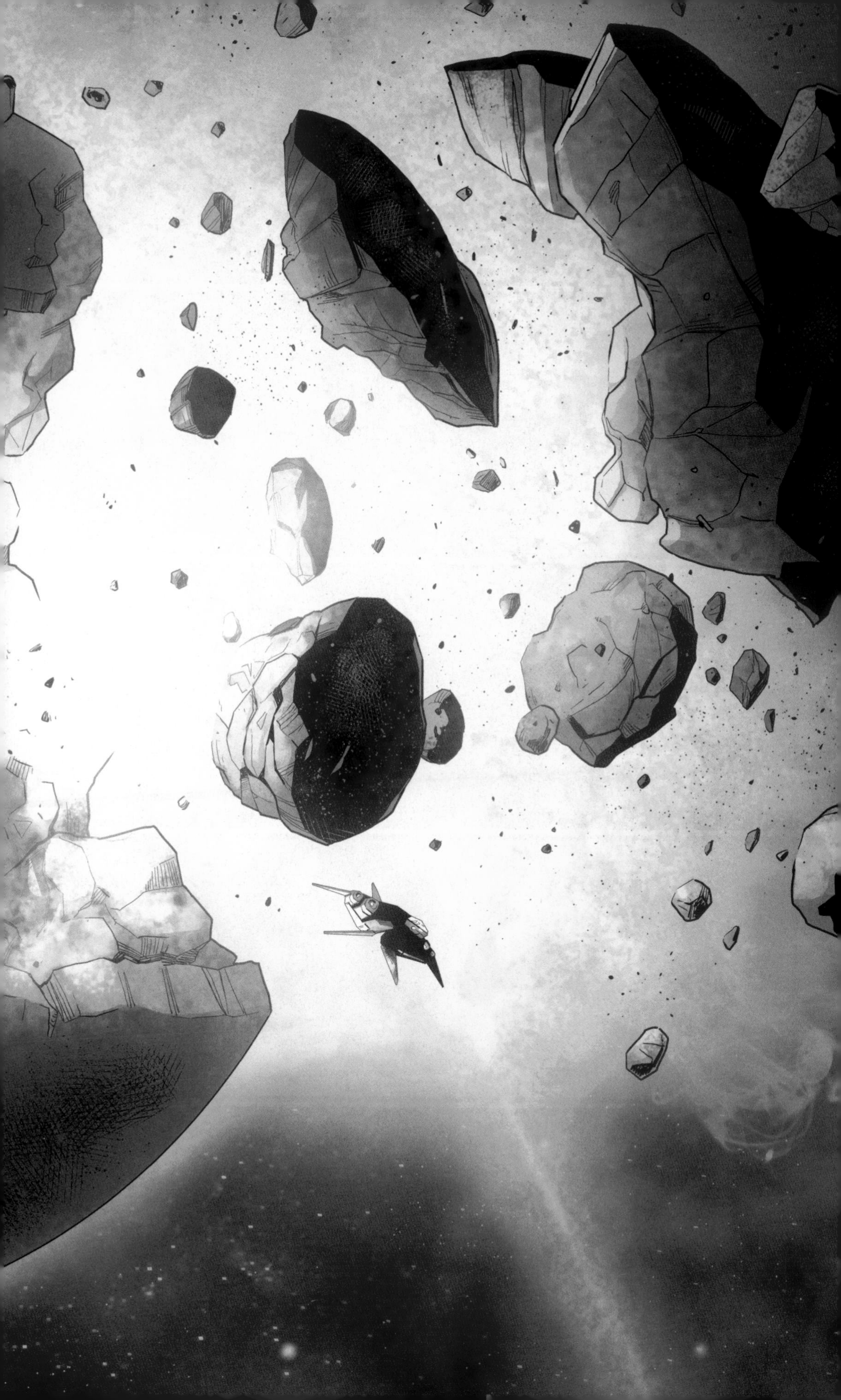

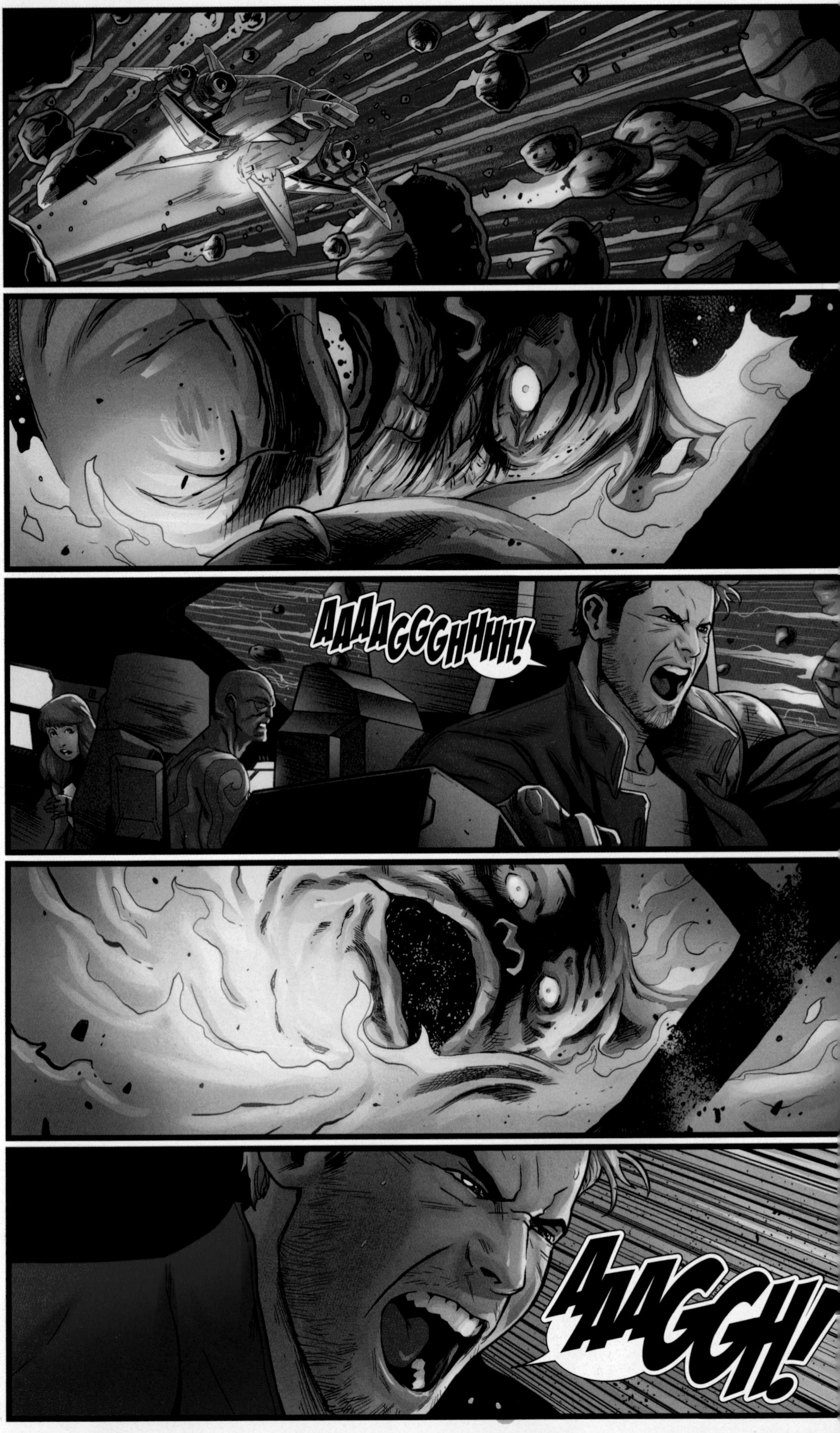
AAAAGGGHHHH!
AAAGGH!

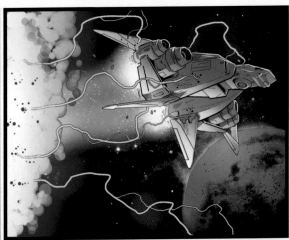

$@*%&#$!

THAT--
THAT ENTIRE
PLANET JUST
DIED?

YEAH...

THE ONE
WE WERE
JUST ON?

IT WAS
ATTACKED.

BY
WHO?

WHO
HAS THAT KIND
OF--?

WAS IT
THE BLACK
VORTEX?

IT CAN
TAKE OUT A
WHOLE
PLANET?

AND
NOVA?

WHAT
ABOUT
NOVA?

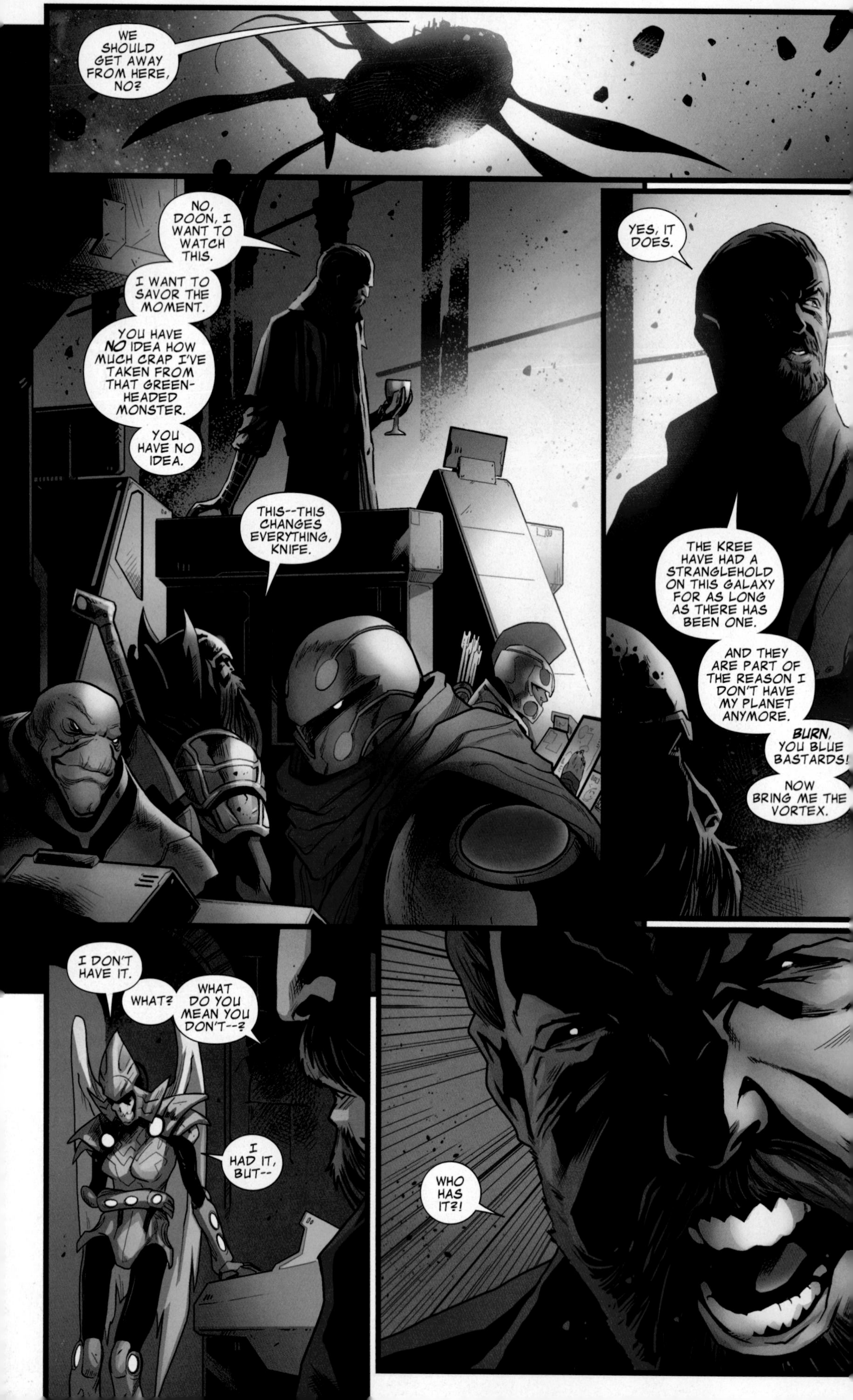
WE SHOULD GET AWAY FROM HERE, NO?
NO, DOON, I WANT TO WATCH THIS.
I WANT TO SAVOR THE MOMENT.
YOU HAVE **NO** IDEA HOW MUCH CRAP I'VE TAKEN FROM THAT GREEN-HEADED MONSTER.
YOU HAVE NO IDEA.
THIS--THIS CHANGES EVERYTHING, KNIFE.
YES, IT DOES.
THE KREE HAVE HAD A STRANGLEHOLD ON THIS GALAXY FOR AS LONG AS THERE HAS BEEN ONE.
AND THEY ARE PART OF THE REASON I DON'T HAVE MY PLANET ANYMORE.
BURN, YOU BLUE BASTARDS!
NOW BRING ME THE VORTEX.
I DON'T HAVE IT.
WHAT?
WHAT DO YOU MEAN YOU DON'T--?
I HAD IT, BUT--
WHO HAS IT?!

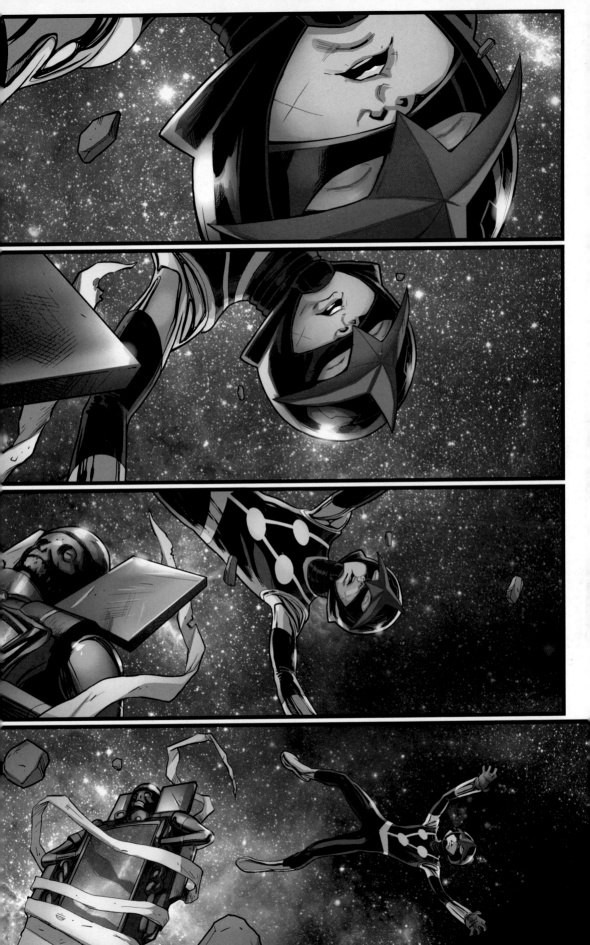

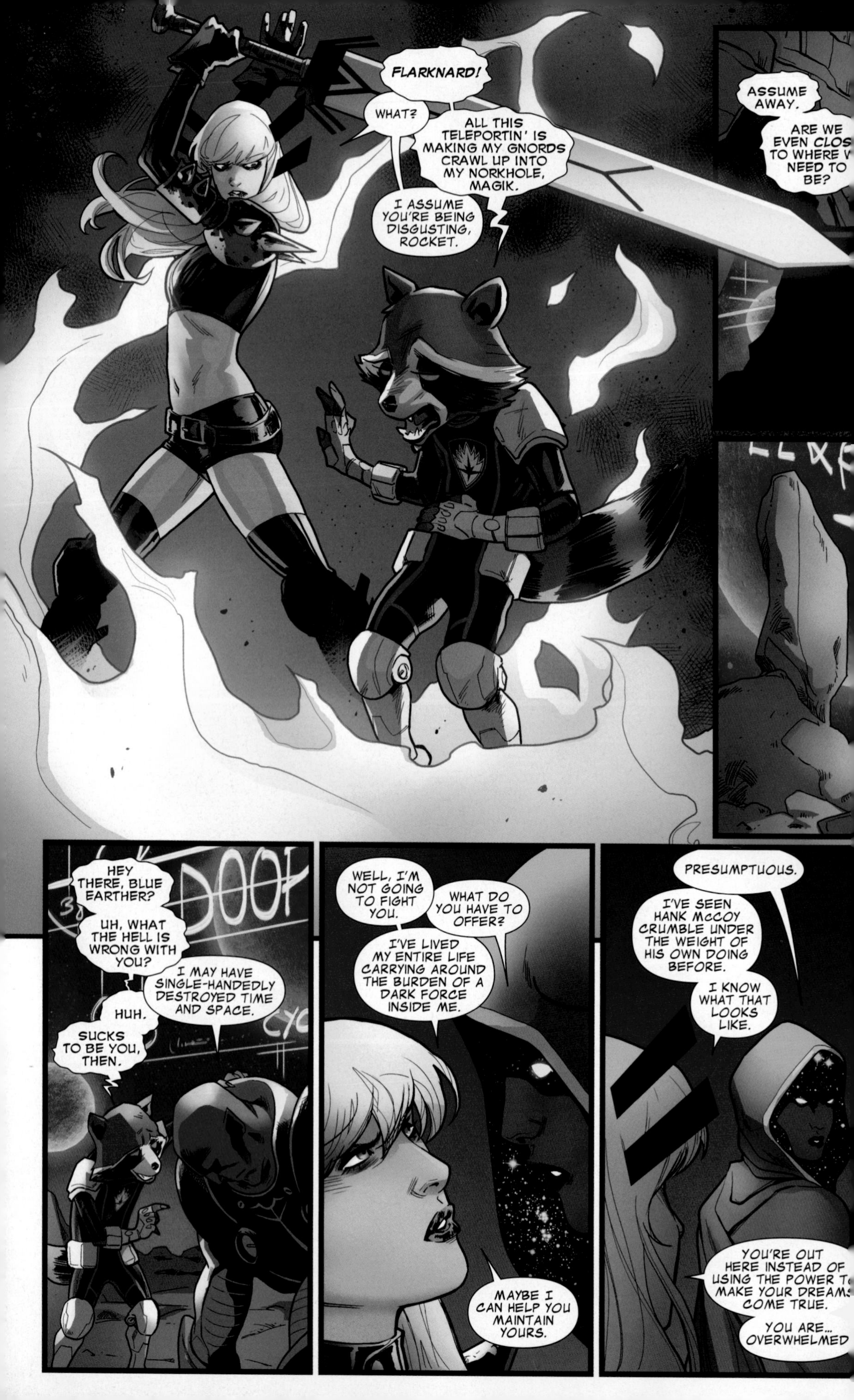
FLARKNARD!
WHAT?
ALL THIS TELEPORTIN' IS MAKING MY GNORDS CRAWL UP INTO MY NORKHOLE, MAGIK.
I ASSUME YOU'RE BEING DISGUSTING, ROCKET.
ASSUME AWAY.
HEY THERE, BLUE EARTHER?
UH, WHAT THE HELL IS WRONG WITH YOU?
I MAY HAVE SINGLE-HANDEDLY DESTROYED TIME AND SPACE.
HUH.
SUCKS TO BE YOU, THEN.
WELL, I'M NOT GOING TO FIGHT YOU.
WHAT DO YOU HAVE TO OFFER?
I'VE LIVED MY ENTIRE LIFE CARRYING AROUND THE BURDEN OF A DARK FORCE INSIDE ME.
MAYBE I CAN HELP YOU MAINTAIN YOURS.
PRESUMPTUOUS.
I'VE SEEN HANK McCOY CRUMBLE UNDER THE WEIGHT OF HIS OWN DOING BEFORE.
I KNOW WHAT THAT LOOKS LIKE.
YOU ARE... OVERWHELMED

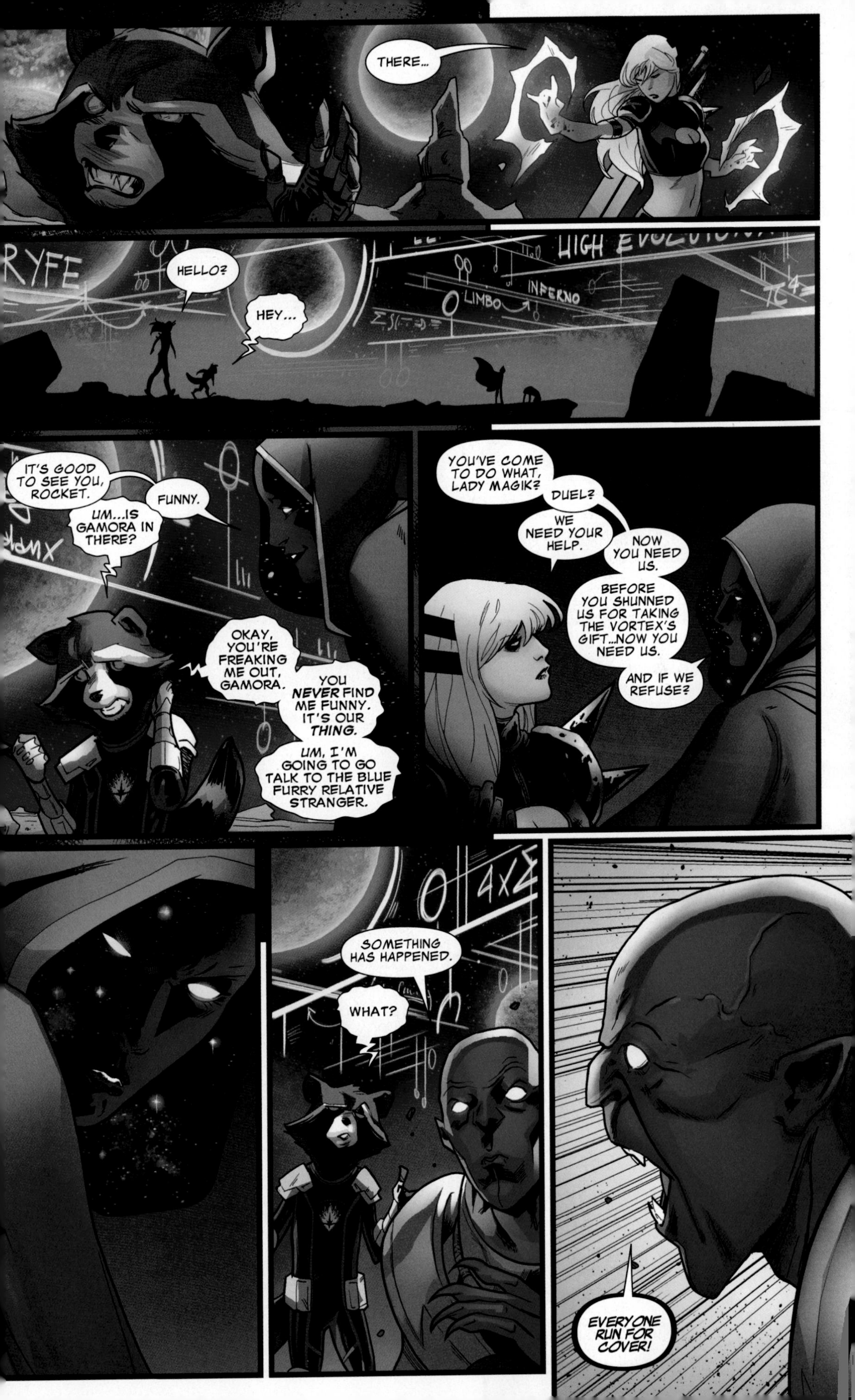
THERE...
RYFE
HIGH EVOLUTION
HELLO?
HEY...
LIMBO
INFERNO
IT'S GOOD TO SEE YOU, ROCKET.
FUNNY.
UM...IS GAMORA IN THERE?
OKAY, YOU'RE FREAKING ME OUT, GAMORA.
YOU NEVER FIND ME FUNNY. IT'S OUR THING.
UM, I'M GOING TO GO TALK TO THE BLUE FURRY RELATIVE STRANGER.
YOU'VE COME TO DO WHAT, LADY MAGIK?
DUEL?
WE NEED YOUR HELP.
NOW YOU NEED US.
BEFORE YOU SHUNNED US FOR TAKING THE VORTEX'S GIFT...NOW YOU NEED US.
AND IF WE REFUSE?
SOMETHING HAS HAPPENED.
WHAT?
EVERYONE RUN FOR COVER!

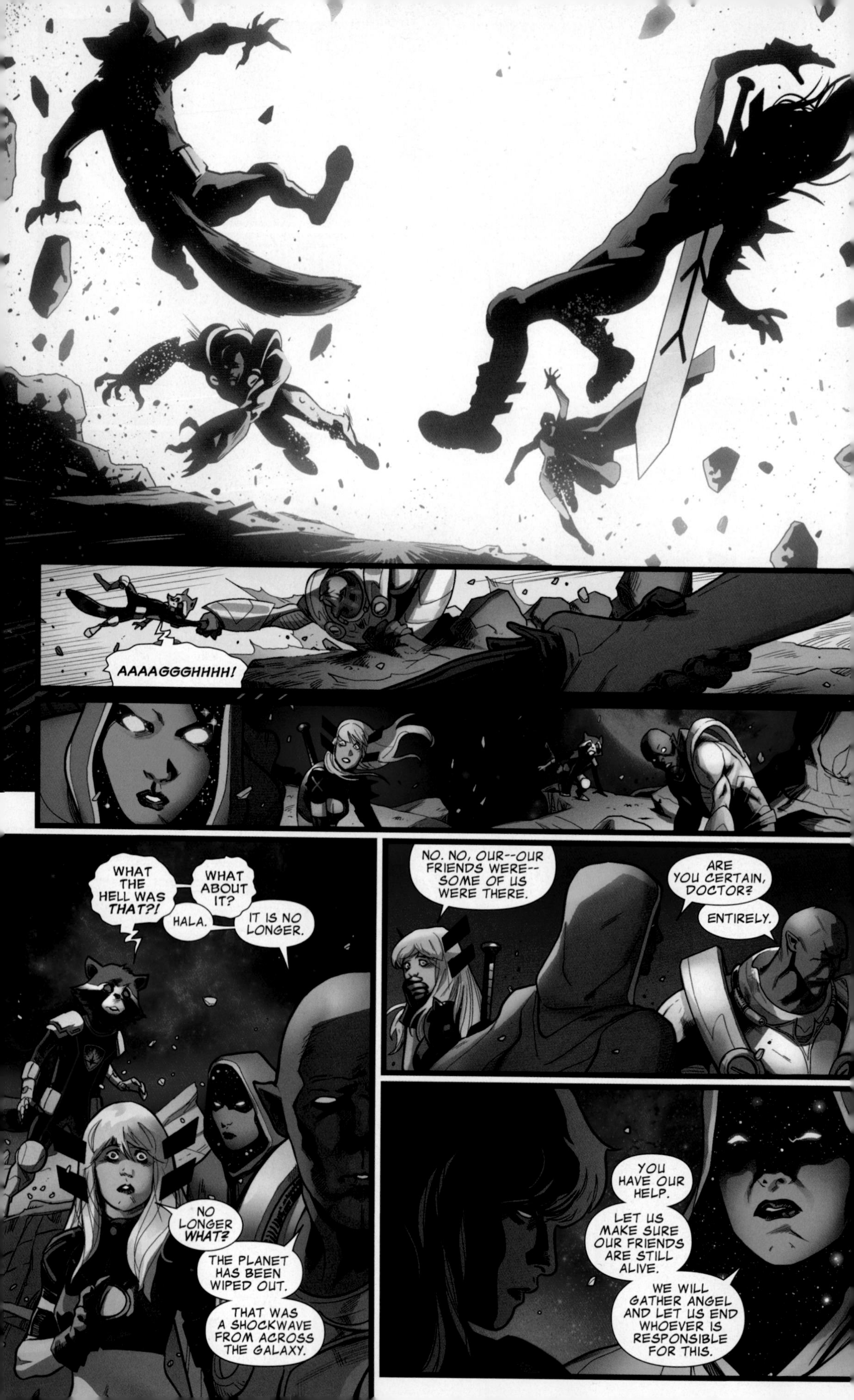
AAAAGGGHHHH!
WHAT THE HELL WAS THAT?!
WHAT ABOUT IT?
HALA.
IT IS NO LONGER.
NO LONGER WHAT?
THE PLANET HAS BEEN WIPED OUT.
THAT WAS A SHOCKWAVE FROM ACROSS THE GALAXY.
NO. NO, OUR--OUR FRIENDS WERE-- SOME OF US WERE THERE.
ARE YOU CERTAIN, DOCTOR?
ENTIRELY.
YOU HAVE OUR HELP.
LET US MAKE SURE OUR FRIENDS ARE STILL ALIVE.
WE WILL GATHER ANGEL AND LET US END WHOEVER IS RESPONSIBLE FOR THIS.

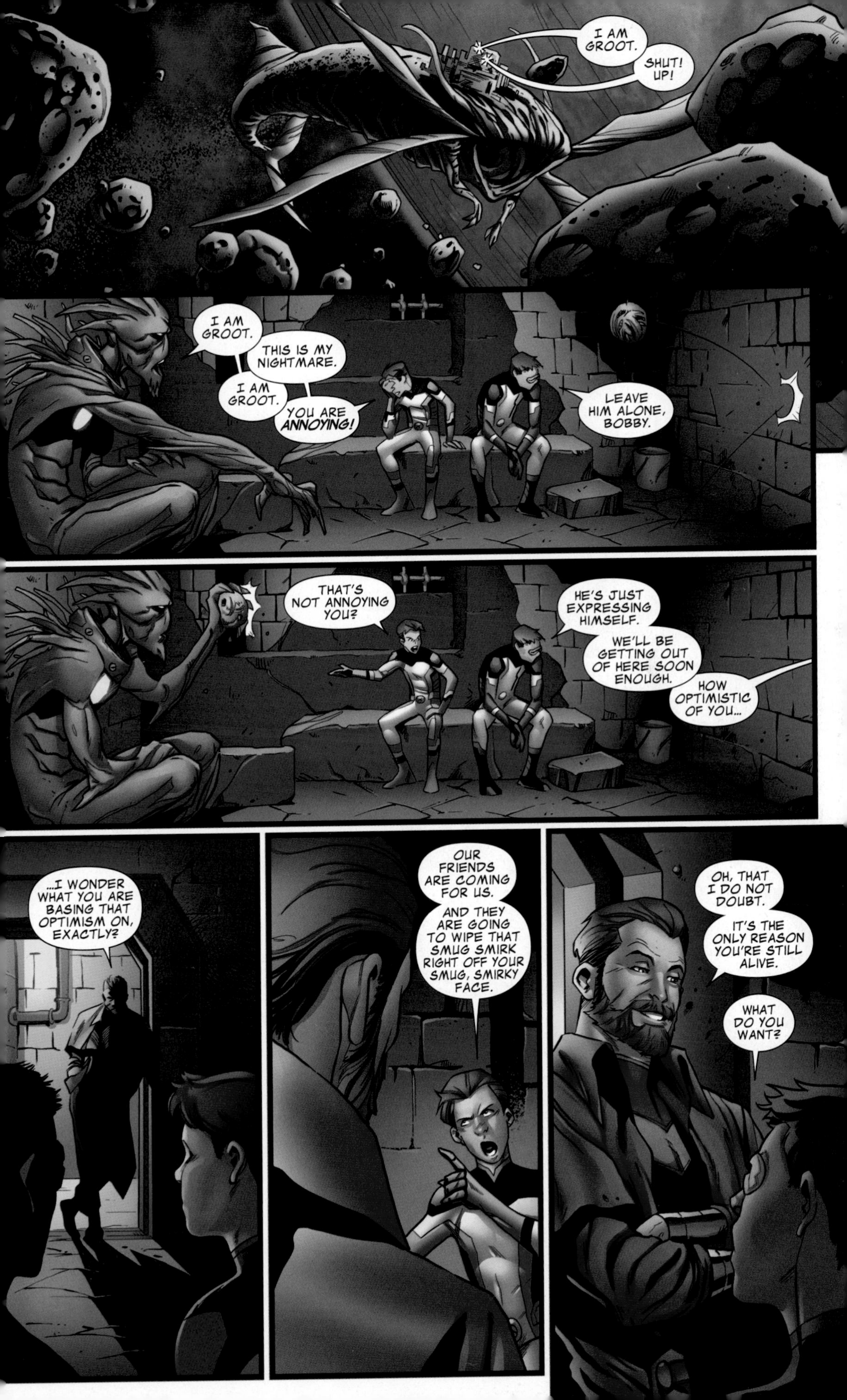
I AM GROOT.
SHUT! UP!
I AM GROOT.
THIS IS MY NIGHTMARE.
I AM GROOT.
YOU ARE ANNOYING!
LEAVE HIM ALONE, BOBBY.
THAT'S NOT ANNOYING YOU?
HE'S JUST EXPRESSING HIMSELF.
WE'LL BE GETTING OUT OF HERE SOON ENOUGH.
HOW OPTIMISTIC OF YOU...
...I WONDER WHAT YOU ARE BASING THAT OPTIMISM ON, EXACTLY?
OUR FRIENDS ARE COMING FOR US.
AND THEY ARE GOING TO WIPE THAT SMUG SMIRK RIGHT OFF YOUR SMUG, SMIRKY FACE.
OH, THAT I DO NOT DOUBT.
IT'S THE ONLY REASON YOU'RE STILL ALIVE.
WHAT DO YOU WANT?

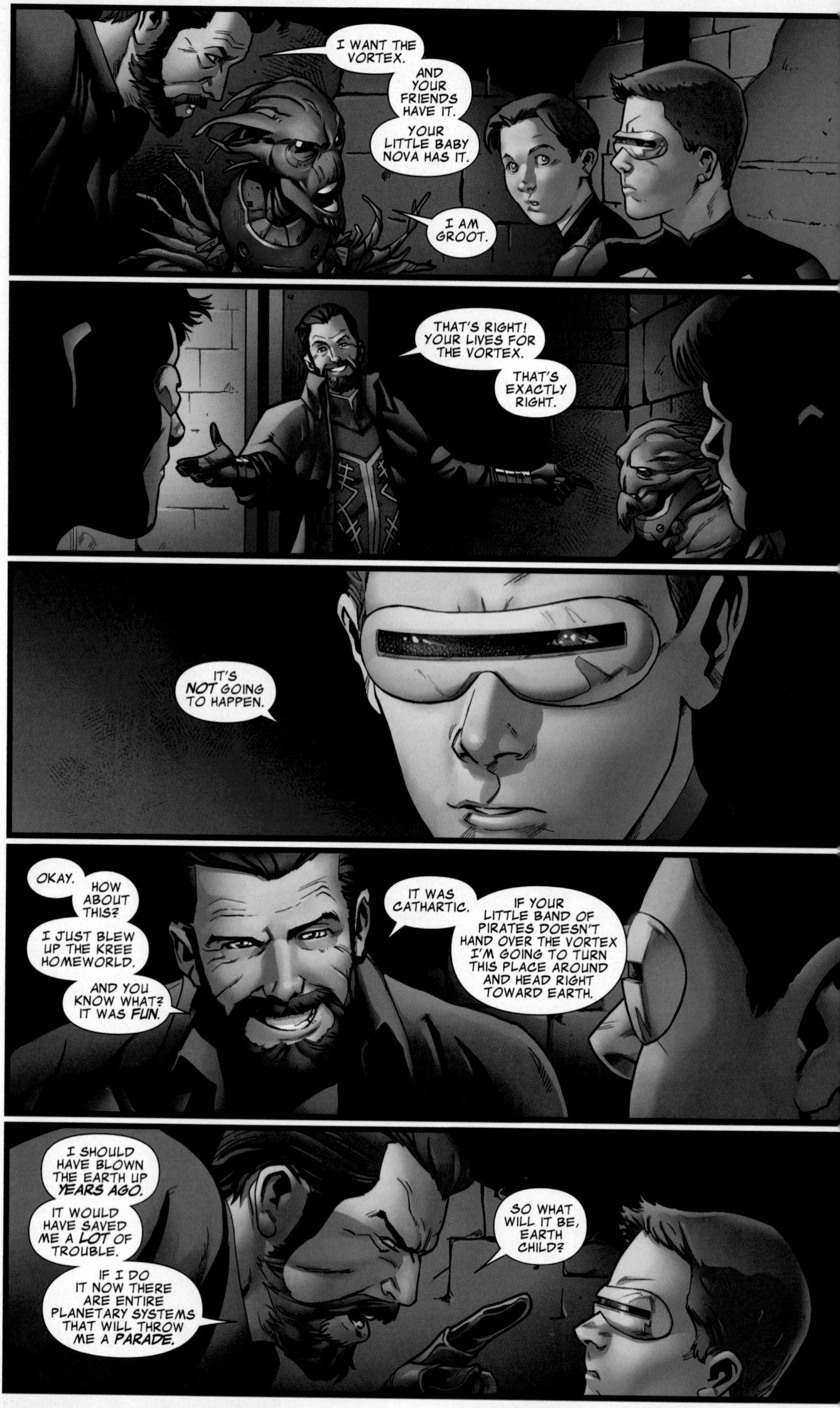
I WANT THE VORTEX.
AND YOUR FRIENDS HAVE IT.
YOUR LITTLE BABY NOVA HAS IT.
I AM GROOT.
THAT'S RIGHT! YOUR LIVES FOR THE VORTEX.
THAT'S EXACTLY RIGHT.
IT'S NOT GOING TO HAPPEN.
OKAY.
HOW ABOUT THIS?
I JUST BLEW UP THE KREE HOMEWORLD.
AND YOU KNOW WHAT? IT WAS FUN.
IT WAS CATHARTIC.
IF YOUR LITTLE BAND OF PIRATES DOESN'T HAND OVER THE VORTEX I'M GOING TO TURN THIS PLACE AROUND AND HEAD RIGHT TOWARD EARTH.
I SHOULD HAVE BLOWN THE EARTH UP YEARS AGO.
IT WOULD HAVE SAVED ME A LOT OF TROUBLE.
IF I DO IT NOW THERE ARE ENTIRE PLANETARY SYSTEMS THAT WILL THROW ME A PARADE.
SO WHAT WILL IT BE, EARTH CHILD?

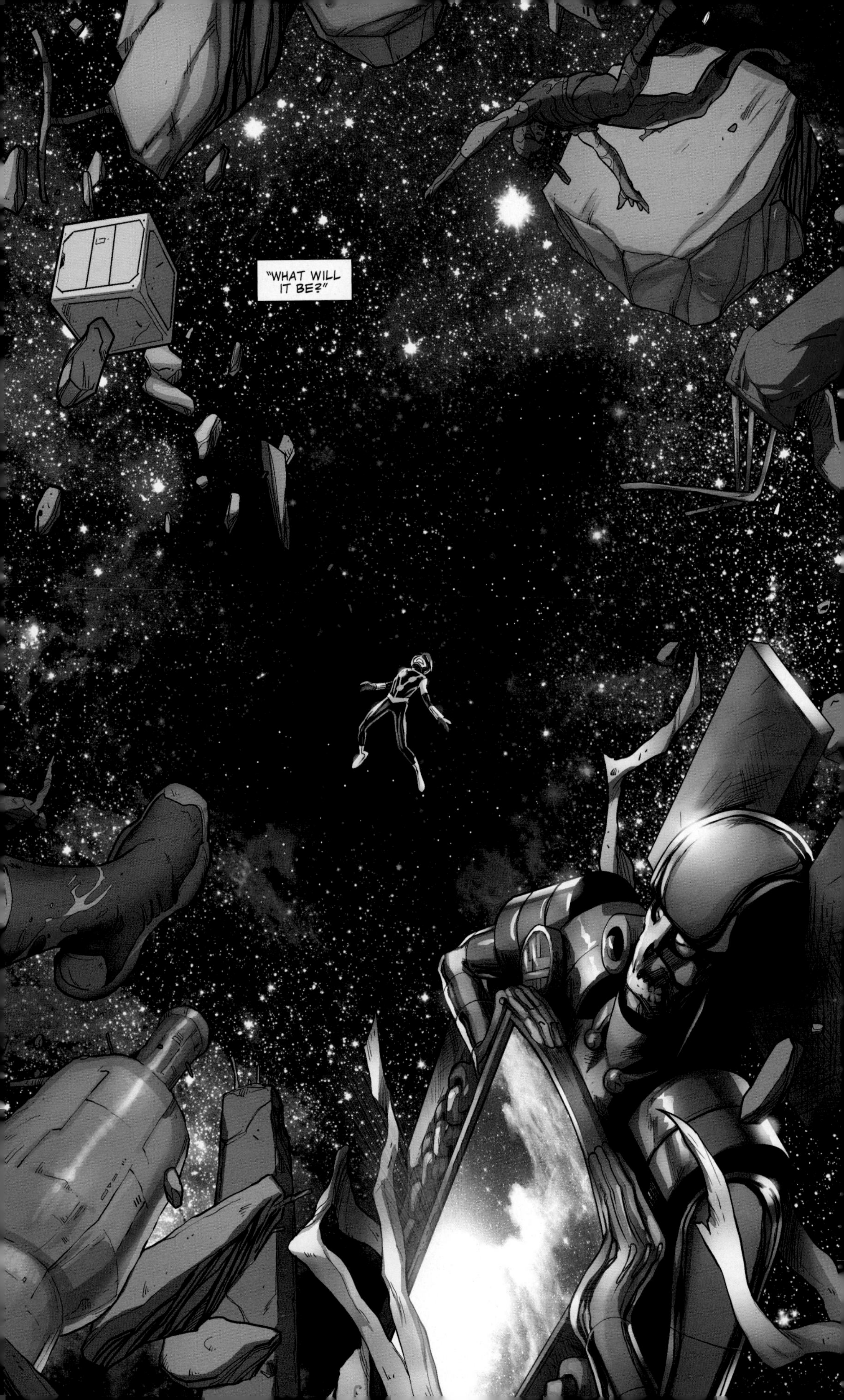
"WHAT WILL IT BE?"

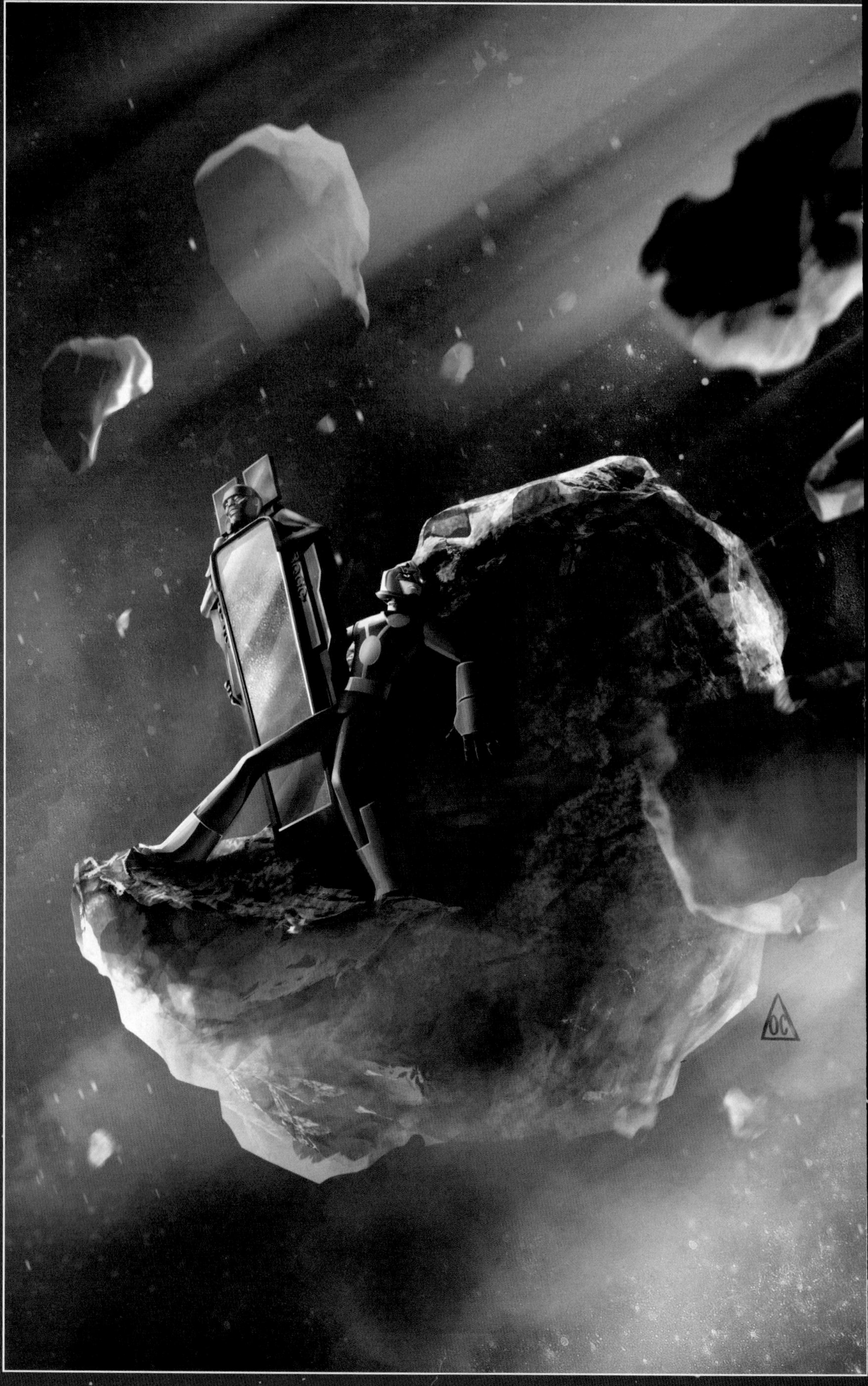

NOVA #28

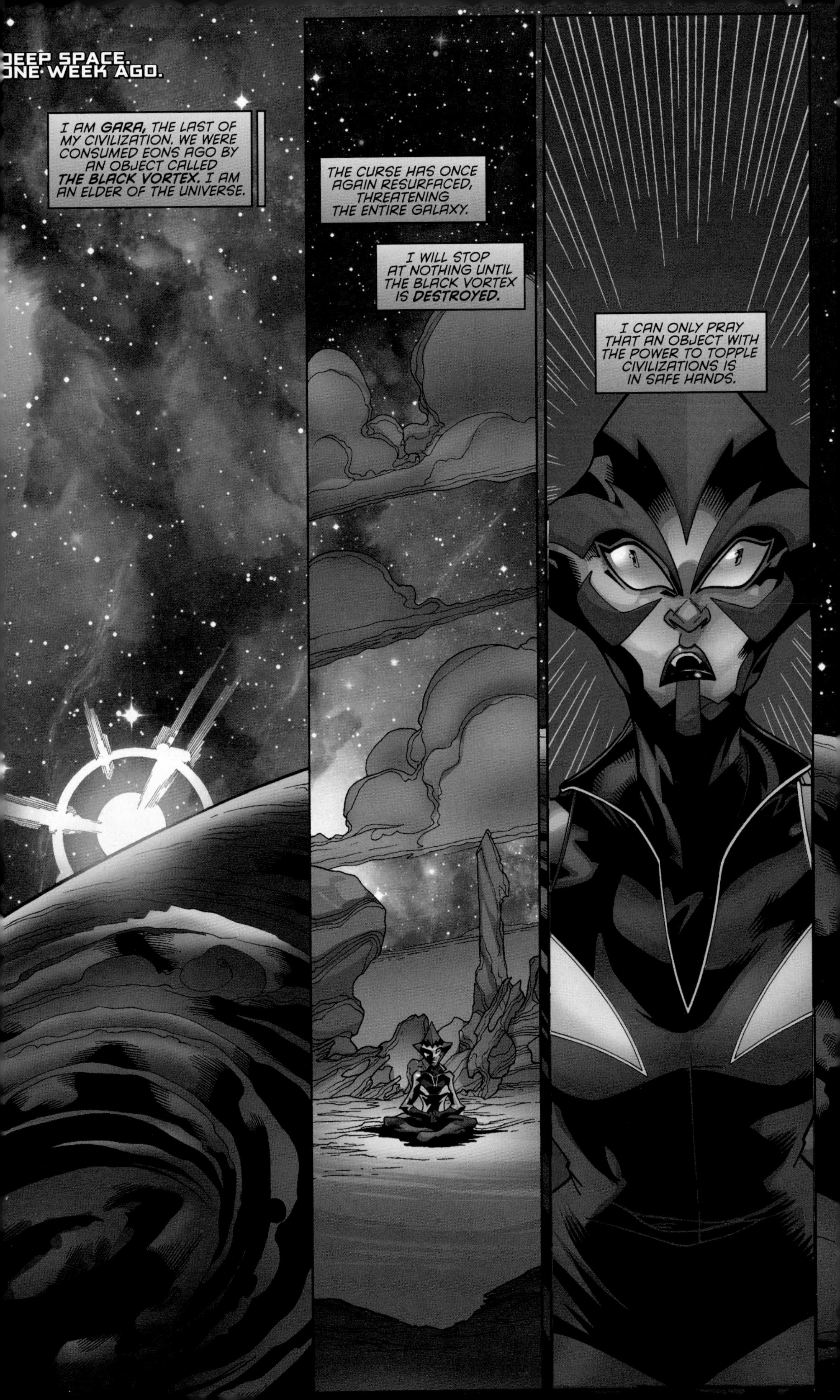
DEEP SPACE.
ONE WEEK AGO.
I AM GARA, THE LAST OF MY CIVILIZATION. WE WERE CONSUMED EONS AGO BY AN OBJECT CALLED THE BLACK VORTEX. I AM AN ELDER OF THE UNIVERSE.
THE CURSE HAS ONCE AGAIN RESURFACED, THREATENING THE ENTIRE GALAXY.
I WILL STOP AT NOTHING UNTIL THE BLACK VORTEX IS DESTROYED.
I CAN ONLY PRAY THAT AN OBJECT WITH THE POWER TO TOPPLE CIVILIZATIONS IS IN SAFE HANDS.

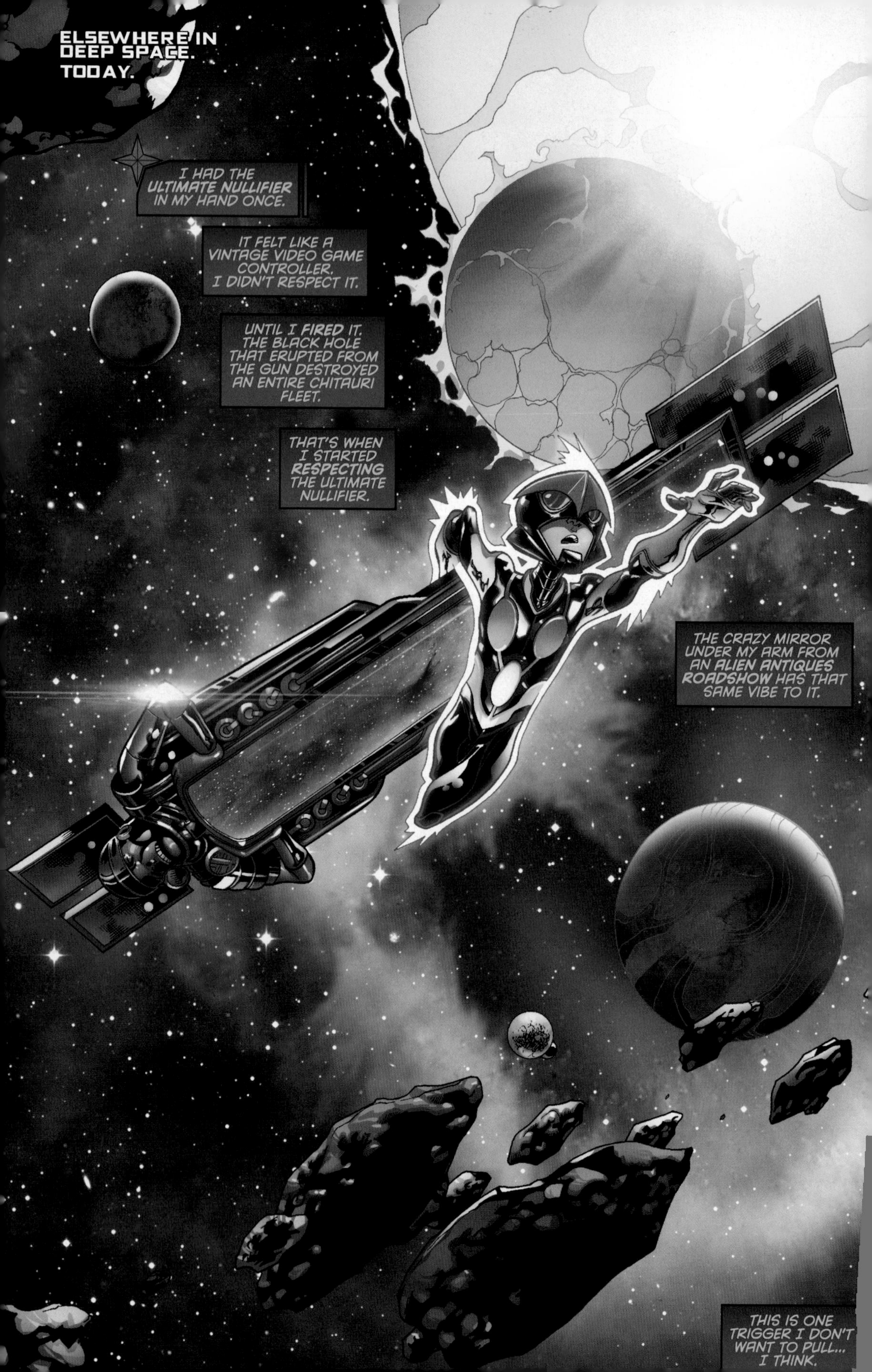
ELSEWHERE IN DEEP SPACE. TODAY.
I HAD THE ULTIMATE NULLIFIER IN MY HAND ONCE.
IT FELT LIKE A VINTAGE VIDEO GAME CONTROLLER. I DIDN'T RESPECT IT.
UNTIL I FIRED IT. THE BLACK HOLE THAT ERUPTED FROM THE GUN DESTROYED AN ENTIRE CHITAURI FLEET.
THAT'S WHEN I STARTED RESPECTING THE ULTIMATE NULLIFIER.
THE CRAZY MIRROR UNDER MY ARM FROM AN ALIEN ANTIQUES ROADSHOW HAS THAT SAME VIBE TO IT.
THIS IS ONE TRIGGER I DON'T WANT TO PULL... I THINK.

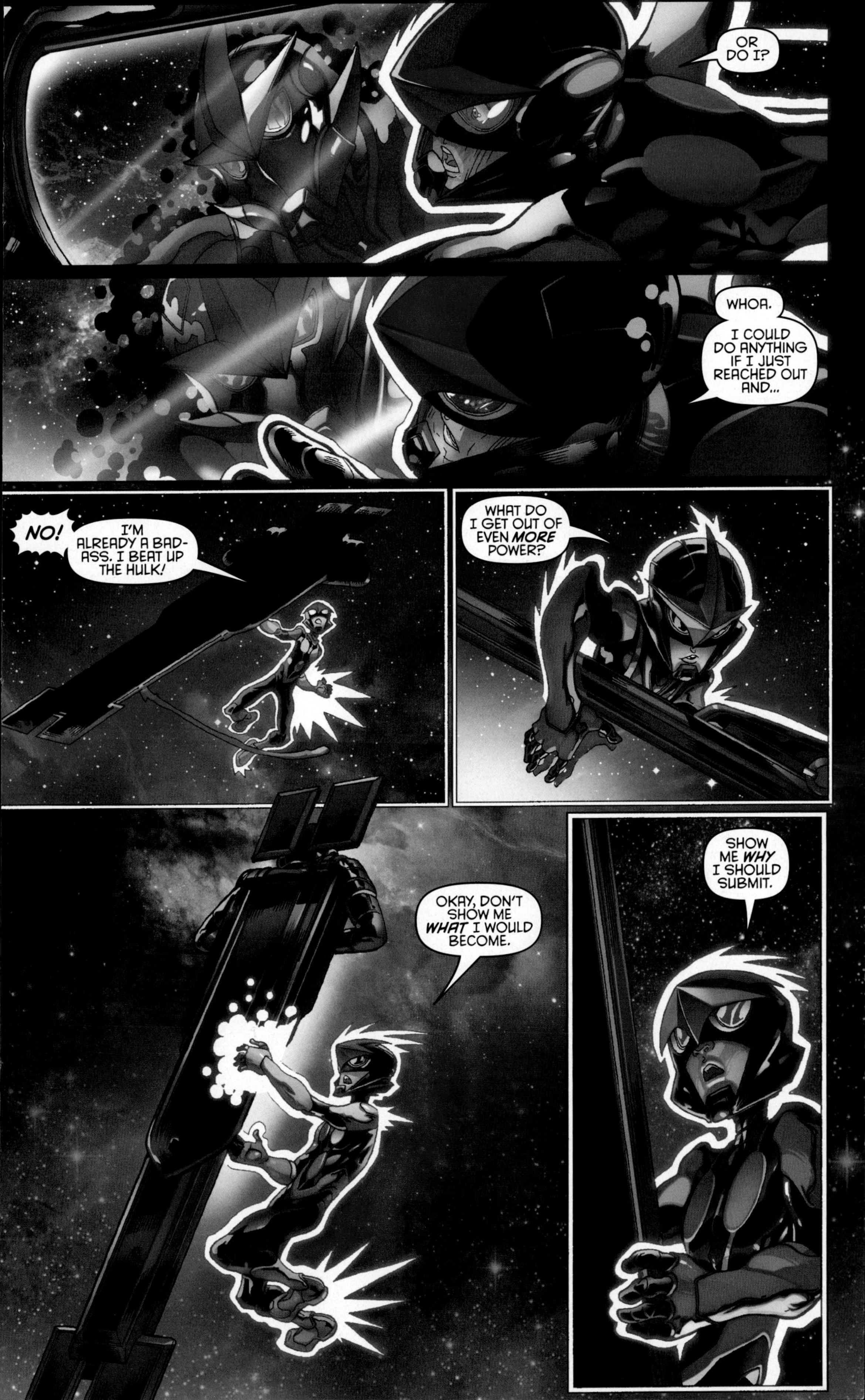
OR DO I?
WHOA.
I COULD DO ANYTHING IF I JUST REACHED OUT AND...
NO!
I'M ALREADY A BAD-ASS. I BEAT UP THE HULK!
WHAT DO I GET OUT OF EVEN MORE POWER?
OKAY, DON'T SHOW ME WHAT I WOULD BECOME.
SHOW ME WHY I SHOULD SUBMIT.

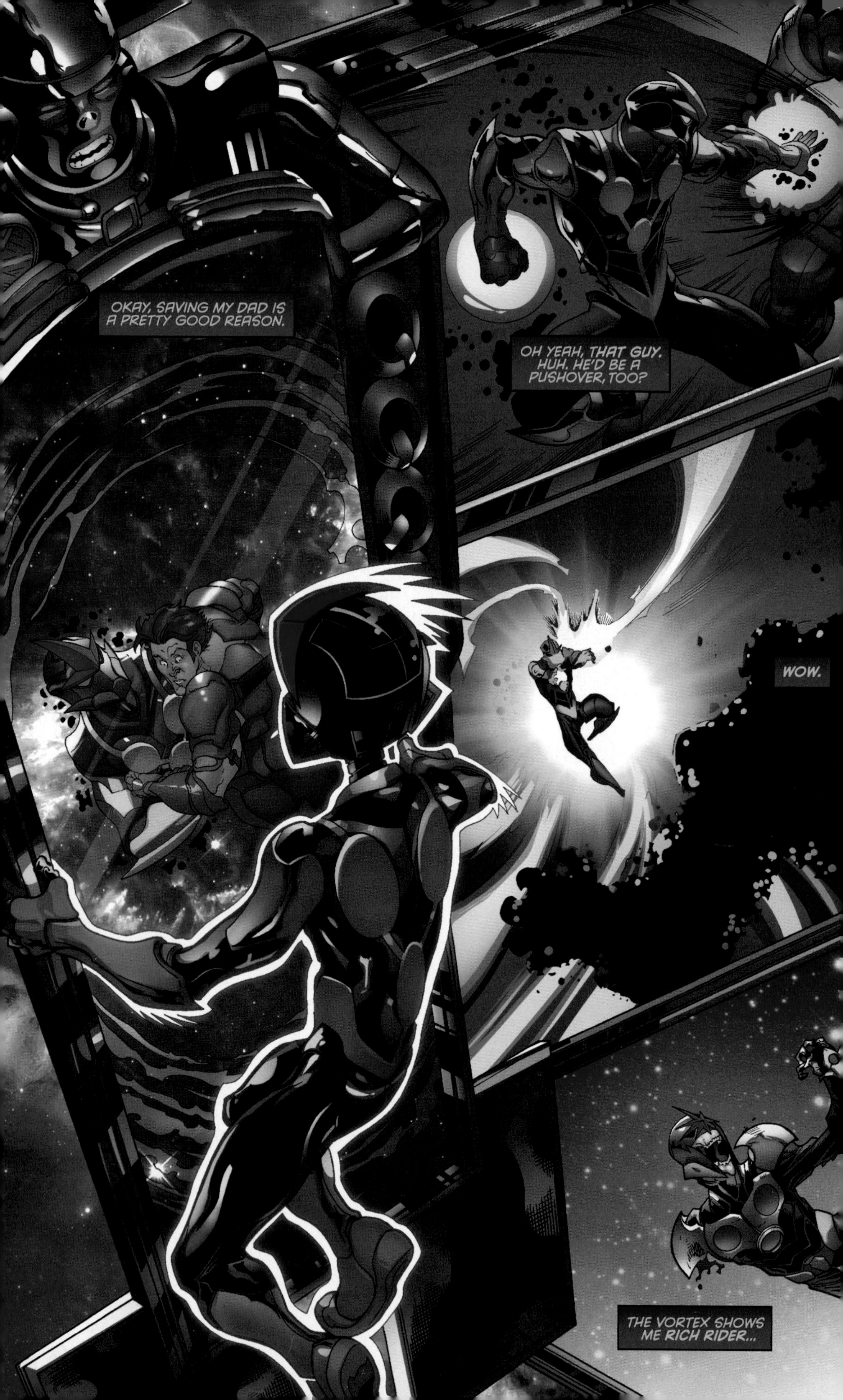
OKAY, SAVING MY DAD IS A PRETTY GOOD REASON.
OH YEAH, THAT GUY. HUH. HE'D BE A PUSHOVER, TOO?
WOW.
THE VORTEX SHOWS ME RICH RIDER...

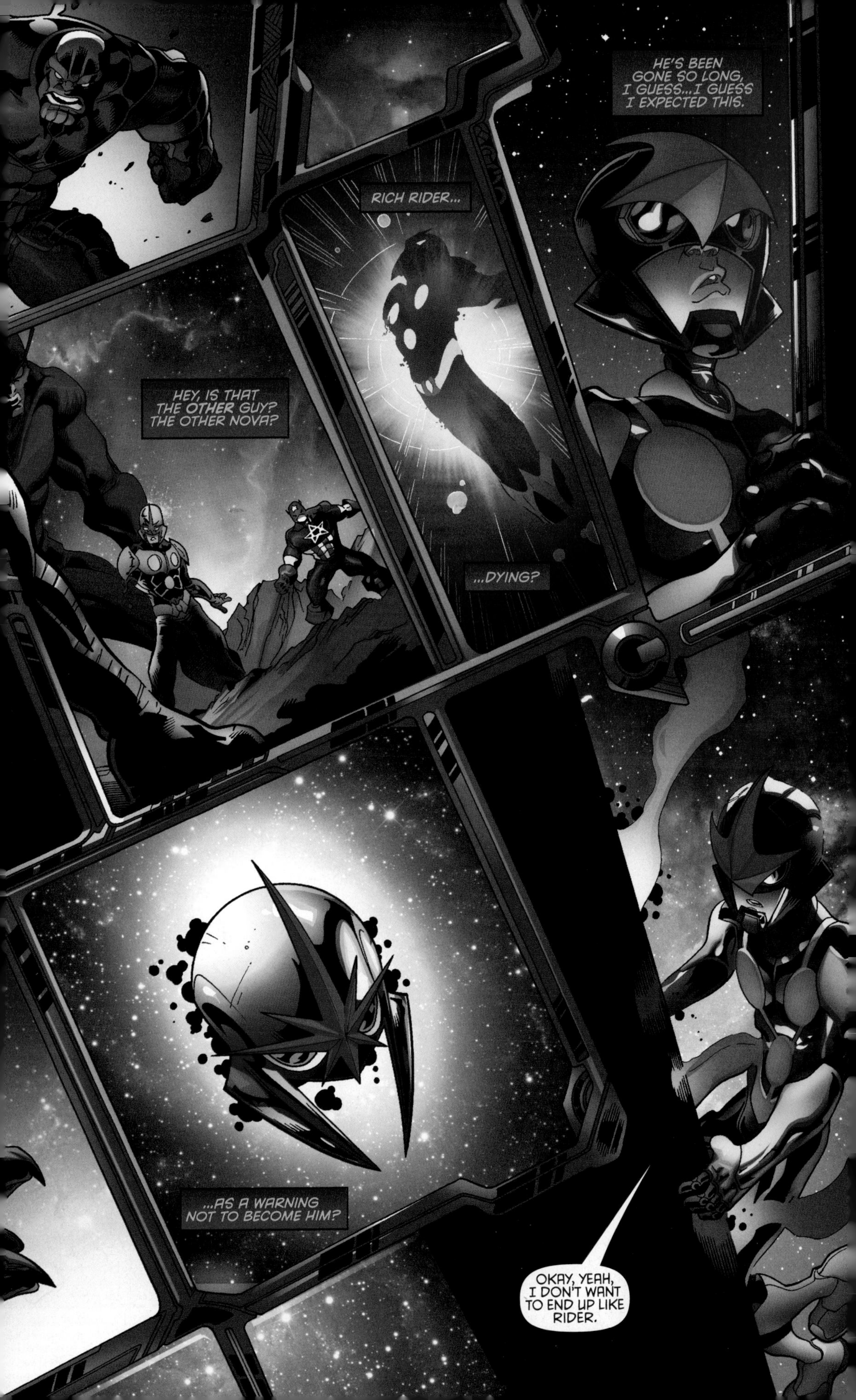
HEY, IS THAT THE OTHER GUY? THE OTHER NOVA?
RICH RIDER...
...DYING?
HE'S BEEN GONE SO LONG, I GUESS...I GUESS I EXPECTED THIS.
...AS A WARNING NOT TO BECOME HIM?
OKAY, YEAH, I DON'T WANT TO END UP LIKE RIDER.

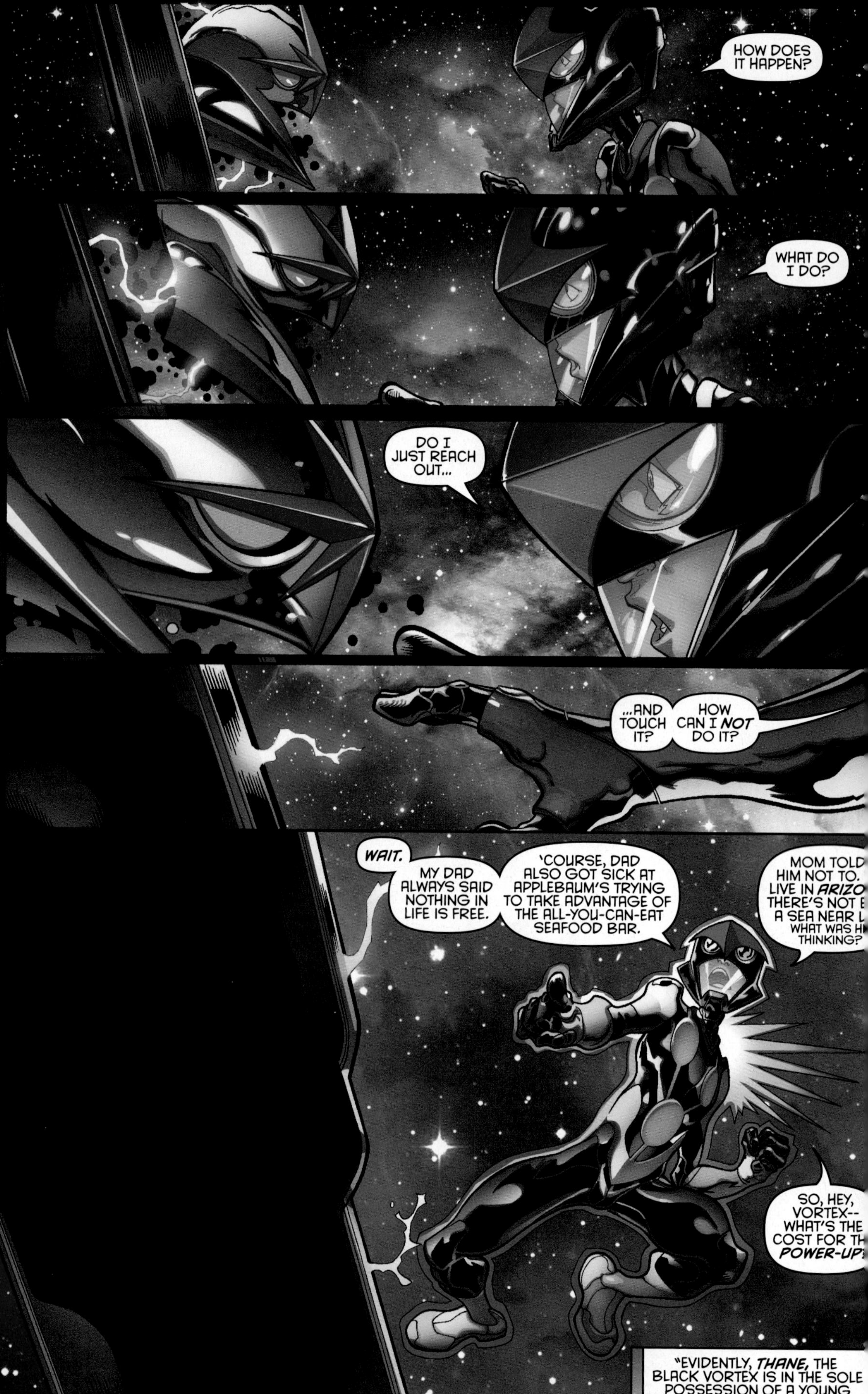
HOW DOES IT HAPPEN?
WHAT DO I DO?
DO I JUST REACH OUT...
...AND TOUCH IT?
HOW CAN I *NOT* DO IT?
WAIT.
MY DAD ALWAYS SAID NOTHING IN LIFE IS FREE.
'COURSE, DAD ALSO GOT SICK AT APPLEBAUM'S TRYING TO TAKE ADVANTAGE OF THE ALL-YOU-CAN-EAT SEAFOOD BAR.
MOM TOLD HIM NOT TO. LIVE IN *ARIZO* THERE'S NOT A SEA NEAR WHAT WAS H THINKING?
SO, HEY, VORTEX-- WHAT'S THE COST FOR TH *POWER-UP*
"EVIDENTLY, *THANE,* THE BLACK VORTEX IS IN THE SOLE POSSESSION OF A YOUNG SIMPLETON FROM EARTH..."

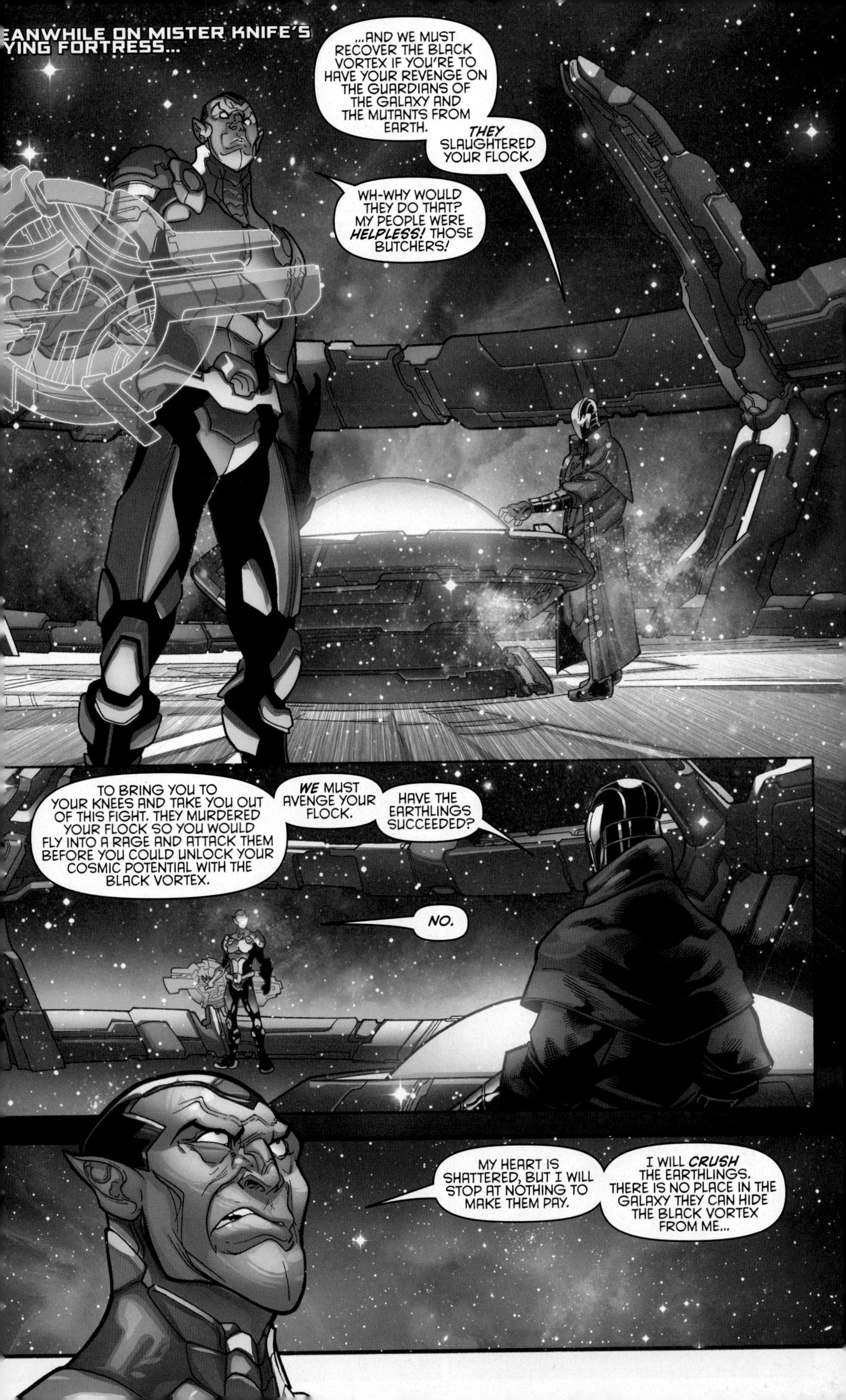
EANWHILE ON MISTER KNIFE'S
YING FORTRESS...
...AND WE MUST RECOVER THE BLACK VORTEX IF YOU'RE TO HAVE YOUR REVENGE ON THE GUARDIANS OF THE GALAXY AND THE MUTANTS FROM EARTH.
THEY SLAUGHTERED YOUR FLOCK.
WH-WHY WOULD THEY DO THAT? MY PEOPLE WERE HELPLESS! THOSE BUTCHERS!
TO BRING YOU TO YOUR KNEES AND TAKE YOU OUT OF THIS FIGHT. THEY MURDERED YOUR FLOCK SO YOU WOULD FLY INTO A RAGE AND ATTACK THEM BEFORE YOU COULD UNLOCK YOUR COSMIC POTENTIAL WITH THE BLACK VORTEX.
WE MUST AVENGE YOUR FLOCK.
HAVE THE EARTHLINGS SUCCEEDED?
NO.
MY HEART IS SHATTERED, BUT I WILL STOP AT NOTHING TO MAKE THEM PAY.
I WILL CRUSH THE EARTHLINGS. THERE IS NO PLACE IN THE GALAXY THEY CAN HIDE THE BLACK VORTEX FROM ME...

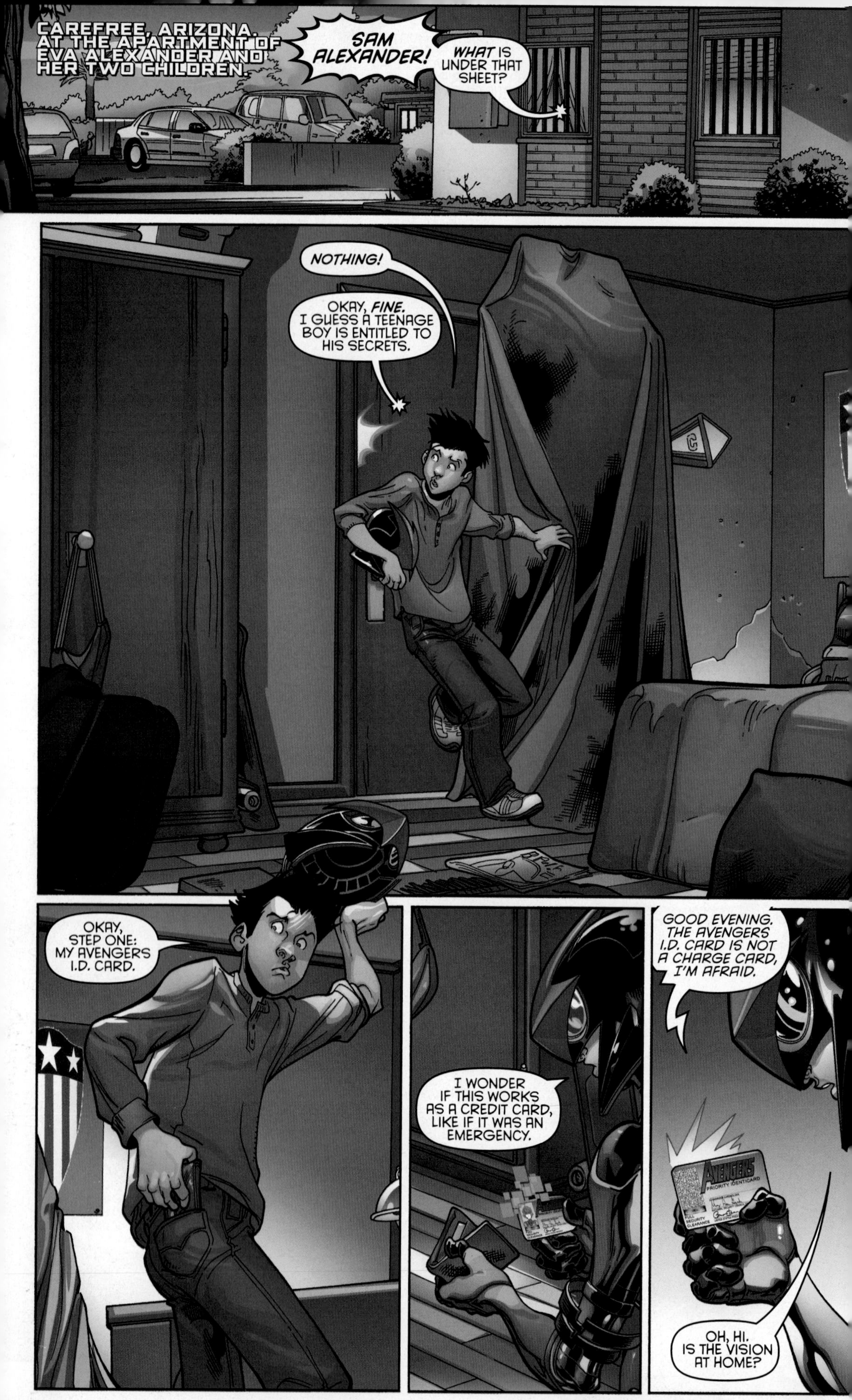
CAREFREE, ARIZONA. AT THE APARTMENT OF EVA ALEXANDER AND HER TWO CHILDREN.
SAM ALEXANDER!
WHAT IS UNDER THAT SHEET?
NOTHING!
OKAY, FINE. I GUESS A TEENAGE BOY IS ENTITLED TO HIS SECRETS.
OKAY, STEP ONE: MY AVENGERS I.D. CARD.
I WONDER IF THIS WORKS AS A CREDIT CARD, LIKE IF IT WAS AN EMERGENCY.
GOOD EVENING. THE AVENGERS I.D. CARD IS NOT A CHARGE CARD, I'M AFRAID.
AVENGERS
PRIORITY IDENTICARD
OH, HI. IS THE VISION AT HOME?

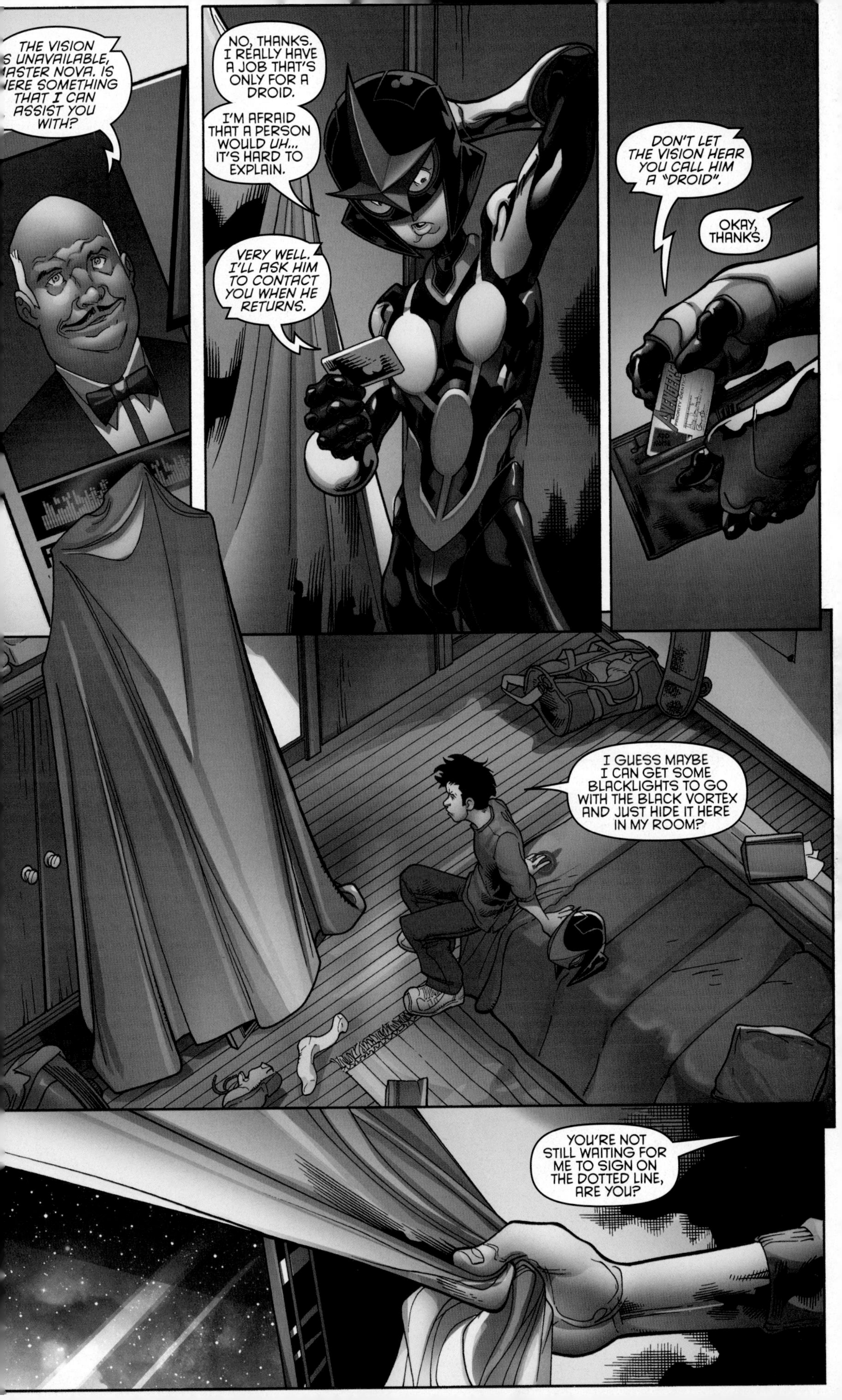

THE VISION S UNAVAILABLE, MASTER NOVA. IS HERE SOMETHING THAT I CAN ASSIST YOU WITH?
NO, THANKS. I REALLY HAVE A JOB THAT'S ONLY FOR A DROID.
I'M AFRAID THAT A PERSON WOULD UH... IT'S HARD TO EXPLAIN.
VERY WELL. I'LL ASK HIM TO CONTACT YOU WHEN HE RETURNS.
DON'T LET THE VISION HEAR YOU CALL HIM A "DROID".
OKAY, THANKS.
AVENGERS
I GUESS MAYBE I CAN GET SOME BLACKLIGHTS TO GO WITH THE BLACK VORTEX AND JUST HIDE IT HERE IN MY ROOM?
YOU'RE NOT STILL WAITING FOR ME TO SIGN ON THE DOTTED LINE, ARE YOU?

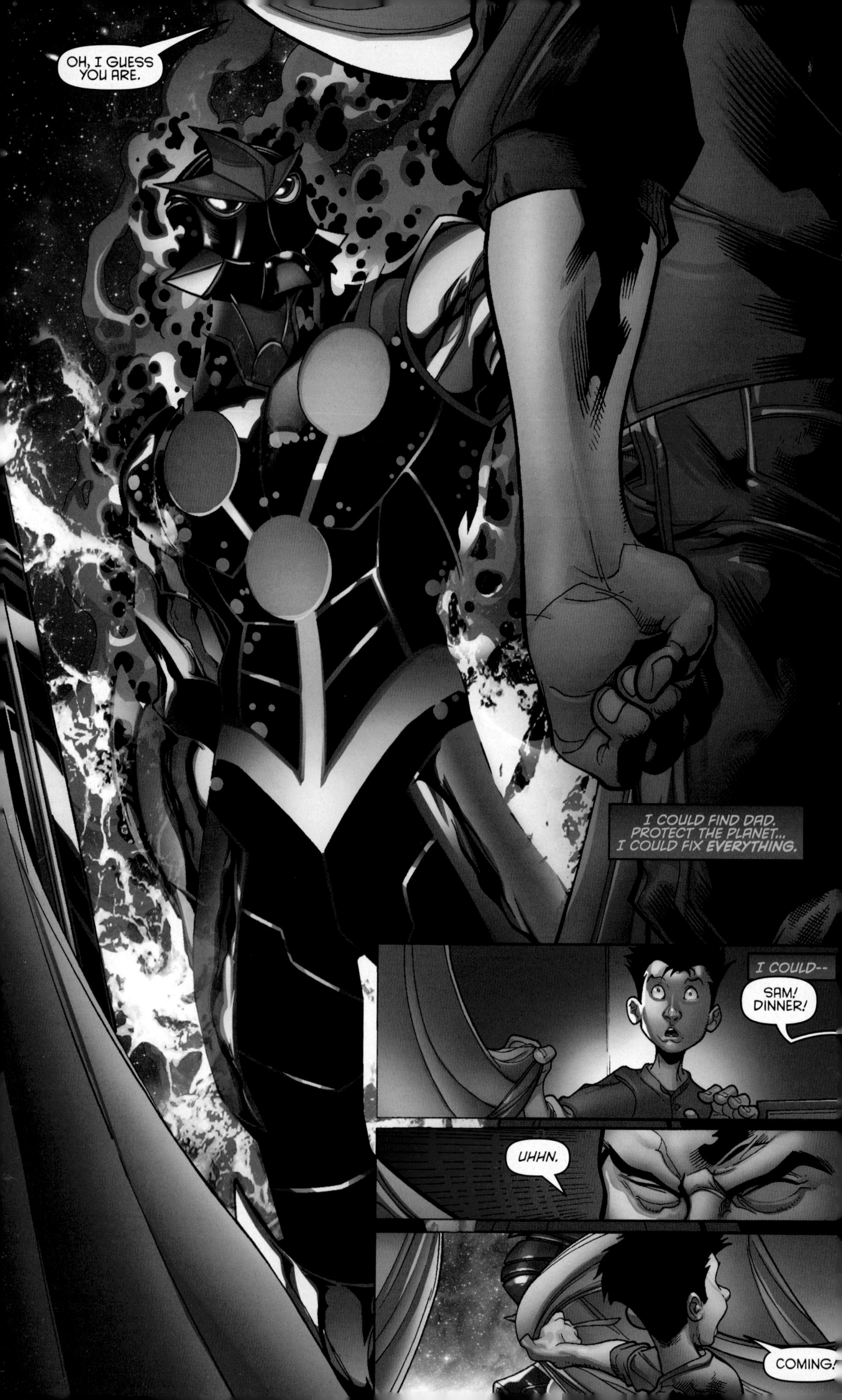
OH, I GUESS YOU ARE.
I COULD FIND DAD. PROTECT THE PLANET... I COULD FIX EVERYTHING.
I COULD--
SAM! DINNER!
UHHN.
COMING!

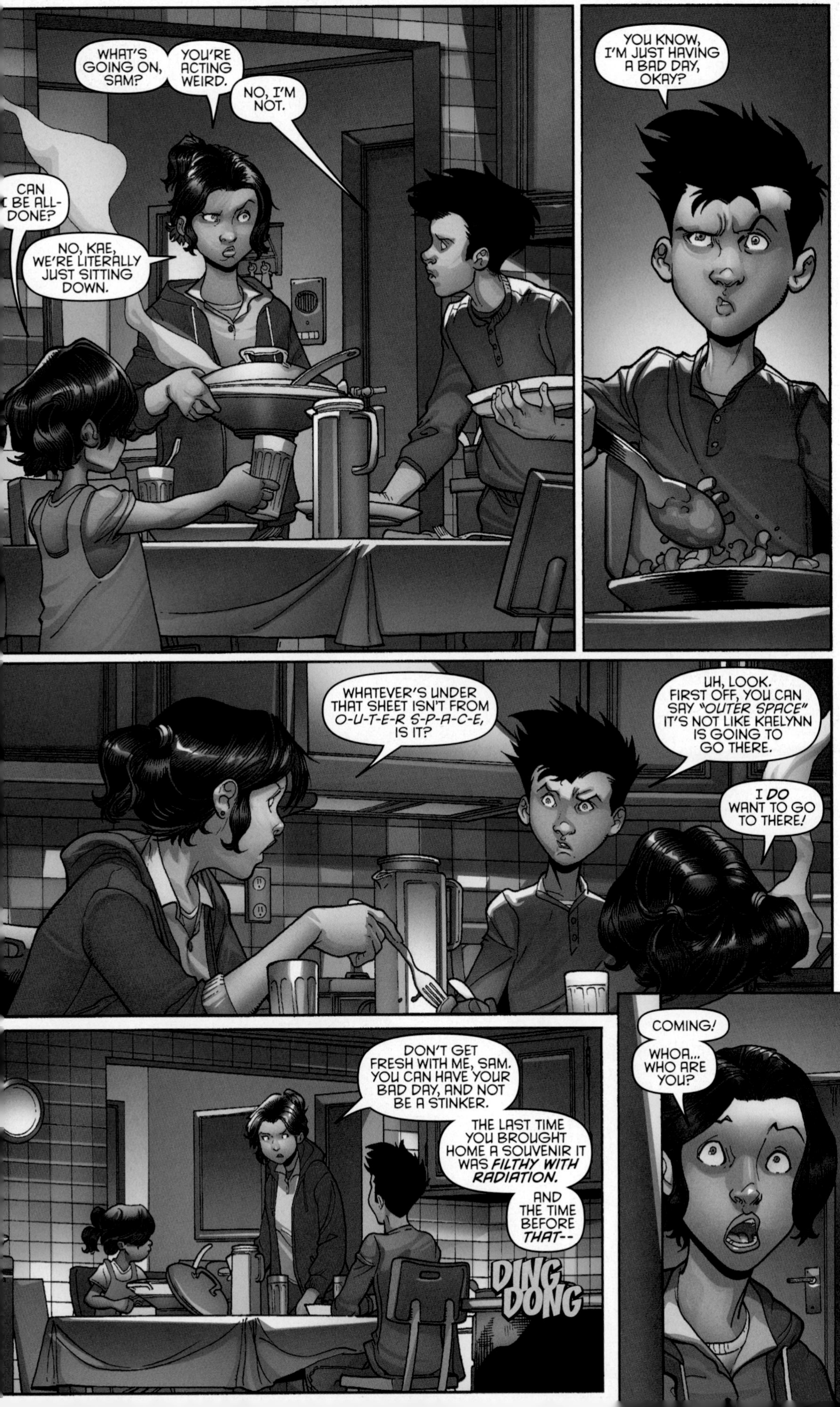
WHAT'S GOING ON, SAM?
YOU'RE ACTING WEIRD.
NO, I'M NOT.
CAN I BE ALL-DONE?
NO, KAE, WE'RE LITERALLY JUST SITTING DOWN.
YOU KNOW, I'M JUST HAVING A BAD DAY, OKAY?
WHATEVER'S UNDER THAT SHEET ISN'T FROM O-U-T-E-R S-P-A-C-E, IS IT?
UH, LOOK. FIRST OFF, YOU CAN SAY "OUTER SPACE" IT'S NOT LIKE KAELYNN IS GOING TO GO THERE.
I DO WANT TO GO TO THERE!
DON'T GET FRESH WITH ME, SAM. YOU CAN HAVE YOUR BAD DAY, AND NOT BE A STINKER.
THE LAST TIME YOU BROUGHT HOME A SOUVENIR IT WAS FILTHY WITH RADIATION.
AND THE TIME BEFORE THAT--
DING DONG
COMING!
WHOA... WHO ARE YOU?

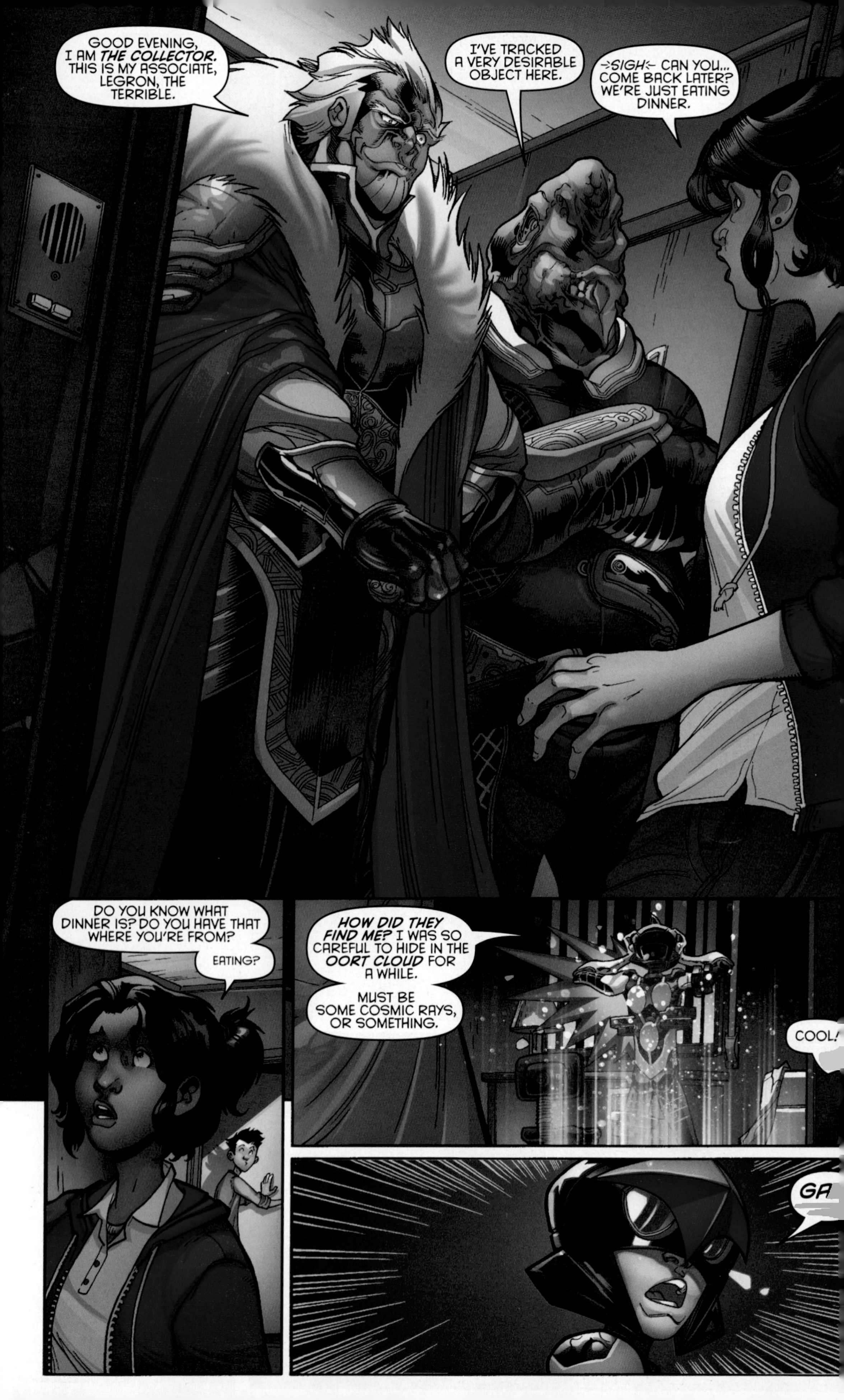
GOOD EVENING, I AM THE COLLECTOR. THIS IS MY ASSOCIATE, LEGRON, THE TERRIBLE.
I'VE TRACKED A VERY DESIRABLE OBJECT HERE.
-SIGH- CAN YOU... COME BACK LATER? WE'RE JUST EATING DINNER.
DO YOU KNOW WHAT DINNER IS? DO YOU HAVE THAT WHERE YOU'RE FROM?
EATING?
HOW DID THEY FIND ME? I WAS SO CAREFUL TO HIDE IN THE OORT CLOUD FOR A WHILE.
MUST BE SOME COSMIC RAYS, OR SOMETHING.
COOL!
GA

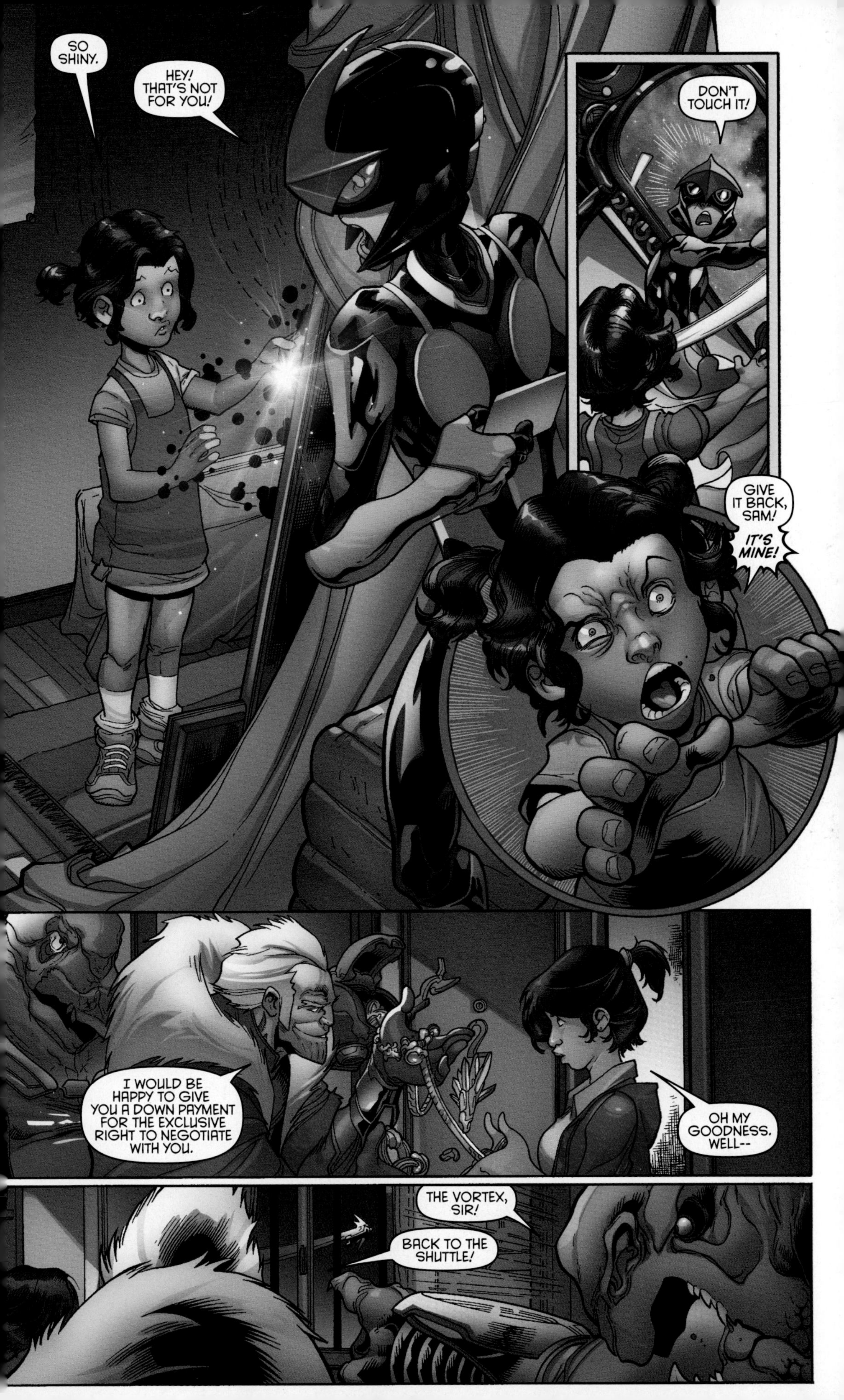
SO SHINY.
HEY! THAT'S NOT FOR YOU!
DON'T TOUCH IT!
GIVE IT BACK, SAM!
IT'S MINE!
I WOULD BE HAPPY TO GIVE YOU A DOWN PAYMENT FOR THE EXCLUSIVE RIGHT TO NEGOTIATE WITH YOU.
OH MY GOODNESS. WELL--
THE VORTEX, SIR!
BACK TO THE SHUTTLE!

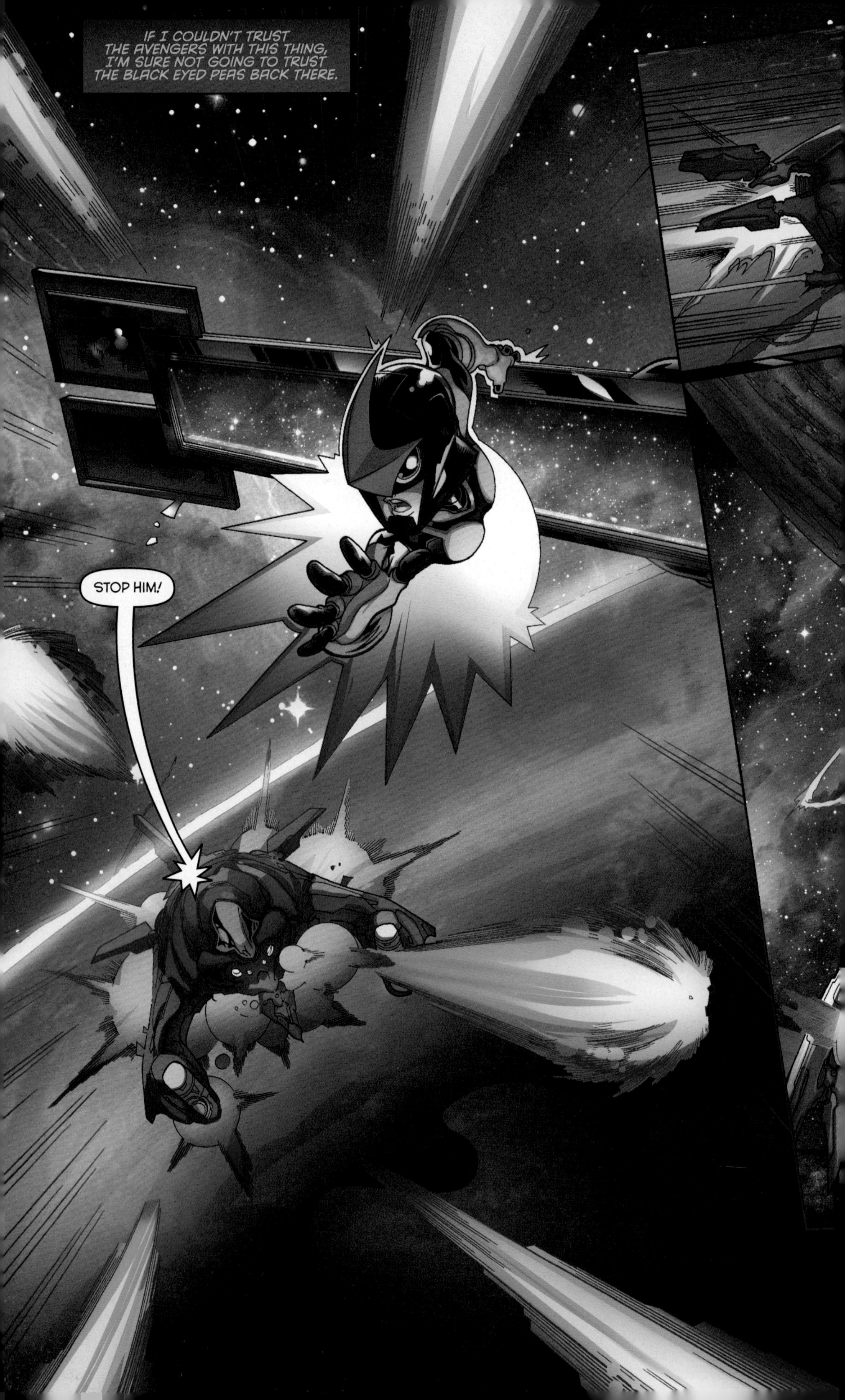
IF I COULDN'T TRUST THE AVENGERS WITH THIS THING, I'M SURE NOT GOING TO TRUST THE BLACK EYED PEAS BACK THERE.
STOP HIM!

WHOA! HEY! HEY!
ALL RIGHT, YOU WANT TO BE JERKS-- FOLLOW ME.
WHERE DID HE GO? DID HE WARP AWAY?
HE'S GOING TO SLINGSHOT AROUND THE MOON!
DID WE LOSE THE BLACK VORTEX?!
NO. FELDERCARB! HE STOPPED SHORT AND NOW HE'S BEHIND US. HANG ON, I CAN TURN AROUND AND--
YOU GUYS HAVEN'T HEARD OF NOVA? I BEAT UP THE HULK! I'M A DOUBLE-SECRET PROBATIONARY AVENGER!
FWABOOM
DON'T TRY TO FOLLOW ME!
DON'T LOSE HIM, AND DON'T WORRY. AVENGERS DON'T KILL. WELL, MOST OF THEM DON'T, ANYWAY.
THERE'S ONE PLACE WHERE I KNOW I CAN FIND SOME FRIENDS...

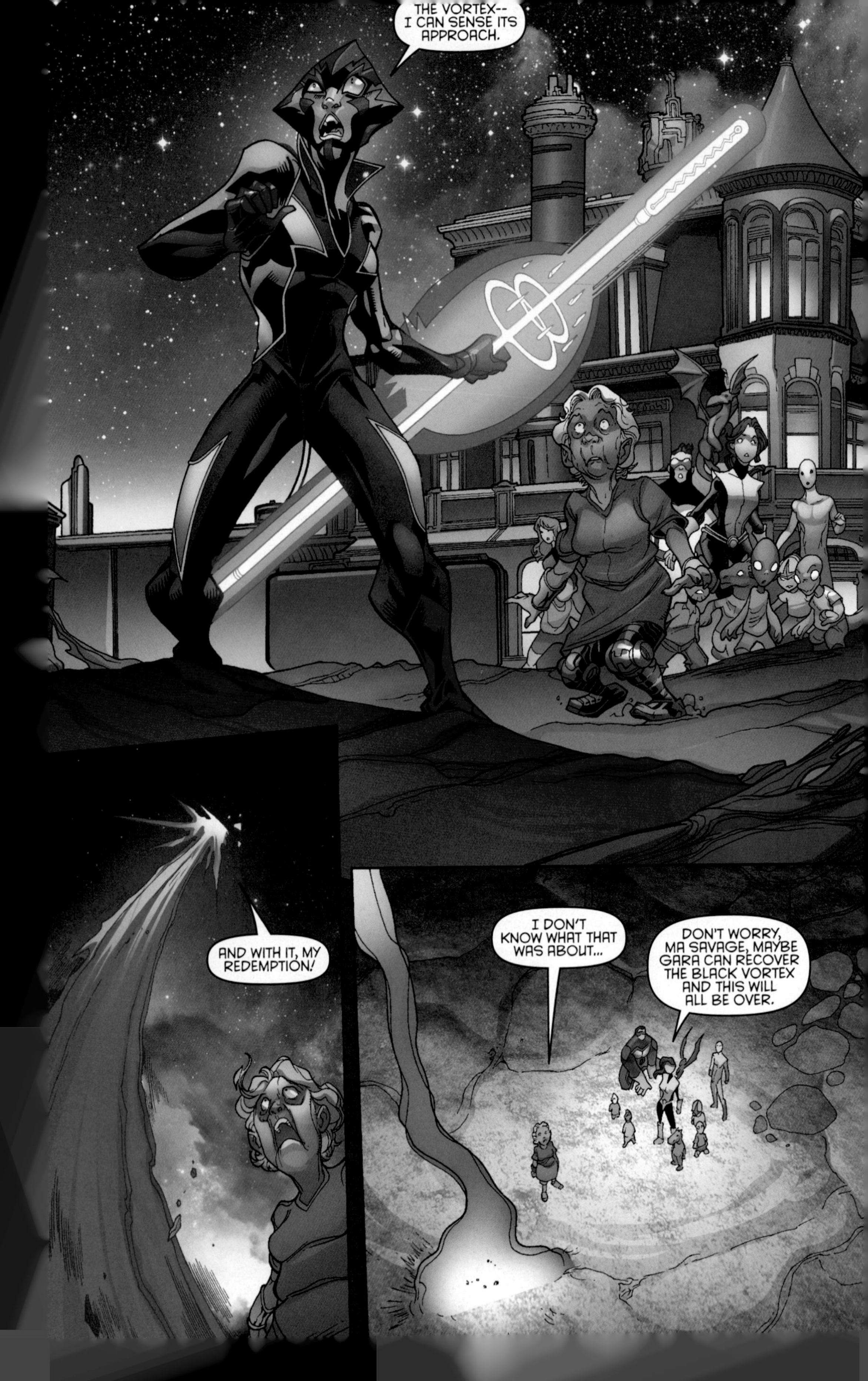
THE VORTEX-- I CAN SENSE ITS APPROACH.
AND WITH IT, MY REDEMPTION!
I DON'T KNOW WHAT THAT WAS ABOUT...
DON'T WORRY, MA SAVAGE, MAYBE GARA CAN RECOVER THE BLACK VORTEX AND THIS WILL ALL BE OVER.

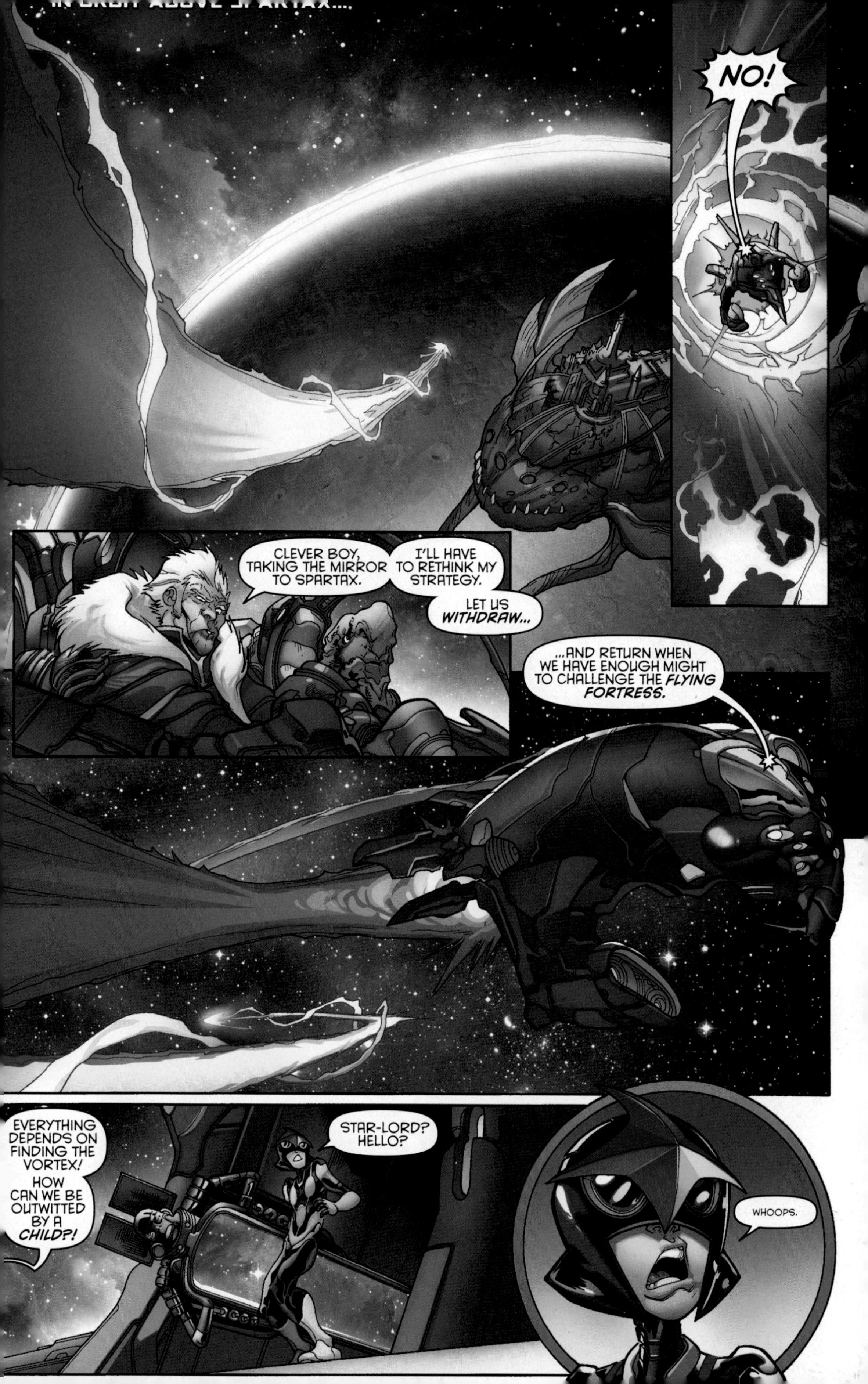
NO!
CLEVER BOY, TAKING THE MIRROR TO SPARTAX.
I'LL HAVE TO RETHINK MY STRATEGY.
LET US *WITHDRAW*...
...AND RETURN WHEN WE HAVE ENOUGH MIGHT TO CHALLENGE THE *FLYING FORTRESS.*
EVERYTHING DEPENDS ON FINDING THE VORTEX!
HOW CAN WE BE OUTWITTED BY A *CHILD?!*
STAR-LORD? HELLO?
WHOOPS.

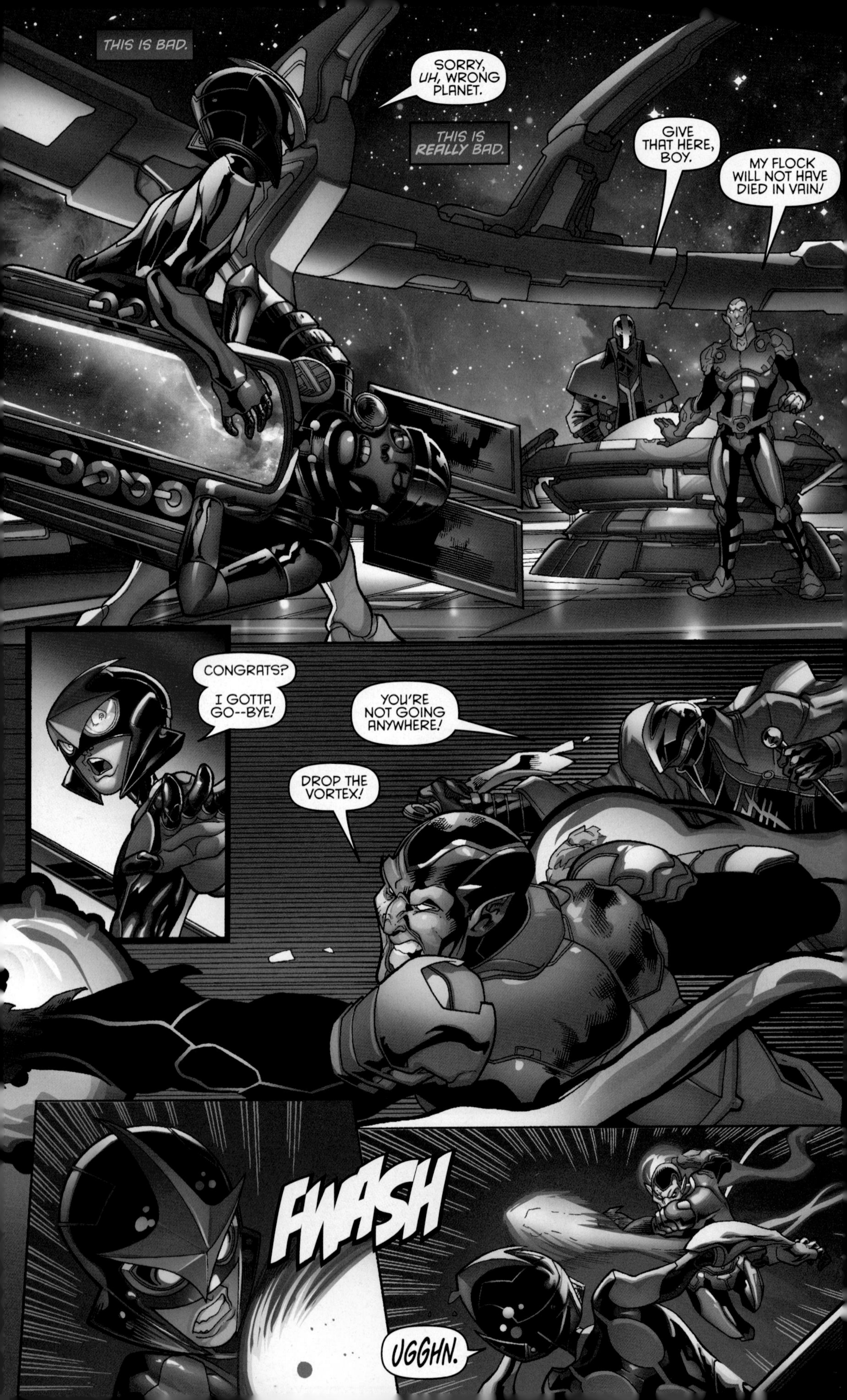
THIS IS BAD.
SORRY, UH, WRONG PLANET.
THIS IS REALLY BAD.
GIVE THAT HERE, BOY.
MY FLOCK WILL NOT HAVE DIED IN VAIN!
CONGRATS?
I GOTTA GO--BYE!
YOU'RE NOT GOING ANYWHERE!
DROP THE VORTEX!
FWASH
UGGHN.

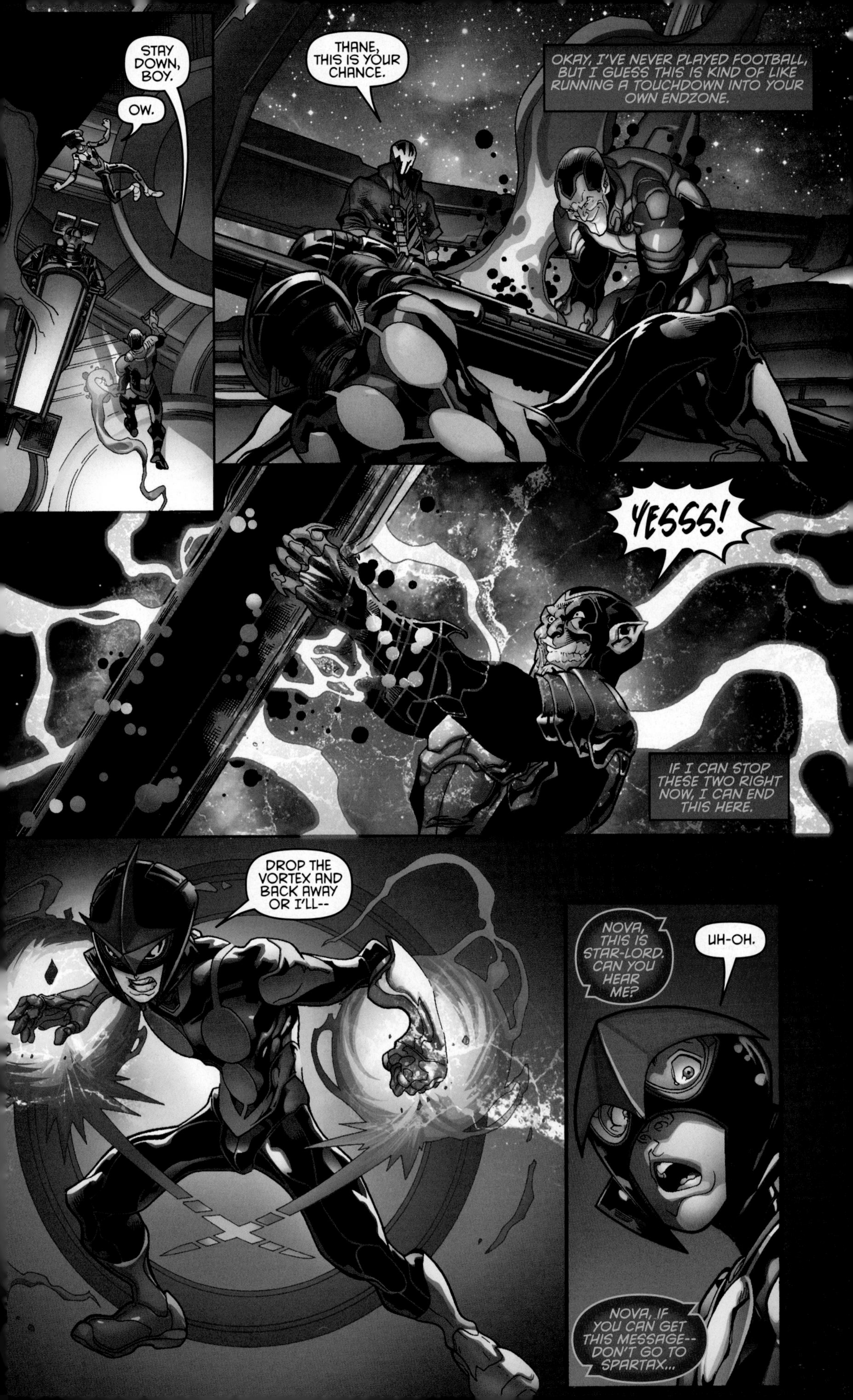
STAY DOWN, BOY.
OW.
THANE, THIS IS YOUR CHANCE.
OKAY, I'VE NEVER PLAYED FOOTBALL, BUT I GUESS THIS IS KIND OF LIKE RUNNING A TOUCHDOWN INTO YOUR OWN ENDZONE.
YESSS!
IF I CAN STOP THESE TWO RIGHT NOW, I CAN END THIS HERE.
DROP THE VORTEX AND BACK AWAY OR I'LL--
NOVA, THIS IS STAR-LORD. CAN YOU HEAR ME?
UH-OH.
NOVA, IF YOU CAN GET THIS MESSAGE-- DON'T GO TO SPARTAX...

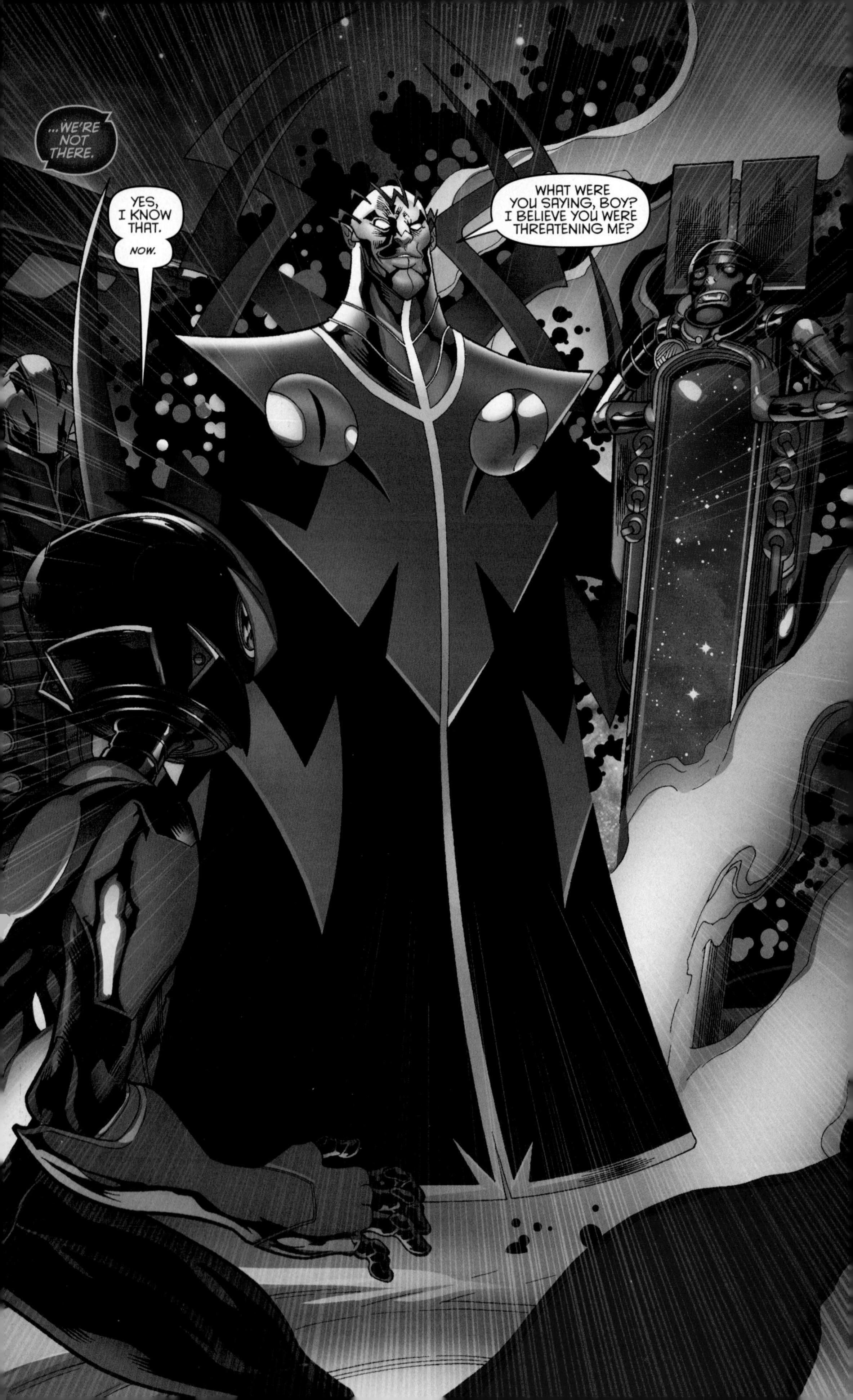
...WE'RE NOT THERE.
YES, I KNOW THAT.
NOW.
WHAT WERE YOU SAYING, BOY? I BELIEVE YOU WERE THREATENING ME?

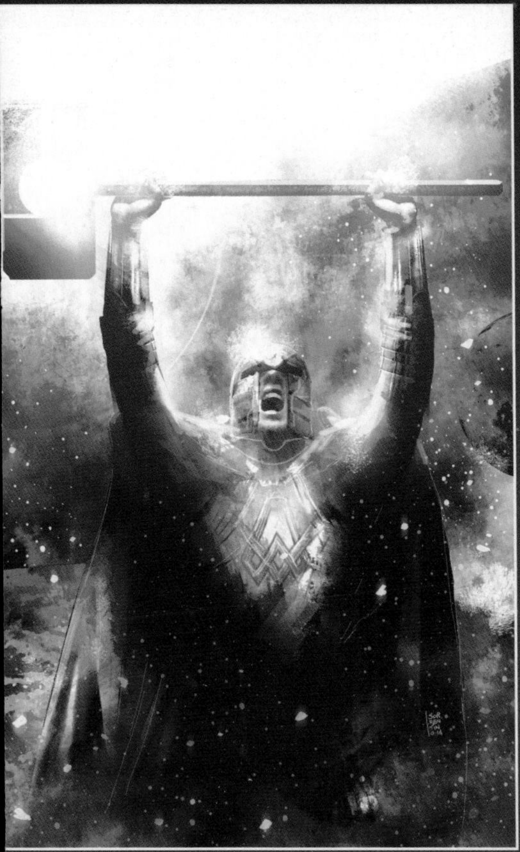

Guardians Team-Up #3 Cosmically Enhanced Variant
by Andrea Sorrentino

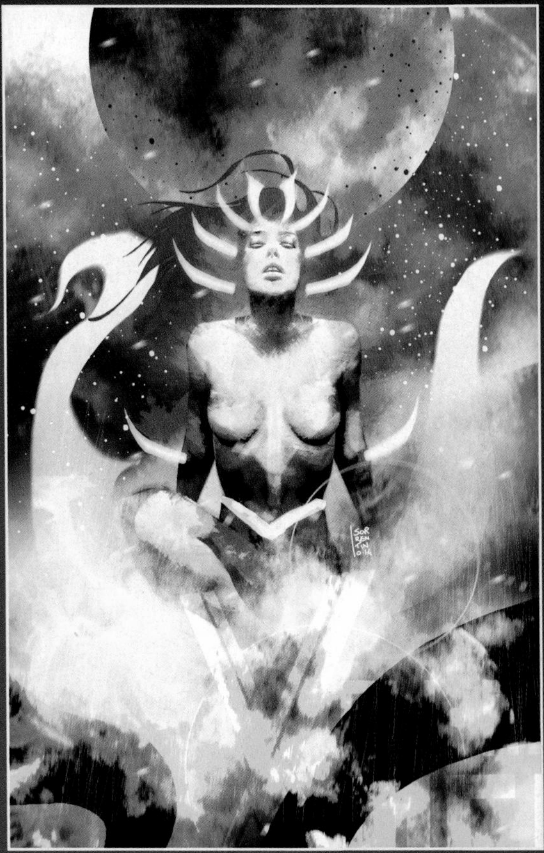

Guardians of the Galaxy #24 Cosmically Enhanced Variant
by Andrea Sorrentino

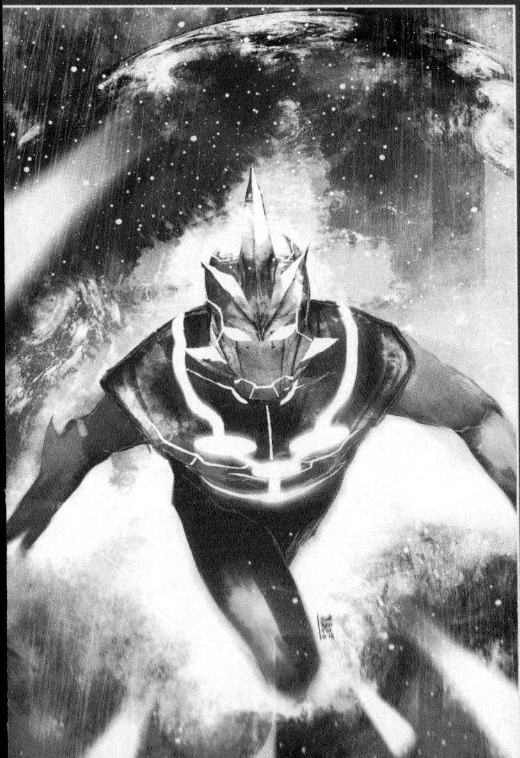

Nova #28 Cosmically Enhanced Variant
by Andrea Sorrentino

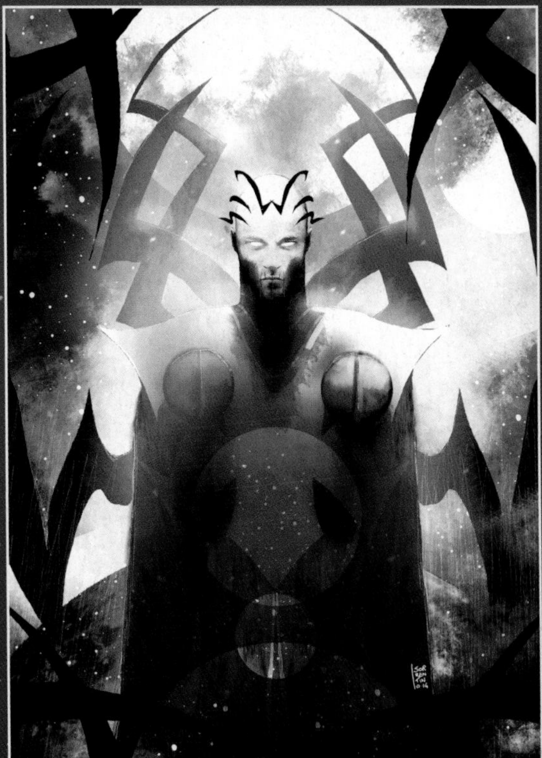

Legendary Star-Lord #9 Cosmically Enhanced Variant
by Andrea Sorrentino

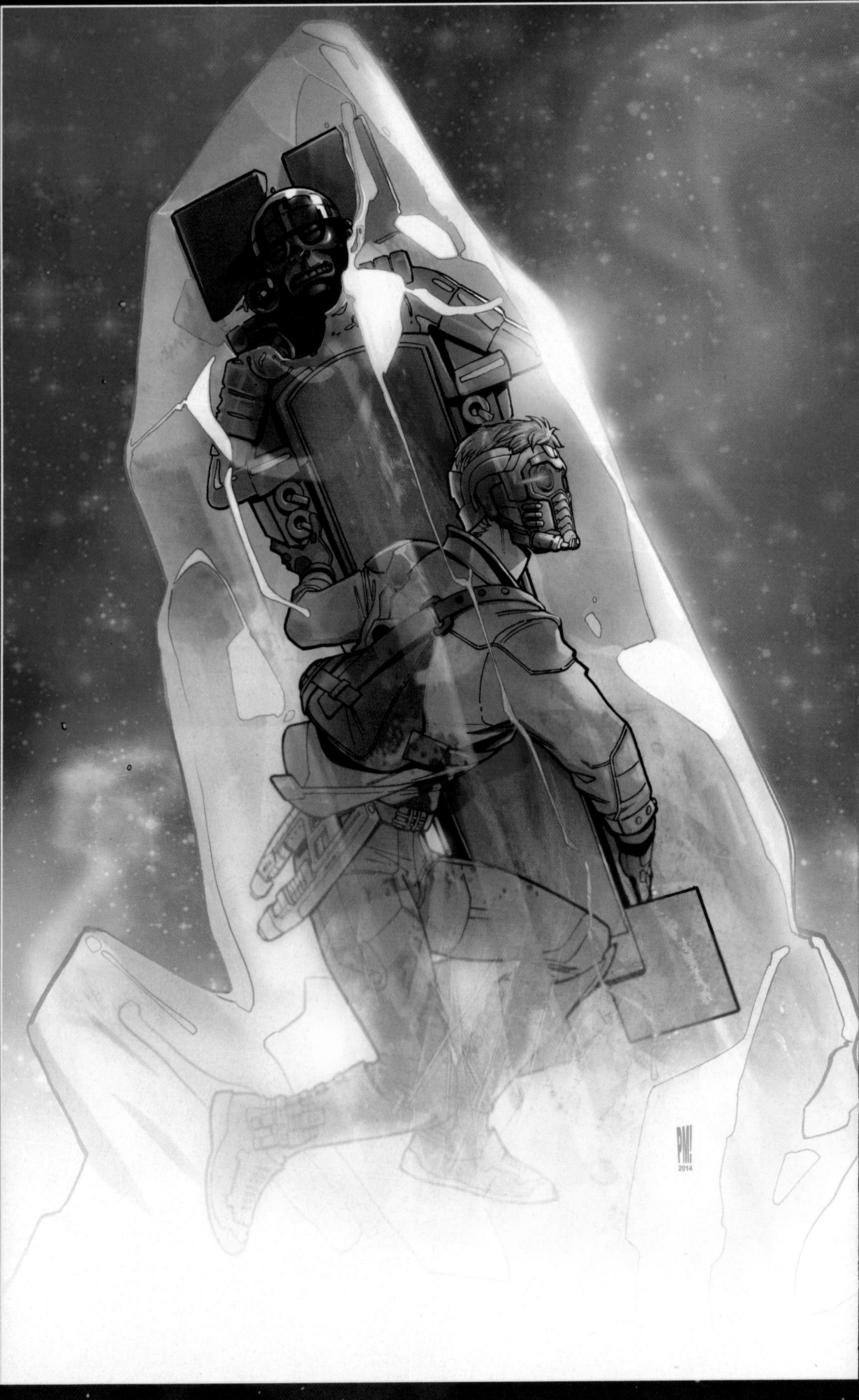

LEGENDARY STAR-LORD #10

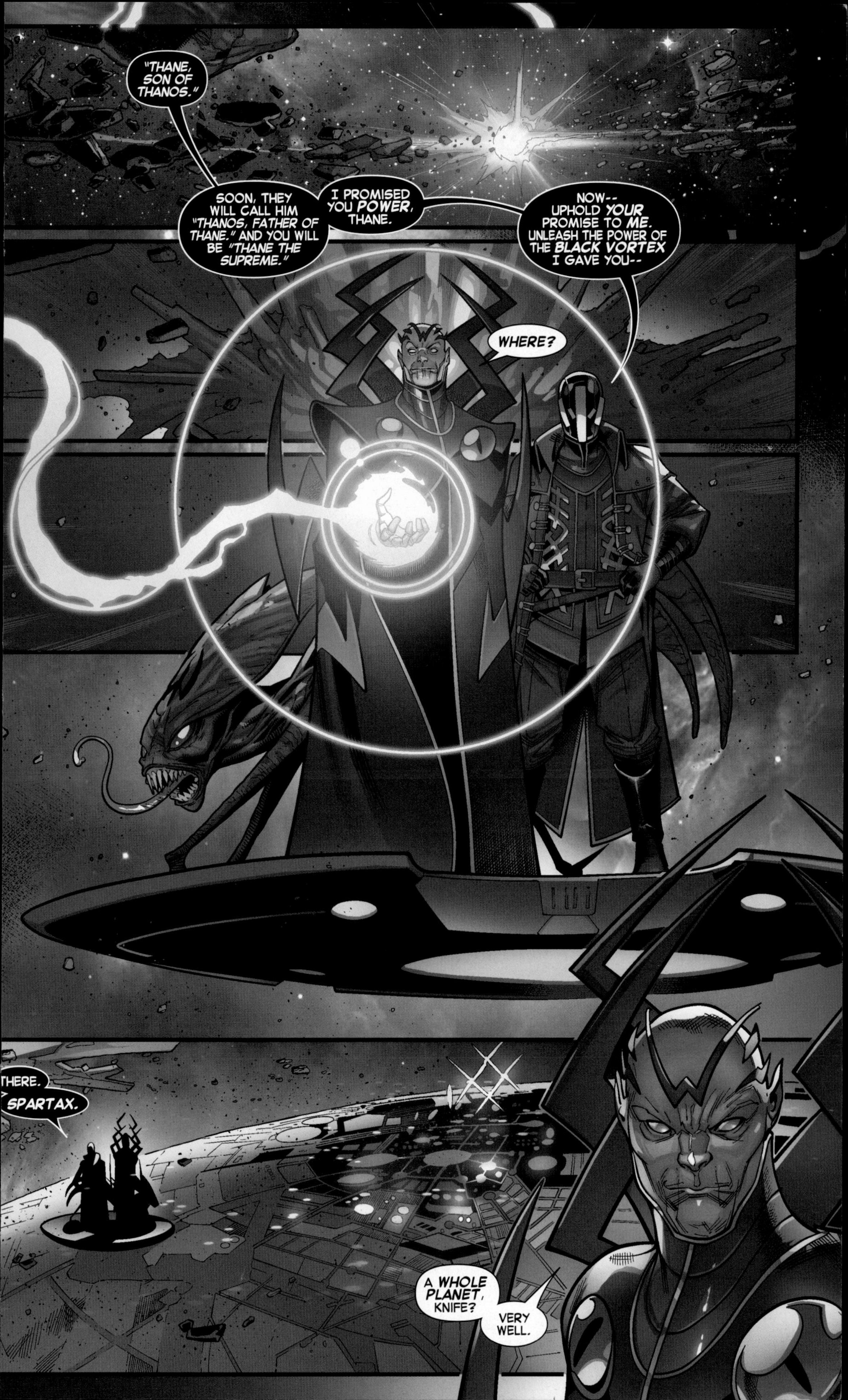
"THANE, SON OF THANOS."
SOON, THEY WILL CALL HIM "THANOS, FATHER OF THANE." AND YOU WILL BE "THANE THE SUPREME."
I PROMISED YOU POWER, THANE.
NOW-- UPHOLD YOUR PROMISE TO ME. UNLEASH THE POWER OF THE BLACK VORTEX I GAVE YOU--
WHERE?
THERE.
SPARTAX.
A WHOLE PLANET, KNIFE?
VERY WELL.

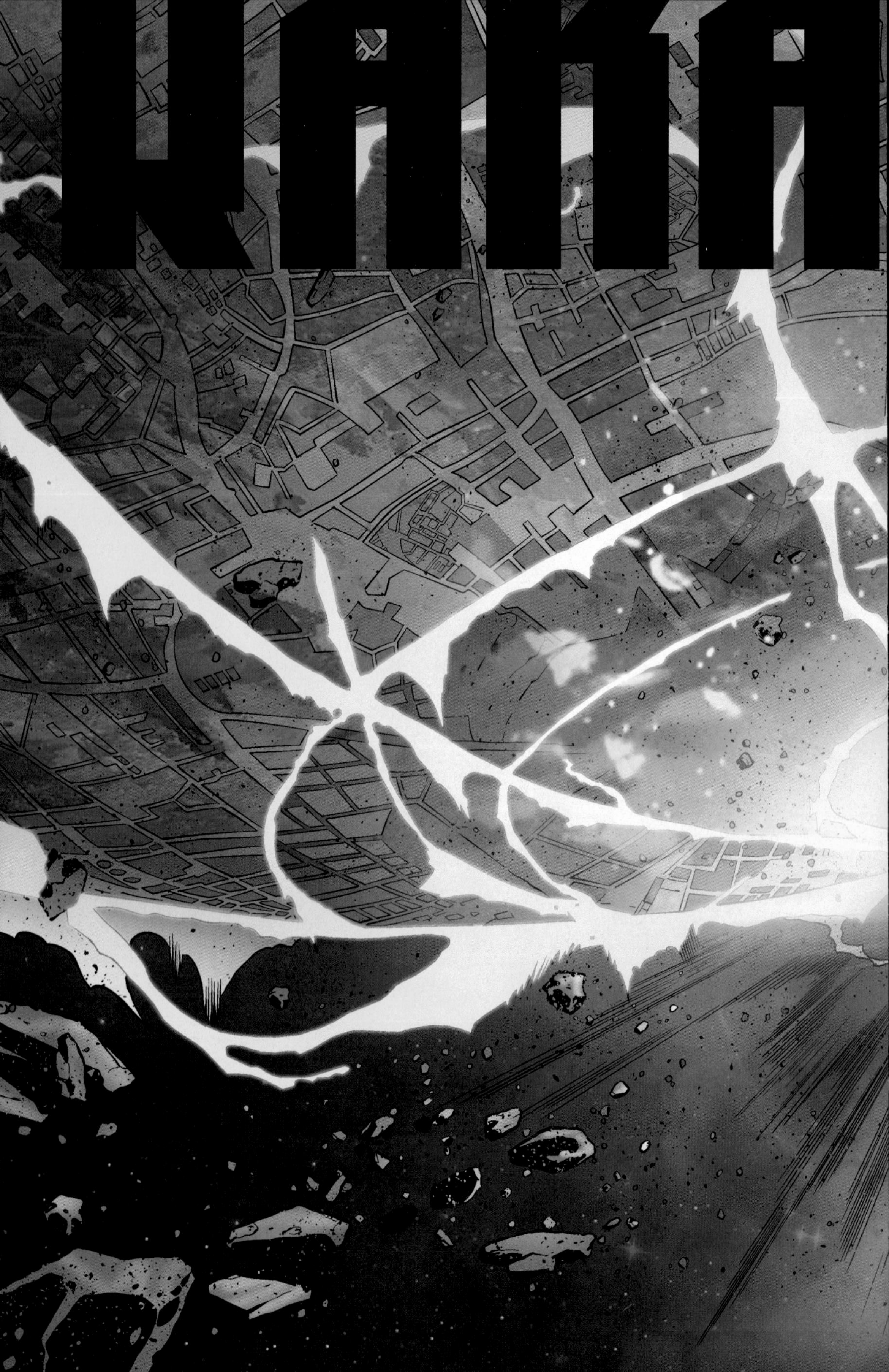
WAKA

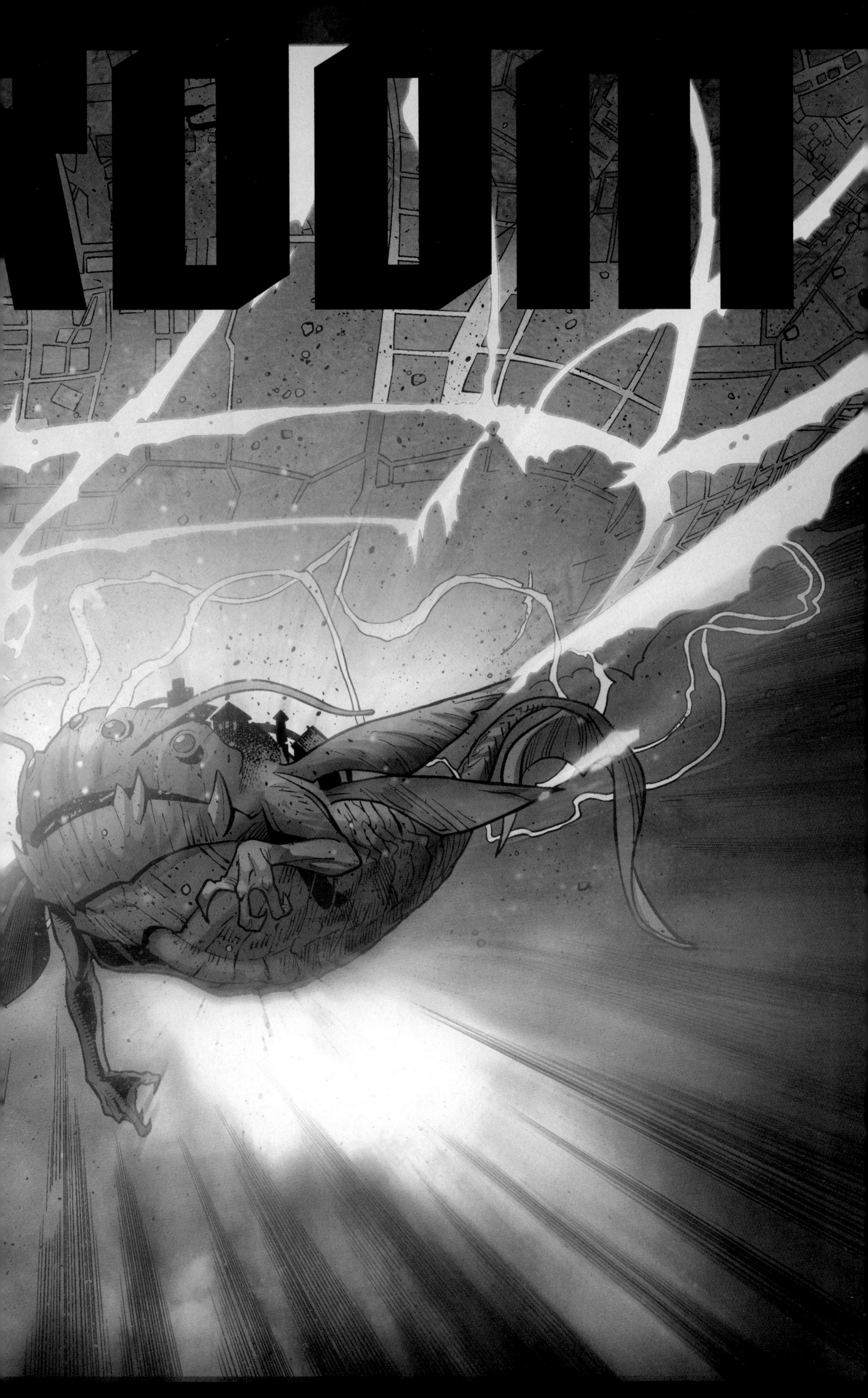

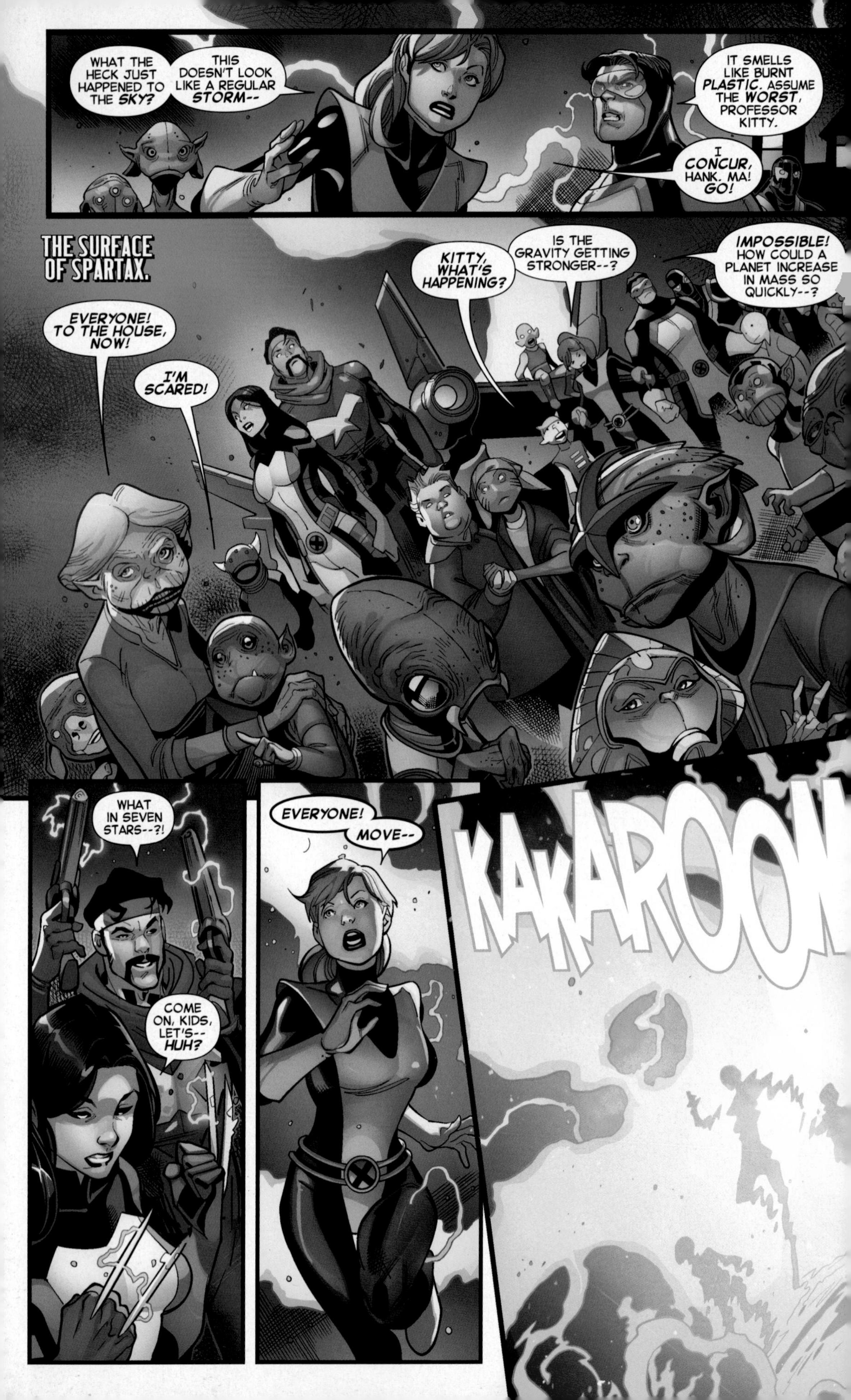

WHAT THE HECK JUST HAPPENED TO THE SKY?
THIS DOESN'T LOOK LIKE A REGULAR STORM--
IT SMELLS LIKE BURNT PLASTIC. ASSUME THE WORST, PROFESSOR KITTY.
I CONCUR, HANK. MA! GO!
THE SURFACE OF SPARTAX.
EVERYONE! TO THE HOUSE, NOW!
I'M SCARED!
KITTY, WHAT'S HAPPENING?
IS THE GRAVITY GETTING STRONGER--?
IMPOSSIBLE! HOW COULD A PLANET INCREASE IN MASS SO QUICKLY--?
WHAT IN SEVEN STARS--?!
COME ON, KIDS, LET'S-- HUH?
EVERYONE!
MOVE--
KAKAROOOM

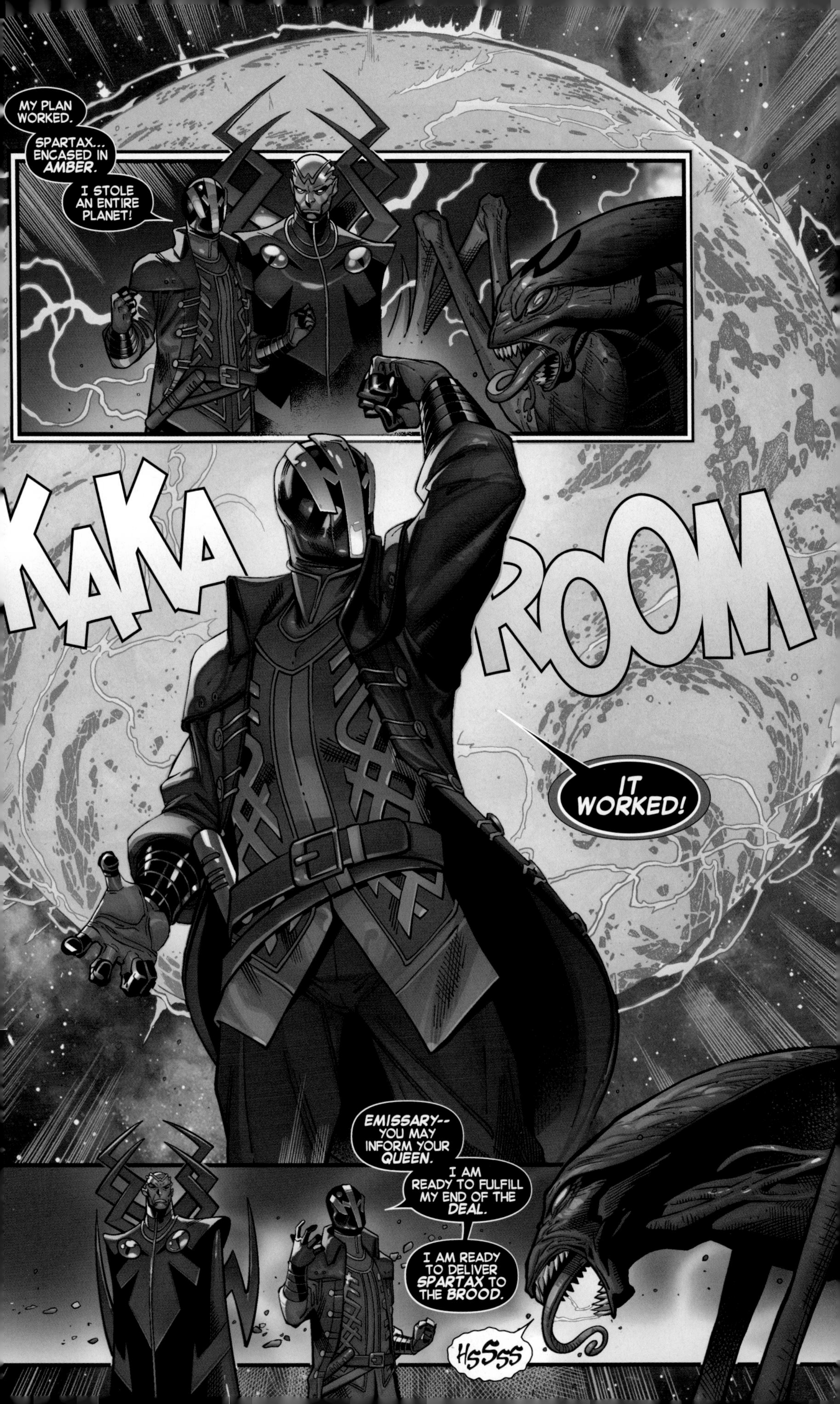
MY PLAN WORKED.
SPARTAX... ENCASED IN AMBER.
I STOLE AN ENTIRE PLANET!
KAKAROOM
IT WORKED!
EMISSARY-- YOU MAY INFORM YOUR QUEEN.
I AM READY TO FULFILL MY END OF THE DEAL.
I AM READY TO DELIVER SPARTAX TO THE BROOD.
HSSSS

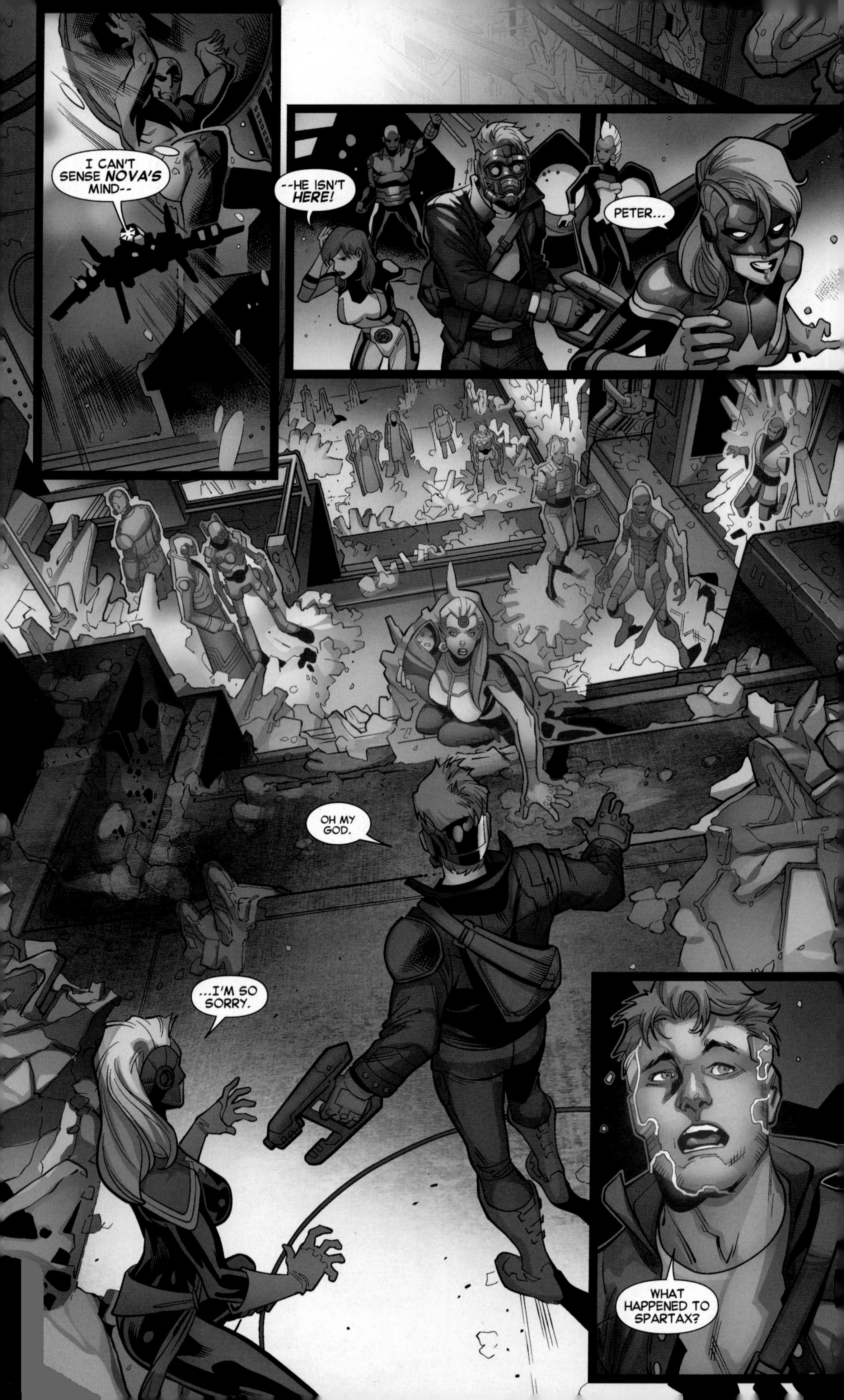
I CAN'T SENSE NOVA'S MIND--
--HE ISN'T HERE!
PETER...
OH MY GOD.
...I'M SO SORRY.
WHAT HAPPENED TO SPARTAX?

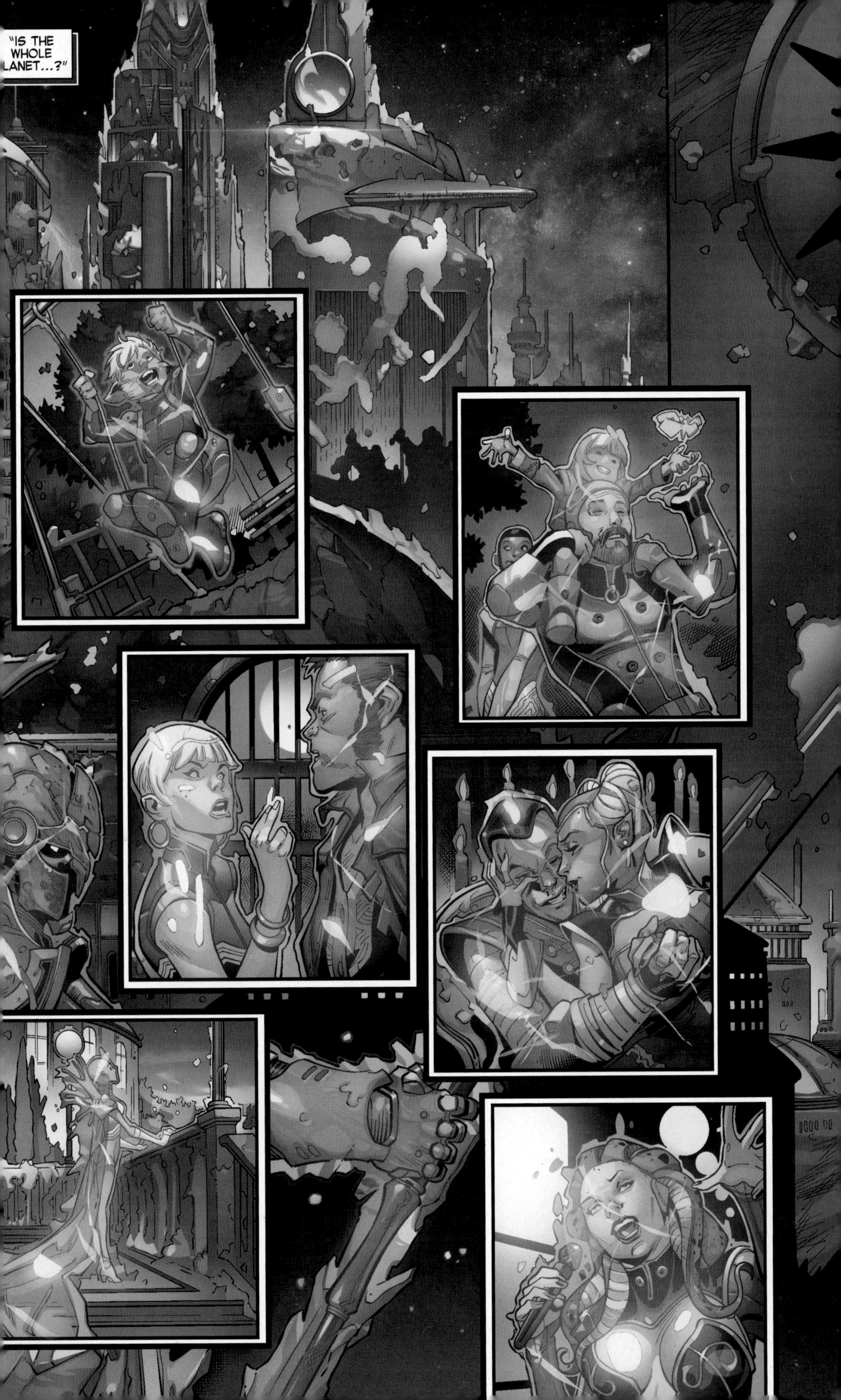
"IS THE WHOLE LANET...?"

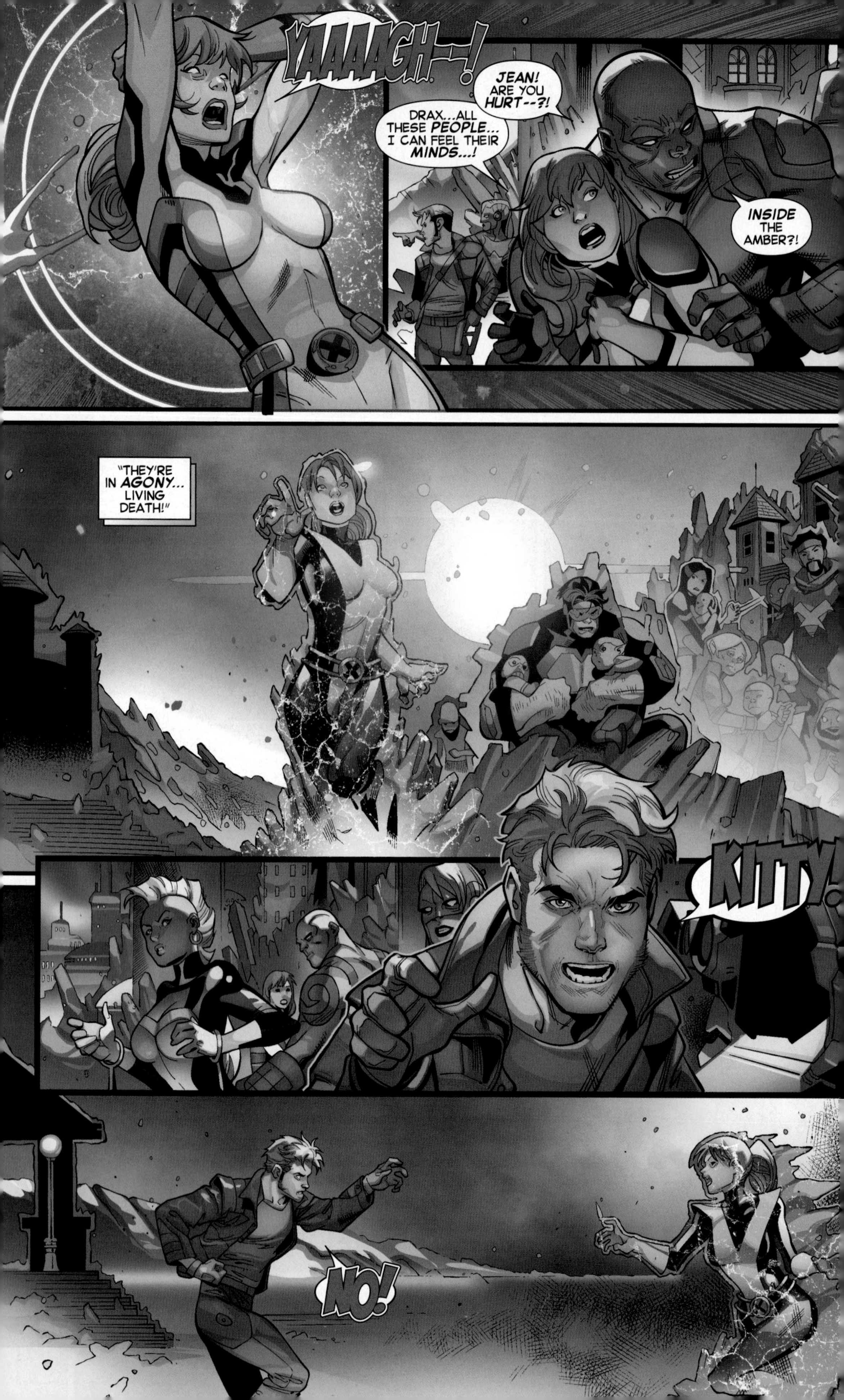
YAAAAGH--!
JEAN! ARE YOU HURT--?!
DRAX...ALL THESE PEOPLE... I CAN FEEL THEIR MINDS...!
INSIDE THE AMBER?!
"THEY'RE IN AGONY... LIVING DEATH!"
KITTY!
NO!

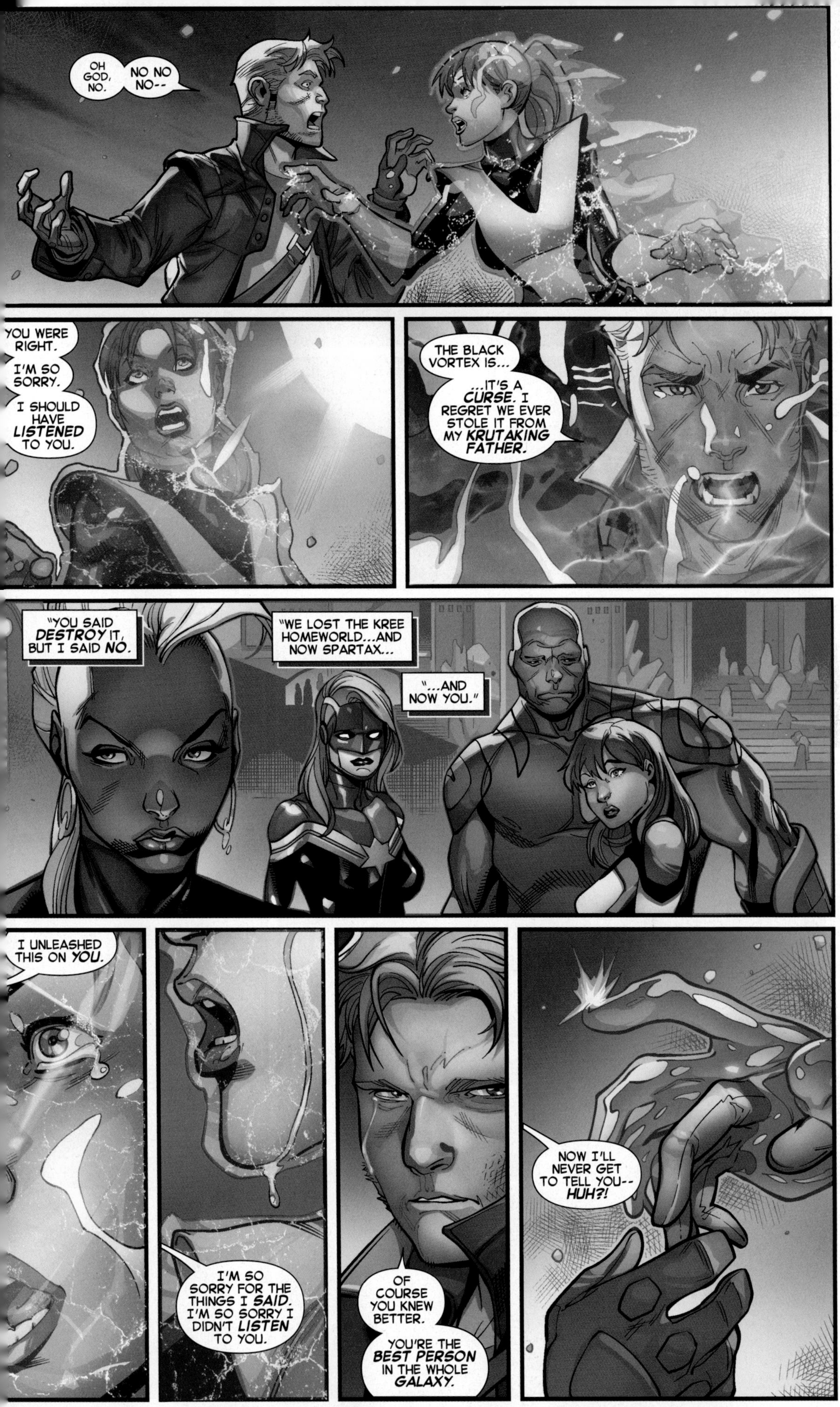
OH GOD, NO.
NO NO NO--
YOU WERE RIGHT.
I'M SO SORRY.
I SHOULD HAVE LISTENED TO YOU.
THE BLACK VORTEX IS...
...IT'S A CURSE. I REGRET WE EVER STOLE IT FROM MY KRUTAKING FATHER.
"YOU SAID DESTROY IT, BUT I SAID NO.
"WE LOST THE KREE HOMEWORLD...AND NOW SPARTAX...
"...AND NOW YOU."
I UNLEASHED THIS ON YOU.
I'M SO SORRY FOR THE THINGS I SAID. I'M SO SORRY I DIDN'T LISTEN TO YOU.
OF COURSE YOU KNEW BETTER.
YOU'RE THE BEST PERSON IN THE WHOLE GALAXY.
NOW I'LL NEVER GET TO TELL YOU-- HUH?!

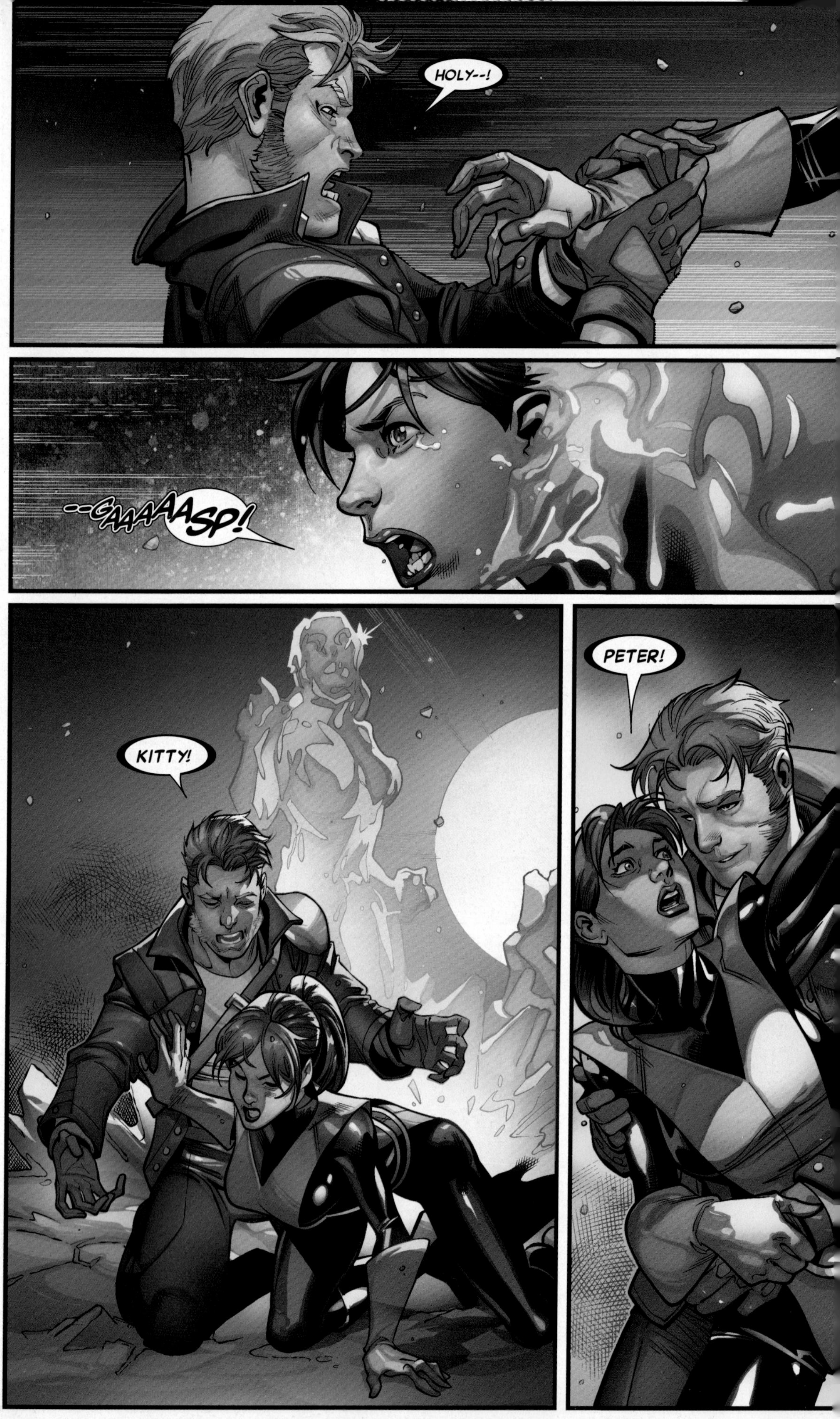
HOLY--!
--GAAAAASP!
KITTY!
PETER!

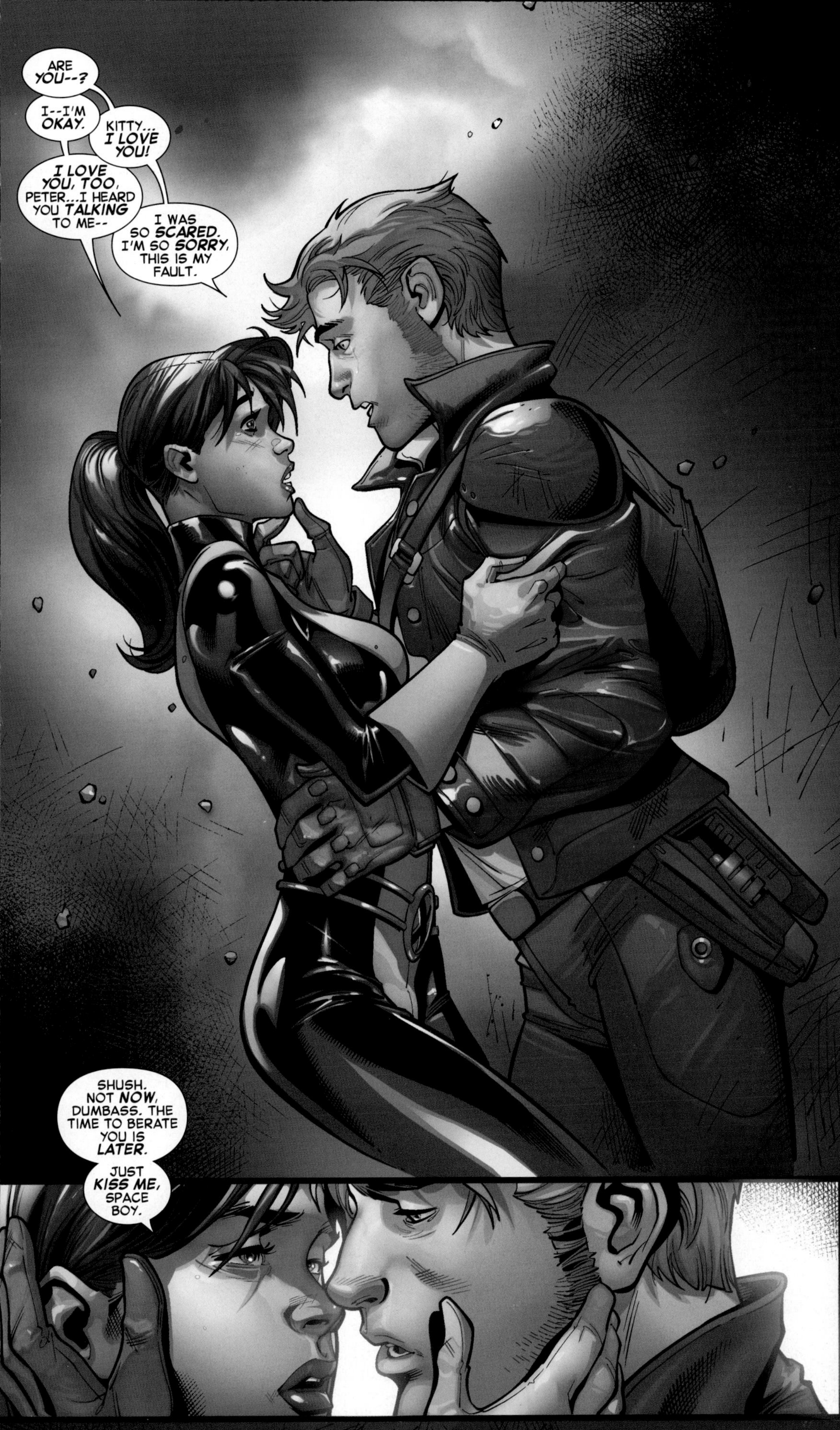
ARE YOU--?
I--I'M OKAY.
KITTY... I LOVE YOU!
I LOVE YOU, TOO, PETER...I HEARD YOU TALKING TO ME--
I WAS SO SCARED. I'M SO SORRY, THIS IS MY FAULT.
SHUSH. NOT NOW, DUMBASS. THE TIME TO BERATE YOU IS LATER.
JUST KISS ME, SPACE BOY.

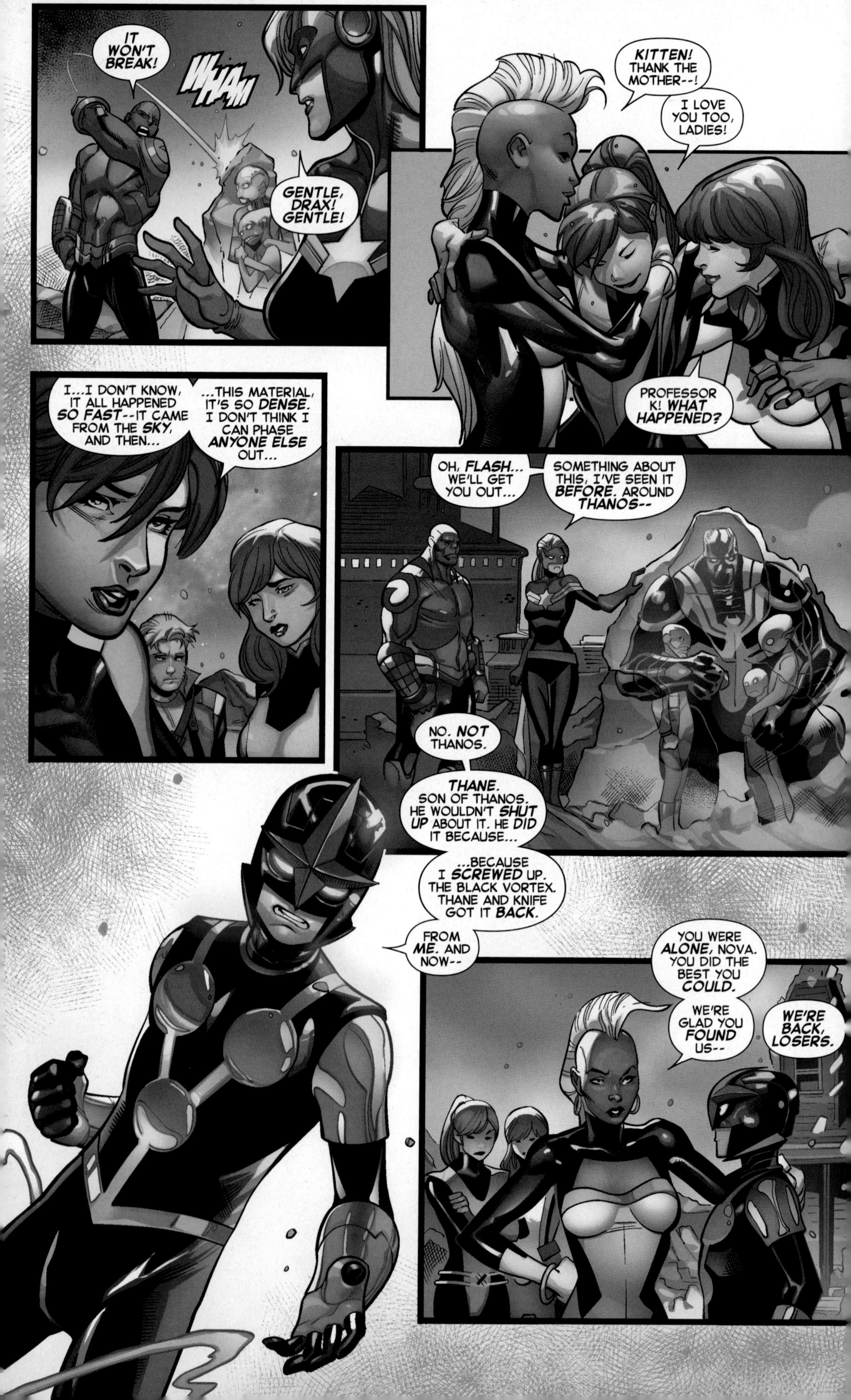
IT WON'T BREAK!
WHAM
GENTLE, DRAX! GENTLE!
KITTEN! THANK THE MOTHER--!
I LOVE YOU TOO, LADIES!
PROFESSOR K! WHAT HAPPENED?
I...I DON'T KNOW, IT ALL HAPPENED SO FAST--IT CAME FROM THE SKY, AND THEN...
...THIS MATERIAL, IT'S SO DENSE. I DON'T THINK I CAN PHASE ANYONE ELSE OUT...
OH, FLASH... WE'LL GET YOU OUT...
SOMETHING ABOUT THIS, I'VE SEEN IT BEFORE. AROUND THANOS--
NO. NOT THANOS.
THANE. SON OF THANOS. HE WOULDN'T SHUT UP ABOUT IT. HE DID IT BECAUSE...
...BECAUSE I SCREWED UP. THE BLACK VORTEX. THANE AND KNIFE GOT IT BACK.
FROM ME. AND NOW--
YOU WERE ALONE, NOVA. YOU DID THE BEST YOU COULD.
WE'RE GLAD YOU FOUND US--
WE'RE BACK, LOSERS.

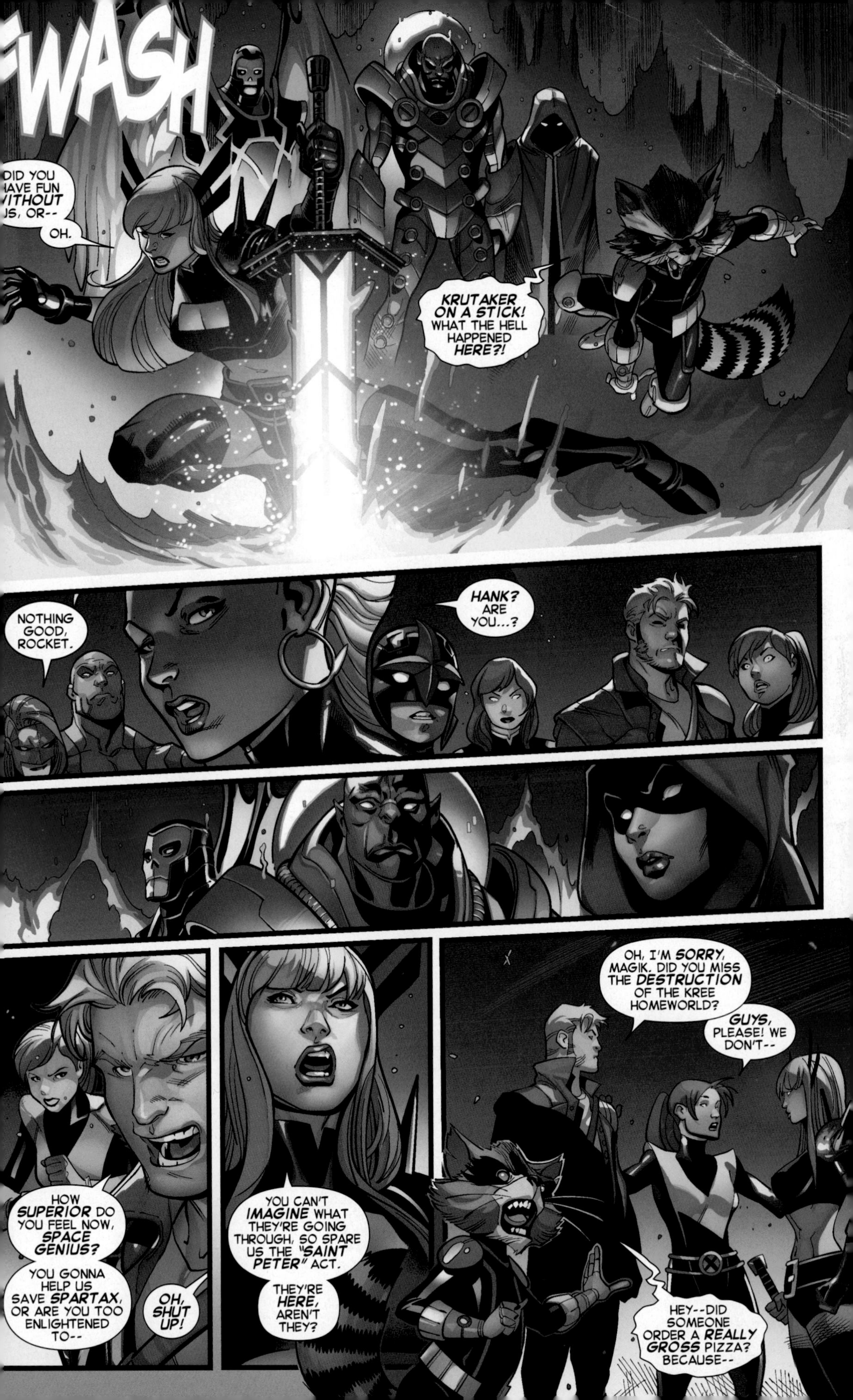
WASH
DID YOU HAVE FUN WITHOUT US, OR--
OH.
KRUTAKER ON A STICK! WHAT THE HELL HAPPENED HERE?!
NOTHING GOOD, ROCKET.
HANK? ARE YOU...?
HOW SUPERIOR DO YOU FEEL NOW, SPACE GENIUS?
YOU GONNA HELP US SAVE SPARTAX, OR ARE YOU TOO ENLIGHTENED TO--
OH, SHUT UP!
YOU CAN'T IMAGINE WHAT THEY'RE GOING THROUGH, SO SPARE US THE "SAINT PETER" ACT.
THEY'RE HERE, AREN'T THEY?
OH, I'M SORRY, MAGIK. DID YOU MISS THE DESTRUCTION OF THE KREE HOMEWORLD?
GUYS, PLEASE! WE DON'T--
HEY--DID SOMEONE ORDER A REALLY GROSS PIZZA? BECAUSE--

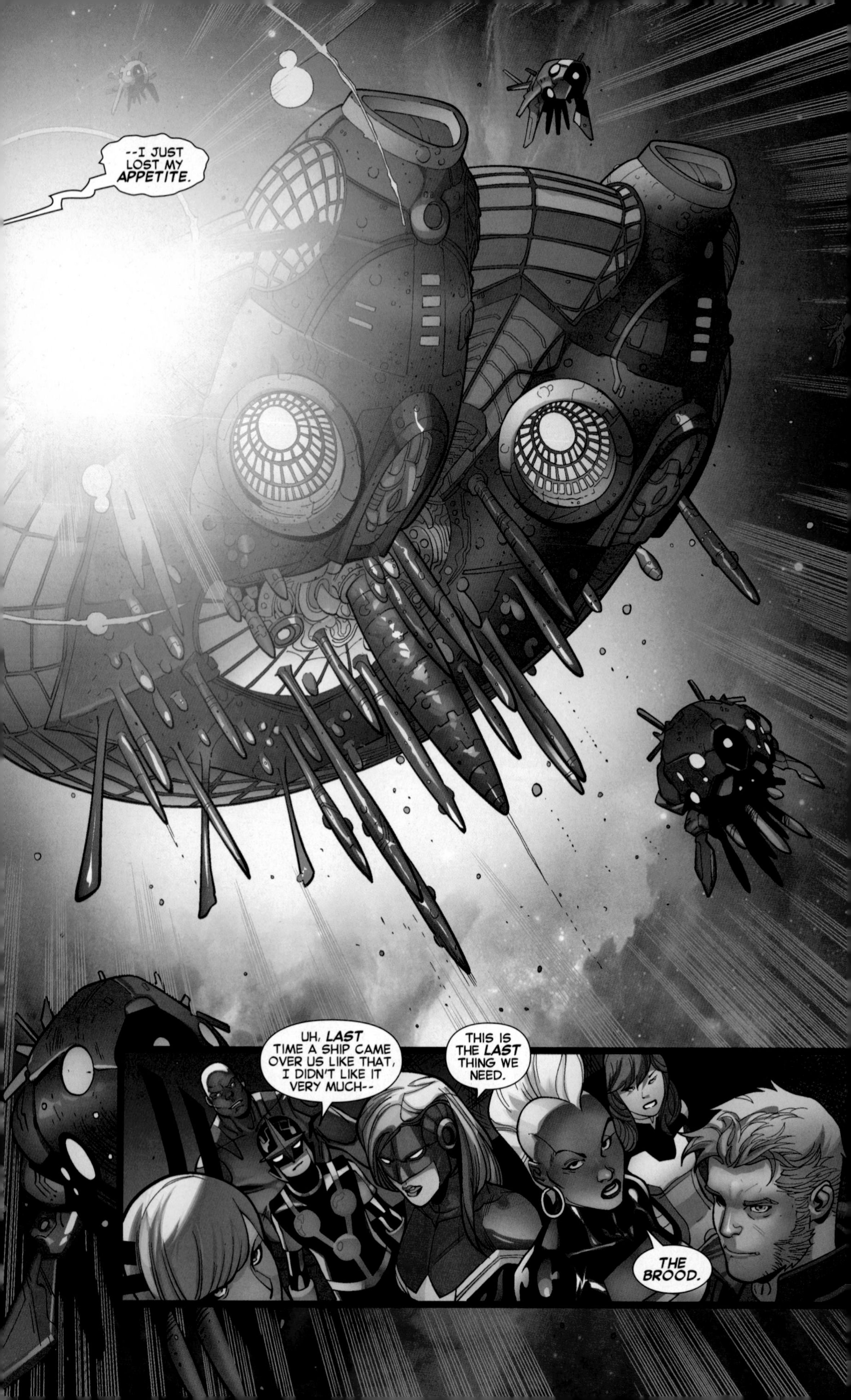
--I JUST LOST MY APPETITE.
UH, LAST TIME A SHIP CAME OVER US LIKE THAT, I DIDN'T LIKE IT VERY MUCH--
THIS IS THE LAST THING WE NEED.
THE BROOD.

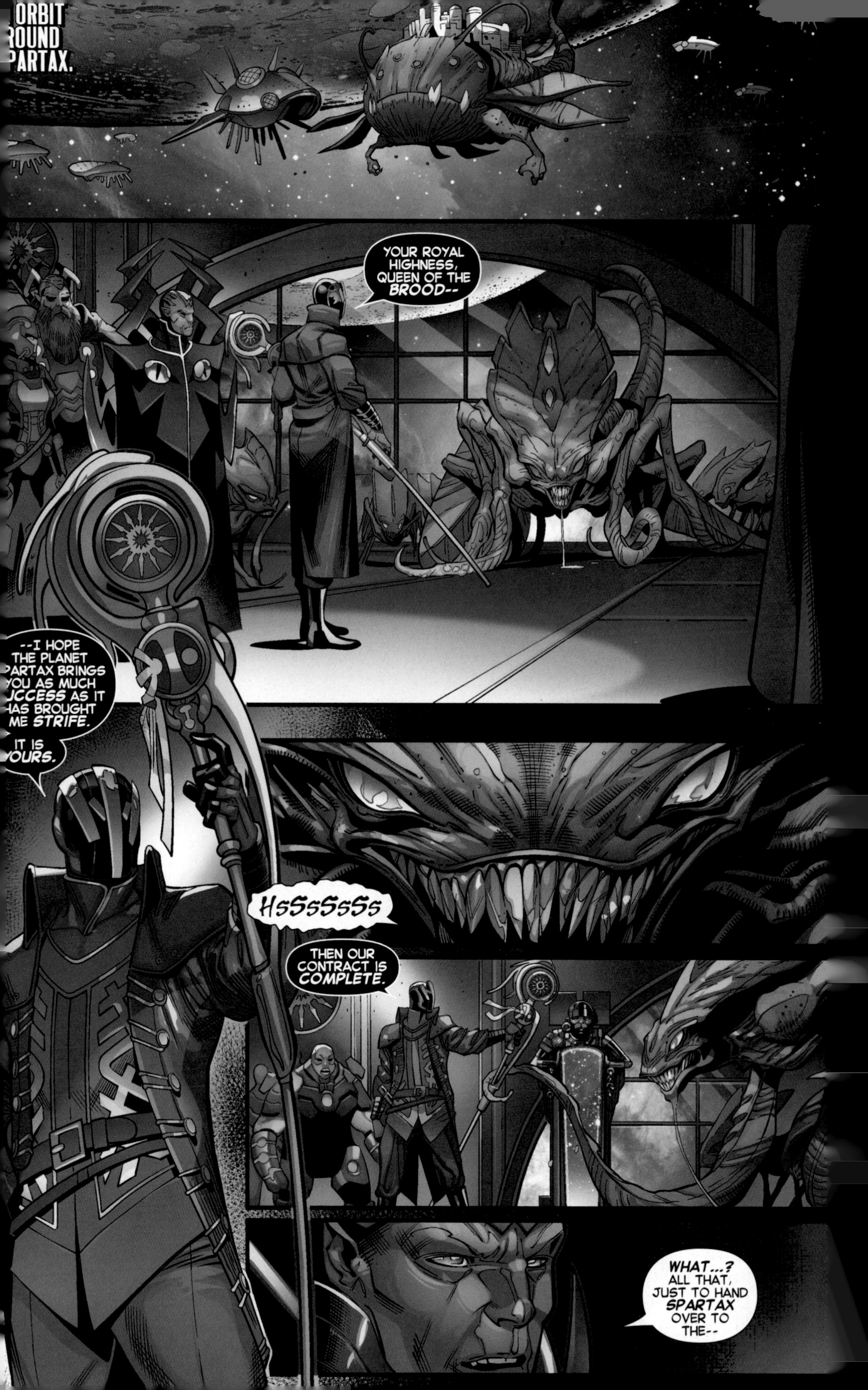
ORBIT
ROUND
PARTAX.
YOUR ROYAL HIGHNESS, QUEEN OF THE BROOD--
--I HOPE THE PLANET PARTAX BRINGS YOU AS MUCH UCCESS AS IT HAS BROUGHT ME STRIFE.
IT IS YOURS.
HsSsSsSs
THEN OUR CONTRACT IS COMPLETE.
WHAT...? ALL THAT, JUST TO HAND SPARTAX OVER TO THE--

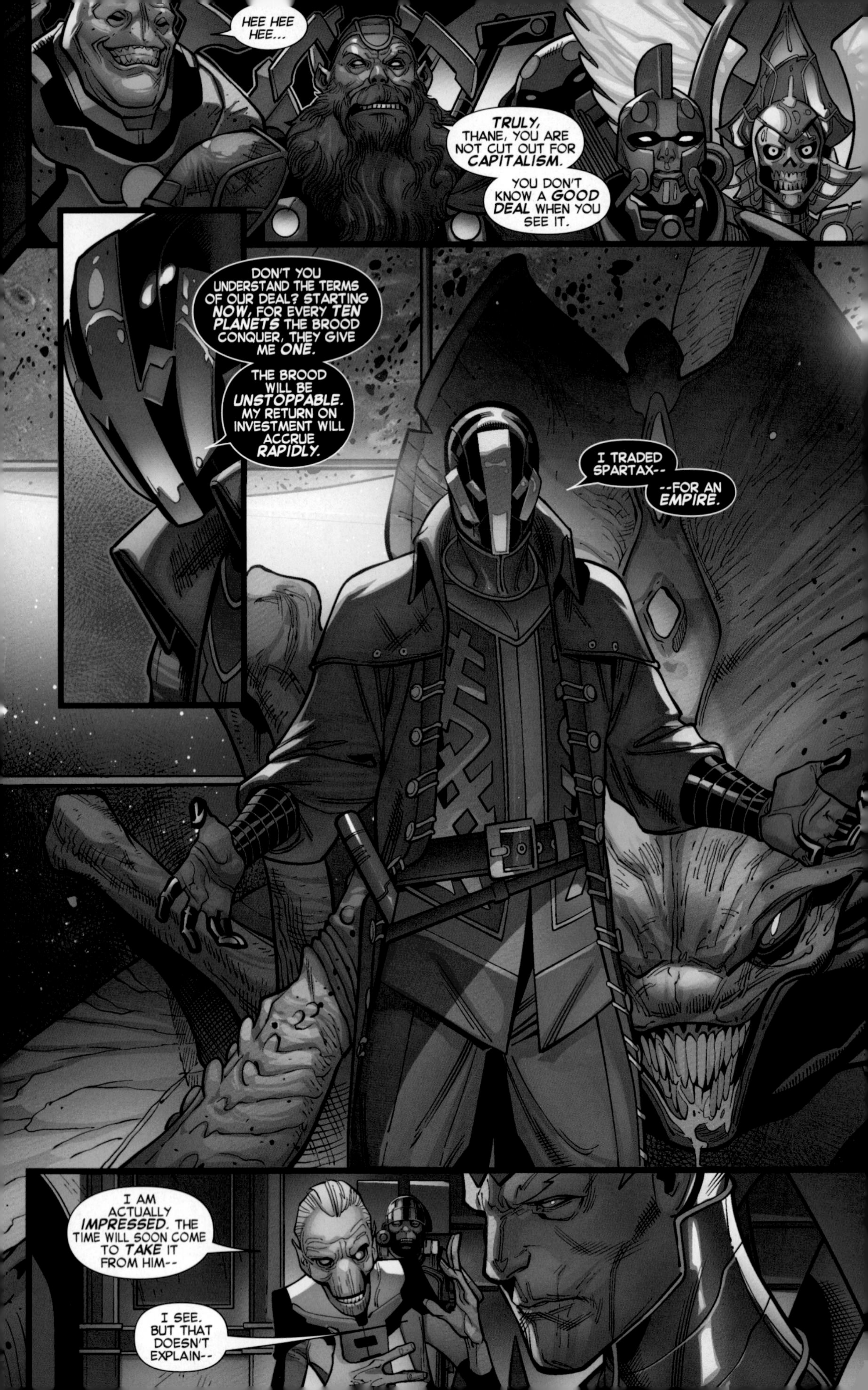

HEE HEE HEE...
TRULY, THANE, YOU ARE NOT CUT OUT FOR CAPITALISM.
YOU DON'T KNOW A GOOD DEAL WHEN YOU SEE IT.
DON'T YOU UNDERSTAND THE TERMS OF OUR DEAL? STARTING NOW, FOR EVERY TEN PLANETS THE BROOD CONQUER, THEY GIVE ME ONE.
THE BROOD WILL BE UNSTOPPABLE. MY RETURN ON INVESTMENT WILL ACCRUE RAPIDLY.
I TRADED SPARTAX--
--FOR AN EMPIRE.
I AM ACTUALLY IMPRESSED. THE TIME WILL SOON COME TO TAKE IT FROM HIM--
I SEE. BUT THAT DOESN'T EXPLAIN--

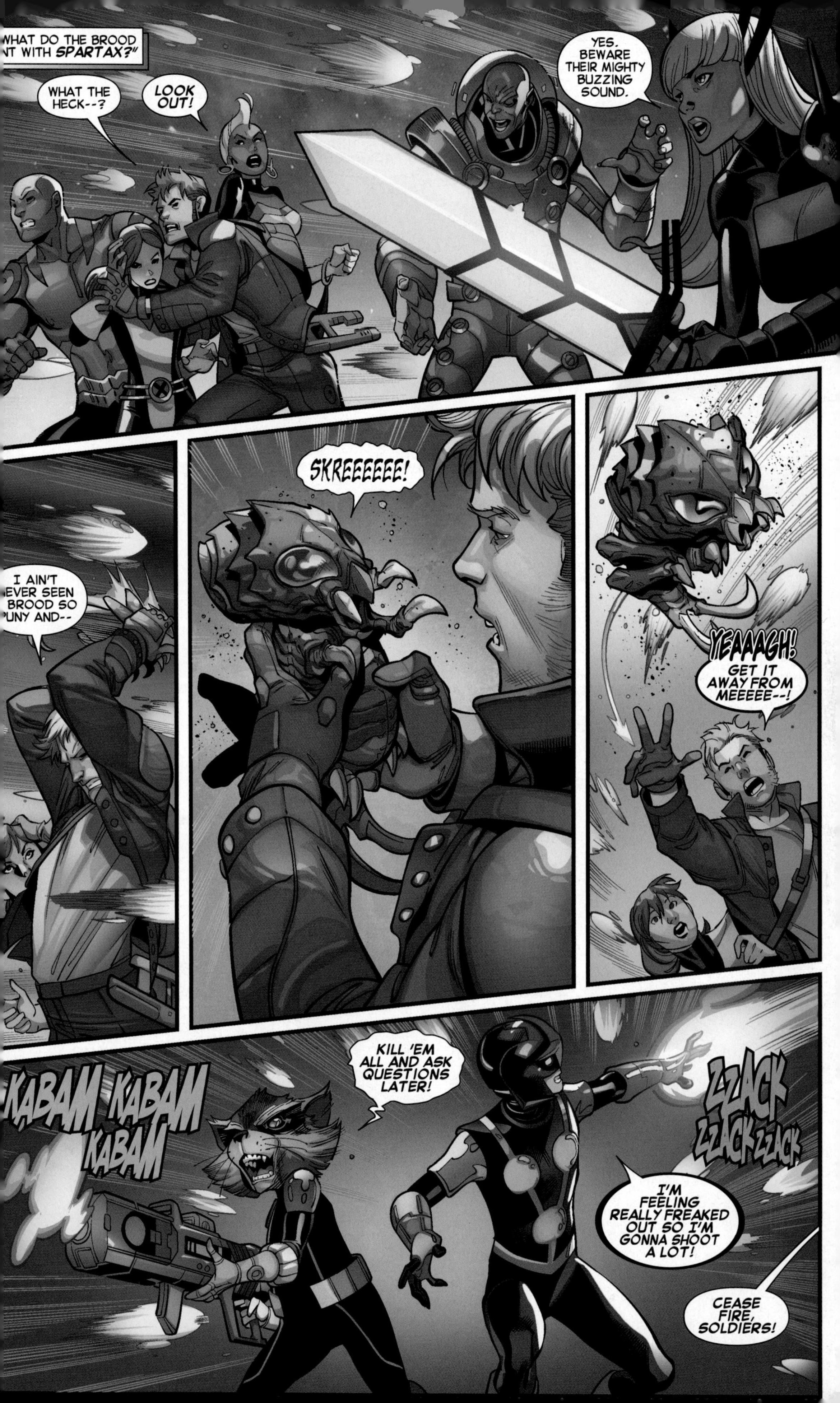
WHAT DO THE BROOD
NT WITH SPARTAX?"
WHAT THE HECK--?
LOOK OUT!
YES. BEWARE THEIR MIGHTY BUZZING SOUND.
I AIN'T
EVER SEEN
BROOD SO
PUNY AND--
SKREEEEEEE!
YEAAAGH!
GET IT AWAY FROM MEEEEE--!
KABAM KABAM KABAM
KILL 'EM ALL AND ASK QUESTIONS LATER!
ZZACK ZZACK ZZACK
I'M FEELING REALLY FREAKED OUT SO I'M GONNA SHOOT A LOT!
CEASE FIRE, SOLDIERS!

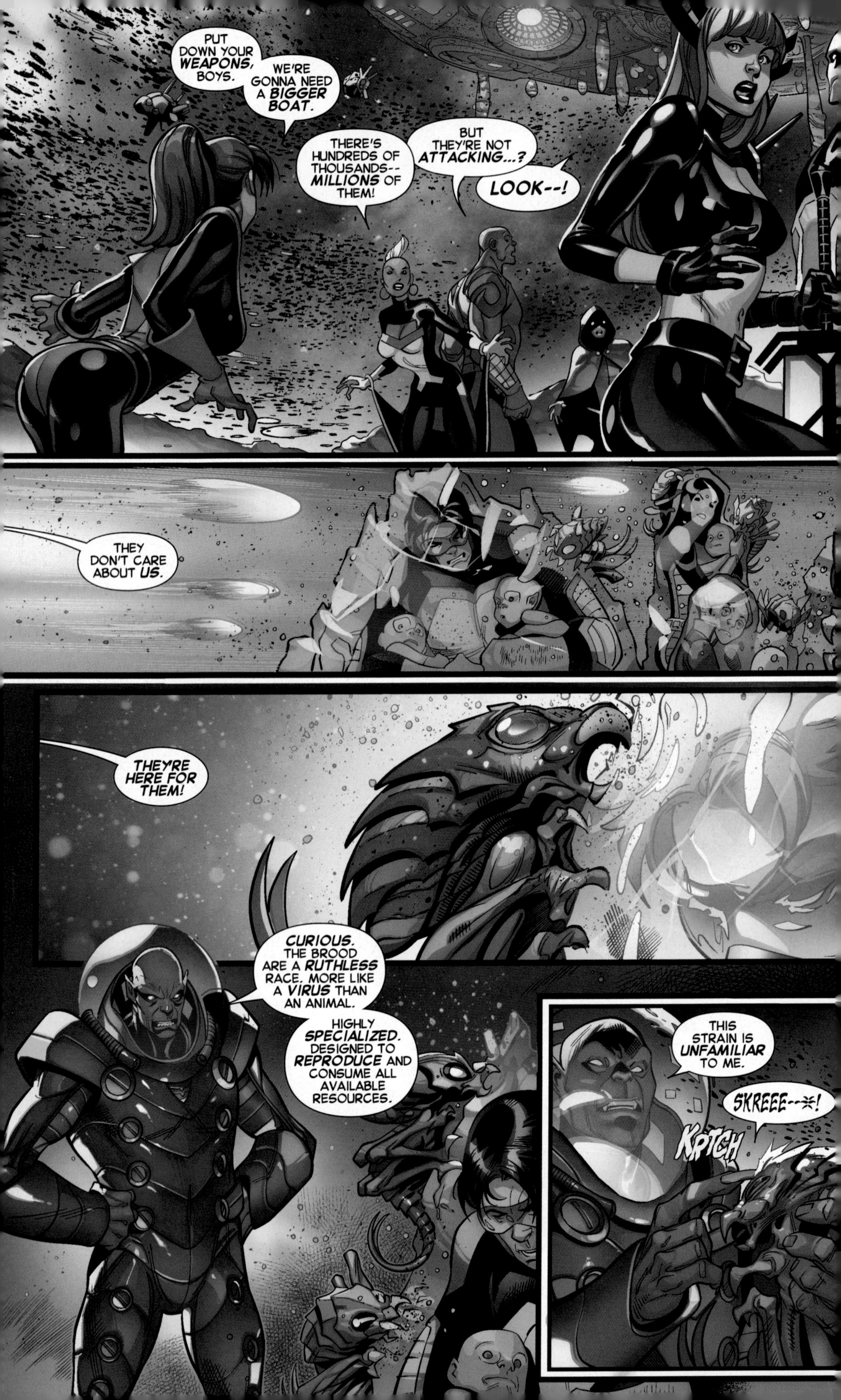

PUT DOWN YOUR WEAPONS, BOYS.
WE'RE GONNA NEED A BIGGER BOAT.
THERE'S HUNDREDS OF THOUSANDS-- MILLIONS OF THEM!
BUT THEY'RE NOT ATTACKING...?
LOOK--!
THEY DON'T CARE ABOUT US.
THEY'RE HERE FOR THEM!
CURIOUS. THE BROOD ARE A RUTHLESS RACE. MORE LIKE A VIRUS THAN AN ANIMAL.
HIGHLY SPECIALIZED. DESIGNED TO REPRODUCE AND CONSUME ALL AVAILABLE RESOURCES.
THIS STRAIN IS UNFAMILIAR TO ME.
SKREEE--*!
KRTCH

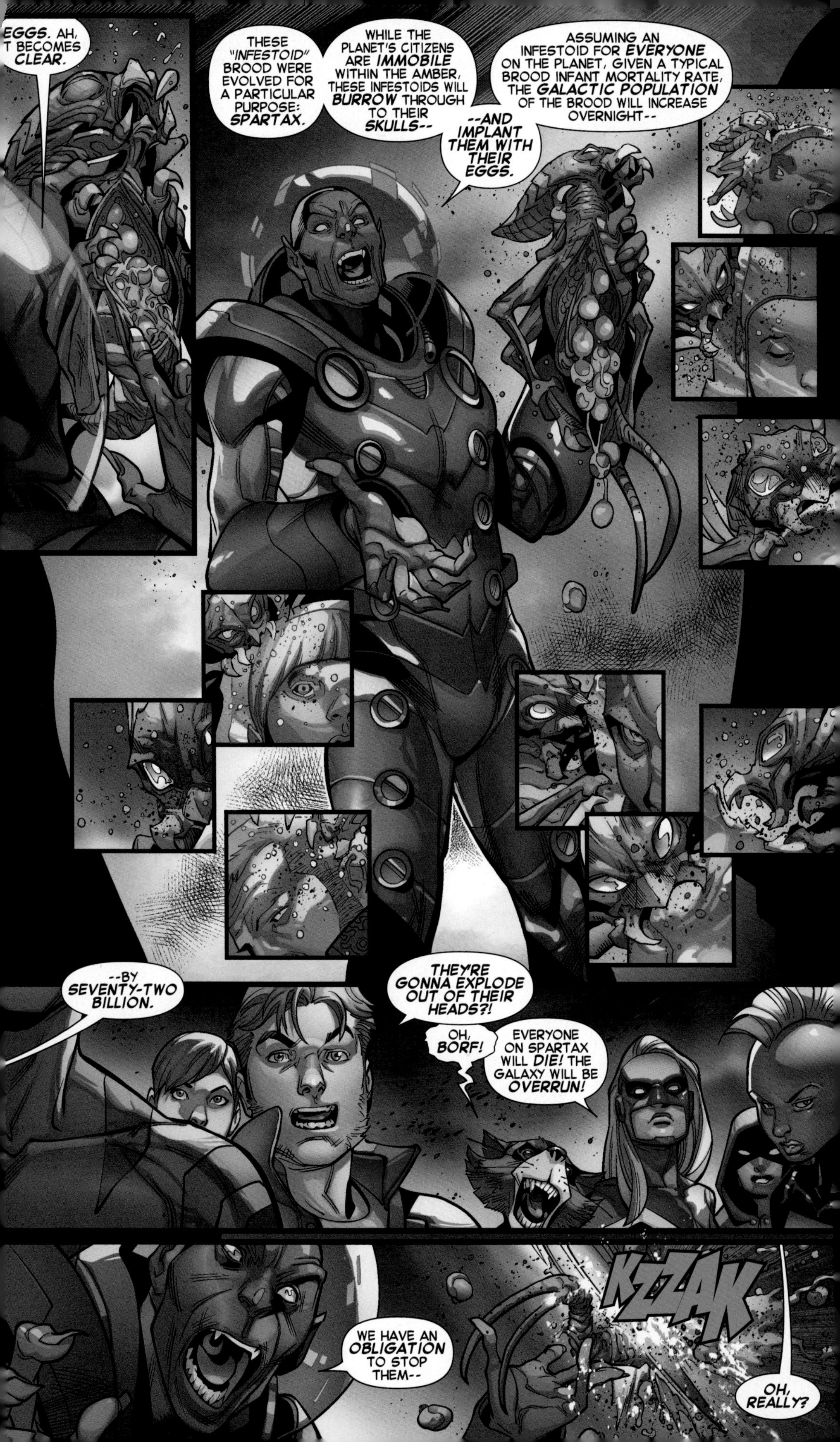
EGGS. AH, IT BECOMES CLEAR.
THESE "INFESTOID" BROOD WERE EVOLVED FOR A PARTICULAR PURPOSE: SPARTAX.
WHILE THE PLANET'S CITIZENS ARE IMMOBILE WITHIN THE AMBER, THESE INFESTOIDS WILL BURROW THROUGH TO THEIR SKULLS--
--AND IMPLANT THEM WITH THEIR EGGS.
ASSUMING AN INFESTOID FOR EVERYONE ON THE PLANET, GIVEN A TYPICAL BROOD INFANT MORTALITY RATE, THE GALACTIC POPULATION OF THE BROOD WILL INCREASE OVERNIGHT--
--BY SEVENTY-TWO BILLION.
THEY'RE GONNA EXPLODE OUT OF THEIR HEADS?!
OH, BORF!
EVERYONE ON SPARTAX WILL DIE! THE GALAXY WILL BE OVERRUN!
WE HAVE AN OBLIGATION TO STOP THEM--
KZZAK
OH, REALLY?

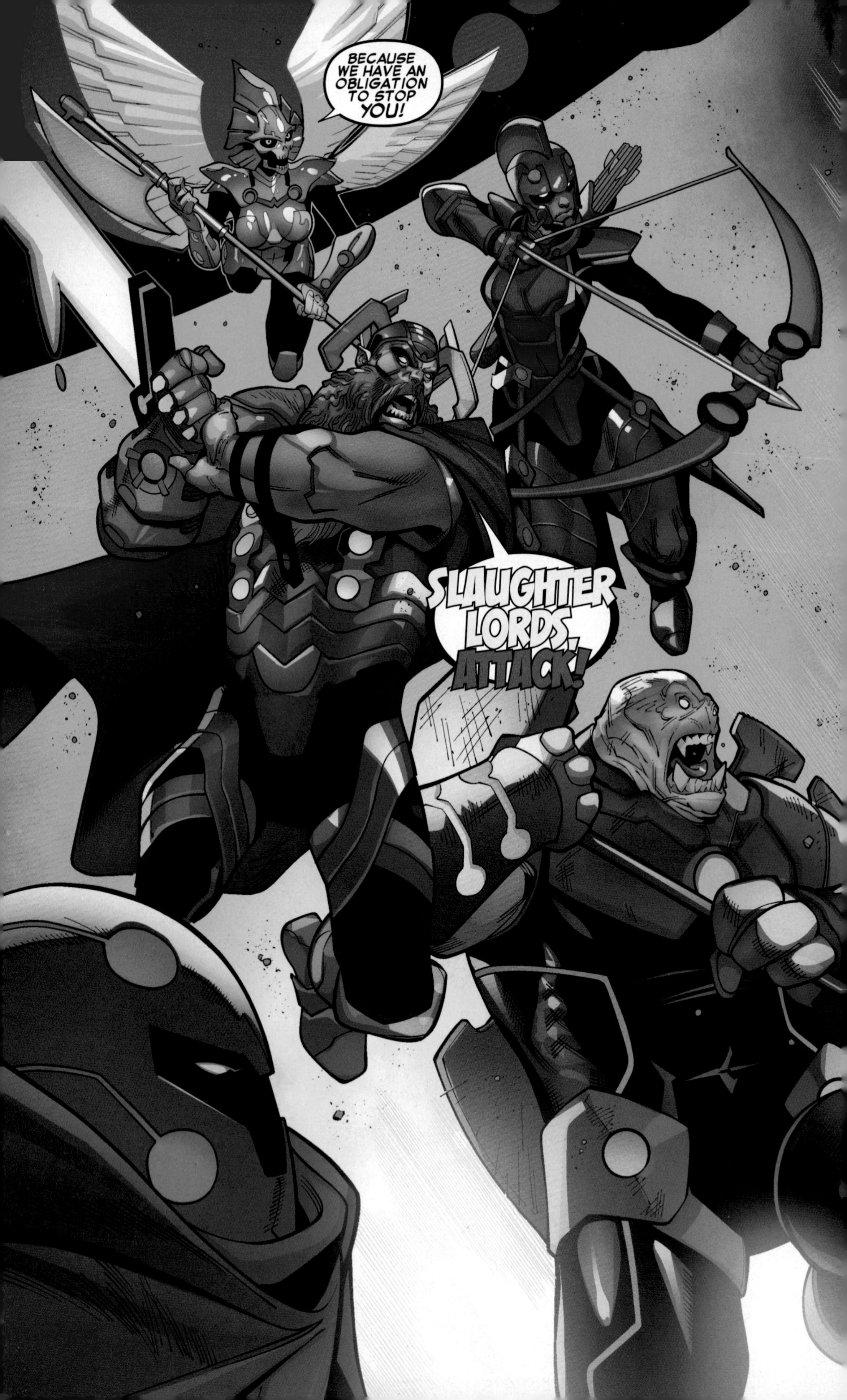
BECAUSE WE HAVE AN OBLIGATION TO STOP YOU!
SLAUGHTER LORDS, ATTACK!

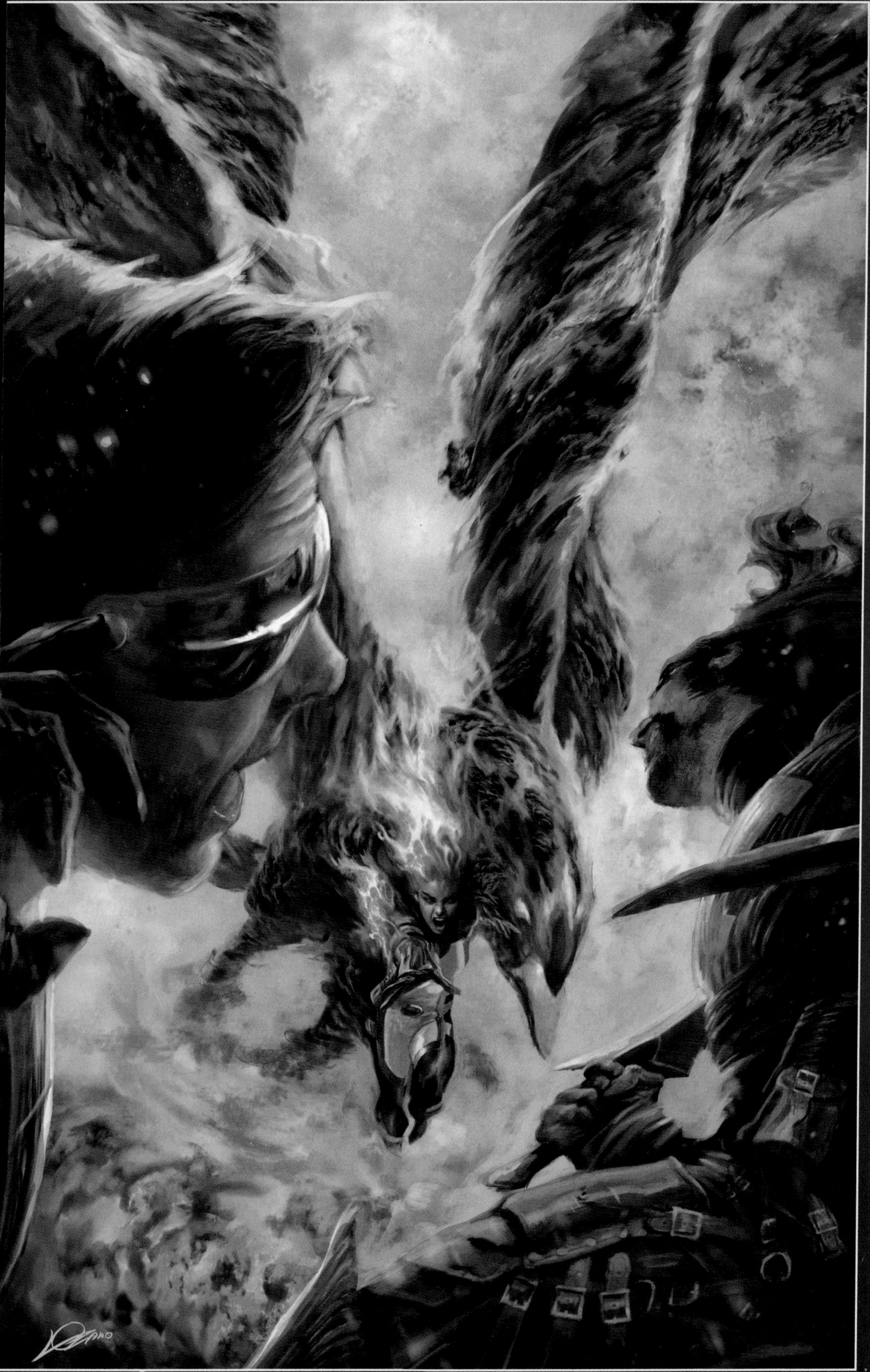

CYCLOPS #12

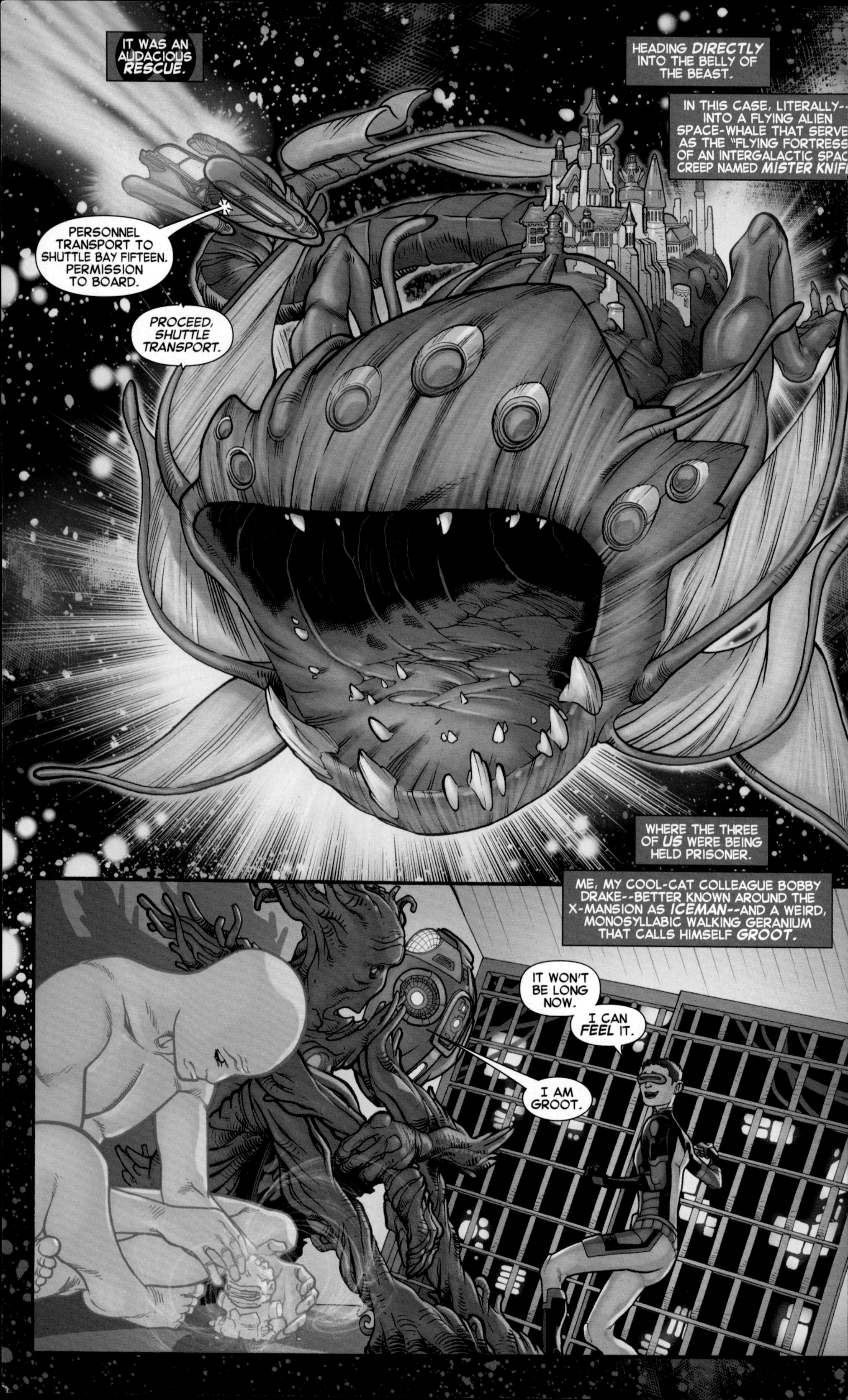
IT WAS AN AUDACIOUS RESCUE.
HEADING DIRECTLY INTO THE BELLY OF THE BEAST.
IN THIS CASE, LITERALLY--INTO A FLYING ALIEN SPACE-WHALE THAT SERVE AS THE "FLYING FORTRESS OF AN INTERGALACTIC SPAC CREEP NAMED MISTER KNIF
PERSONNEL TRANSPORT TO SHUTTLE BAY FIFTEEN. PERMISSION TO BOARD.
PROCEED, SHUTTLE TRANSPORT.
WHERE THE THREE OF US WERE BEING HELD PRISONER.
ME, MY COOL-CAT COLLEAGUE BOBBY DRAKE--BETTER KNOWN AROUND THE X-MANSION AS ICEMAN--AND A WEIRD, MONOSYLLABIC WALKING GERANIUM THAT CALLS HIMSELF GROOT.
IT WON'T BE LONG NOW.
I CAN FEEL IT.
I AM GROOT.

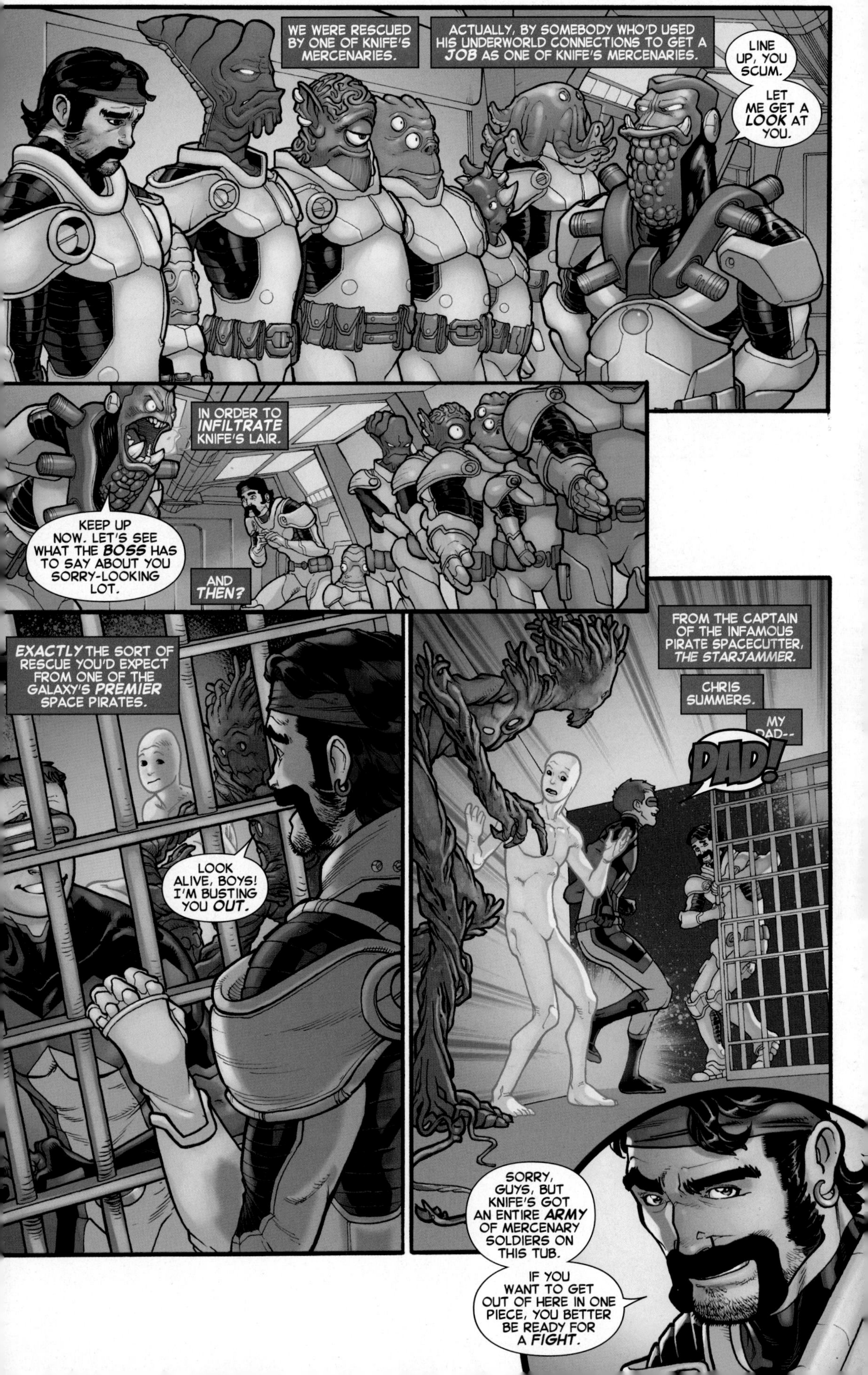
WE WERE RESCUED BY ONE OF KNIFE'S MERCENARIES.
ACTUALLY, BY SOMEBODY WHO'D USED HIS UNDERWORLD CONNECTIONS TO GET A JOB AS ONE OF KNIFE'S MERCENARIES.
LINE UP, YOU SCUM.
LET ME GET A LOOK AT YOU.
IN ORDER TO INFILTRATE KNIFE'S LAIR.
KEEP UP NOW. LET'S SEE WHAT THE BOSS HAS TO SAY ABOUT YOU SORRY-LOOKING LOT.
AND THEN?
EXACTLY THE SORT OF RESCUE YOU'D EXPECT FROM ONE OF THE GALAXY'S PREMIER SPACE PIRATES.
LOOK ALIVE, BOYS! I'M BUSTING YOU OUT.
FROM THE CAPTAIN OF THE INFAMOUS PIRATE SPACECUTTER, THE STARJAMMER.
CHRIS SUMMERS.
MY DAD--
DAD!
SORRY, GUYS, BUT KNIFE'S GOT AN ENTIRE ARMY OF MERCENARY SOLDIERS ON THIS TUB.
IF YOU WANT TO GET OUT OF HERE IN ONE PIECE, YOU BETTER BE READY FOR A FIGHT.

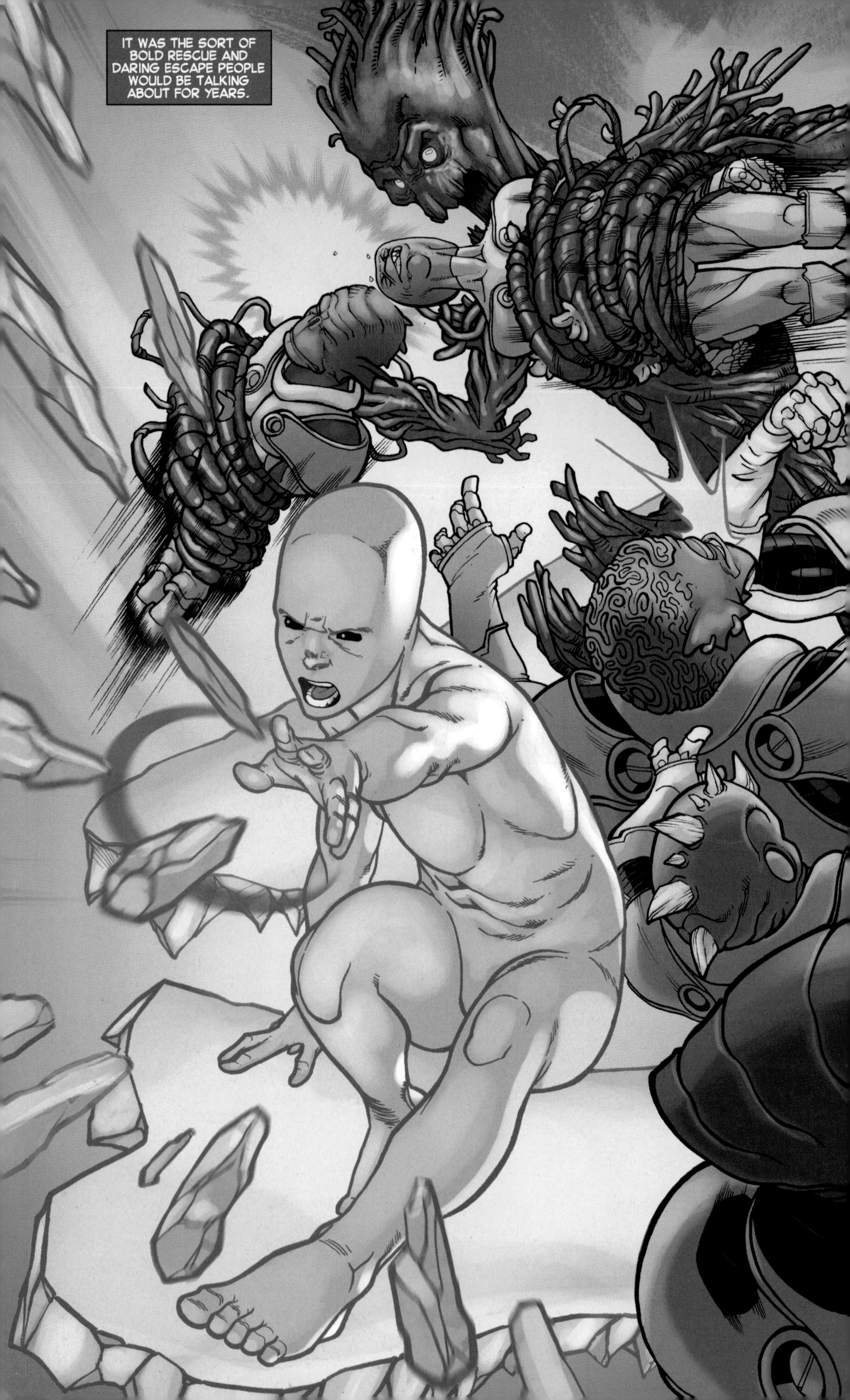
IT WAS THE SORT OF BOLD RESCUE AND DARING ESCAPE PEOPLE WOULD BE TALKING ABOUT FOR YEARS.

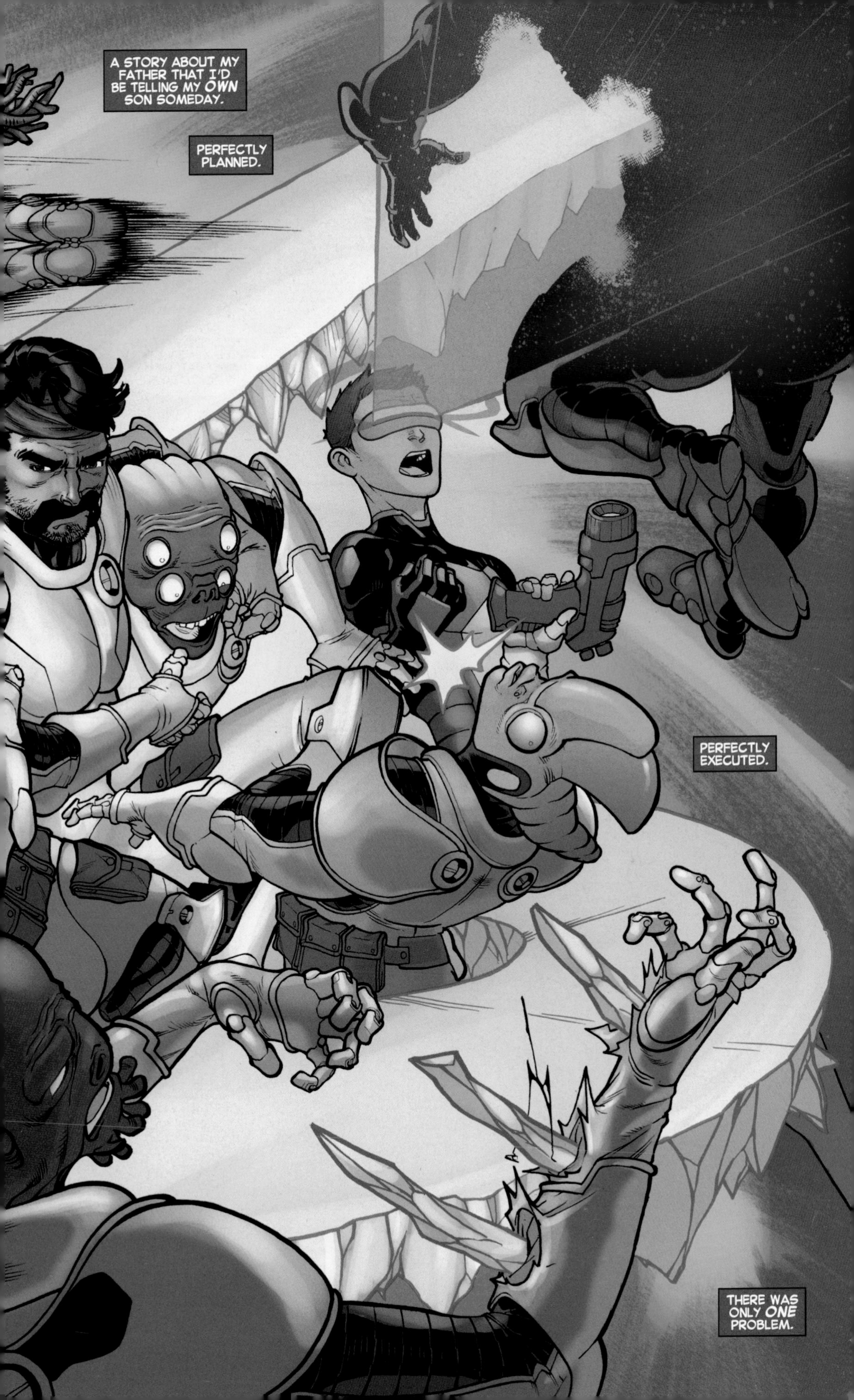
A STORY ABOUT MY FATHER THAT I'D BE TELLING MY OWN SON SOMEDAY.
PERFECTLY PLANNED.
PERFECTLY EXECUTED.
THERE WAS ONLY ONE PROBLEM.

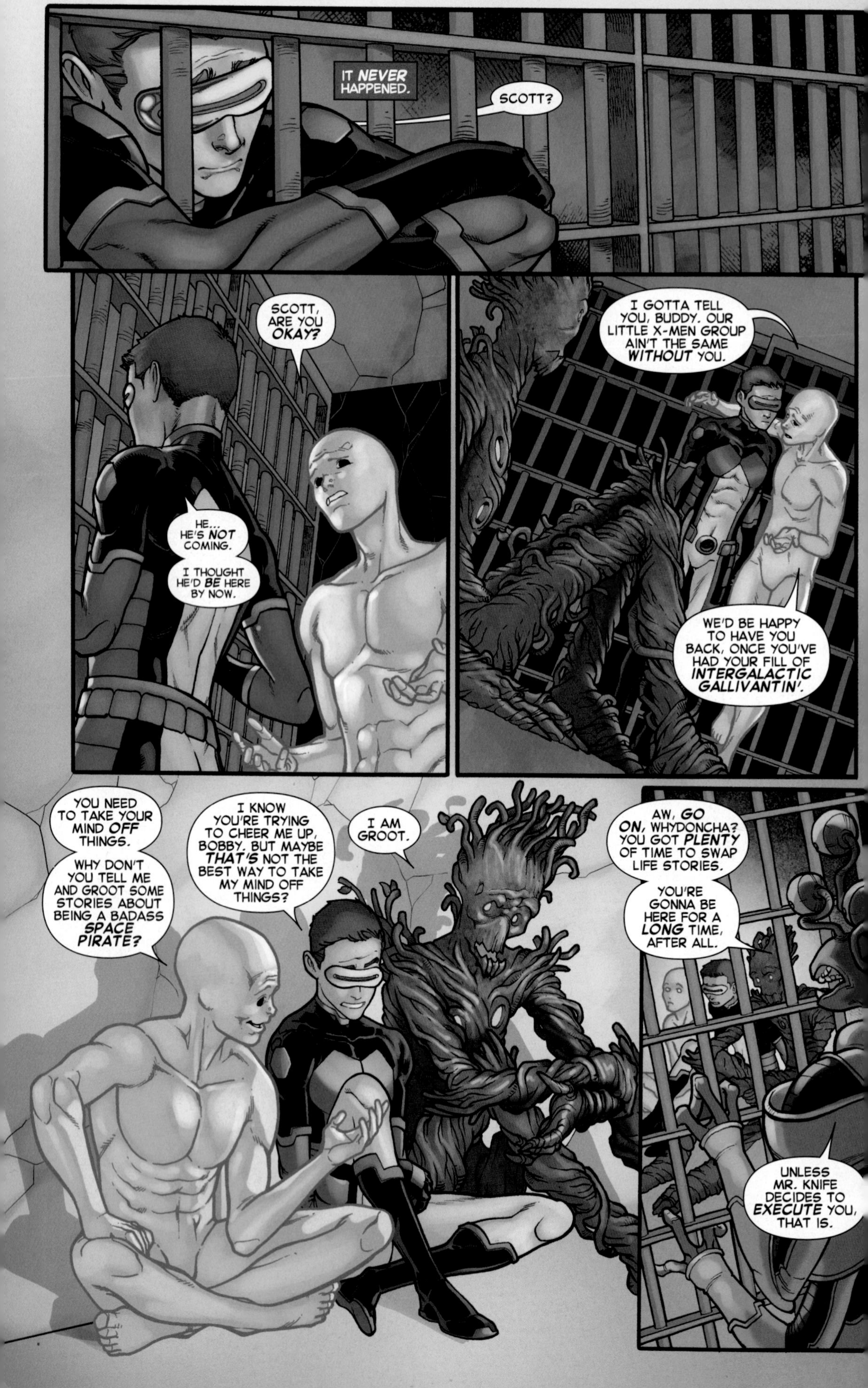
IT NEVER HAPPENED.
SCOTT?
SCOTT, ARE YOU OKAY?
HE... HE'S NOT COMING.
I THOUGHT HE'D BE HERE BY NOW.
I GOTTA TELL YOU, BUDDY. OUR LITTLE X-MEN GROUP AIN'T THE SAME WITHOUT YOU.
WE'D BE HAPPY TO HAVE YOU BACK, ONCE YOU'VE HAD YOUR FILL OF INTERGALACTIC GALLIVANTIN'.
YOU NEED TO TAKE YOUR MIND OFF THINGS.
WHY DON'T YOU TELL ME AND GROOT SOME STORIES ABOUT BEING A BADASS SPACE PIRATE?
I KNOW YOU'RE TRYING TO CHEER ME UP, BOBBY. BUT MAYBE THAT'S NOT THE BEST WAY TO TAKE MY MIND OFF THINGS?
I AM GROOT.
AW, GO ON, WHYDONCHA? YOU GOT PLENTY OF TIME TO SWAP LIFE STORIES.
YOU'RE GONNA BE HERE FOR A LONG TIME, AFTER ALL.
UNLESS MR. KNIFE DECIDES TO EXECUTE YOU, THAT IS.

SPEAKING OF WHICH, THE BOSS HAS CALLED AN ALL-HANDS MEETIN' TO ADDRESS SOME OF THE STUFF GOING DOWN.

I'D TELL YOU NOT TO MAKE *TROUBLE* WHILE I'M *GONE*--

--BUT WITH THIS CELL'S *POWER INHIBITORS* GOING, YOU COULDN'T IF YOU *TRIED*.

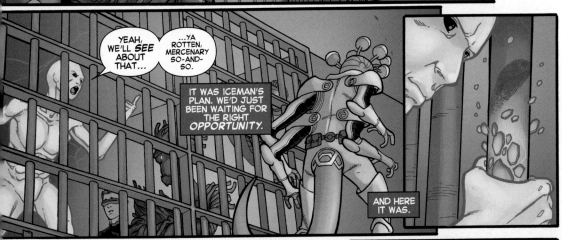

YEAH, WE'LL *SEE* ABOUT THAT...

...YA ROTTEN, MERCENARY SO-AND-SO.

IT WAS ICEMAN'S PLAN. WE'D JUST BEEN WAITING FOR THE RIGHT *OPPORTUNITY*.

AND HERE IT WAS.

YOU SURE YOU CAN *DO* THIS, SCOTT?

I CAN *BARELY* CHILL METAL WITH THESE INHIBITORS GOING. DOUBT YOUR OPTIC BLASTS ARE STRONG ENOUGH TO *KNOCK OVER* ANYTHING MORE THAN A *FEATHER*.

YEAH, WELL, I DON'T REMEMBER YOUR POWERS BEING *THIS* PRECISE, SCOTTY.

IT'S NOT ABOUT FORCE. IT'S ABOUT *PRECISION*.

THEY *WEREN'T*.

I *COULD* TELL BOBBY ABOUT HOW MUCH *TRAINING* I DID WITH MY DAD.

FINGERPRINT RECOGNIZED.

INHIBITORS DEACTIVATED.

BUT SUDDENLY OUR TIME WAS UP!

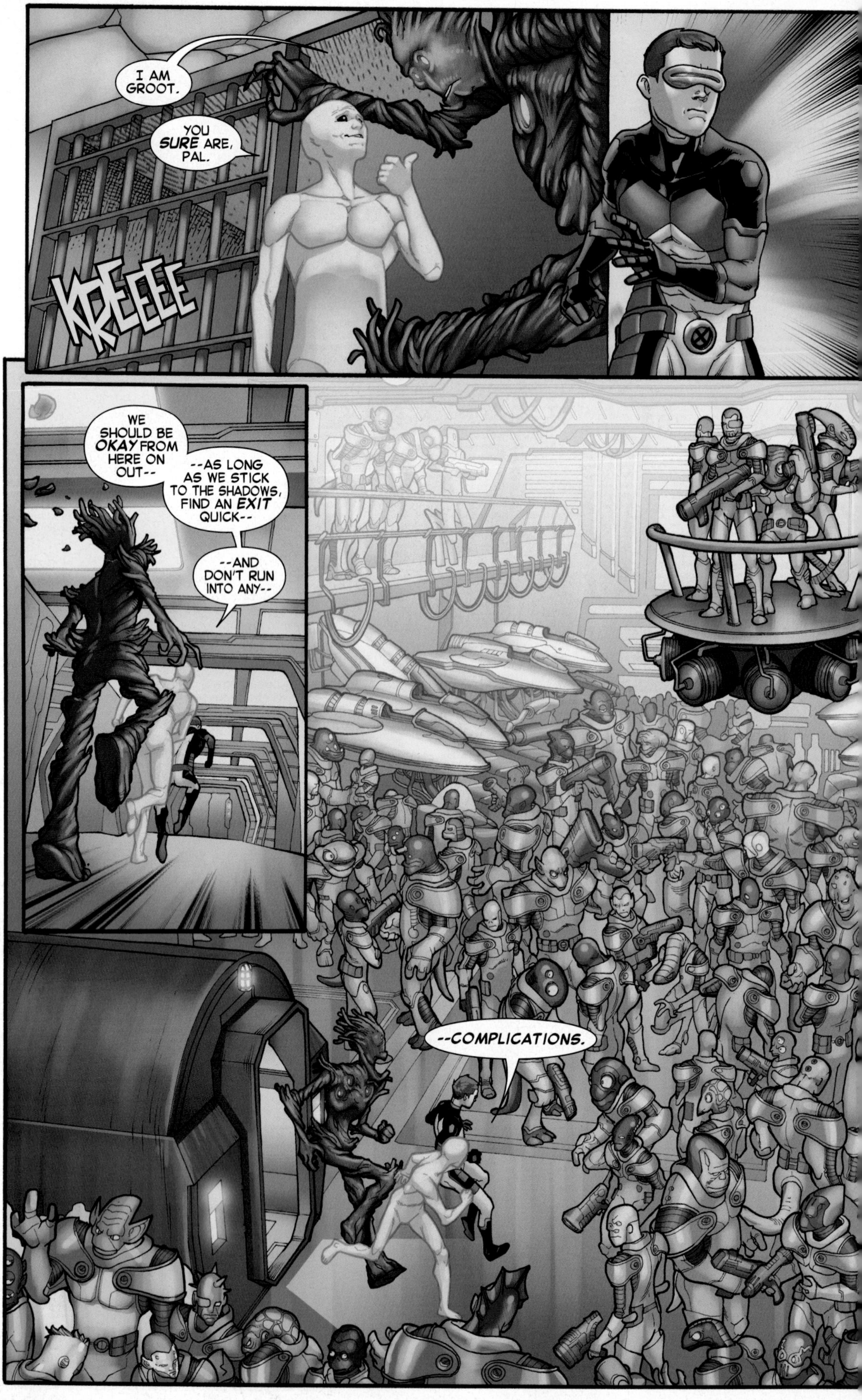
I AM GROOT.
YOU SURE ARE, PAL.
KREEEE
WE SHOULD BE OKAY FROM HERE ON OUT--
--AS LONG AS WE STICK TO THE SHADOWS, FIND AN EXIT QUICK--
--AND DON'T RUN INTO ANY--
--COMPLICATIONS.

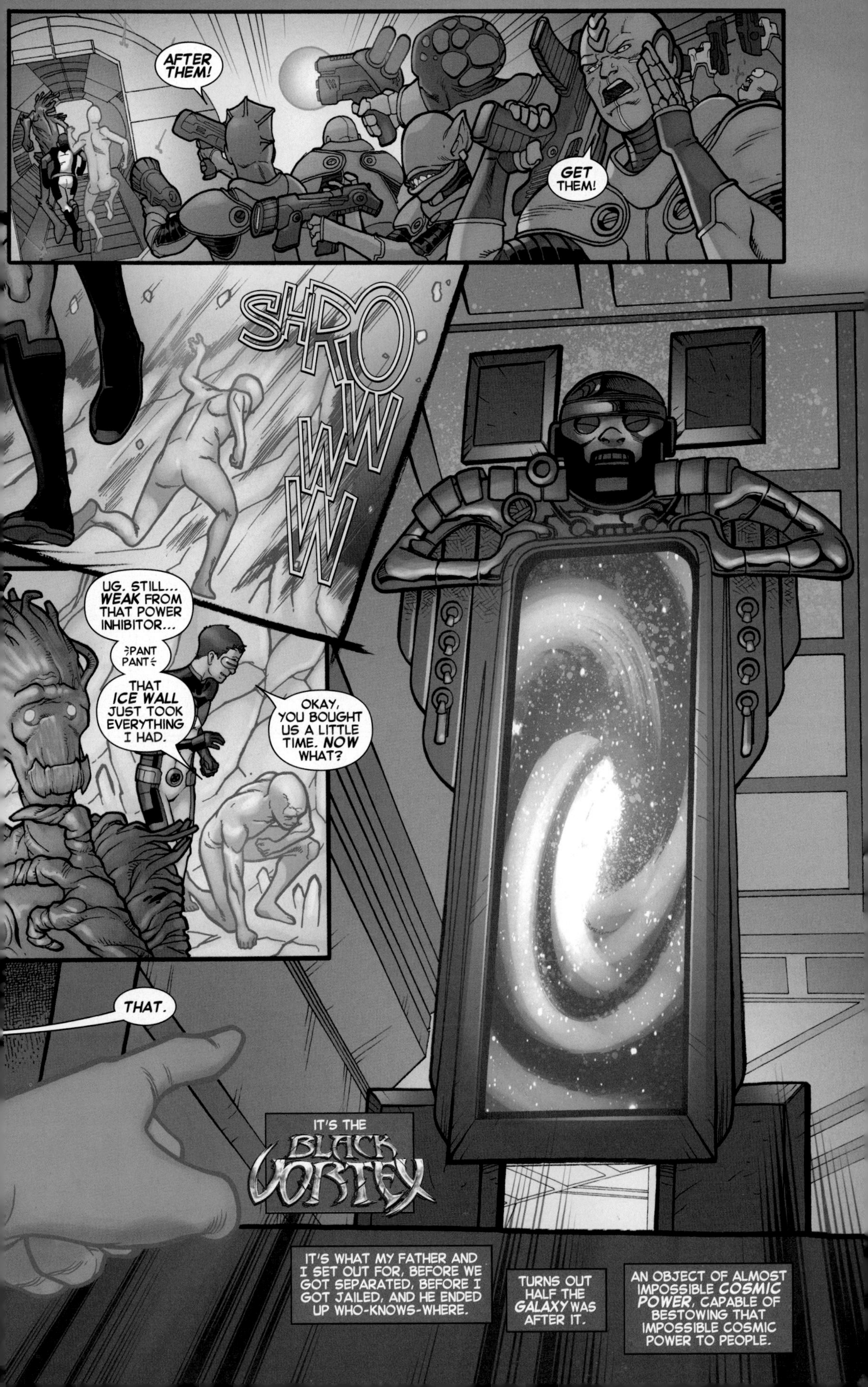
AFTER THEM!
GET THEM!
SHROWWWW
UG. STILL... WEAK FROM THAT POWER INHIBITOR...
PANT PANT
THAT ICE WALL JUST TOOK EVERYTHING I HAD.
OKAY, YOU BOUGHT US A LITTLE TIME. NOW WHAT?
THAT.
IT'S THE BLACK VORTEX
IT'S WHAT MY FATHER AND I SET OUT FOR, BEFORE WE GOT SEPARATED, BEFORE I GOT JAILED, AND HE ENDED UP WHO-KNOWS-WHERE.
TURNS OUT HALF THE GALAXY WAS AFTER IT.
AN OBJECT OF ALMOST IMPOSSIBLE COSMIC POWER, CAPABLE OF BESTOWING THAT IMPOSSIBLE COSMIC POWER TO PEOPLE.

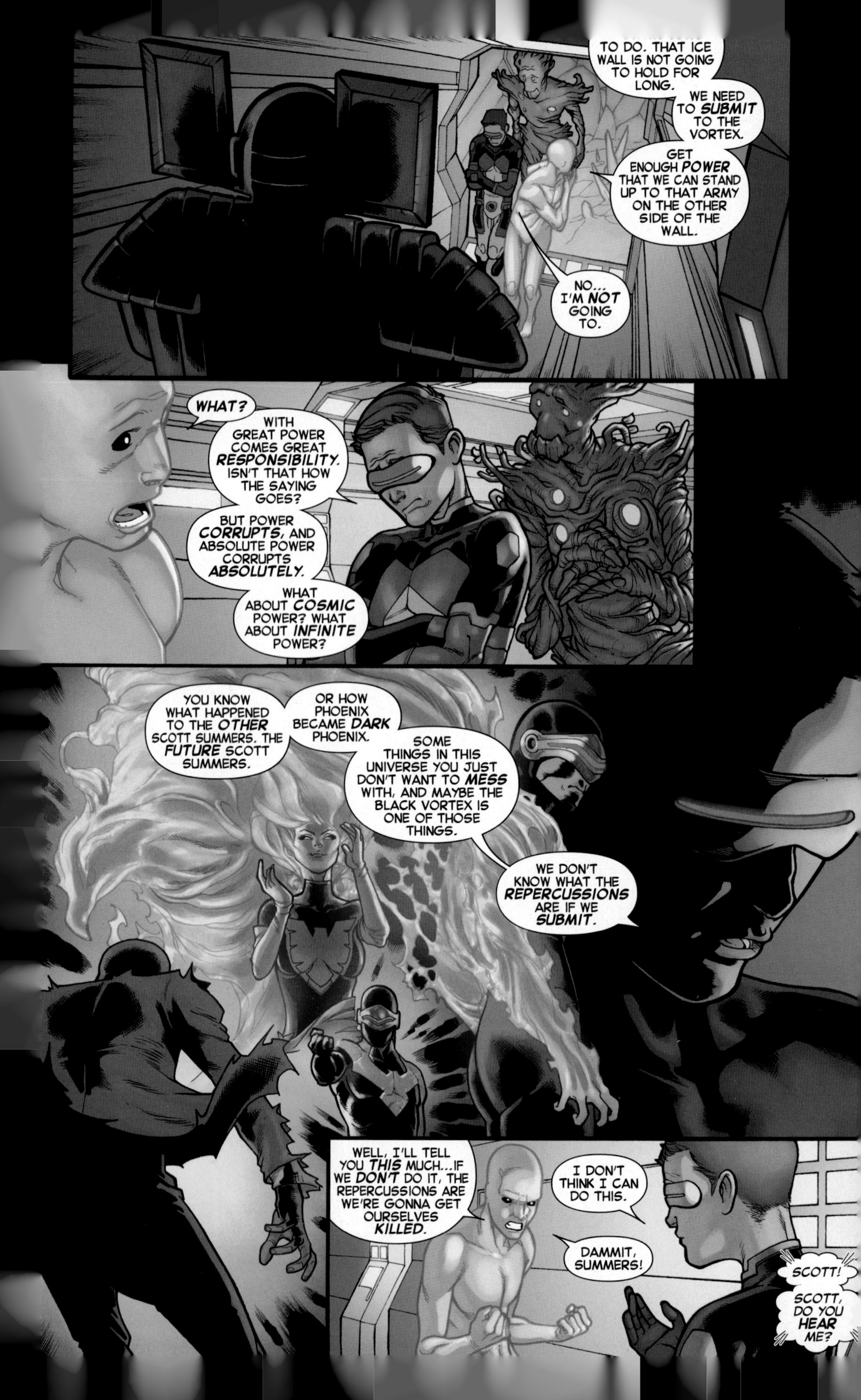

TO DO. THAT ICE WALL IS NOT GOING TO HOLD FOR LONG.
WE NEED TO SUBMIT TO THE VORTEX.
GET ENOUGH POWER THAT WE CAN STAND UP TO THAT ARMY ON THE OTHER SIDE OF THE WALL.
NO... I'M NOT GOING TO.
WHAT?
WITH GREAT POWER COMES GREAT RESPONSIBILITY. ISN'T THAT HOW THE SAYING GOES?
BUT POWER CORRUPTS, AND ABSOLUTE POWER CORRUPTS ABSOLUTELY.
WHAT ABOUT COSMIC POWER? WHAT ABOUT INFINITE POWER?
YOU KNOW WHAT HAPPENED TO THE OTHER SCOTT SUMMERS. THE FUTURE SCOTT SUMMERS.
OR HOW PHOENIX BECAME DARK PHOENIX.
SOME THINGS IN THIS UNIVERSE YOU JUST DON'T WANT TO MESS WITH, AND MAYBE THE BLACK VORTEX IS ONE OF THOSE THINGS.
WE DON'T KNOW WHAT THE REPERCUSSIONS ARE IF WE SUBMIT.
WELL, I'LL TELL YOU THIS MUCH...IF WE DON'T DO IT, THE REPERCUSSIONS ARE WE'RE GONNA GET OURSELVES KILLED.
I DON'T THINK I CAN DO THIS.
DAMMIT, SUMMERS!
SCOTT!
SCOTT, DO YOU HEAR ME?

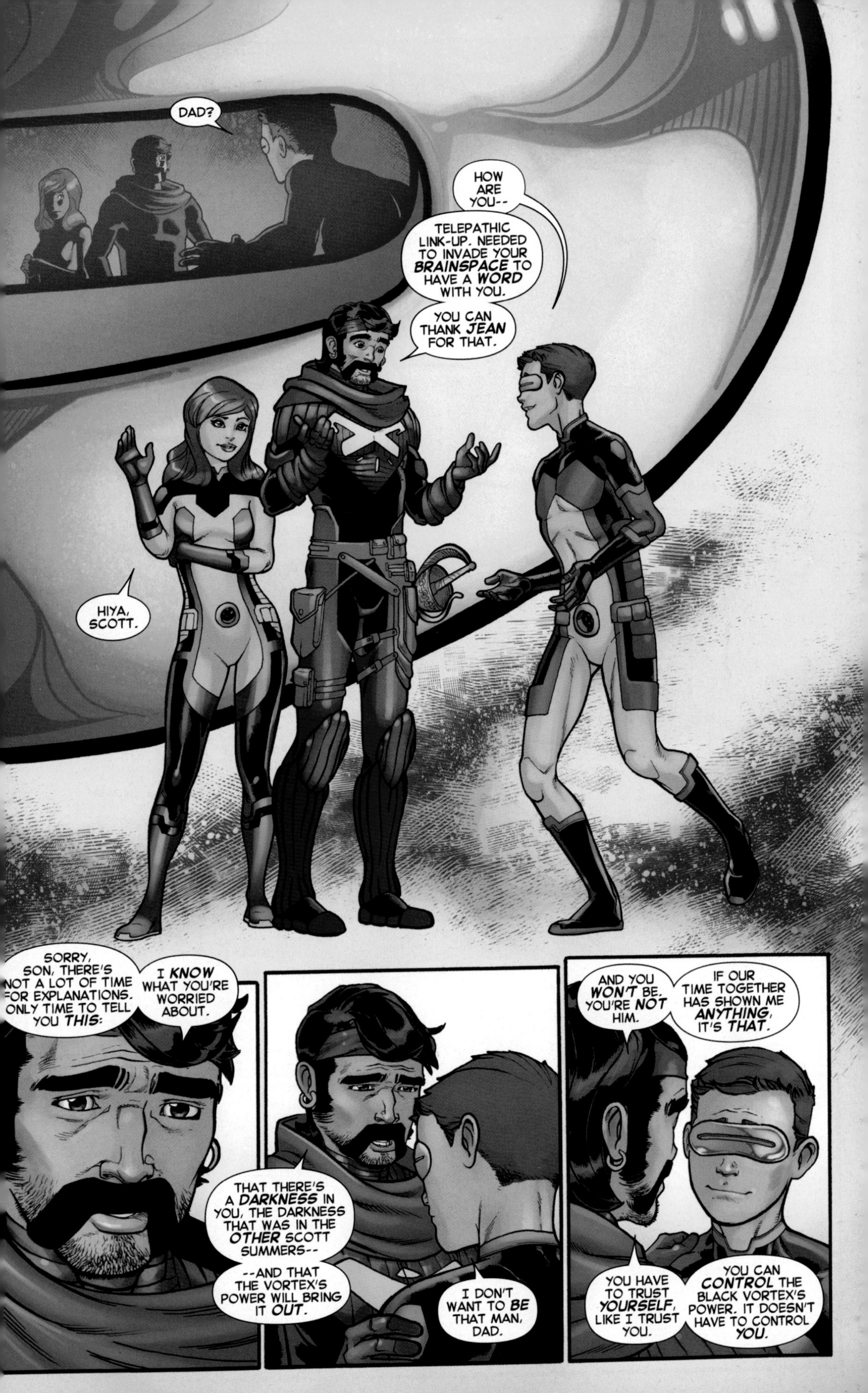

DAD?
HOW ARE YOU--
TELEPATHIC LINK-UP. NEEDED TO INVADE YOUR BRAINSPACE TO HAVE A WORD WITH YOU.
YOU CAN THANK JEAN FOR THAT.
HIYA, SCOTT.
SORRY, SON, THERE'S NOT A LOT OF TIME FOR EXPLANATIONS. ONLY TIME TO TELL YOU THIS:
I KNOW WHAT YOU'RE WORRIED ABOUT.
THAT THERE'S A DARKNESS IN YOU, THE DARKNESS THAT WAS IN THE OTHER SCOTT SUMMERS--
--AND THAT THE VORTEX'S POWER WILL BRING IT OUT.
I DON'T WANT TO BE THAT MAN, DAD.
AND YOU WON'T BE. YOU'RE NOT HIM.
IF OUR TIME TOGETHER HAS SHOWN ME ANYTHING, IT'S THAT.
YOU HAVE TO TRUST YOURSELF, LIKE I TRUST YOU.
YOU CAN CONTROL THE BLACK VORTEX'S POWER. IT DOESN'T HAVE TO CONTROL YOU.

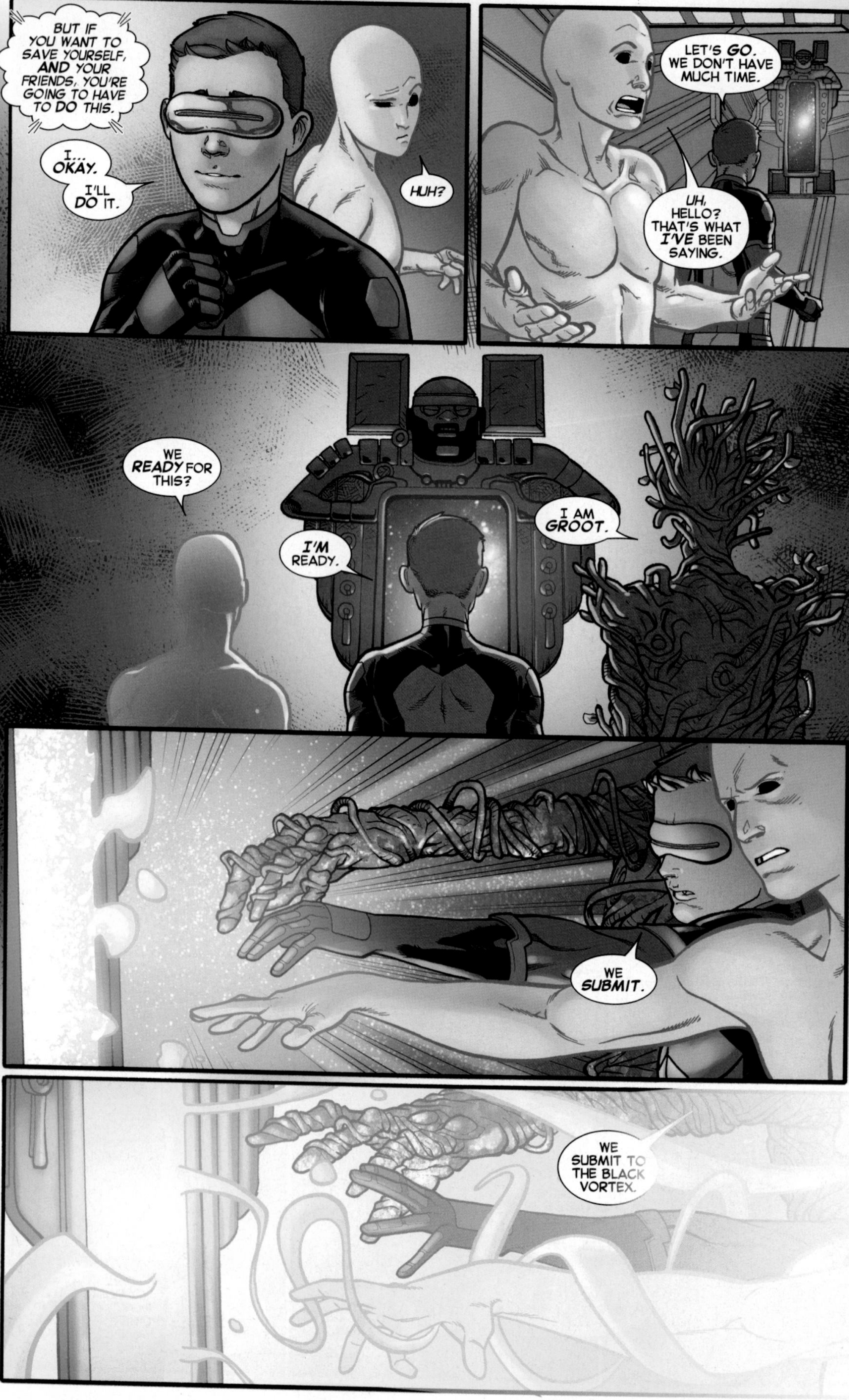

BUT IF YOU WANT TO SAVE YOURSELF, AND YOUR FRIENDS, YOU'RE GOING TO HAVE TO DO THIS.
I... OKAY.
I'LL DO IT.
HUH?
LET'S GO. WE DON'T HAVE MUCH TIME.
UH, HELLO? THAT'S WHAT I'VE BEEN SAYING.
WE READY FOR THIS?
I'M READY.
I AM GROOT.
WE SUBMIT.
WE SUBMIT TO THE BLACK VORTEX.

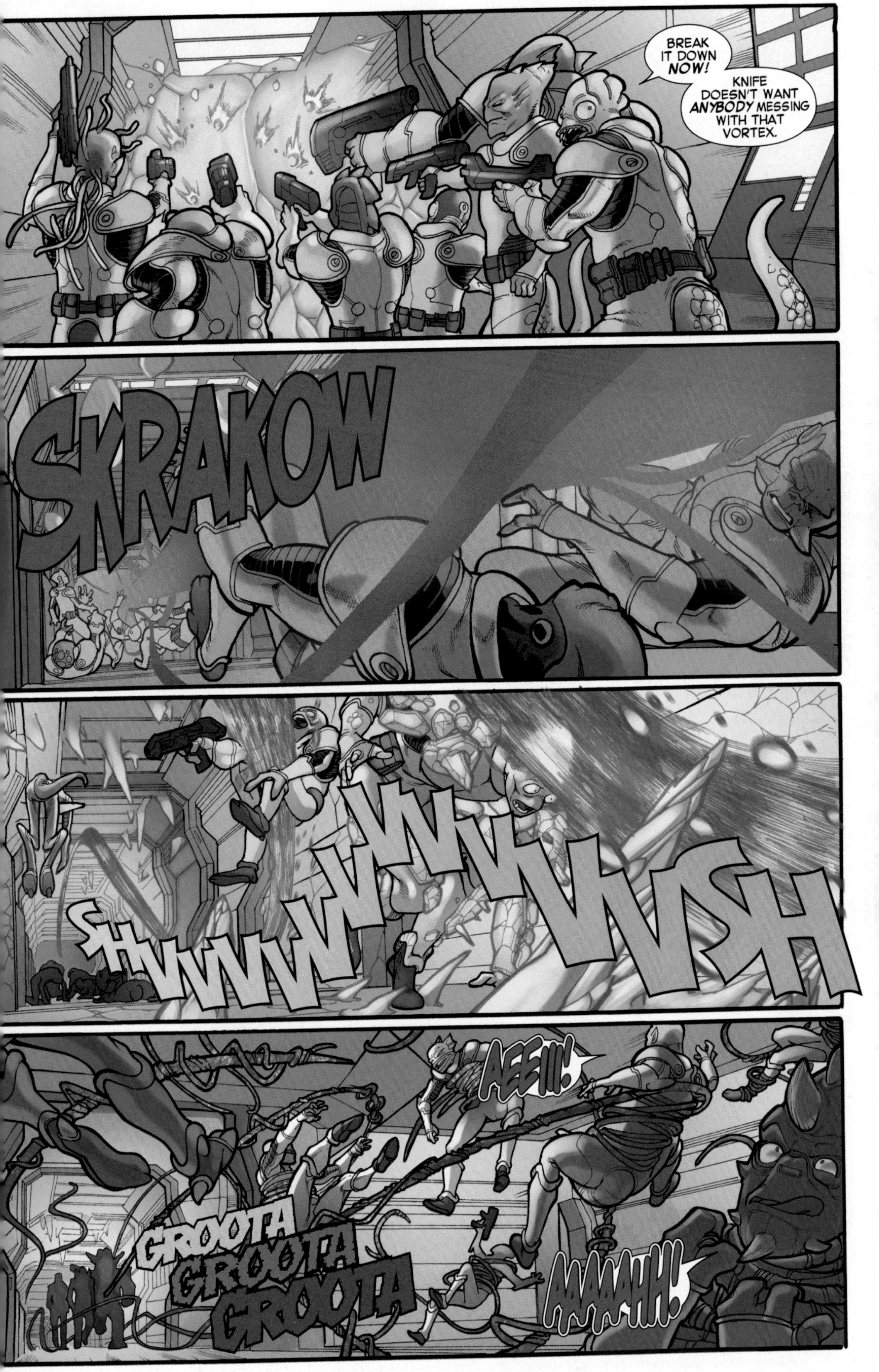
BREAK IT DOWN NOW!
KNIFE DOESN'T WANT ANYBODY MESSING WITH THAT VORTEX.
SKRAKOW
SHVVVVVVVVVVVVSH
AEEIII!
GROOTA GROOTA GROOTA
AAAAAHH!

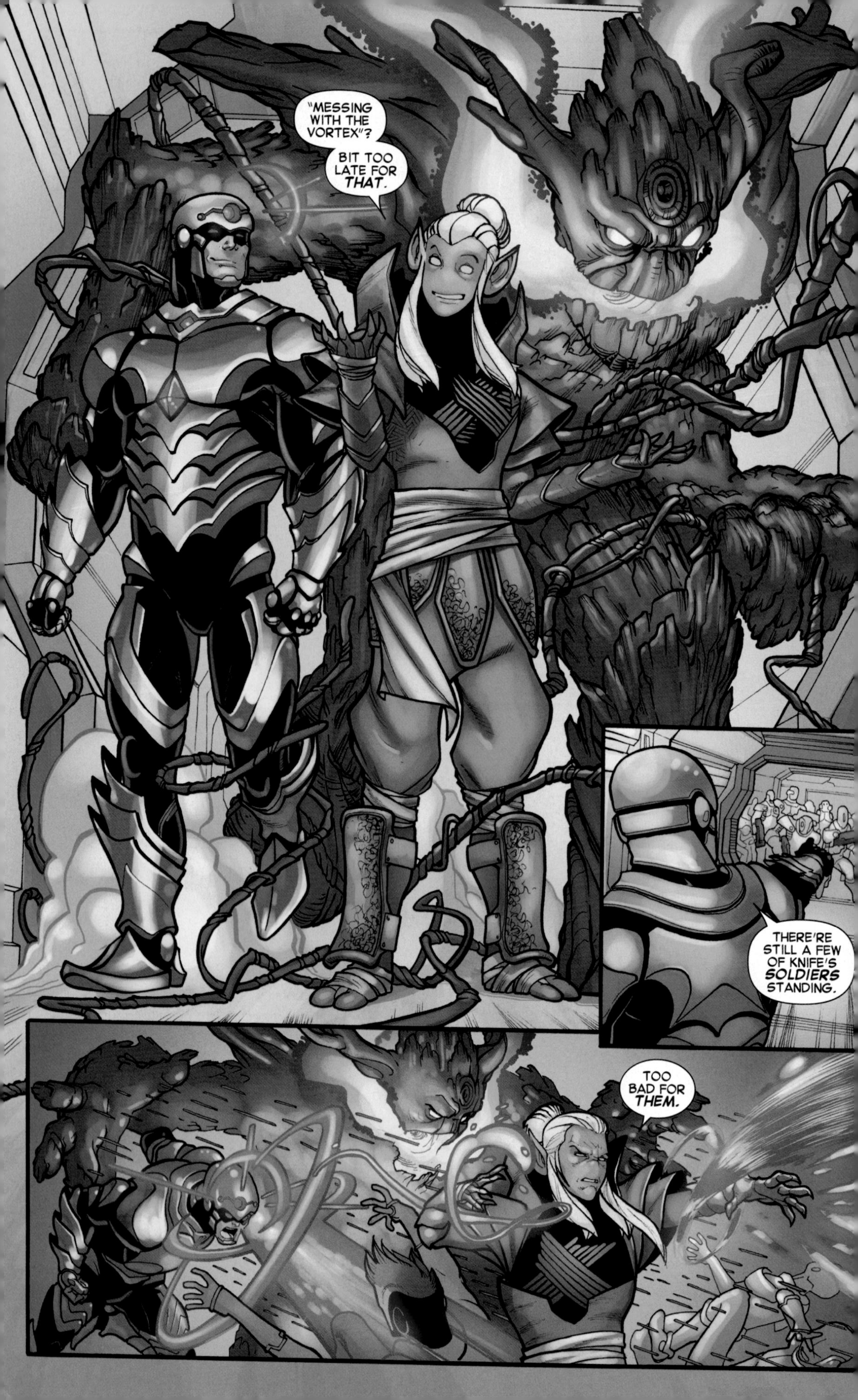
"MESSING WITH THE VORTEX"?
BIT TOO LATE FOR THAT.
THERE'RE STILL A FEW OF KNIFE'S SOLDIERS STANDING.
TOO BAD FOR THEM.

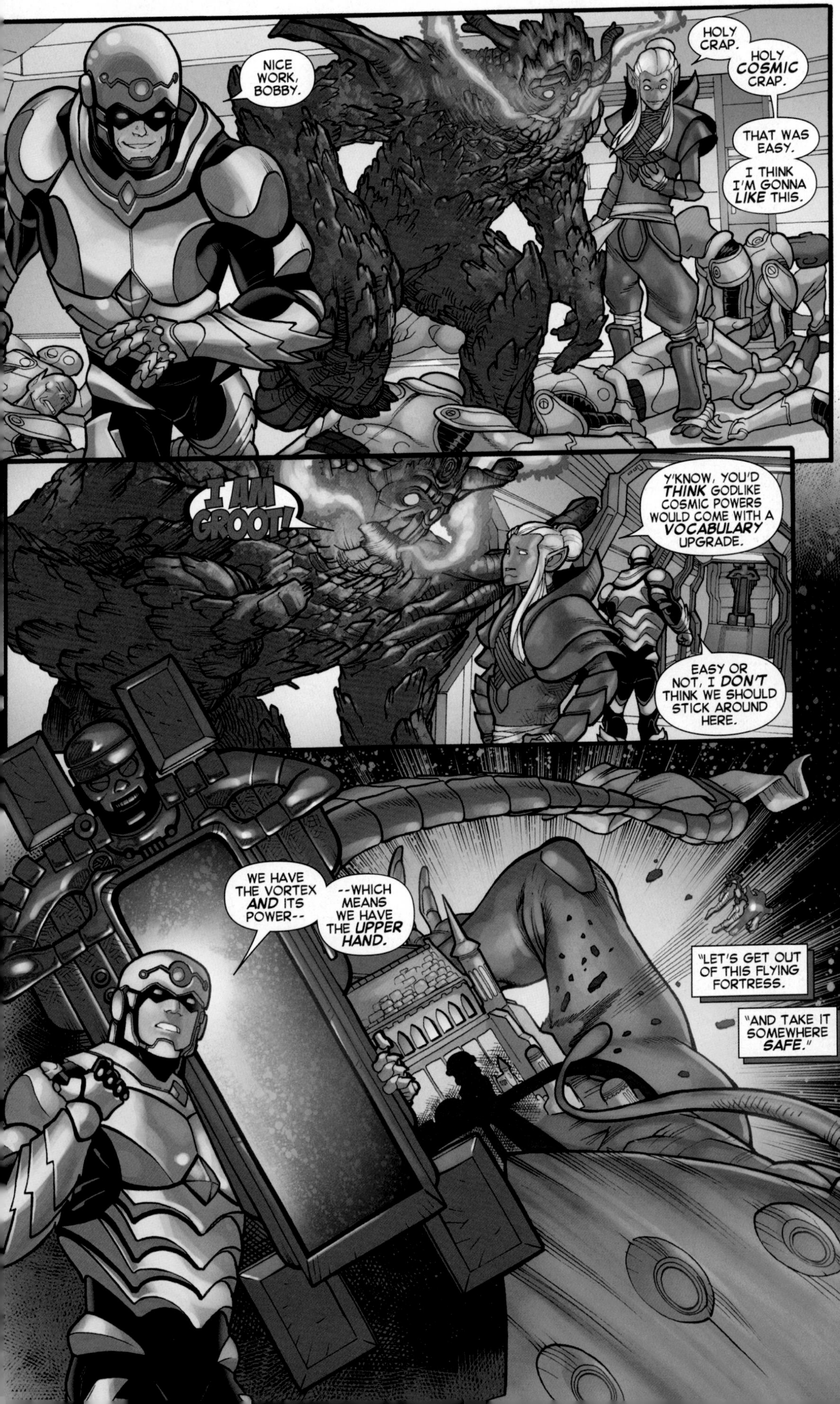
NICE WORK, BOBBY.
HOLY CRAP.
HOLY COSMIC CRAP.
THAT WAS EASY.
I THINK I'M GONNA LIKE THIS.
I AM GROOT!
Y'KNOW, YOU'D THINK GODLIKE COSMIC POWERS WOULD COME WITH A VOCABULARY UPGRADE.
EASY OR NOT, I DON'T THINK WE SHOULD STICK AROUND HERE.
WE HAVE THE VORTEX AND ITS POWER--
--WHICH MEANS WE HAVE THE UPPER HAND.
"LET'S GET OUT OF THIS FLYING FORTRESS.
"AND TAKE IT SOMEWHERE SAFE."

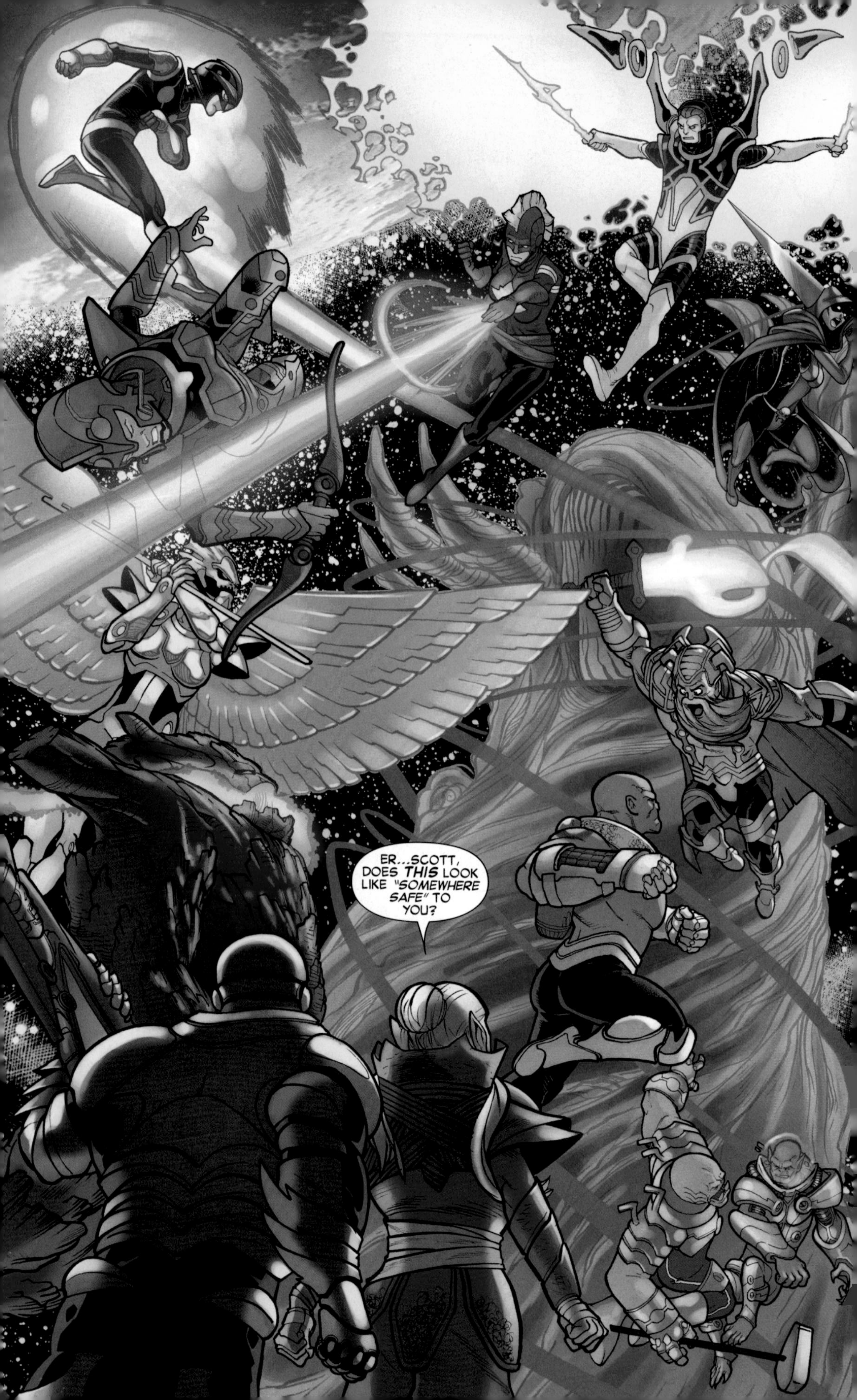
ER...SCOTT, DOES *THIS* LOOK LIKE "SOMEWHERE SAFE" TO YOU?

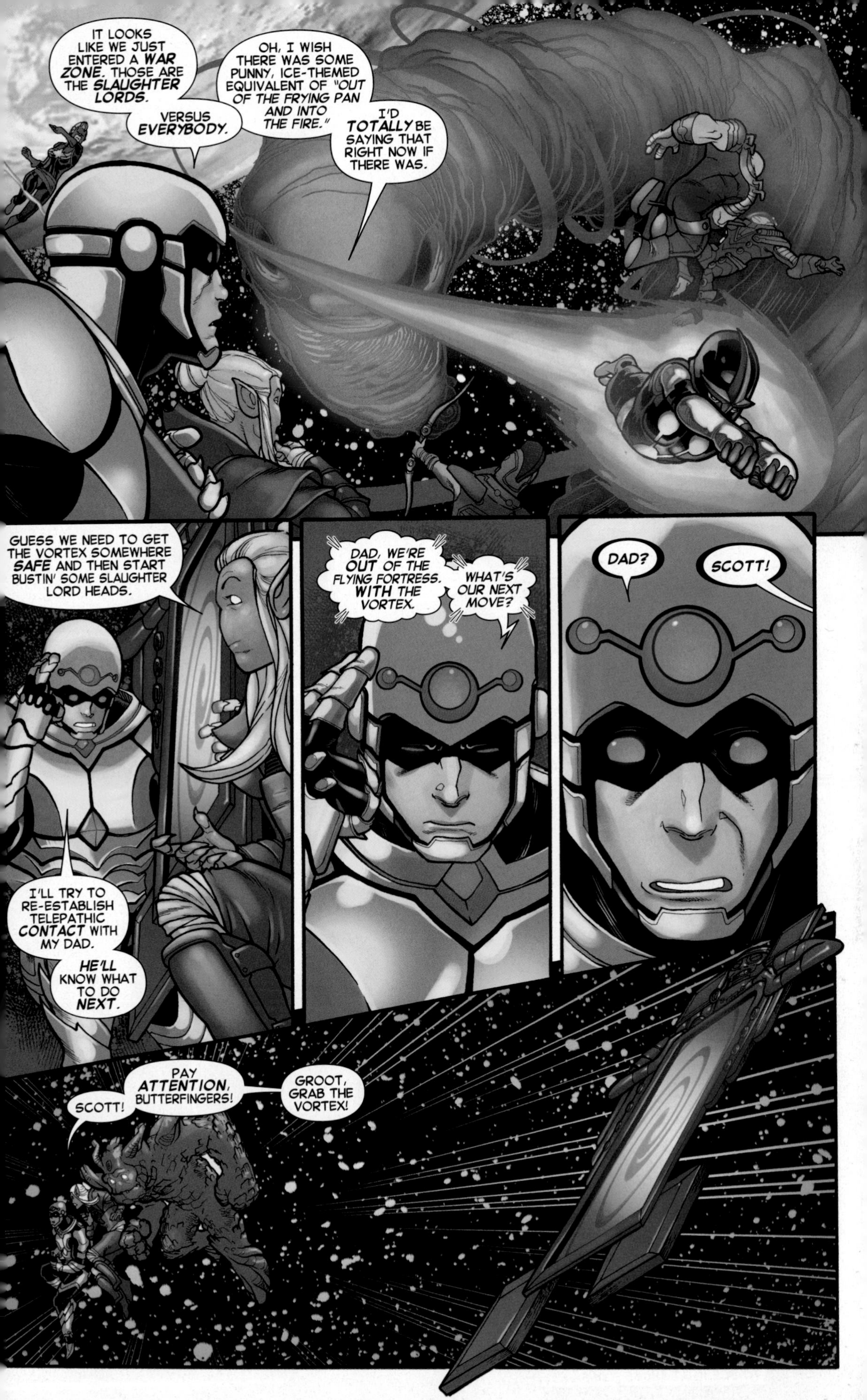
IT LOOKS LIKE WE JUST ENTERED A WAR ZONE. THOSE ARE THE SLAUGHTER LORDS.
VERSUS EVERYBODY.
OH, I WISH THERE WAS SOME PUNNY, ICE-THEMED EQUIVALENT OF "OUT OF THE FRYING PAN AND INTO THE FIRE."
I'D TOTALLY BE SAYING THAT RIGHT NOW IF THERE WAS.
GUESS WE NEED TO GET THE VORTEX SOMEWHERE SAFE AND THEN START BUSTIN' SOME SLAUGHTER LORD HEADS.
I'LL TRY TO RE-ESTABLISH TELEPATHIC CONTACT WITH MY DAD.
HE'LL KNOW WHAT TO DO NEXT.
DAD, WE'RE OUT OF THE FLYING FORTRESS. WITH THE VORTEX.
WHAT'S OUR NEXT MOVE?
DAD?
SCOTT!
SCOTT!
PAY ATTENTION, BUTTERFINGERS!
GROOT, GRAB THE VORTEX!

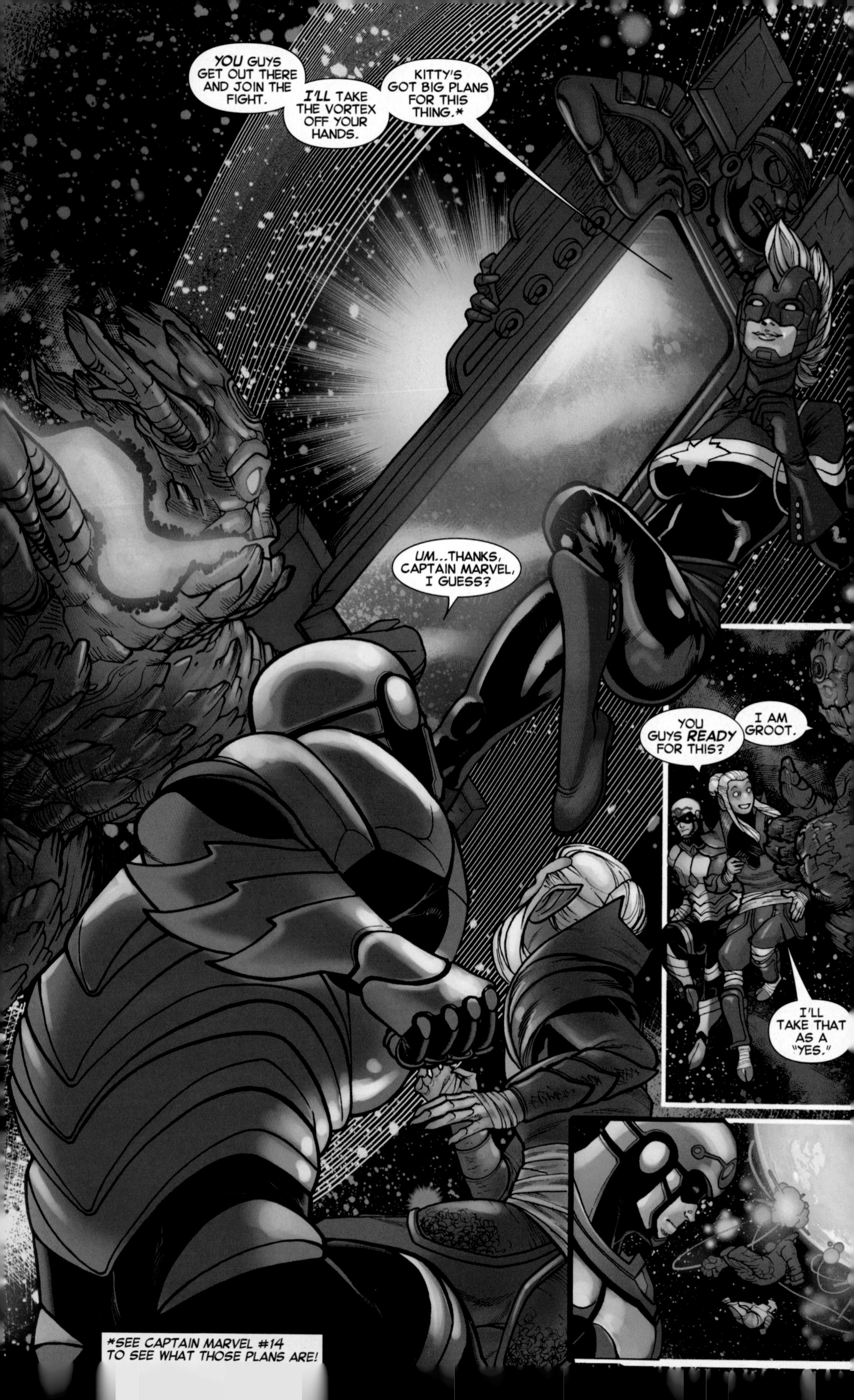
YOU GUYS GET OUT THERE AND JOIN THE FIGHT.
I'LL TAKE THE VORTEX OFF YOUR HANDS.
KITTY'S GOT BIG PLANS FOR THIS THING.*
UM...THANKS, CAPTAIN MARVEL, I GUESS?
YOU GUYS READY FOR THIS?
I AM GROOT.
I'LL TAKE THAT AS A "YES."
*SEE CAPTAIN MARVEL #14 TO SEE WHAT THOSE PLANS ARE!

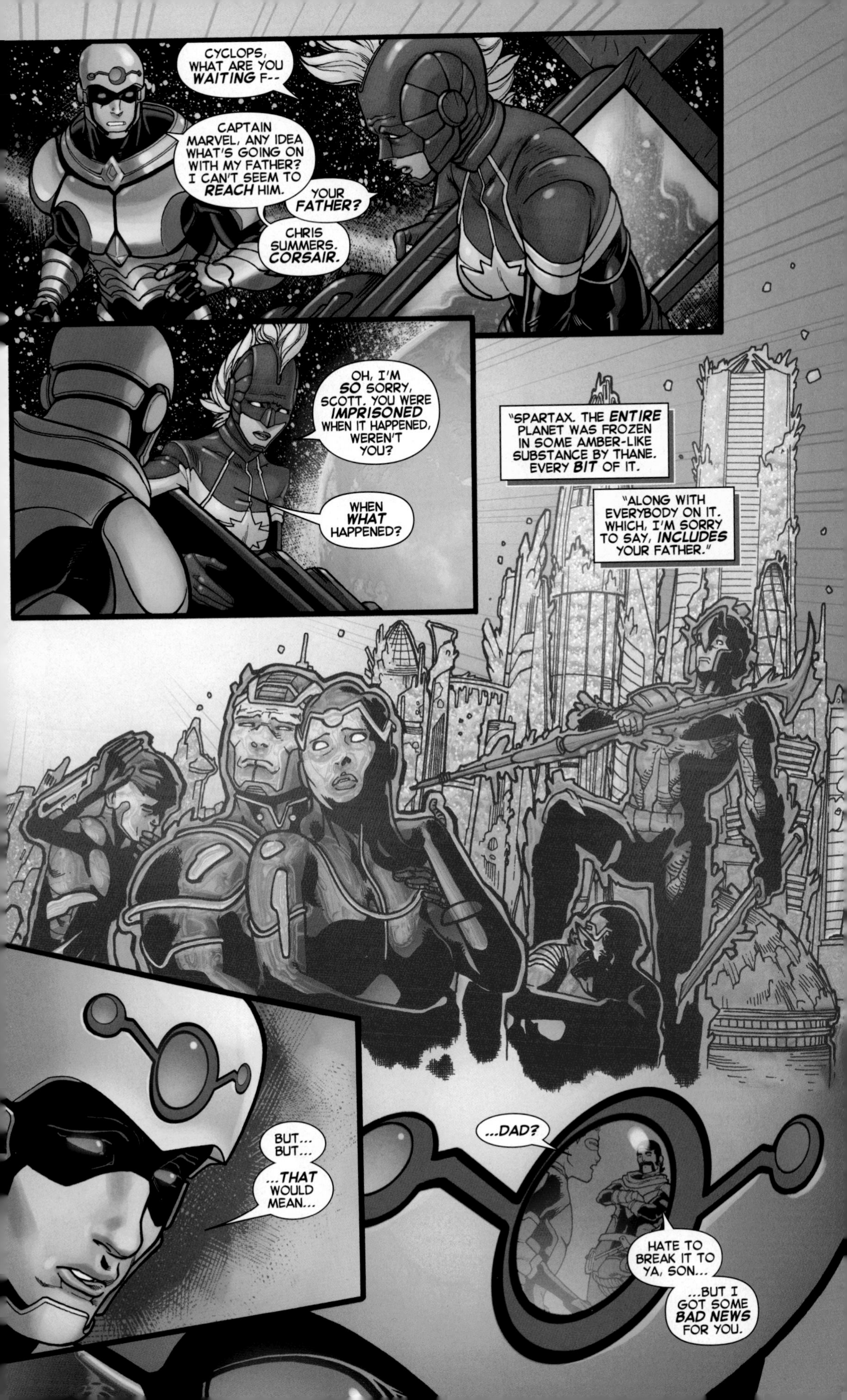
CYCLOPS, WHAT ARE YOU WAITING F--
CAPTAIN MARVEL, ANY IDEA WHAT'S GOING ON WITH MY FATHER? I CAN'T SEEM TO REACH HIM.
YOUR FATHER?
CHRIS SUMMERS. CORSAIR.
OH, I'M SO SORRY, SCOTT. YOU WERE IMPRISONED WHEN IT HAPPENED, WEREN'T YOU?
WHEN WHAT HAPPENED?
"SPARTAX. THE ENTIRE PLANET WAS FROZEN IN SOME AMBER-LIKE SUBSTANCE BY THANE. EVERY BIT OF IT.
"ALONG WITH EVERYBODY ON IT. WHICH, I'M SORRY TO SAY, INCLUDES YOUR FATHER."
BUT... BUT... ...THAT WOULD MEAN...
...DAD?
HATE TO BREAK IT TO YA, SON...
...BUT I GOT SOME BAD NEWS FOR YOU.

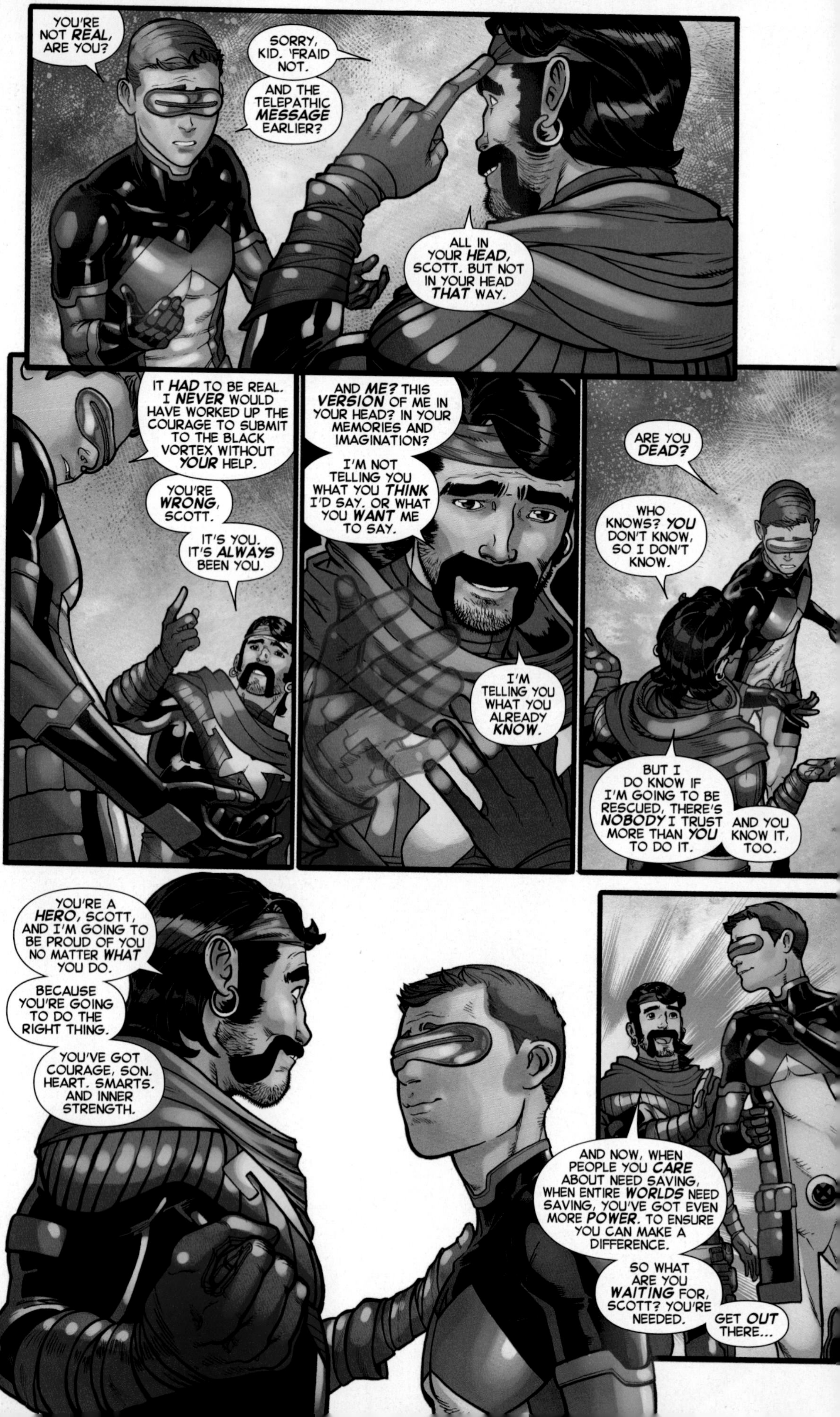
YOU'RE NOT REAL, ARE YOU?
SORRY, KID. 'FRAID NOT.
AND THE TELEPATHIC MESSAGE EARLIER?
ALL IN YOUR HEAD, SCOTT. BUT NOT IN YOUR HEAD THAT WAY.
IT HAD TO BE REAL. I NEVER WOULD HAVE WORKED UP THE COURAGE TO SUBMIT TO THE BLACK VORTEX WITHOUT YOUR HELP.
YOU'RE WRONG, SCOTT.
IT'S YOU. IT'S ALWAYS BEEN YOU.
AND ME? THIS VERSION OF ME IN YOUR HEAD? IN YOUR MEMORIES AND IMAGINATION?
I'M NOT TELLING YOU WHAT YOU THINK I'D SAY. OR WHAT YOU WANT ME TO SAY.
I'M TELLING YOU WHAT YOU ALREADY KNOW.
ARE YOU DEAD?
WHO KNOWS? YOU DON'T KNOW, SO I DON'T KNOW.
BUT I DO KNOW IF I'M GOING TO BE RESCUED, THERE'S NOBODY I TRUST MORE THAN YOU TO DO IT.
AND YOU KNOW IT, TOO.
YOU'RE A HERO, SCOTT, AND I'M GOING TO BE PROUD OF YOU NO MATTER WHAT YOU DO.
BECAUSE YOU'RE GOING TO DO THE RIGHT THING.
YOU'VE GOT COURAGE, SON. HEART. SMARTS. AND INNER STRENGTH.
AND NOW, WHEN PEOPLE YOU CARE ABOUT NEED SAVING, WHEN ENTIRE WORLDS NEED SAVING, YOU'VE GOT EVEN MORE POWER. TO ENSURE YOU CAN MAKE A DIFFERENCE.
SO WHAT ARE YOU WAITING FOR, SCOTT? YOU'RE NEEDED.
GET OUT THERE...

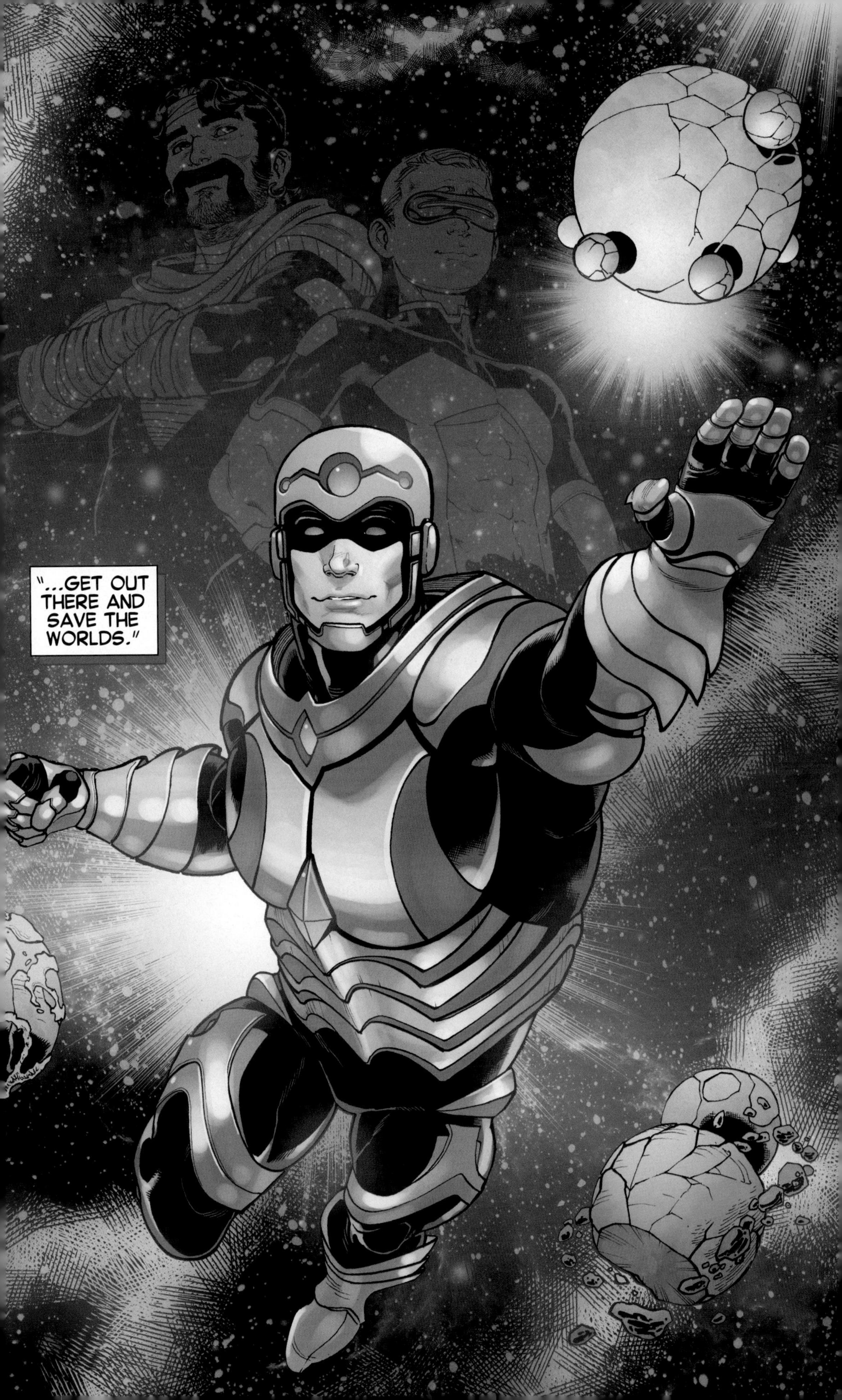
"...GET OUT THERE AND SAVE THE WORLDS."

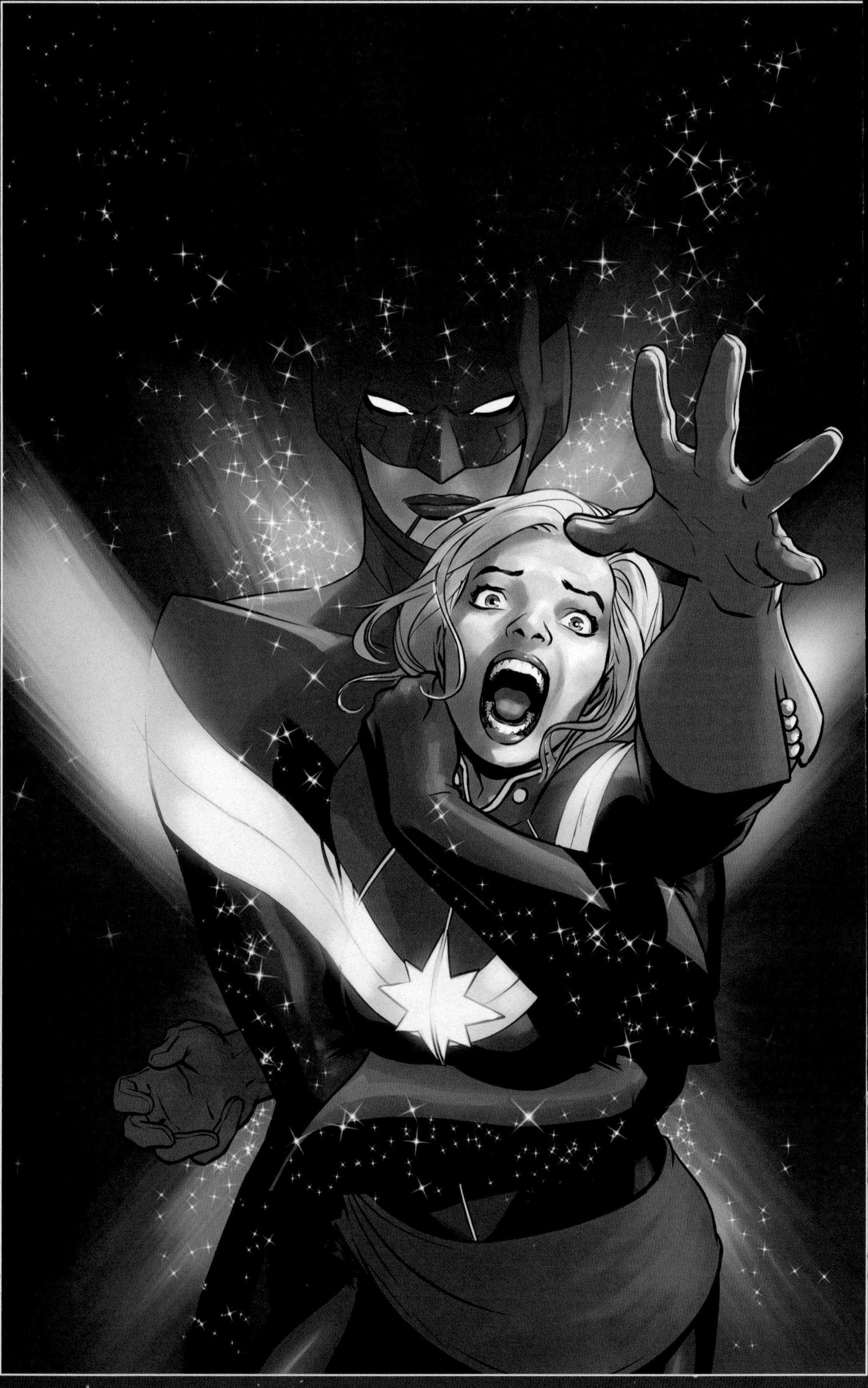

CAPTAIN MARVEL #14

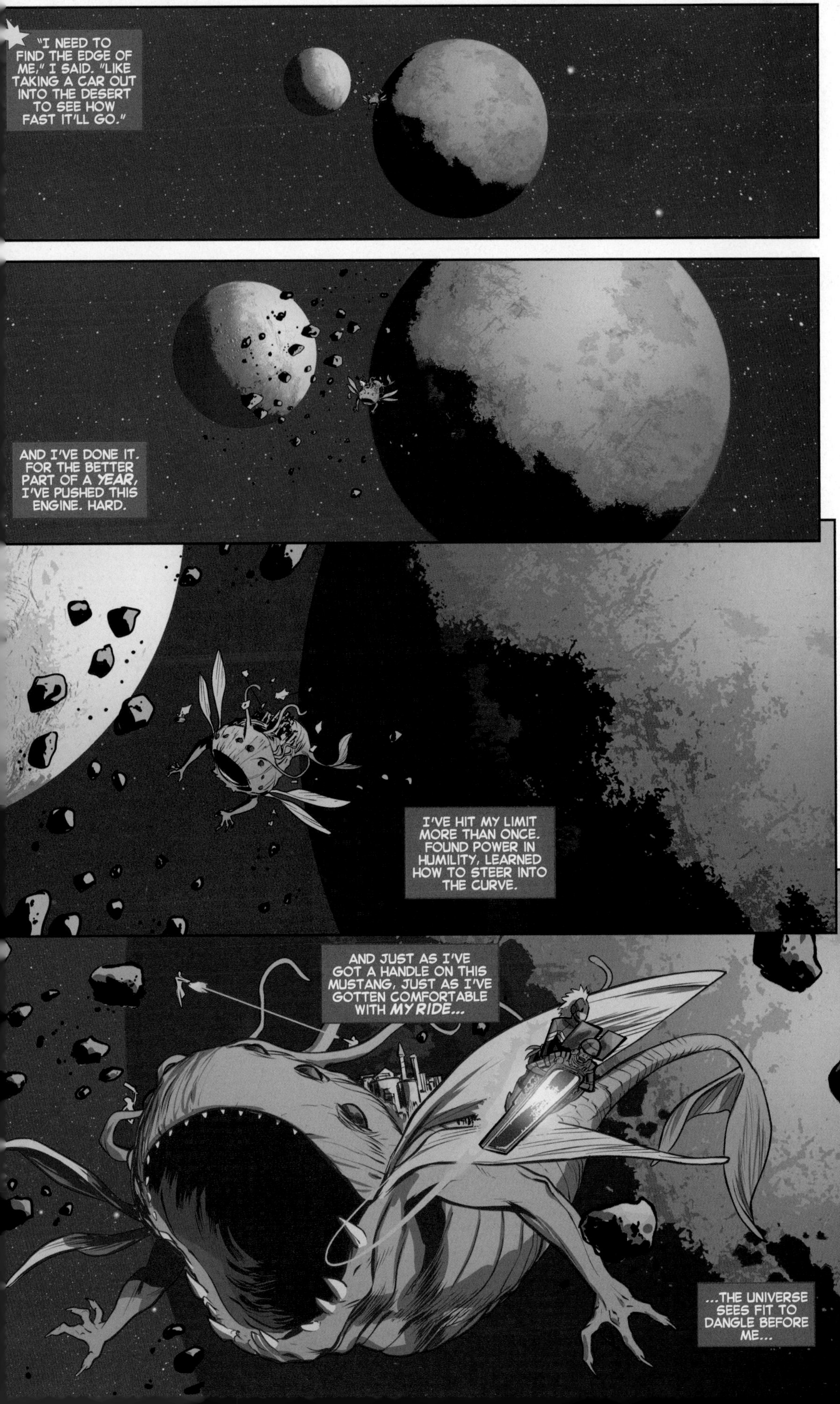
"I NEED TO FIND THE EDGE OF ME," I SAID. "LIKE TAKING A CAR OUT INTO THE DESERT TO SEE HOW FAST IT'LL GO."
AND I'VE DONE IT. FOR THE BETTER PART OF A *YEAR*, I'VE PUSHED THIS ENGINE. HARD.
I'VE HIT MY LIMIT MORE THAN ONCE. FOUND POWER IN HUMILITY, LEARNED HOW TO STEER INTO THE CURVE.
AND JUST AS I'VE GOT A HANDLE ON THIS MUSTANG, JUST AS I'VE GOTTEN COMFORTABLE WITH *MY RIDE*...
...THE UNIVERSE SEES FIT TO DANGLE BEFORE ME...

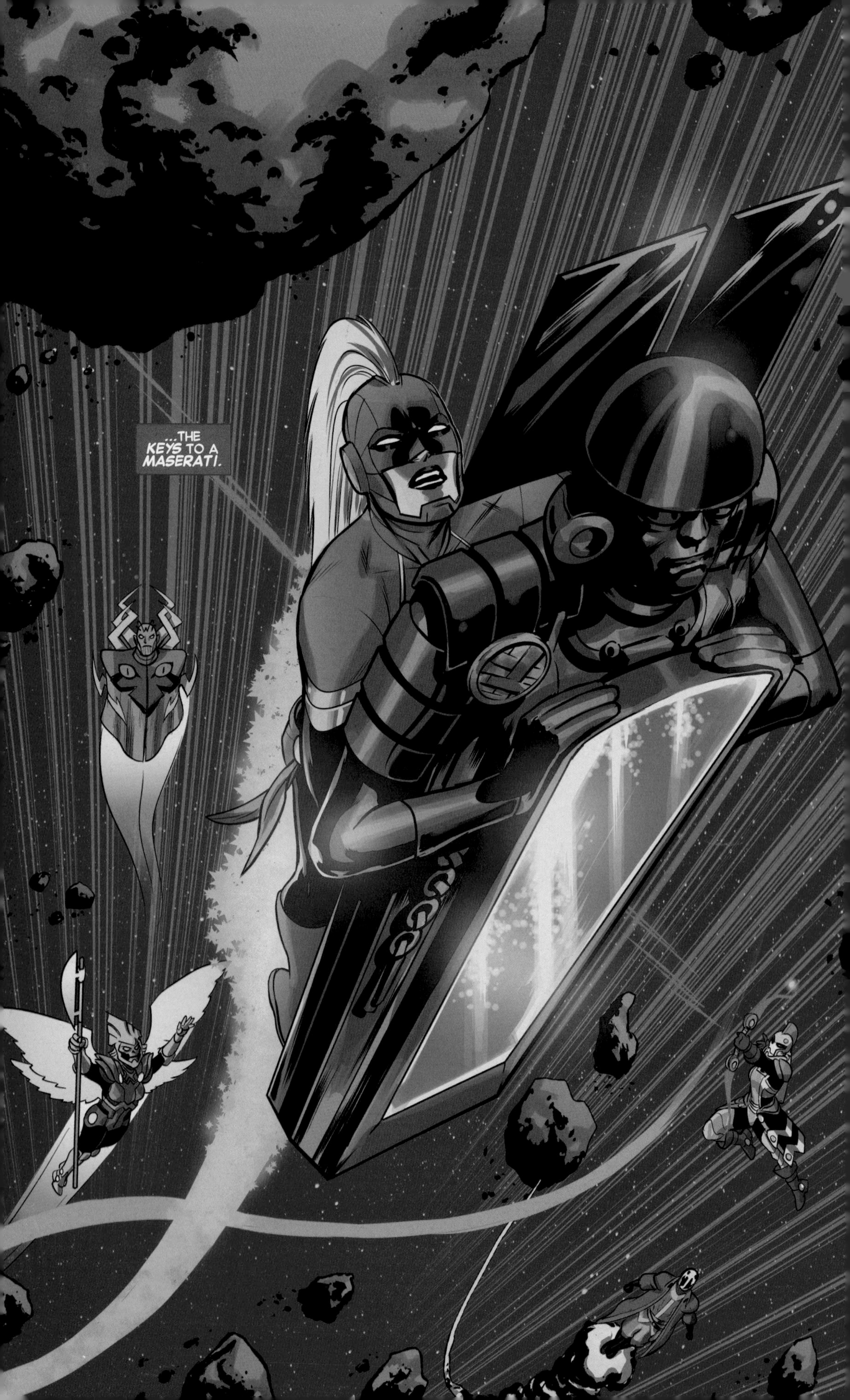
...THE KEYS TO A MASERATI.

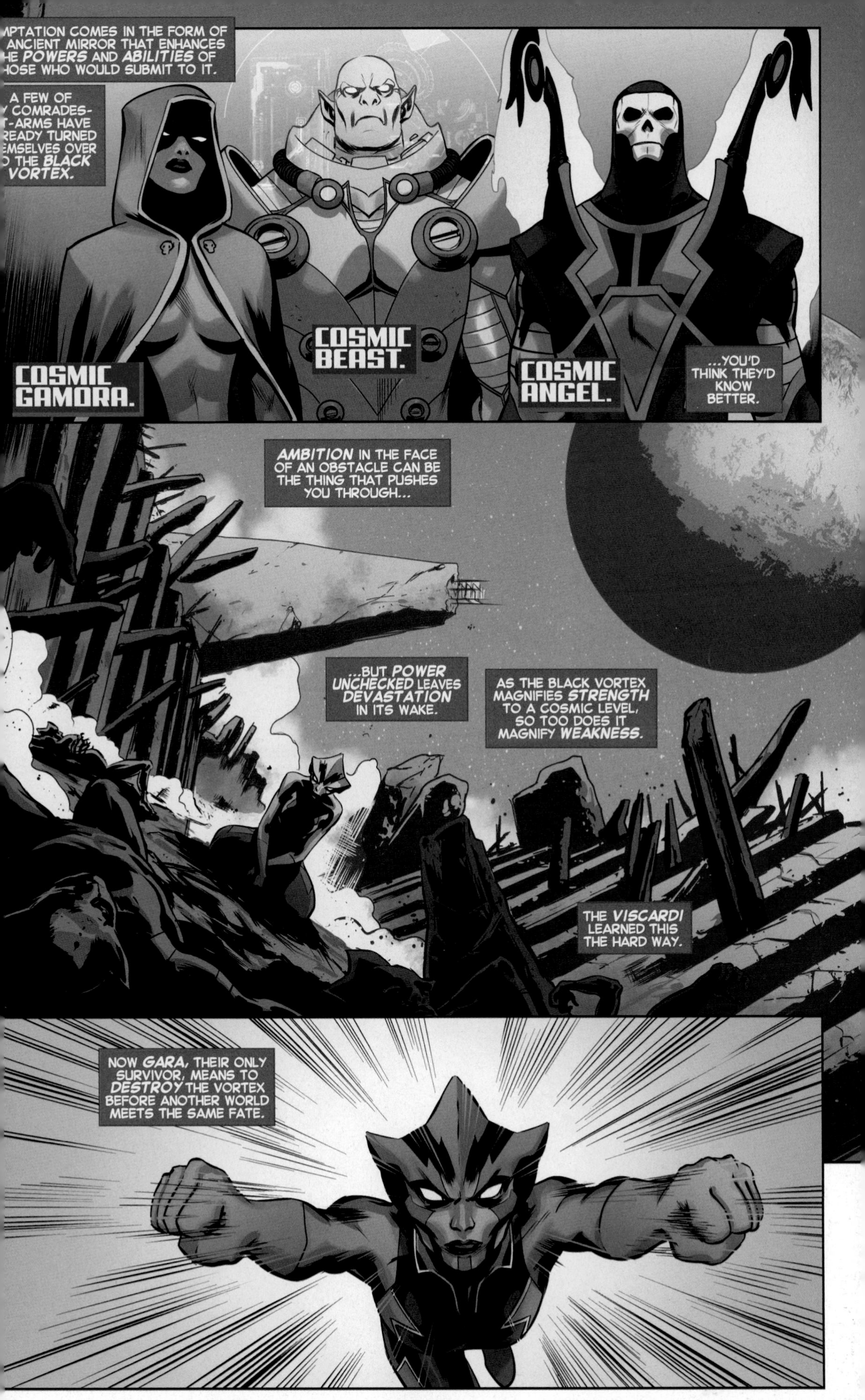
MPTATION COMES IN THE FORM OF ANCIENT MIRROR THAT ENHANCES HE POWERS AND ABILITIES OF HOSE WHO WOULD SUBMIT TO IT.
A FEW OF Y COMRADES- T-ARMS HAVE READY TURNED EMSELVES OVER O THE BLACK VORTEX.
COSMIC GAMORA.
COSMIC BEAST.
COSMIC ANGEL.
...YOU'D THINK THEY'D KNOW BETTER.
AMBITION IN THE FACE OF AN OBSTACLE CAN BE THE THING THAT PUSHES YOU THROUGH...
...BUT POWER UNCHECKED LEAVES DEVASTATION IN ITS WAKE.
AS THE BLACK VORTEX MAGNIFIES STRENGTH TO A COSMIC LEVEL, SO TOO DOES IT MAGNIFY WEAKNESS.
THE VISCARDI LEARNED THIS THE HARD WAY.
NOW GARA, THEIR ONLY SURVIVOR, MEANS TO DESTROY THE VORTEX BEFORE ANOTHER WORLD MEETS THE SAME FATE.

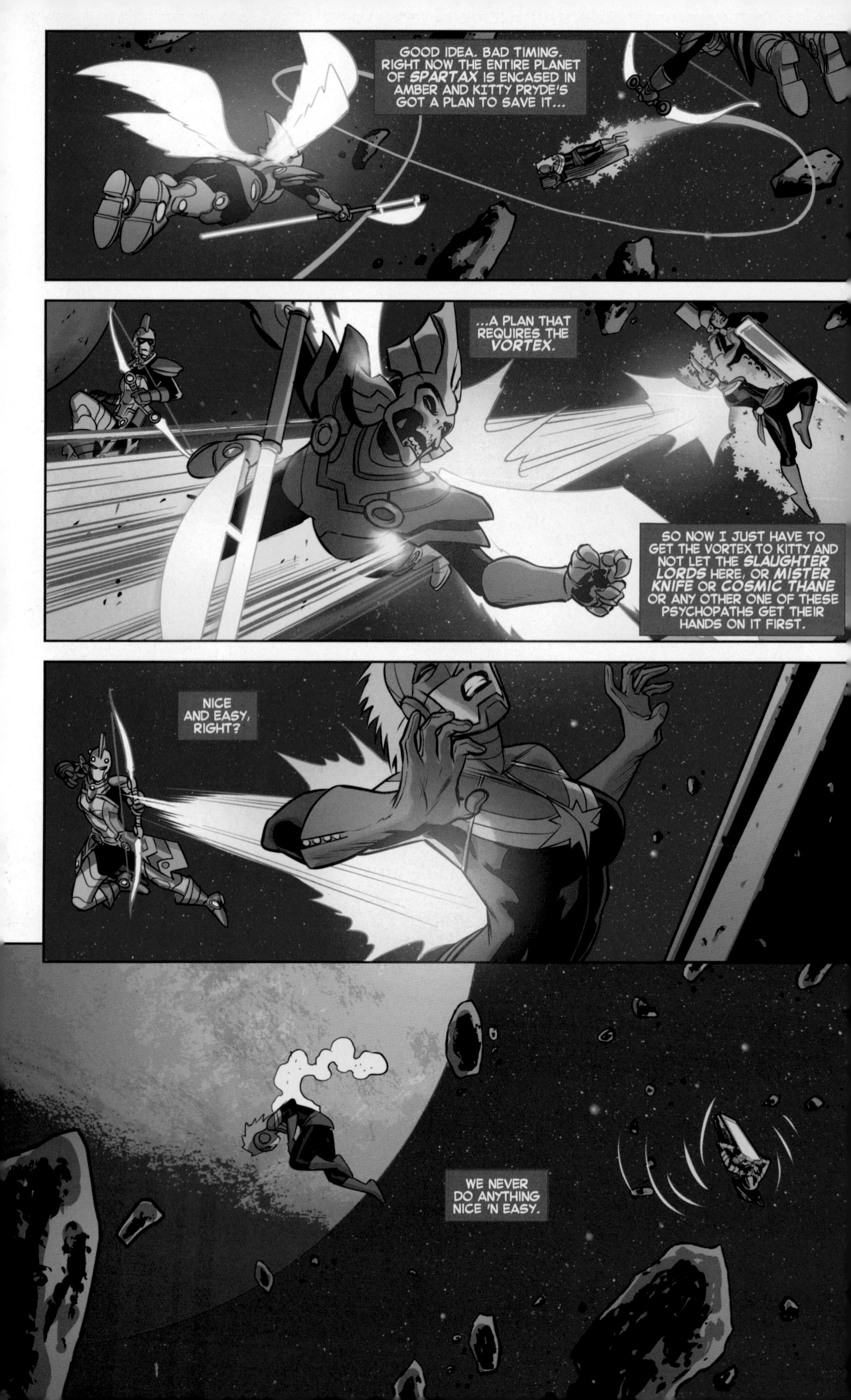
GOOD IDEA. BAD TIMING. RIGHT NOW THE ENTIRE PLANET OF SPARTAX IS ENCASED IN AMBER AND KITTY PRYDE'S GOT A PLAN TO SAVE IT...
...A PLAN THAT REQUIRES THE VORTEX.
SO NOW I JUST HAVE TO GET THE VORTEX TO KITTY AND NOT LET THE SLAUGHTER LORDS HERE, OR MISTER KNIFE OR COSMIC THANE OR ANY OTHER ONE OF THESE PSYCHOPATHS GET THEIR HANDS ON IT FIRST.
NICE AND EASY, RIGHT?
WE NEVER DO ANYTHING NICE 'N EASY.

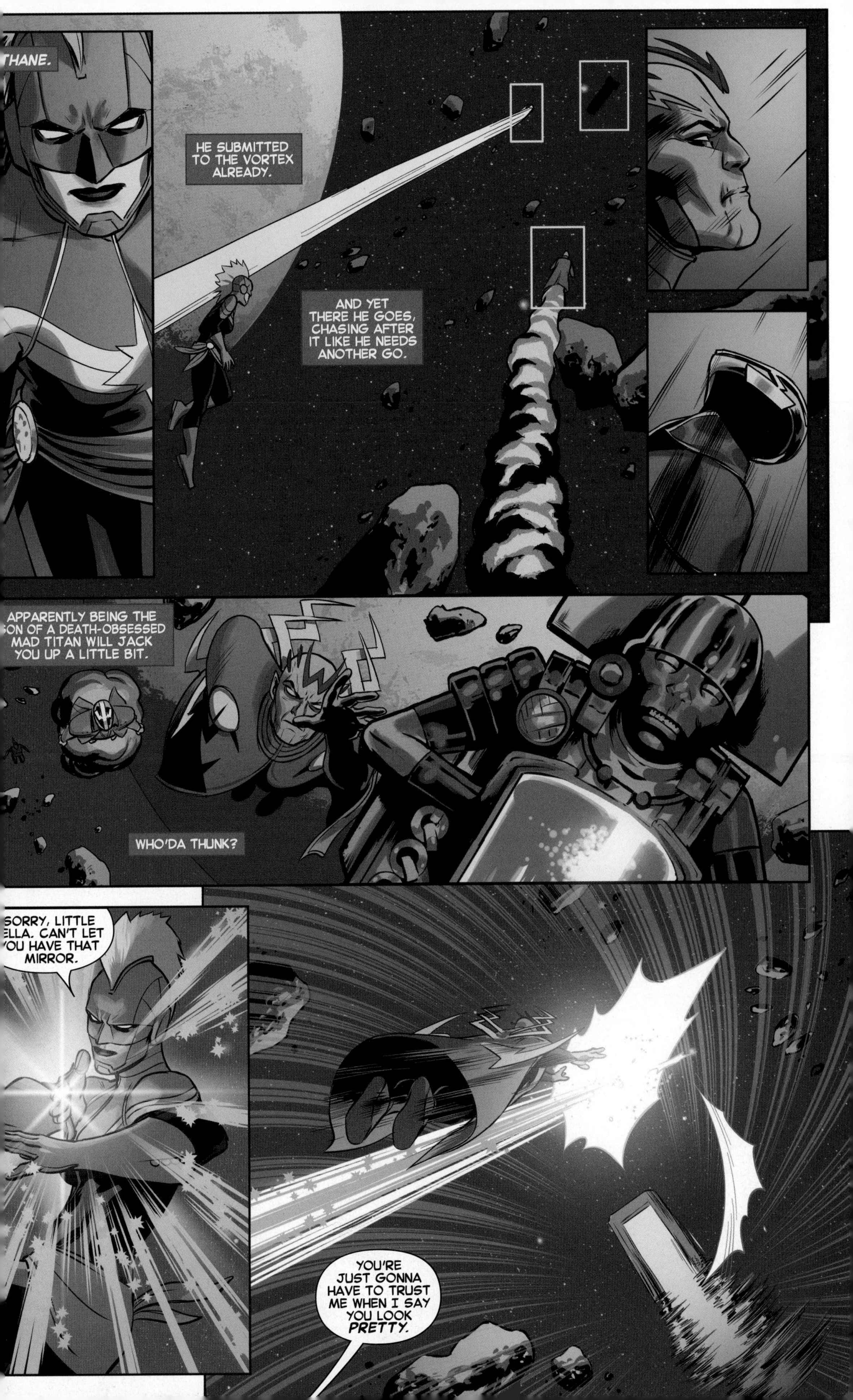
THANE.
HE SUBMITTED TO THE VORTEX ALREADY.
AND YET THERE HE GOES, CHASING AFTER IT LIKE HE NEEDS ANOTHER GO.
APPARENTLY BEING THE SON OF A DEATH-OBSESSED MAD TITAN WILL JACK YOU UP A LITTLE BIT.
WHO'DA THUNK?
SORRY, LITTLE ELLA. CAN'T LET YOU HAVE THAT MIRROR.
YOU'RE JUST GONNA HAVE TO TRUST ME WHEN I SAY YOU LOOK PRETTY.

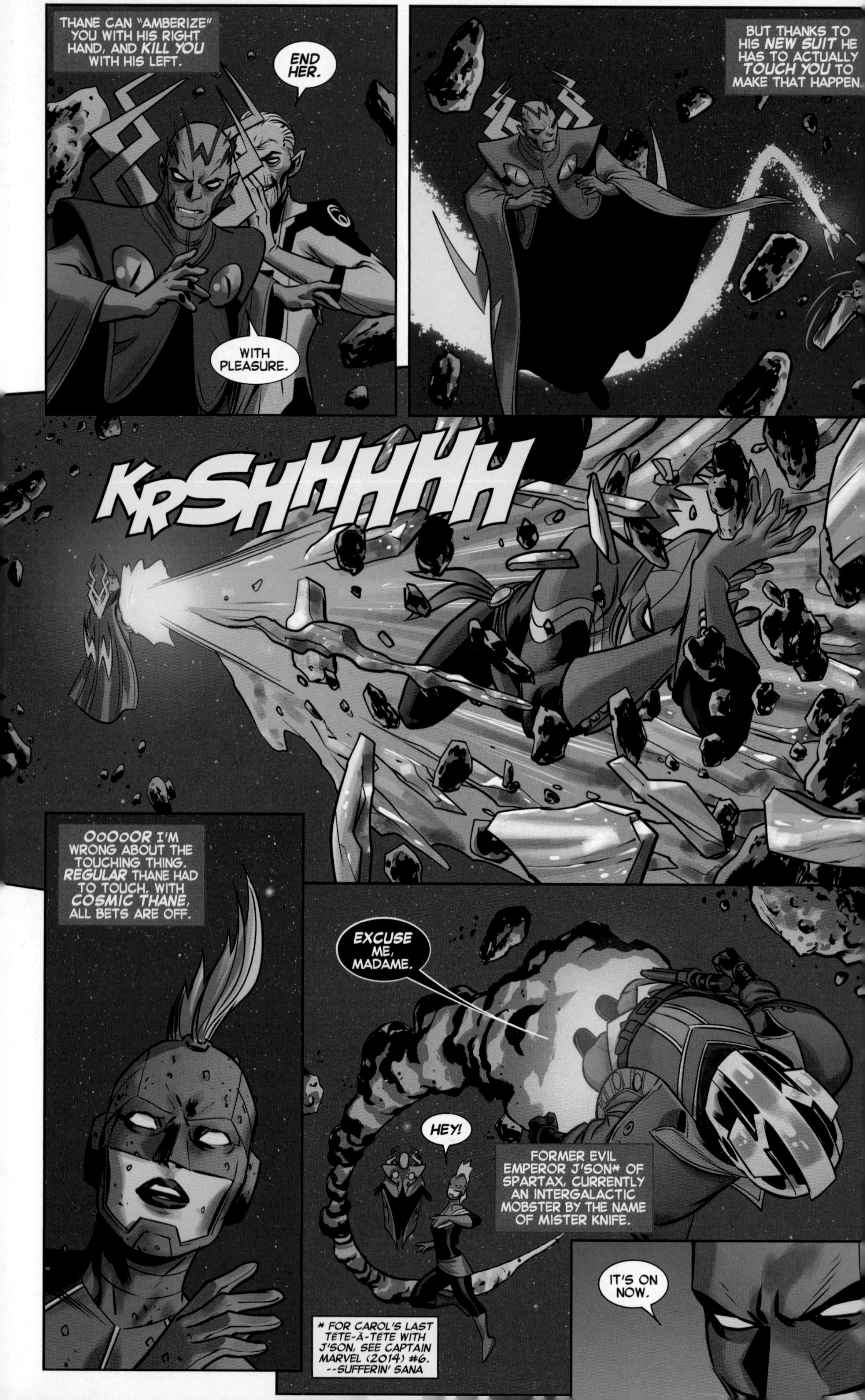
THANE CAN "AMBERIZE" YOU WITH HIS RIGHT HAND, AND KILL YOU WITH HIS LEFT.
END HER.
WITH PLEASURE.
BUT THANKS TO HIS NEW SUIT HE HAS TO ACTUALLY TOUCH YOU TO MAKE THAT HAPPEN.
KRSHHHHHH
OOOOOR I'M WRONG ABOUT THE TOUCHING THING. REGULAR THANE HAD TO TOUCH. WITH COSMIC THANE, ALL BETS ARE OFF.
EXCUSE ME, MADAME.
HEY!
FORMER EVIL EMPEROR J'SON* OF SPARTAX, CURRENTLY AN INTERGALACTIC MOBSTER BY THE NAME OF MISTER KNIFE.
* FOR CAROL'S LAST TÊTE-À-TÊTE WITH J'SON, SEE CAPTAIN MARVEL (2014) #6. --SUFFERIN' SANA
IT'S ON NOW.

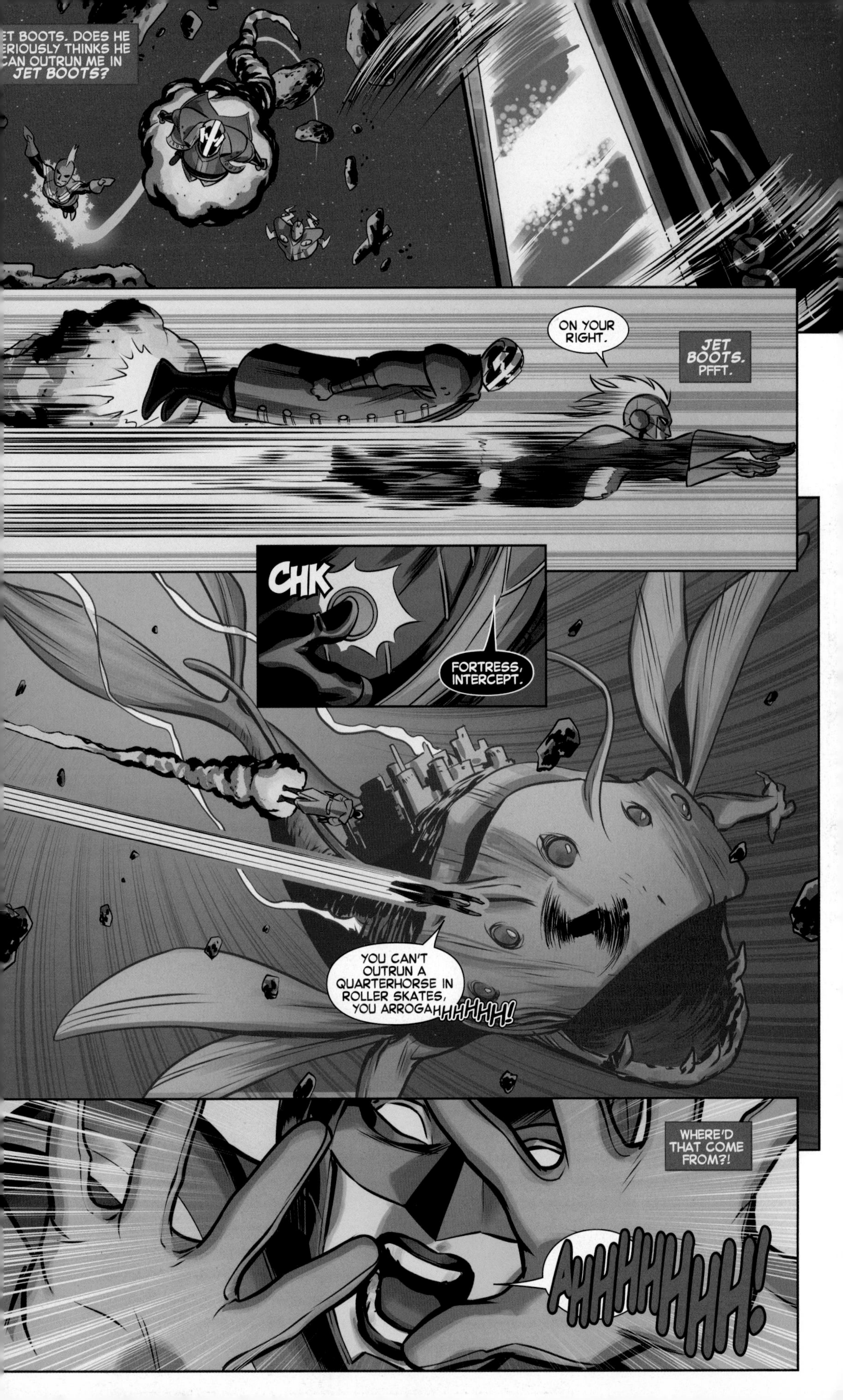
JET BOOTS. DOES HE SERIOUSLY THINKS HE CAN OUTRUN ME IN JET BOOTS?
ON YOUR RIGHT.
JET BOOTS. PFFT.
CHK
FORTRESS, INTERCEPT.
YOU CAN'T OUTRUN A QUARTERHORSE IN ROLLER SKATES, YOU ARROGAHHHHHH!
WHERE'D THAT COME FROM?!
AHHHHHHH!

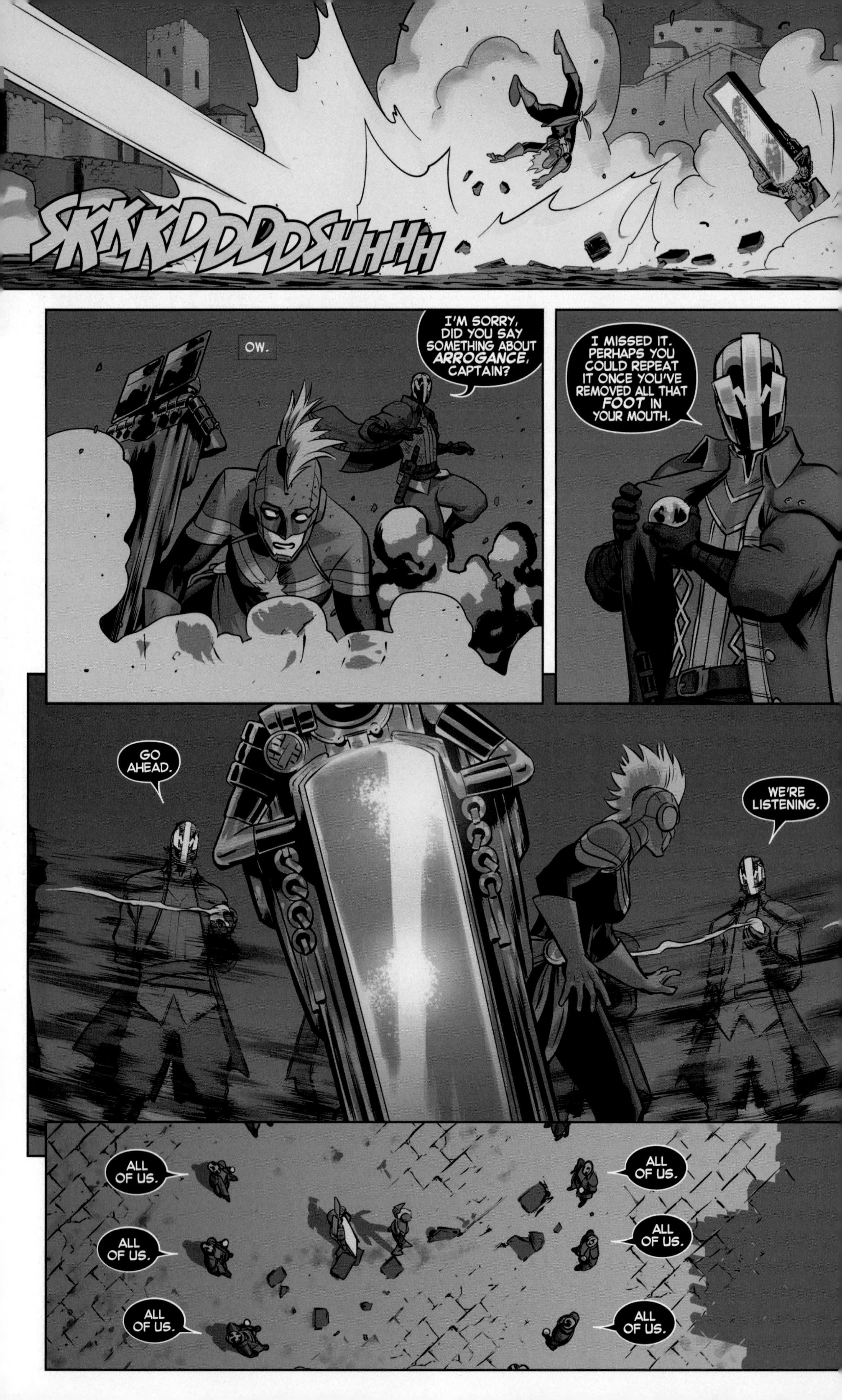
SKKKDDDDSHHHH
OW.
I'M SORRY, DID YOU SAY SOMETHING ABOUT ARROGANCE, CAPTAIN?
I MISSED IT. PERHAPS YOU COULD REPEAT IT ONCE YOU'VE REMOVED ALL THAT FOOT IN YOUR MOUTH.
GO AHEAD.
WE'RE LISTENING.
ALL OF US.
ALL OF US.
ALL OF US.
ALL OF US.
ALL OF US.
ALL OF US.

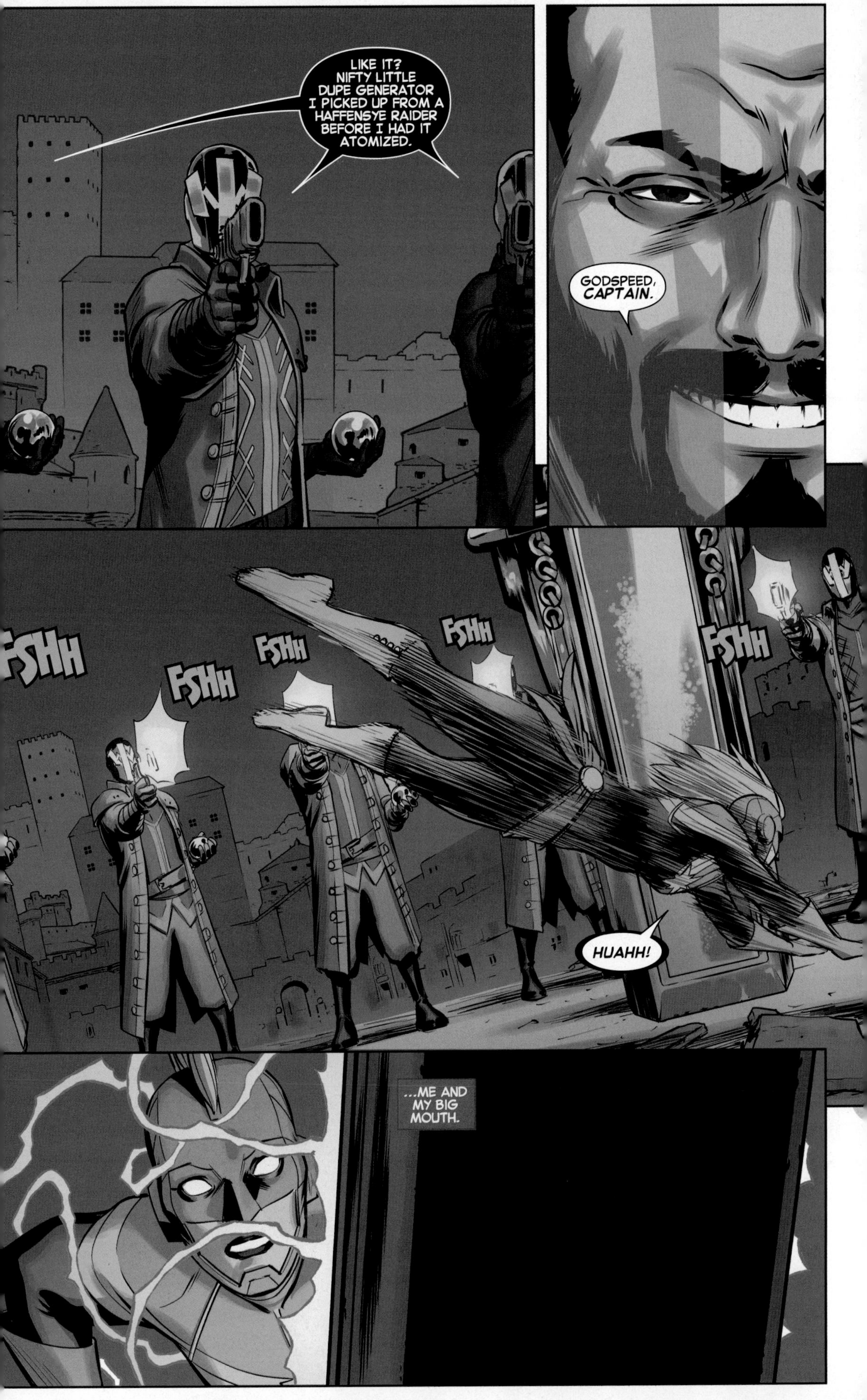
LIKE IT? NIFTY LITTLE DUPE GENERATOR I PICKED UP FROM A HAFFENSYE RAIDER BEFORE I HAD IT ATOMIZED.
GODSPEED, CAPTAIN.
FSHH
FSHH
FSHH
FSHH
FSHH
HUAHH!
...ME AND MY BIG MOUTH.

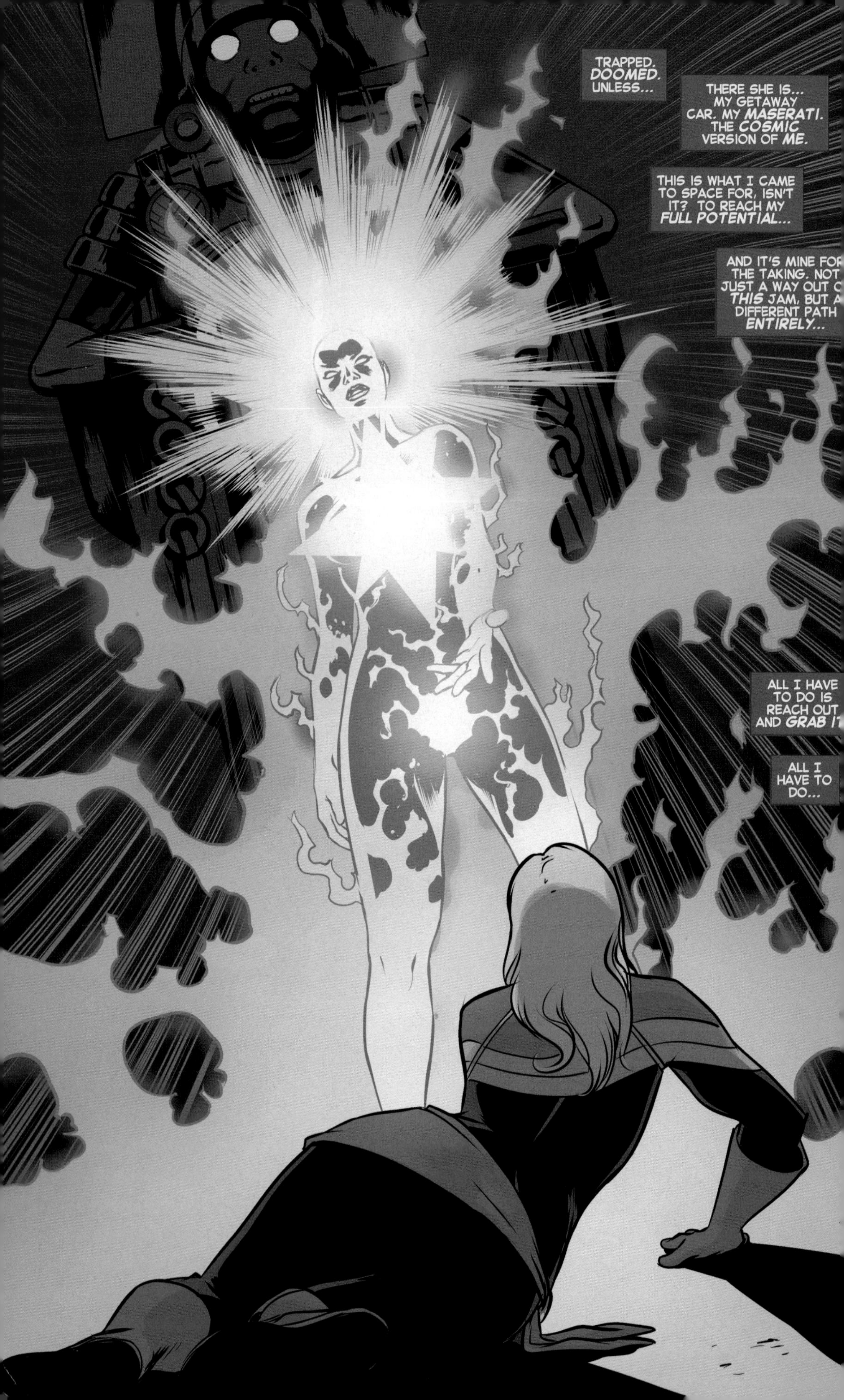

TRAPPED. DOOMED. UNLESS...
THERE SHE IS... MY GETAWAY CAR. MY MASERATI. THE COSMIC VERSION OF ME.
THIS IS WHAT I CAME TO SPACE FOR, ISN'T IT? TO REACH MY FULL POTENTIAL...
AND IT'S MINE FOR THE TAKING. NOT JUST A WAY OUT O THIS JAM, BUT A DIFFERENT PATH ENTIRELY...
ALL I HAVE TO DO IS REACH OUT AND GRAB IT
ALL I HAVE TO DO...

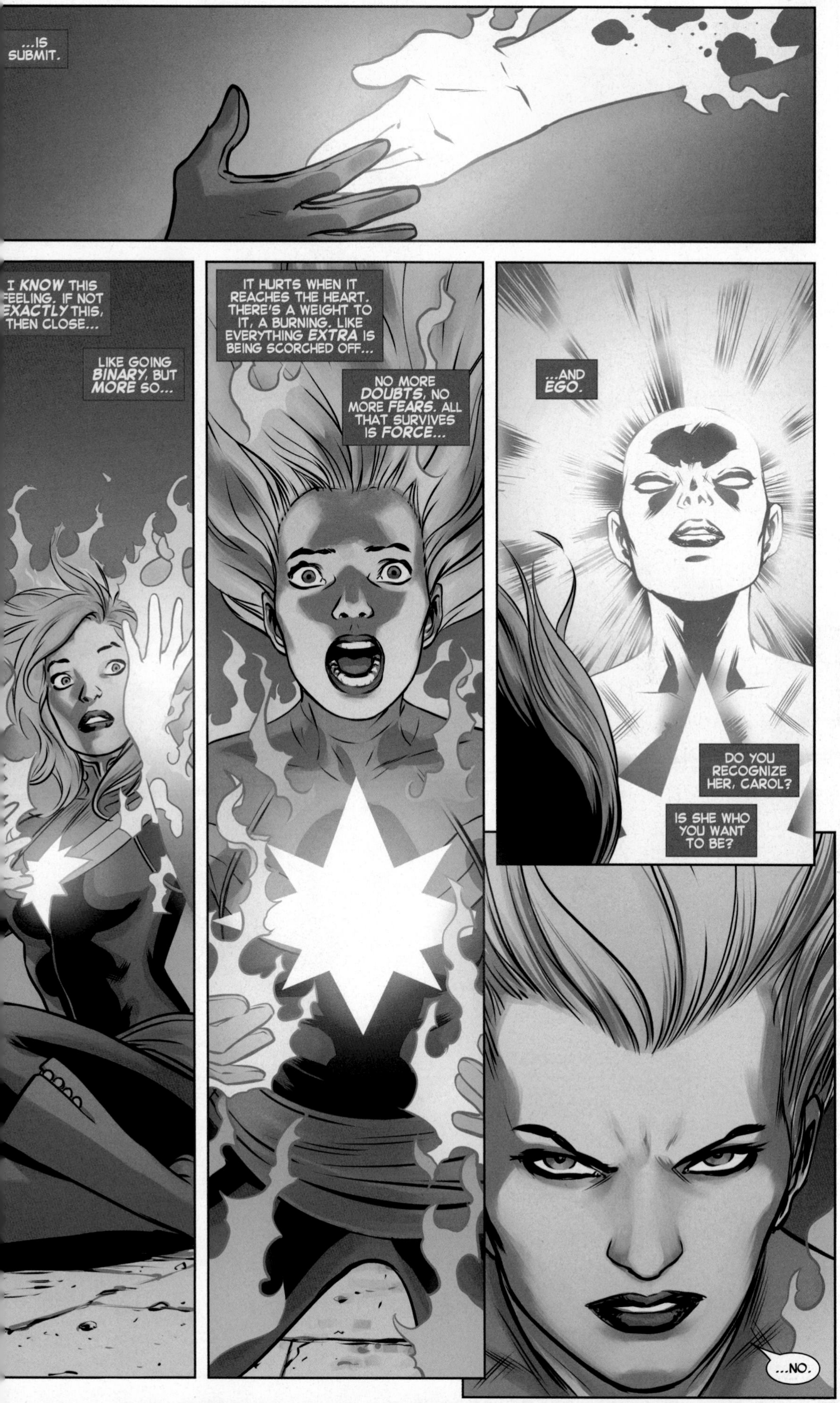

...IS SUBMIT.
I KNOW THIS FEELING. IF NOT EXACTLY THIS, THEN CLOSE...
LIKE GOING BINARY, BUT MORE SO...
IT HURTS WHEN IT REACHES THE HEART. THERE'S A WEIGHT TO IT, A BURNING. LIKE EVERYTHING EXTRA IS BEING SCORCHED OFF...
NO MORE DOUBTS, NO MORE FEARS. ALL THAT SURVIVES IS FORCE...
...AND EGO.
DO YOU RECOGNIZE HER, CAROL?
IS SHE WHO YOU WANT TO BE?
...NO.

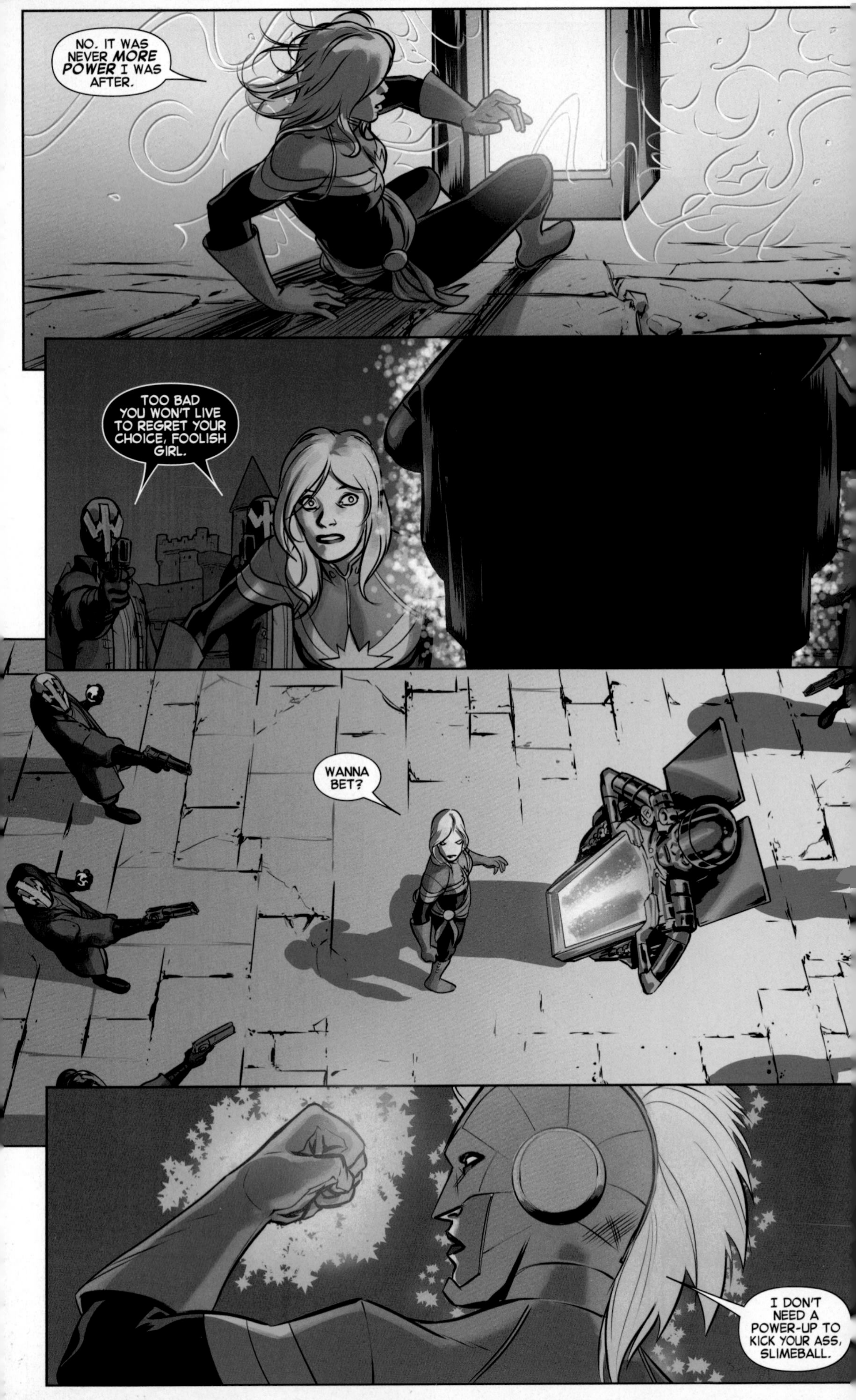
NO. IT WAS NEVER MORE POWER I WAS AFTER.
TOO BAD YOU WON'T LIVE TO REGRET YOUR CHOICE, FOOLISH GIRL.
WANNA BET?
I DON'T NEED A POWER-UP TO KICK YOUR ASS, SLIMEBALL.

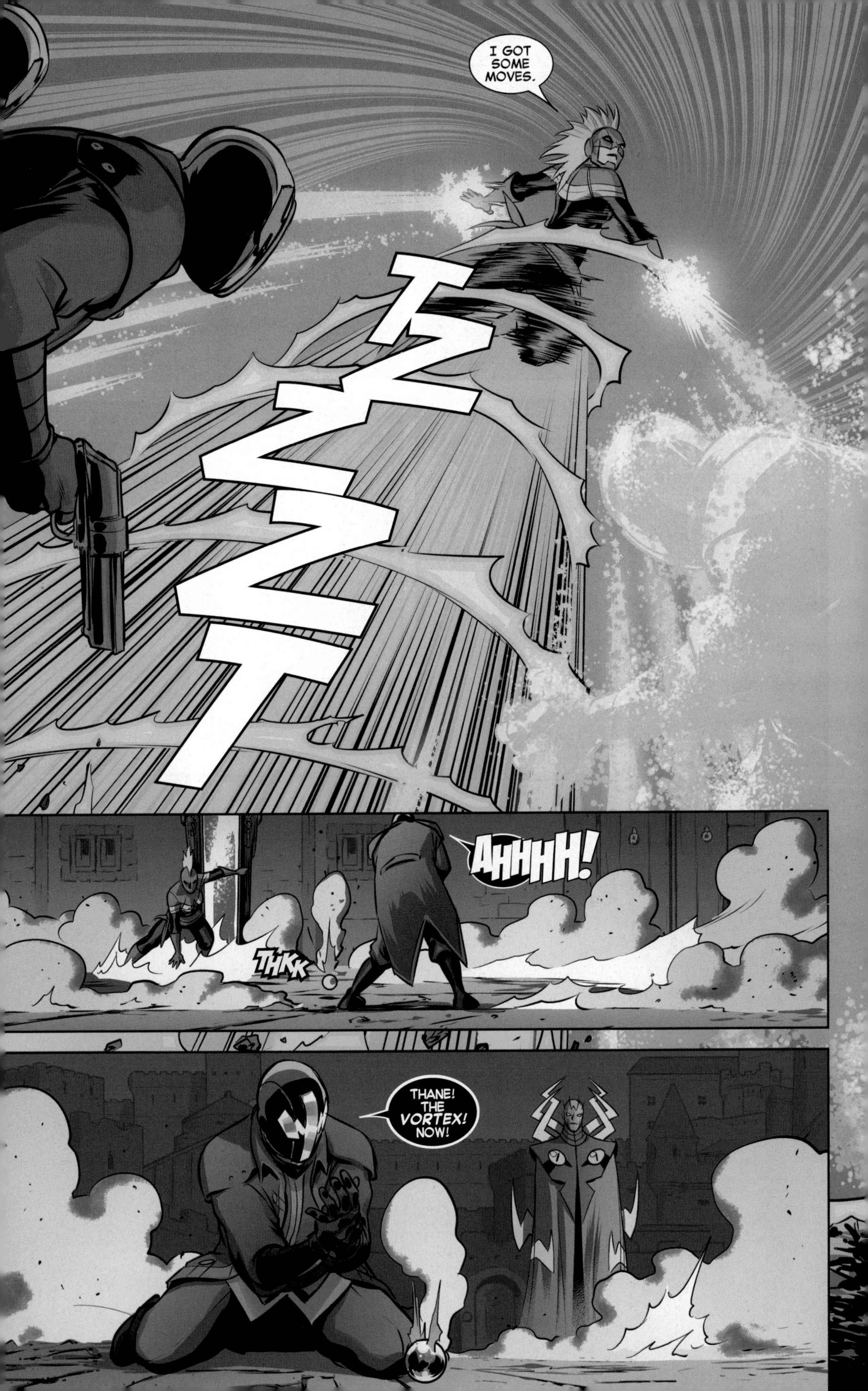
I GOT SOME MOVES.
TZZZZT
AHHHH!
THKK
THANE! THE VORTEX! NOW!

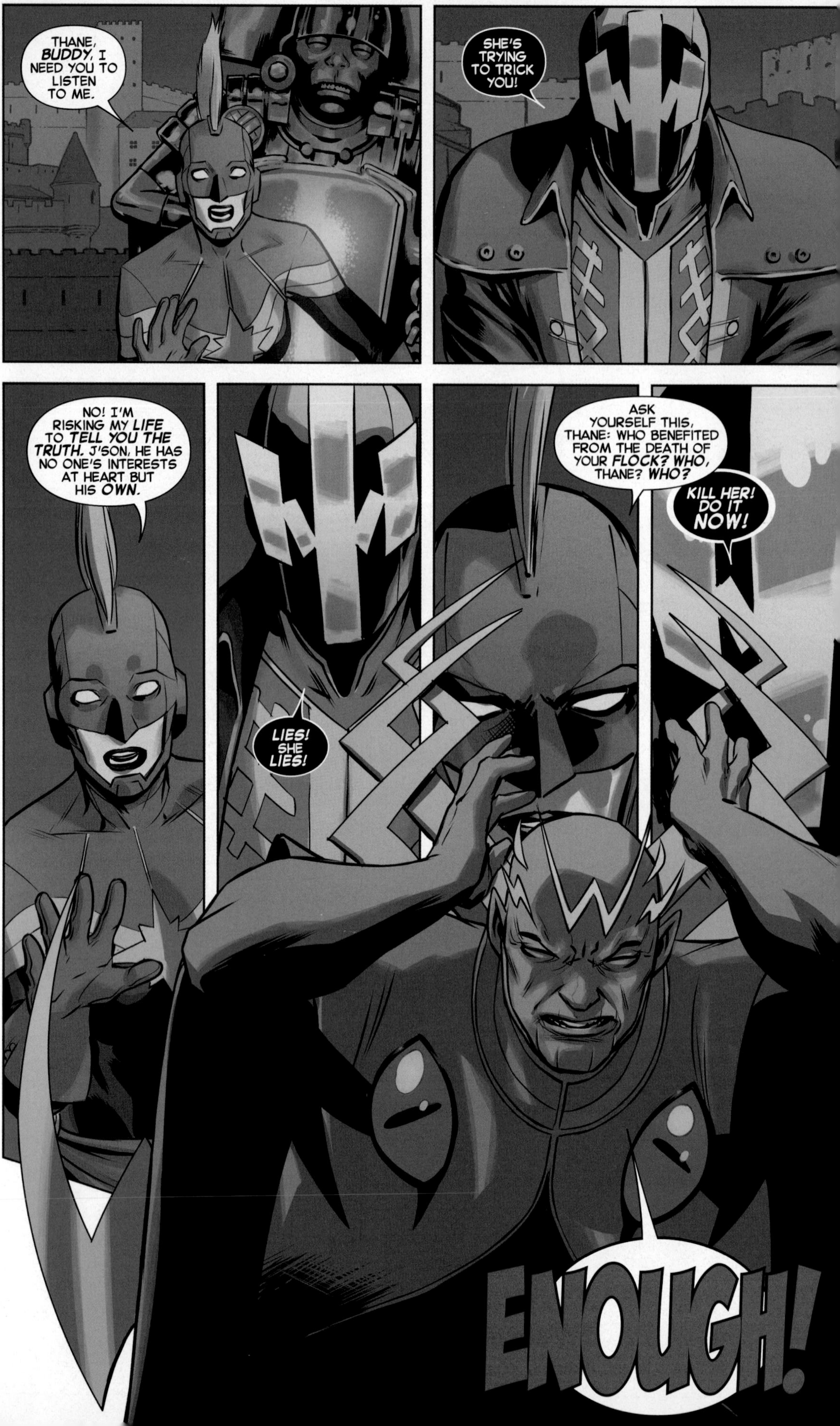
THANE, BUDDY, I NEED YOU TO LISTEN TO ME.
SHE'S TRYING TO TRICK YOU!
NO! I'M RISKING MY LIFE TO TELL YOU THE TRUTH. J'SON, HE HAS NO ONE'S INTERESTS AT HEART BUT HIS OWN.
LIES! SHE LIES!
ASK YOURSELF THIS, THANE: WHO BENEFITED FROM THE DEATH OF YOUR FLOCK? WHO, THANE? WHO?
KILL HER! DO IT NOW!
ENOUGH!

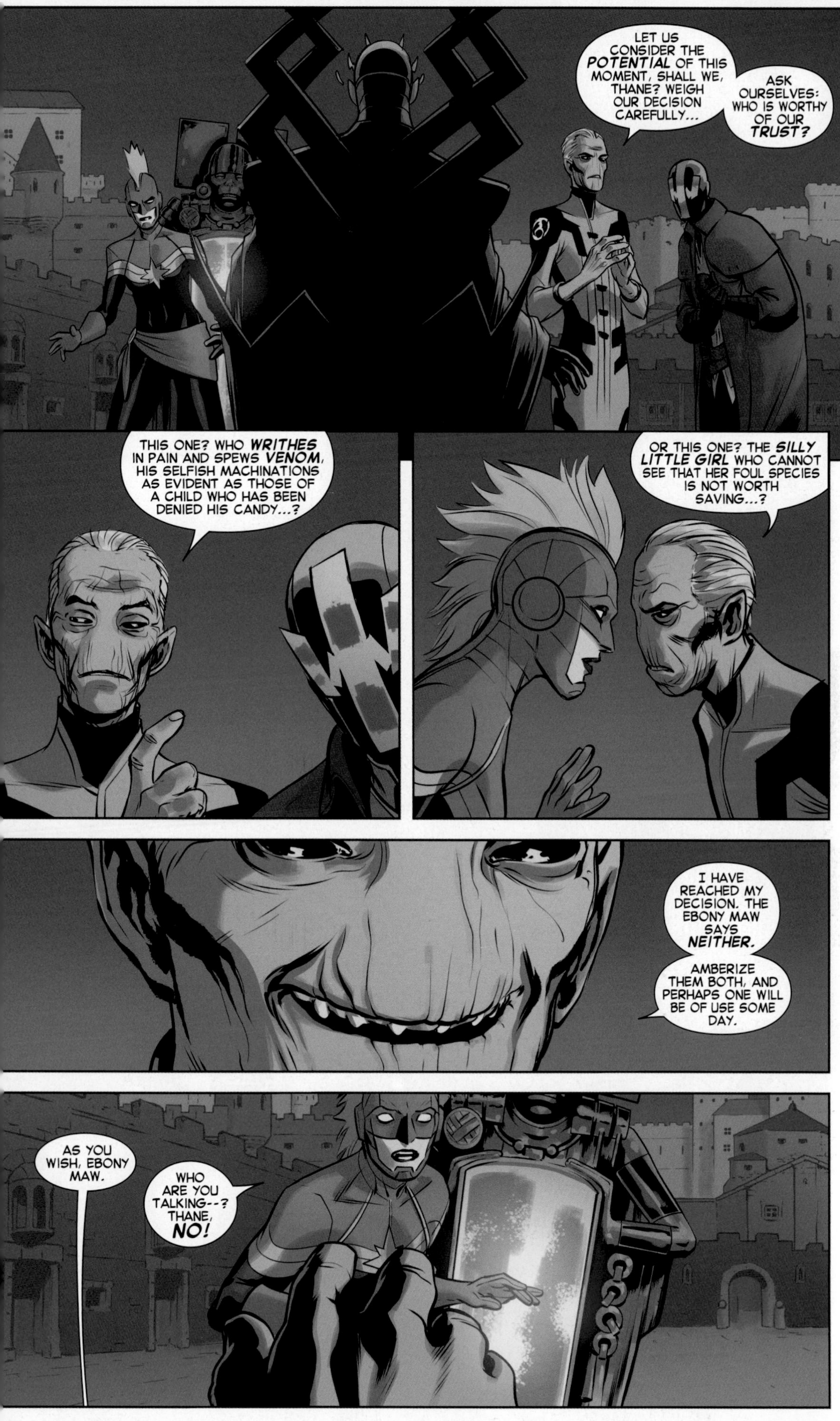
LET US CONSIDER THE POTENTIAL OF THIS MOMENT, SHALL WE, THANE? WEIGH OUR DECISION CAREFULLY...
ASK OURSELVES: WHO IS WORTHY OF OUR TRUST?
THIS ONE? WHO WRITHES IN PAIN AND SPEWS VENOM, HIS SELFISH MACHINATIONS AS EVIDENT AS THOSE OF A CHILD WHO HAS BEEN DENIED HIS CANDY...?
OR THIS ONE? THE SILLY LITTLE GIRL WHO CANNOT SEE THAT HER FOUL SPECIES IS NOT WORTH SAVING...?
I HAVE REACHED MY DECISION. THE EBONY MAW SAYS NEITHER.
AMBERIZE THEM BOTH, AND PERHAPS ONE WILL BE OF USE SOME DAY.
AS YOU WISH, EBONY MAW.
WHO ARE YOU TALKING--? THANE, NO!

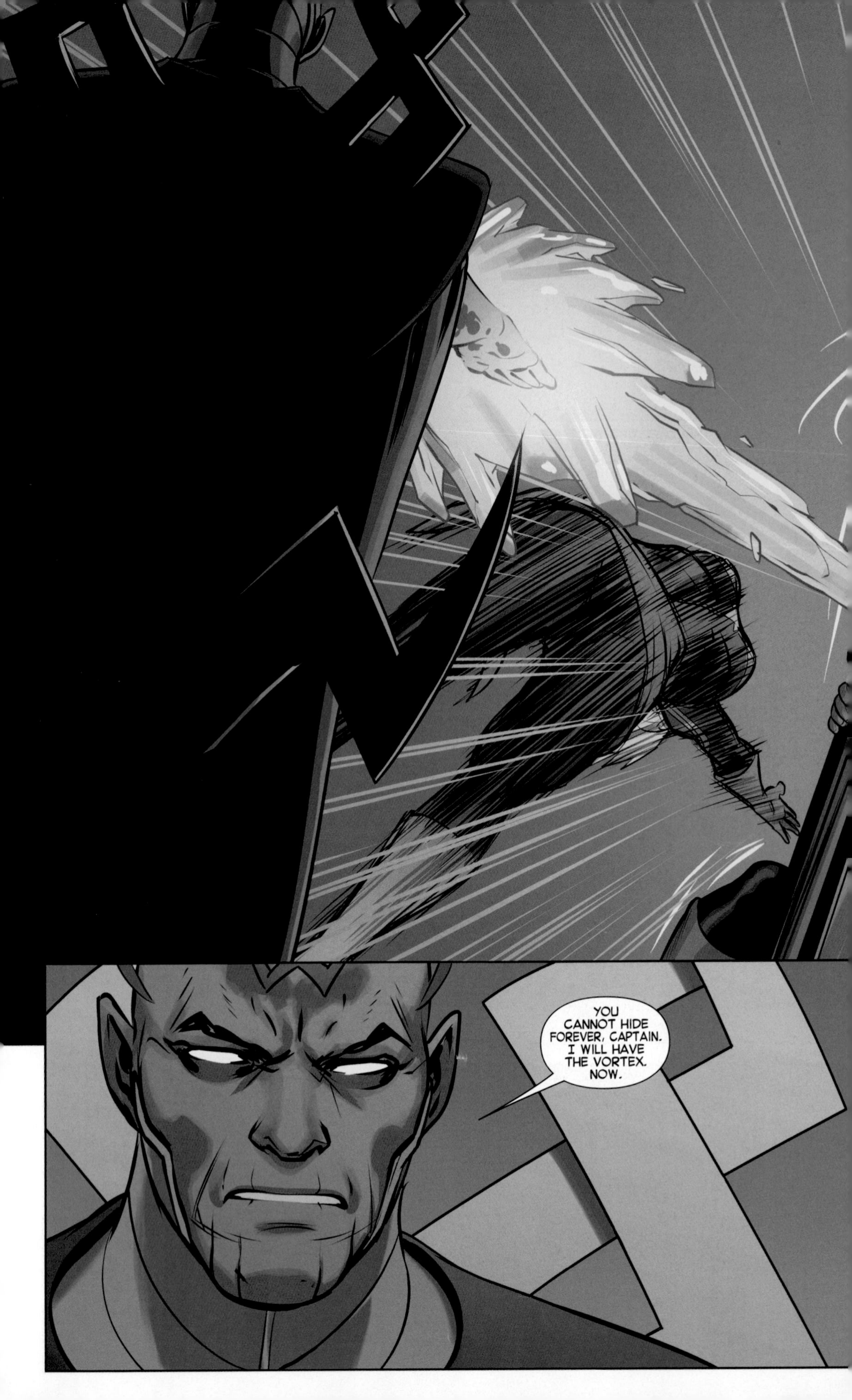
YOU CANNOT HIDE FOREVER, CAPTAIN. I WILL HAVE THE VORTEX. NOW.

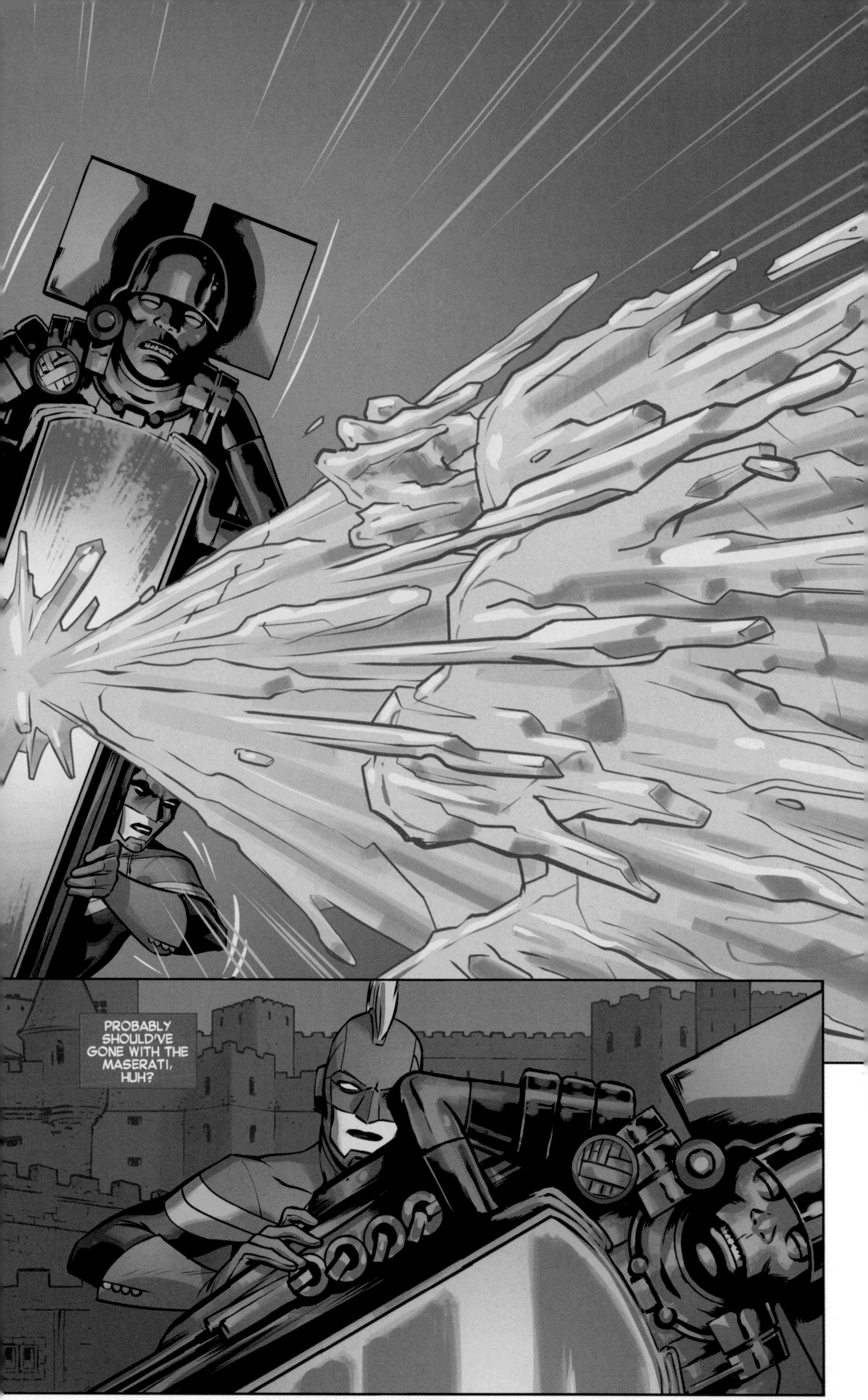
PROBABLY SHOULD'VE GONE WITH THE MASERATI, HUH?

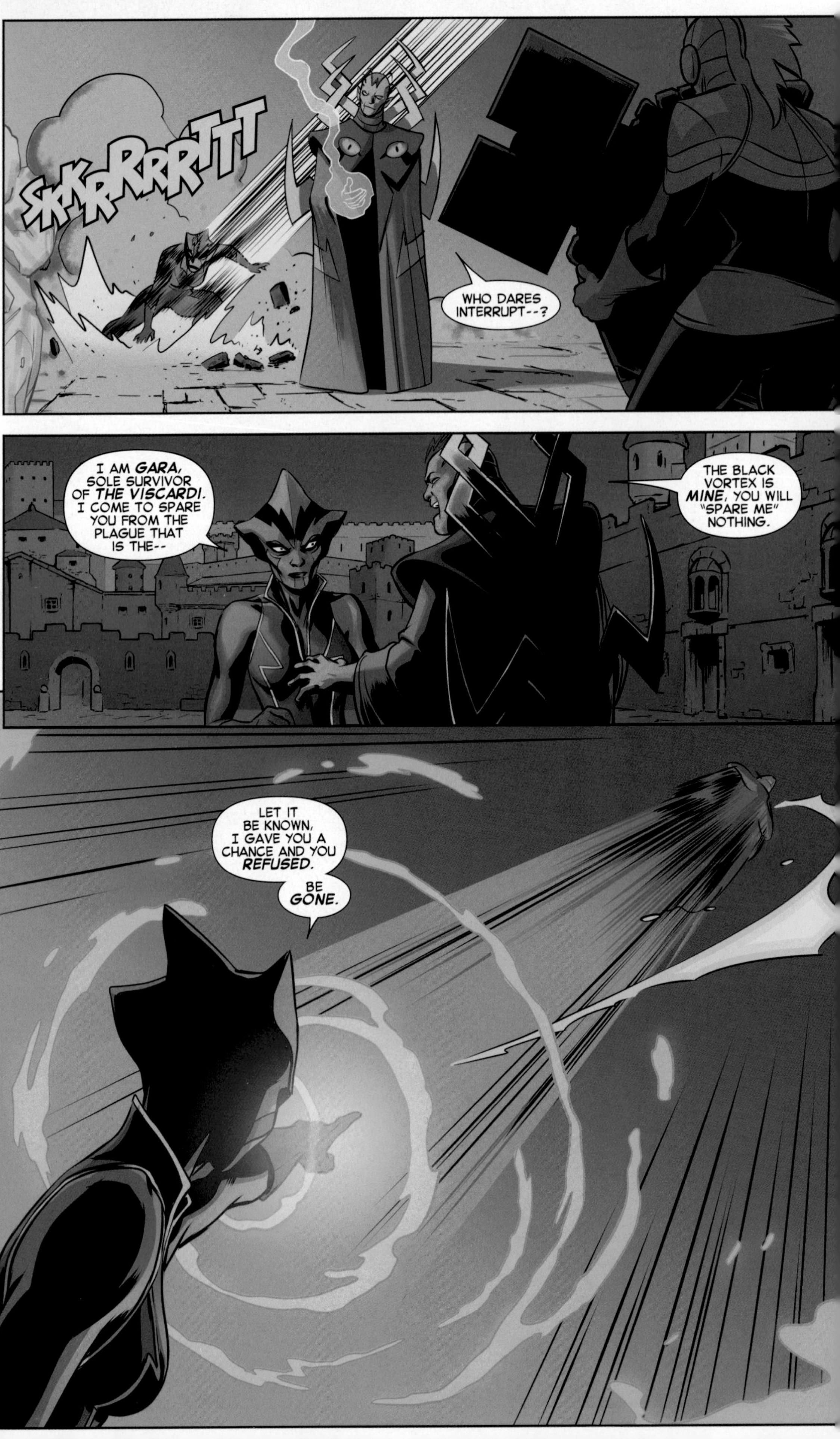
SKKRRRRRTTT
WHO DARES INTERRUPT--?
I AM GARA, SOLE SURVIVOR OF THE VISCARDI. I COME TO SPARE YOU FROM THE PLAGUE THAT IS THE--
THE BLACK VORTEX IS MINE, YOU WILL "SPARE ME" NOTHING.
LET IT BE KNOWN, I GAVE YOU A CHANCE AND YOU REFUSED.
BE GONE.

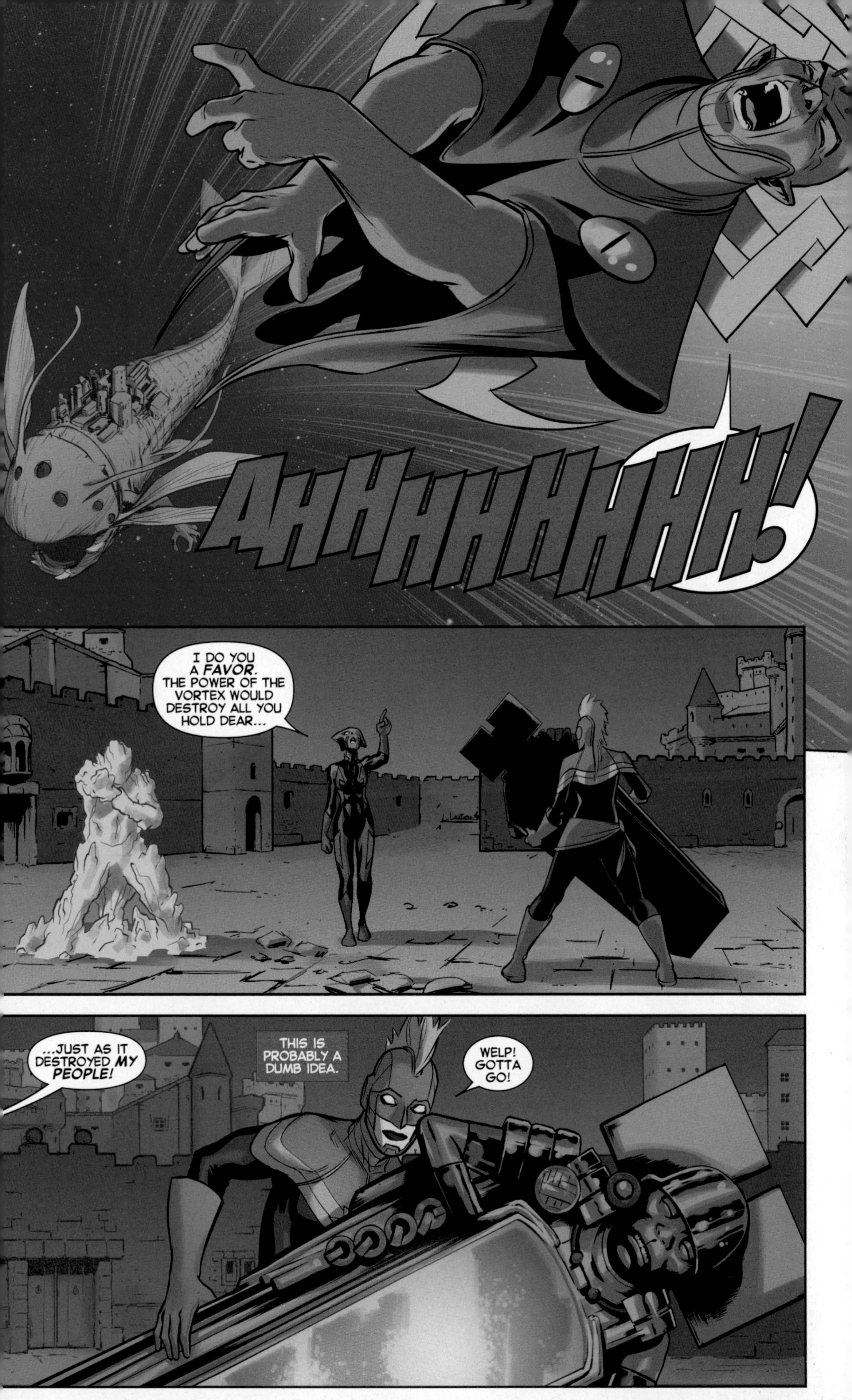
AHHHHHHHHHH!
I DO YOU A *FAVOR*. THE POWER OF THE VORTEX WOULD DESTROY ALL YOU HOLD DEAR...
...JUST AS IT DESTROYED *MY PEOPLE!*
THIS IS PROBABLY A DUMB IDEA.
WELP! GOTTA GO!

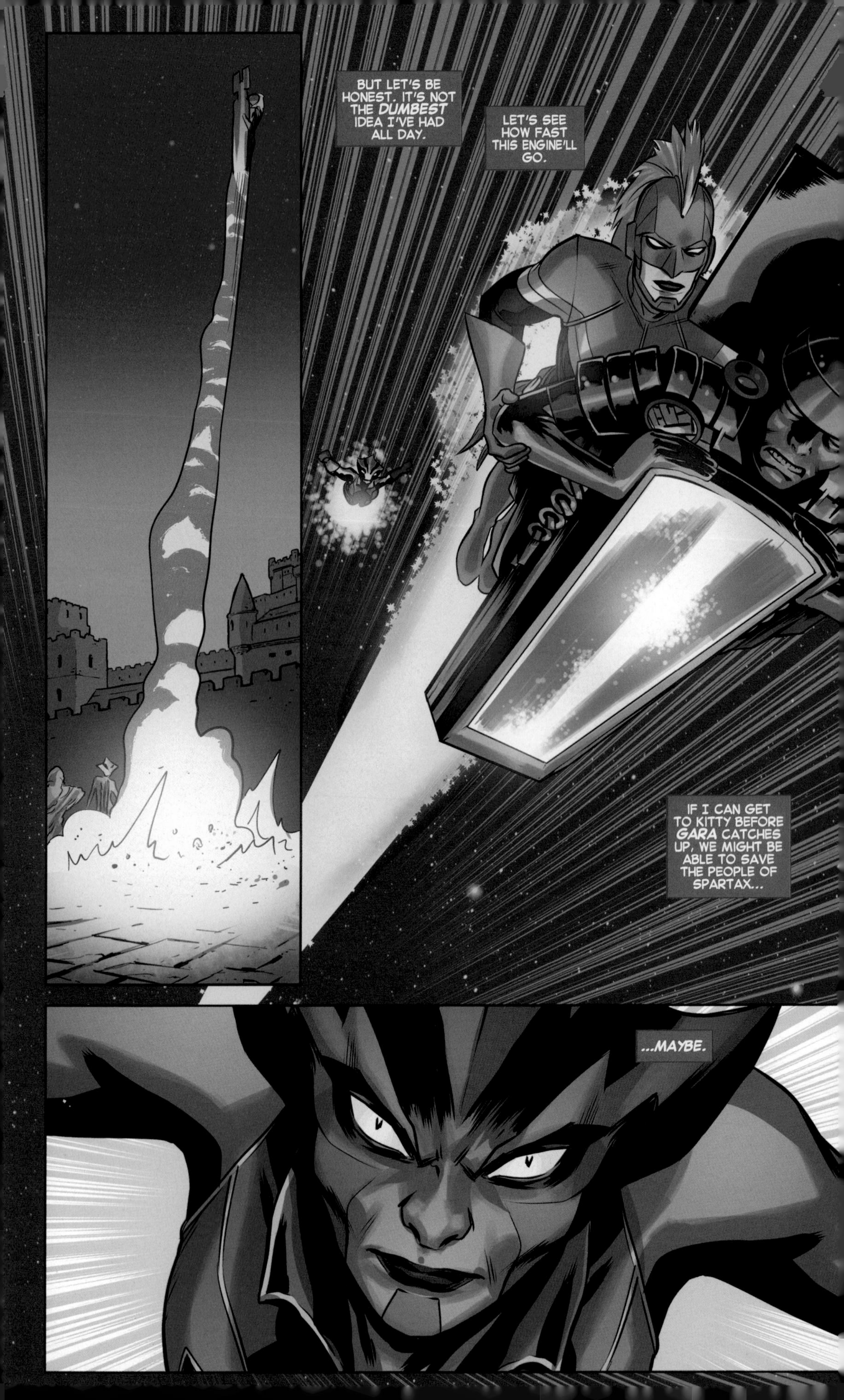
BUT LET'S BE HONEST. IT'S NOT THE DUMBEST IDEA I'VE HAD ALL DAY.
LET'S SEE HOW FAST THIS ENGINE'LL GO.
IF I CAN GET TO KITTY BEFORE GARA CATCHES UP, WE MIGHT BE ABLE TO SAVE THE PEOPLE OF SPARTAX...
...MAYBE.

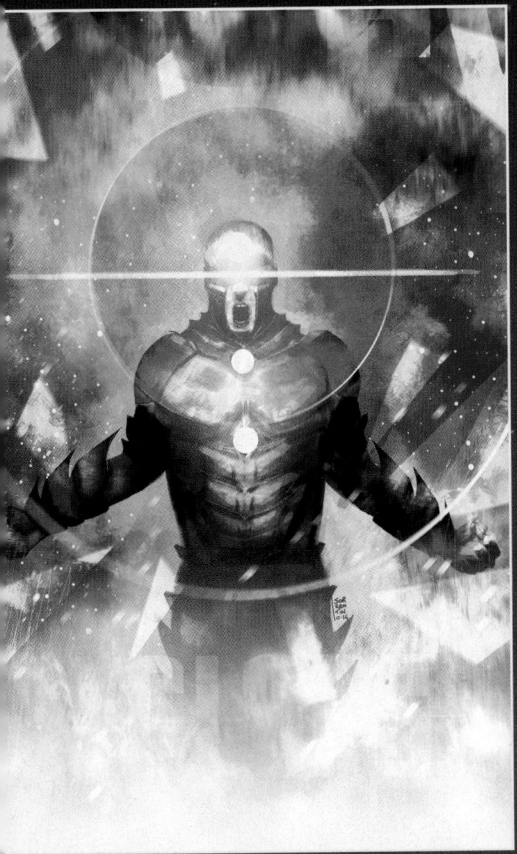

CYCLOPS #12 COSMICALLY ENHANCED VARIANT
BY ANDREA SORRENTINO

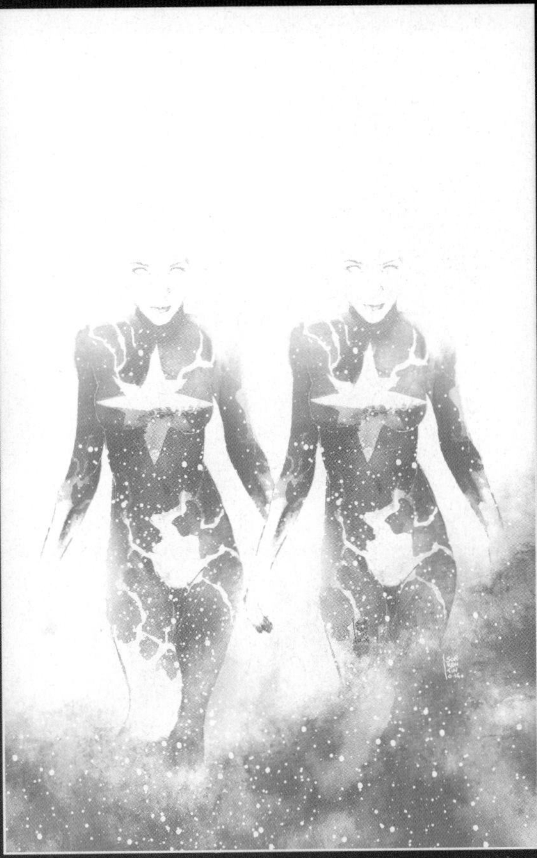

CAPTAIN MARVEL #14 COSMICALLY ENHANCED VARIANT
BY ANDREA SORRENTINO

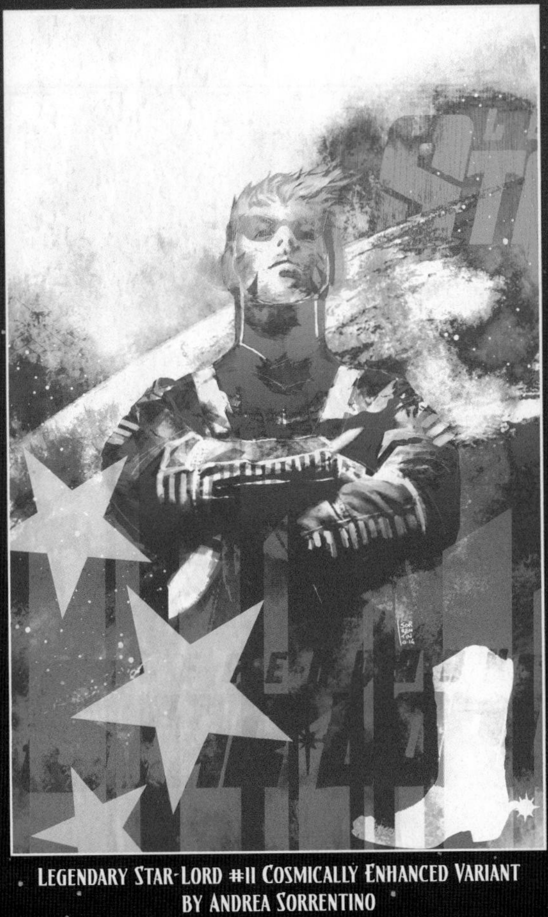

LEGENDARY STAR-LORD #11 COSMICALLY ENHANCED VARIANT
BY ANDREA SORRENTINO

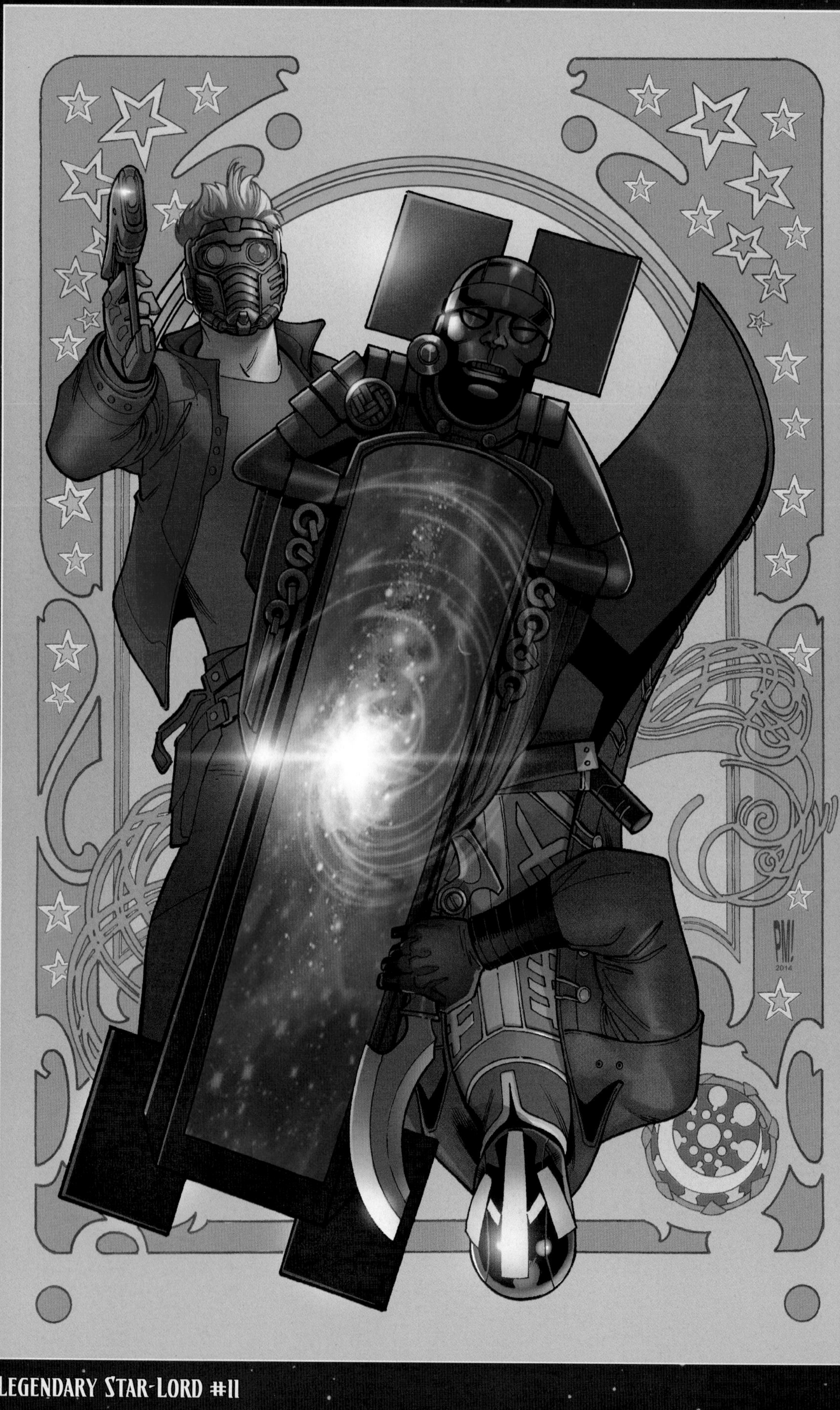

LEGENDARY STAR-LORD #11

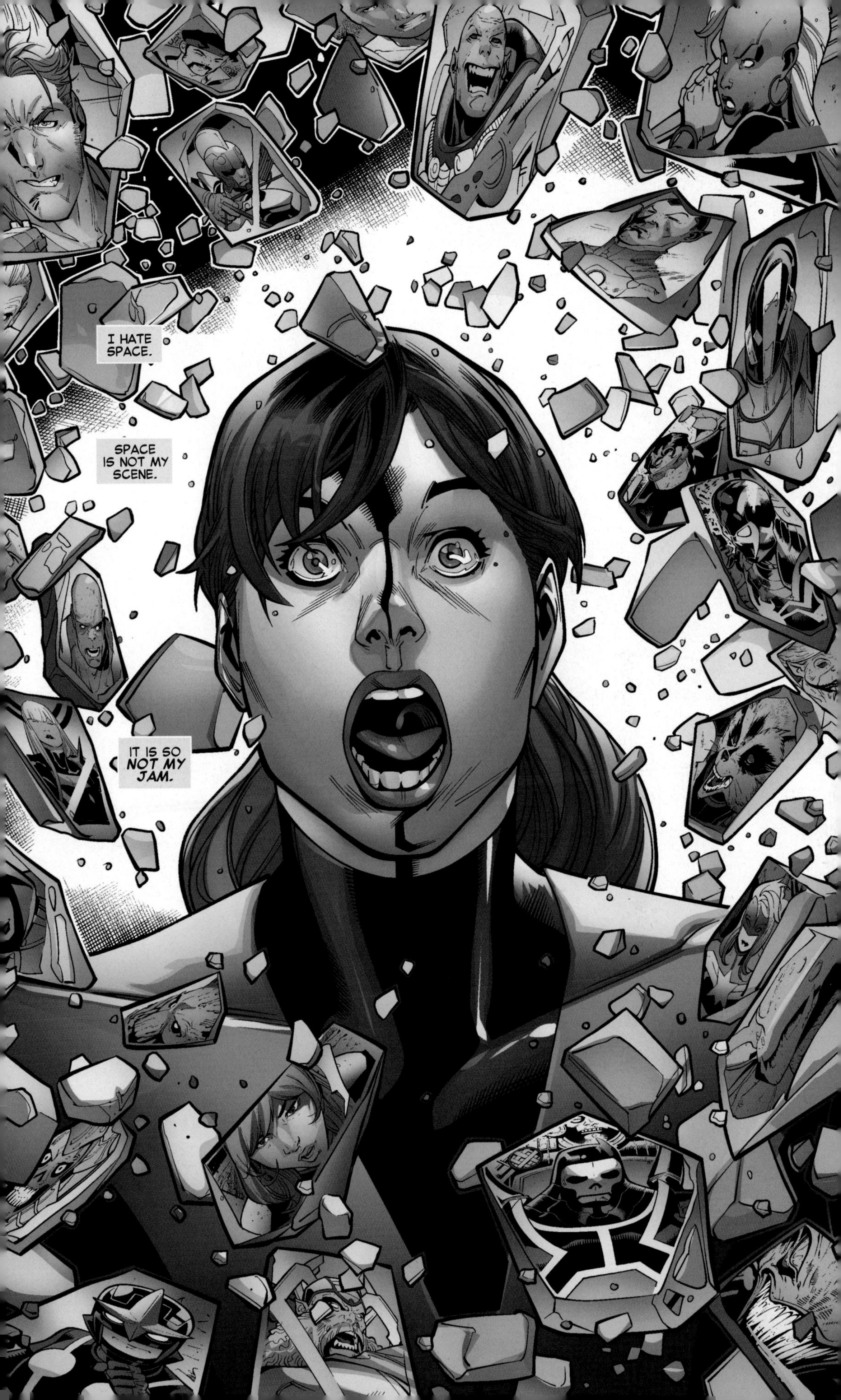
I HATE SPACE.
SPACE IS NOT MY SCENE.
IT IS SO *NOT MY JAM*.

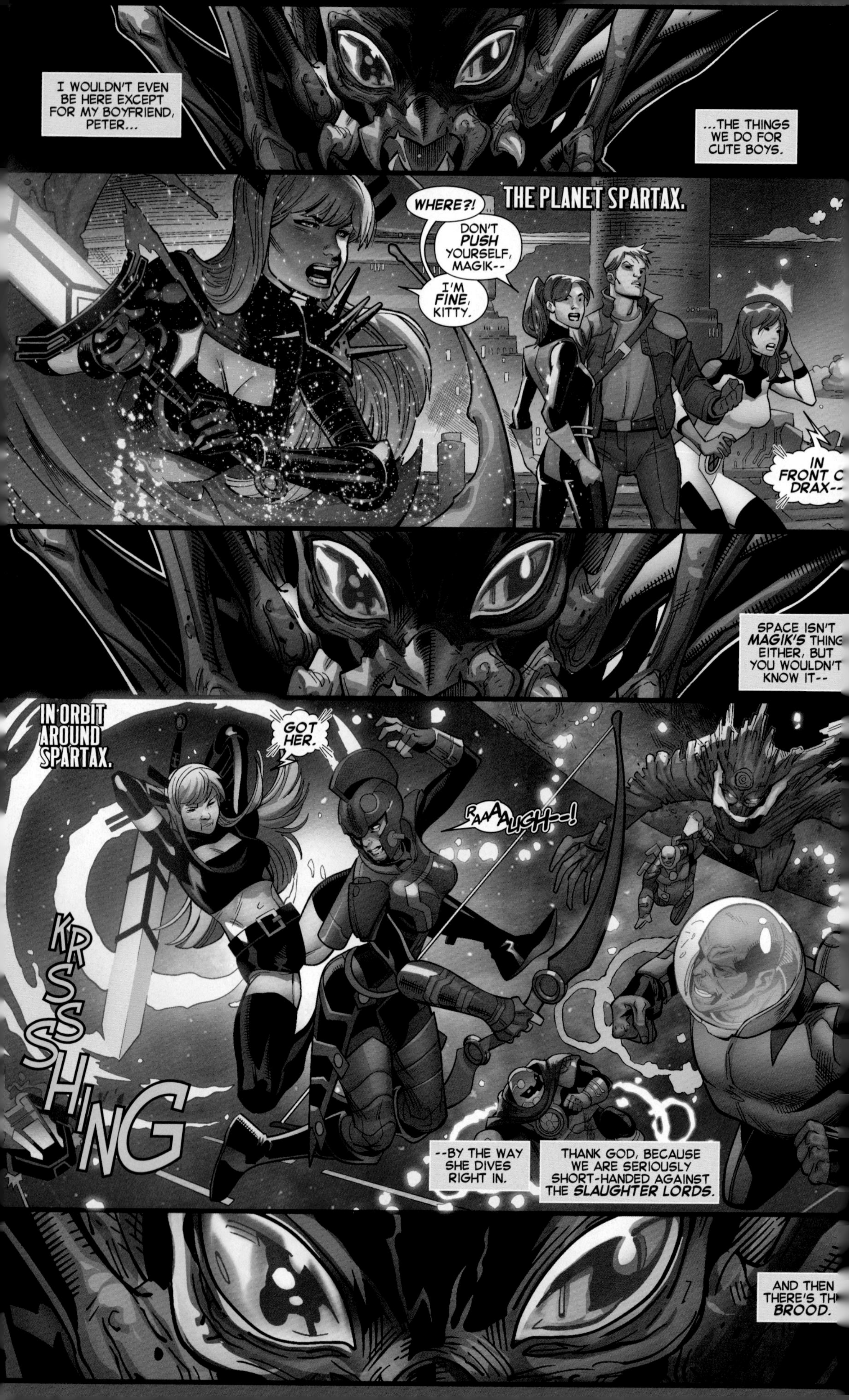

I WOULDN'T EVEN BE HERE EXCEPT FOR MY BOYFRIEND, PETER...
...THE THINGS WE DO FOR CUTE BOYS.
THE PLANET SPARTAX.
WHERE?!
DON'T PUSH YOURSELF, MAGIK--
I'M FINE, KITTY.
IN FRONT O DRAX--
SPACE ISN'T MAGIK'S THING EITHER, BUT YOU WOULDN'T KNOW IT--
IN ORBIT AROUND SPARTAX.
GOT HER.
RAAAAUGH--!
KRSSSHING
--BY THE WAY SHE DIVES RIGHT IN.
THANK GOD, BECAUSE WE ARE SERIOUSLY SHORT-HANDED AGAINST THE SLAUGHTER LORDS.
AND THEN THERE'S TH BROOD.

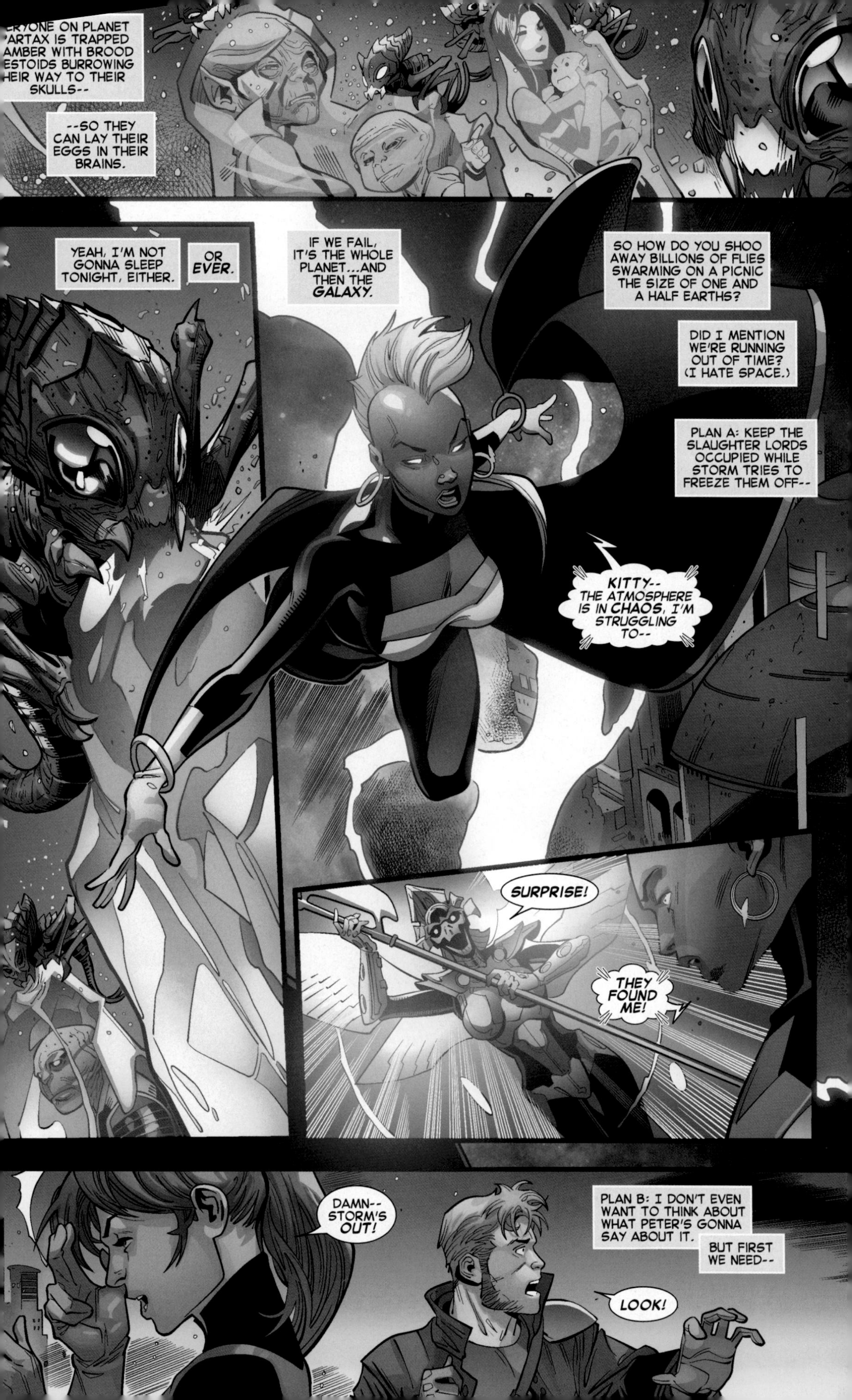
ERYONE ON PLANET 'ARTAX IS TRAPPED AMBER WITH BROOD ESTOIDS BURROWING HEIR WAY TO THEIR SKULLS--
--SO THEY CAN LAY THEIR EGGS IN THEIR BRAINS.
YEAH, I'M NOT GONNA SLEEP TONIGHT, EITHER.
OR *EVER*.
IF WE FAIL, IT'S THE WHOLE PLANET...AND THEN THE *GALAXY*.
SO HOW DO YOU SHOO AWAY BILLIONS OF FLIES SWARMING ON A PICNIC THE SIZE OF ONE AND A HALF EARTHS?
DID I MENTION WE'RE RUNNING OUT OF TIME? (I HATE SPACE.)
PLAN A: KEEP THE SLAUGHTER LORDS OCCUPIED WHILE STORM TRIES TO FREEZE THEM OFF--
KITTY-- THE ATMOSPHERE IS IN *CHAOS*, I'M STRUGGLING TO--
SURPRISE!
THEY FOUND ME!
DAMN-- STORM'S *OUT*!
PLAN B: I DON'T EVEN WANT TO THINK ABOUT WHAT PETER'S GONNA SAY ABOUT IT.
BUT FIRST WE NEED--
LOOK!

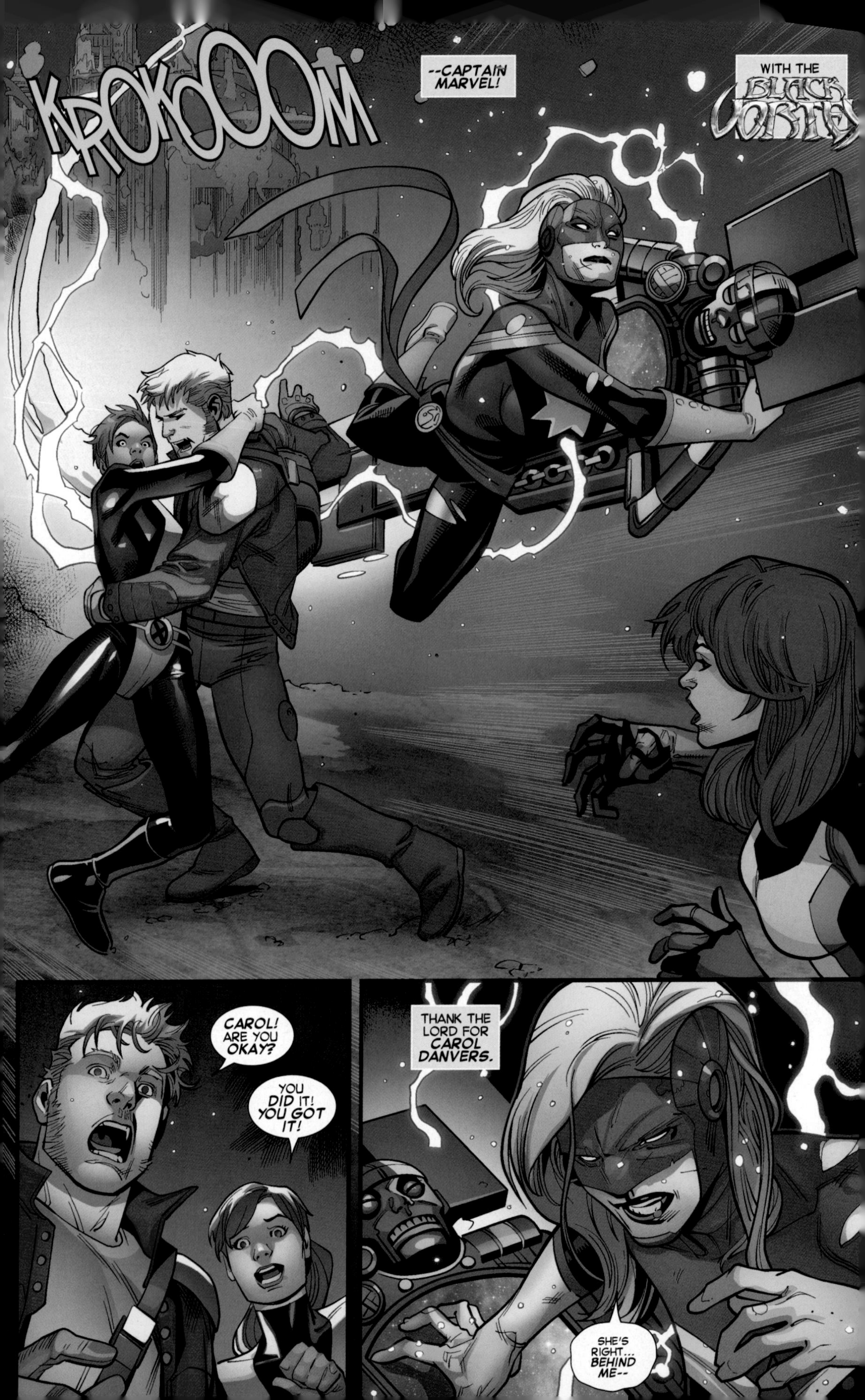
KROKOOOM
--CAPTAIN MARVEL!
WITH THE BLACK VORTEX
CAROL! ARE YOU OKAY?
YOU DID IT! YOU GOT IT!
THANK THE LORD FOR CAROL DANVERS.
SHE'S RIGHT... BEHIND ME--

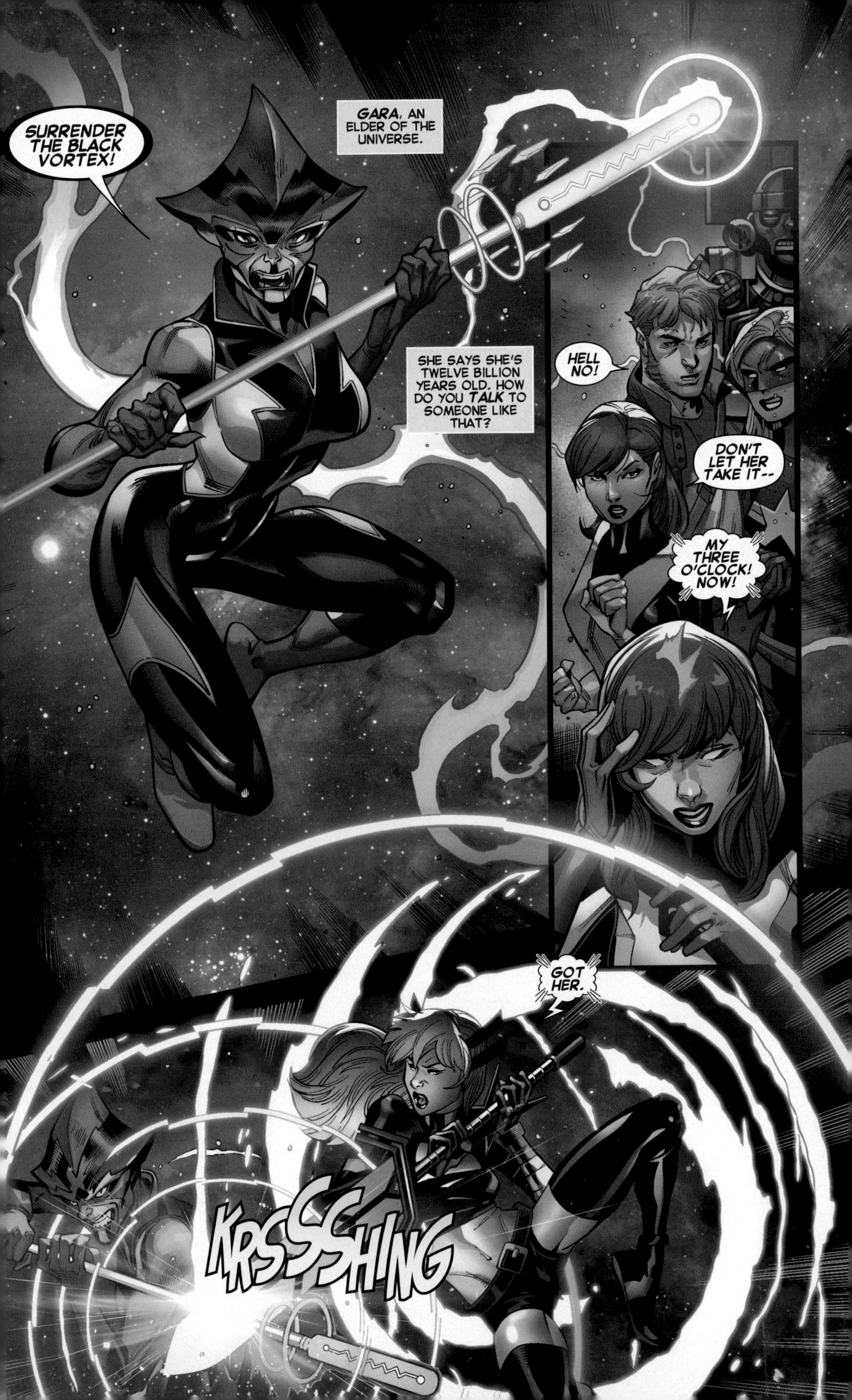
SURRENDER THE BLACK VORTEX!
GARA, AN ELDER OF THE UNIVERSE.
SHE SAYS SHE'S TWELVE BILLION YEARS OLD. HOW DO YOU TALK TO SOMEONE LIKE THAT?
HELL NO!
DON'T LET HER TAKE IT--
MY THREE O'CLOCK! NOW!
GOT HER.
KRSSSHING

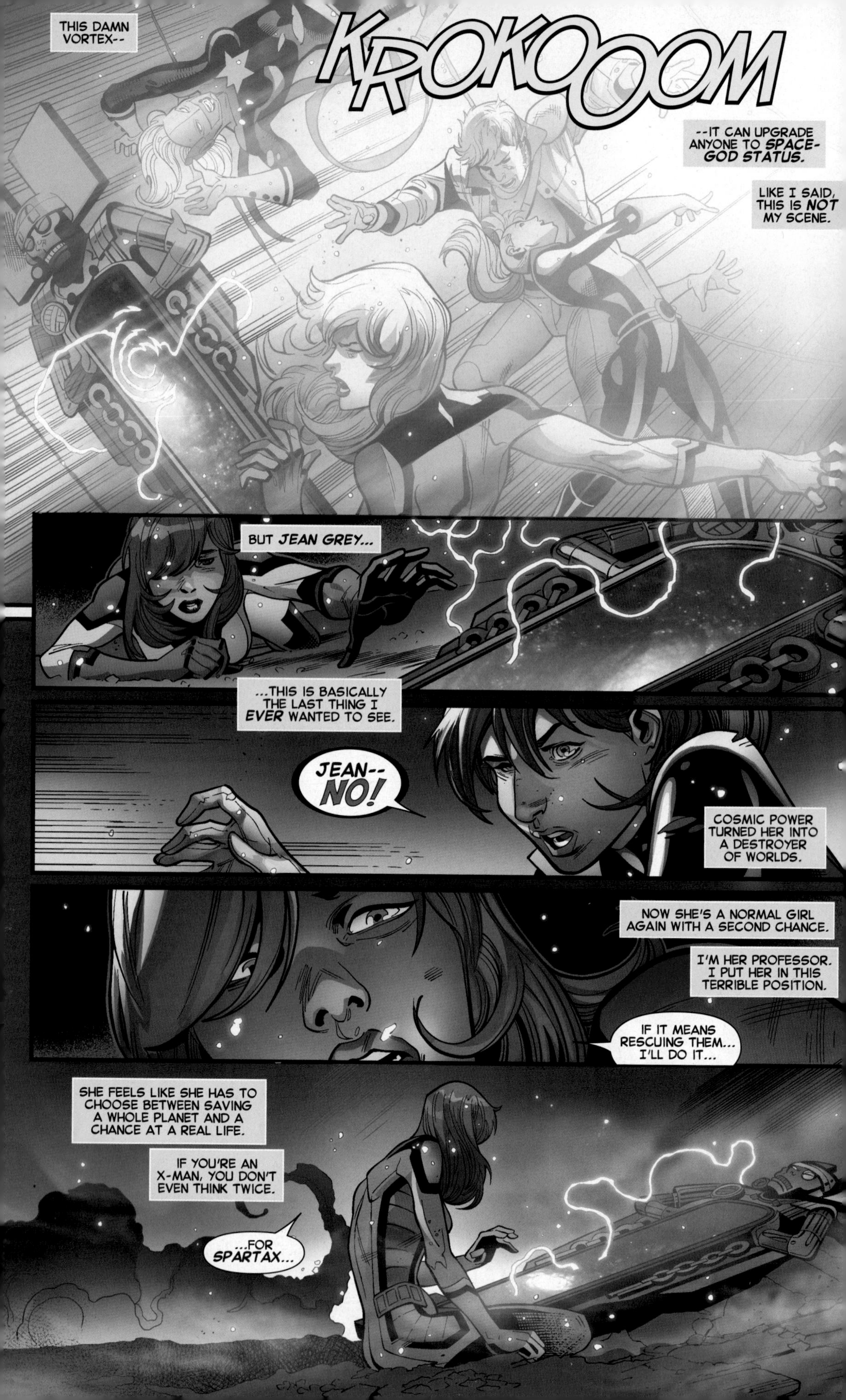
THIS DAMN VORTEX--
KROKOOOOM
--IT CAN UPGRADE ANYONE TO SPACE-GOD STATUS.
LIKE I SAID, THIS IS NOT MY SCENE.
BUT JEAN GREY...
...THIS IS BASICALLY THE LAST THING I EVER WANTED TO SEE.
JEAN-- NO!
COSMIC POWER TURNED HER INTO A DESTROYER OF WORLDS.
NOW SHE'S A NORMAL GIRL AGAIN WITH A SECOND CHANCE.
I'M HER PROFESSOR. I PUT HER IN THIS TERRIBLE POSITION.
IF IT MEANS RESCUING THEM... I'LL DO IT...
SHE FEELS LIKE SHE HAS TO CHOOSE BETWEEN SAVING A WHOLE PLANET AND A CHANCE AT A REAL LIFE.
IF YOU'RE AN X-MAN, YOU DON'T EVEN THINK TWICE.
...FOR SPARTAX...

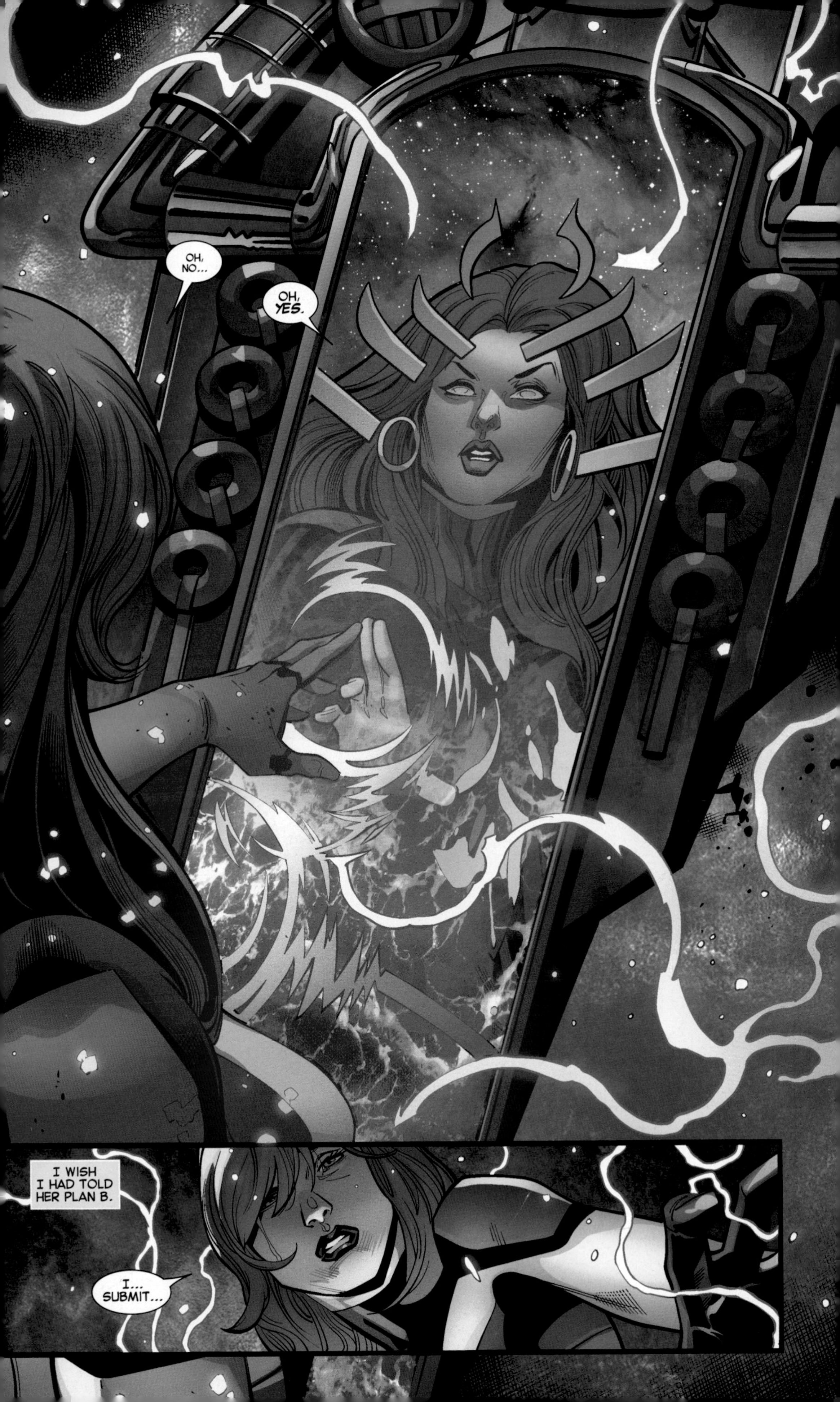
OH, NO...
OH, YES.
I WISH I HAD TOLD HER PLAN B.
I... SUBMIT...

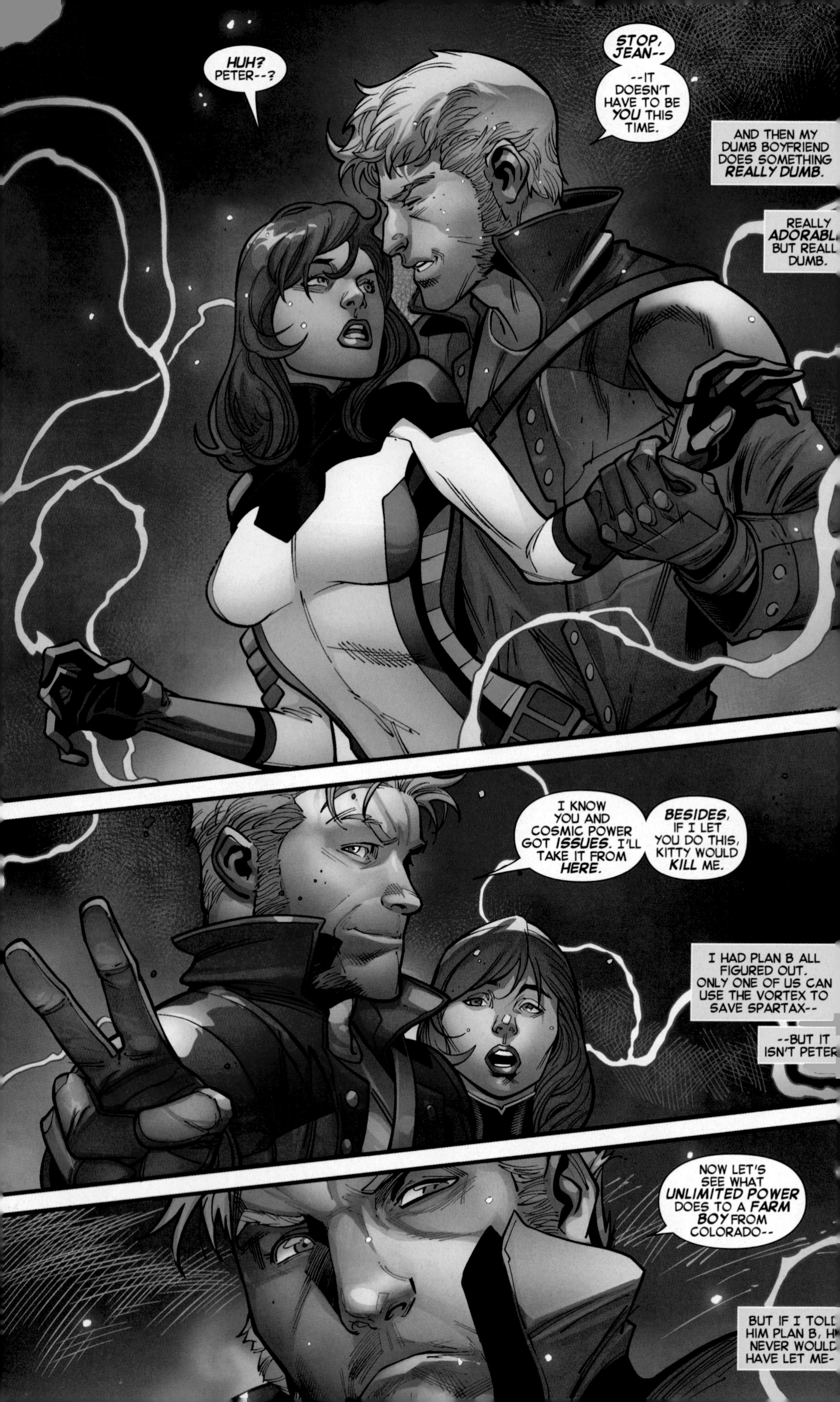
HUH? PETER--?
STOP, JEAN--
--IT DOESN'T HAVE TO BE YOU THIS TIME.
AND THEN MY DUMB BOYFRIEND DOES SOMETHING REALLY DUMB.
REALLY ADORABL BUT REALL DUMB.
I KNOW YOU AND COSMIC POWER GOT ISSUES. I'LL TAKE IT FROM HERE.
BESIDES, IF I LET YOU DO THIS, KITTY WOULD KILL ME.
I HAD PLAN B ALL FIGURED OUT. ONLY ONE OF US CAN USE THE VORTEX TO SAVE SPARTAX--
--BUT IT ISN'T PETER
NOW LET'S SEE WHAT UNLIMITED POWER DOES TO A FARM BOY FROM COLORADO--
BUT IF I TOLD HIM PLAN B, H NEVER WOULD HAVE LET ME-

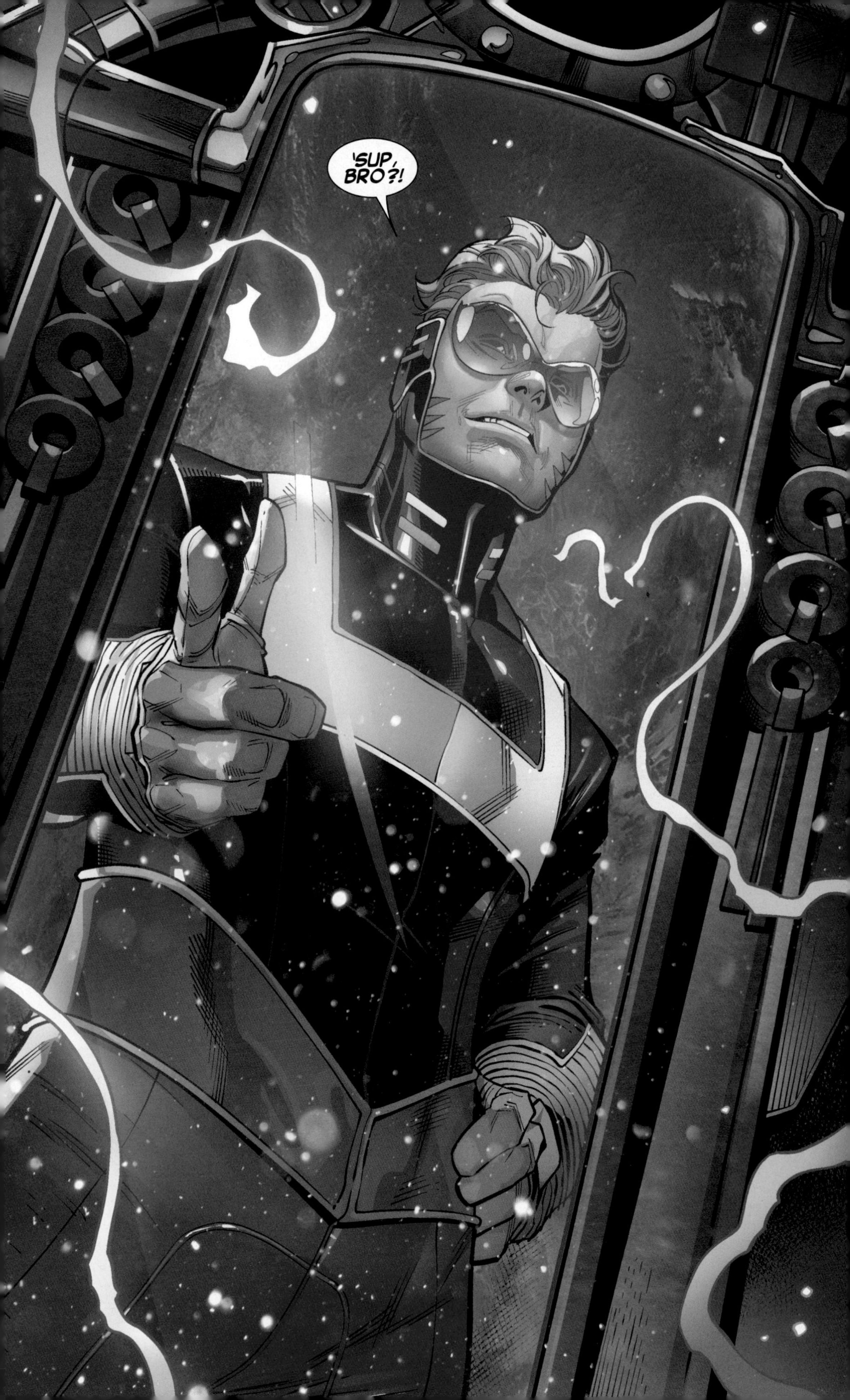
'SUP, BRO?!

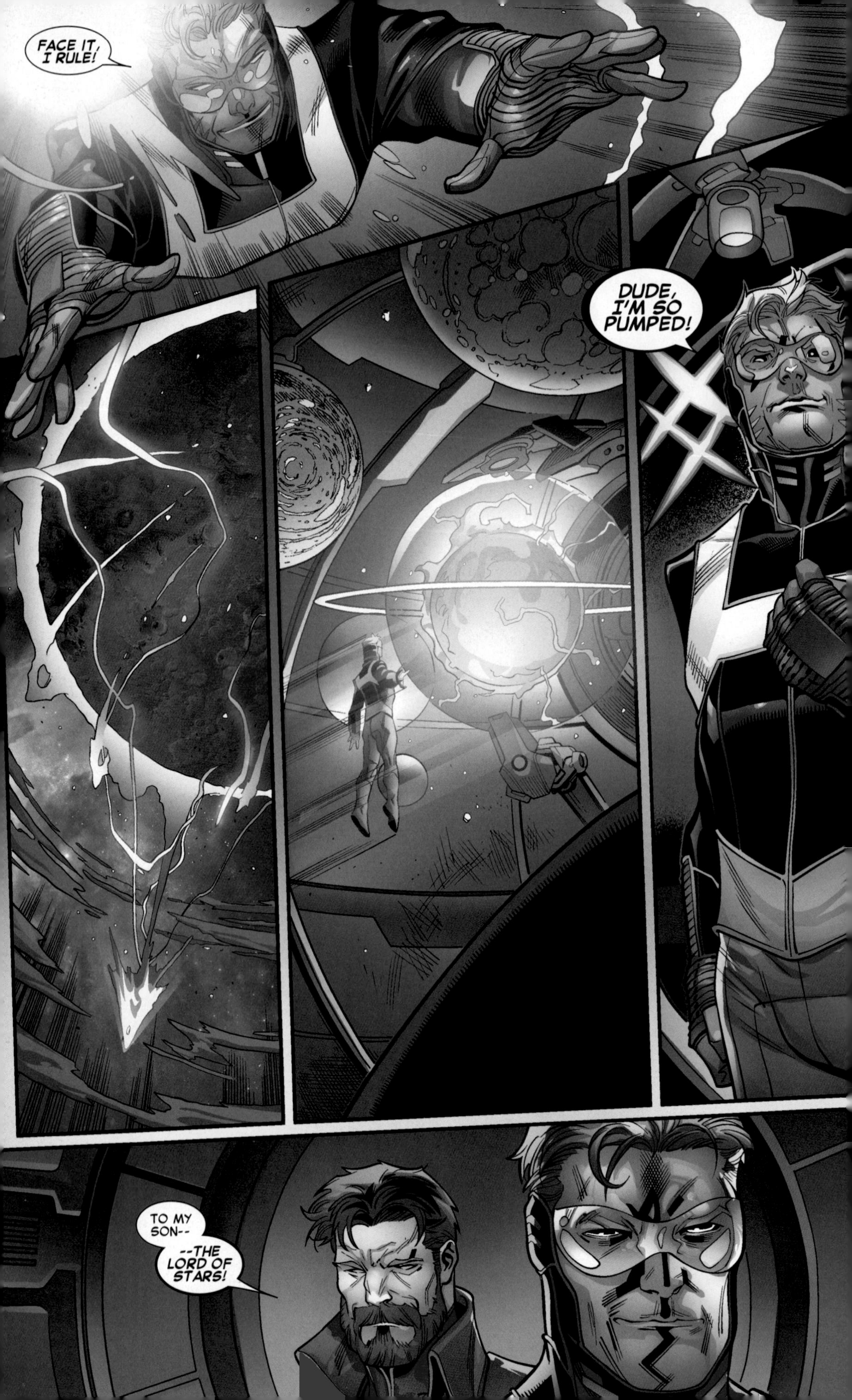
FACE IT, I RULE!
DUDE, I'M SO PUMPED!
TO MY SON--
--THE LORD OF STARS!

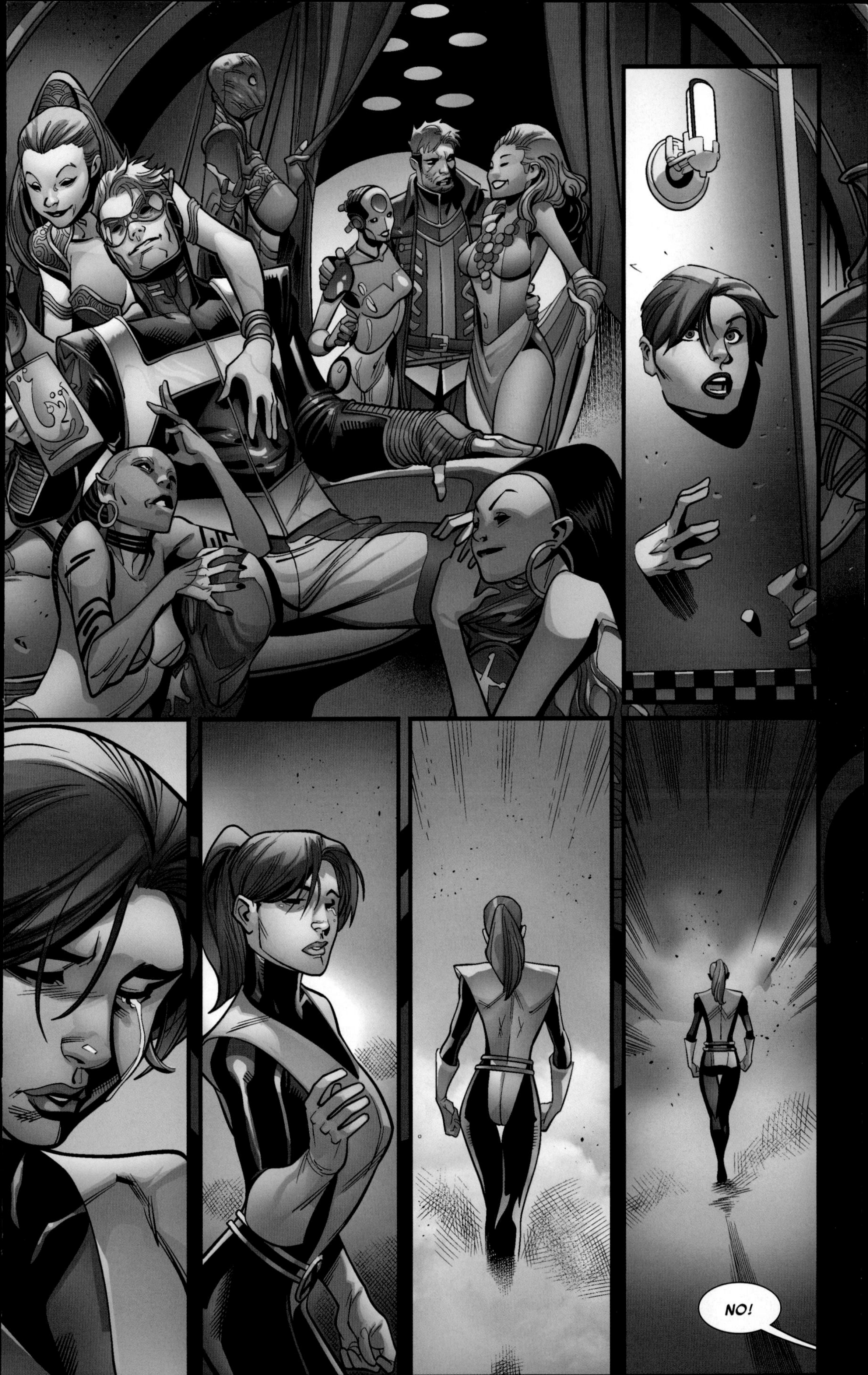
NO!

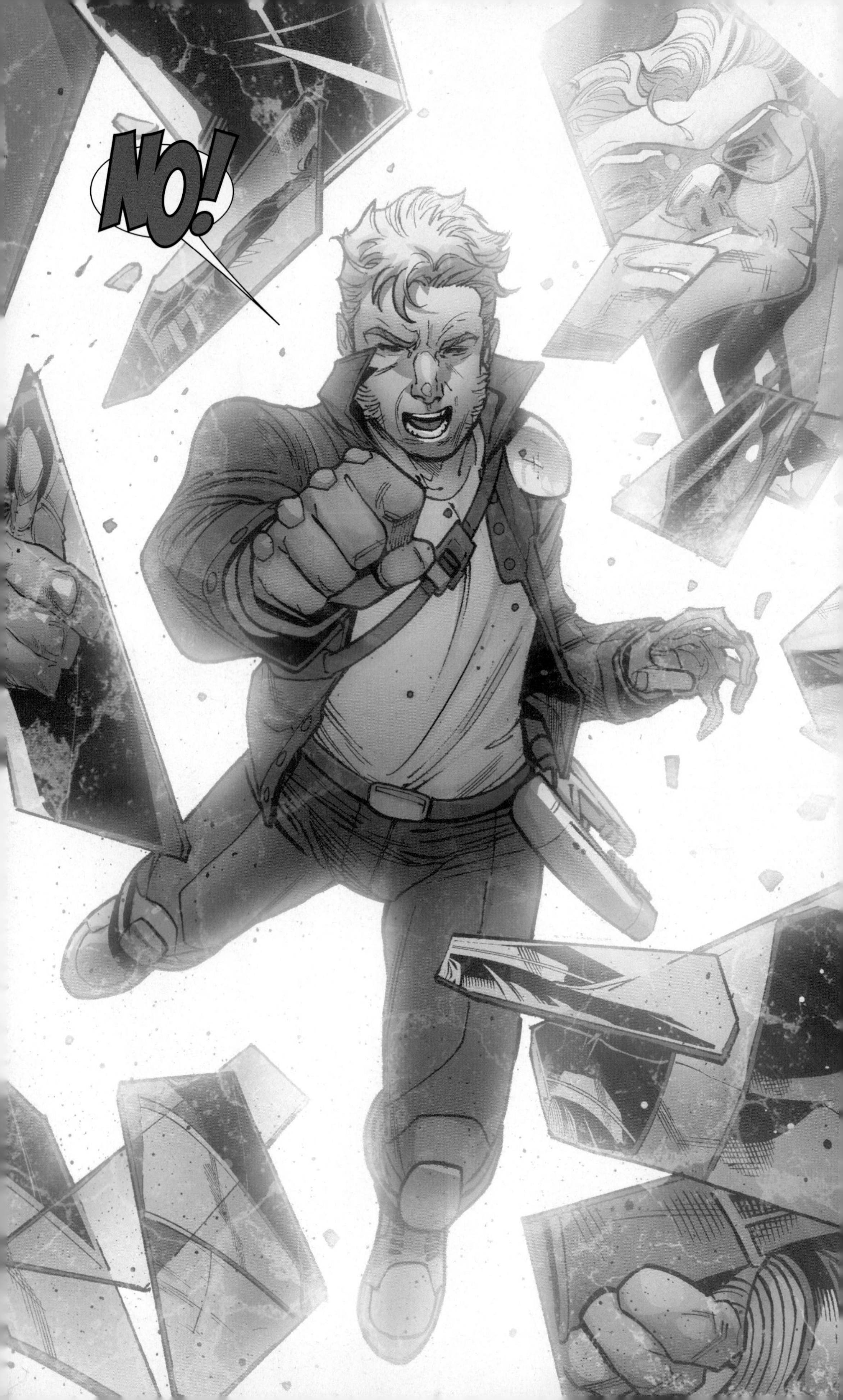
NO!

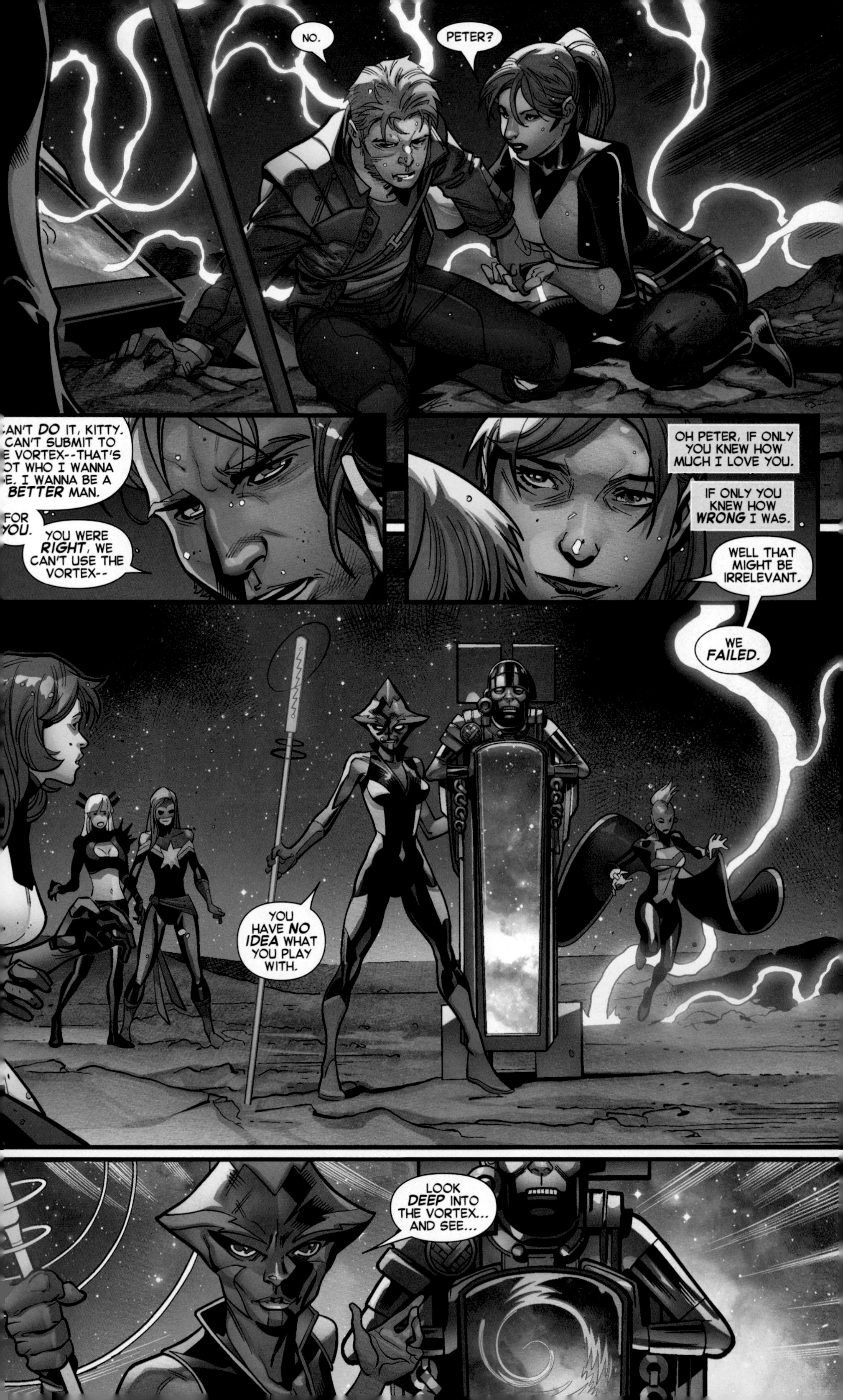
NO.
PETER?
...AN'T DO IT, KITTY. ...CAN'T SUBMIT TO ...E VORTEX--THAT'S ...OT WHO I WANNA ...E. I WANNA BE A BETTER MAN.
FOR YOU.
YOU WERE RIGHT, WE CAN'T USE THE VORTEX--
OH PETER, IF ONLY YOU KNEW HOW MUCH I LOVE YOU.
IF ONLY YOU KNEW HOW WRONG I WAS.
WELL THAT MIGHT BE IRRELEVANT.
WE FAILED.
YOU HAVE NO IDEA WHAT YOU PLAY WITH.
LOOK DEEP INTO THE VORTEX... AND SEE...

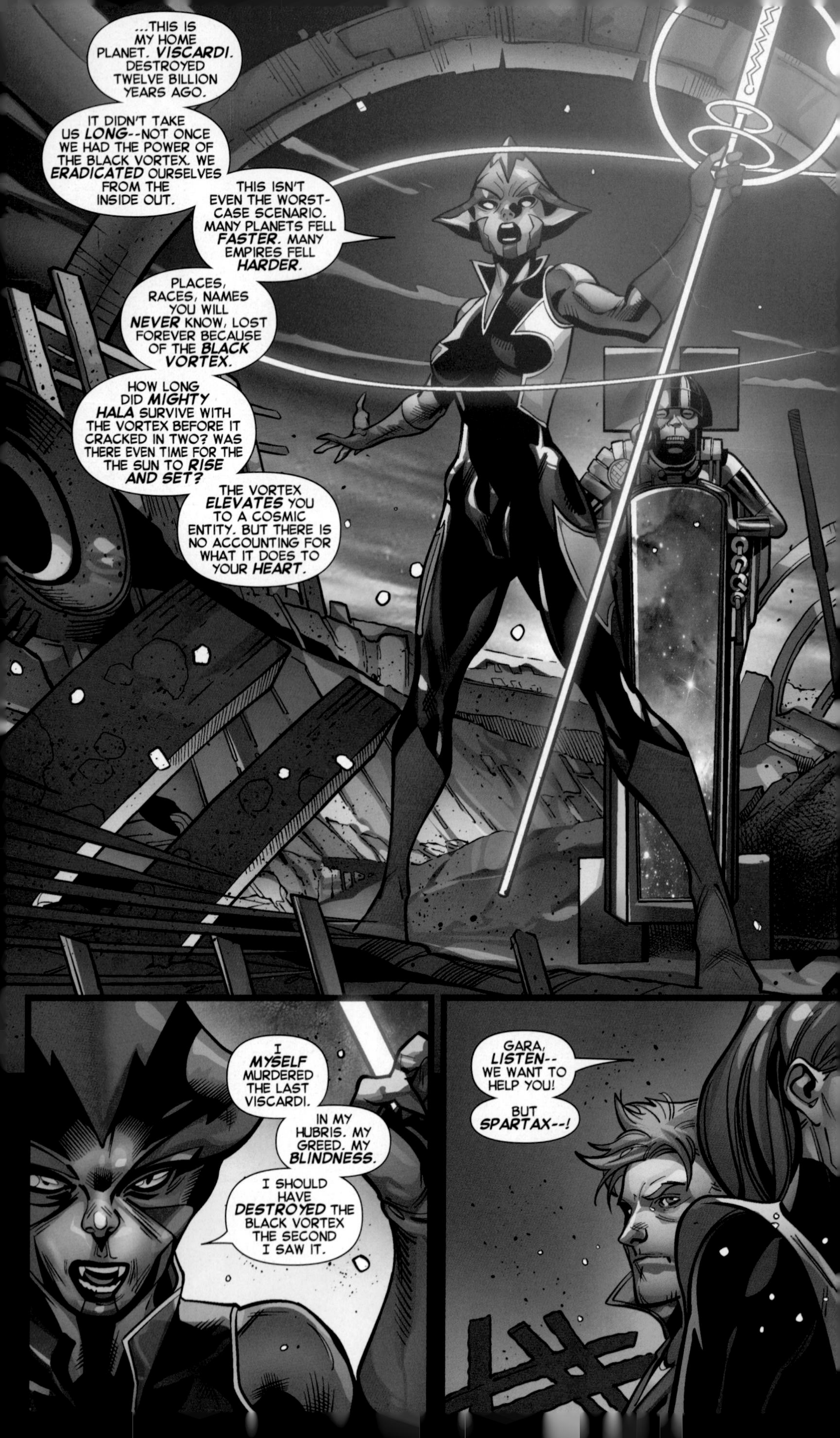
...THIS IS MY HOME PLANET. VISCARDI. DESTROYED TWELVE BILLION YEARS AGO.
IT DIDN'T TAKE US LONG--NOT ONCE WE HAD THE POWER OF THE BLACK VORTEX. WE ERADICATED OURSELVES FROM THE INSIDE OUT.
THIS ISN'T EVEN THE WORST-CASE SCENARIO. MANY PLANETS FELL FASTER. MANY EMPIRES FELL HARDER.
PLACES, RACES, NAMES YOU WILL NEVER KNOW, LOST FOREVER BECAUSE OF THE BLACK VORTEX.
HOW LONG DID MIGHTY HALA SURVIVE WITH THE VORTEX BEFORE IT CRACKED IN TWO? WAS THERE EVEN TIME FOR THE THE SUN TO RISE AND SET?
THE VORTEX ELEVATES YOU TO A COSMIC ENTITY. BUT THERE IS NO ACCOUNTING FOR WHAT IT DOES TO YOUR HEART.
I MYSELF MURDERED THE LAST VISCARDI.
IN MY HUBRIS. MY GREED. MY BLINDNESS.
I SHOULD HAVE DESTROYED THE BLACK VORTEX THE SECOND I SAW IT.
GARA, LISTEN-- WE WANT TO HELP YOU!
BUT SPARTAX--!

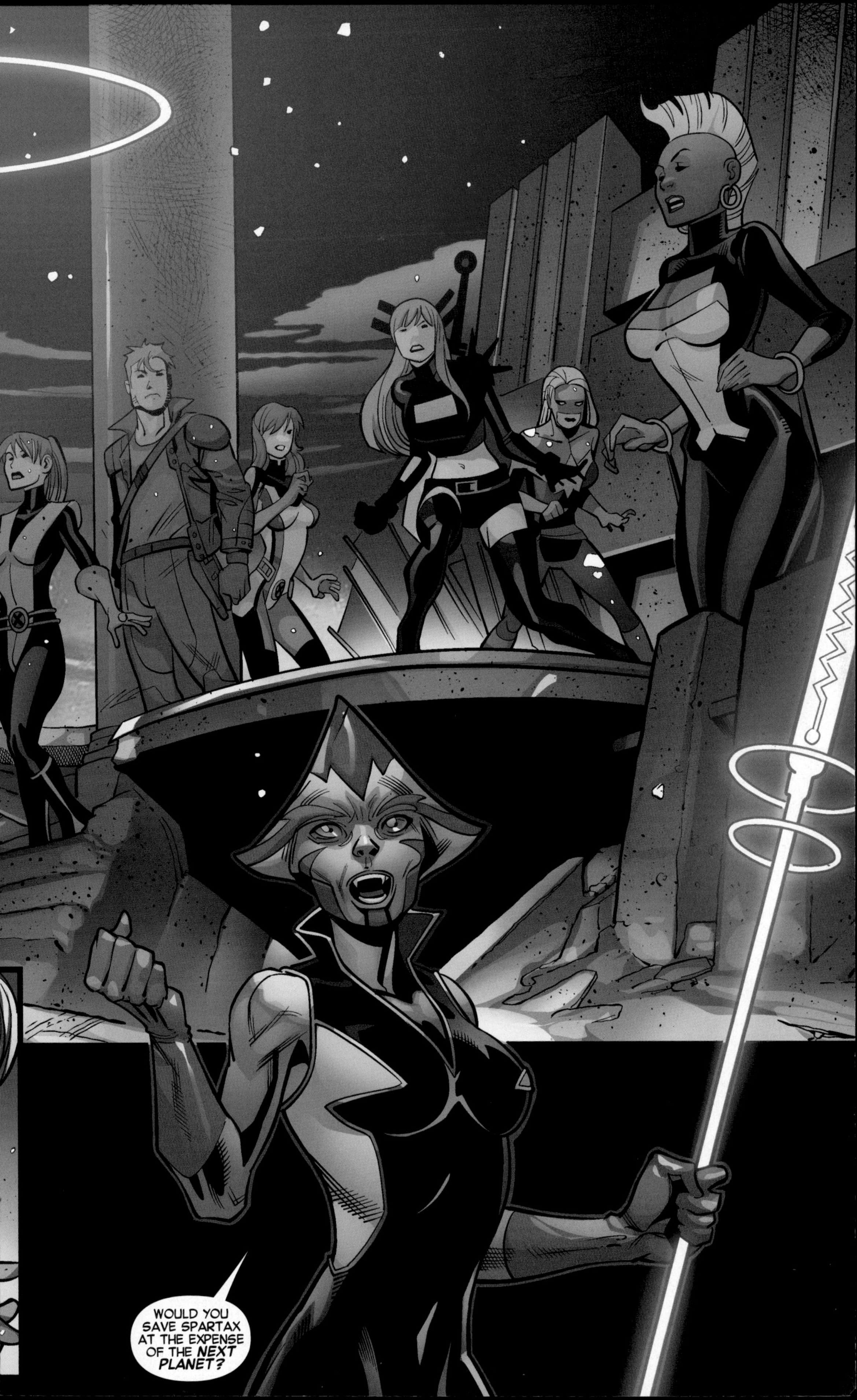
WOULD YOU SAVE SPARTAX AT THE EXPENSE OF THE NEXT PLANET?

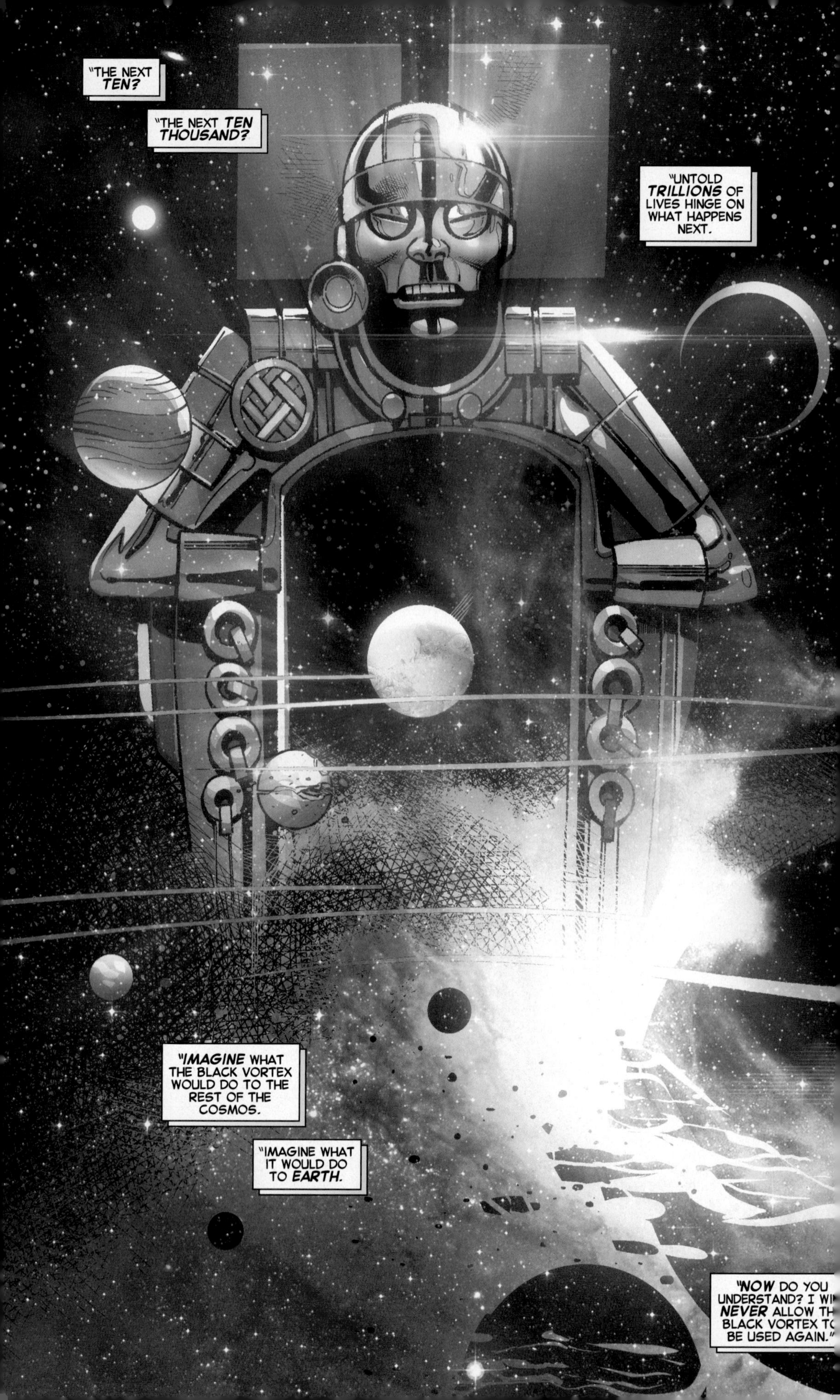
"THE NEXT *TEN?*
"THE NEXT *TEN THOUSAND?*
"UNTOLD *TRILLIONS* OF LIVES HINGE ON WHAT HAPPENS NEXT.
"*IMAGINE* WHAT THE BLACK VORTEX WOULD DO TO THE REST OF THE COSMOS.
"IMAGINE WHAT IT WOULD DO TO *EARTH*.
"*NOW* DO YOU UNDERSTAND? I WI *NEVER* ALLOW TH BLACK VORTEX TO BE USED AGAIN."

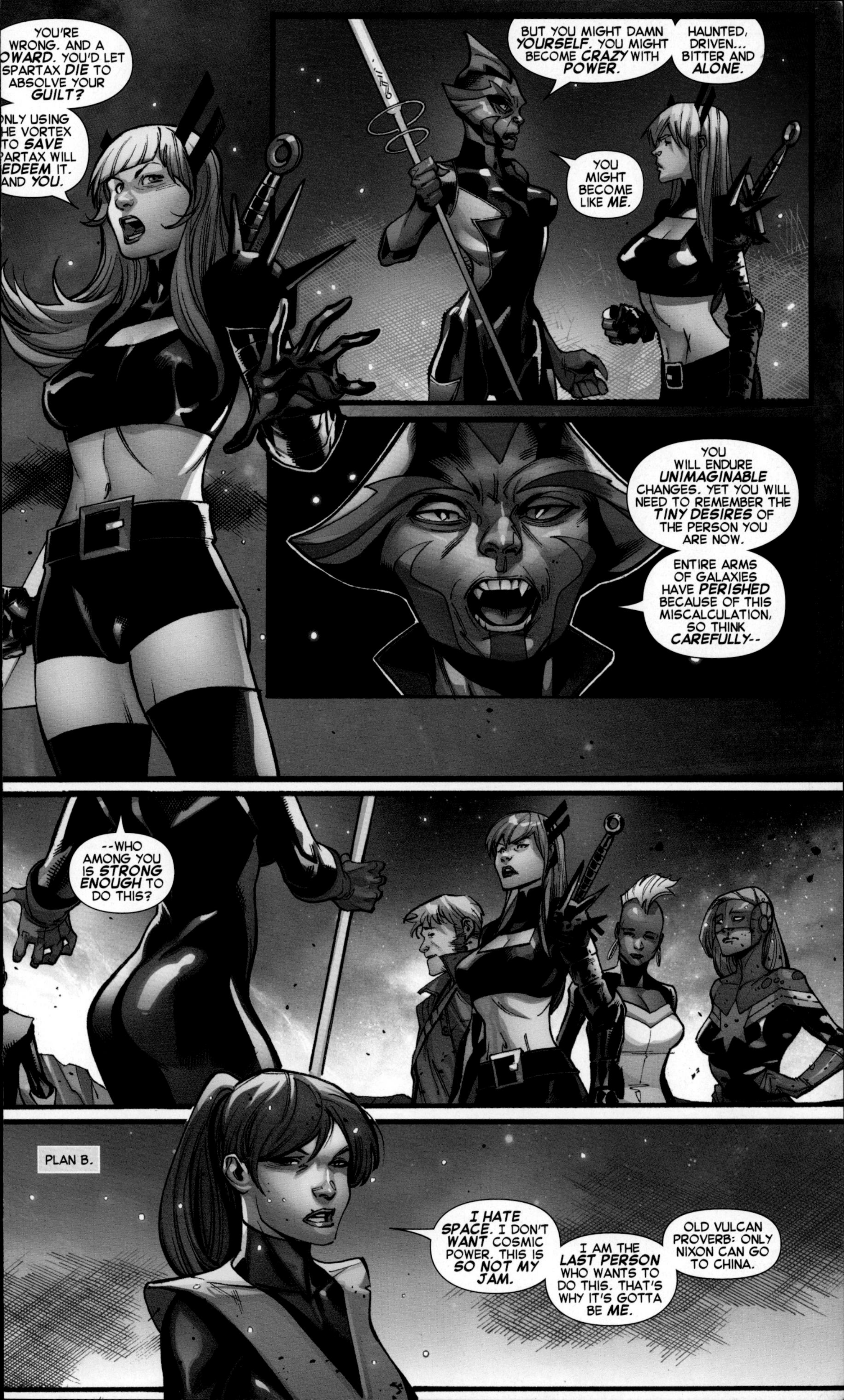
YOU'RE WRONG. AND A OWARD. YOU'D LET SPARTAX DIE TO ABSOLVE YOUR GUILT?
NLY USING HE VORTEX TO SAVE PARTAX WILL EDEEM IT. AND YOU.
BUT YOU MIGHT DAMN YOURSELF. YOU MIGHT BECOME CRAZY WITH POWER.
HAUNTED, DRIVEN... BITTER AND ALONE.
YOU MIGHT BECOME LIKE ME.
YOU WILL ENDURE UNIMAGINABLE CHANGES. YET YOU WILL NEED TO REMEMBER THE TINY DESIRES OF THE PERSON YOU ARE NOW.
ENTIRE ARMS OF GALAXIES HAVE PERISHED BECAUSE OF THIS MISCALCULATION, SO THINK CAREFULLY--
--WHO AMONG YOU IS STRONG ENOUGH TO DO THIS?
PLAN B.
I HATE SPACE. I DON'T WANT COSMIC POWER. THIS IS SO NOT MY JAM.
I AM THE LAST PERSON WHO WANTS TO DO THIS. THAT'S WHY IT'S GOTTA BE ME.
OLD VULCAN PROVERB: ONLY NIXON CAN GO TO CHINA.

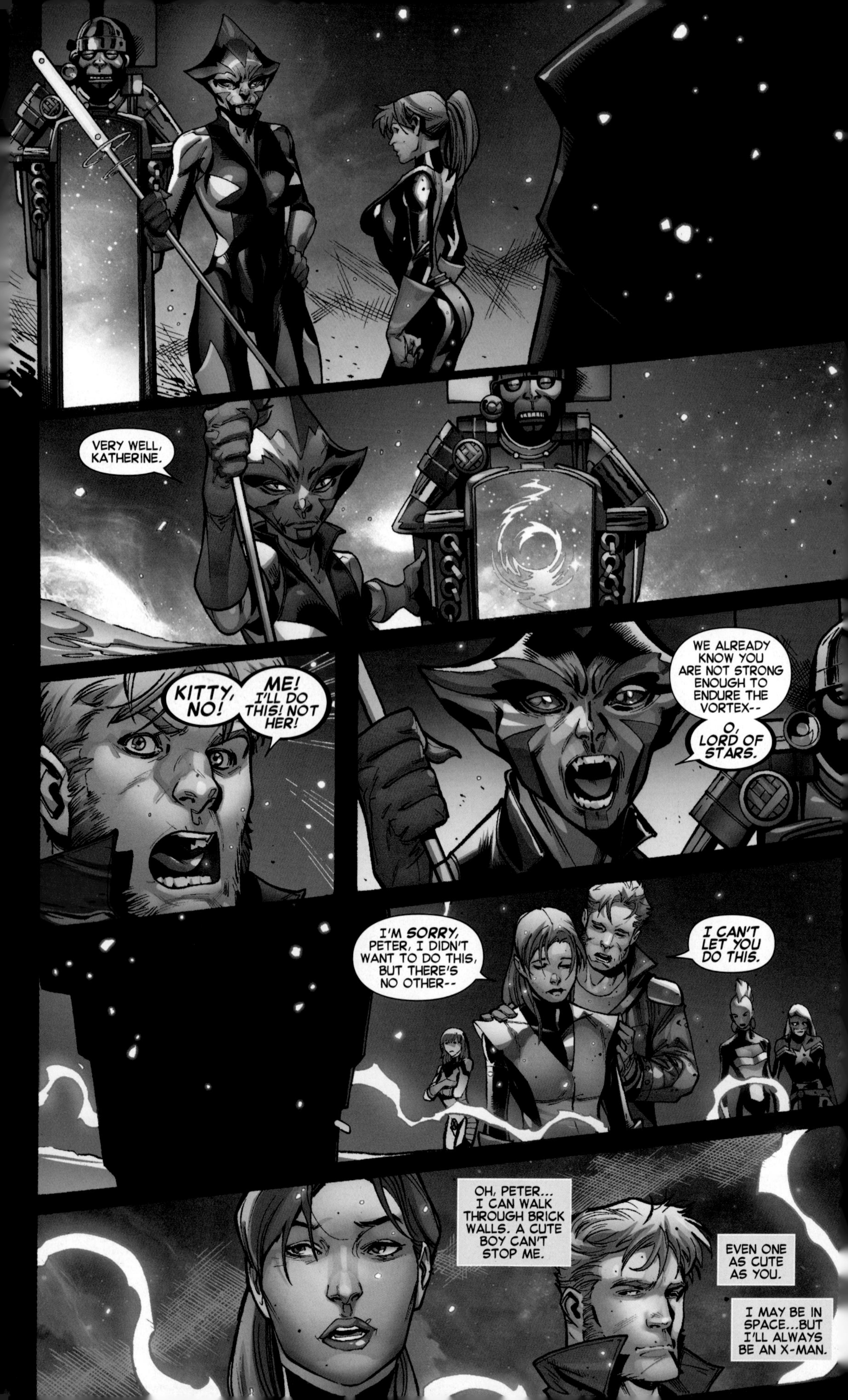
VERY WELL, KATHERINE.
KITTY, NO!
ME! I'LL DO THIS! NOT HER!
WE ALREADY KNOW YOU ARE NOT STRONG ENOUGH TO ENDURE THE VORTEX--
O, LORD OF STARS.
I'M SORRY, PETER, I DIDN'T WANT TO DO THIS, BUT THERE'S NO OTHER--
I CAN'T LET YOU DO THIS.
OH, PETER... I CAN WALK THROUGH BRICK WALLS. A CUTE BOY CAN'T STOP ME.
EVEN ONE AS CUTE AS YOU.
I MAY BE IN SPACE...BUT I'LL ALWAYS BE AN X-MAN.

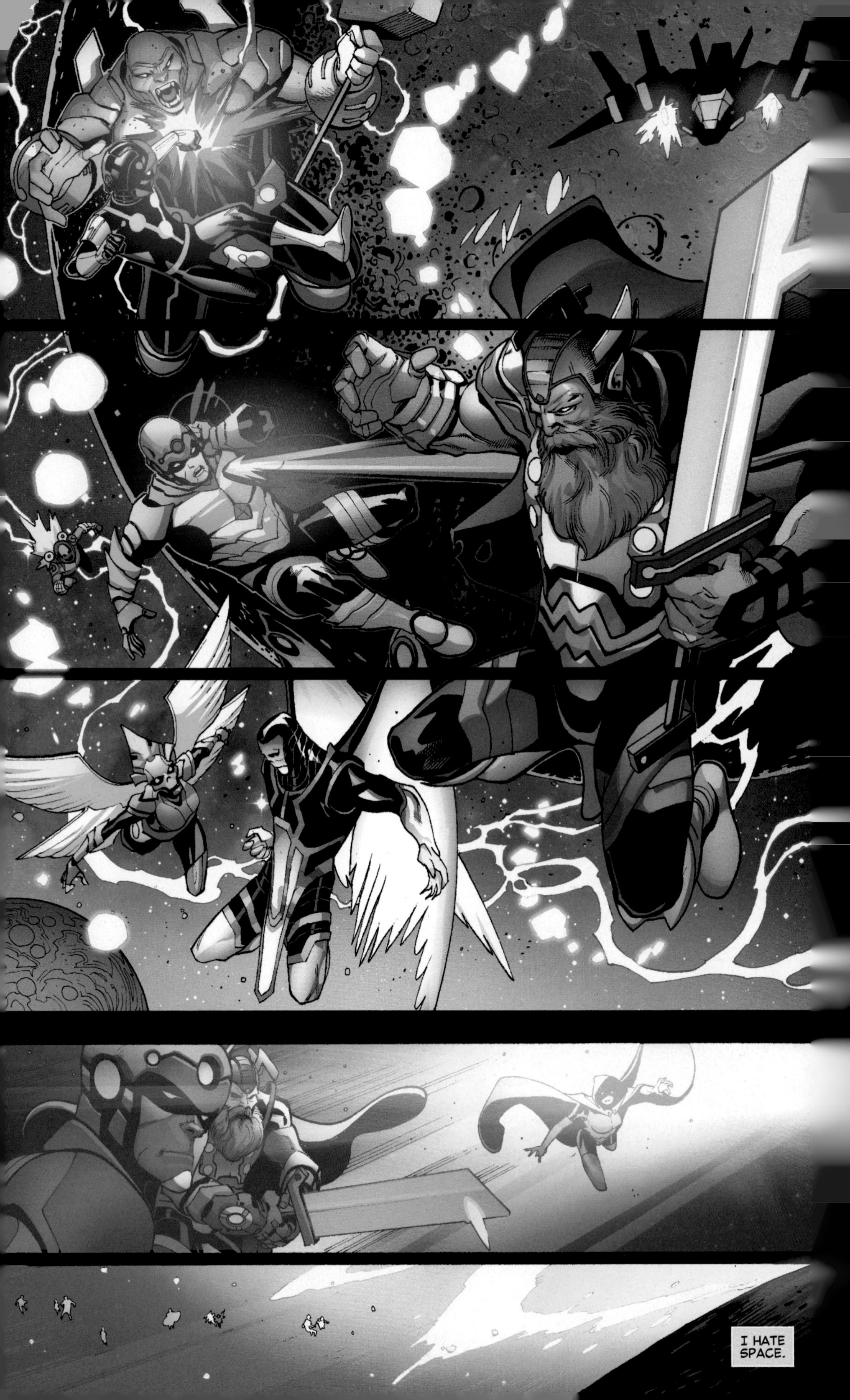
I HATE SPACE.

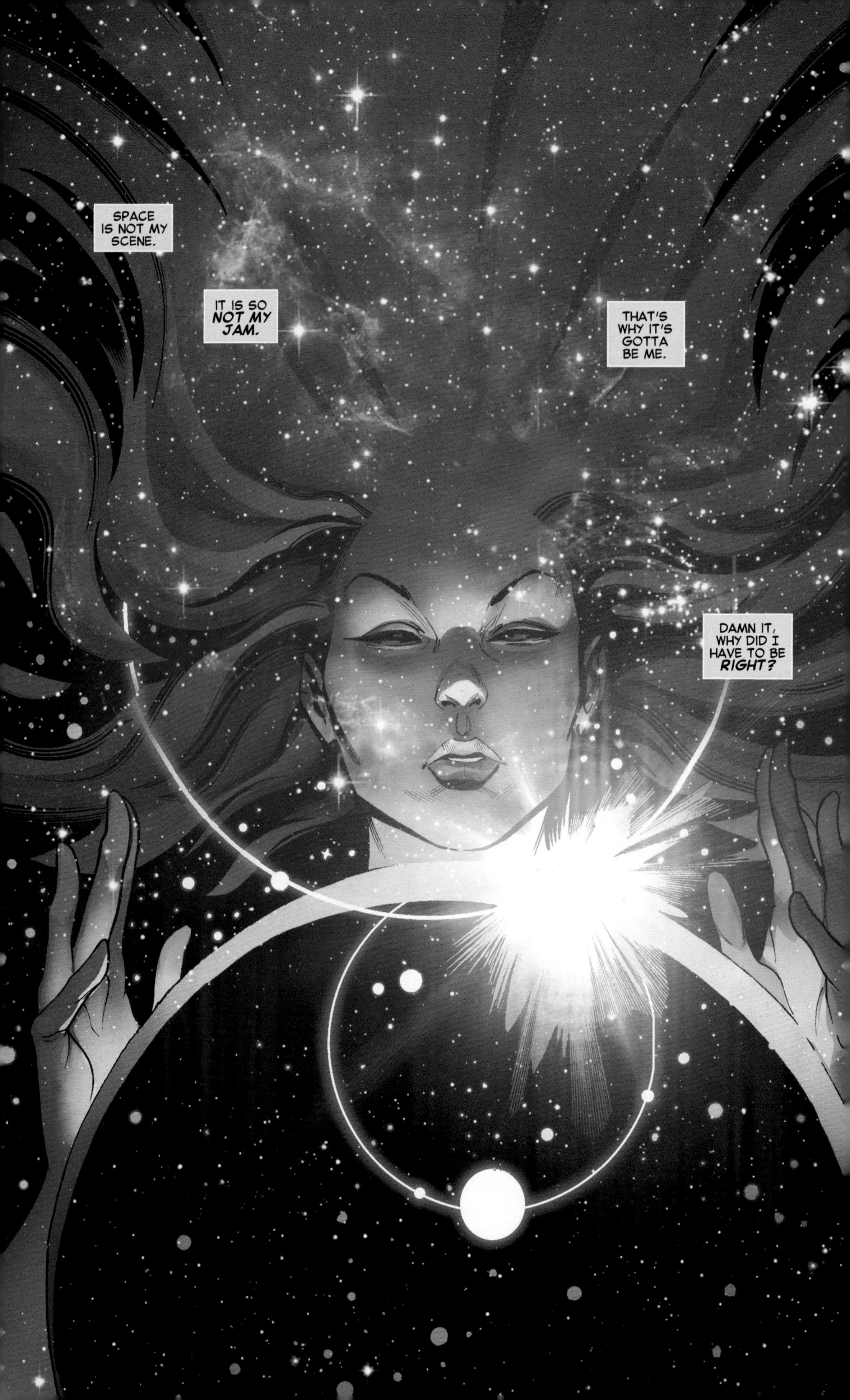
SPACE IS NOT MY SCENE.
IT IS SO NOT MY JAM.
THAT'S WHY IT'S GOTTA BE ME.
DAMN IT, WHY DID I HAVE TO BE RIGHT?

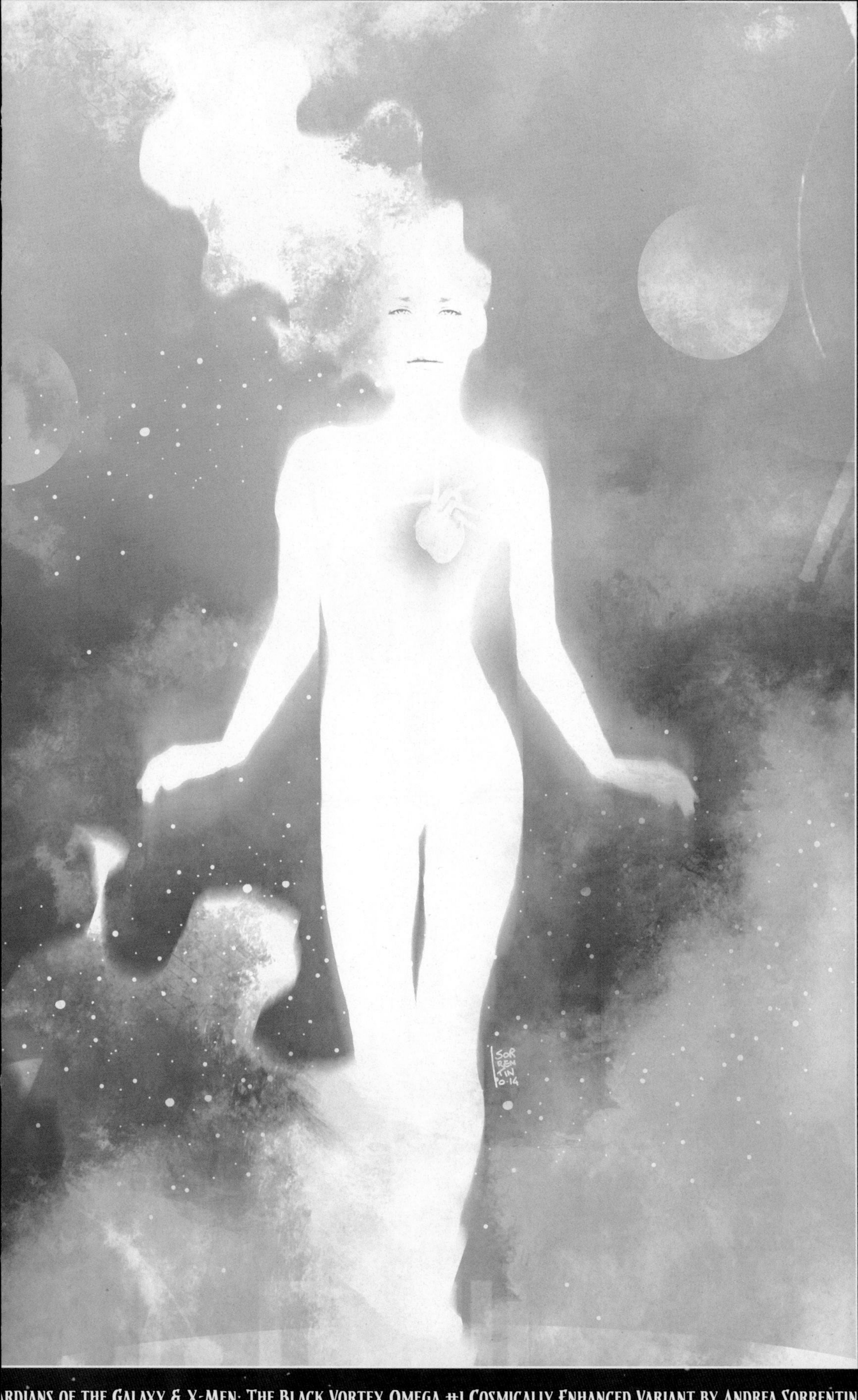

ARDIANS OF THE GALAXY & X-MEN: THE BLACK VORTEX OMEGA #1 COSMICALLY ENHANCED VARIANT BY ANDREA SORRENTIN

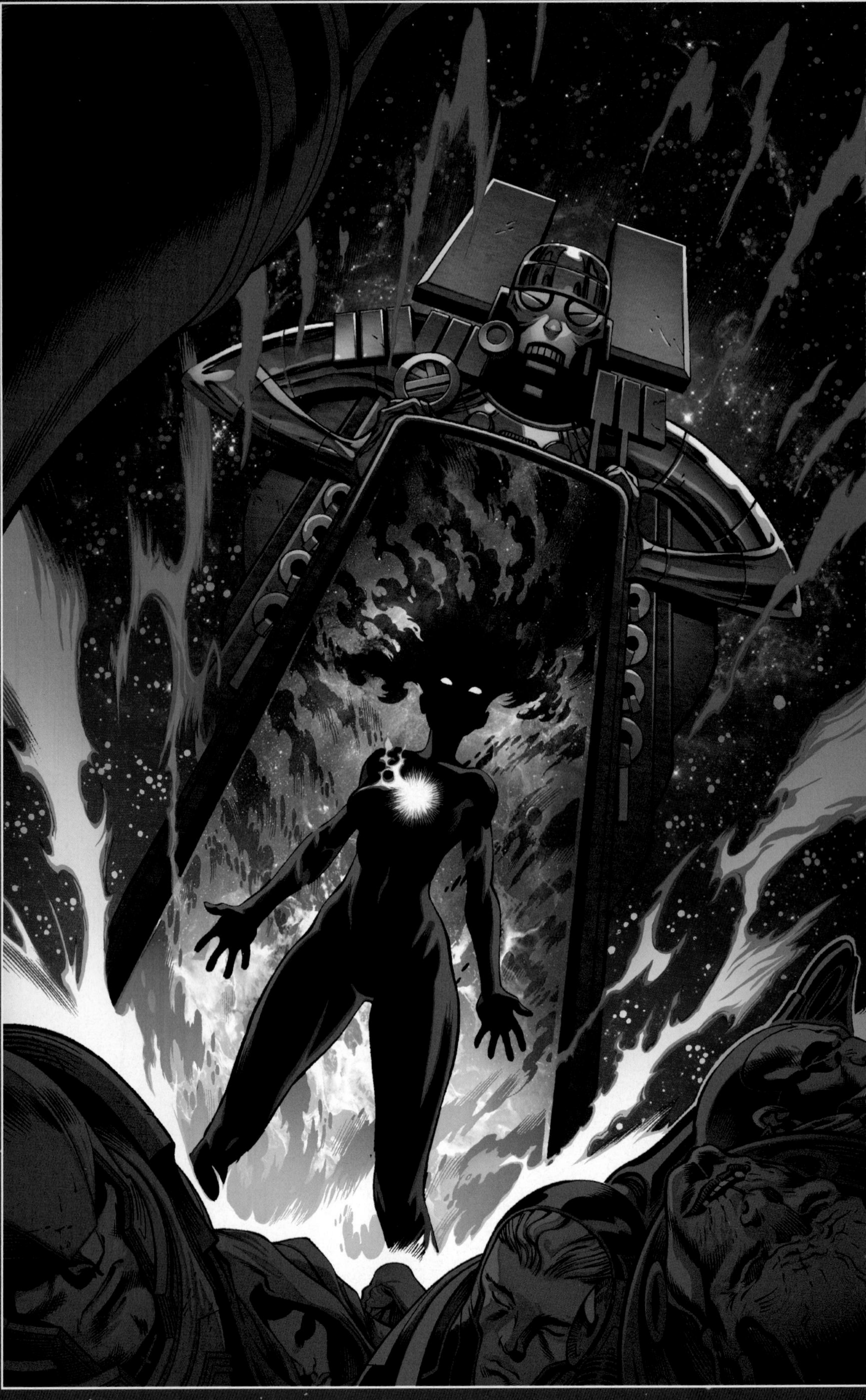

GUARDIANS OF THE GALAXY & X-MEN: THE BLACK VORTEX OMEGA #1

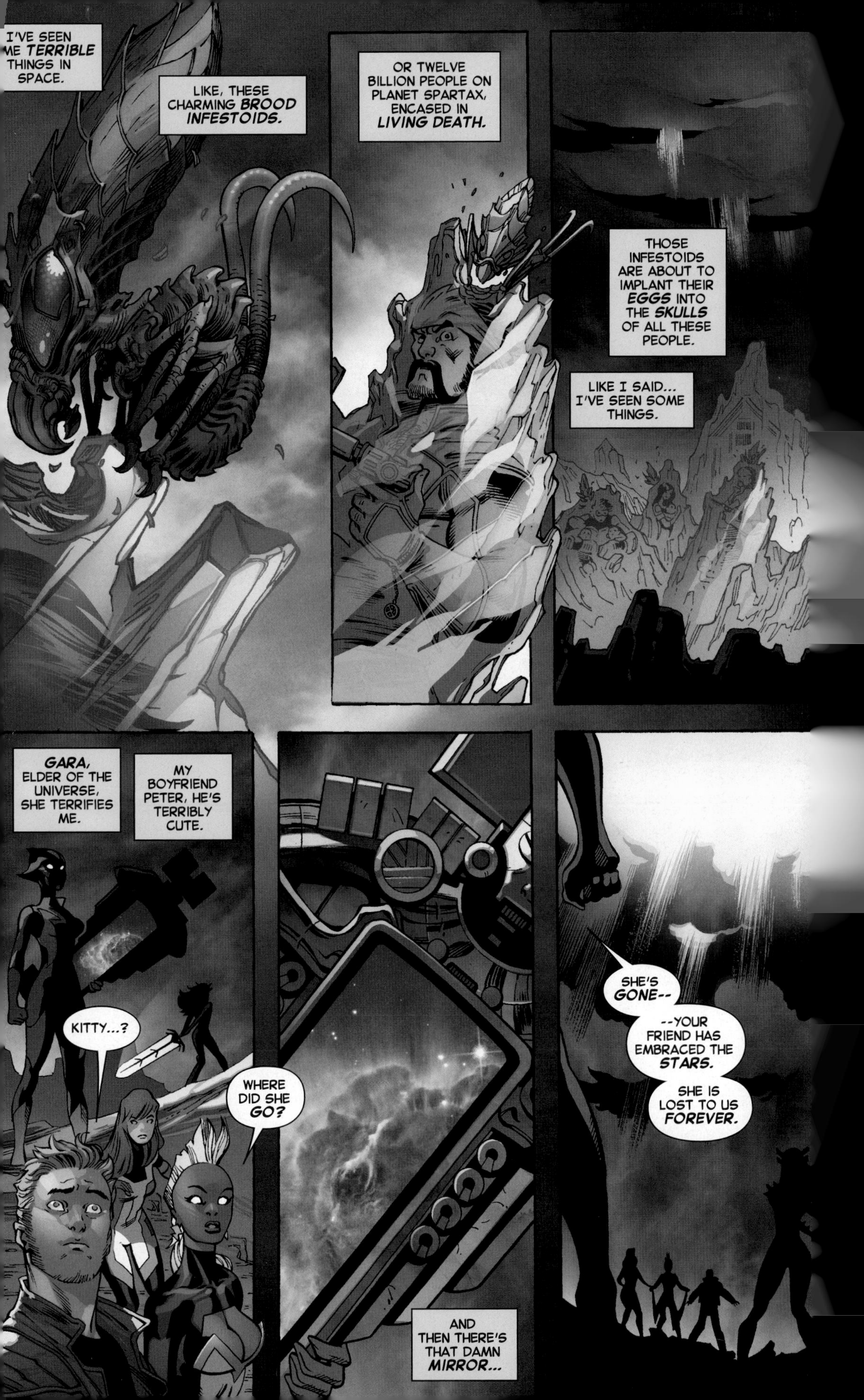
I'VE SEEN
ME TERRIBLE
THINGS IN
SPACE.
LIKE, THESE CHARMING BROOD INFESTOIDS.
OR TWELVE BILLION PEOPLE ON PLANET SPARTAX, ENCASED IN LIVING DEATH.
THOSE INFESTOIDS ARE ABOUT TO IMPLANT THEIR EGGS INTO THE SKULLS OF ALL THESE PEOPLE.
LIKE I SAID... I'VE SEEN SOME THINGS.
GARA, ELDER OF THE UNIVERSE, SHE TERRIFIES ME.
MY BOYFRIEND PETER, HE'S TERRIBLY CUTE.
KITTY...?
WHERE DID SHE GO?
AND THEN THERE'S THAT DAMN MIRROR...
SHE'S GONE--
--YOUR FRIEND HAS EMBRACED THE STARS.
SHE IS LOST TO US FOREVER.

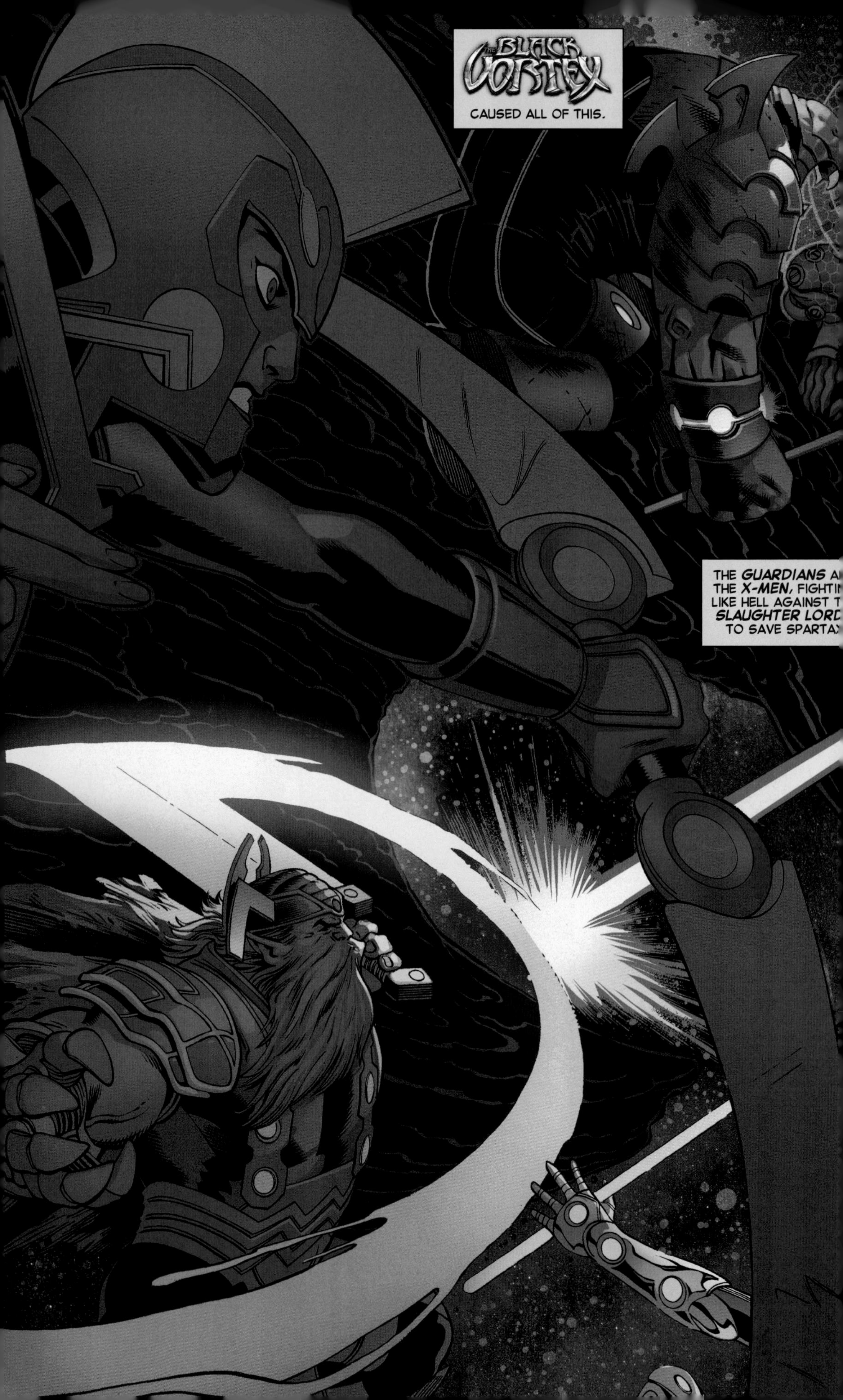
THE BLACK VORTEX
CAUSED ALL OF THIS.
THE GUARDIANS A
THE X-MEN, FIGHTI
LIKE HELL AGAINST T
SLAUGHTER LORD
TO SAVE SPARTA

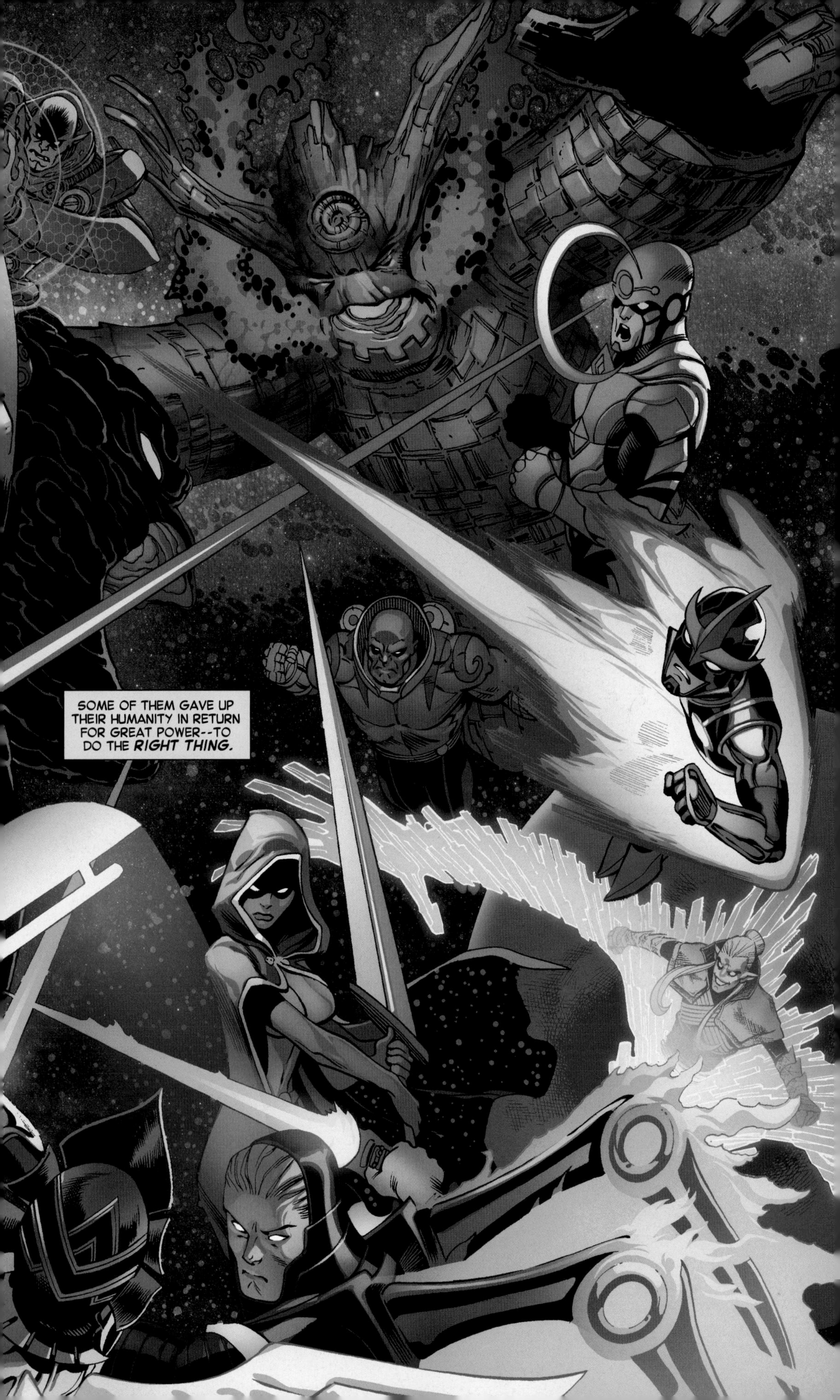
SOME OF THEM GAVE UP THEIR HUMANITY IN RETURN FOR GREAT POWER--TO DO THE RIGHT THING.

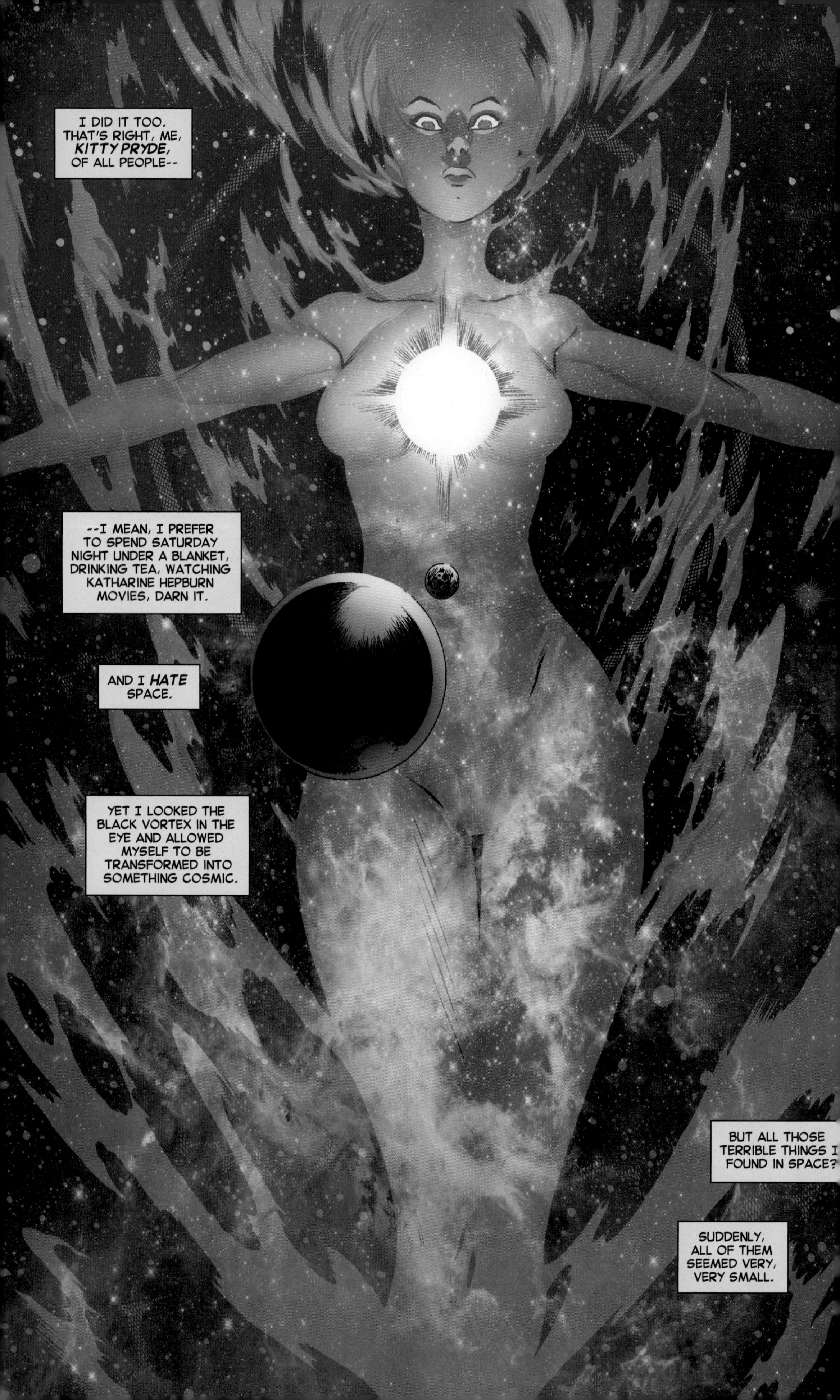

I DID IT TOO. THAT'S RIGHT, ME, *KITTY PRYDE,* OF ALL PEOPLE--
--I MEAN, I PREFER TO SPEND SATURDAY NIGHT UNDER A BLANKET, DRINKING TEA, WATCHING KATHARINE HEPBURN MOVIES, DARN IT.
AND I *HATE* SPACE.
YET I LOOKED THE BLACK VORTEX IN THE EYE AND ALLOWED MYSELF TO BE TRANSFORMED INTO SOMETHING COSMIC.
BUT ALL THOSE TERRIBLE THINGS I FOUND IN SPACE?
SUDDENLY, ALL OF THEM SEEMED VERY, VERY SMALL.

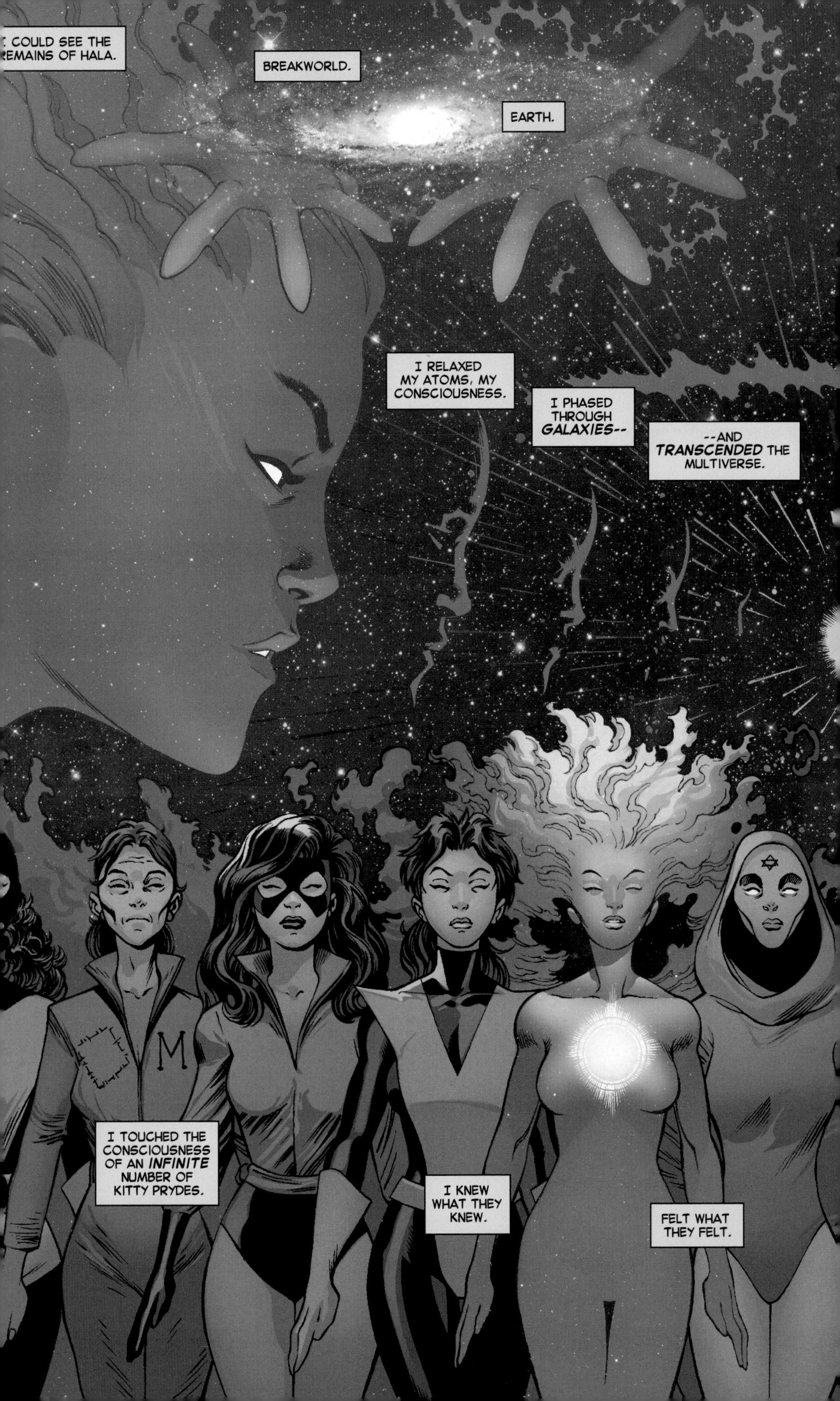
I COULD SEE THE REMAINS OF HALA.
BREAKWORLD.
EARTH.
I RELAXED MY ATOMS, MY CONSCIOUSNESS.
I PHASED THROUGH GALAXIES--
--AND TRANSCENDED THE MULTIVERSE.
I TOUCHED THE CONSCIOUSNESS OF AN INFINITE NUMBER OF KITTY PRYDES.
I KNEW WHAT THEY KNEW.
FELT WHAT THEY FELT.

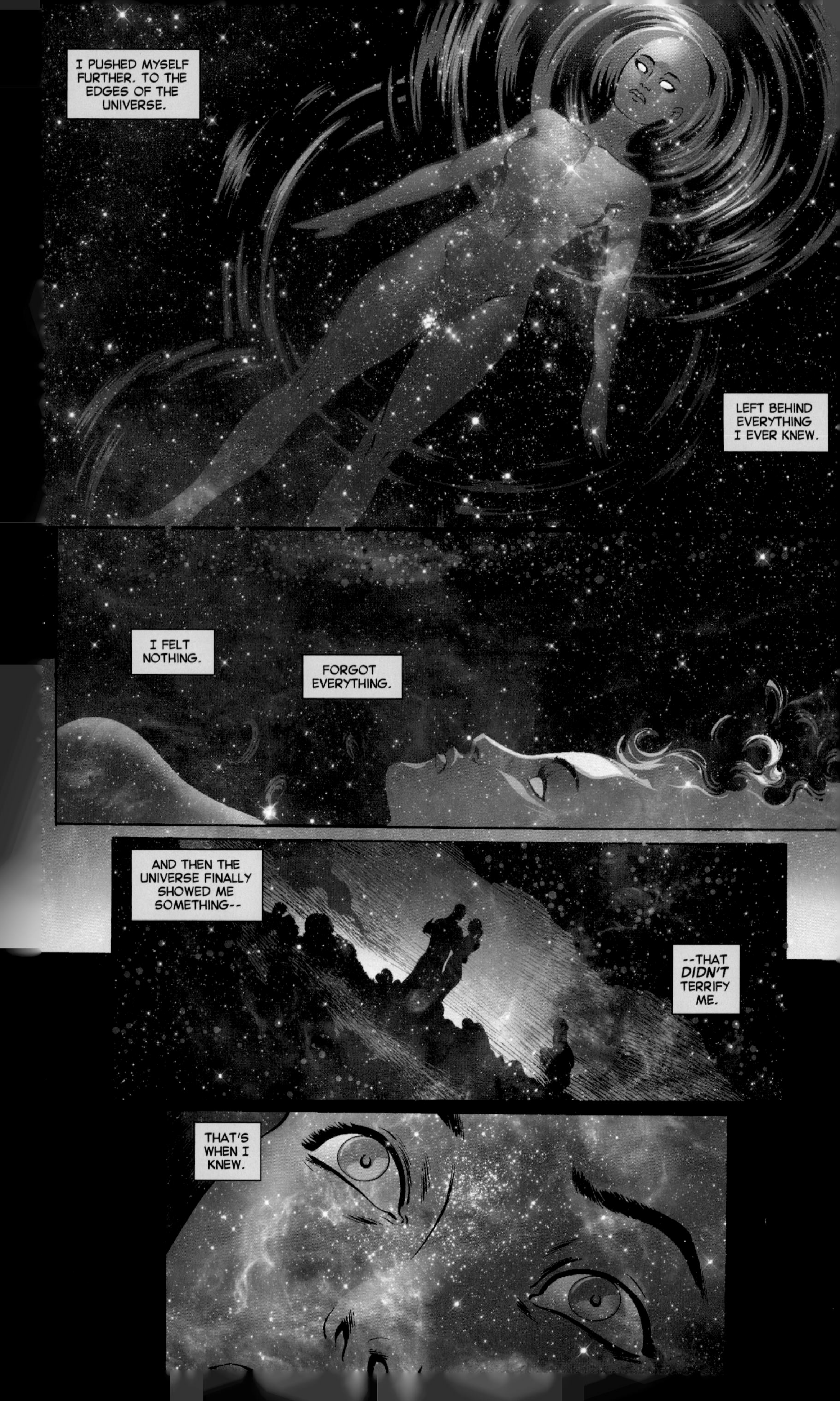
I PUSHED MYSELF FURTHER. TO THE EDGES OF THE UNIVERSE.
LEFT BEHIND EVERYTHING I EVER KNEW.
I FELT NOTHING.
FORGOT EVERYTHING.
AND THEN THE UNIVERSE FINALLY SHOWED ME SOMETHING--
--THAT DIDN'T TERRIFY ME.
THAT'S WHEN I KNEW.

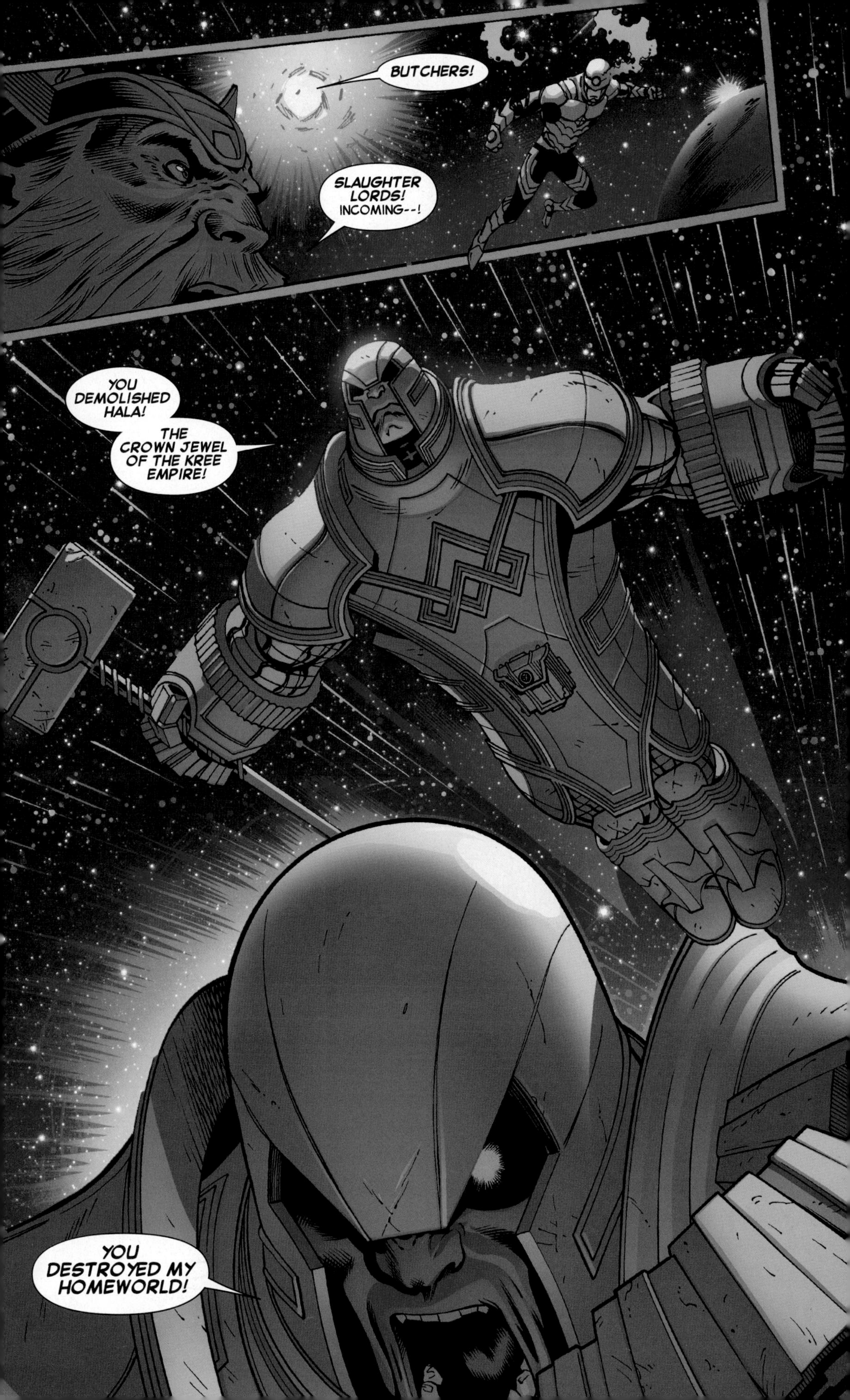
BUTCHERS!
SLAUGHTER LORDS! INCOMING--!
YOU DEMOLISHED HALA!
THE CROWN JEWEL OF THE KREE EMPIRE!
YOU DESTROYED MY HOMEWORLD!

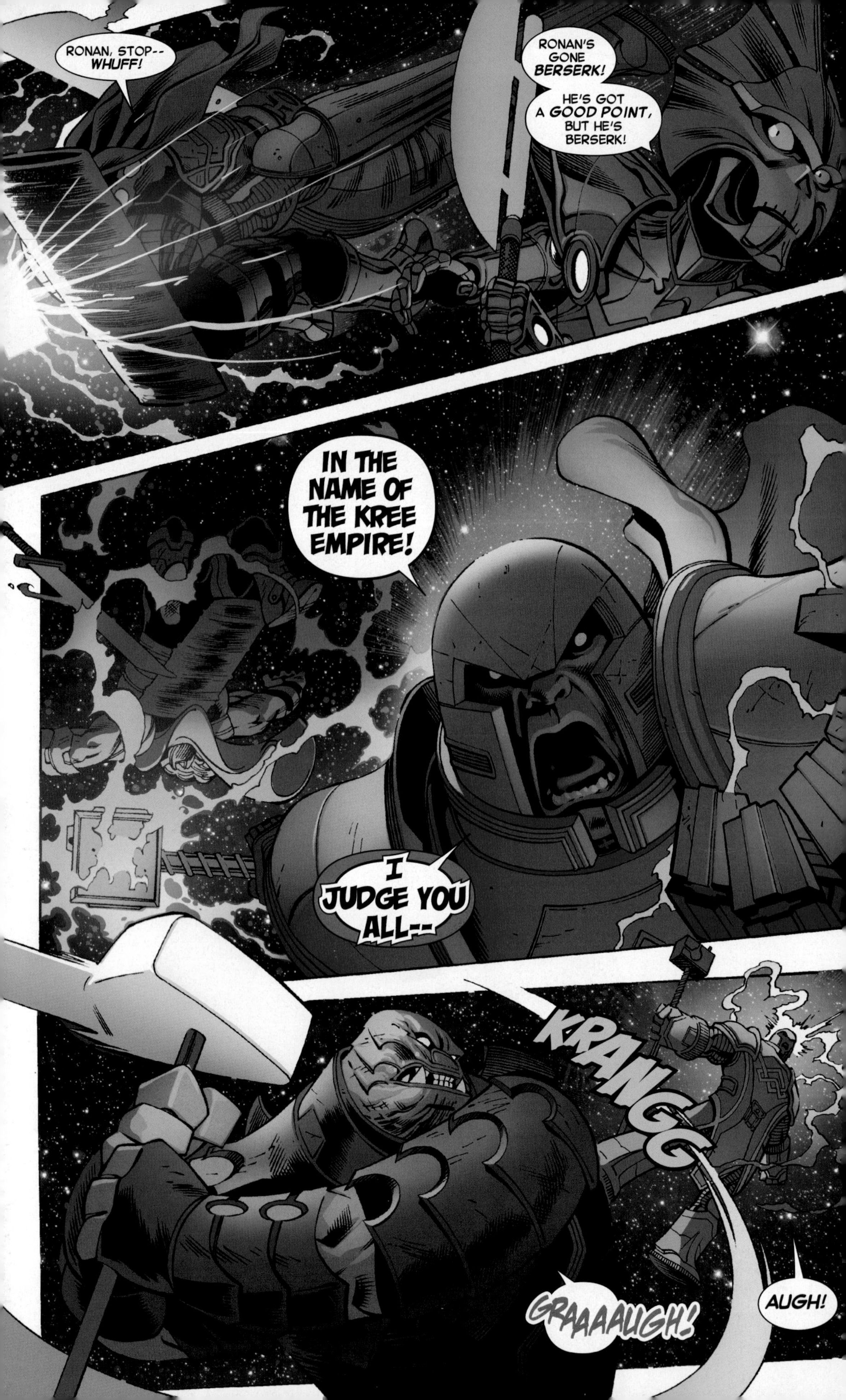
RONAN, STOP-- WHUFF!
RONAN'S GONE BERSERK!
HE'S GOT A GOOD POINT, BUT HE'S BERSERK!
IN THE NAME OF THE KREE EMPIRE!
I JUDGE YOU ALL--
KRANGG
GRAAAAUGH!
AUGH!

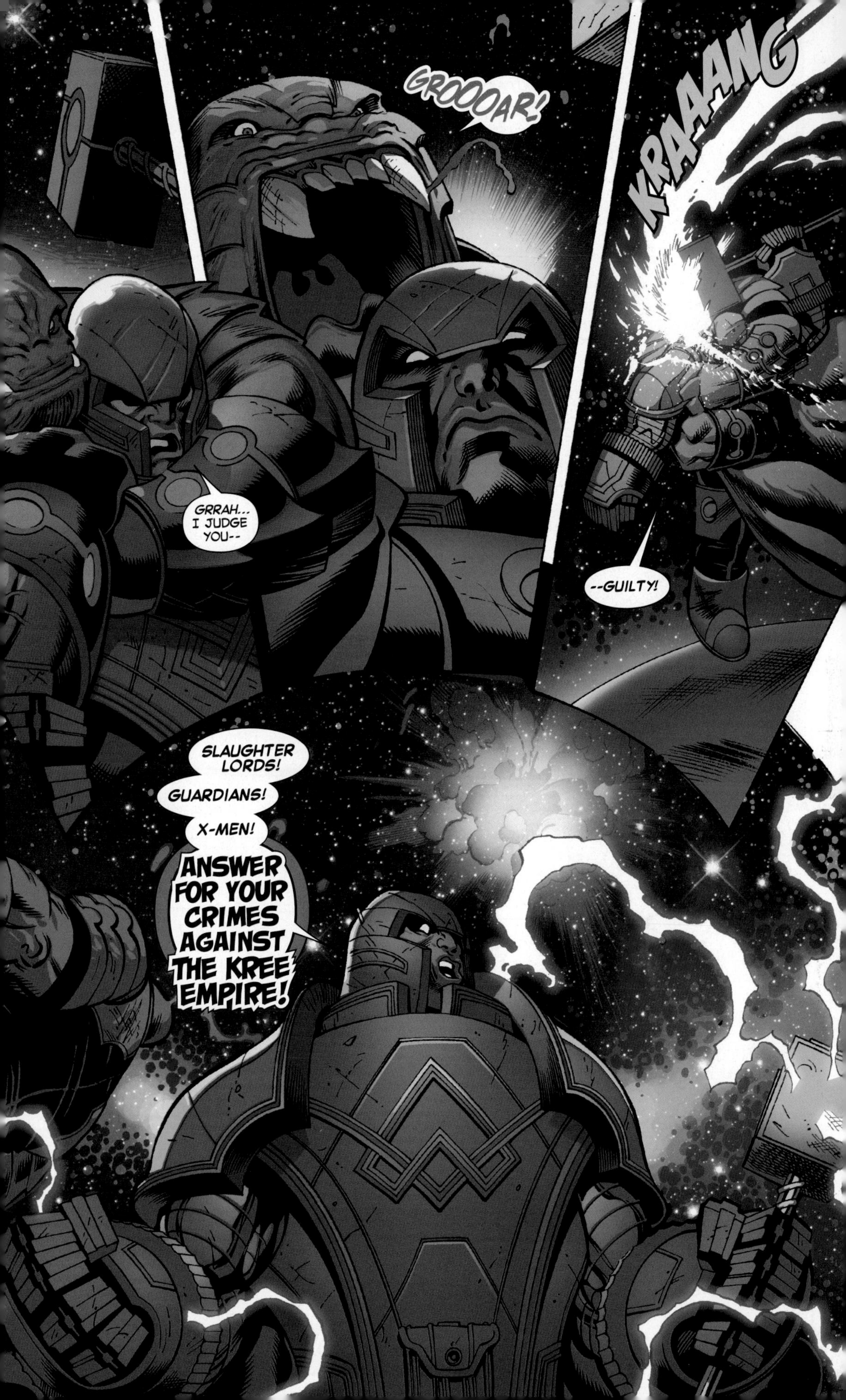
GROOOAR!
KRAAAANG
GRRAH... I JUDGE YOU--
--GUILTY!
SLAUGHTER LORDS!
GUARDIANS!
X-MEN!
ANSWER FOR YOUR CRIMES AGAINST THE KREE EMPIRE!

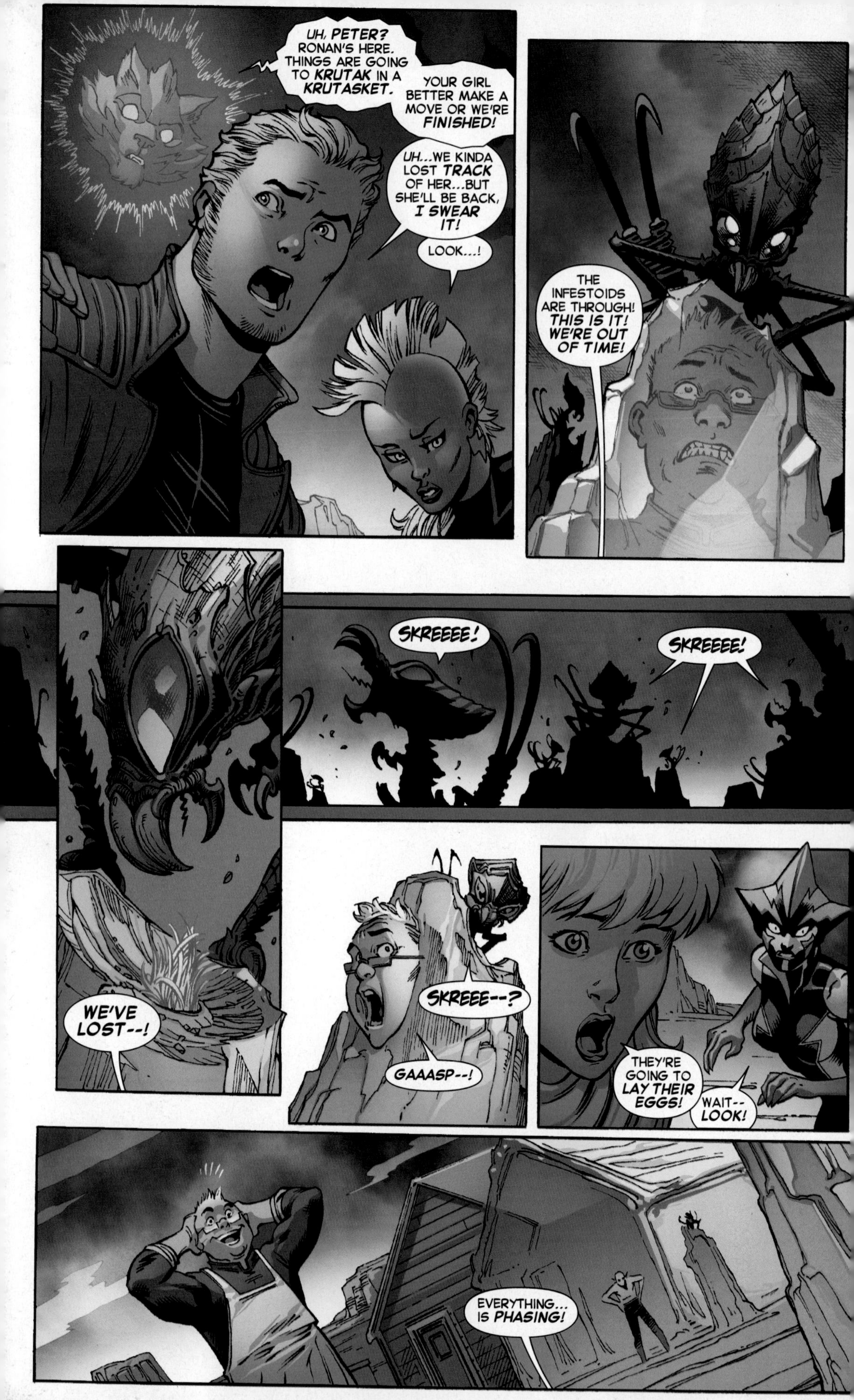
UH, PETER? RONAN'S HERE. THINGS ARE GOING TO KRUTAK IN A KRUTASKET.
YOUR GIRL BETTER MAKE A MOVE OR WE'RE FINISHED!
UH...WE KINDA LOST TRACK OF HER...BUT SHE'LL BE BACK, I SWEAR IT!
LOOK...!
THE INFESTOIDS ARE THROUGH! THIS IS IT! WE'RE OUT OF TIME!
SKREEEE!
SKREEEE!
WE'VE LOST--!
SKREEE--?
GAAASP--!
THEY'RE GOING TO LAY THEIR EGGS!
WAIT-- LOOK!
EVERYTHING... IS PHASING!

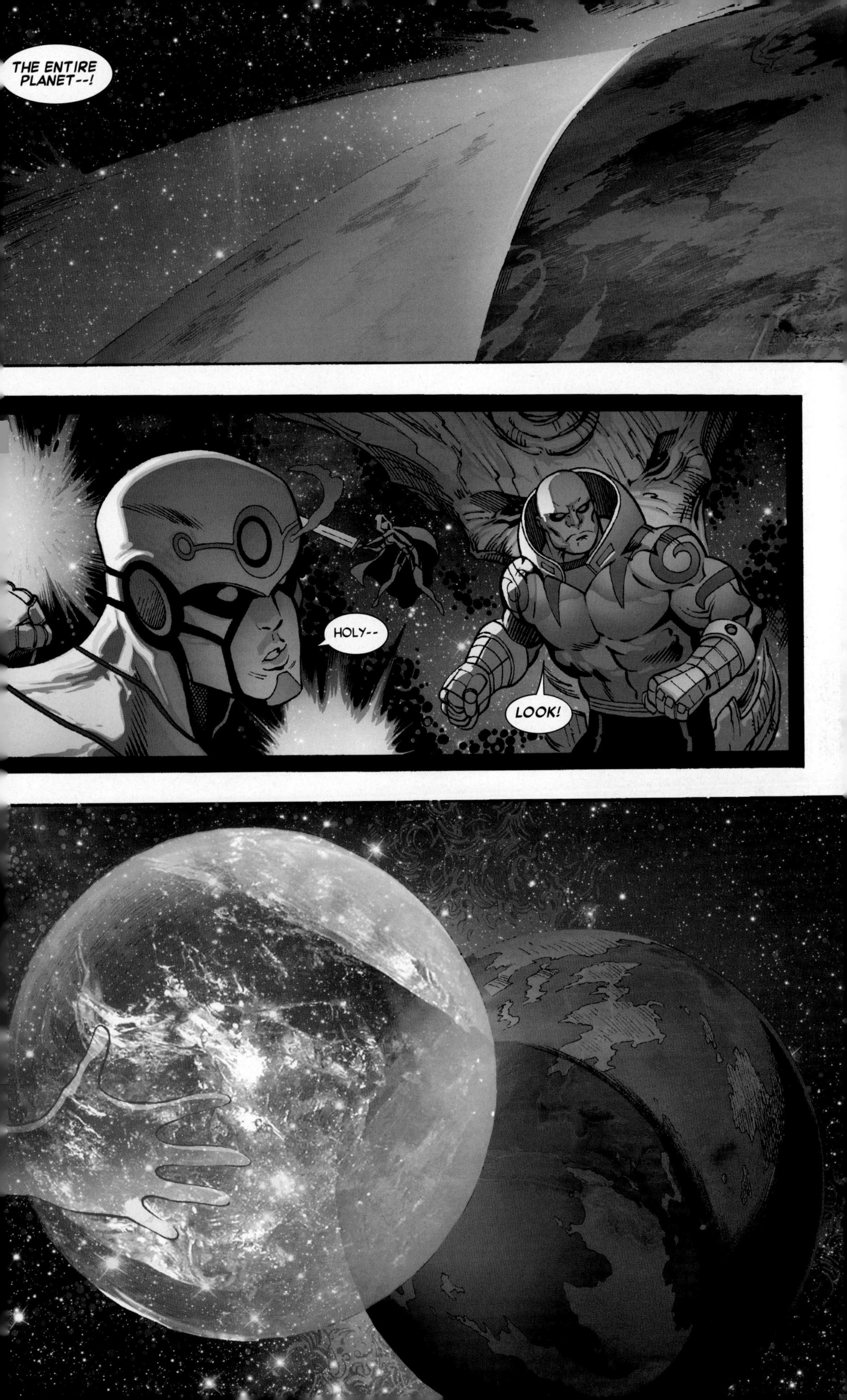
THE ENTIRE PLANET--!
HOLY--
LOOK!

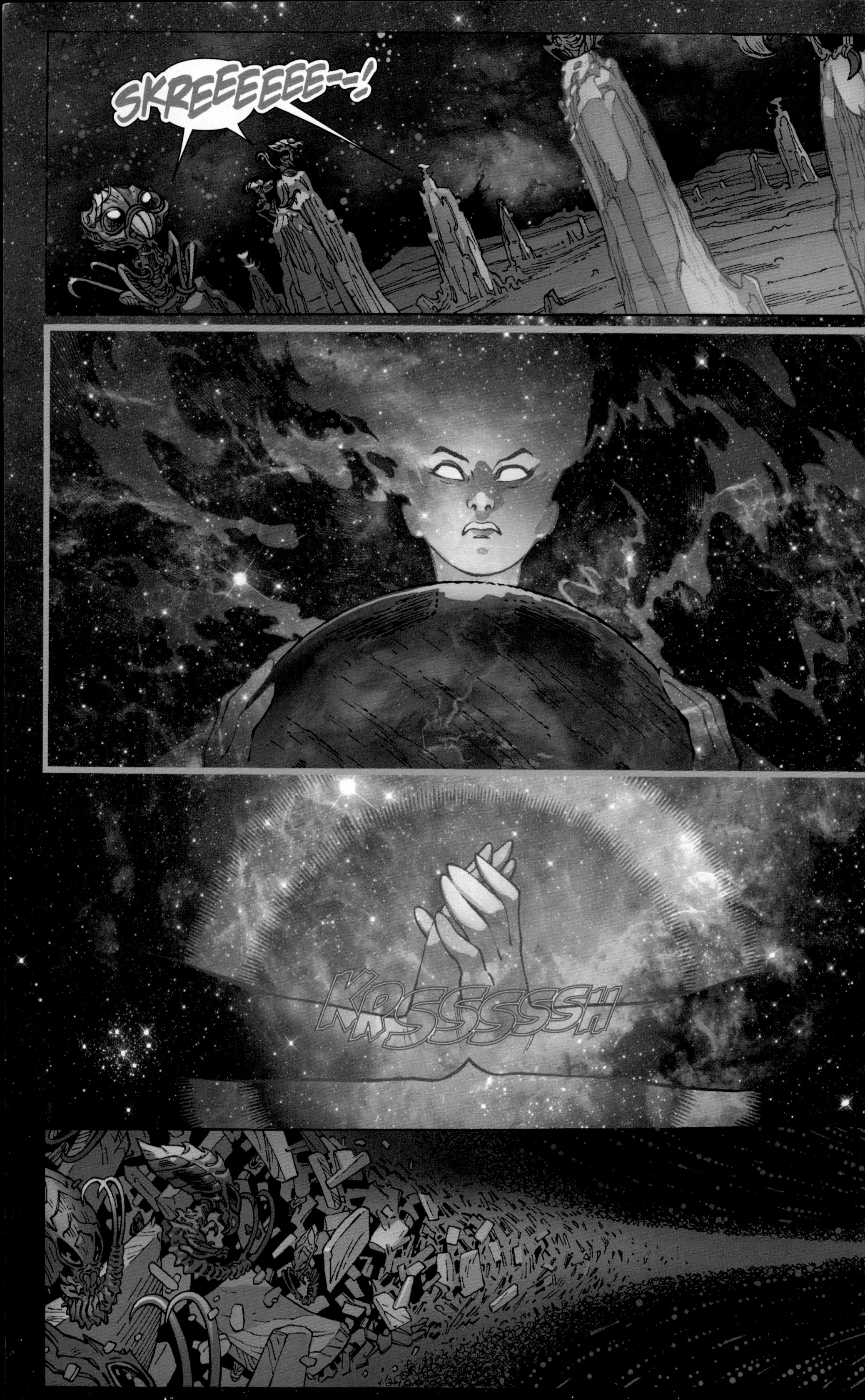
SKREEEEEEE--!
KRSSSSSSH

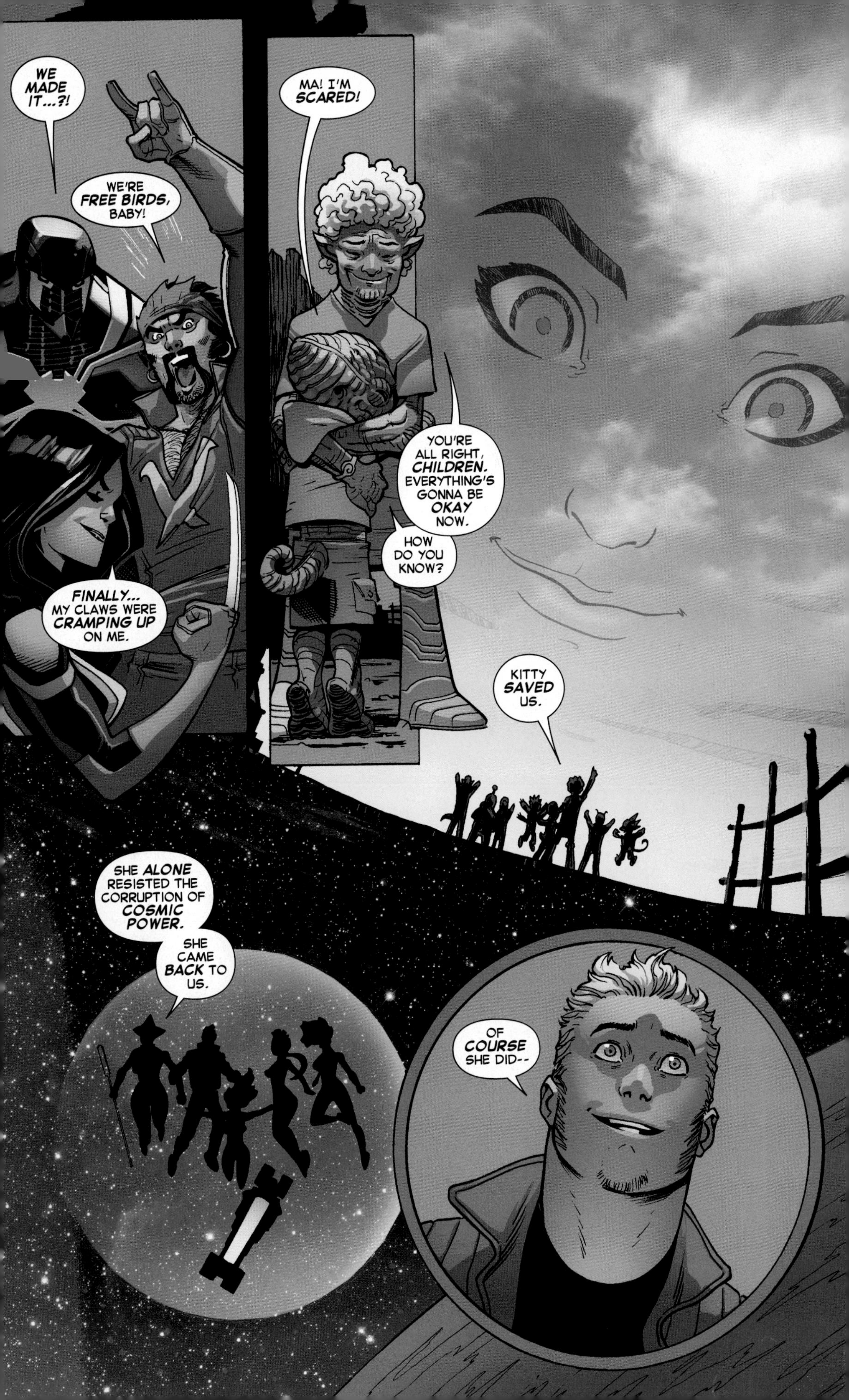
WE MADE IT...?!
WE'RE FREE BIRDS, BABY!
FINALLY... MY CLAWS WERE CRAMPING UP ON ME.
MA! I'M SCARED!
YOU'RE ALL RIGHT, CHILDREN. EVERYTHING'S GONNA BE OKAY NOW.
HOW DO YOU KNOW?
KITTY SAVED US.
SHE ALONE RESISTED THE CORRUPTION OF COSMIC POWER.
SHE CAME BACK TO US.
OF COURSE SHE DID--

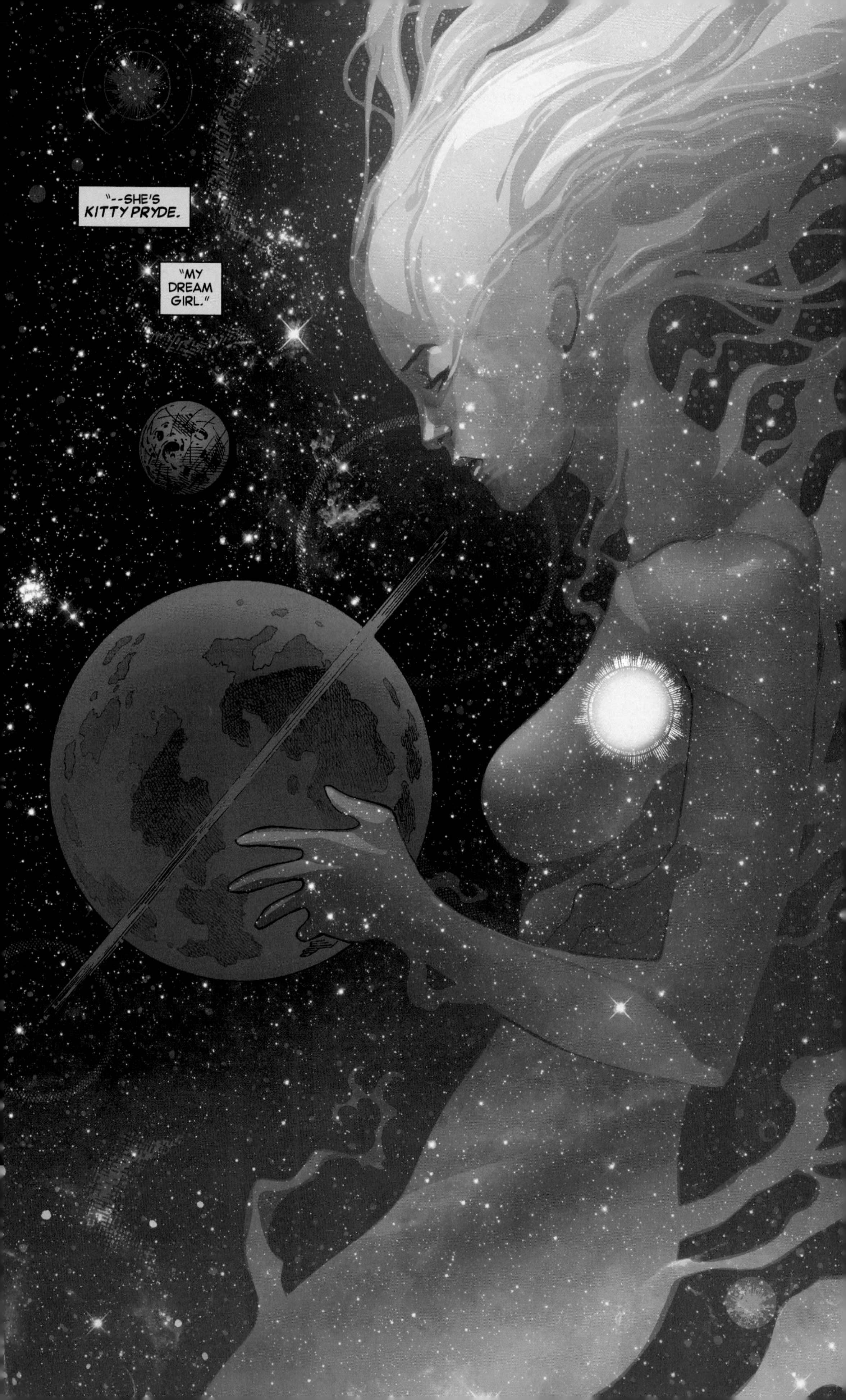
"--SHE'S KITTY PRYDE.
"MY DREAM GIRL."

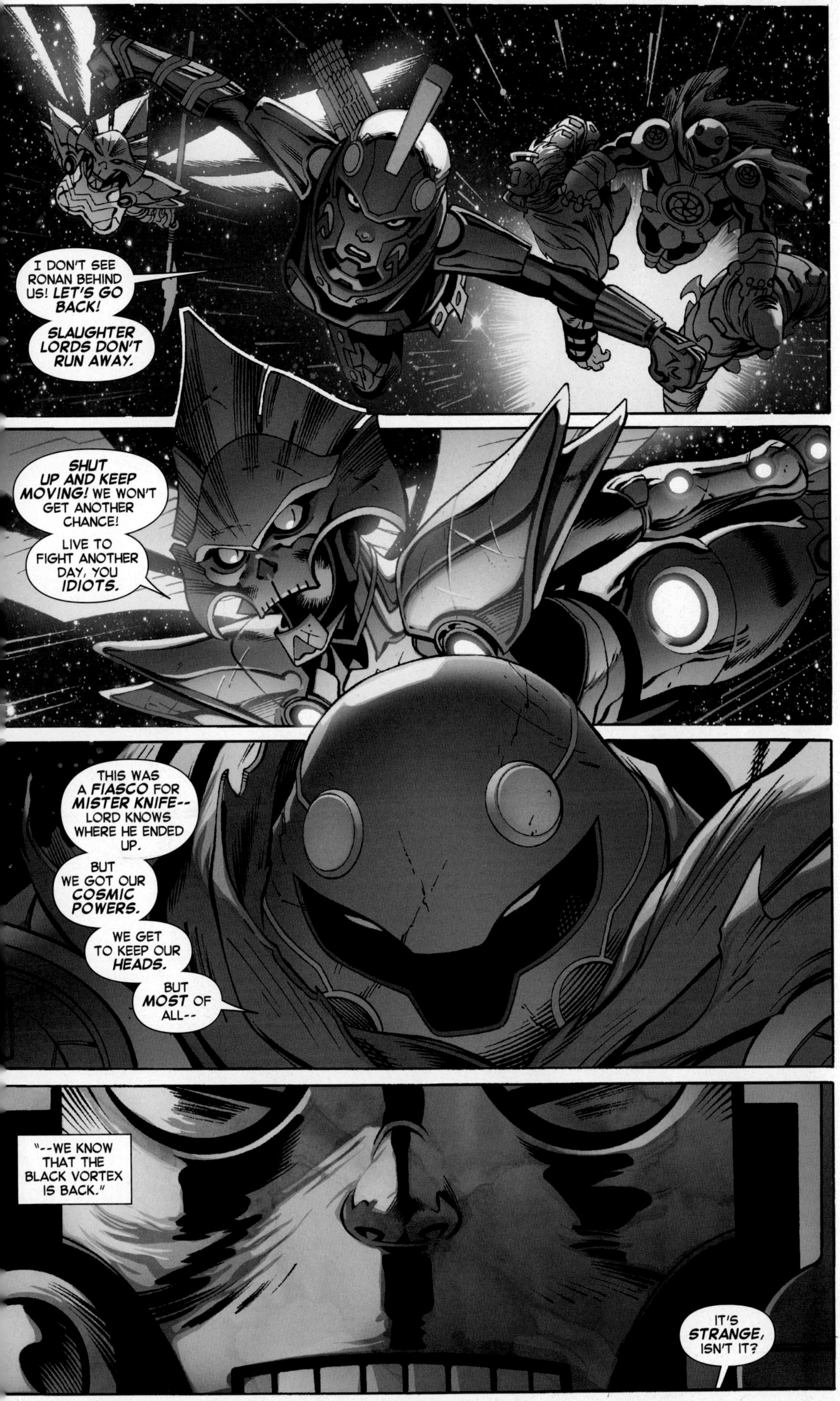

I DON'T SEE RONAN BEHIND US! **LET'S GO BACK!**
SLAUGHTER LORDS DON'T RUN AWAY.
SHUT UP AND KEEP MOVING! WE WON'T GET ANOTHER CHANCE!
LIVE TO FIGHT ANOTHER DAY, YOU ***IDIOTS.***
THIS WAS A ***FIASCO*** FOR ***MISTER KNIFE--*** LORD KNOWS WHERE HE ENDED UP.
BUT WE GOT OUR ***COSMIC POWERS.***
WE GET TO KEEP OUR ***HEADS.***
BUT ***MOST*** OF ALL--
"--WE KNOW THAT THE BLACK VORTEX IS BACK."
IT'S ***STRANGE,*** ISN'T IT?

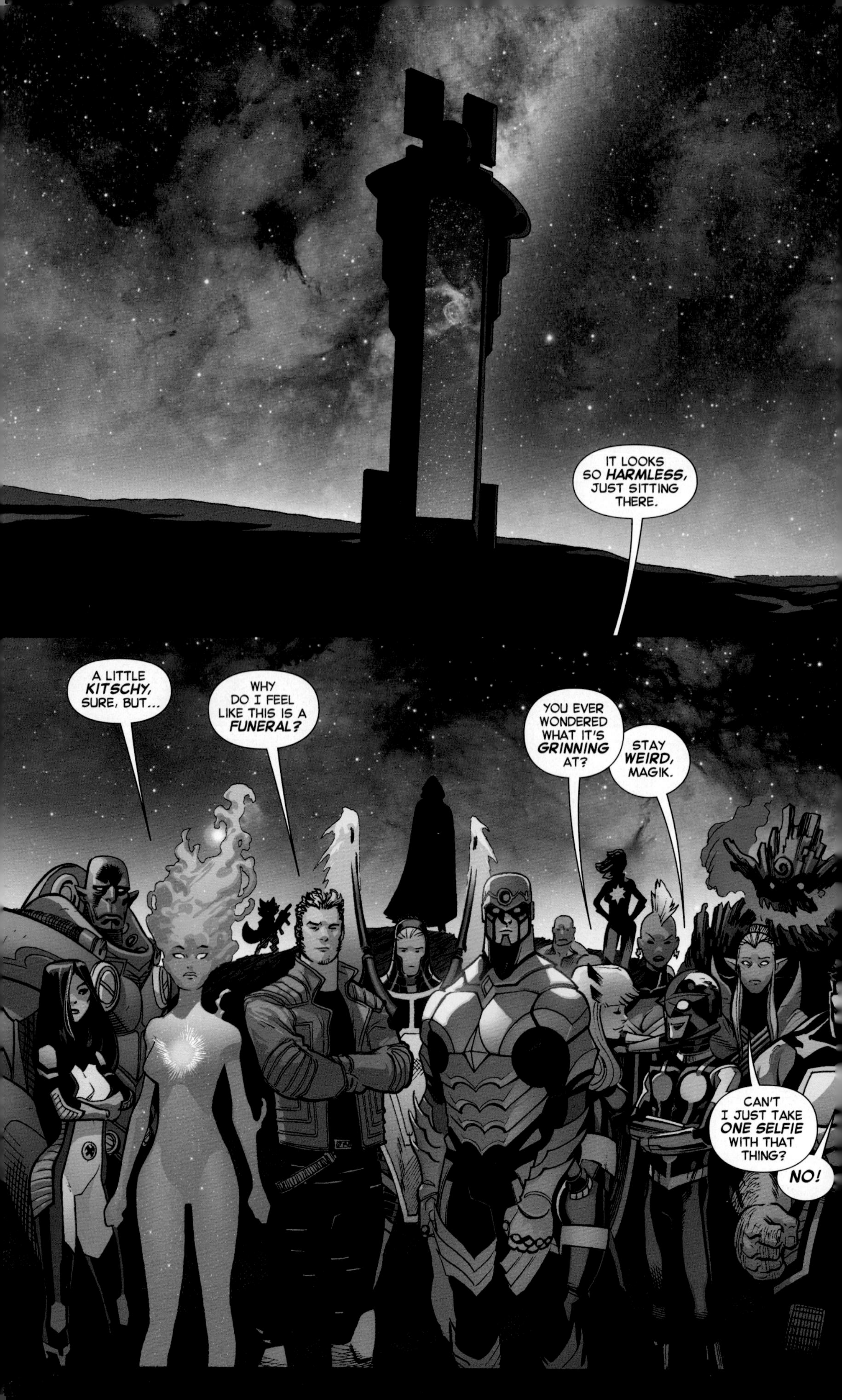
IT LOOKS SO HARMLESS, JUST SITTING THERE.
A LITTLE KITSCHY, SURE, BUT...
WHY DO I FEEL LIKE THIS IS A FUNERAL?
YOU EVER WONDERED WHAT IT'S GRINNING AT?
STAY WEIRD, MAGIK.
CAN'T I JUST TAKE ONE SELFIE WITH THAT THING?
NO!

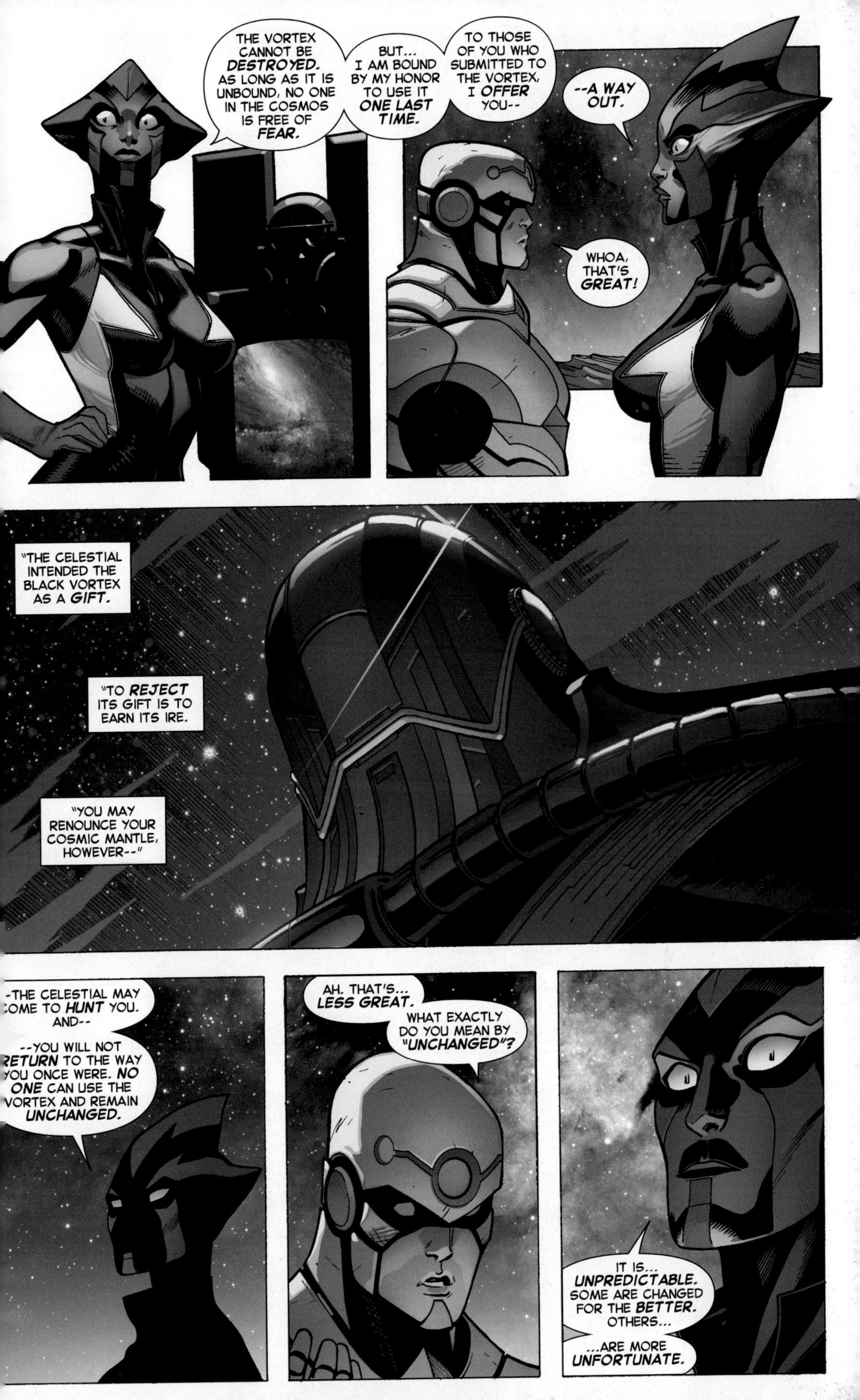
THE VORTEX CANNOT BE DESTROYED. AS LONG AS IT IS UNBOUND, NO ONE IN THE COSMOS IS FREE OF FEAR.
BUT... I AM BOUND BY MY HONOR TO USE IT ONE LAST TIME.
TO THOSE OF YOU WHO SUBMITTED TO THE VORTEX, I OFFER YOU--
--A WAY OUT.
WHOA, THAT'S GREAT!
"THE CELESTIAL INTENDED THE BLACK VORTEX AS A GIFT.
"TO REJECT ITS GIFT IS TO EARN ITS IRE.
"YOU MAY RENOUNCE YOUR COSMIC MANTLE, HOWEVER--"
-THE CELESTIAL MAY COME TO HUNT YOU. AND--
--YOU WILL NOT RETURN TO THE WAY YOU ONCE WERE. NO ONE CAN USE THE VORTEX AND REMAIN UNCHANGED.
AH. THAT'S... LESS GREAT.
WHAT EXACTLY DO YOU MEAN BY "UNCHANGED"?
IT IS... UNPREDICTABLE. SOME ARE CHANGED FOR THE BETTER. OTHERS...
...ARE MORE UNFORTUNATE.

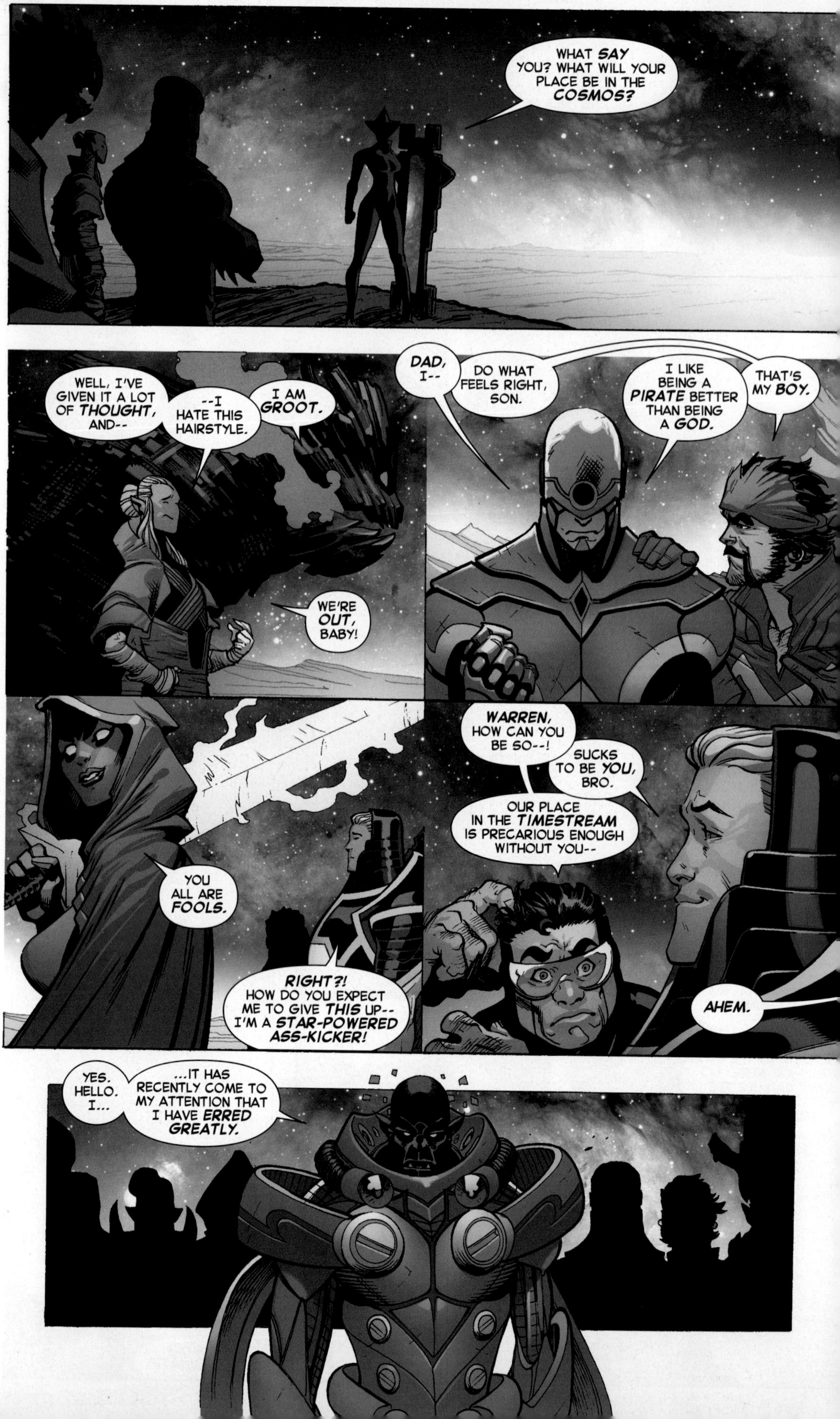
WHAT SAY YOU? WHAT WILL YOUR PLACE BE IN THE COSMOS?
WELL, I'VE GIVEN IT A LOT OF THOUGHT, AND--
--I HATE THIS HAIRSTYLE.
I AM GROOT.
WE'RE OUT, BABY!
DAD, I--
DO WHAT FEELS RIGHT, SON.
I LIKE BEING A PIRATE BETTER THAN BEING A GOD.
THAT'S MY BOY.
YOU ALL ARE FOOLS.
RIGHT?! HOW DO YOU EXPECT ME TO GIVE THIS UP-- I'M A STAR-POWERED ASS-KICKER!
WARREN, HOW CAN YOU BE SO--!
SUCKS TO BE YOU, BRO.
OUR PLACE IN THE TIMESTREAM IS PRECARIOUS ENOUGH WITHOUT YOU--
AHEM.
YES. HELLO. I...
...IT HAS RECENTLY COME TO MY ATTENTION THAT I HAVE ERRED GREATLY.

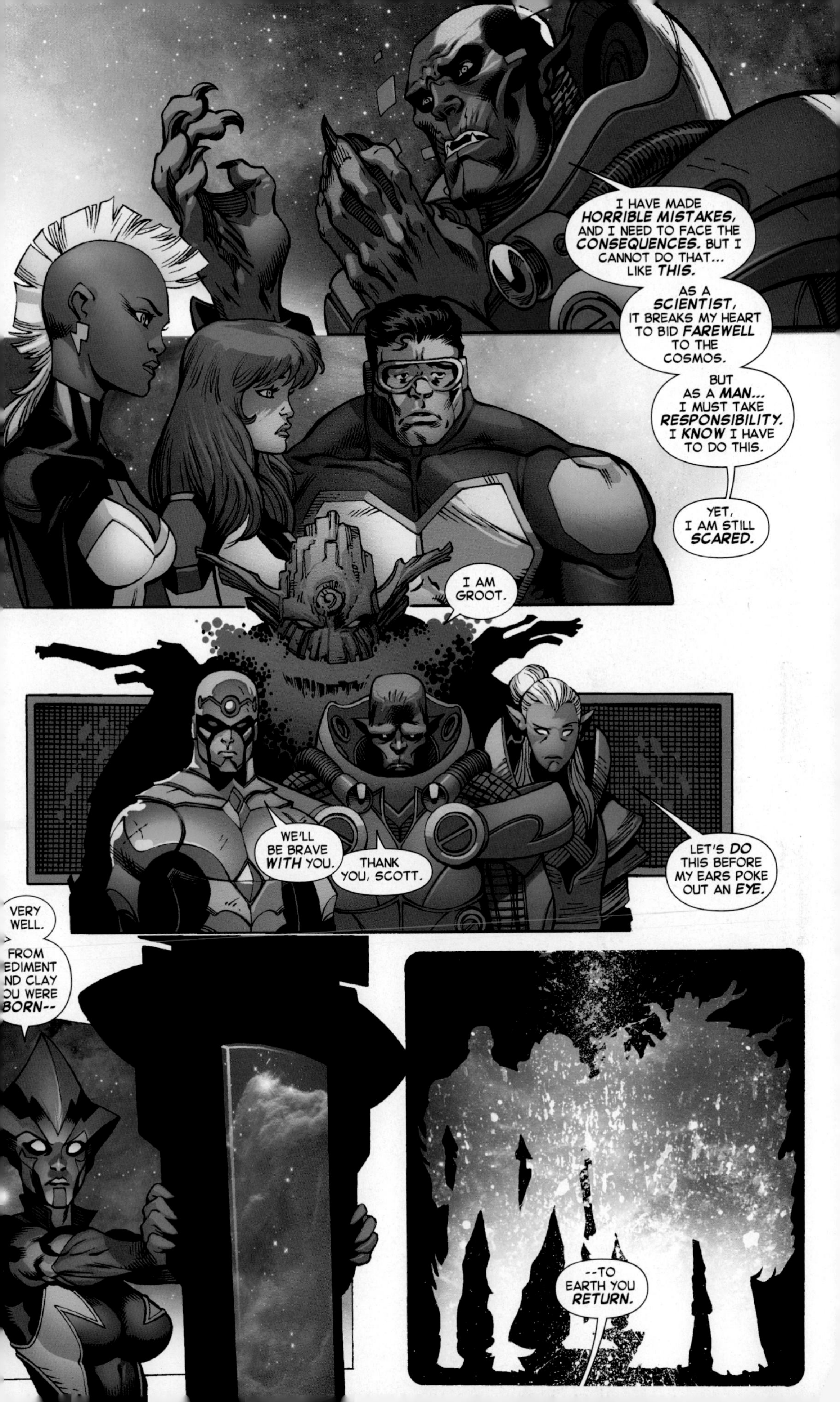

I HAVE MADE HORRIBLE MISTAKES, AND I NEED TO FACE THE CONSEQUENCES. BUT I CANNOT DO THAT... LIKE THIS.
AS A SCIENTIST, IT BREAKS MY HEART TO BID FAREWELL TO THE COSMOS.
BUT AS A MAN... I MUST TAKE RESPONSIBILITY. I KNOW I HAVE TO DO THIS.
YET, I AM STILL SCARED.
I AM GROOT.
WE'LL BE BRAVE WITH YOU.
THANK YOU, SCOTT.
LET'S DO THIS BEFORE MY EARS POKE OUT AN EYE.
VERY WELL.
FROM EDIMENT ND CLAY OU WERE BORN--
--TO EARTH YOU RETURN.

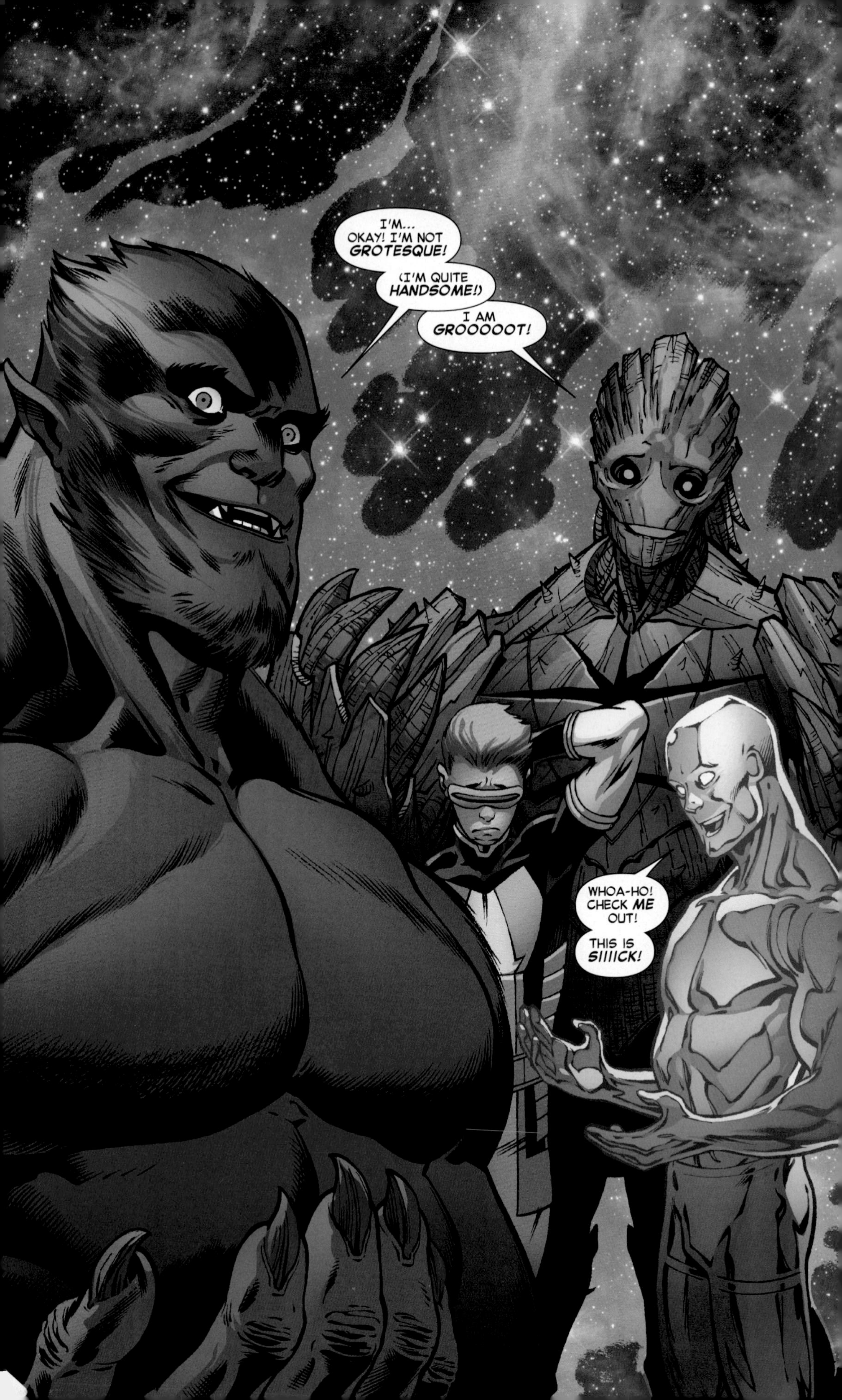
I'M... OKAY! I'M NOT GROTESQUE!
(I'M QUITE HANDSOME!)
I AM GROOOOOT!
WHOA-HO! CHECK ME OUT!
THIS IS SIIIICK!

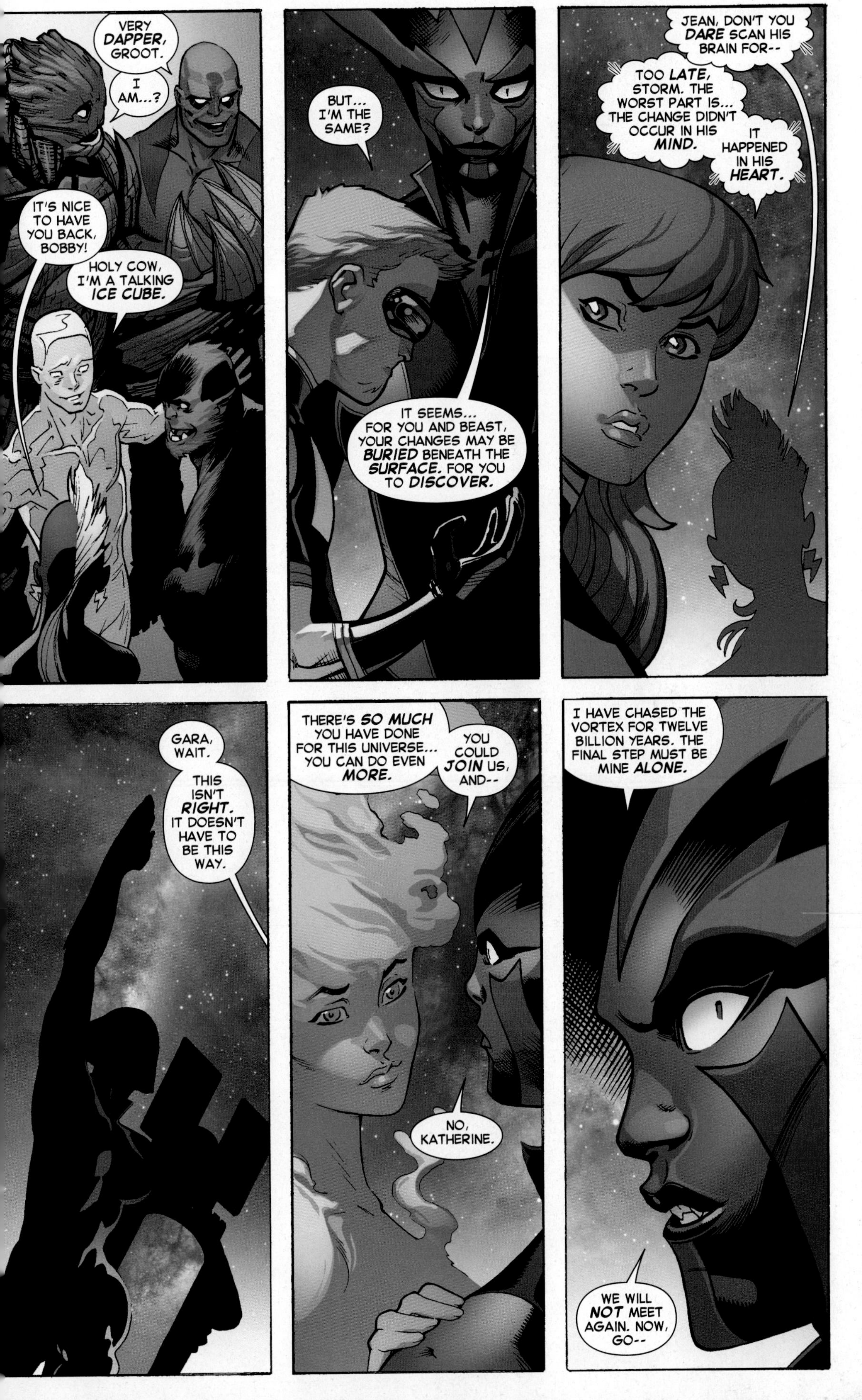

VERY DAPPER, GROOT.
I AM...?
IT'S NICE TO HAVE YOU BACK, BOBBY!
HOLY COW, I'M A TALKING ICE CUBE.
BUT... I'M THE SAME?
IT SEEMS... FOR YOU AND BEAST, YOUR CHANGES MAY BE BURIED BENEATH THE SURFACE. FOR YOU TO DISCOVER.
JEAN, DON'T YOU DARE SCAN HIS BRAIN FOR--
TOO LATE, STORM. THE WORST PART IS... THE CHANGE DIDN'T OCCUR IN HIS MIND.
IT HAPPENED IN HIS HEART.
GARA, WAIT.
THIS ISN'T RIGHT. IT DOESN'T HAVE TO BE THIS WAY.
THERE'S SO MUCH YOU HAVE DONE FOR THIS UNIVERSE... YOU CAN DO EVEN MORE.
YOU COULD JOIN US, AND--
NO, KATHERINE.
I HAVE CHASED THE VORTEX FOR TWELVE BILLION YEARS. THE FINAL STEP MUST BE MINE ALONE.
WE WILL NOT MEET AGAIN. NOW, GO--

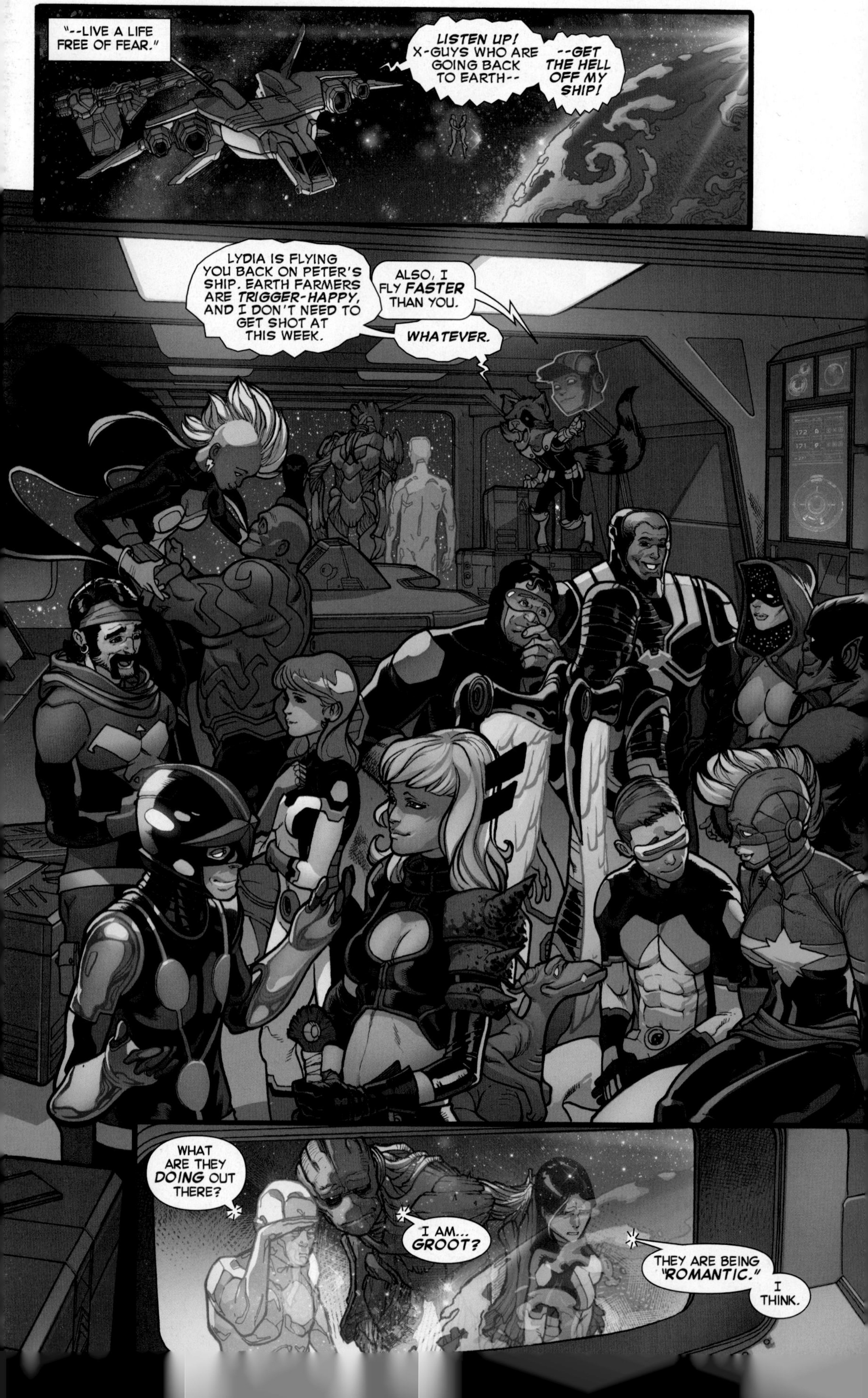
"--LIVE A LIFE FREE OF FEAR."
LISTEN UP! X-GUYS WHO ARE GOING BACK TO EARTH--
--GET THE HELL OFF MY SHIP!
LYDIA IS FLYING YOU BACK ON PETER'S SHIP. EARTH FARMERS ARE TRIGGER-HAPPY, AND I DON'T NEED TO GET SHOT AT THIS WEEK.
ALSO, I FLY FASTER THAN YOU.
WHATEVER.
WHAT ARE THEY DOING OUT THERE?
I AM... GROOT?
THEY ARE BEING "ROMANTIC."
I THINK.

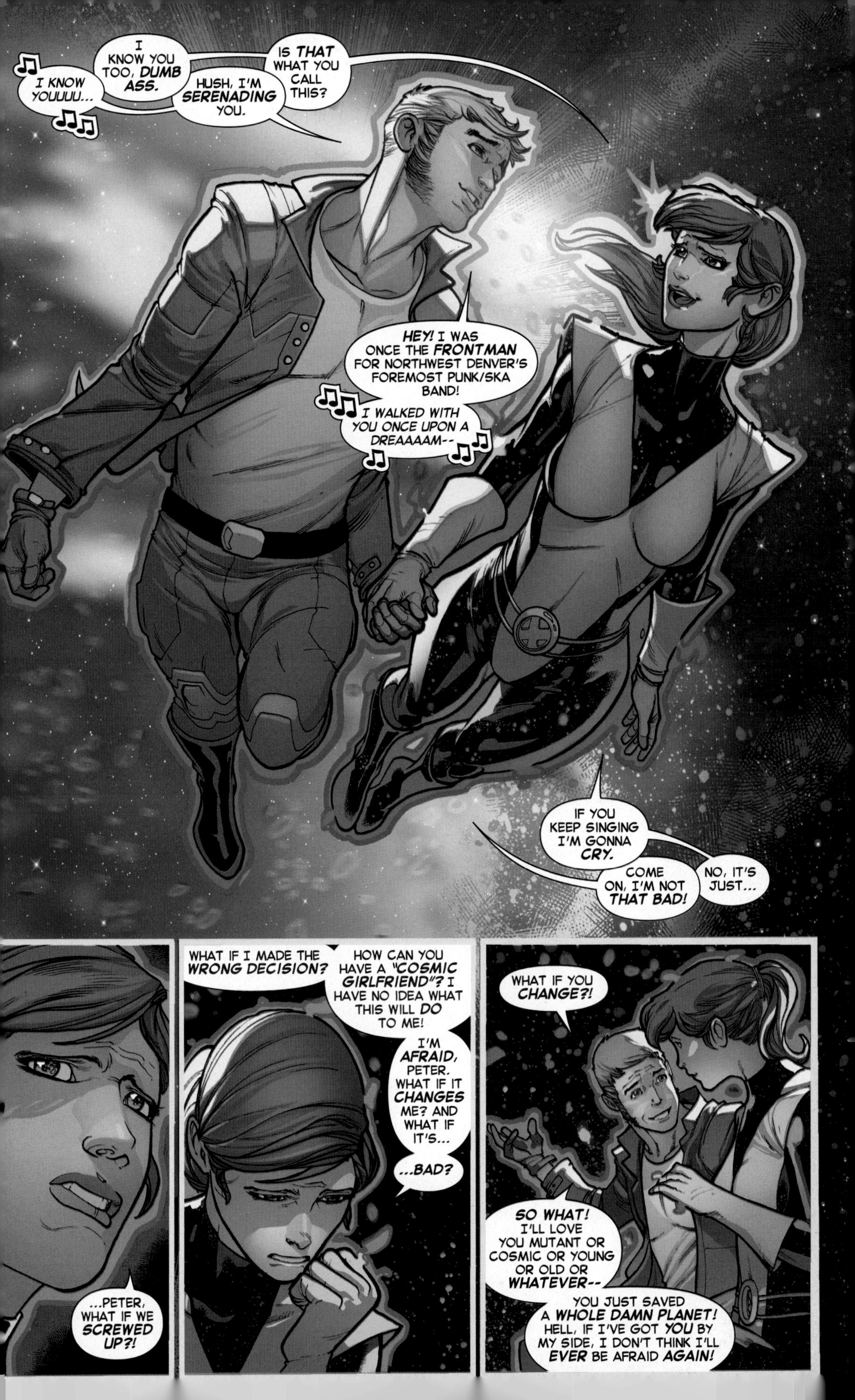
I KNOW YOUUUU...
I KNOW YOU TOO, DUMB ASS.
HUSH, I'M SERENADING YOU.
IS THAT WHAT YOU CALL THIS?
HEY! I WAS ONCE THE FRONTMAN FOR NORTHWEST DENVER'S FOREMOST PUNK/SKA BAND!
I WALKED WITH YOU ONCE UPON A DREAAAAM--
IF YOU KEEP SINGING I'M GONNA CRY.
COME ON, I'M NOT THAT BAD!
NO, IT'S JUST...
...PETER, WHAT IF WE SCREWED UP?!
WHAT IF I MADE THE WRONG DECISION?
HOW CAN YOU HAVE A "COSMIC GIRLFRIEND"? I HAVE NO IDEA WHAT THIS WILL DO TO ME!
I'M AFRAID, PETER. WHAT IF IT CHANGES ME? AND WHAT IF IT'S...
...BAD?
WHAT IF YOU CHANGE?!
SO WHAT! I'LL LOVE YOU MUTANT OR COSMIC OR YOUNG OR OLD OR WHATEVER--
YOU JUST SAVED A WHOLE DAMN PLANET! HELL, IF I'VE GOT YOU BY MY SIDE, I DON'T THINK I'LL EVER BE AFRAID AGAIN!

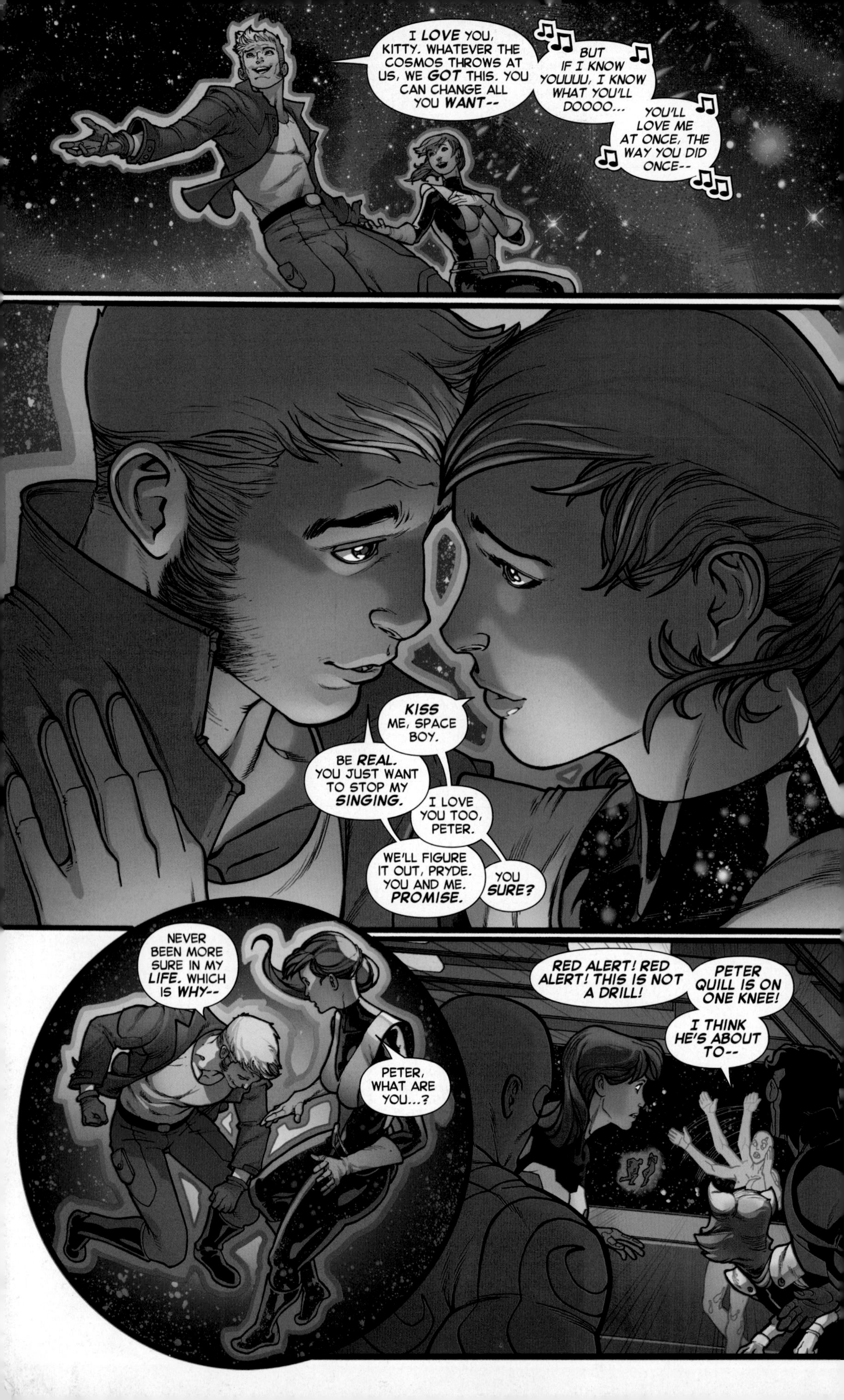
I LOVE YOU, KITTY. WHATEVER THE COSMOS THROWS AT US, WE GOT THIS. YOU CAN CHANGE ALL YOU WANT--
BUT IF I KNOW YOUUUU, I KNOW WHAT YOU'LL DOOOO...
YOU'LL LOVE ME AT ONCE, THE WAY YOU DID ONCE--
KISS ME, SPACE BOY.
BE REAL. YOU JUST WANT TO STOP MY SINGING.
I LOVE YOU TOO, PETER.
WE'LL FIGURE IT OUT, PRYDE. YOU AND ME. PROMISE.
YOU SURE?
NEVER BEEN MORE SURE IN MY LIFE. WHICH IS WHY--
PETER, WHAT ARE YOU...?
RED ALERT! RED ALERT! THIS IS NOT A DRILL!
PETER QUILL IS ON ONE KNEE!
I THINK HE'S ABOUT TO--

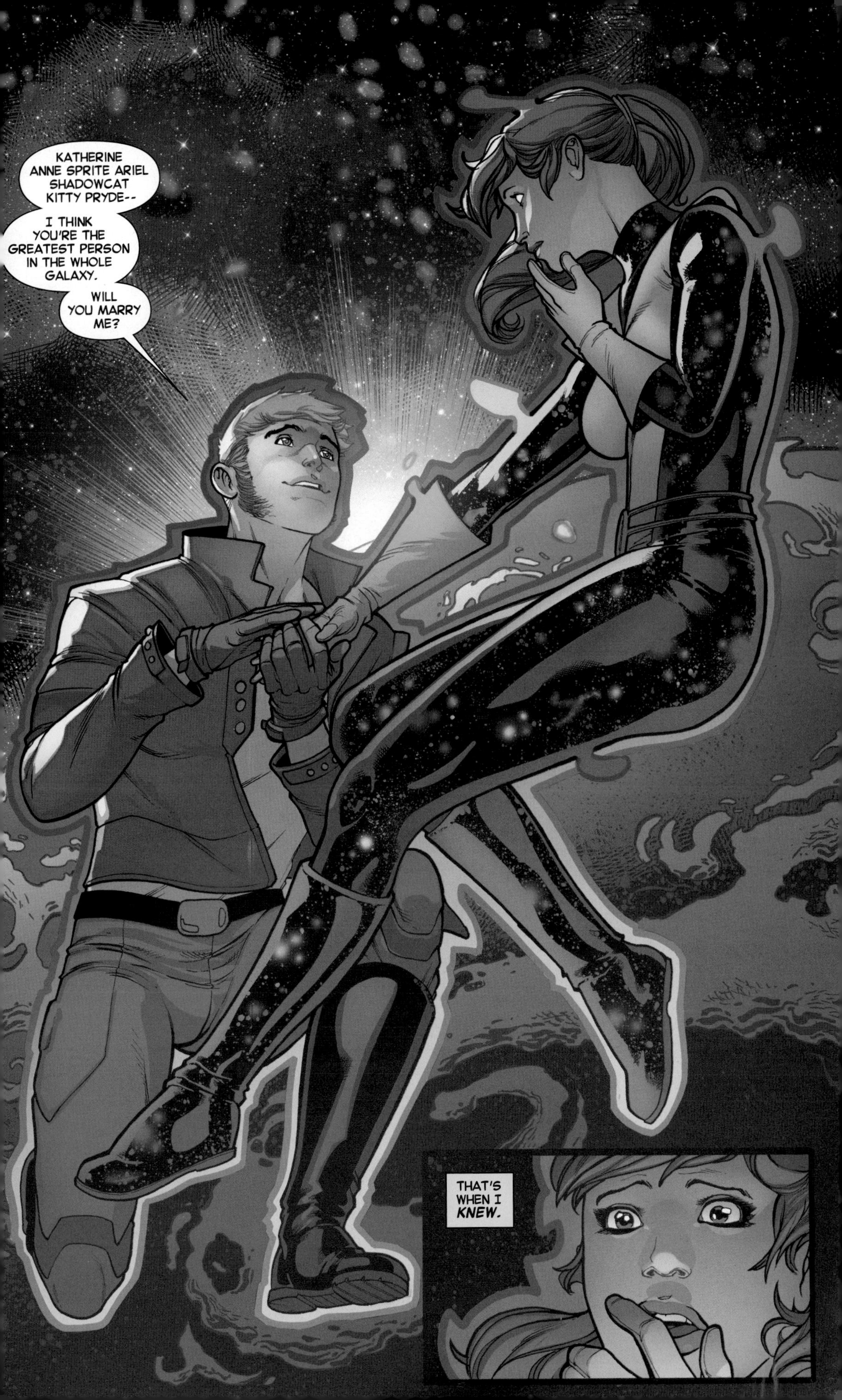
KATHERINE ANNE SPRITE ARIEL SHADOWCAT KITTY PRYDE--
I THINK YOU'RE THE GREATEST PERSON IN THE WHOLE GALAXY.
WILL YOU MARRY ME?
THAT'S WHEN I KNEW.

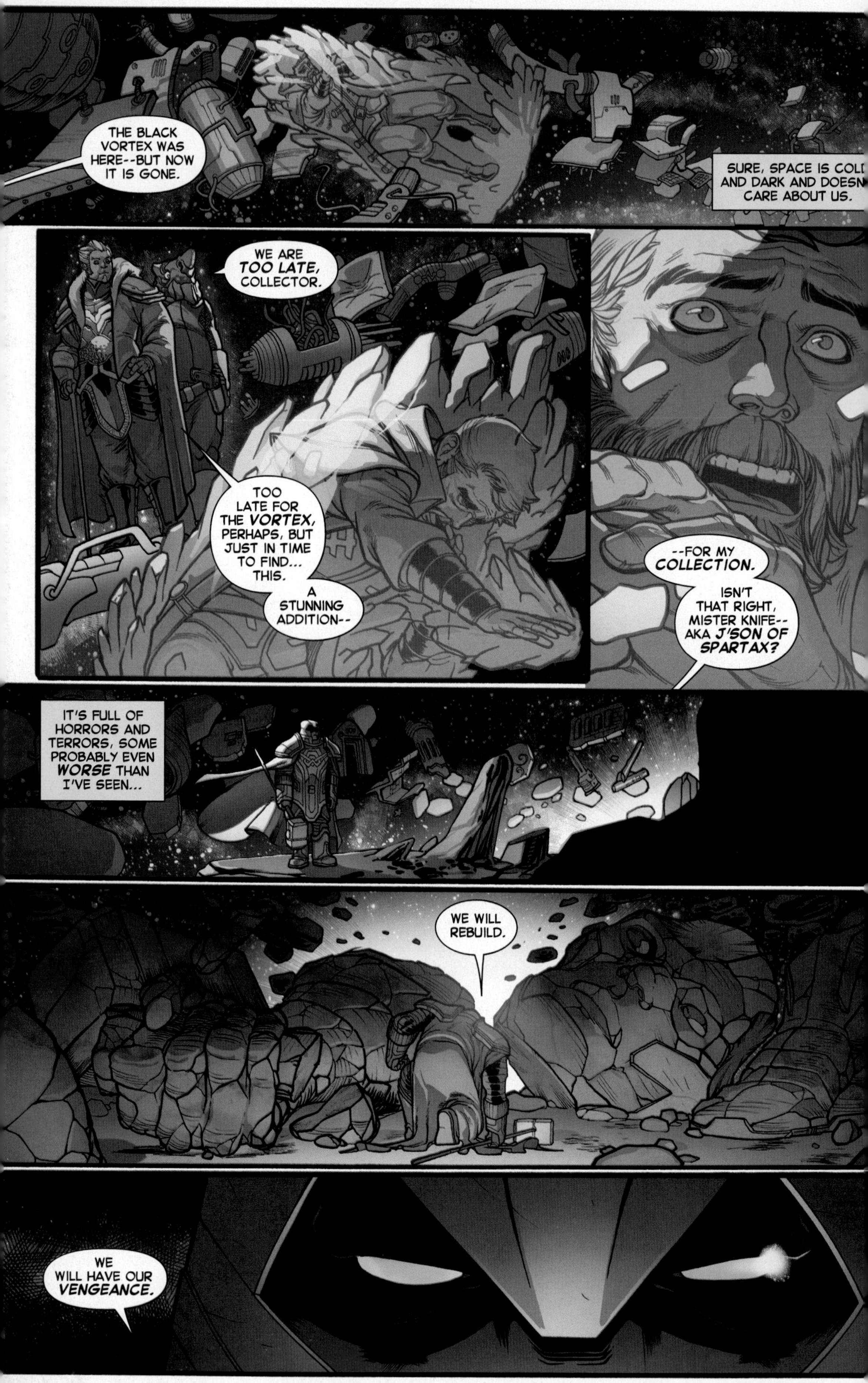
THE BLACK VORTEX WAS HERE--BUT NOW IT IS GONE.
SURE, SPACE IS COLD AND DARK AND DOESN'T CARE ABOUT US.
WE ARE TOO LATE, COLLECTOR.
TOO LATE FOR THE VORTEX, PERHAPS, BUT JUST IN TIME TO FIND... THIS.
A STUNNING ADDITION--
--FOR MY COLLECTION.
ISN'T THAT RIGHT, MISTER KNIFE--AKA J'SON OF SPARTAX?
IT'S FULL OF HORRORS AND TERRORS, SOME PROBABLY EVEN WORSE THAN I'VE SEEN...
WE WILL REBUILD.
WE WILL HAVE OUR VENGEANCE.

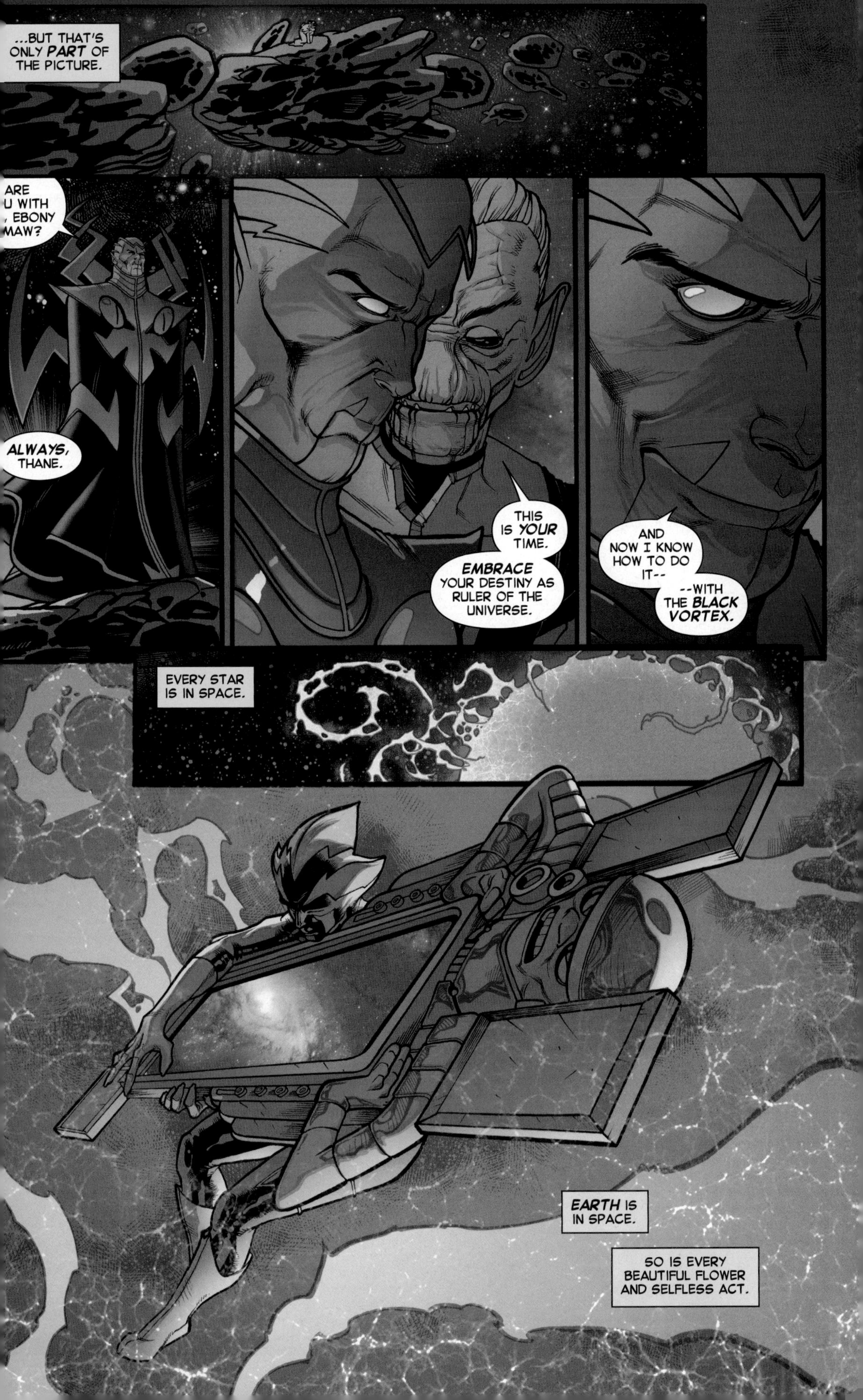
...BUT THAT'S ONLY PART OF THE PICTURE.
ARE U WITH , EBONY MAW?
ALWAYS, THANE.
THIS IS YOUR TIME.
EMBRACE YOUR DESTINY AS RULER OF THE UNIVERSE.
AND NOW I KNOW HOW TO DO IT--
--WITH THE BLACK VORTEX.
EVERY STAR IS IN SPACE.
EARTH IS IN SPACE.
SO IS EVERY BEAUTIFUL FLOWER AND SELFLESS ACT.

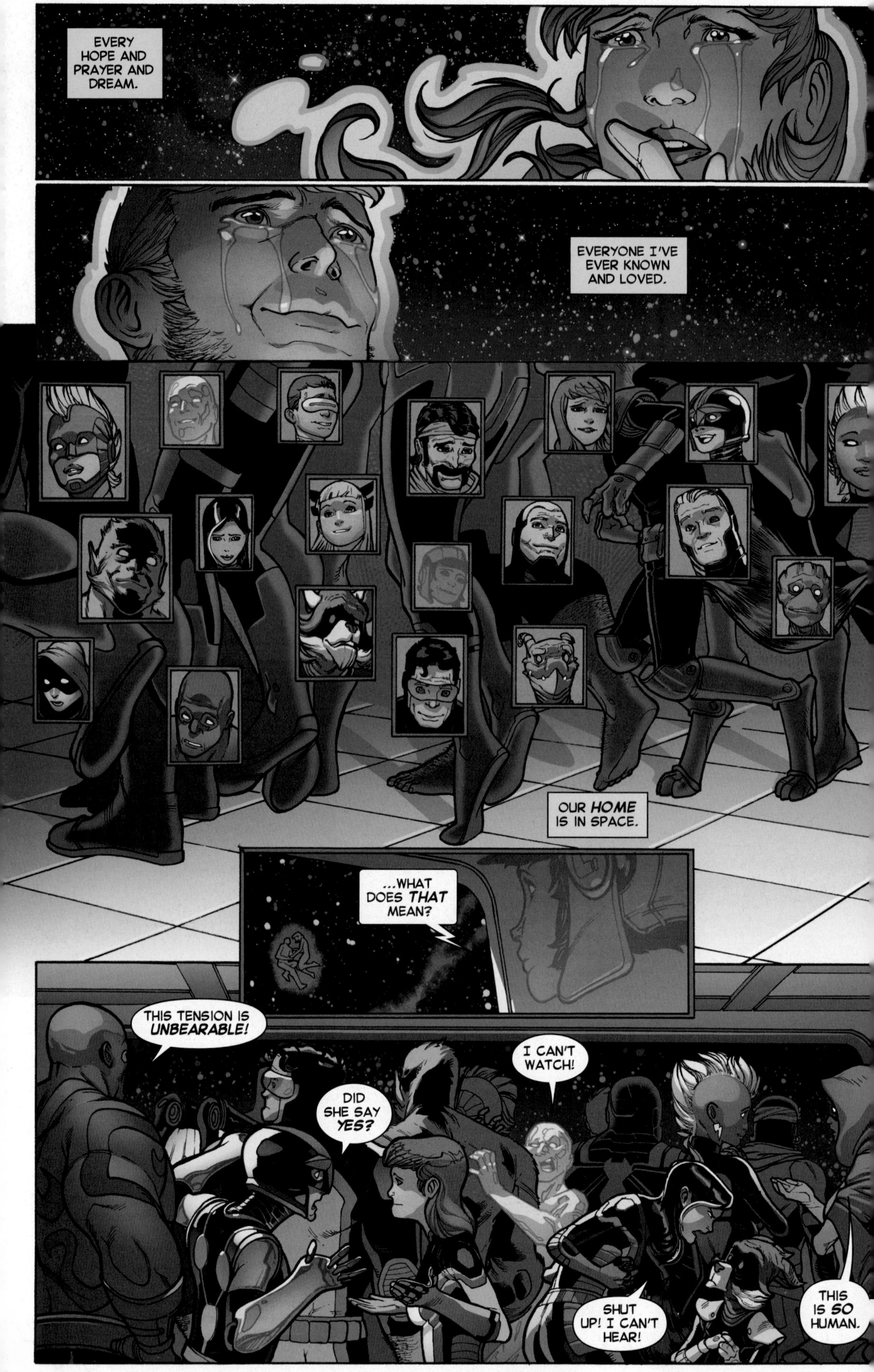
EVERY HOPE AND PRAYER AND DREAM.
EVERYONE I'VE EVER KNOWN AND LOVED.
OUR *HOME* IS IN SPACE.
...WHAT DOES *THAT* MEAN?
THIS TENSION IS *UNBEARABLE!*
DID SHE SAY *YES?*
I CAN'T WATCH!
SHUT UP! I CAN'T HEAR!
THIS IS *SO* HUMAN.

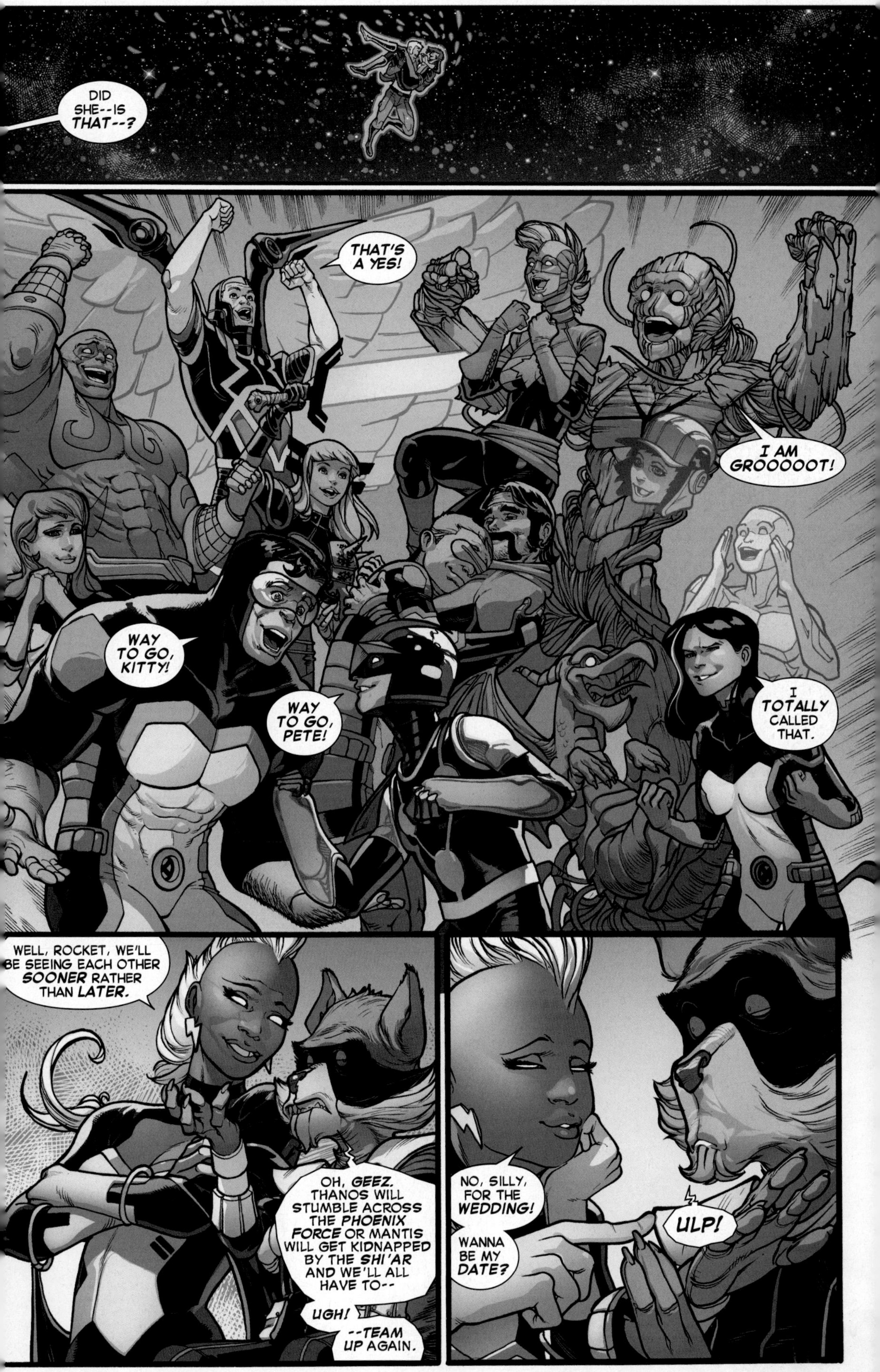

DID SHE--IS THAT--?
THAT'S A YES!
I AM GROOOOOT!
WAY TO GO, KITTY!
WAY TO GO, PETE!
I TOTALLY CALLED THAT.
WELL, ROCKET, WE'LL BE SEEING EACH OTHER SOONER RATHER THAN LATER.
OH, GEEZ. THANOS WILL STUMBLE ACROSS THE PHOENIX FORCE OR MANTIS WILL GET KIDNAPPED BY THE SHI'AR AND WE'LL ALL HAVE TO--
UGH!
--TEAM UP AGAIN.
NO, SILLY, FOR THE WEDDING!
WANNA BE MY DATE?
ULP!

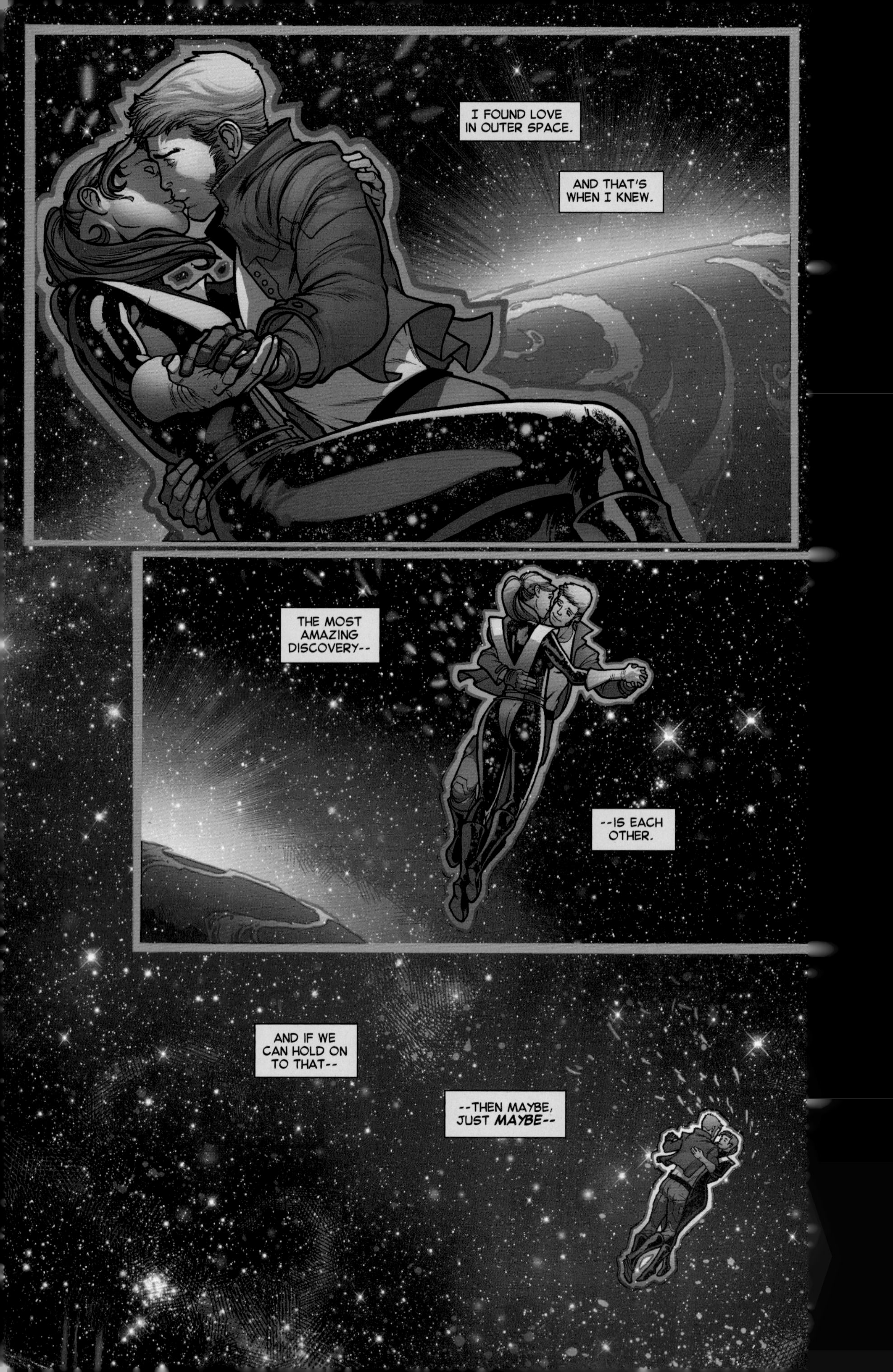
I FOUND LOVE IN OUTER SPACE.
AND THAT'S WHEN I KNEW.
THE MOST AMAZING DISCOVERY--
--IS EACH OTHER.
AND IF WE CAN HOLD ON TO THAT--
--THEN MAYBE, JUST *MAYBE*--

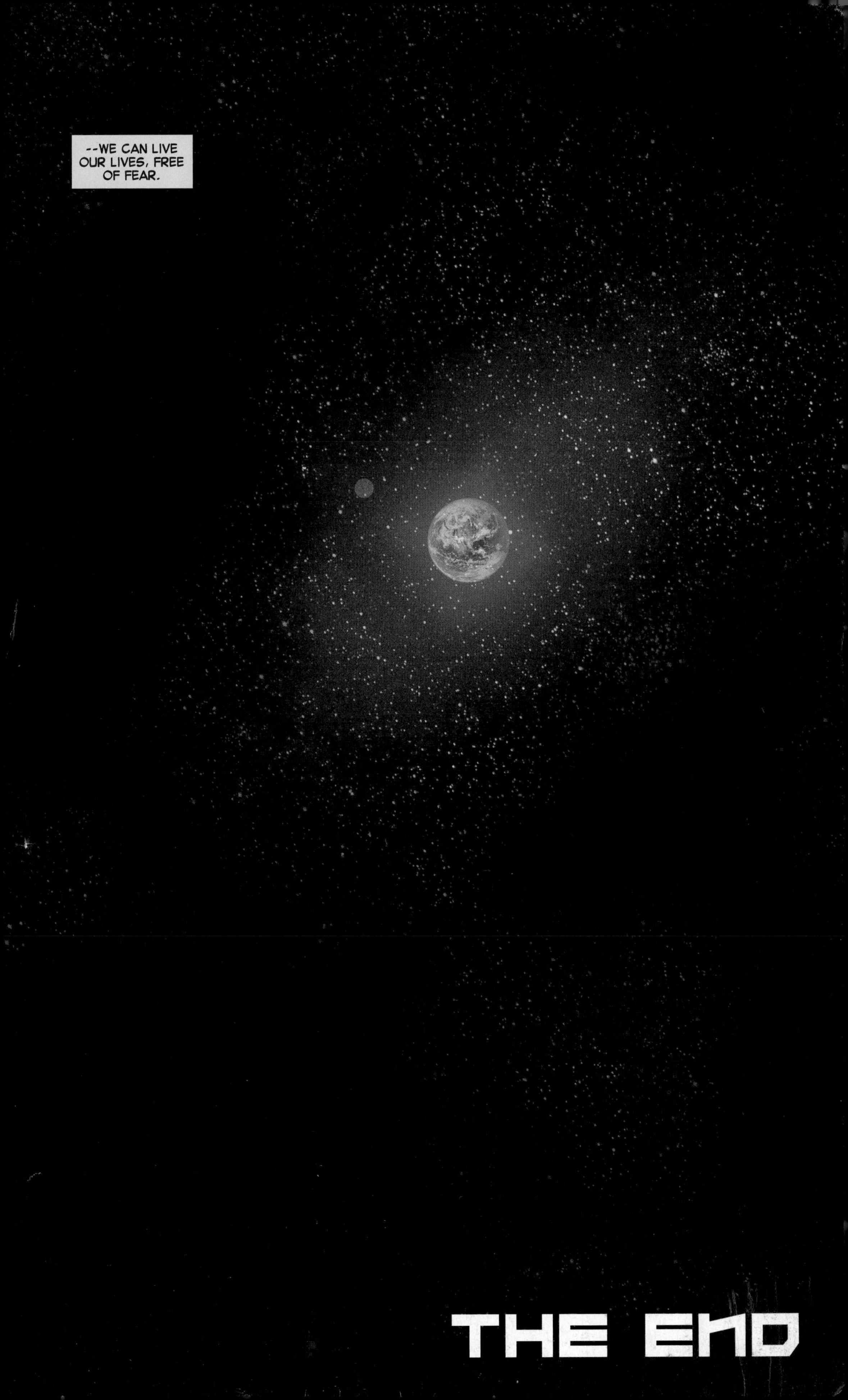
--WE CAN LIVE OUR LIVES, FREE OF FEAR.
THE END

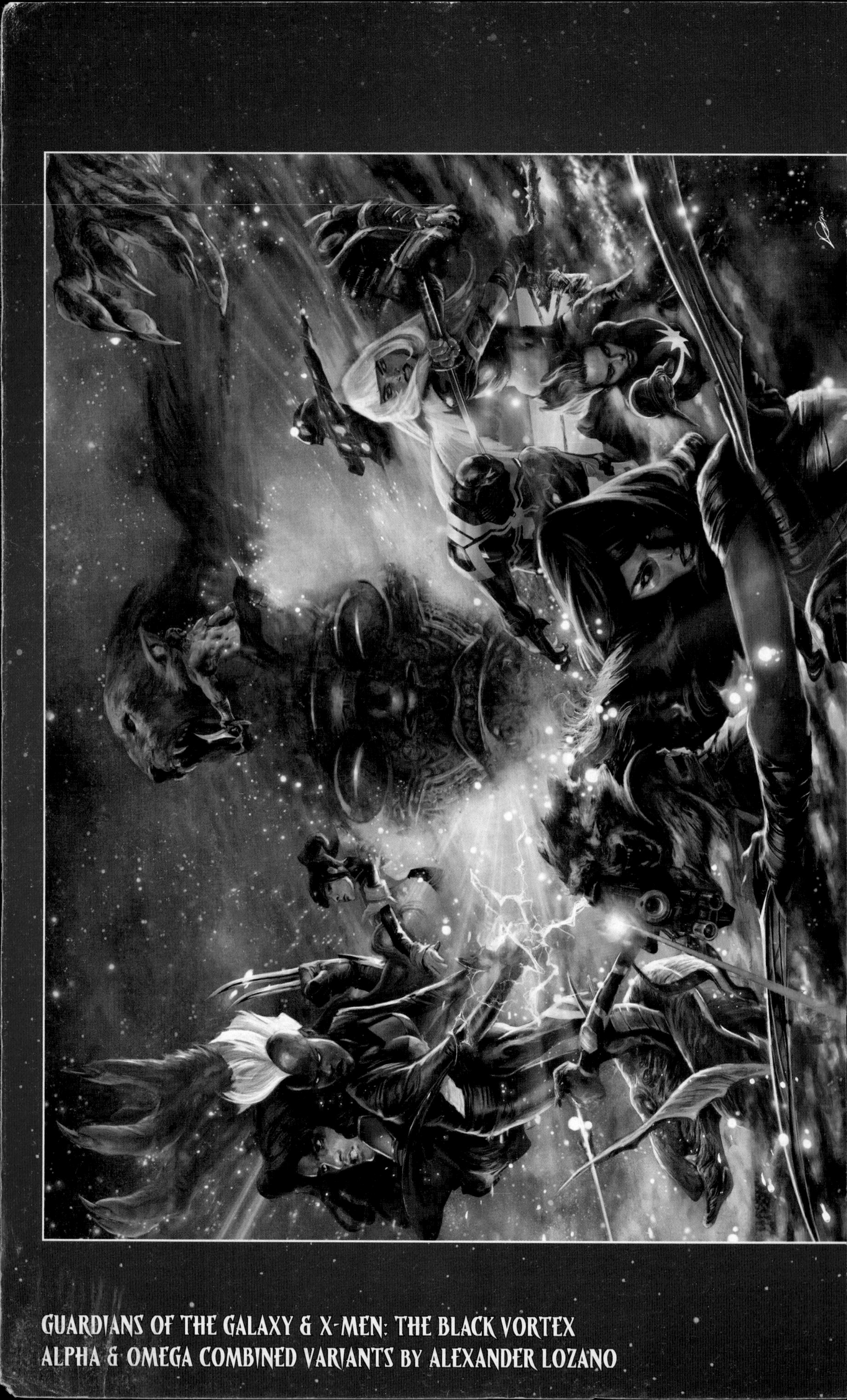

GUARDIANS OF THE GALAXY & X-MEN: THE BLACK VORTEX
ALPHA & OMEGA COMBINED VARIANTS BY ALEXANDER LOZANO